W9-BXN-394

Gerald Ford
and the Challenges
of the 1970s

Gerald Ford

and the Challenges of the

1970s

YANEK MIECZKOWSKI

THE UNIVERSITY PRESS OF KENTUCKY

Publication of this volume was made possible in part
by a grant from the National Endowment for the Humanities.

Scholarly publisher for the Commonwealth,
serving Bellarmine University, Berea College, Centre
College of Kentucky, Eastern Kentucky University,
The Filson Historical Society, Georgetown College,
Kentucky Historical Society, Kentucky State University,
Morehead State University, Murray State University,
Northern Kentucky University, Transylvania University,
University of Kentucky, University of Louisville,
and Western Kentucky University.

Editorial and Sales Offices: The University Press of Kentucky
663 South Limestone Street, Lexington, Kentucky 40508-4008
www.kentuckypress.com

All photographs are courtesy of the Gerald R. Ford Library,
unless otherwise specified.

09 08 07 06 05   5 4 3 2 1

Library of Congress Cataloging-in-Publication Data

Mieczkowski, Yanek.
 Gerald Ford and the challenges of the 1970s / Yanek Mieczkowski.
  p. cm.
 Includes bibliographical references and index.
 ISBN 0-8131-2349-6 (hardcover : alk. paper)
 1. Ford, Gerald R., 1913- 2. Presidents–United States–Biography. 3. United States–
Politics and government–1974-1977. 4. United States–Economic conditions–1971-
1981. 5. United States–Social conditions–1960-1980. I. Title.
 E866.M54 2005
 973.925'092–dc22   2004026890

To my parents,
Dr. Bogdan and Seiko Mieczkowski

Contents

Part Three: The Energy Challenge

Part Four: Diplomatic and Political Challenges

Illustrations follow page 228

Acknowledgments

This work began in a grape vineyard overlooking Seneca Lake in Central New York. While attending graduate school in Manhattan, I returned to my hometown, Ithaca, for an early autumn weekend, along with a classmate, Mike Green. I was planning to begin my doctoral dissertation, and I knew that I wanted to study Gerald Ford's presidency. Ford, I felt, was a thoughtful and steady leader who had never received enough credit for his stewardship—especially in economic matters—during difficult years in our country's history. People familiar with the Finger Lakes region know that its beauty can act as a tonic, and it did for me that weekend. As Mike and I discussed Ford's presidency—picking Niagara, Concord, and Catawba grapes, of all things—I felt a work begin to crystallize in my mind.

Over the next few years, my dissertation adviser, Alan Brinkley, gave me enormous encouragement and guidance, helping to shape the thesis into a study of not only Ford's presidency but America in the 1970s. The other members of my dissertation committee, David Farber, Joshua Freeman, Robert Shapiro, and James Shenton, gave valuable advice to prepare the work for publication. David Farber expressed interest in this project from the start, and three other graduate school professors, Mark Carnes, John Garraty, and Alden Vaughan, greatly influenced my training as a researcher and writer, as did several classmates, including Ed O'Donnell of Holy Cross College.

The Gerald R. Ford Foundation awarded a generous grant to conduct research at the Gerald R. Ford Presidential Library in Ann Arbor, Michigan. I have made numerous trips there and found the staff peerless in efficiency and helpfulness. Supervisory archivist David Horrocks has been wonderfully supportive; Geir Gundersen answered many questions by telephone and e-mail over the years; audio-visual archivist Kenneth Hafeli fulfilled numerous video requests and gave generous assistance in selecting photographs for the picture section. I want to thank all other staff members as well: Director

Acknowledgments

Dennis Daellenbach, Stacy Davis, Donna Lehman, William McNitt, Nancy Mirshah, Helmi Raaska, recent retirees Dick and Karen Holtzhausen, and archives technicians Brooke Clement and Joshua Cochran. Donald Holloway of the Gerald R. Ford Museum in Grand Rapids proofread the manuscript and gave me access to museum holdings in storage, and Jamie Draper helped me to assemble them for photographs. Jennifer Sternaman, now at the Ronald Reagan Presidential Library, was very helpful during my early years of research at the Ford Library.

I got to know many libraries well while researching this book. I want to pay homage to the libraries and librarians of Dowling College, Ithaca College, Columbia University, and Brevard Community College at Cocoa. Especially helpful have been those institutions that keep paper volumes of older periodicals; digging up 1970s articles on paper was much easier than on microfilm, and the portraits of this nation and individual Americans in the pages that follow came in part from my poring over the bound paper collections of a few libraries.

A number of institutions offered financial assistance to mine their archival collections. I received grants from the Lilly Library of Indiana University at Bloomington, the Rockefeller Archive Center of Sleepy Hollow, New York, and the Carl Albert Congressional Research and Studies Center at the University of Oklahoma, where archivist Todd Kosmerick gave great assistance. Diane Windham Shaw of the David Bishop Skillman Library at Lafayette College helped me considerably during visits to review the William Simon papers.

Faculty, staff, and administration colleagues at Dowling College have been extraordinarily supportive, and the college's Long Range Planning and Development Committee has facilitated my research by granting course releases, for which I am deeply grateful. During the spring 2003 semester, I assigned an earlier draft of this work to my "America in the 1970s" class at Dowling. The students were very encouraging, and their reactions and insights informed my thinking not only on the Ford presidency but the entire decade. During 2003–2004, I was lucky to have two Dowling students working as research assistants, John Conroy and Darren Large, who helped to transcribe the interviews that I conducted from 2002–2004.

I owe a huge debt of gratitude to members of Gerald Ford's administration and the Ninety-forth Congress who granted interviews and patiently answered questions that probed their memories of decades-old events and emotions. A number of Ford administration and congressional alumni proofread chapters, offering valuable comments, and gave me access to their personal papers. I would like to thank Roy Ash, Charles Curtis, Barber Conable, Max Friedersdorf, John Hill, Russell Freeburg, Ken Glozer, Paul MacAvoy, Ron Nessen, Robert Nordhaus, L. William Seidman, Paul and Nancy Theis, and Frank Zarb. Charles DiBona and William Johnson, energy advisors during the Nixon administration, spent considerable time in explaining the origins of the energy crisis, giving me a wealth of recollections as well as books and articles. I owe special thanks to James Lynn and Glenn Schleede, who proofread chapters and, more than that, have been wonderful friends, directing me to colleagues and showing a patience and generosity for which I am profoundly grateful.

President Ford has been more than a good sport as I researched and wrote this work; he has lived up to his reputation as one of the most open and accessible of modern presidents. Few works have benefited from as much cooperation from a former president as this one, as President Ford hosted me at his California and Colorado homes to answer many questions and explain the decisions that he made while he led the country. I would also like to thank Chief of Staff Penny Circle and Judi Risk for arranging my interviews with President Ford and making me feel welcome whenever I visited.

Although no longer with the University Press of Kentucky, John Ziegler made it clear that he wanted me to publish with them from the moment I approached. My editors, Gena Henry and Nichole Lainhart, were excellent: always kind and helpful, they accommodated many last-minute changes and guided this project to completion. Freelance copyeditor Bob Burchfield and freelance proofreader Bethany Easter made numerous insightful comments and corrections that improved the book. Rick Perlstein read the manuscript thoroughly—twice, in fact—and made valuable recommendations for improvement, which led me to write new chapters. I greatly appreciate his encouragement and shrewd judgment.

Mike Green, who teaches at the Community College of Southern Nevada, has done marvelous work as a proofreader, tightening prose, pointing out errors, and showing unstinting generosity with his time and ideas. In countless ways, this work has benefited from Mike's insights and immense knowledge of history.

The deepest debt I owe is to my parents, Bogdan and Seiko Mieczkowski. I wrote the manuscript at their home in Ithaca and continued to revise the manuscript during extended visits with them. Dedicated professors and scholars, they proofread, directed me to sources, and had long conversations with me about the topics that this book comprises. As always, they have my greatest admiration and appreciation.

Introduction

Presidential Leadership in Post-Watergate America

"What do you think is the most important problem facing this country today?"

Think about it for a minute. Pollsters have posed this question to Americans throughout the post–World War II era. In the summer of 1974, shortly before Gerald Ford became president, three issues stood out. Respondents overwhelmingly ranked the "high cost of living" as their chief worry. Then came a pair of concerns associated with the Watergate scandal, "lack of trust in government" and "corruption in government." Third came the nation's energy crisis.[1]

Gerald Ford saw these problems as the greatest of his presidency. In July 1975, after almost a year as chief executive, he sat in the Oval Office as *New York Times* reporters interviewed him. They asked him what goals he had set for his administration and how he had fared in accomplishing them. He cited three: reducing inflation and unemployment, restoring public confidence in the White House after Watergate, and redressing the country's energy vulnerability. These challenges became themes of the Ford presidency and the 1970s, and he believed that he had taken the right steps toward solving them.[2]

These responses, from Americans and their president, typified the decade. Today, if you ask people about the 1970s, you might hear something about disco, pet rocks, or polyester. But these fads were more blips on the cultural radar screen than true national concerns. Instead, inflation dominated Americans' thoughts like few phenomena did during the post–World War II era. Energy shortages also haunted daily life for most of the decade. Americans viewed a national energy policy as a higher priority than national health insurance or public job programs. By May 1979, 57 percent of respondents still considered inflation the nation's most important problem, and 33 percent picked the energy crisis.[3] The economy and energy were such important

1

concerns that, in negotiating presidential debates during the 1976 campaign, some of Ford's advisers pressed for one debate devoted exclusively to these two matters. Ultimately, trust in public leaders, another critical issue of the era, helped to determine that election's outcome. The integrity of public officials continued to be a driving force in politics for the rest of the decade (and into the 1980s, when character issues torpedoed Ronald Reagan's 1987 nomination of Douglas Ginsburg to the Supreme Court and Senator Gary Hart's 1988 campaign for the presidency).[4] Two of these defining issues were inextricably linked, because high energy prices fueled inflation. In early 1975, Ford's principal economic adviser, Alan Greenspan, surveyed how much the economy had changed since the 1960s and concluded that the "immediate problem is oil."[5] Richard Nixon's presidency bequeathed all three issues to Ford in far worse condition than when Nixon took office.

These concerns were striking for another reason. Almost never surfacing during previous cold war decades, they uniquely defined the 1970s. In the 1950s and early 1960s, Americans generally trusted their leaders. They considered their presidents trustworthy men who skillfully managed the economy and protected their national security, which oil embargoes never threatened. Aided by low energy prices, the economy hummed along so well during these decades that Americans took its health for granted. With domestic issues under control, they scoped out the world. International issues—the containment of communism, the Korean and Vietnam wars, the arms race—dominated the nation's agenda before the 1970s. Presidents Dwight Eisenhower and John Kennedy devoted their inaugural addresses almost entirely to foreign affairs, and a 1964 survey showed that the top five issues on Americans' list of concerns were all foreign policy issues.[6]

What a difference a decade made. During the 1970s, Americans looked inward. This domestic focus—especially on the three overriding challenges that Ford confronted—helped to define the decade and distinguish it from the previous two decades. Gone was the buoyant optimism of before, when Americans enjoyed prosperity without galloping prices, contained communism abroad, and even landed men on the moon. In part, the reversal of fortune was prompted by the Vietnam War, which ate away at Americans' trust in their leaders, increased budget deficits and economic instability, and made Americans question whether the country should lead the free world so actively. By 1973, fewer young men described themselves as willing to go to war to defend America's interests or maintain its world power.[7] A neo-isolationist mood gripped the country, and it tightened as the economy deteriorated and Americans encountered difficulty in finding fuel to run their cars and heat their homes.[8] Then came Watergate and Nixon's resignation, and the country felt shattered.

These untoward circumstances help to explain a sentence on a display at the Gerald R. Ford Presidential Museum in Grand Rapids, Michigan: "Gerald Ford may have been among the unluckiest presidents of the 20th century." The nation's only unelected president, he came to the Oval Office during a constitutional crisis, without a mandate, and amid horrendous economic conditions. The country suffered double-digit inflation and soon fell into a deep recession. Preoccupation with domestic issues reduced the presidential authority of previous post–World War II decades, because in foreign policy presidents carried the greatest prestige and enjoyed a rally-around-the-flag effect. With domestic problems, Americans voiced more dissenting views. To make matters worse, Americans were cynical after Watergate, yet Ford had to summon their support while negotiating with aggressive opposition in Congress. The treacherous political environment was one of the worst that any chief executive has ever faced. How Ford addressed these challenges furnishes a compelling story of presidential leadership.

Cleaning Up Messes

Watergate and the "credibility gap" left from previous presidential administrations presented a personally demanding challenge to Ford. Although Watergate was shocking, Americans had been losing confidence in government for several years. They had grown frustrated, even frightened by the social conflicts of the 1960s, which the government failed to quell and, indeed, even contributed to, as Lyndon Johnson's and Richard Nixon's deceptive conduct of the Vietnam War generated deep mistrust of the presidency.

Nixon's behavior, especially in his second term, further crippled public trust. Nixon concentrated power in his office and blocked access to himself, nearly shutting down the lines of communication between the White House and Congress. Nixon never got along with the Democratic Congress; he never really intended to, and he ignored constitutional limits on presidential power. Trust in the presidency plummeted when Nixon resigned from office in disgrace. William Hungate, a Democratic congressman from Missouri who had decided on a career in government service after returning from World War II, opted to retire in 1975. His passion for the job had burned out, and he felt disappointed by the distrust and disillusionment toward politicians: "Politics has gone from an age of 'Camelot' when all things were possible to the age of 'Watergate' when all things are suspect."[9]

The constitutional crisis coincided with economic decline. Since the end of World War II, most Americans had known prosperity. The U.S. economy was the most powerful in the world, enabling millions to experience rising standards of living, low inflation, and low unemployment. Economic expansion seemed limitless; indeed, the liberal tenets that dominated American political thought during the 1960s preached the belief that this growth would continue unabated. Government planners were primarily concerned with ensuring full employment; inflation was of secondary importance.[10]

Yet by the late 1960s, the post–World War II economic boom slowed down; by the 1970s, it had ended. Labor productivity slumped after the late 1960s, and manufacturing employed a declining share of workers, reflecting deindustrialization. The country's share in world markets slipped, especially in mainstay industries like automobiles and steel. In 1951, the sixteen leading industrial nations of the world did 30 percent of their business with the United States; by 1971, the United States accounted for 18 percent of their world trade.[11] Other parts of the world, like Japan and Western Europe, competed successfully with the United States for slices of the world market. Americans could see signs of this change in their streets, as peppy, fuel-thrifty imported cars began to outsell clunky American models.

The worst sign of economic decline was inflation. Averaging only 1.6 percent annually between 1948 and 1965, inflation increased steadily and topped 12 percent in 1974.[12] Americans wondered if high inflation would stay forever. And again, the federal government failed. Nixon's policies, such as wage and price controls, were feckless, even counterproductive, and by 1973 he was too embroiled in the Watergate scandal to pay enough attention to the economy. Compounding the inflation, economic growth became sluggish and unemployment relatively high. This combination of high inflation laced with anemic economic performance marked a bewildering phenomenon, "stagflation." Ford saw the worst of it. When he took office, inflation was over 12 percent; just a few months later, the picture was entirely different. As Ford recalled, "By early December [1974], our economy was having a tremendous change. We went from inflationary problems to unemployment problems. And by January of 1975, we were in the worst post–World War II economic recession. . . . And the net result was, instead of fighting inflation, we were fighting a recession."[13]

A major contributor to the economic downturn was the energy crisis. U.S. oil consumption had increased dramatically in the post–World War II years, rising from 6.5 million barrels a day in 1950 to 13.9 million barrels in 1970.[14] Meanwhile, domestic oil production peaked in 1970, then began to decline, and the United States relied increasingly on imported oil, so that by the 1970s the United States imported one-third of its oil. The government adopted disastrous policies that reduced the country's oil supplies, setting the stage for a devastating display of American vulnerability during the Arab oil embargo of 1973–74, which some observers called an "economic Pearl Harbor." That winter the country suffered fuel shortages, long lines at gas stations, and frayed tempers. Americans chastised themselves for a gluttonous appetite for energy. Ominously, they believed assessments like that from economist Walter Heller, who stated that "the era of cheap oil and gasoline is rapidly slipping into history, never to return."[15]

The challenges of the 1970s were disorienting. Americans had never experienced such domestic problems in the post–World War II era. The president of Ohio State University, Harold Enarson, worried about declining confidence and faith. "The energy shortage is the least important of the shortages in our life," he said. "The American society is now short of those attributes that, mattering the most, undergird all else: integrity, high purpose, confidence in one another, faith in a brighter future."[16]

Many cultural phenomena of the 1970s owed their popularity to the troubled times, as Americans needed some way to escape or soften the difficult reality of life. The popular music of the decade was more mellow and lighthearted than that of the 1960s, typified by recording artists such as the Captain and Tennille, the Carpenters, Barry Manilow, and Neil Sedaka. The top-rated television program of the mid-1970s was ABC's *Happy Days* comedy, set in 1950s Milwaukee. The popularity of the series, its *Laverne and Shirley* spin-off, director George Lucas's motion picture *American Graffiti* (1973), and the Broadway musical *Grease* showed a nostalgia for the 1950s, a prosperous decade and a more innocent, tranquil time before the turmoil of Vietnam and Watergate.[17]

Some cultural commentators have explained the success of the 1970s' highest grossing film, *Star Wars* (1977), by describing it as an antidote to the national malaise. With the country buffeted by forces that seemed evil, *Star Wars* offered an escapist reaffirmation of the nation's virtues. Americans wanted their country once again to have the determination and force of Jedi knight Luke Skywalker, battling the evil Darth Vader. *Los Angeles Times* writer Eric Harrison observed, "America was tired of complications in 1977 when the first *Star Wars* was released. Vietnam, Watergate, and social unrest had rattled our brains. The oil embargo showed us how weak we had become. We'd lost our sense of who we were. George Lucas reminded us."[18]

Perhaps Lucas could inspire Americans, but could a president? Gerald Ford took office under extraordinary circumstances. He had to lead a country whose morale had been battered by rude shocks—assassinations, social unrest and fragmentation, the Vietnam War, Watergate, the energy crisis, stagflation, and runaway government spending. Ford navigated the country through uncharted waters and could not repair to any tested, proven doctrines.[19] No president ever had to confront simultaneously what Ford called the "three domestic devils"—inflation, recession, and the energy crisis. Any one of the devils, by itself, would have been trouble enough. Coming together, they constituted a tangled skein, each related to the other yet requiring separate attention and treatment.[20]

Making Ford's challenges particularly significant, the political and economic landscape shifted under his feet. By the 1970s, Keynesian economic orthodoxy, which government fiscal planners had practiced almost religiously for decades, crumbled under the weight of stagflation and uncontrollable government spending and deficits. Massachusetts Institute of Technology professor Paul Samuelson's economics textbook, standard college reading for much of the post–World War II era, claimed, "Economic science knows how to use monetary and fiscal policy to keep any recessions that break out from snowballing into lasting chronic slumps."[21] But in 1974, the country slipped into a recession so deep that some Americans feared it would deteriorate into a depression.

The debate over how best to deal with these problems was divided into two camps, separated by just one mile in Washington. Capitol Hill, which Democrats had controlled since 1955, squared off against the White House, which Republicans had occupied since 1969. As Ford raced to develop programs to deal with the nation's challenges, the debate sharpened. In explaining what had gone wrong with the economy, the fiscally conservative Ford blamed excessive government activity and federal deficits. On Capitol Hill, the Democratic Congress sought to ameliorate joblessness through government assistance programs, which Ford targeted for reduction.

Ford's struggles were difficult not just because of the nature of the crises. He operated against an environment that resisted his policies. The public and the press had entered an era of diminishing trust and confidence in government leaders. The media, Congress, and even the right wing of Ford's own party challenged his authority and never accepted his approach to the country's problems. In addition, Ford had difficulty in making his ideas attractive and inspiring. He could not convince Americans of the logic of his ideas, the economic achievements of his administration, or the importance of his goals.

Although criticized for lacking visionary leadership, Ford had clear priorities and a guiding philosophy. His first objective involved calming the country and repairing relations between the White House and Capitol Hill.

But Ford also focused on economic objectives, such as lowering federal expenditures and the deficit to contain his cardinal foe, inflation. He also had to reassure America's allies that the country remained an active world player, recent setbacks notwithstanding, and he had to revitalize a Republican Party so fragmented and weak that it bore the stench of death.

Ford's press secretary, Ron Nessen, reflected that "Ford's role in history was to clean up other people's messes." In a coarse metaphor, Nessen recounted an incident during one Christmas with the First Family in Vail, Colorado. A family dog had an accident on the floor, and when a White House steward went to scoop up the mess, Ford rose from the family dinner table and cleaned it himself. "No man should have to clean up after another man's dog," he told the steward. On a national level, Nessen thought that the "messes [Ford] inherited included: the shattered faith of the people in their president as a result of Watergate . . . [and] a sick economy ready to plunge precipitously because of mismanagement by earlier presidents and Congresses."[22] This work will examine how Ford fared in cleaning up the messes of the 1970s.

At the time, the view of Ford's performance was unkind. Liberal reporters pummeled him, his public approval ratings were stuck below 50 percent, and he lost the 1976 election. The view has begun to change. Two decades after Ford left office, against the backdrop of the scandal-tainted presidency of Bill Clinton, pundits reevaluated their harsh assessments of Ford. In 1996, journalist Richard Reeves, whose scathing 1975 book *A Ford Not a Lincoln* inflamed negative perceptions of Ford, offered an unusual mea culpa. In an article entitled "I'm Sorry, Mr. President," Reeves admitted that he had been needlessly cruel toward Ford, who "had done a much better job than I had predicted or imagined." Reeves acknowledged that Ford generated trust while in office and "checked or slowed the slide toward today's foul public cynicism."[23] In a similar vein, after Ford suffered a small stroke at the 2000 Republican National Convention, Anthony Lewis of the *New York Times* wrote, "One of my greatest regrets as a newspaper columnist is how I underrated Gerald Ford when he was in the White House. It is time, past time, to say what a model of decency and respect for the law he has been."[24] As this book will illustrate, the new appreciation for Ford has considerable merit.

Who Was Gerald Ford?

Susan Ford was happy. The sixteen-year-old daughter of House minority leader Gerald Ford had just won a $5 bet with her mother. Susan had wagered that President Nixon would pick her father to be the next vice president, to succeed

Spiro Agnew. Nixon loved pulling surprises, so he kept his choice confidential, and speculation ran rampant throughout the nation's capital. Thinking the president might be calling them, many Republican politicians in Washington stood by their telephones the evening Nixon was to notify his nominee. Congressman Ford just finished swimming laps in his pool when the phone rang. Susan answered it and yelled, "Dad, the White House is calling." In a private Oval Office meeting earlier that day, Nixon had informed Ford that he would be the vice-presidential nominee but asked him to keep that information secret, not even telling his family. Now, Nixon telephoned to make it official, and congratulatory calls flooded the Ford house. At one point, when a well-wisher called, Susan was on one telephone line, telling her friends the exciting news. "Tell her to get off the phone," her father said. He thought for a moment and added, "Tell her the Vice President told her to get off. That's the only way to impress a teenager."[25]

From that evening in October 1973, the Fords' lives changed quickly and dramatically. Their quiet Virginia home became the center of activity and media attention. The garage was transformed into a Secret Service command center, staffed twenty-four hours a day, and the driveway had to be ripped up and rebuilt with reinforced concrete to withstand the weight of armored limousines.[26] That was just the beginning. In accepting the vice presidency, Ford assumed that he would merely serve out the balance of Agnew's term. Instead, his appointment as vice president sent him on a trajectory that, within less than a year, landed him in the presidency.

The man charged with leading the country through the challenges of the 1970s was described by admirers and detractors alike as an ordinary man in extraordinary circumstances.[27] Gerald Rudolph Ford Jr. came from humble beginnings. He was born Leslie Lynch King Jr. on July 14, 1913, in Omaha, Nebraska, and his parents divorced when he was two years old. He was raised in Grand Rapids, Michigan, his mother's hometown. There his mother remarried, and the young boy was renamed after his stepfather, Gerald R. Ford Sr. Jerry Ford was later compared to the furniture produced in that city — solid and plain, possessed of the virtues of middle America.[28] At Grand Rapids's South High School, Ford was a serious student who concentrated on his studies, part-time work, and football. The young Ford was a star football center, played basketball, and ran track. His parents, with four children to raise, were always pressed for money and wanted the gifted athlete to take part-time jobs while he was in school, so Ford mowed lawns and grilled hamburgers at a restaurant across the street from his high school.

After high school, Ford attended the University of Michigan, where he pursued his passion for football, playing for two national championship teams and named the team's most valuable player his senior year in addition to All–Big Ten honors. In 1935, he graduated in the top 25 percent of his class, majoring in economics. Passing up offers to play professional football with the Detroit Lions and the Green Bay Packers, Ford set his sights on law school. He took a position as an assistant football coach at Yale University and, by his second year, grew determined to enroll in the law school. But the faculty was dubious: here was a former college athlete, now a coach, who wanted a place in a law school where more than two-thirds of the students had achieved Phi Beta Kappa status as undergrads. Ford persuaded the law school faculty to allow him to take courses part-time, and he performed well enough to be admitted as a fully matriculated student. While working full-time as a coach, Ford earned his law degree, graduating in 1941 in the top quarter of a class that included such talents as future secretary of state Cyrus Vance, future Supreme Court justice Potter Stewart, future Pennsylvania governor William Scranton, and future Peace Corps director Sargent Shriver. Returning to Grand Rapids, Ford started a law practice with a college friend, Philip Buchen, but after just one year left to join the U.S. Navy and fight in World War II.[29]

Returning home after the war, Ford joined a law firm, but in 1948 he made a decision that changed his life. He decided to enter the Republican primary to challenge Congressman Bartel Jonkman for Michigan's fifth district seat. At the time, foreign affairs dominated the political landscape. The primary contrasted Jonkman's fervent isolationism—he opposed the Marshall Plan, for example—with Ford's internationalism. Ford ran against heavy odds. A political novice, he faced a Dutch man in a Dutch town, not to mention a ten-year House veteran and protégé of Frank McKay, a Grand Rapids political boss. Moreover, in the conservative fifth district, Ford's internationalism and moderate Republicanism carried less appeal than Jonkman's views. But the overconfident Jonkman took Ford lightly and exerted little effort against him.[30] Endorsed by Michigan's senator Arthur Vandenberg, Ford won the primary and cruised to an easy victory in the general election. That same year, he also married Betty Bloomer, a Grand Rapids resident who had studied at Martha Graham's dance school in New York City.

One of Congressman Ford's first big breaks came in 1950, when he received a seat on the powerful House Appropriations Committee. Ford's work on the committee tutored him on the intricacies of the federal budget. He stressed fiscal discipline and supported President Eisenhower's drive to balance the federal budget.[31] In 1963, Ford gained national exposure when President Johnson appointed him to the Warren Commission investigating the Kennedy assassination. When Johnson asked him, Ford at first demurred, saying that his congressional duties were already demanding, but the president practically ordered him to serve on the commission as a national duty. Ford worked tirelessly, reviewing graphic autopsy photos and x-rays of the slain president, visiting Dallas, retracing and timing the steps of Lee Harvey Oswald from the sixth floor of the book depository to the street below, and interviewing Jack Ruby (who told Ford that he shot Oswald to spare Jacqueline Kennedy from returning to Dallas to testify at a trial). In the end, Ford supported the Warren Commission's conclusion that no evidence of a conspiracy existed, and Ford and his first campaign manager, Jack Stiles, authored a book, *Portrait of the Assassination*, detailing the commission's findings.[32]

Ford's House career spanned a quarter of a century. Never regarded as a brilliant innovator in the House, Ford compensated with diligence and amiability for what he lacked in creative fire.[33] His 90 percent attendance record was one of the best on Capitol Hill. His reputation for congeniality and his absence of enemies, combined with hard work and an ability to compromise sensibly, also propelled him to the top of the Republican House leadership. In 1964, by a slim margin, Ford's colleagues elevated him to chairman of the House Republican Conference. After Barry Goldwater's disastrous defeat and the calamitous Republican losses in the 1964 elections, the GOP hungered for an image makeover, seeking to build a reputation as a more progressive party. A disgruntled group of House Republicans banded together and selected Ford as a candidate to depose the minority leader, Charles Halleck of Indiana, whose stodgy and truculent ways did the party little good.[34] In January 1965, their coup succeeded: Ford defeated Halleck to become the new minority leader. His ultimate political goal, the House speakership, was one step closer.

As minority leader, Ford earned a reputation as a conciliator, mending the breach between the conservative and moderate wings of his party, stressing compromise and collegiality. He once explained, "You have to give a little, take a little, to get what you really want, but you don't give up your principles." No great orator, he spoke simply, with little inflection in his voice and no bombast, avoiding grand ideas or abstractions, instead relying on facts and figures that some audiences considered boring. Ford belonged to an unlucky generation of congressional Republicans, almost always in the minority, never able to muster the votes to advance new or bold programs. To avoid the GOP's being branded as negative or obstructionist, he opposed President Johnson's programs largely for fiscal reasons, not just for the sake of opposing, urging Democrats to recognize the expense of their programs. "The minority has the responsibility of pointing out 'the other side' and this includes the cost of the program or project," he said.[35]

As minority leader in the 1960s, Ford sounded the tenets of moderate Republican conservatism that he would repeat as president in the 1970s. He wanted less government intervention in people's lives and more reliance on private initiative and the workings of the free market. He warned against the "explosion of federal spending" and worried about the "haunting image of inflation" caused by federal deficits and federal borrowing. He believed that "private ownership and free enterprise best serve economic progress" and argued that government—like any household—should be forced to live within its budget. In the thousands of votes he cast during his congressional career, Ford established himself as a solid fiscal conservative. (The conservative Americans for Constitutional Action gave him an overall 77 percent rating.)[36]

A quarter-century of friendship and conservative kinship translated into the minority leader's firm support for Richard Nixon. As chairman of the Republican National Convention in 1968, Ford backed his friend against rivals Ronald Reagan and Nelson Rockefeller. Once Nixon was elected, the minority leader loyally supported the president, whose controversial policies often forced Ford into uncomfortable positions. At various times, Ford found himself defending wage and price controls, Nixon's conduct of the Vietnam War, the supersonic passenger jet, and the doomed Supreme Court nominations of Clement Haynsworth and G. Harrold Carswell.[37] In 1973, Ford recorded the second-highest rate of support for Nixon in the House and voted to sustain all of Nixon's vetoes.[38] Nixon's landslide 1972 reelection victory, however, failed to translate to broader political gains; the Republicans held just 192 seats in the House. The continuing minority status of the GOP forced Ford to reevaluate his career. He wanted the House speakership so badly that he turned down opportunities to run for governor of Michigan, and in 1968 he casually dismissed suggestions that he make a bid to be Nixon's running mate, gambling that the Republicans would soon win the House. With the GOP unlikely to gain control of the chamber, Ford faced bitter reality. His goal of the speakership was beyond reach. So, early in 1973, he agreed with his wife, Betty, that he would run for one more term and then retire.[39]

National events propelled Ford's career plans onto a different path. In a scandal unrelated to Watergate, Vice President Spiro Agnew was accused of accepting bribes while governor of Maryland and even while vice president. In October 1973, he resigned from office, only the second vice president in history to do so.[40] The vice presidency was vacant, and with Watergate transfixing the country and with mounting revelations of criminal behavior within the White House, the Agnew resignation prompted Ford to despair privately, "I just wonder how much more of this the country can take."[41]

In light of his stormy relations with Capitol Hill and the brewing scandal, Nixon needed an uncontroversial replacement for the pugnacious, corrupt Agnew. Operating under the Twenty-fifth Amendment, ratified in 1967, he chose Ford.[42] Ford was not Nixon's first choice. Nelson Rockefeller, Ronald Reagan, and John Connally all ranked higher on the president's list of possibilities.[43] But Ford was the least offensive, a decent man who could add ballast to Nixon's foundering presidency. He could win easy confirmation by Congress, thanks to his popularity and reputation for honesty, and he could work to repair Nixon's troubled relationship with the legislative branch. House Speaker Carl Albert told Nixon that Ford was probably the only potential nominee that his Democratic colleagues would find acceptable.[44] Upon learning of Nixon's choice of Ford, Democratic senator Frank Church of Idaho commented, "It's a very good thing for the country we're not likely to have a protracted [confirmation] struggle."[45]

Congress approved Ford by resounding margins, 387–35 in the House and 92–3 in the Senate, and on December 6, 1973, he was sworn in as the nation's fortieth vice president. His acceptance speech, short and modest, had a typically self-deprecating touch. The new vice president told his Capitol Hill audience, "I am a Ford, not a Lincoln. My addresses will never be as eloquent as Mr. Lincoln's. But I will do my very best to equal his brevity and plain speaking."[46] Ford's swearing-in was greeted with a standing ovation and a palpable sense of relief in the Capitol rotunda. Representatives of both parties felt that they finally had a friend in the increasingly bunkered Nixon White House.[47]

Vice President Ford believed Nixon's assurances that he was innocent of the Watergate affair, and he publicly defended the president. But as Nixon's presidency sank, Ford distanced himself from the chief executive. He had a fine line to tread: he could not continue to support a president guilty of wrongdoing, yet he could not appear eager to push Nixon out so that he could become president. Ford recalled, "If I was critical of Nixon, people would have said, 'He's trying to get his job.' If I were not critical, people were saying I was part of a conspiracy."[48] Because of this delicate predicament, Ford spent as little time as possible in the capital. Since the embattled president could do no campaigning, the responsibility fell upon Ford to be the GOP's leader and chief spokesman.[49] He traveled extensively during his eight months as vice president, logging more than five hundred personal appearances in forty states.[50] "I'm trying to do everything I can to put the party back together," he explained.[51]

Nixon's demise was a distinct possibility, and members of Congress felt more comfortable about hastening his exit with Ford as vice president. In October

1973, at the reception following Nixon's naming of Ford as his vice-presidential nominee, House majority leader Thomas P. "Tip" O'Neill alluded to the probable in a conversation with Secretary of Housing and Urban Development (HUD) James Lynn. Lynn approached O'Neill and said, "Tip, what do you think of this? History is being made tonight. The Twenty-fifth Amendment is being enacted for the first time. I bet we'll never see another night like this one." In his deep, gruff voice, O'Neill replied, "Don't count on it."[52]

It took eight more months for events to overtake Ford.

Part One
The Leadership Challenge

Chapter 1

Hungering for Heroes

In the mid-1970s, feeling betrayed by their president after Watergate, Americans hungered for new national heroes. They found Evel Knievel. The motorcycle stuntman wore a red, white, and blue jumpsuit; spoke openly of his love of country; denounced the Hell's Angels motorcycle gang; and urged his young fans to avoid drugs and wear helmets when motorcycling. Most important, Knievel performed stunts that demanded superhuman courage, leaping over cars, trucks, buses, and even the fountains at Las Vegas's Caesars Palace. A legend grew around him; awestruck children claimed that he had broken every bone in his body (in reality, his crashes had caused around thirty-five fractures).

On September 8, 1974, the daredevil performed what was supposed to be his greatest stunt. He tried to jump Idaho's Snake River Canyon on his Sky-Cycle X-3, a rocket-motorcycle hybrid. The steam-powered machine was to shoot off a ramp and fly at 200 miles per hour across the 1,600-foot canyon. On that day, when Knievel pressed the ignition button, the Sky-Cycle roared up the ramp, but as it tried to sail across the enormous chasm, the safety parachute unfurled and the bike and rider floated slowly to the Snake River below. Rescuers plucked Knievel safely from the canyon floor. The daredevil received only scrapes and bruises; no broken bones this time. But he fractured his reputation. These were cynical times, and skeptics denounced the whole affair as a hoax, even accusing Knievel of intentionally deploying the parachute early.[1] The charges were untrue, but Knievel's hero status was tarnished for good.

On the same day that Knievel made his notorious Snake River Canyon jump, more than 2,000 miles away in Washington, D.C., Gerald Ford took the most controversial action of his presidency by pardoning Richard Nixon. There were some parallels. Knievel crashed and enraged fans and detractors alike, who felt that they had been cheated; Ford's public support crashed, and he, too, enraged supporters and opponents alike, who said that justice had been cheated, even accusing Ford of conspiratorial behavior. His presidency never fully recovered.

Post-Watergate Cynicism

On the morning of August 8, 1974, Vice President Ford had an appointment with the president. He walked into the Oval Office alone, unsure what Nixon would say. For months, the Nixon presidency had been hanging by a thread. On August 5, the thread snapped. The Supreme Court rejected Nixon's claim of executive privilege, which he had used in refusing to turn over taped recordings of Oval Office conversations. Nixon was compelled to release transcripts of Oval Office conversations indicating that he had wanted the Central Intelligence Agency (CIA) to obstruct the Federal Bureau of Investigation's (FBI) inquiry into the 1972 break-in at the Democratic Party headquarters in the Watergate office-apartment-hotel complex. This evidence became the "smoking gun" implicating the president in an attempt to cover up the scandal. The release of the transcripts cost Nixon what little support he had left in Congress and with the public. Impeachment was a certainty.

Yet rumors circulated that the battle-scarred president might hang on and fight for his political life. When Ford entered the room, Nixon was sitting behind his desk. After Ford sat down, the tired president spoke solemnly and slowly. "I have made the decision to resign," he began. "It's in the best interests of the country. I won't go into the details pro and con. I have made my decision." After a pause, Nixon added, "Jerry, I know you'll do a good job."[2] Ford would become the thirty-eighth president of the United States, at the helm of a country in crisis. His most pressing goal was to reestablish trust in government, which had evaporated during Watergate.

On August 9, 1974, as he assumed the presidency on a wave of goodwill, Ford offered words of reconciliation. Since the development of voice recording, a few presidential inaugural addresses have been powerful enough to be preserved almost as a historical archive that many citizens carry in their heads. Franklin Roosevelt's and John Kennedy's stand out, and Ford's became a classic as well. After taking the oath of office in the White House East Room, the new president spoke earnestly to the nation, his voice occasionally cracking with emotion. He declared, "My fellow Americans, our long national nightmare is over," which became the most quoted and best-remembered line of his presidency.[3] "Our Constitution works; our great Republic is a government of laws and not of men. Here the people rule," Ford continued. He reassured the nation, "I believe that truth is the glue that holds government together, not only our government, but civilization itself," and he pledged,

"In all my public and private acts as your President, I expect to follow my instincts of openness and candor with full confidence that honesty is always the best policy in the end."[4] These were words that Americans wanted—and needed—to hear.

By 1974, a series of presidential tragedies had brutalized Americans' political sensibilities, and Watergate was the coup de grâce. Kennedy had been murdered, Johnson had led the country into a painful war in Vietnam, and Nixon had prolonged the war. For Americans, Vietnam was tragic not just in its outcome but in how it was conducted. Johnson, Nixon, and government officials withheld critical information from the public. During the 1964 presidential campaign, Johnson preached restraint in Vietnam yet secretly planned more bombing raids and troop commitments against North Vietnam and misled the public and Congress about attacks on American destroyers in the Gulf of Tonkin. After deploying ground troops, Johnson tried to conceal from public view the enormous cost of the military effort. Taking their cue from the White House, top officials dissembled about the war. One assistant secretary of defense was even candid about government mendacity. In 1966, when a reporter questioned the credibility of "official" information on the war, he bluntly replied, "Look, if you think any American official is going to tell the truth, then you're stupid. Did you hear that—stupid." The 1968 Tet Offensive, during which the Viet Cong scored swift victories throughout South Vietnam, destroyed the credibility of American assessments that the enemy was almost vanquished and helped to drive Johnson from office. But Nixon followed Johnson's pattern of prevarication, continuing wildly optimistic assurances, exaggerating enemy losses and the effects of American bombing, and ordering secret bombing raids into Cambodia.[5] (Nixon's diplomatic efforts throughout the world depended on secrecy and deception, sometimes leading to breakthroughs, as with his 1972 visit to China, but always surprising the public.)

Because of the deceptive conduct of the war, Americans increasingly distrusted presidential actions and decried a growing "credibility gap," which became a euphemism for presidential lies.[6] In a 1967 speech, Congressman Gerald Ford attacked Johnson's war leadership, saying that "Vietnam gave rise to the credibility gap. Various Administration statements and actions involving Vietnam initially established the credibility gap and then widened it. This . . . has produced the deep frustration felt by the American people, a crisis of confidence at a time of international crisis for the Nation."[7] The trend toward distrusting the president had a corrosive influence on public approval ratings. During much of the post–World War II era, presidents won public approbation almost effortlessly. From 1953 to 1965, presidents usually scored an average of at least 60 percent in public approval, especially as Americans supported the president against the menace of communism. But Vietnam chipped away at this remarkable consensus, and as partisan sniping increased, Americans' regard for their presidents fell. Beginning in 1966, approval ratings slid, and presidents had a difficult time even cracking the 50 percent mark.[8]

The Nixon presidency dragged the public's trust in government down to a new low. (Ironically, Nixon had promised to be a healing president. During the turmoil of 1968, one of his campaign themes was "bring us together"; in a further irony, he promised that his administration would represent "law and order.")[9] Offenses of many different stripes continually assaulted the nation's moral sensibilities. The president underpaid and made questionable deductions on his income taxes, and at taxpayers' expense, he spent millions of dollars on additions to his California and Florida homes. Nixon also used the presidency for politicalcombat. He tarred political opponents as unpatriotic and kept track of them with an "Enemies List." He ordered freeze-outs of reporters who published unfavorable stories, barring them from communicating with administration officials. Some tactics were squalid. In early 1970, when the Senate debated Nixon's nomination of the undistinguished G. Harrold Carswell to the Supreme Court, the White House tried to sully the reputation of senators who opposed the nomination, spreading word that Birch Bayh once failed his bar exam and that Hubert Humphrey and George McGovern had restrictive covenants in the deeds to their houses forbidding their sale to blacks. (The Senate ultimately rejected Carswell's nomination.) When Senators McGovern and Mark Hatfield introduced an amendment to force American withdrawal from Vietnam, the Nixon administration oppugned their patriotism. By fighting so dirtily, the Nixon White House cut political lacerations that would not heal as long as he remained in office.[10]

Watergate gouged the deepest wounds. After a long, bitter battle over the Watergate tapes in the spring of 1974, Nixon released edited transcripts. Most Americans recoiled at what they read. The transcripts revealed the president as a man of mean moral character, with private behavior sharply at variance with his public image. Senate minority leader Hugh Scott of Pennsylvania called them "shabby, disgusting, immoral."[11] Small and petty men may commit small and petty crimes, but Nixon's peccadilloes, like cursing in private conversation, were offensive simply by the nature of his position. He disgraced not only himself but the presidency, an office that Americans revered.[12]

What damages a president damages the nation, and that was true with Watergate. Democratic senator Sam Ervin of North Carolina, who chaired the Senate committee investigating the scandal, hyperbolically called Watergate "the greatest tragedy this country has ever suffered, [worse than] the Civil War."[13] Watergate changed how Americans saw their government and their president more radically than any other event since the New Deal. But while the New Deal prompted Americans to view the federal government as a benevolent force and the president as their friend, Watergate convinced most Americans that their president was evil.[14] Heretofore, they thought that some sheriffs or mayors could be corrupt, but their president was somehow above seaminess. Watergate shattered the assumption of presidential decency.[15] At a dinner party in 1973, *Newsweek* writer Shana Alexander overheard CBS News anchorman Walter Cronkite saying, "I think we ought to take Lysol and scrub out the Oval Office." Alexander agreed, reflecting that Americans "share [Cronkite's] disgust and contempt for the soiled presidency; they too want to scrub it clean again."[16]

Public opinion polls reflected the plummeting confidence in government. Whereas trust in government stood at 76 percent in 1964—the highest rate in the world—it had dropped to 36 percent a decade later.[17] A 1975 poll revealed that 68 percent of Americans thought that the government had consistently lied to the American people over the past ten years. Irving Crespi of the Gallup Organization predicted, "If this trend persists, it is within the realm of possibility that the United States will in the near future experience its greatest crisis of confidence since 1933 [a Great Depression year]."[18]

One measure of American disgust with politicians and government was the low voter turnout in the 1974 elections, when only 38 percent of eligible voters cast ballots, the worst showing in three decades.[19] Surveys indicated a limited public confidence not just in the executive branch but in Congress. In 1975, one question from Maryland senator J. Glenn Beall's survey of constituents asked, "Do you have confidence in the ability of Congress to deal with today's problems?" Marylanders answered "no" by nearly 2 to 1. One Baltimore couple scoffed, "We don't have enough confidence—or trust—in our congressmen to let them take out the garbage." In Indiana, a woman wrote to Birch Bayh to tell him that all incumbents should resign from office. A popular bumper sticker simply read: IMPEACH SOMEONE.[20] This mood persisted when Ford ran for president in 1976, and in preparing the president for his debates against Jimmy Carter, adviser Doug Bailey suggested that Ford avoid mentioning his congressional experience—normally a political asset.[21]

Their moral fiber rubbed raw after Watergate, Americans had little stomach for shenanigans. In the mid-1970s, political careers lay ruined after revelations of scandal, like wreckage strewn across a field of ethical land mines. In October 1974, Washington Park police found Democratic congressman Wilbur Mills of Arkansas drunk in the Tidal Basin in the company of a spectacularly buxom stripper. The erudite Mills, who served as Ways and Means Committee chairman for more than a decade, was forced to relinquish the chairmanship and declined to run for reelection in 1976. That year the career of veteran Democratic congressman Wayne Hays of Ohio was ruined by scandal. Hays's twenty-seven-year-old secretary, Elizabeth Ray, made the stunning revelation, "I can't type, I can't file, I can't even answer the phone," yet she was on the House payroll for two years. The only services that she performed were sexual favors for the congressman. After initially denying the affair, Hays confessed and resigned in disgrace.[22]

The 1970s became an era of distrust in government. Presidents—indeed, the entire executive and legislative branches—faced relentless scrutiny by the public and press.[23] Republican congressman John B. Anderson of Illinois remarked that Ford "presided as our chief magistrate under the shadow—under the overpowering ethos of the time—which was that we had a president who had defiled his oath."[24] A clear signal of the times came with the 1975 investigations into the CIA. A firestorm in the media and on Capitol Hill broke out after a December 1974 New York Times article alleged that the CIA carried out "a massive, illegal domestic intelligence operation during the Nixon administration." Ford responded by forming a presidential commission to investigate the CIA. When the commission generally exonerated the agency, dissatisfied senators sprang into action, creating their own committee to look into the matter. It concluded that the agency needed congressional oversight, which was immediately implemented, signaling a dramatic change in the nation's intelligence operations. The CIA, notorious for spying, would itself be under surveillance to guard against illegal or improper activities.[25]

The post-Vietnam, post-Watergate suspicion was highly visible in the media. After covering the Vietnam War and Watergate and trapping the president in lies during both events, the press would not let presidential statements go unexamined. Reporters, hunting for fame, fortune, and Pulitzer Prizes, engaged in "investigative journalism" both in print and on television. (CBS's news magazine, 60 Minutes, became a top-rated program during the 1970s and spawned imitations such as ABC's 20/20.)[26] Ford became the subject of the more aggressive and cynical journalistic code. An example occurred in early 1975, when NBC White House correspondent Tom Brokaw interviewed him at the White House. The young reporter asked Ford if he was "intellectually up to the job of being president." The audacious question at once illustrated three phenomena: the new, bold press behavior; the diminished reverence that the media felt toward the presidency and its occupant; and the negative public image plaguing Ford. Ford replied by mentioning his solid academic performance at the University of Michigan and Yale Law School. But this was not enough. The next day, reporters demanded that the White House furnish transcripts of Ford's grades.[27] Jerald terHorst, Ford's first press secretary, commented that the "distrust was deep and almost endemic. . . . You couldn't talk about policy and the need for continuity without someone questioning whether there was a devious plot behind it all. The press had been feeding on Watergate and Vietnam for so long that it was hard to shift gears." Government officials, journalist Bob Woodward believed, were usually guilty as charged, which gave the press additional incentive to pursue aggressively allegations of wrongdoing.[28]

Candidates for public office tried various methods to inoculate themselves against charges of dishonesty. In the 1974 elections, for the first time ever, many candidates voluntarily disclosed information on their personal finances and released income tax records. Some set voluntary limits on the size of political contributions, often just $100.[29] As Birch Bayh ran for reelection in 1974, his campaign strategists emphasized the need to depict him as "honest, forthright, conscientious and hardworking. . . . Projecting honesty and accomplishment should be our primary goal."[30] The 1976 presidential primaries displayed candidates' devotion to the new "integrity chic"; many White House aspirants portrayed themselves as Washington outsiders or as unusually honest men ready to rush in and clean up the town. In challenging Ford for the Republican nomination, former California governor Ronald Reagan looked good because he had spent his entire career outside Washington. Bayh entered the lists promising to provide "moral leadership" for the country, and Arizona representative Morris Udall unabashedly trumpeted his own "integrity." Jimmy Carter was the most unblushing of all. A former peanut farmer and one-term governor of Georgia, Carter was the consummate Washington outsider and forged an impressive drive for the Democratic nomination with promises like "I will never lie to you." He strategically repeated phrases like the "Nixon-Ford" era to link Ford with his disgraced predecessor and bemoaned the "deep hunger" for reassurance that Americans felt after Vietnam and Watergate. Carter went so far as to vow that he would withdraw from the race if he were ever caught in a lie.[31] By winning the Democratic nomination and the presidency, Carter proved that he had struck a responsive chord.

"An Age of Nonheroes"

The national malaise of the 1970s produced a quest for new heroes. The first half of the twentieth century had been an exciting and sometimes terrifying age, with the rise of the automobile and the airplane, two world wars, the dawn of the nuclear era, and the onset of the cold war. With these historic developments came a line of immortals broad and deep: Henry Ford, the Wright brothers, Amelia Earhart, Franklin and Eleanor Roosevelt, Jackie Robinson, and Dwight D. Eisenhower. During the 1970s, the line had few additions.

U.S. News and World Report called the 1970s an "age of nonheroes" and noted, "In much of the world, an uneasy awareness is dawning among ordinary mortals that a shortage is developing in a much needed commodity: heroes. Nowhere in sight at this moment are replacements for the Lindberghs, the Pasteurs, the Babe Ruths, the Churchills and others who have given humanity its household words to utter, its feats to emulate and its leaders to follow." When Charles Lindbergh died in September 1974, Time regretted that "America lost not only one of its pioneers of the machine age but perhaps its last authentic hero." Especially lacking were leaders who could steer the nation through troubled times. During the summer of 1974, a Time cover story entitled "In Quest of Leadership" noted the dearth of not just heroes but leaders.[32]

The laments were understandable. Leaders had recently failed Americans, sometimes spectacularly. Even Dwight Eisenhower, a trusted, grandfatherly figure, had been caught in an embarrassing lie during the U-2 incident, when he initially denied that a U.S. plane captured by the Soviet Union was a reconnaissance jet. The episode marred his last year as president. Nixon's disgraceful exit was all the more shocking because he had been widely respected during his first years in office. The presidential prospects of Senator Edward Kennedy, the last surviving Kennedy brother, were ruined as a result of his Chappaquiddick scandal. In September 1974, Kennedy ended speculation about his plans for 1976 by declaring that he would not run. In a way, Kennedy became a victim of not just his own behavior but also the heightened concern over morality and integrity.[33]

As contemporary political idols fell, icons from history also tumbled to the ground. The faults of previously untouchable heroes were exposed, especially by journalists exercising more aggressive reporting. A spate of new newspaper accounts and books sullied John Kennedy, a legend whose idolatry had reached almost religious dimensions. Journalists began to give lurid accounts of Kennedy's dalliances, prescription drug use, and hidden illnesses. Washington Post executive editor Benjamin Bradlee published Conversations with Kennedy, which showed the slain president as a flawed human being— often vulgar, weak for vices like porn films, and disposed to make catty comments about other politicians. *The Search for JFK*, by naval historians Joan Blair and Clay Blair Jr., further debunked the Kennedy myth by assailing the callow lieutenant's behavior during the PT-109 incident of World War II, which the Kennedy clan embellished into an act of heroism.[34] Once larger than life, political heroes like Kennedy were reduced to smaller dimensions, destroying the ideals they represented and leaving Americans further adrift about whom they admired and whether they could any longer find leaders to respect and trust.

Americans anxiously groped about for new idols, and unlikely ones emerged. The 1976 film *Rocky* became a sleeper hit partly because the underdog boxer appealed to American's yearning for new heroes. The most improbable one to surface in the 1970s (besides Evel Knievel) was a politician—Harry Truman. "Trumania," a renewed admiration for the thirty-third president, swept the nation. Just two decades earlier, such sentiments would have been inconceivable. While president, Truman steadily lost popularity, and by his term's end many Americans despised him for "losing" China, dragging the country into the Korean War, and mishandling the economy. While campaigning for Congress in 1948, Gerald Ford unleashed harsh language on Truman, declaring that he "has neither the mental capacity nor the historical perspective to understand what is going on [in today's world]," and as a congressman, Ford blasted the president's record as "one which smacked of scandal and extreme partisanship."[35]

But after the sins of Watergate, Truman's appeal shot skyward. Truman bumper stickers and T-shirts appeared. Merle Miller's *Plain Speaking*, a book of Truman reminiscences, sold more than two million copies. The hit play *Give 'Em Hell, Harry* ran in major cities, and President Ford himself caught a performance in Washington. In 1974, the rock group Chicago released a song simply entitled "Harry Truman," with lyrics that captured the disillusionment of the times, bemoaning the country's condition and saying that Truman would "know what to do" to save the nation.

Ford became one of the new Truman fans, calling him one of his favorite presidents. He said he now admired the Missourian because he "had guts, he was plain-talking, he had no illusions about being a great intellectual, but he seemed to make the right decisions." Upon assuming office, Ford asked that a portrait of Truman be placed in the Cabinet Room, along with those of his two other favorite presidents, Lincoln and Eisenhower.[37] Americans reflected nostalgically on the hard-nosed, straightforward president who cared more about principles than polls. The Missourian spat in the eye of public opinion surveys, once scoffing, "I wonder how far Moses would have gone, if he had taken a poll in Egypt." Truman's blunt talk and forward manners, seen as flaws while he was in office, became virtues. (Prophetic and particularly appealing was his assessment of Richard Nixon as "a shifty-eyed, goddamn liar.") As Truman's daughter Margaret explained, "In our day, honesty was taken for granted."[38] By the 1970s, no longer.

Trumania showed that Americans hungered not just for leadership but for basic honesty. After Watergate, it was not enough to lead; one had to do so honestly. Ford knew that his primary task in government would be to reestablish Americans' confidence in their leaders. While vice president, Ford was asked what he would do for America if he could do but one thing. He thought for a moment and replied, "As I look at our problems, [it would be] anything I could do to restore public credibility and faith in our government. Why do I pick that? Because if the American people have full and strong faith in their government, it gives the leaders of our government bigger clout both at home and abroad." This objective became even more critical after Nixon's resignation. Ford believed that to be a successful president, "integrity is mandatory."[39]

Since his childhood in Michigan, Ford had learned the importance of honesty, which his stepfather had emphasized in three ironclad rules of conduct for Ford and his half brothers: work hard, speak the truth, and come to dinner on time.[40] During his congressional career, Ford built a reputation for honesty by, for example, refusing to put his wife on the congressional payroll. Many other members of Congress were less scrupulous. What Ford lacked in eloquence on the House floor, he tried to make up for with what he termed "straight talk." Jean McKee, a Grand Rapids lawyer who ran unsuccessfully for Ford's House seat in 1970 and 1972, commented, "You'd have to catch Jerry Ford smuggling heroin into the country to make people in Grand Rapids think he was dishonest."[41] After Ford's nomination for the vice presidency, an investigative microscope put Ford's reputation for honesty to a stiff test. Congress and the FBI conducted one of the most thorough searches into the background of a nominee in the history of American politics. The FBI assigned an army of 350 special agents nationwide to work on the investigation, checking everything imaginable. Agents even interviewed a football player from an opposing high school in Grand Rapids, whom Ford had once tackled during a game after the whistle, to ascertain whether the young Ford had played dirty. Agents also visited the Grand Rapids tailor shop that Ford had frequented for twenty-five years to inquire about his sartorial tastes and payment habits.[42] In all, the FBI interviewed more than a thousand people across the country—childhood friends, football teammates and opponents, college friends, professors, military officers, and politicians. The result was staggering: a 1,700-page file on Ford. When the investigations were done, Ford emerged clean, his reputation even enhanced.[43] The evidence indicated that Ford was a rare commodity: an honest politician. Yet Americans soon suffered a wrenching letdown.

The High and the Crash

During the twentieth century, vice presidents who succeeded to the presidency labored to fulfill the mandate of popular predecessors and follow their policies. Most notably, Johnson ran for election in 1964 pledging "Let us continue," a reference to the work that Kennedy had started. Theodore Roosevelt, Calvin Coolidge, and Harry Truman, while imprinting individual styles of presidential leadership, built on the their predecessors' personalities, either trying to equal their energy and expand the use of the modern communications at their disposal, as with Roosevelt and Truman, or emulating a laissez-faire, low-profile approach to the job, as with Coolidge. Unlike these men, Ford could not continue his predecessor's leadership style; he had to make a sharp break from it.[44]

Ford moved to reestablish public confidence in the White House. As the executive branch collectively held its breath after Nixon's departure, Ford's steady, calm demeanor provided reassurance. Budget Director Roy Ash recalled that after Nixon's helicopter lifted off from the White House lawn for the final time, White House staffers returned to their offices and, with a self-assured new president holding the reins, "it was business as usual." Ash called it a "seamless transition."[45] The stability that Ford projected was critical to maintaining morale among civil service workers throughout the executive branch. The public felt relief, too. James Cavanaugh, an associate director of the Domestic Council for both Nixon and Ford, recalled when, early in the Ford administration, the president's motorcade traveled to Capitol Hill for a bill-signing ceremony. As Cavanaugh looked at the citizens lining the streets, "There were smiles on their faces and greetings and waves. It was a sharp contrast to the last few weeks of the Nixon administration, when there were people mingling at the White House gates, all with sad faces, if not protest signs. It was if a new beginning had arrived."[46]

One of Ford's most important early decisions was his vice-presidential nomination of Nelson Rockefeller, the liberal Republican who had served as governor of New York for sixteen years. By selecting the eminent and well-respected Rockefeller, Ford hoped to reassure the country that the executive branch was in good hands again. Ford ordered that the Oval Office be swept clean of all listening devices, and he also graciously reached out to groups that Nixon had shunned. When Ford learned of Nixon's "Enemies List," he observed that a person "who can't keep his enemies in his head has got too many enemies." "During my first two weeks in office," he explained, "I made a strenuous attempt to show critics that an 'open' White House meant exactly that."[47] Noting that AFL-CIO president George Meany had not been a guest in the White House in over a year, Ford invited him for a chat. Other groups that Nixon had given the cold shoulder met with the new president, like the Congressional Black Caucus and a group of congresswomen supporting the Equal Rights Amendment, which to their great satisfaction Ford endorsed.[48] Ford opened the White House to so many of Nixon's old foes that humorist Art Buchwald quipped that when the Fords compiled their dinner guest lists, "they're working from an old Nixon enemies folder, which they mistakenly believe was the president's social list."[49]

At the conclusion of Ford's first week in office, he and Betty hosted a lively party for King Hussein and Queen Alia of Jordan that signaled the break from the morose last years of the Nixon reign. The dinner guests included several notorious Nixon "enemies," including World Bank president and former defense secretary Robert McNamara, anti-Nixon congressman Pete McCloskey of California, and reporters who had been in Nixon's doghouse. Ford happily recalled dancing to Jim Croce's "Bad, Bad Leroy Brown," and during the dancing Republican senator Mark Hatfield of Oregon yelled out an expression of emotion that many shared on that August night: "Happy New Year." As McNamara and his wife were leaving, they approached Ford and said, "Boy, what a change."[50] Paul O'Neill, associate director of the Office of Management and Budget, said that later in the year, at the 1974 White House Christmas reception, Ford announced to those present, "Welcome to *your* house." O'Neill recalled, "I'll never forget thinking, 'It's just the right touch.'"[51]

Ford had to repair damaged relations in many areas and especially with the media. Nixon had despised the press. Regularly referring to reporters as "the enemy," he thought that the liberal media constituted "the greatest concentration of power in the United States," and his administration singled out for special harassment reporters and newspapers that he considered hostile. The Nixon White House had Jack Anderson put under surveillance and browbeat *Newsday*, the *Boston Globe*, and the president's arch nemesis, the *Washington Post*, with tactics such as tax audits and exclusion from diplomatic trips. Ford generally liked reporters. He restored the practice of inviting reporters to the White House as social guests, which conveyed to the entire executive branch the attitude that the media were to be treated as friends. *Time* correspondent Hugh Sidey wrote of how differently the Ford White House regarded reporters: "The few times I was allowed into the back corridors of the White House during the Nixon years, the atmosphere was repressive — one of fear. . . . On my first pilgrimage into the sanctums of Ford, there was genial confusion. . . . I was given several handshakes and made to feel welcome."[52]

Ford's first press secretary, Jerald terHorst, wanted a clear break from the Nixon press conferences, in which a defensive, sometimes sweaty president faced a battery of reporters in the East Room, his back against the wall on the room's far side. As terHorst explained, "I did *not* want Jerry Ford standing behind a huge, bullet-proof podium with his back to the wall . . . as Richard Nixon and Lyndon Johnson did. That set-up made them look like caged men, surrounded by cameras and reporters, with the press in a feeding frenzy, almost like sharks. Jerry Ford agreed to let me fashion something that would be different, more open." TerHorst decided to reverse the seating arrangement, putting the president before the doorway of the great White House hallway, with the doors symbolically swung open. Gone was the massive podium that Nixon had used, replaced by a slender pedestal shaped like an hourglass, which gave a less obstructed view of the president and the hallway behind him. TerHorst explained that the new arrangement "was cosmetic, but it was also symbolic. It reinforced Ford's promise to be an open, accessible president."[53] (Presidents have used this seating arrangement ever since.) Moreover, at his first press conference Ford appeared without makeup, which signaled that he intended to remain the same man reporters had known in the House.[54]

Reporters responded enthusiastically, even excessively, to Ford's unpretentious style. During his first month as president, they indulged in an orgy of praise, exulting that Ford had restored the presidency to the people, tickling themselves over his common touch. The media seemed agog that the nation had a president human enough to engage in everyday tasks like fixing his own English muffins for breakfast or appearing in pajamas on the front porch of his Alexandria, Virginia, home, looking for the morning newspaper. (In a thoughtful gesture to allow the Nixon family time to move out of the White House, for his first two weeks as president, Ford continued to live at his suburban home. Like thousands of other federal employees, the president commuted daily to Washington.) *Newsweek* paid homage to Ford in almost messianic terms, commenting that "the manner of his coming felt as cool and cleansing to a soiled Capital as a freshening Lake Michigan breeze."[55] *Time* gave a similarly glowing tribute: "Last week Washington and the nation seemed satisfied to rejoice in such simplicities as having a Chief Executive who worked in his shirtsleeves, who said what he meant and meant what he said, who by his honesty and accessibility was swiftly exorcising the pinched ghosts of the Nixon era from the White House." Naturally, Ford felt flattered. "In the first month of my Presidency," he wrote, "I had received the kind of press coverage that every politician loves but almost never gets." But with a dose of realism, he added, "I'd been in politics long enough to realize that popularity of this magnitude wouldn't continue forever."[56] The media praise of Ford was like a giant, overblown balloon, just waiting to be popped.

It burst on September 8, 1974. That Sunday, Ford went to a church across Lafayette Square from the White House. Strangely, he went without his family and sat alone in a pew. After receiving Holy Communion, he returned to the Oval Office.[57] From there, Ford addressed the nation on television and announced a shocker. He decided to grant Nixon "a full, free, and absolute pardon" for all offenses he had committed "or may have committed" while president. Ford believed the action was in the country's best interests. After just one month in office, he found that he had to devote inordinate time and energy to the lingering problems of the former president. Exasperated, he wanted to sweep these problems aside and focus his and the nation's attention on urgent issues, especially the economy, the energy crisis, and foreign policy. Ford recalled that he was devoting "about 25 percent of my time listening to lawyers argue what I should do with Mr. Nixon's papers, his tapes, et cetera. At the very same time, our country was faced with serious economic problems, inflation, higher interest rates, unemployment going up. And we had allies that were uncertain as to what would happen. And the Soviet Union—we never knew what they might do in this change of presidency." Confronted by such challenges, Ford decided that "the right thing for me to do was to spend one hundred percent of my time on the problems of 240 million Americans and not 25 percent of my time on the problems of one man."[58] Despite Ford's eloquent inaugural words, the long national nightmare was not over. It lingered on, and Ford thought that pardoning Nixon would finally end it.[59]

Most Americans did not see it that way. An avalanche of criticism buried the White House, as more than 30,000 messages poured in, running six-to-one against Ford's decision. When the president appeared in Pittsburgh the next day, protesters chanted, "Jail Ford, jail Ford."[60] Ford's rating in the Gallup opinion poll plummeted from 66 percent to 49 percent, the worst single drop in the history of that poll.[61] One constituent telegrammed House Speaker Carl Albert, "Ford gutted justice. Do something," while another called on

Albert to impeach Ford.[62] Angry critics fumed that Ford allowed Nixon to escape not only punishment but even a trial. The most powerful man in the disgraced administration went free, while subordinates—more than forty in all—received indictments or marched off to prison.

Amid the furor, Ford received a blow that hurt personally as much as politically. The morning that Ford was to pardon Nixon, Jerald terHorst entered the Oval Office to discuss arrangements for the upcoming telecast. Ford could tell that something was on terHorst's mind, and the press secretary finally pulled out an envelope and handed him a letter. The message explained to Ford that terHorst opposed the decision to pardon Nixon. It concluded, "Thus it is with a heavy heart that I hereby tender my resignation as Press Secretary to the President, effective today." Ford was stunned. He stared outside the window for a moment, and then turned to face his friend of twenty-five years. "I hope that you will reconsider and change your mind," he said. TerHorst replied, "My decision is final." His startling departure only poured more fuel on the fire, aggravating the president's attempts to explain the pardon. Ford felt hurt and betrayed by his longtime friend.[63]

Politics is a fickle business, and while almost every president begins his term with a honeymoon, many eventually get burned by public opinion. (One of the only presidents who had no honeymoon, remaining unpopular throughout his term, was Abraham Lincoln, whose controversial election triggered the secession of Southern states and, one month after he took office, civil war.) As Franklin Roosevelt wryly noted, the legendary Mr. Dooley, a humorous Irish-brogued character created by journalist Finley P. Dunne, commented that people build triumphant arches for their heroes only to pull bricks from the arches and hurl them at the heroes. The list of twentieth-century presidents who left office defeated or discredited included many whom the public initially embraced: Hoover, Truman, Johnson, Nixon, Carter, and George H.W. Bush. All of these men were broken on the wheel of public opinion and left office either by resigning, losing an election, or wisely declining to seek another term. But the political destruction of all of these men was gradual, lasting months or years. Ford's fall was instantaneous, and it illustrated the converse of Lyndon Johnson's coarse principle that "in politics, overnight chicken shit can turn to chicken salad."[64]

For a brief moment, some Americans had felt that they found a "hero" in their new president, a forthright leader in whom they could repose their trust. By pardoning Nixon so abruptly, Ford punctured those feelings. The pardon reignited the cynicism pervading the country. The angry accusations and the jolting end to Ford's honeymoon reflected the national mood after Watergate, when Americans thought that all political motives were morally bankrupt.[65]

Ford's plunge down the cataract of public opinion showed that the media benediction of his young presidency rested on shaky ground. Reporters still held a large reservoir of distrust for politicians and stood ready to give vent at any moment.[66] In his highly critical 1975 book, *A Ford Not a Lincoln*, journalist Richard Reeves scored Ford and his ilk, writing that all politicians were "in the information-deploying, image-making business. Their stock-in-trade is favorable partial truths."[67]

Some reporters chastised themselves for having been too quick and fulsome in praising the new president. Columnist Mary McGrory noted that the press was responsible for the euphoria over Ford: "The Washington press corps lost its head over Gerald Ford. A thousand reporters turned overnight into flacks for Jerry Ford. They raved about his decency, his smile, his English muffins, his peachy dancing. . . . He perhaps did us all a favor by slapping us awake that Sunday morning."[68] As for "the exhilarating atmosphere of honesty and belief that surrounded Gerald Ford in his first month in office," a *Time* staff writer commented, "that unreal glow is gone, and it will probably never return." The magazine was right. Never again did the press view Ford in a generous light, nor did he ever again enjoy public opinion ratings over 70 percent; indeed, his ratings seldom crept above 50 percent. As Reeves commented, after the pardon "reporters just turned a full 180 degrees and began to pound Ford and his lousy English muffins."[69]

Ford was shocked at the public outcry that the pardon engendered. "I thought the public would understand my reasons for the decision, which I tried to explain. I thought perhaps the public would consider the resignation of a president as sufficient public punishment, shame, and disgrace," he said. He had expected an understanding and forgiving public and instead got an angry one. The adverse public reaction was one of Ford's greatest disappointments while in office.[70]

Most damaging to Ford was speculation that as vice president, he had cooked up a secret "deal" with Nixon to trade the presidency for a pardon. Outside the White House, protesters hoisted a bedsheet that read, "Promise Me a Pardon and I'll Make You a President."[71] Ford sincerely believed that he had made no deal. (The charges echoed the accusations of a "corrupt bargain" that haunted John Quincy Adams immediately after the House of Representatives elected him president in 1825, as supporters of the defeated Andrew Jackson claimed that Adams had fashioned a secret deal with Henry Clay to exchange Clay's support for Adams in the House with Clay's appointment as secretary of state. The charges were never substantiated, but Adams began his presidency under a cloud of suspicion that he never could dispel. He subsequently lost the 1828 election to Jackson.) A week before

Nixon resigned, White House chief of staff Alexander Haig met with Ford to inform him that the president might resign. At this meeting, Haig presented Ford with six possible scenarios for a Nixon resignation (including, incredibly, the president's pardoning himself and then resigning). The sixth option was for Nixon to resign and then have Ford pardon him. Ford refused to agree to any of the options, but when he told speechwriter and longtime friend Robert Hartmann about the sixth option, Hartmann was furious. Ford should have immediately rebuffed Haig at the mention of that scenario, he insisted. At Hartmann's urging, Ford telephoned Haig to confirm explicitly that he had agreed to no deals.[72]

But just a few weeks later, the new president informed his aides that he wanted to pardon Nixon. Ford believed that, in his conversations with Haig, he had set no preconditions for Nixon's resignation nor committed himself to a pardon. No evidence ever surfaced to suggest any collusion between Ford and Nixon. Years later, Ford acknowledged that some observers may interpret his discussion with Haig as involving "a deal," but he never agreed to Haig's proposals and made his decision independently, using his own judgment and appraisal of a pardon's merits.[73] The most convincing construction of Ford's action was that he indeed viewed it as a way to put Nixon and his crimes behind and concentrate on more important national issues.[74] The pardon was critical if Ford were ever to dispel the miasma of Watergate and begin his own presidency. Republican congressman Elford Cederburg of Michigan commented that a pardon "was the only thing Ford could do that made any sense. He could have chewed on that problem for all the time he was there [as president]. He had to get rid of it."[75] A Nixon trial would have kept the former president in the headlines for months, even years, diverting attention from more pressing issues, poisoning political dialogue, and damaging America's image throughout the world.[76] Moreover, finding an impartial jury was impossible, and the former president's health was so poor that he may not have survived a trial. Instead, Ford extracted from Nixon an agreement to turn over to the government his tapes and papers, which have continued to provide more valuable information than a trial would have, dribbling out new insights into his words and actions while in office.[77]

Many decisions that Ford made while in office involved a high political cost in the short term while taking years for critics and the public to appreciate; the Nixon pardon was a classic example. Journalist Bob Woodward recalled how dismayed he was to hear of the pardon; he awoke that Sunday morning to a phone call from Carl Bernstein, his *Washington Post* colleague, who angrily barked, "The son of a bitch pardoned the son of a bitch." Yet over the years, after interviewing Ford and viewing his action through the prism of time, Woodward concluded, "Ford was wise to act. What at first and perhaps for many years looked like a decision to protect Nixon was instead largely designed to protect the nation."[78] Though Ford acknowledged that the pardon may have cost him the 1976 presidential election, he maintained that "the decision was right and I don't feel badly about it."[79] Ironically, while many observers might count the pardon as one of Ford's failures as president, he considered it a signal achievement.[80]

But anger can cloud people's vision, and infuriated Americans were in no mood to see the logic from the president's perspective. Ford exacerbated the public fallout by not vetting his decision. He informed only a small cadre of advisers and members of Congress, then dropped the bomb on the American public. Press assistant John Hushen said that the pardon "was delivered to the country like Pearl Harbor."[81] It was an unfortunate way to make such a momentous decision. The pardon caught the country off guard, and for many Americans it was an event frozen in time, one of those immortal moments when they can remember precisely what they were doing when the news came. The blow was unpleasantly similar to the Watergate shocks during Nixon's second term. Presidential adviser David Gergen wrote, "Just as I can vividly remember coming out of a restaurant in downtown Washington when word hit of Nixon's Saturday Night Massacre, I can recall careening off a back road in Virginia when our car radio reported on the pardon."[82] It came too soon after Nixon's resignation, before the public had digested that historic event. When Ford informed close associates that he would pardon Nixon, some expressed shock at the timing. "Jesus, don't you think it's kind of early?" Tip O'Neill blurted out. Hartmann implored, "What's the rush? Why must it be tomorrow? Why not Christmas Eve, or a year from now, when things quiet down?"[83]

As great a president as Lincoln waited until a propitious moment, when the Union had won a battle victory at Antietam, before issuing the preliminary Emancipation Proclamation. To prepare the public, Lincoln also dropped intimations in a letter to newspaper editor Horace Greeley. The Nixon pardon was, likewise, a decision of such magnitude that the president needed to brace the public beforehand and then wait for the right moment. Melvin Laird, Nixon's defense secretary and a close Ford friend, recalled telling Ford that he had made a disastrous mistake by pardoning Nixon so hastily. If Ford had given him advance warning, Laird would have had time to lobby for bipartisan support in Congress. "I would have had them begging him to do it," Laird believed.[84] Ford should have consulted widely and frequently before issuing the pardon. He should have sent up trial balloons, hinting at what he contemplated, and shored up the political and public support needed to sustain him in the face of a possible outcry. By handling the decision in a politically clumsy way, he damaged his image of rectitude.

In a sense, Ford's popularity and the media adulation during his first month in office established conditions that made his poor handling of the pardon possible. When awash in public support, presidents experience an almost heady feeling of infallibility that makes them prone to lapses in judgment. The resulting errors explode like political powder kegs, blackening the president's image and damaging public trust in him. Some of the most invidious executive actions or scandals have occurred after a president has experienced a whopping electoral victory or high numbers at the polls. Thus Franklin Roosevelt promoted a misbegotten "court packing" scheme after his resounding 1936 reelection; Kennedy approved the disastrous Bay of Pigs invasion during his rosy first weeks in office; Johnson deepened American involvement in Vietnam after his 1964 landslide; Nixon pursued a Watergate cover-up after his 1972 reelection triumph; Reagan stumbled through the Iran-Contra scandal after he pounded Walter Mondale in the 1984 election; Bill Clinton, still popular despite the Monica Lewinsky scandal, granted egregious pardons just before leaving office; and George W. Bush, riding stratospheric approval rating after the September 11, 2001, terrorist attacks, ordered a dangerous and controversial invasion of Iraq.[85] High approval ratings breed a sense of presidential hubris or carelessness; it is difficult to imagine Ford granting the Nixon pardon so abruptly had he suffered from lower poll ratings and rougher media treatment. In a more adverse political climate, he likely would have been more cautious. Had he waited until after the 1974 midterm elections—which might have helped spare the GOP a drubbing— campaign politics would have naturally ended his honeymoon by that time, and he would have had the opportunity to act more circumspectly. As it was, Republicans suffered; Senator Bob Dole of Kansas, locked in a difficult reelection battle, called the pardon "premature" and begged the White House not to spring any more "surprises" before November.[86]

Ford worked hard to contain the damage from the pardon and restore his image of integrity. In a dramatic move, he went personally to Capitol Hill to testify before the House Judiciary Committee's Subcommittee on Criminal Justice. No president since George Washington had taken the extraordinary measure of appearing in person before Congress to testify. Many of Ford's advisers urged him not to risk the testimony, fearing the appearance would only unleash demands for more such personal testimonies.[87] Appearing alone at the witness table, he explained to the committee that the purpose of the pardon "was to change our national focus. I wanted to do all I could to shift our attentions from the pursuit of a fallen President to the pursuit of the urgent needs of a rising nation." At one point committee member Elizabeth Holtzman, a Democratic congresswoman from New York, brusquely challenged Ford about a "deal." He responded angrily, pounding the table and exclaiming, "There was no deal, period, under no circumstances."[88]

Ford did not mention his aides' belief that Haig had indeed broached the idea of a "deal," and his testimony did not completely allay suspicions.[89] Yet his appearance before the committee was courageous and won praise. *U.S. News and World Report* said that Ford "impressed viewers as unflustered, forthright, a man with nothing to hide." A writer for the *Washington Post* editorialized: "The President was categorical and compelling, in our view, in refuting the allegation that his pardon of Richard Nixon was part of a prearranged 'deal.' His mere presence, as well as his ease and good temper, said a lot about the restoration of civil relations and a sensible balance between the executive branch and Congress." Other journalists disagreed. The *Washington Post*'s William Raspberry wrote, "Anybody who previously had suspicions about a 'deal' between President Ford and his predecessor has exactly the same suspicions now. There is no way that [the] namby-pamby session between the President and the House Judiciary Subcommittee could have eased anyone's doubts."[90]

Despite Ford's attempts at damage control, the pardon irreparably harmed his presidency. Since the famous "Hundred Days" of Franklin Roosevelt's presidency, when Congress passed a whirlwind of New Deal legislation, observers have used the first hundred days as a benchmark to judge a new president's activity and success in office. Frequently, those days are a period when a president enjoys high public opinion ratings and congenial relations with Congress. Because of the pardon, Ford's presidency was already in trouble by the thirty-day mark, making his the rockiest beginning for any modern president. Although Ford brought a welcome change of atmosphere to the White House and restored a sense of trust to government, the pardon exploded the delicately emerging image of a savior president, and lingering suspicion sapped his presidency of strength. Republican congressman Barber Conable of New York recalled that after the pardon, Congress sensed that the president "was a wounded fish," and the Democrats became sharks "circling on the floor of the House. There was no question about it—they were determined to put him away because he was vulnerable. And he was vulnerable because he had pardoned Nixon."[91]

The Nixon pardon was a defining event of the Ford presidency. In another era, it might have seemed a salutary move for the country. But Ford was a victim of the times. A cynical Congress, public, and press viewed a politically courageous decision as an act of malfeasance. By damaging Ford's reputation and political strength, the pardon hampered his ability to promote the policies that he later introduced. Ultimately, it may have also cost him election to a full term.

Chapter 2

The Congenial Presidency

On October 11, 1975, at 11:30 P.M., a new program debuted on television. NBC's *Saturday Night* (later renamed *Saturday Night Live*) became a hit partly because it was so different. It aired live, which infused energy and spontaneity into its antics. Unlike other television comedies, it welcomed a different guest host each week. It starred fresh, raw talent; most cast members were younger than thirty. It featured a so-called cold opening that dove straight into a comedic sketch, skipping the prefatory title and credits. The show came at a good moment, too, since the nation needed laughter after the morose days of Watergate and Vietnam. *Saturday Night* also succeeded by tapping into a new market, baby boomers, who had grown up watching television. By the 1970s, many of them were in college, staying up late, and they wanted more risqué, irreverent comedy than what aired on prime time. The show's first guest host, George Carlin, set the tone with cracks like, "God can't be perfect; everything he makes dies." God was fair game on the show; so were presidents. *Saturday Night* regularly poked fun at the nation's chief executives. Young viewers, who embraced television as their main source of political information, shaped their views accordingly.

Among the *Saturday Night* cast, one standout was a thirty-two-year-old comedy writer with a heavy cocaine habit, Cornelius Chase. His grandmother called him "Chevy," and with the same name as an affluent Washington suburb, he had an instant trademark. Chase also had a standard gag: the fall. "The fall is my favorite thing," he said. "I love making people think I've killed myself." He did it well, too. The sight of his tall, six-foot-four frame hitting the floor and creating chaos made studio audiences shriek with laughter.[1] In Gerald Ford, Chase found the perfect marriage between his love for falls and the show's presidential satire. Chase launched his career and left *Saturday Night* after just one season to pursue movie roles. But his buffoonery indelibly marred Ford's image.

"Pleasant Plainness"

One irony of Ford's presidency was that although he tried to maintain good press relations, reporters often ignored substance for the sake of an entertaining caricature. That misfortune had not happened while he was in Congress. Although some reporters found Minority Leader Ford to be dull, they liked the affable and accessible Michigander. In 1965, the National Press Club formally recognized Ford's good relationship with the media by awarding him their prestigious Meritorian Award.[2] Congressman Ford appreciated the press's importance to the proper functioning of government; once president, he thought that the press was one of the chief executive's few links to the outside world, preventing insularity and providing reality checks by continually critiquing his job performance. Thus he invited reporters to White House social functions and even attended dinners at reporters' homes.[3]

Ford said that he was "well aware that the trust between the media and the White House had been severely battered" during the Nixon administration. In addition to cosmetic innovations like the East Room's new seating arrangement, Ford introduced substantive changes to improve his dialogue with the media, such as allowing reporters to ask follow-up questions at press conferences.[4] Press Secretary Ron Nessen permitted *Time* and *Newsweek* writers to interview the president during quieter moments, such as weekends, so that they could get more detail for their stories. Ford took the unprecedented step of appearing as a guest on a weekend public affairs program, CBS's *Face the Nation*. Nessen recalled other innovations in the president's relations with the media: "When Ford traveled, he would have news conferences out of town, and we would have half the questions from the White House press corps and half from the local press corps. We tried different locations for the news conferences; he would sometimes have news conferences in the Rose Garden."[5] As Nessen observed, "One of the things about Ford was that when you came to him and said, 'Here is an idea of how to improve relations with the press,' he always had the same answer, which was: 'Let's try it!'"[6]

Ford's official photographer, Pulitzer Prize–winning David Kennerly, enjoyed unprecedented access and arranged for other photographers to shadow the president. One notable example was Fred Ward, a freelance photographer who enjoyed two months of nearly unrestricted access to White House offices, First Family quarters, and Camp David, eventually producing an elegant picture book of the Ford presidency, *Portrait of a President*. Ford granted other reporters similar treatment. He allowed Pulitzer Prize–winning author John Hersey to spend a week at the White House, interviewing and observing him at work; the result was a book, *The President*. Mark Rozell's appraisal of

Ford's relations with the media, *The Press and the Ford Presidency*, offers a charitable view: "Ford knew what journalists wanted from the White House after Richard Nixon: more press conferences, more access to the President, more 'straight talk.' He no doubt helped ease press cynicism and rancor by stressing the 'open' presidency theme."[7]

The Office of Public Liaison (OPL) was a Ford administration innovation that underscored his attempt to conduct an "open" White House. Its purpose was to get Ford out of the Oval Office and bring the president and the people together again. William Baroody, director of the OPL, recalled, "I had previously pitched the idea [of an OPL] to President Nixon but he was only about 25 percent behind the idea. . . . I made the proposal for such an office to Jerry Ford and, almost immediately, he was one hundred percent behind the idea."[8] The OPL held meetings every Wednesday at the White House, during which invited guests met with administration officials and sometimes with the president himself. Consumer advocate Ralph Nader was invited to one such meeting, and one of his assistants marveled, "Can you imagine? [Nader] couldn't have gotten in the White House door with an ax during [the Nixon presidency]."[9]

The most innovative OPL program was the "townhouse meetings" held across the country with audiences comprising a cross section of the host community. Baroody recalled that Ford attended almost every townhouse meeting, which far exceeded original expectations of presidential participation. Reporter Sarah McClendon praised the OPL as "an effective and original idea," and Budget Director James Lynn admired Ford's performances during the OPL conferences: "If you wanted to see Ford at his best, he was really good in those. I used to come away from those with my jaw down in awe. . . . He'd talk for 10 to 15 minutes. And then he'd spend two hours answering questions" from a diverse crowd often at odds with presidential policy.[10]

Ford's accessibility marked a welcome departure from Nixon's presidency. The difference was like that between a narrow artery and a wide one. Access to the Nixon White House had been constricted, at times even closed. Nixon limited the flow of persons seeing him to only a few privileged and powerful. Still the shy Quaker, he made decisions alone, avoided face-to-face meetings, and preferred written comments to oral discussions. By contrast, Ford widened access, seeing a variety of persons, encouraging participation, enjoying face-to-face discussions, and relishing the give-and-take of debate.[11] Speechwriter Robert Orben marveled that administration members enjoyed "amazing access to the President." Chief of Staff Donald Rumsfeld, who functioned as the keeper of the Oval Office's open door, explained that Ford's philosophy was that "you can gain a lot from reading and thinking, but you're more likely to acquire a sense of the mood of the country by meeting with people." About every six weeks, Ford met with a kitchen cabinet comprising friends from government and industry, which gave him feedback and brought an infusion of ideas from different political and ideological backgrounds.[12] Ford communicated with the academic community through Robert Goldwin, a University of Chicago constitutional scholar who described his role in the administration as "an outsider on the inside" and who brought in academic groups to confer with the president.[13] Goldwin observed that Ford "was very good at listening to other people's ideas, and in any meeting he seemed to be able to get everybody to speak. And if somebody didn't volunteer, he would seek him out, and get him to comment. And he listened to the lower-ranking people as he did to the highest-ranking ones."[14] One important difference, both symbolic and substantive, was that Nixon traveled on Air Force One with his compartment door shut; Ford kept it open.[15] Nessen believed that "a lot of what Ford's administration did was designed to demonstrate both substantively and symbolically that this was not the Nixon administration. This is the White House that did things differently, did everything they could differently than the Nixon White House."[16]

The psychological differences between Nixon and Ford significantly affected their presidencies. Where Nixon was insecure, plagued by inner demons that made him hypersensitive to criticism, Ford was more at ease with critics, a disposition that he credited in part to his background in sports. (As a football star, he grew used to columnists critiquing his performance.) During discussions, Ford tolerated a wide range of viewpoints. Chief of Staff Dick Cheney described Ford as "a man who was able to sit down and listen to debates. He never cut off an individual's access because that person disagreed with him."[17] Alan Greenspan, chairman of the Council of Economic Advisors (CEA), said he would sometimes feel guilty after talking to the president in what he later realized was an excessively contentious manner. Ford knew his own strengths and weaknesses and felt comfortable with himself, a psychological security that Nixon lacked and that enabled Ford to share conflicting ideas with others and to forge political compromises.[18]

Shortly after Ford assumed the presidency, he called Barber Conable to the Oval Office to solicit the congressman's recommendations for a vice-presidential nominee; one possibility they discussed was Nelson Rockefeller, whom Ford eventually nominated. Conable believed that Ford wanted to make certain that he had fully explored his range of possible selections, that he had not overlooked any potential nominee. Conable observed in his diary,

"The president really invites vigorous exchanges, participates in them himself, and thus carries on his tradition of wanting a good, collective input before he makes up his mind about matters of policy and strategy. This was his pattern when he was minority leader, and he appears to continue it as president." This openness to new ideas was one of Ford's greatest strengths, and it was a quality Conable seldom found in presidents. "Most presidents think they know it all," he regretted. "That's partly because they're elected, and they know they're anointed by God and the American people to do their thing. Jerry knew he wasn't. And he invited debate . . . because he wanted to be sure that he had all inputs on which he could base his decision. He knew he didn't know it all." Conable found that "very, very refreshing" in a president.[19]

By communing with a range of people, Ford brought the presidency down to earth. He thought that one of the best ways to reestablish trust in the presidency was to remain a part of the people and avoid elevating himself to a rarefied atmosphere. As he commented, "A President has to have the backing, faith, and trust of the American people. I don't think a President can get that by adopting an attitude that maybe he is better than they. As a matter of fact, my feeling is that a President ought to be a part of the American people." This kind of perspective allowed journalist David Broder, who knew presidents from Lyndon Johnson to Bill Clinton, to call Ford "the least neurotic president I've known."[20]

Ford's uncommonly human behavior as president may be partly ascribed to his having bypassed the normal route to the White House. The path to the presidency, usually involving grueling primaries followed by a rigorous general campaign, is pitted with traps and snares and demands a degree of meanness. Ford's personality had never endured the tough, annealing process of a national campaign. Thus his "nice guy" touch was unaffected by the rigors that normally test and winnow presidential aspirants. Unusual circumstances had resulted in an unusual president.

Douglas Bennett, who served as director of the President's Personnel Office, recalled members of the Ford administration were conscious of the arrogance that marked previous administrations. Ford worked studiously to avoid it. Bennett noted that when Ford selected his appointees, he was meticulous about one condition: "He didn't want arrogance. He didn't want this condescending attitude [just] because you're in the White House." To ensure that potential administration members were approachable and congenial, he took an active role in choosing his staff and met with Bennett three to four times a week to review candidates.[21]

This care in staff selection yielded an administration whose members have enjoyed long careers in public service. Ford biographer James Cannon pointed out that in contrast to preceding and succeeding administrations, no prominent Ford cabinet member or appointee finished his or her political career in disgrace or, worse, in jail. On the contrary, many went on to high positions in government or industry (most notably Dick Cheney, Donald Rumsfeld, and Paul O'Neill, who all worked as CEOs of corporations and then served as vice president, defense secretary, and treasury secretary, respectively, in George W. Bush's administration, and Federal Reserve chairman Alan Greenspan).[22] David Broder observed, "By the end, when he'd replaced Nixon's people with his own, Ford had one of the most competent staffs any of us have seen."[23]

A subtle element of presidential leadership involves when to hold back: when to refrain from using power, issuing public comment, or acting regally and above the hoi polloi. Acutely conscious of the last, Ford dismantled many of the ostentatious trappings of the presidency before Jimmy Carter excited public comment with the same goal. Ford's longtime friend and White House Counsel Philip Buchen thought that he "humanized the presidency after it had gained the reputation of being almost an imperial office. . . . Yet, I don't think he demeaned the office. . . . Ford did not carry his own suitcase, but he showed in other, more natural ways that a person in the position of President can act in a very human fashion."[24] Ford instructed the White House band to limit playing of "Hail to the Chief," replacing it instead with the rousing University of Michigan fight song, "The Victors."[25] Friends commented on his ability to remain unchanged, despite the power of his position. He wanted close friends to continue calling him Jerry rather than Mr. President.[26] The open and relaxed atmosphere at Ford's Vail, Colorado, rented chalet contrasted sharply with Lyndon Johnson's sprawling Texas ranch and Nixon's cloistered homes in San Clemente, California, and Key Biscayne, Florida. Ford's retreat was within easy eyeshot of neighbors' homes, and on Vail's slopes, reporters and townspeople caught glimpses of the president skiing with his family.[27]

Ford's sense of humor tended toward self-effacement, a welcome contrast to presidents who took themselves too seriously and another crucial aspect of his approach. One of the best examples of Ford's ability to poke fun at himself came after his November 1974 trip to Japan, where he was photographed next to Emperor Hirohito wearing embarrassingly short trousers that ended above his ankles. The sartorial fiasco received considerable media derision. After he returned from the trip, during a speech at the Boy Scouts Annual Awards Dinner, Ford—an Eagle Scout who remembered his oath by heart—opened with the line: "They say once a Scout always a Scout, and I can tell you from my own experience that is true. After all these years I still love the outdoors. I still know how to cook for myself, at least breakfast. And as anyone who saw those pictures of me in Japan will know, on occasion I still go around in short pants."[28]

While Johnson and Nixon had penchants for big moves and drama, often with disagreeable results, Ford adopted a style that journalist Joseph Alsop described as "pleasant plainness."[29] For example, after Cambodia's Khmer Rouge seized the U.S. merchant ship *Mayaguez*, reporters noted that the crisis atmosphere of the Johnson and Nixon days was remarkably absent as Ford planned reprisals against Cambodia. The calm reaction reflected his character and presidential style, which was frequently described as boring and bland.[30] Political cartoonist Jules Feiffer said that Ford "fills space like vacuum," and Ford once conceded that he lacked "that kind of electrifying leadership FDR gave."[31] He hoped to compensate by capitalizing on attributes that he felt the country needed at that time: "straightforwardness, complete honesty, and just talking straight."[32] Ford believed that an unpretentious style was a virtue. As vice president, he once declared, "It's the quality of the ordinary, the straight, the square that accounts for the great stability and success of our nation."[33]

The Ford brand of leadership left its mark on the 1970s. By the summer of 1975, his quiet, undramatic style translated into something that the nation's capital had not felt for years: boredom. The summer was so serene that *Newsweek* dubbed Washington "Dullsville, U.S.A." A slogan began to wend its way around town that residents could "stay bored with Ford." The press had no White House scandals to pursue, no protests to cover, no dramatic presidential moves. Former Democratic senator J. William Fulbright of Arkansas likened the atmosphere to the halcyon days of Eisenhower's presidency, and political comedian Mark Russell wisecracked that the summer was "so boring that the kids sit around in circles and get high on Scoop Jackson speeches" (a reference to Senator Henry Jackson of Washington, known for a soporific speaking style).[34] With the nation's cities and campuses at peace, the political turmoil of the past decade was easy to forget. In an essay simply entitled "Sigh!" columnist Russell Baker wrote, "The nineteen-seventies are boring. The decade is already half over and its chief legacy is an engulfing swamp of boredom." Baker noted that "President Ford is boring, which is his chief political strength." But Baker added, "In the nineteen-sixties, of course, Americans hungered for boredom. A sleepy Government, some peace in the streets. . . . In all that turbulence, it seemed an unattainable dream of paradise. Now we may have it, and may even be enjoying it."[35]

The serenity, which was a welcome relief, was evident again the following summer during celebrations commemorating the nation's bicentennial. Douglas Bennett recalled that in 1976, while campaigning for Ford, he reminded audiences that less than two years earlier Americans "were angry . . . we trusted nobody, and in the course of two years this president has restored a confidence. And this past Fourth of July was the bicentennial, hundreds and hundreds of people gathered at places around this nation *without incident*—and I think that is a direct tribute to the leadership of President Ford and the restoration of confidence, tranquility, and trust in our nation."[36] Ford himself spoke proudly of "a new spirit" in America that he observed during bicentennial celebrations.[37]

During Nixon's term, observers spoke of an "imperial presidency." Ford's was a congenial presidency, the antidote to Nixon's reign. But the pleasant style did not guarantee political success. Americans love a president who leads with style and panache; for this reason, their affection for John Kennedy far exceeds his modest achievements in office. Ford offered stability, a quality that was virtuous yet unlikely to generate fervent support. Moreover, he had to cope with domestic crises, especially regarding the economy and energy, and furnish a blueprint for the nation's future. And he had to convince the public and the press that his policies measured up to the nation's challenges.[38]

A Vision for America

The distrust of government was one of the greatest challenges that the nation faced during the 1970s. At the end of his presidency, Ford won bipartisan praise for quelling the anxiety and mistrust that the public had developed toward the executive branch. Tip O'Neill gave Ford high praise in his memoirs, suggesting that Ford's presidential ascension owed something to divine guidance: "God has been good to America, especially during difficult times. At the time of the Civil War, he gave us Abraham Lincoln. And at the time of Watergate, he gave us Gerald Ford—the right man at the right time who was able to put the nation back together again."[39]

At a time when Americans bemoaned the dearth of heroes, it may have been easy to overlook Gerald Ford because of his undramatic leadership style. Americans sought a hero of Homeric dimensions. Yet Ford's leadership may have satisfied a deeper yearning that Americans felt. As Ford was about to leave office, David Broder wrote, "In an odd, inexplicable way, the truth has begun to dawn on people in the final days of Gerald R. Ford's tenure that he was the kind of President Americans wanted—and didn't know they had." What Americans wanted, after a decade of presidents who aggrandized power, was "a man of modesty, good character, honesty, and openness. They wanted a President who was human and prudent, peaceable but firm. Especially, they wanted one uncorrupted by the cynicism and lust for power that they had come to associate with Washington politicians." Ford, Broder reminded readers, was exactly this kind of leader.[40] Presidents before Ford, especially his two immediate predecessors, used power extraconstitutionally and turned the presidency into an instrument that weakened public confidence and divided the country. By contrast, as Democratic congressman James Hanley of New York pointed out, Ford used the presidency as an instrument to unify the nation.[41]

But when Ford left office, many media assessments tempered their praise for his decency by criticizing his inability to articulate an inspiring vision or activist agenda. Dennis Farney of the *Wall Street Journal*, commenting that "'decency' was not enough," believed that "Gerald Ford never seemed to have a clear idea of just what he wanted to do with the vast powers he inherited." *Time* faulted Ford for failing to provide inspirational leadership, while the *New York Times* declared that Ford "never persuaded the public that he was firmly in charge or keenly determined to lead the nation toward specific objectives."[42]

Because he wanted to reduce the size of government, Ford avoided bold new paths and major projects. Moreover, lacking an election mandate, he would have found it rough sledding to get sweeping new programs accepted by Congress and the people and could have exacerbated political tensions if he had tried.[43] Republican senator Henry Bellmon of Oklahoma recalled, "I think it would have been wrong at that time to have a president who proposed a great many innovative things. The Democratic Congress was not too receptive to much input from a Republican president, anyway."[44]

Rather than propose new programs, Ford wanted to restore normal political relations in a troubled capital and provide a sense of stability. According to Bennett, Ford "felt his greatest challenge was to restore integrity and confidence in the office of the president, in the White House, and in the leadership of our country. I think that prevailed over everything. That was a vision, an objective that he felt was critically important."[45] While Ford may have been criticized for lacking a broad presidential vision, Nixon's CEA chairman Paul McCracken commented that Ford "had a vision of a country regaining its self-confidence, and he helped it do that. And that was quite a legacy. A greater legacy than most presidents leave."[46]

This objective, coupled with Ford's inherently unassuming personality, gave the nation a presidency that, while not spectacular, was steady. This leadership style was a fitting corrective to the unhappier attributes of his predecessors, for it helped to defuse the cynicism that permeated the land after Vietnam and Watergate. As Ford reflected on his mission in office and the circumstances surrounding his stewardship, he remembered the "unhappy condition of the country" when he took office. "My main concern was to overcome that crisis, to restore trust in government, to restore confidence that our country had weathered the storm."[47] Ford turned his energies toward restoring a sense of decency and probity to the executive branch. This, in John B. Anderson's words, Ford did "with grace, with dignity, and with honesty and integrity at a difficult time—when we were teetering on the brink of a constitutional crisis. And for that I think he will and should deserve a place in the affection of his countrymen."[48] In many political aspects of his presidency, Ford fared unevenly, landing in the maw of controversy after the Nixon pardon, enduring stiff resistance from Congress, and failing to win a full term. But in his role as a healing president, Ford provided a personal and institutional stability that allayed national cynicism.

The Image Problem

Although Ford helped to dispel post-Watergate animosities, his leadership had a less felicitous aspect. He never achieved a high popularity rating in public opinion polls. His average approval rating for his two and a half years in office was just 46 percent. An even more devastating reflection of how the public perceived Ford's presidential performance came in a poll taken during his last weeks in office. When asked to name Ford's greatest achievement, 24 percent of those questioned said that he had no great achievement, while another 24 percent replied that they did not know. A quarter of respondents had positive appraisals: 10 percent credited Ford with restoring faith in the presidency, 7 percent with improving the economy, 6 percent with uniting the nation, and 5 percent with having "cleaned up Watergate."[49]

Clearly, many respondents had an underwhelming view of Ford's accomplishments, which may have stemmed from his difficulties in appearing "presidential." In late 1974, as the country slipped into a deep recession, Barber Conable wrote, "Increasing doubts are arising as to whether Gerald Ford can administer the government. . . . The impression he has created so far is that of a nice man struggling manfully in the deep water far over his head."[50] Two years later, the president suffered the same image problem. After Ford won the 1976 Republican nomination, Dick Cheney's aides and pollster Bob Teeter prepared an assessment of Ford's chances of winning the race. In blunt terms, they told the president: "You are not perceived as being a strong, decisive leader by anywhere near a majority of the American people."[51] Ford struck the public as a nice, decent man, but not presidential timber.

Any politician thrown into the post-Watergate presidency might have suffered in public opinion standings. The 1970s was a difficult era for presidents because public confidence in the economy and American institutions was shaky and because cold war concerns over communism, which rallied Americans around the commander in chief in the 1950s and 1960s, had lost their urgency. With economic concerns taking precedence, a majority of Americans grew impatient, thought that inflation might never end, and doubted the country's future prosperity.[52] Moreover, the stench of the Vietnam War and Watergate still hung heavily in the air. After visiting his home district during the summer of 1975, Democratic representative Edward Mezvinsky of Iowa reported, "I discovered disillusionment with the whole political process. I thought the disillusionment would dissipate after the war and Watergate, but it hasn't." Ford labored under the additional burden of the Nixon pardon.[53] Ford's low public approval ratings translated into decreased congressional support for his programs because, as Lyndon Johnson noted, "presidential popularity is a major source of strength in gaining cooperation from Congress."[54]

Ford's public image suffered for other reasons. Notably, the press was more aggressive after Watergate. White House reporters had been frustrated by the deceptions of five and a half years of Johnson's presidency and the five and a half years of the Nixon presidency. Nessen recalled, "So you had two presidents in a row spanning over ten years, in which this relationship [with the White House media] had grown absolutely poisonous, and Ford inherited that."[55] The Nixon pardon aggravated reporters' levels of distrust. After depicting Ford's homespun values during the first few weeks of his presidency, the press felt betrayed after the pardon and reacted with more hard-hitting scrutiny.[56] The caricatured portrayals that resulted worked against Ford's efforts to be perceived as an earnest, capable leader. The White House press corps trailed their subject with a sense of hard-bitten skepticism; anything was fair game for attack.[57]

In June 1975, the media hit their mark. That month, something happened to Ford that irrevocably altered press portrayals of him. He slipped. Ford was on a diplomatic swing through Europe, and Air Force One landed in Salzburg, Austria, where it had just rained. Ford had slept poorly the night before—a pitfall of frequent travel—and the damp weather stiffened his arthritic football knees. As he helped Betty down the airplane's slick metal steps—one arm around his wife and the other clutching an umbrella—he lost his footing and tumbled to the tarmac. Unfortunately, it happened with reporters' cameras trained on him, and thus began a media carnival. After this incident, they magnified and replayed any incident of Ford falling, stumbling, or bumping his head.[58] For example, Ford fell while skiing in Vail, and the mishap made the evening news and newspaper front pages. While swimming laps, he crashed his head into the end of a pool and cut himself; he bumped his head on the entry hatch of the presidential helicopter; working a crowd, he tripped over the outstretched leg of a woman in a wheelchair.[59] The impression was that

Ford, the accidental president, was accident prone. The press was all too happy to cover such incidents; Assistant Press Secretary Larry Speakes remarked, "The press was determined to make him look like a klutz."[60] Indeed, some of the press corps seemed disappointed if, on any given day, nothing physically untoward happened to Ford. After a 1976 campaign stop that went without incident, a reporter for the Oklahoma *Morning Press* wrote, "I kept wishing the president would bump his head or skin his shins or suffer some small mishap for me to peg a paragraph on."[61]

Irreverent jokes depicting a maladroit president became standard comic fare. One wisecrack concerned a "Jerry Ford doll" that, after being wound up, lurched into something. Another was that the Secret Service forbade Ford from throwing out the first pitch of the baseball season because they feared that he would hit himself with the ball. Ford had the misfortune of serving as president when *NBC's Saturday Night* premiered. The program's presidential spoofs were hilarious, and Chevy Chase rose to national prominence through his slapstick impressions of Ford. The dopey comedian stumbled into lecterns, hit golf balls with tennis rackets, and even pretended to staple his ear to his head. The impressions were primitive, as Chase made no attempt to parrot Ford's mannerisms or speaking style. Instead, he fell down wildly, once accidentally smashing his testicles on a podium so badly that he had to miss two weeks of the show. The routines, however crude, had a lasting impact on millions of amused viewers.[62]

The bumbler depictions of Ford toppled a lifetime of sports achievement. Ford had always been proud of his athletic interests; he sprinkled speeches with sports metaphors (calling colleagues "team players" or "60-minute players" or talking about "huddling" on an issue) and as both participant and spectator enjoyed this human endeavor with a zest that exceeded his love of politics. (In reading the newspaper, he liked to turn to the sports pages first, partly because, he reasoned, a fan has at least a fifty-fifty chance of being right.) Jimmy Carter observed that Ford "was the best athlete who ever lived in the White House," and indeed his athletic past and present were impressive. As president, he enjoyed tennis, swimming, and golf while in his early sixties. He was one of the only chief executives ever to ski while in office, and he did so avidly. (Painful football knees did not deter him from vigorous activity, even after a 1972 operation on his right knee.)[63] *Sports Illustrated*, in ranking the most overrated and underrated athletes in history, declared Ford the most underrated "jock politician." Noting the relentless ribbing Ford received from comedians, the magazine commented, "The irony is that no president has come close to Ford in athletic ability."[64] The press knew how athletic Ford was. They followed him playing sports; they once tried to tag along when he skied in Vail, and only two reporters could keep up with him.[65] During the fall of 1974, caricaturists often drew Ford as a muscular ex-football-player-turned-president. But after the June 1975 tarmac tumble, all that changed. The press focused not on Ford's athletic prowess but on mishaps.

Ford believed that he generally received fair press treatment during his presidency, and he tried to shrug off the media's new obsession. "Anyone who competed in college athletics, football particularly, got used to what the sports writers wrote, and they were a lot more hard-nosed than even the White House people," he explained. "So although it bothered me, it didn't affect my attitude on substantive matters or the operations in the White House."[66] Sometimes, though, the bumbler depictions got under his skin. Hearing some of the jokes about his alleged clumsiness "kind of hurts your pride a little because you know it isn't true," he admitted, and in Vail he complained privately that many of the reporters who were lampooning his skiing were half his age, got most of their exercise on bar stools, and could not even ski down the beginners' slope.[67]

Administration members tried to defend the president. J. William Roberts, an assistant press secretary, explained that Ford's bumping his head on the helicopter could be easily understood, "because he was a tall guy and he had this habit of waving just before getting into the helicopter and then not ducking before turning around to get in. Well, that's just human."[68] Discerning reporters chastised their colleagues. Journalist Martin Schram described the bumbler stories as "an example of the media at its very worst." After all, everybody trips and falls occasionally, and they can only hope that nobody sees it. Unfortunately, Schram observed, "Jerry Ford had the whole world watching him" whenever he took a spill.[69] Ford's staff was worried enough about the image problem to mention as a 1976 campaign objective that Ford should avoid self-deprecating remarks (such as "I'm a Ford, not a Lincoln") and actions (they made a specific reference to Ford wearing cowboy hats, as he did at one appearance).[70] When the unflattering depictions first appeared, the president told a worried Nessen that the ribbing would soon stop. As Ford recalled, "There was no doubt in my mind that I was the most athletic President to occupy the White House in years. 'I'm an activist,' I said. 'Activists are more prone to stumble than anyone else. If you don't let their questions get under your skin, they'll realize that they're just wasting time, and they'll start to focus on something else.'"[71]

But the image of a klutz stuck to Ford like glue, and the White House could never peel it off. It became so deeply embedded that often it was the prevailing image that people had of the president. When advertising executive Malcolm MacDougall was asked to work for the 1976 Ford election campaign, he admitted that "the first thought that popped into my mind was that President Ford bumped into things. The press had done that to him. As I thought about it, I felt that here was a guy who had been given a bum rap."[72]

These portrayals did more than just convey an impression of clumsiness. More seriously, they implied a congruence between Ford's athletic missteps and his intellectual powers. Entertainers and less responsible members of the media translated the klutz depictions into the image of a man who was mentally obtuse, prone to making policy blunders as well as physical ones.[73] Ford's critics mused with condescension as his energy programs got entangled in a web of congressional committees and subcommittees; his vetoes created a sense of legislative impasse; his moderate policies were attacked by liberals and conservatives; and his 1976 presidential campaign struggled. Was Ford somehow given to political accidents as well as physical ones?[74] When Ford took a spill while skiing, CBS correspondent Bob Pierpoint commented that such pratfalls "have been almost symbolic of the Ford administration."[75]

The image of a genial oaf took shape, further riveted in place by wisecracks that President Johnson had made against Ford. The House minority leader was one of Johnson's chief political opponents, and, along with Senate minority leader Everett Dirkson of Illinois, Ford appeared on a weekly television show to promote Republican positions and assail the president. Johnson grew irritated, and he vented with crude, scatological remarks. He once tapped his head and remarked that Ford played too much football without a helmet; he also famously said that Ford "is so dumb he can't walk and fart at the same time."[76] In 1976, a *Jerry Ford Joke Book* appeared in paperback, full of cracks not only about the president's alleged clumsiness but also about purported mental lapses. "During the 1976 primary in frigid New Hampshire Mr. Ford in his absentminded way kissed a snowball and threw a baby," went one joke.[77] When Ford visited Kansas in 1975 to promote his economic and energy programs, he referred to the Wizard of Oz, prompting reporters to parody the scarecrow's song:

> I could overcome inflation
> Put gas in every station
> And we would feel no pain.
> I could make the Arabs cower
> I could be an Eisenhower
> If I only had a brain.[78]

Charges that a president lacked brainpower were nothing new. Andrew Jackson's critics pointed to his lack of schooling and ridiculed his numerous mistakes in pronunciation and diction. Lincoln's detractors questioned his intellectual qualifications for the job; the *New York World* called him "the obscene ape of Illinois," a "third-rate" lawyer who was "ignorant" and "boorish."[79] More recently, liberal critics have challenged the intellectual credentials of Republican presidents, variously implying that Eisenhower, Ford, Reagan, and George W. Bush lacked mental powers. With Ford, the charges were particularly incongruous. One of the best-educated men to serve as president, Ford earned a bachelor's degree from the University of Michigan and was only the second president to hold a graduate degree from an Ivy League institution, a law degree from Yale.[80] Yet time and again the White House was forced to defend the president against allegations that his intellectual credentials were substandard. The charges were, by their very nature, difficult to counter: How does one "prove" how smart one is?

In April 1976, Nessen attempted to dispel Ford's klutz image by accepting an invitation to host *Saturday Night* and good-naturedly joining in Chevy Chase's spoofs of the president. His participation in the charade, Nessen hoped, would demonstrate the administration's sense of humor and neutralize Ford's growing image problem. But the gambit seemed only to feed the fire, and stories immediately surfaced reporting the First Family's displeasure with the press secretary's appearance on the program. While Ford said that Nessen's appearance "wasn't a major problem," he admitted, "I wish in retrospect he hadn't done it."[81] Nessen agreed, conceding that "it's obvious that my attempt to smother the ridicule of Ford by joining the laughter on 'Saturday Night' was a failure."[82] Later, Nessen reflected that his greatest shortcoming as press secretary was that "I could never change Ford's image; I could never convince the press that he wasn't clumsy and a bumbler."[83]

The ridicule reduced respect. Carter wryly admitted that during the 1976 campaign he "thoroughly enjoyed" the jokes about Ford's clumsiness but acknowledged that the depictions were unfair and wounded Ford politically.[84] The parodies, while fun for the press and comedians, damaged Ford's public image irreparably, adversely affecting his policies and his ability to promote them. After the Nixon and Johnson administrations, the president was no longer a sacred figure, spared from savage satire. "Gone was all the reverence for the No. 1 position in the land," wrote columnist and radio commentator Earl Wilson. *New York Times* reporter Philip Shabecoff felt that reporters less frequently invoked regal language to depict the presidency and portrayed Ford more as court jester than as king. Yet, Shabecoff noted, Ford was in much better physical and mental condition than his predecessors, and he delved into complex issues from fiscal and monetary policy to strategic arms control.

But the media glossed over such complex issues. Presidential scandals and blunders attract more attention, and if a president is low in the polls, such news constitutes a theme consistent with his public standing. As presidential scholar George Edwards III observed, Ford's administration was "especially plagued by the press' emphasis on the superficial. Coverage of trivial shortcomings, such as his skiing and golf mishaps [i.e., hitting a spectator with a golf ball], his awkwardness on plane steps . . . regularly appeared on the front pages of America's newspapers. . . . The substance of speeches or meetings were ignored or superficially covered in a few second paragraphs."[85]

Ford's public persona was bland and inoffensive, but the post-Watergate journalistic ethos inspired reporters to search for spectacular sins. In Ford, they found none of the chicanery or character defects of past presidents. *Washington Post* publisher Ben Bradlee admitted, "There wasn't all that much to investigate, nor that much time to investigate it, during the Ford administration."[86] Finding no serious moral shortcomings, the media focused instead on visual pratfalls and used them to create excitement. Comedians did the same, as Chase explained: "Ford is so inept that the quickest laugh is the cheapest laugh, and the cheapest laugh is the physical joke."[87] (More liberal comedians also had a political interest in lampooning Ford. Chevy Chase, for example, called him a "terrible president" and declared, "He's never supported any legislation to help people in his life. He is a totally compassionless man." Three days before the 1976 election, *Saturday Night* took a shot at Ford by rebroadcasting his speech announcing his pardon of Nixon, just to remind voters.)[88] The "trip-and-fall" stories were the lowest common denominator for lazy reporters. They were easy to cover, made entertaining copy, and obviated the need to understand complex economic or energy issues. A herd mentality took hold, too, as reporters wanted to avoid being left behind on a growing media obsession. So they pounced on the untoward image of Ford, Nessen explained, "because it's easy and fun, and everybody else is doing it."[89]

The press criticism of Ford came from other, more substantive angles as well. In *The Press and the Ford Presidency*, Mark Rozell argued persuasively that journalists faulted Ford for not articulating a leadership vision. They wanted Ford to use government resources munificently to solve domestic problems. When Ford instead preached fiscal austerity and vetoed Democratic initiatives, journalists criticized him as merely a "reactive" president who lacked innovative public policies. Rozell wrote that journalists faulted Ford "for not responding to the nation's problems in a Rooseveltian fashion. . . . [Ford] wanted to be Ford. They wanted Roosevelt."[90] By fundamentally clashing with Ford's public policy, the press weakened Ford's ability to build support for it and detracted from an image of a strong leader who had serious programs to offer.

While the lash of a liberal media came down hard on Ford, his problem had another, more subtle aspect. Lyndon Johnson's domestic agenda may be fairly described as the most liberal of any president's in history, yet the media often treated him roughly. Nixon believed more strongly in an activist government than did Ford and was far less physically coordinated, even needing help from Secret Service agents to open prescription medicine bottles. But the media focused on the Nixon administration's combativeness and corruption rather than his surprisingly moderate domestic agenda or his awkwardness. At bottom, one of Ford's problems was that he was too easygoing and psychologically secure to produce front-page copy or the lead on the evening news. Reporters hoping to emulate Woodward and Bernstein wanted action and conflict, while Ford had—by comparison—a steady style and modest goals, reducing activist governance and providing stable economic growth.

Then, too, there was the eloquence problem. Leaders often lead through well-spoken words and, by doing so, can parry media thrusts using journalists' own weapon, the English language. Theodore Roosevelt, a media darling, trumpeted the presidency as a "bully pulpit," from which the chief executive could promulgate new programs. Yet the Ford White House failed to develop some of his themes—like fiscal austerity—in a way that appealed to the public and the media. It did not, for example, use a name or catchphrase like the "New Deal." Paul O'Neill admitted to frustration that Ford "was never able to communicate [his values] in a way which the general public could understand and respect."[91] Ford could not, as British prime minister Margaret Thatcher said of Ronald Reagan, take words and send them out to fight for his cause.[92] Ford's verbal blandness prevented his programs from catching fire. He came across as a president without a program, a leader of a rudderless administration. No reporter could make flashy headlines or win a Pulitzer Prize by investigating these objectives.

Ford was capable of a simple eloquence; his inaugural address stands as one of the most earnest and reassuring in history. Often, though, his speaking style was slow and uninspiring. Television cameras turned him to stone; he seemed to freeze before them, becoming rigid and unspontaneous. His pronunciation was labored, as he turned "judgment" into three syllables and flubbed words like "serendipity," saying "ser-a-binity." The problem may have stemmed from stuttering that afflicted Ford as a small child; Robert Hartmann, additionally, suspected that Ford may have been tone-deaf, for he never heard the president hum or sing a tune. But Hartmann also felt that Ford never understood how critical a well-delivered speech was to his presidency's success.[93] Ford hoped to make up for his lack of eloquence and charisma by substituting a commonsense and plain style that might appeal to Americans jaded by slick politics. He once conceded, "I am the first to admit that I am no great orator or no person that got where I have gotten by any William Jennings Bryan technique. But I am not sure that the American people want that."[94]

Over time, Ford's court jesters appreciated the virtues of his style, regretting their cruelty and in their own ways belatedly apologizing. On a Saturday morning at the end of Lyndon Johnson's term, Ford was at home when the White House suddenly dispatched a car to take him to see the president. Ford figured that an international crisis had broken out. Instead, he found Johnson sitting alone upstairs in the Lincoln bedroom. He sat down close to the president, who put his hand on Ford's knee and said, "I'm going to leave here in a couple of days, and I've been thinking about it. . . . I said some pretty mean things about you." Johnson admitted that he had been wrong, that Ford had been a loyal supporter who had the nation's best interests in mind; the big Texan said he was sorry. Chevy Chase also regretted his insensitivity to Ford. One of Ford's sons told Chase that his *Saturday Night* sketches sometimes hurt his father's feelings. At first, Chase did not understand. He believed that, as a public figure, the president could endure any kind of mockery. Years later, though, Chase conceded, "Of course, now my feelings have been hurt so much, I know exactly what he means."[95] But these apologies neither received public attention nor undid the damage to Ford's image.

In January 1976, as Ford prepared to kick off his election campaign, he expressed hope that the public would look beyond the bad imagery and discern the essence of his presidency. His administration's achievements "have not yet been understood by the majority of the American people. But I am encouraged because I believe these are accomplishments the American people in the long run will recognize and respond to."[96] As Ford spoke, the economy was rebounding from a deep recession. Real gross national product (GNP) was increasing at a robust rate of more than 8 percent. Unemployment had dropped for the third straight month. The number of Americans holding jobs increased by 800,000 in January 1976, a near-record monthly gain. Perhaps most significant, inflation was running at an annual rate of 4.8 percent, substantially down from the double-digit rate when Ford took office. But these auspicious statistics did little to change perceptions of Ford. Despite the good economic news, his approval rating was just 46 percent.[97]

Chapter 3

Gerald Ford and the Ninety-fourth Congress

January 20, 1977, was Gerald Ford's last day as president. After Jimmy Carter was inaugurated, Ford and his wife, Betty, now private citizens, strode through the Capitol rotunda, walked down the building's rear steps, and boarded a helicopter to fly to Andrews Air Force Base. It was a sunny winter day in Washington, and Ford asked the helicopter pilot to circle over the Capitol so that he could take one last look at the building where he had spent a huge part of his career. As the chopper flew over the dome, Ford gazed down and said, "That's my real home."[1]

Years after he left Washington and the presidency, Ford's thoughts often came back to his life on Capitol Hill—and one unfulfilled goal. "I still would have liked to be speaker [of the House]. . . . It would have been a great achievement," he reflected. "To be speaker is the number one job in the country."[2] Ford felt that his innate talents were as a legislator, and he knew Congress well, after twenty-five years in the House and eight months presiding over the Senate as vice president. But for all his fondness for the legislative branch, when Ford was in the White House, his perspective of Congress changed dramatically. He still loved the institution, but the people in it— and its revolutionary changes—proved trying.

Repairing the Rift

Gerald Ford thought of himself as a "healing president," and one area badly needing the palliative touch was relations between the White House and Congress, where Nixon did much damage. Throughout his presidency, Nixon had complained that he was stuck with a Democratic Congress, which was true, but he did little to help his plight. He joylessly went through the motions of flattering, cajoling, and horse-trading with Congress. He poisoned the dialogue between the two branches with his secretive conduct of the Vietnam

War, impoundment of budget money appropriated by Congress, and the abuses and mendacity of Watergate. At times, he treated Congress with contempt and recoiled from joining hands with Capitol Hill in a necessary partnership. By 1974, as his presidency unraveled and Congress debated impeachment, Nixon privately joked about dropping a nuclear bomb on Capitol Hill.[3]

Institutionally, Nixon thought that he could govern without Congress, but he was also by nature a loner, shutting himself up at the White House, Camp David, or his vacation homes, sometimes for weeks at a time. Legislative aide Max Friedersdorf recalled that if an issue involving Congress cropped up, Nixon "didn't want to see the congressman or senator. That was the last thing that he wanted to do. We had to really work to get somebody in to see him. . . . He much preferred that we wrap it up in a memo . . . and he would act on the memo without ever seeing anybody. I think if we left him to his own devices he would never, ever see a congressman or senator." The mercurial president so isolated himself that in 1973 Republican senator Barry Goldwater of Arizona wrote to him to warn, "You have to stop living alone. You have to tear down that wall you have built around you." Goldwater's letter contained a blunt conclusion: "No one whom I know feels close to you . . . you've got to become the warm-hearted Nixon and not the Cold Nixon, which you are now."[4]

Using hard-bitten aides like H. R. Haldeman and John Ehrlichman, Nixon kept legislators a country mile away. The two men presented so formidable a barrier that detractors called them the "Berlin Wall" and "the German Shepherds." Haldeman and Ehrlichman ignored the basic courtesies essential to congenial relations between the White House and Capitol Hill. Minority leader Ford disliked both men, whom he called "obnoxious when it came to their dealings with the Congress." He complained that "Haldeman, Ehrlichman, and a few of their associates on the White House staff viewed Congress in much the same way that the chairman of the board of a large corporation regards his regional sales managers. We existed, they seemed to believe, only to follow their instructions and we had no right to behave as if we were a coequal branch of government." Haldeman seldom took the trouble to visit Capitol Hill and on one occasion stated, "I don't think Congress is supposed to work with the White House." When Ehrlichman—who once claimed, "The President *is* the government"—came to Ford's Capitol Hill office to meet with Senate and House Republican leaders, Ford recalled, "Ehrlichman sat over in a corner in a big chair, obviously bored to death. He was silent, totally disdainful of the serious effort we were making to work out an accommodation. I'm not sure he didn't sleep; he had his hands over his eyes. I was disgusted." Senate minority leader Hugh Scott felt that after Nixon's 1972 reelection landslide, the president's advisers acted even more arrogantly, as though they could ride roughshod over Congress. At one meeting, Ehrlichman told senators to support a Nixon veto. Scott expressed doubts and asked how he could get other senators to support the president. Ehrlichman suggested, "Well, hit them in the face." The odd remark underscored Ehrlichman's complete failure to understand the subtleties of congressional relations.[5]

Ford had to restore normal executive-legislative relations. Nixon had selected him as vice president not only because he could win swift confirmation from Congress but also because he could help build and repair bridges between the Nixon White House and the Ninety-third Congress. Upon becoming vice president, Ford declared, "Working with Congress will be my major responsibility, as I see it."[6]

As president, Ford wasted no time to begin a ritual of healing. He gathered Nixon's few friends and many foes from Congress in the White House East Room for his swearing in. The invitees included men long banished from Nixon's White House, like Republican senator Robert Griffin of Michigan, who had helped to force Nixon from office, and former New York senator Charles Goodell, a liberal Republican whom Vice President Agnew had gleefully watched lose a 1972 reelection bid. Just three days into his presidency, Ford hastened to Capitol Hill to address a joint session of Congress. Pledging that his motto toward Congress would be "communication, conciliation, compromise, and cooperation," he told his colleagues, "I do not want a honeymoon with you. I want a good marriage."[7]

Ford's repair work showed in his legislative liaison staff. A key ingredient for successful relations between the Oval Office and the Capitol is the president's legislative liaisons, who function as the telegraph lines that convey the president's wishes to Congress, marshal votes, and keep information and the traffic of ideas moving smoothly. Patrick O'Donnell, a legislative assistant for Nixon and Ford, thought that "there was no sense of personal warmth between [Nixon] and his legislative people. He was not comfortable dealing with Congress on a daily basis, and that showed in his attitude toward us." Indeed, Nixon did not even know the name of one of his most important congressional liaisons. At a 1972 presidential campaign stop in Indiana, a large sign amid the airport crowd read, "Welcome Home, Max Friedersdorf." Nixon whispered to Ehrlichman, "Who the heck is Max Friedersdorf?" Not only was Friedersdorf a key aide, he was on the plane.[8]

The contrast between Nixon and Ford was striking. Ford elevated his legislative liaison staff to his most trusted inner circle. O'Donnell said that when Ford "had his frequent meetings with congressional leaders he made it a practice to have the liaison people sit right up at the table." Friedersdorf had a prominent profile in the Ford administration as a senior political assistant. Vernon Loen, the liaison for the House under both Nixon and Ford, recalled, "I served under President Nixon for almost exactly a year. I was with him in the Oval Office exactly three times, always when I escorted a member of Congress to see him. I saw him only at public ceremonies like bill signings. When President Ford came in, I would see him four or five times a day." Ford telegraphed to congressional leaders his trust in his legislative staff, thereby reaffirming their credibility. With Ford's closeness to them so clearly defined, the liaisons found that representatives and senators respected them and called on them directly.[9]

Ford's Oval Office became the site of frequent and friendly meetings between the president and members of Congress. Just after assuming power, Ford invited Barber Conable for a private Oval Office meeting, where he was shocked when the congressman told him that it was the first time he had been there. Here was one of Nixon's most steadfast supporters in the House, the chairman of the House Republican Policy Committee, and the second-ranking Republican on the Ways and Means Committee, yet a complete stranger to the president's office. That would change starting now, the new president assured Conable, telling him that he would see plenty more of the Oval Office.[10]

Ford remained a true creature of Congress and "was in his element when he was around congressmen or senators," Friedersdorf remembered. "So it made my job and our congressional relations staff's job just such a ball after Nixon. It was like night and day."[11] Every week Ford set aside "congressional hours," during which a steady stream of congressional visitors flowed into the Oval Office. William Kendall, who served both Nixon and Ford as the deputy assistant to the president for legislative affairs, contrasted the two presidents: "When Nixon brought in people from the Congress for a meeting there was no opportunity for feedback. He told them in no uncertain terms what he had to sell. The members of Congress knew Jerry Ford and respected him. Much of that respect had to do with the fact that he would take the time to listen to them."[12] Democratic congressman James Hanley of New York found Ford "a very open person who . . . tried hard to maintain an open door and enjoy good relations with the members [of Congress]."[13] In the estimation of presidential scholar George Edwards, among recent presidents Ford ranked second only to Johnson in the strength of his congressional relations.[14]

Instrumental to his relations with Congress was the equanimity with which Ford accepted partisan scraps. Political struggle was normal and inevitable, he believed, and he never let policy disagreements interfere with his personal relations. He regretted the "us versus them" mentality among Nixon's White House aides and believed that their inability to live by former House Speaker Sam Rayburn's adage—"disagree without being disagreeable"—constituted "one of the worst failings of [Nixon's] Administration."[15] Ford reflected that "all my political life I have believed that when you're in office you have an obligation to get things done, and you can't get things done if you just are an extremist and refuse to work out a solution." He recalled that "whenever a problem arose, even though I might have a disagreement with a Democrat or another Republican, I was always looking for a way to resolve the difference and get the problem solved."[16]

One of Ford's favorite refrains was that he had "many adversaries, but not one enemy" in Congress.[17] When Ford's House colleagues sought a new minority leader, they debated whether to put forward Ford or Melvin Laird to challenge Charles Halleck. They settled on Ford because he had fewer enemies than Laird. *Time* magazine's Hugh Sidey wrote admiringly of Ford's political sportsmanship: "Ford plays hard, but when the contest is over and it is time to walk off the field, the battle is left behind." Sidey noted that Ford "had founded his successful congressional career on the idea that good fights did not make permanent enemies." Forgiving by nature, Ford refused to dwell on yesterday's scraps. During his long career as a congressional liaison, Friedersdorf said that the best advice he received came when he was a new lobbyist on Capitol Hill. The Republicans had just lost a crucial series of votes, and Friedersdorf recalled, "I was actually sick at my stomach, really sick." The disheartened aide entered minority leader Ford's office and disparaged his political foes. "I'll never forget his reaction," Friedersdorf said. "He looked at me and said, quite sternly, 'Forget today's vote and look to tomorrow.'"[18]

During his presidency, Ford maintained close relations with Democrats as well as Republicans. He continued to golf with Democratic friends from Congress and invited Democrats to accompany him during presidential trips. Long-standing friendships with influential congressmen were important. Ford maintained close contact with Tip O'Neill from the first moments of his presidency, calling the House majority leader to invite him to the inauguration. "Jerry, isn't this a wonderful country?" O'Neill asked as the two chatted on the phone. "Here we can talk like this and we can be friends, and 18 months from now I'll be going around the country kicking your ass in." O'Neill was true to his word, but he admitted that under Ford's presidency, the political atmosphere in Washington was "much more congenial and relaxed" than under Nixon.[19]

The Democratic Landslide

Despite Ford's good relations with Congress, the reality of politics intruded; the 1974 midterm elections approached soon after he took office. Even if the Nixon pardon had not squashed Ford's popularity, the elections would have ended his honeymoon with Congress. Friedersdorf believed that it ended even before the pardon, only days after Ford's inauguration, as partisan bickering resumed over issues such as the economy. "If it hadn't been an election year, we might have gotten more of a honeymoon," Friedersdorf speculated. "But all the congressmen were fighting for their political lives."[20]

Without the benefit of a vice president to share in the fall campaigning (Nelson Rockefeller's nomination was hanging fire in Congress), Ford had to invest considerable time and energy on the hustings for Republican candidates. The party was in serious trouble after Watergate, and Ford plugged extensively for GOP candidates, delivering eighty-five speeches in twenty-eight states. But the 1974 elections were a disaster for Republicans. Discontented Americans vented their anger and frustration toward the GOP over a raft of complaints: Watergate, the Nixon pardon, double-digit inflation, rising unemployment, and the absence of an energy policy. The Democratic landslide was the most resounding since the depression days of 1932, when economic stresses propelled Democrats to huge victories and sank the Republican Party to its knees. For twenty years, voters identified the GOP with a single calamitous event—the Great Depression—and the party was shut out of the White House. In 1974, the question was whether Watergate would do the same.[21]

Golfing with Ford a few weeks before the election, Tip O'Neill warned him, "It's going to be an avalanche," and predicted Democratic gains of forty to sixty seats in the House. O'Neill was right. The Democrats picked up forty-three seats in the House, far greater than the average of twenty-five seats that the party out of power has gained in midterm elections after World War II. The victories brought the Democratic advantage in the House to 291–144, better than two-to-one. Ninety-two freshmen joined the chamber, the most since 1949, when a class of 118—including Ford—entered. In the Senate, the Democrats picked up three more seats, giving them a 61–39 advantage. Democrats also gained four governorships and thus controlled thirty-six states.[22] Even Ford's former Fifth District congressional seat in Michigan nestled into the Democratic fold, as Richard Vander Veen, a liberal Democrat who won the seat when Ford vacated it for the vice presidency, kept it by an even greater majority.

The midterm elections were a thundering rebuke of the GOP. Ford tried to put the disappointment in perspective, saying, "I don't know of an

Administration that faced more potentially adverse problems on Election Day than this one—with inflation at 11 percent, unemployment at 6 percent, and Watergate. Now, that's a pretty tough combination." The Nixon pardon also contributed mightily to the Democratic landslide. In retrospect, Chief of Staff Dick Cheney wished that Ford had pardoned Nixon after the fall elections. The pardon, Cheney regretted, "did cost us seats. . . . If we had had 20 or 30 more House Republicans during the two years of the Ford presidency, we would have been in much better shape than we were from a legislative standpoint."[23] The one act that did so much to damage Ford's popularity also drained Republican strength in Congress.

The 1974 elections tarnished Ford's prestige. His campaign efforts availed little, and the lopsided losses made Republicans question his effectiveness as party leader. Larry Speakes later commented that it was Ford's nature to help out his friends in Congress, but he added that Ford "should not have staked so much of his prestige on the congressional elections."[24] Historically, presidential campaigning in midterm elections has been ineffective, and for Ford, the November calamity was a chilling reminder of how a president's reputation gets tarnished when his party suffers deep losses.

More important for Ford was the election's meaning for his presidency. The Ninety-fourth Congress would be emphatically Democratic, and Ford's base of support on Capitol Hill would be narrower and weaker. His struggles against this Congress would be a defining theme of his presidency, a source of great political hardship to him, and an obstacle to his policies.

The sheer size of the Democratic majority was only part of Ford's problem. The seventy-five first-term Democrats in the Ninety-fourth Congress were cut from different cloth than the usual new arrivals on Capitol Hill. They were inexperienced, with thirty-one of the seventy-five holding elective office for the first time, and they were young; the incoming class helped to drop the average age of House members below fifty for the first time in the postwar era. Galvanized by public disillusionment with government, these "Watergate babies" promised their constituents that they would fix what was wrong in Washington and stormed into the capital with activism and iconoclasm on their minds.[25]

An unwritten rule on Capitol Hill was that new members of Congress should be seen but not heard. The 1974 freshman class wanted to rewrite the rule. Many new members were fiercely independent, resistant to the traditional seniority concepts of Congress, and eager to defy authority.[26] The president and the majesty of his office failed to awe these rebellious new Democrats. Charles Leppert, a deputy assistant for legislative affairs in the House, recounted a display of appalling effrontery. "I will always remember the

President's first State of the Union [address] in 1975," Leppert said. "Several of the Watergate babies just got up and walked out of the House chamber before the President even began to speak. . . . I can't recall such disrespect for the President of the United States in any other era." Democratic representative Christopher Dodd of Connecticut, the deputy House whip, commented that in the 1970s he found it "awfully hard" to mobilize Democrats on legislative issues. The younger members "don't want to feel as though they have to be responsible to the leadership," Dodd felt. "They see *themselves* as being leaders." As a result, he dared not tell younger members to vote a particular way just to follow the Speaker's instructions.[27]

The maverick spirit among the freshmen made it difficult for Democratic leaders to control them, which in turn made it hard for the White House to use Democratic leaders as levers of influence. Tip O'Neill called the newcomers "weak Democrats" because of their soft support for the party.[28] The Watergate babies accelerated the breakdown of party cohesion among both Democrats and Republicans, and Ford had to work with a Congress that cabinet secretary Jerry Jones called "an unpredictable, lurching mechanism."[29] But this mechanism was sure-footed enough to try to regain political strength in Washington.

The Presidency Weakened

"I think what happens in our country is not really controlled by the President. It's controlled by Congress," said a Baltimore civil engineer in 1976. The 1970s was one of the few times in postwar history that Americans could hear such a statement. During the decade, power drained away from the presidency, so that some Americans thought the president had become a mere figurehead, unable to carry out his duties before congressional opposition. Overseas observers were surprised to see Congress coerce the president. The Soviet people, wrote Ambassador Anatoly Dobrynin, "could not imagine an American president who was not exactly a supreme ruler" and were "shocked" at incidents when Capitol Hill dictated diplomacy.[30]

The situation of a politically weak president facing an ascendant Congress was not new; indeed, in the nineteenth century it was common. Whig Party presidents in the 1840s and 1850s (William Henry Harrison, John Tyler, Zachary Taylor, and Millard Fillmore) were far more restrained in using presidential power than Andrew Jackson had been, partly because their party opposed Jackson's vigorous use of power; in fact, the Whig Party had even been born to challenge it. The last half of the century saw presidents come to office by succession or through elections in which they lost the popular vote, and they lacked a strong political base (most notably Andrew Johnson, Rutherford B. Hayes, Chester Arthur, and Benjamin Harrison); the period from Andrew Johnson to William McKinley was an age of congressional ascendancy. While Ford's predicament might not have been unusual a hundred years earlier, the twentieth century was the era of the strong executive. The nation had come to expect a colorful, activist chief executive, and Ford's situation contrasted with those of his recent predecessors.[31]

Since the days of Franklin Roosevelt, the presidency had steadily accumulated power far beyond that envisaged by the nation's founders, and the trend accelerated during the cold war. In the nuclear age, the president had devastating military power at his fingertips. In the face of Communist threats, the national sentiment was to allow him to be unencumbered by constraints on his decision-making powers and free to make rapid responses to any international crisis. Congress also depended more on the president to propose major policy initiatives. Ironically, the president—not Congress— often assumed the dominant role in the legislative process. With the growth of domestic programs, the president also acted as the final arbiter among the competing local and state interests voiced in Congress.[32] Thus the president's concentration of power and authority came at the expense of Congress. But after Congress investigated the president so effectively during Watergate, it emerged from the crisis self-assured, revitalized, and eager to restore the constitutional balance of power. It had challenged not just Nixon but the presidency itself.

The Ninety-fourth Congress ached to reclaim some of the power lost to the executive branch before the 1970s. With a hefty Democratic majority and a president lacking an electoral mandate, the moment for congressional resurgence was ripe. After the 1974 elections, John Brademas of Indiana, the House Democratic deputy whip, declared, "We have a White House weakened by Watergate, occupied by a President who is not elected, who campaigned hard for his party at the polls and was overwhelmingly repudiated."[33]

To be sure, the presidency remained an office of awesome power. But by the mid-1970s, its power was less awesome. Never in the country's history had the office been so controversial. There were limitations—even if temporary in nature—to Ford's presidential power. Obviously, the unprecedented circumstances under which he assumed office diminished his claim to power. Elected to neither the vice presidency nor the presidency, Ford had a weakened sense of political legitimacy. He had less influence over Congress, since no member of Congress arrived on Capitol Hill on his coattails, and his 1974 midterm campaign efforts proved unavailing. Some members of Congress painted Ford's unusual ascension to office as a blotch on his political legitimacy. When protesting administration policy, Democratic senator Robert Byrd of West Virginia pointed out that Ford "doesn't have a national constituency, and his is an inherited presidency. . . . It doesn't have the national support that it should have." Columnist Russell Baker observed of Ford, "I saw a president with no mandate to govern being treated like a president with no mandate to govern."[34] Congressional Democrats regarded Ford's claim to office, while legal and legitimate, as tenuous.

Party dynamics further circumscribed Ford's power. After Americans punished Republicans during the 1974 elections, Ford found himself at the helm of a party ravaged by deep disaffection and defection. Claiming 38 percent of American voters in 1940, the Republican Party's share of the electorate slipped to just 18 percent after the 1974 elections; the Democrats, by contrast, claimed 46 percent.[35] With the GOP hemorrhaging members, Ford's task was not merely to lead the party but to resurrect it.

It was no small order. Although an effective House minority leader, Ford lacked a national constituency. When he became president, he had less than one year of widespread exposure to politics at the national level, and until he became vice president most Americans had never heard of him. Moreover, he was trying to unite and strengthen a party deeply divided between conservatives and moderates. These handicaps became all too clear during the 1976 primaries, when conservative Ronald Reagan almost wrenched the party's nomination from Ford.

With an incumbent president laboring under so many hardships, Congress saw an opportunity to reclaim power at his expense. Ford did not find a stronger Congress necessarily bad. While in the House, he recognized that the pendulum of power had swung too far toward the presidency. As minority leader, Ford complained about "an erosion of power and prestige of the legislative branch" juxtaposed with "an awesome buildup of strength and the use of this power in the executive arm." He added, "In this situation, there is a modern-day parallel with the story of David and Goliath. Congress, the legislative branch, David. The executive, the White House and all its agencies, is Goliath." He complained of Johnson's "presidential arrogance" and said, "I believe the power of the presidency has become so intoxicating for Lyndon Johnson that he believes he can accomplish anything he sets his mind to."[36] Ford was acutely aware of past presidential encroachment on the power and prerogatives of Congress, saying that "both [Johnson and Nixon] used presidential power, I think, more than can be justified."[37]

Ford wanted to observe the proper constitutional powers of the presidency and avoided the heavy-handed or flashy leadership of some of his predecessors.

He maintained a low-key, congenial leadership style with members of Congress. Republican senator Henry Bellmon of Oklahoma said that Ford "realized his ascension to the presidency was somewhat unusual, so he didn't throw his weight around."[38] Legislative aide O'Donnell commented that "Ford was firm but always personable," adding that he "was not of the LBJ mold where you grabbed someone by the lapels of their jacket and gave them the hard sell. Arm twisting was not his style and if he found out about people on his team using such tactics he would always investigate the situation carefully."[39] Ford demanded that his staff respect congressional opinions, even if they differed from the administration's, and ordered the firing of aide Vern Loen after he publicly criticized Republican congressman Larry Pressler of South Dakota for voting against the president on a bill.[40]

During the 1970s, many members of Congress felt that Capitol Hill, after languishing for decades in the presidential penumbra, had become the dominant branch of national government. Senate majority leader Mike Mansfield remarked, "For the time being, at least, Congress is resurgent." In the year before Ford became president, the Ninety-third Congress had been unusually active in tilting the balance of power away from the president. One example was the War Powers Act (WPA), which symbolized Congress's struggle to regain control over foreign policy after Nixon had shut Congress out of virtually every major diplomatic decision of his administration, especially Vietnam. The act, designed as a safety valve in case the president deployed troops abroad, required the president to give Congress an accounting of presidential actions and gave Congress the right to withdraw the troops after sixty days. In 1973, Congress overrode Nixon's veto to make the WPA law. In the decades since its passage, every president has skirted the WPA, easily deploying U.S. troops abroad. But the WPA showed how Vietnam and Watergate had shattered the political thinking of the postwar era. Before these two synergistic events, a WPA would have been improbable; in their aftermath, Congress resolved to reduce the scope of the president's foreign policy powers.[41]

Foreign policy was not the only area where Congress chipped away at presidential power. The Budget Impoundment and Control Act, passed in 1974, expressed Congress's determination to put itself on equal footing with the president on budgetary matters. Nixon impounded funds, refusing to spend money that Congress appropriated, and he used the tactic heavy-handedly, often to starve or dismantle Great Society programs. Whereas Eisenhower, Kennedy, and Johnson impounded an average of $7.15 billion a year, Nixon withheld an average of $11.10 billion a year in his first term and, in 1973, about $20 billion. The Budget Impoundment and Control Act allowed

Congress to intervene if the president cut spending or cancelled a program. The act also created the Congressional Budget Office, which submitted a budget draft of its own so that the president's budget draft was not the only one considered. The Congressional Budget Office soon became one of the most trusted and accurate sources of economic forecasting in the federal government. The days when Congress simply accepted administration fiscal numbers were gone. Now armed with its own arsenal of experts, figures, and facts, Congress could put the executive branch on the defensive with independent budget analyses and estimates.[42]

Changes within Congress made it more resistant to presidential authority and more difficult to control. On a structural level, traditional power preserves like seniority were under attack. In 1971, the House began to dislodge senior Democrats from key subcommittees by ruling that no representative could chair more than one subcommittee and further dispersed power two years later by adopting a party rule that guaranteed each Democrat a major committee assignment. In the Senate, a 1975 rule encouraged power distribution by granting junior senators the assistance of committee staff, a privilege previously reserved for senior senators.[43]

The sheer number of congressional subcommittees posed a problem for presidents by diluting power. In the 1960s and early 1970s came a proliferation of subcommittees that Ford called "unbelievable" and blamed for an adverse effect on Congress's ability to function. In 1955–56, the Eighty-fourth Congress had 83 subcommittees in the House and 88 in the Senate. By 1975–76, the Ninety-fourth Congress had 151 subcommittees in the House and 140 in the Senate.[44] The subcommittees were of virtually every possible size and for every imaginable subject, including the Special Subcommittee on the Freight Car Shortage and the Subcommittee on Small Business Problems in Smaller Towns and Urban Areas. Congressman Morris Udall joked that since there were so many subcommittee chairmen, he could greet any new Democratic congressman whose name he did not know by saying "Good morning, Mr. Chairman."[45]

Committees and subcommittees are the loci of congressional power; they control legislation, for bills are born and take shape there. With the growth of this system, each congressman became his own lord, ruling over a fiefdom. They jealously guarded power within their committee, competing with other members of Congress, other committees, and the president. Fellow representatives and senators and even the president were averse to challenging committees, not only because they lacked the expertise in a committee's bailiwick but also out of traditional courtesy.[46] By the mid-1970s, the wealth of committees and subcommittees dispersed power among more members, making each harder to control, especially since each committee and subcommittee was vulnerable to interest-group pressures. The nature of the committee system also gave a fragmented feel to legislation. Each committee claimed one patch of policy, and bills were parceled out among committees. Yet there was no way to coordinate the hodgepodge of legislation that resulted. Ford suffered the frustration of this legislative patchwork when his 1975 State of the Union energy proposals splintered among four committees in the House and nine in the Senate.[47]

These complications led to legislative torpor. During a bill's tortuous path through Congress, lawmakers put their feet in concrete and rigidly held their positions, supported by their immense staffs and lobbying groups. Committee and subcommittee majorities were hard to achieve, and each member had to be supplicated and placated individually, which often required marathon bargaining.[48] Thus Democratic leaders in Congress had trouble controlling the party's members, and the president had trouble securing legislation. No longer could a president simply cut a deal with the big fishes on Capitol Hill and expect all the little fishes to swim along.[49] Constituents grew frustrated with the intra-Congress gridlock; one woman complained to House Speaker Carl Albert in 1974, "We urgently need a reformed House of Representatives with viable, strong, responsive committees—not as present committees with competitive, parochial, divisive leadership."[50]

Congressional leaders of the 1970s failed to meet the challenge. Neither Democratic leader, Carl Albert or Mike Mansfield, was effective, especially compared to assertive predecessors such as Sam Rayburn, John McCormack, and Lyndon Johnson. Mansfield had a passive approach to leadership and dispersed power by giving more say to junior senators.[51] Complaints about Albert were common. Democratic congressman Bob Carr of Michigan wanted Albert to resign because he "doesn't have the dynamic leadership personality to inspire the party to march solidly behind him." In 1975, a handful of Democrats even started a "Dump Albert" movement.[52]

The approaching election year made Congress even more obstreperous. Some of Ford's most vociferous critics in Congress—notably Senators Henry Jackson and Robert Byrd—eyed the 1976 Democratic nomination, which tinged their actions with political ambition. Lyndon Johnson believed that when a president dealt with Congress, "you've got just one year when they treat you right, and before they start worrying about themselves. The third year, you lose votes. . . . The fourth's all politics. You can't put anything through when half the Congress is thinking about how to beat you."[53] Since he was completing Nixon's second term, Ford worked with a Congress during the third and fourth year of a presidency.

Many of the structural changes in Congress took place between 1970 and 1975, so Ford was the first president to face the "new Congress." These changes and the charged political environment made Congress much more difficult to bring to heel. Ford complained that "Congress was more rebellious, more assertive of its rights and privileges—and also more irresponsible—than it had been for years." During his first months in office, he was angered that the Ninety-third Congress petulantly delayed the confirmation of Rockefeller as his vice president. He considered the legislative branch especially intrusive in foreign policy. The legislative branch had became so aggressive that Ford warned not of an imperial presidency but an "imperiled presidency."[54]

Ford believed that many of Congress's actions were not just imprudent but unconstitutional. "Congress tried to, in my opinion, do certain things that extended their influence. I happen to think that the War Powers Resolution was a clear case of unconstitutional action, not only unconstitutional but unwise." Ford later noted that in the years since Congress enacted the WPA, presidents have repeatedly defied it. "So it's a meaningless piece of legislation, but it does show that Congress was trying to encroach on a president's prerogatives," he observed. Ford also saw the Budget Reform and Anti-Impoundment Act as "a case where Congress was encroaching on the presidential prerogatives of the right of impoundment. So in these two cases particularly, Congress—over the veto of President Nixon in the War Powers [Act], and over a lot of objection in the Budget Reform [Act]—moved in, and those powers are still in the hands of Congress."[55]

Congressional resurgence became a theme of 1970s Washington. Jimmy Carter was frustrated with the atrophied strength of the presidency and the growing power of Congress. During the first year of Carter's presidency, a reporter asked him if he found his presidential powers more limited than he expected. Carter "nodded his head instantly, almost like an 'amen.'" Carter found the new Congress unruly and wrote that Speaker O'Neill "had a nearly impossible job of trying to deal with a rambunctious Democratic majority that had been reformed out of any semblance of discipline or loyalty to him, and on many occasions he and I were to commiserate about the almost anarchic independence of the House."[56] It took the decisive 1980 election victory of Ronald Reagan and his ability to communicate directly with the American people for the pendulum of power to swing back toward the White House.

The Congenial President and Congress

To a small extent, Ford's warm personal relations with Congress helped him win political support. Representative Charles Mosher of Ohio, a liberal

Republican ideologically more at odds with Ford than with the more moderate Nixon, nonetheless voted the Republican line more often during Ford's term "because I liked Jerry Ford so much." But despite the vastly improved dialogue between the White House and Capitol Hill, political stalemate was often the victor in Washington, leading to Carter's charge during the 1976 campaign, "This is government by stalemate. . . . there has been a constant squabbling between the President and the Congress, and that's not the way this country ought to be run."[57]

The legislative struggle between Ford and Congress was essentially a draw. As Barber Conable summed it up at the end of the Ninety-fourth Congress, "The [Democratic] majority repeatedly locked itself unproductively into a clash with the White House that resulted in the enactment of neither party's programs." A new term was coined to describe the legislative standoff in Washington — gridlock.[58] Congress blocked Ford's attempts to move the nation on a more conservative path, especially in fiscal and social policy. But, especially by using the veto, Ford prevented the large Democratic majority in Congress from enacting programs to increase entitlements. Budget Director James Lynn thought that, given Ford's political predicament, Ford's ability to nullify the will of the opposition testified to his skill in marshaling presidential power. "Sure, there was a resurgence of congressional power," Lynn observed. "But what amazes me is with the resurgence, [the Democrats] would reject our programs, but they didn't get any adopted of their own. I mean, how [Ford] can do that sitting where he is, with those kinds of majorities on the other side, is a real feat."[59] Stalemate represented a small victory, keeping Democrats from enacting legislation that Ford deemed wasteful. Douglas Bennett said that during Ford's term, "there was a sense of stalemate but I think what it had the effect of, at least to some degree, [was] holding down spending."[60]

Ford found congressional resistance to his authority a formidable obstacle, and he complained that the Ninety-fourth Congress was the least productive Congress he had ever seen.[61] The experience altered Ford's view of Capitol Hill. As he explained, "When I was in Congress myself, I thought it fulfilled its constitutional obligations in a very responsible way, but after I became President, my perspective changed. It seemed to me that Congress was beginning to disintegrate as an organized legislative body. It wasn't answering the nation's challenges domestically because it was too fragmented."[62] Dick Cheney recalled that Ford "was capable, after he had been in the White House for a few months, of going behind the closed doors of the Oval Office and saying some very tough things about his former colleagues. It was a very different perspective when he got down to 1600 Pennsylvania Avenue." In his fiery speech accepting the Republican presidential nomination in 1976, Ford blasted Congress. He repeated the phrase "Congress won't act" three times and stated that his administration's achievements came about "in spite of the majority who run the Congress of the United States."[63] Ford's campaign message centered largely on his struggles with Congress, attacking the legislators for wasteful spending and trumpeting his role in restraining them.

Ford could not build a governing coalition in Congress, a prerequisite to winning legislative victories. As a result, he achieved no grand, sweeping programs. Instead, one of his most notable accomplishments was his extraordinary string of vetoes and his ability to have most sustained.[64] Although more congenial than Nixon, Ford faced an even more Democratic Congress than the ones Nixon faced, and he was more conservative than Nixon. Philosophical clashes were sharp. Democratic congressman Frank Thompson of New Jersey said that compared to Nixon, "there was more personal acceptance of Ford, because people in Congress were very fond of Jerry Ford. But in the end, it came down to the same thing—Ford was at least as conservative as Nixon, if not more conservative." Even members of Ford's administration acknowledged that his relations with Congress were personally congenial but, due to philosophical disagreement, substantively thin. O'Donnell conceded, "The Ford Administration will probably not be remembered for what it pulled off in the legislative arena. Ford had good congressional relations because of his personal attitude and experience . . . but a good attitude and comfortable approach just didn't have much to do with making a measurable impact on the bigger policy picture."[65]

Ford's relations with Congress were better than those of his successor, who had the advantage of having a Congress of his own party. Jimmy Carter never hit it off well with Congress. Alien to the practice of striking deals and trading favors, Carter neither fully understood nor enjoyed the political game of dealing with Congress. He once admitted that "horse-trading and compromising and so forth have always been very difficult for me to do," while one of his chief speechwriters commented that Carter's "skin crawled at the thought of the time consuming consultations and persuasion that might be required to bring a legislator around."[66] Instead of bargaining, Carter preferred taking a pious stand on issues. Members of Congress complained that Carter never consulted with them enough and resented his self-portrayal as a political detergent sent to clean up Washington.[67] Ford was better suited than Carter to succeed Nixon and carry out the task of improving the political atmosphere. He appreciated the mechanics of personal relations and was good at it. Under Ford, the president and Congress once again governed together.

"All politics is personal," says an old adage, and Ford treated the members of what he considered his "real home" respectfully and affably. Given the wide philosophical gap between Ford and the Ninety-fourth Congress and their clashes on substantive issues—like the economy, energy, and foreign policy—his comity with Capitol Hill was vitally important in post-Watergate Washington. The *New York Times* praised Ford for "a better working relationship" with Congress than either of his Republican predecessors, Eisenhower and Nixon. Ford never resorted to extralegal methods to advance his agenda, even when he had difficulty in promoting it. He respected the balance of power, consulted with Congress frequently, and dared not govern without it. Political scientist James Reichley wrote that by promoting his policies "in a spirit of amity and civility, rather than through attempted intimidation and aggression, Ford advanced the healing, not only of the executive, but of the entire governmental system."[68] He salved raw wounds between Congress and the president, reduced the post-Watergate animosities and suspicions, and restored civility to political conflict. In an era of disillusionment with government, Ford's accomplishment was a great feat. While some of his successors developed rabid enemies by the time they left the presidency, when Ford finished his term he could make the same claim as during his congressional career: he had adversaries, but not a single enemy, in Washington.

Chapter 4

Ford's Vision for America

G erald Ford went to college during the Great Depression. Coming from a modest, middle-class background, he faced a great challenge in simply finding the money to attend the University of Michigan. The Wolverine gridiron coach heavily recruited Ford, who captained his high school football team as a senior, leading it to an undefeated season and state championship; but in the 1930s there were no athletic scholarships. Still, help came down various avenues. Ford's high school principal created a special scholarship for him. Ford waited tables at the university hospital and gave blood every two to three months for money. Although always on a tight budget, he managed to pay for his Michigan education.[1]

For meals, Ford turned to the center of his college social life, Delta Kappa Epsilon. Ford recalled that being in a fraternity "was the thing to do in those days." During his freshman year, he pledged, washed dishes at "Deke" for meals, and was inducted as a sophomore.[2] The frat brothers grew to respect the star football center, one of them remembering that Ford took "tough courses like economics and got excellent grades."[3] They appreciated another Ford achievement. As a junior and senior, Ford served as the Deke house manager. He recalled that "when I became house manager, we straightened out the fraternity's fiscal problems, and instead of being in the red, we became solvent."[4] When Ford graduated in 1935, the University of Michigan yearbook credited him with having "put the D.K.E. house back on a paying basis."[5]

Forty years later, Ford found himself managing a much larger budget, that of the United States. But his principles remained the same; once again, he fought for solvency.

The Definition of a Statesman

In December 1973, when Ford's nomination as vice president came before Congress, just three senators voted against his confirmation. Two of them,

Democrats Thomas Eagleton of Missouri and Gaylord Nelson of Wisconsin, explained that they did not think that Ford could provide what Nelson called "inspirational leadership" were he to succeed Nixon.[6] From the moment Ford stepped into the executive branch, liberals in Congress decried his vision for the country, or lack of one. As president, Ford's views ignited ideological opposition from Congress. Democrats took a traditional liberal approach to correcting the country's economic ills, emphasizing full employment and an active role for the federal government, with less concern about inflation and budgetary deficits.

Ford had been a fiscal conservative throughout his career, and since he had not campaigned for the presidency, he transformed his political beliefs into a presidential program, making his ideas a nostrum for the nation's challenges. This process was critical; to lead, a president must articulate a philosophy and establish policies to implement it. For his vision of a good America, Ford repaired to the Constitution and the idea of limited government. As Philip Buchen recalled, Ford was "very realistic about how government works and the effects of its action; he knew what its limitations were."[7] Buchen explained that his longtime friend and colleague "was not a great one for initiating a wide variety of programs. He limited his so-called 'agenda' to what really concerned him, and to what he thought government had the opportunity to do something about. He was a minimalist as far as the government was concerned."[8] This outlook was a key component in Ford's battle against inflation. Excessive government spending and budget deficits fueled inflation, he believed, and the Democratic pursuit of "full employment" contributed to higher prices.[9]

Ford was trying to change, even reverse, a trend in social and economic policies that had been entrenched for nearly half a century. Skeptical of grand federal programs with catchy names like the New Deal or the Great Society, Ford couched his language in simple terms and eschewed a lofty vision. "Ford wasn't a theme type of man. He wasn't someone who attempted to sell things by packaging them for the media," Assistant for Ecomonic Affairs William Seidman recalled. As a congressman, Ford opposed such Great Society initiatives as Medicare, federal aid to education, and subsidized housing.[10] He believed that they were often wasteful and did little to assist those they were designed to help, instead reaping benefits for the professionals who planned and administered them. "The trouble with a lot of these programs, where compassion ought to be the main thrust, is that they get well beyond the properly intended scope," Ford maintained. "You can't be compassionate for the ones who get cut out, because they shouldn't have been in the program in the first place."[11] In Ford's view, much of the 1970s disillusionment with government came because Americans grew disgusted with the sheer size and scope of government social programs.[12]

A mainspring of Ford's principles was that federal resources and spending capacities were limited. He was determined to end what he saw as the social experimentation of the 1960s, which, in his view, increased the burden on the taxpayer and created disincentives to work and a dependence on welfare.[13] Instead, Ford set much store by the adage that the government that governs least governs best. "A government big enough to do everything for you is a government big enough to take everything away from you" was a standard Ford refrain.[14]

Ford thought that government spending also increased the tax burden on the private sector. He believed that "federal tax rates on corporate profits are too excessive for us to accumulate capital and expand our economy to provide jobs. I don't accept the premise that profits are excessive in this country, across the board. An industry or a particular corporation might do extremely well, but over the years those profits will average out."[15] In addition to creating a heavy tax burden, government spending had diverted savings and credit from the private sector and discouraged capital investment. As a result, among the world's industrialized countries, the United States devoted a disturbingly small share of its economic output toward capital goods.[16] Consistent with Ford's focus on long-term economic growth, he wanted more resources to go toward savings and investment—the crux of long-term growth—and less toward consumption. Combined with a prudent paring of government expenditures, Ford hoped that this policy could reduce aggregate demand, decrease inflation, and promote stable economic growth.[17]

Ford's concept of an activist president was that of a budget cutter. The administration's constitutional scholar, Robert Goldwin, recalled that the "closest [Ford] came, in my view, [to enunciating] something far-reaching and broad was a simple formulation: no new spending programs. He said that over and over again, trying to get a grip on the budget." Goldwin credited Ford with realizing long before other public officials did that "unless there were some powerful restraint exercised, that the budget would just run away without anyone being able to control it."[18] Yet this position carried political risks. When the president pledged that he would support no new spending programs, he immediately deprived himself of potential constituents and weakened his political base.[19]

This concept of presidential leadership was neither popular nor innovative. Ford admitted, "If 'vision' is to be defined as inspirational rhetoric describing how this or that new government program will better the human condition in the next 60 days, then I'll have to confess I didn't have it." Instead, Ford emphasized the long term. "As President," he believed, "it was my job to identify the trends that were emerging in American society, and then to determine what decisions could affect those trends and put the country in better shape ten or twenty years from now. That's why I kept saying the rate of growth of federal expenditures should stay below the rate of growth of the economy as a whole." Ford thought the 1970s could mark a watershed for the federal government's role. As the United States entered its third century as a nation, he stated, "We are at a critical point in our history, a point where we can either allow federal spending and federal deficits to mushroom, or we can decide to restrain the growth of federal spending and restore the vitality of our private economy." During the nation's bicentennial year, Ford often urged consecrating America's next hundred years to the individual, shifting focus away from government: "Now we are on the threshold of our third century. I see this as the century of individual freedom. . . . [That] means liberty from oppressive, heavy-handed bureaucratic government. . . . That is a goal we must achieve in our third century."[20]

Ford was a legislator-turned-executive, and his disinclination to propose new programs reflected his political training. Accustomed to seeing individual bills, he viewed issues separately, looking at components rather than a large program.[21] Moreover, for all but six of Ford's twenty-five years in Congress, he served in the minority, blocking Democratic initiatives, often without offering counterproposals. Hugh Carey, a Democratic congressman before becoming governor of New York, charged, "In my 14 years in Congress I never saw Gerald Ford advocate a constructive program." Because Ford was in the minority, Senator Henry Bellmon said, "He didn't have to do things that were innovative or creative. . . . I think that's a problem when you spend so much time in the minority—you begin to have a negative mindset, and Ford had that."[22]

Lack of time also prevented Ford from developing and articulating a sweeping new vision for America. Political agendas are usually developed and fine-tuned during a presidential campaign, and an election mandate endows a president with an additional sense of mission. Ford had no time to plot an ambitious course once in office. His short presidency was an irony, because he believed that his actions would transcend his term in office and affect future presidents, just as his predecessors' decisions affected him. George Reedy, Lyndon Johnson's press secretary, observed the many problems that Ford inherited as president and commented, "Ford is paying for the mistakes of the last four decades. He's been run over by history."[23]

Wary of programs offering short-term gains while hiding long-term costs, Ford preferred action that proposed future benefits despite immediate, sometimes painful, costs, such as reducing the deficit and ensuring Social Security's solvency (even pardoning Nixon).[24] He believed that this distinction separated a statesman from a politician. "A politician is interested in the next election. A statesman is concerned about the next generation," he wrote. "No statesman approves short term benefits if they undermine long range progress."[25] Programs to help individuals and special interest groups often passed on costs to future generations. Ford declared, "It is my judgment that we have to stop trading today for tomorrow in our government spending programs. Unless we do, when tomorrow comes, the nation will pay a terrible price for yesterday's expediencies." By focusing on the long term, Ford wanted to foster steady if slow economic growth, so as to eliminate the cycles of steep inflation and deep recession that the country suffered during the 1970s.[26] His modest but salutary long-term economic goal could be summarized as "3 percent, 3 percent, 3 percent," meaning rates of 3 percent inflation, unemployment, and gross domestic product (GDP) growth. Such a steady growth rate would keep inflation in check while allowing the economy to absorb new entrants into the labor force.[27]

Democrats bristled at Ford's approach, which they considered slow and painful. When Ford proposed a ceiling on cost-of-living increases and Social Security benefits, the voluble Hubert Humphrey called the plan "immoral, cheap, unforgivable, unacceptable, and unconscionable." On another occasion the Minnesota senator remarked, "Ford is like a 17th-century physician bleeding his patients in an attempt to cure them." Indeed, Ford's eagerness to limit government benefit programs created an image that he lacked sympathy for the disadvantaged. Ralph Nader called him "a smiling man who makes cruel decisions."[28]

This dichotomy between Ford's kind disposition and his political behavior, which seemed insensitive, surprised observers. Liberal writer John Hersey was shocked that in discussing a Democratic bill to provide jobs, Ford wanted foremost to limit spending. Hersey glimpsed "another side of the man who has been so considerate, so open and so kind to me as an individual—what seems a deep, hard, rigid side. Talking here, he has seemed a million miles away from many Americans who . . . are now feeling the cruel pinch of hard times."[29] Jerald terHorst believed that Ford would give the shirt off his back to help a child who needed clothes and then would "go right into the White House and veto a school-lunch bill."

But terHorst explained that Ford learned tight-fisted habits at an early age. The young Ford worked at his stepfather's Grand Rapids paint company during summers. Gerald Ford Sr. operated on a strict budget, paying bills every ten days, taking few risks to expand the company because he feared debt. The future president's introduction to the principles of strict fiscal management made a lasting impression on him, which his long experience on the House Appropriations Committee reinforced. TerHorst summed up this experience as "twenty-five years of complaining about Democratic budgets." Ford instinctively looked at the cost of a proposal in weighing its merits. Compassionate on a face-to-face basis, Ford believed that he had to take a different perspective with government programs. He explained, "I think some of the people who go for all these social programs don't understand that what they're doing is sometimes *not* compassionate, and helps to undercut and destroy some of the strong fabric of this country."[30]

In 1975, government spending accounted for a third of the national output. If the trend continued, Ford believed, within the next two decades government expenditures would account for more than half of the GDP, resulting in onerous taxes. The federal government "cannot, in my judgment, overspend year after year without doing drastic damage to the economy and harm [to] every one of our citizens," Ford warned.[31]

"Sewers and Mundane Things"

In avoiding new programs, Ford's presidency seemed barren of new ideas, opening Ford to charges that he had no "vision" for America's future. Democratic senator William Proxmire of Wisconsin had a name for Ford's political agenda: "do-nothingism."[32] To those Americans accustomed to more forceful presidential leadership, Ford's approach wasted the office's magnificent powers.

Ford and his detractors had contrasting perspectives and looked at different problems. To him, the presidency meant more than just unveiling new entitlement programs. Paul O'Neill voiced frustration that the media failed to look deeply at the issues that Ford emphasized, such as the need to reduce spending and the danger of deficits. O'Neill said the media find the details of the federal budget "mind-numbing" and "don't want to know about or suffer the intellectual energy drain of understanding the nuances or complexity of important public policy issues."[33]

Ford's understanding of such economic issues was better than that of any other president in recent history. Paul McCracken, who worked with Eisenhower, Nixon, Ford, and Reagan, believed that Ford's grasp of economics and the federal budget was the best among them.[34] Federal Reserve chairman Arthur Burns, who frequently discussed economic and fiscal policy with Ford when he was president, later remarked, "I had no problem talking economics with Ford. He had a better grasp of economics than any other President I served." (Burns was Federal Reserve chairman under Presidents Nixon, Ford, and Carter and CEA chairman under Eisenhower.) Moreover, Burns believed that Ford dealt with the Federal Reserve discreetly, respecting its independence and studiously avoiding any meddling. Burns called Ford "truly angelic" in his relationship with the Fed. Observers who witnessed Ford's grasp of fiscal data invariably came away impressed. Democratic governor Dan Walker of Illinois said that he had rarely seen a chief executive with such a prepossessing knowledge of economic facts and statistics.[35] Yet Ford had trouble translating his mastery of economic policy into a well-known public trait.

Perhaps the best demonstration of Ford's knowledge and skills was his media briefing for the 1977 fiscal year budget. When Budget Director James Lynn was once leaving the Oval Office after discussing the fiscal 1977 budget with Ford, he turned and asked the president if he knew that Truman—one of Ford's presidential favorites—was the last president to give his own budget briefing. No, Ford replied, he was not aware of that. The next time the two met, Ford asked Lynn, "Would you mind if I gave the budget briefing myself?" Having planted the seed, Lynn was only too happy to agree, knowing that Ford would give a sterling show.[36]

The site was the State Department auditorium. The president stood at a podium on the stage. Cabinet members sat at small tables positioned in an arc behind him. Ford was appearing personally to acquaint the media with the intricacies of his proposed federal budget. His appearance underscored his involvement in formulating the budget, to which Ford devoted even more time than crucial legislative proposals. The move was also daring, because the budget was vast and complex, loaded with facts and figures that could become verbal landmines. The budget had grown in size and complexity since Truman's day. Most presidents dared not conduct their own briefing; as O'Neill said, "Even for those who spend a lifetime studying [the federal budget], it is crammed full of details and nuances in areas where one could get tripped up."[37] Ford recalled that when he decided to do the briefing himself, "Some of my aides were aghast. If I tried to respond to specific questions about complex items in the budget, they said, I'd slip. *Anyone* would. And if I had to refer questions to my assistants, it would appear to the public that I didn't know what the budget was all about. I'd reinforce the image of an amiable bumbler not quite up to the job."[38]

Yet Ford's performance was, in the words of prior Budget Director Roy Ash, "amazing."[39] He briefed the entire budget and in doing so showed a staggering command of the information. Awestruck administration members conceded that some cabinet officers did not know their department's budget with the intimacy that Ford demonstrated.[40] Robert Goldwin watched Ford deftly answer specific questions about the budget without relying on the cabinet or Office of Management and Budget (OMB) officers present to provide assistance. "The questions came from all these journalists, some of whom were specialists in one part of the budget or other, and Ford answered all the questions without asking help from all the people behind him. It went on for about an hour," Goldwin recalled. Later Goldwin asked some OMB economists to appraise Ford's performance. They said, "He answered some of those questions that I couldn't have answered. The parts of the budget that I know, he answered, and he got it right. And there were other parts that I couldn't have answered—I don't know those things. But he knew the whole thing."[41]

Yet few reporters acknowledged Ford's impressive grasp of the budget. O'Neill was exasperated: "Here was a person who knew more about the intricacies of policies and programs than anyone since Harry Truman, and the press was portraying him as a stumblebum, and I must say it was a great aggravation to me."[42] Ron Nessen thought that the federal budget failed to sate the media's hunger for sensational stories. "It was difficult for many journalists to come down from the high of Watergate," he wrote. "They were addicted. Lies! Tapes! Exposures! Drama! . . . Who could be happy again covering mundane matters like budgets, energy, and legislative proposals?"[43] The public never appreciated Ford's understanding of the federal government or understood his political vision, which was well enunciated in his budget messages. For the media, James Lynn lamented, "These things are too technical. They're boring."[44]

Ford's extensive knowledge of the federal budget was no accident; it was rooted in his long service on the House Appropriations Committee, which decides how the federal government spends money. When first appointed, Ford recalled, "Appropriations was where the power was, and I said to myself, 'That's going to be my specialty—how the government spends money.'" Ford's quarter century on the committee allowed him to observe and partake in decisions on the government's day-to-day operations. Ford parlayed his experience into a hands-on approach to budget formulation, which contrasted with that of previous presidents, who found such detail dull. Lyndon Johnson's eyes glazed over during budget discussions, and he interrupted only to ask bizarre questions such as the crotch size in air force uniform pants. Nixon grew irritated when Budget Director Richard Mayo bored him with details and numbers. One reason that Ford invested so much time and energy in formulating his budget was that it defined his approach to executive leadership. The budget was the engine room of government, and there Ford liked to tinker.[45]

Few presidents have the opportunity to lead during moments of true national crisis, such as major wars. Presidential leadership involves spectacular action only occasionally. Instead, as William Seidman observed, "It's about sewers and welfare and taxes and mundane things, and it needs somebody who knows how to . . . make government work. Ford had the ability to make government work, and he was well along on his way of doing that. And that is not inspirational."[46] Ford once reflected, "Too often 'vision' is just a fancy word people use to justify spending a lot of money. You can spend an awful lot of money on some pretty unattainable goals. That's why I'm a firm believer in the pragmatic approach. I'm more concerned with the nuts and bolts of getting from here to there." He explained, "My idea of vision is ensuring that we're making progress on a day-to-day basis. I want to know the accounting figures for how we did today and how we're going to do tomorrow—and how we're going to get there, in practical terms."[47] Ford's political philosophy never attracted a devoted following in part because this idea of making government work and remain in the black was a mundane matter that Americans expected, even took for granted. According to Seidman, Ford believed that "the presidency is not a matter of a great crusade. It's a matter of providing sound government to people on every level. [That] is a wonderful legacy which unfortunately isn't recognized."[48] Instead, history defines twentieth-century presidential greatness in terms of dramatic accomplishments, such as wartime victories or innovative domestic programs that involve spending federal money.

Yet in fostering public understanding of his political philosophy, Ford also handicapped himself. His oratorical skills were unspectacular, and he never articulated a persuasive theme or idea to capture the essence of his presidency, especially important since the idea of fiscal integrity was hard for the public to understand. Although he gave many speeches and communicated with the press, Ford never convincingly stated his presidency's central purpose. After Ford had been in office for just over a year, William Baroody told him of "the need for an articulation of your basic philosophy and your definition of the Administration's larger objective."[49] The perceived absence of a theme was disconcerting, especially as the 1976 campaign approached. Seeking to redress the problem, Goldwin tried to elicit from Ford a verbal picture of the goals he had set for his presidency and the country, an effort that was largely unsuccessful.[50]

To get Americans—a people accustomed to speedy service and instant gratification—to understand the need for short-term pain for long-term gain, Ford had to summon a critical presidential power, persuasion. His modest, uninspiring oratory contributed to his inability to advertise his knowledge of government and his failure to win a full term. Paradoxically, Ford lost the

1976 election even though the economy was healthier after two years of his presidency. Had he been able to popularize his approach to governing and his success in ameliorating economic ills, he might have won the election.[51] His failure was not economic but political. Ford's dilemma also reflected troubled times, especially compared to earlier postwar decades, such as the 1950s.

Ford and Eisenhower

Gerald Ford was once asked who he thought was the best president of the twentieth century. His answer was Dwight D. Eisenhower. He greatly admired Eisenhower, and in his outlook on the federal budget and the presidency, Ford echoed the views of the thirty-fourth president. Ford called Eisenhower "one of my presidential heroes . . . he was a far, far better, more astute president than the public thought."[52]

Like Ford, Eisenhower wanted to exercise restraint in presidential authority. The former general thought that Franklin Roosevelt and Harry Truman had expanded the president's power and authority beyond constitutional bounds, outleaping Congress, and he wanted to redress the imbalance.[53] Eisenhower tried to limit spending, reduce taxes, and balance the budget. Time and again he preached "fiscal responsibility." He wanted to convince Americans that "thrift is not a bad word" and railed against "political radicals" in the Democratic Party who "mangled and mushroomed" his frugal proposals and whom he charged with spending huge sums of government money. Throughout his presidency, Eisenhower struggled to curb congressional spending but often felt stymied by Congress. "The Congress, as a whole, has never been sufficiently committed to frugality and efficiency," he lamented.[54]

Both Ford and Eisenhower saw balanced budgets as vital for one major reason: containing inflation. Eisenhower once dismissed the claim that moderate inflation benefited the economy by arguing that it was "like saying that being a little bit pregnant was good for you."[55] In embracing fiscal integrity, Eisenhower took a long-term perspective; he peered into the future and felt disturbed by contemporary trends, especially deficit spending. Eisenhower wanted to brace the economy for the "long haul," as he often called it. In the 1950s, he predicted that the cold war would last a half century and argued that America's ultimate success in the struggle depended on its ability to husband economic resources.[56] That meant restraint in spending. In comparing his own focus to Eisenhower's, Ford explained, "My whole life I've looked at goals. . . . I always felt that you had to have a long-term goal, you had to have a strategy to achieve it, you had to have discipline to accomplish it. And my feeling is that was Eisenhower's approach."[57]

To hold down government spending, Eisenhower introduced few domestic initiatives, contributing to the tranquility, even boredom, of the 1950s. Critics charged that he failed to realize the heroic potential of his office; one pundit cracked, "His smile was his philosophy." The same charges badgered Ford.[58] Both preferred to sacrifice large-scale federal initiatives for balanced budgets and long-term growth. But neither could eloquently explain his philosophy to the people or develop a well-defined, enduring party constituency.

No Republican rushed to claim the Eisenhower or Ford mantles and carry on their missions. Both the right and left assailed Eisenhower. His conservative fiscal policy was anathema to liberals, his moderate "modern Republicanism" had little appeal to conservatives. He once remarked, "I feel pretty good when I'm attacked from both sides . . . it makes me feel more certain I'm on the right track."[59] Eisenhower was also lucky. With a winning smile and personality, he rode a crest of goodwill that followed his World War II military accomplishments. It was easy to like Ike, and millions did. The war hero won thumping election victories in 1952 and 1956 and presided over a prosperous economy.

Jerald terHorst called Ford "an Eisenhower without medals."[60] Like the general, Ford had a warm smile and kind personality. But the public loved Eisenhower; Ford generated no such deep affection. Ford also led the country in a more difficult era. The 1970s economy was buffeted by an ill never seen during the 1950s—stagflation—and the public was more cynical and unforgiving. Moreover, the GOP's conservative wing was much stronger and more rebellious, and the locus of party power had shifted not only toward the right but toward the West Coast, creating more difficulty for a moderate, Washington-based midwesterner like Ford. While he espoused ideals similar to those of Eisenhower and fostered a similar, if shorter, period of tranquility, Ford never captured the public and party backing that the war hero did. In part, he was a victim of the era.

The Veto Strategy

Ford labored against another burden that did not afflict Eisenhower, a rebellious opposition Congress. But Ford had the advantage of intimate knowledge of Capitol Hill, and his conflict with Democrats, who largely opposed his philosophy of fiscal restraint, produced a shrewd strategy: using the veto. He set the pattern early. After just one week as president, he had already vetoed two bills. It was more than some presidents reject in a year and a harbinger of more to come.

Ford was not the first president to use the veto so vigorously or to cause so much chagrin among opponents in the process. Andrew Jackson, whose twelve vetoes totaled more than those of his six predecessors combined, earned the nickname "King Veto" from adversaries, who charged that his use of the veto enlarged presidential powers and reflected a pugnacious personality. They were right on both counts. But through his vetoes, Jackson exerted a check on Congress and established presidential influence in the legislative process. The veto also allowed Jackson to express his political philosophy, one that embraced limited federal power and the Jeffersonian ideal of "a wise and frugal government."

The veto enabled a president in Ford's predicament to restrain congressional spending. With limited political resources, Ford considered the veto the only tool that he could really employ.[61] Its use could preserve the balance of power between the chief executive and Congress. As he explained, the veto strategy "was an outgrowth of my understanding of how to deal with Congress. Too many presidents think you gain respect and favor with Congress by rolling over and playing nice with them. Congress has to learn to respect you, and they learn to respect you when you tell them 'no.' And after you tell them 'no' enough, then they'll sit down and talk with you."[62]

With the veto, Ford also found a way to express his philosophy and concerns for the country. Phil Buchen said, "Ford just didn't want any proposal that expanded the role of government. He was very much worried about deficit financing that was beginning [to accentuate itself in the 1970s]. . . . And that's why he took to vetoing so many bills."[63] Administration members believed that without presidential restraint, Congress could spend too much money. As Ford explained, "Congress passes a lot of bad legislation without really thinking about it. And every once in a while a president has to say, 'You made a mistake. Now go back and think about it.' And often, when they think about it, they change."[64]

Ford's vetoes led to charges that his was a negative presidency. Tip O'Neill said with incredulity, "The amazing thing about President Ford's record on vetoes is that he's proud of it. He is proud of the negativism that has kept Americans out of work and slowed our economy." Ford's staff feared that a veto strategy reinforced the image of a presidency in stasis.[65] Ford recalled that Democrats in Congress accused him of "obstructionism" and "thwarting the will of the majority." Critics "kept saying when I'd veto, 'It's a negative attitude, it's a negative attitude.'" "That's just not true," he argued. "A president has a constitutional responsibility and authority to veto. And if he doesn't use that tool he's neglecting his presidential responsibility." Ford used the veto not just to block bills but to mold legislation, and he maintained that it had a positive rather than negative influence in shaping fiscal policy.[66] After leaving office, Ford wrote that a veto "is an affirmative decision by a President in that it is an action telling the Congress that perhaps the House and Senate have moved too rapidly or in error. A veto gives the Congress an opportunity to review carefully what it has done and to possibly seek an agreeable compromise with the President."[67] Members of Congress would think twice about a bill and try to improve it if they knew that Ford would veto it.

James Lynn spoke admiringly of Ford's veto strategy, saying the president applied it "like a scalpel" to trim fat off the budget.[68] By using the veto, Ford could force Congress to modify its "irresponsible spending schemes," as he saw them, thereby inducing it to adopt legislation that he found acceptable.[69] In early 1976, Ford commented that the veto strategy helped to fashion legislation more consonant with his philosophy: "We used vetoes several times this year to produce constructive legislation in place of legislation that I think would have been unwise. Take housing. Congress sent down a bill that was loaded for all the special-interest groups in the housing industry, and everybody else, virtually. I vetoed it. They came back with a bill that was 90 percent or 95 percent good." Ford's veto messages resonated with the theme of fiscal responsibility. When he pocket vetoed a nurse training bill, Ford's veto message explained that the measure proposed to authorize more than $650 million over three years, a spending level that he called "intolerable." Ford saw the veto as the "single most powerful weapon at my disposal to force Congress to recognize fiscal restraint and keep the economy on track."[70]

Under Ford, the OMB developed a meticulous process to ensure that legislation stayed within spending limits. After the president's budget went to Capitol Hill, the OMB staff tracked bills as they made their way through Congress. "We'd track every appropriation bill, from the [levels of] subcommittee, to the full committee, full House, full Senate," recalled Ken Glozer, the OMB's deputy associate director for energy and food. "Every piece of legislation, every week." If a bill exceeded an appropriation level—or "wandered off the reservation," as the OMB termed it—the administration sent veto threats to subcommittee or committee chairmen. The process represented a rigorous attempt to control an opposition Congress and contain spending, and Glozer (who later served in the Carter, Reagan, and Bush [senior] administrations) reflected that Ford's OMB "did an excellent job . . . in terms of managing the government to conform to the administration's goals, priorities, and policies."[71]

Seidman thought that most members of Congress, rather than sensing stalemate from Ford's vetoes, voiced relief that Ford rejected a costly bill.

Seidman remembered, "I don't know how many congressmen I heard say, 'Boy, that's great. You vetoed that turkey, we never should have spent that much. . . . now I'll send it up to you with the right amount.'" By failing to override—sometimes not even trying—Congress signaled tacit agreement with the president's action. An example was a 1975 bill to increase tobacco price supports for farmers. In vetoing it, Ford expressed sympathy for tobacco growers; however, he asserted that increased price supports would make American tobacco less competitive in world markets and increase budget outlays by $157 million: "I believe this bill would adversely affect our tobacco exports, lower farm income in the long run and increase federal spending at a critical time in our economic recovery." Congress made no attempt to override his veto.[72]

Seidman explained that "most of the Congress was very pleased to let him take the heat for cutting stuff, and they could claim they voted for the higher thing and then support the lower thing." Seidman observed that Ford, as a former congressman, "had it figured out very well and the Congress behaved exactly the way he expected they would. They would all holler about his veto, then they would support a lower thing." Max Friedersdorf shared the view of many administration members that Ford's vetoes were "the highlight of his two-and-a-half years in office," and he remarked that Ford "could have rolled over and signed those bills, and he could have saved himself a lot of grief. But he chose not to, and I think it took a lot of courage."[73] No postwar president used the veto as effectively as Ford. Even Ronald Reagan, whose sweeping mandates and communication skills gave him far more influence on Capitol Hill, was criticized by conservatives and businesspeople for not using the veto enough, and Bill Clinton did not issue his first veto until June 1995, more than two years into his presidency.[74]

Ford's veto of the emergency housing bill illustrated his ability to force Congress to rework fiscal follies into legislation more in keeping with his fiscal philosophy. Poor economic conditions led to a severe housing industry contraction in 1974. By January 1975, unemployment in the industry stood at 15 percent, almost twice the national rate, and by May 1975 increased to 22 percent, with housing starts at their lowest levels in twenty-eight years. In response, Congress developed a bill for HUD to make loans to homeowners. But the bill included two major subsidy programs that Ford found unacceptable: one would have offered middle-income home buyers cash grants of $1,000 for down payments on houses; another would have given subsidies to middle-income families to reduce mortgage rates to just 6 percent. Even some Democrats considered the bill extravagant. Democratic congressman Albert Ashley of Ohio, regarded as the most knowledgeable

House member on housing issues, called the bill "a turkey" and "a loser." Warning his colleagues that a presidential veto was justified, he sputtered with outrage, "I do not understand why we insist on serving up these veto pitches that come over the plate the size of a pumpkin. I do not understand the surprise, frustration, the little shrieks of anger when the President picks on these fat cripples and drives them out of the ball park. What on earth can we expect?" Ford vetoed the bill and specifically cited the two subsidies as "excessive." By vetoing the bill, Ford forced Congress back to the drawing board, and within two weeks it sent him a new bill that eliminated both major subsidies and made other cost-saving modifications. Ford signed the compromise version and praised Congress for its cooperation.[75]

As potentially inflammatory as Ford's veto strategy was, the executive and legislative branches still functioned effectively. No paralyzing enmity resulted because Ford's style created a political atmosphere that allowed him to veto bills without generating deep umbrage. Ford's congeniality made healthy, even heated, legislative confrontation possible again. John B. Anderson remembered that while he sometimes heard complaints that Ford ran a government by veto, "I don't recall that [the charge] stuck very well to Ford. He was too well liked."[76]

Some critics charged that Ford used the veto promiscuously. But the relative number of vetoes was surprisingly small. In 1975, Congress passed 1,436 measures; Ford vetoed 13 of them, and was overridden three times.[77] During his presidency, Ford vetoed 66 bills (50 regular vetoes and 16 pocket vetoes), more than Nixon, Carter, Bush (senior), and Clinton, all of whom served longer.[78] Among presidents since Ford, only Reagan, with 78 over eight years, vetoed more than Ford. Ford's average of 26.4 vetoes a year gave him the fourth-highest annual average among all presidents in history. (Grover Cleveland heads this list with 73 per year; Franklin Roosevelt is second with 53; and Truman comes in third with 31.3.)[79]

Congress overrode 12 of Ford's 66 vetoes, or 18 percent, much higher than the 4 percent average for all presidents.[80] The only president overridden more times than Ford was Andrew Johnson, Lincoln's embattled successor and one of only two presidents ever to be impeached, who had 15 of his 29 vetoes overridden. Even Nixon, whose effectiveness during his last year in office was crippled by Watergate, managed a lower percentage of veto overrides (16 percent) than Ford. Yet in light of the Democratic opposition, Ford felt successful in sustaining vetoes: "Bearing in mind that I had to deal with a better than two-to-one Democrat-controlled House and Senate, [I had] a pretty good track record," he reflected.[81] That Congress upheld 54 of Ford's 66 vetoes was a notable achievement. After their landslide in 1974, congressional

Democrats relished the prospect of overriding his vetoes at will. First-term Democrats, in particular, expecting to ride roughshod over the White House, were shocked to find they could not. Ironically, they themselves offered part of the explanation. Notoriously intractable, the freshmen Democrats were difficult to bring in line with the majority, leaving it splintered and unable to muster the votes for an override. Ford capitalized on the traditional Democratic inability to agree and even contributed to the fractiousness, as his legislative team cultivated Democrats with briefings and invitations to the White House.[82]

Tip O'Neill marveled at Ford's ability to elude veto overrides: "President Ford has to be the best as far as sustaining vetoes is concerned. I would call him 'King Veto.' . . . He knows every trick in the trade. Nobody has been able to sustain a veto like Jerry Ford can. He's the champion." Democrats in and out of Congress expressed frustration at their inability to beat his vetoes. In 1975, Speaker Carl Albert received a letter from a man who complained, "It is so difficult for a lifelong Democrat to believe what is taking place in Congress these days, with a two to one Democratic majority. The failure to override a veto is unbelievable. The President handles Congress like puppets on a string."[83] The weak congressional leadership of the 1970s, which hurt Ford by hindering his attempts to pass his energy legislation speedily, also helped him by allowing his vetoes to be sustained. After leaving office, Ford spoke with obvious satisfaction over his vetoes: "The hallmark of my administration is that even though I was tough on Congress, I ended up getting a lot more . . . of my views [out of Congress] than anybody anticipated."[84]

Ford used the veto as an instrument to shape national policy. Many of the bills he rejected concerned economic or foreign policy or entitlement programs. Throughout American history, most vetoes had been of private bills that provided special privileges to constituents, naming a particular person such as a veteran receiving benefits or an immigrant being granted citizenship. Ford vetoed public bills, which dealt with broad issues and large constituencies such as the unemployed, elderly, or farmers and which had greater ramifications on society than private bills. To a greater extent than any president, Ford used the veto to make public policy.[85]

Sometimes Ford vetoed bills if an override seemed certain. Kenneth Cole, director of his Domestic Council, remarked that Ford vetoed a veterans' education bill because he thought it would be inflationary, even though he knew Congress could effortlessly override: "He was advised that it was political suicide. But he said: 'I'm going to make my decision on what I think is right for the country, not on the basis of what Congress will do.'"[86] In such situations, Ford's vetoes assumed symbolic importance, expressing his conviction to limit government spending. "There were some things he wouldn't sign his name to," Robert Goldwin recalled. "He thought they were wrong and he knew it was going to be enacted whether he signed or not. He wanted to voice his objection to it."[87] By using the veto, Ford attracted attention to costly bills that otherwise would have passed unnoticed.[88]

Democrats believed that they had found an easy campaign issue for 1976. One union group urged its members to "Veto Ford!" in November. Warned Democratic presidential aspirant Birch Bayh, "Every unmet social need in this country today—from child care to aid to our senior citizens—stands at the mercy of Gerald Ford's overworked veto stamp."[89] But during the campaign, Ford extolled his veto strategy, telling supporters, "I have held the line on government spending with 66 vetoes and saved you—and I emphasize 'you'—the hard-pressed taxpayers, more than $9 billion." He claimed that the $9 billion translated to $200 for each American family. (By the end of Ford's presidency, his vetoes had translated to a savings of $41 billion.)[90] The veto strategy was Ford's method to demonstrate firm presidential leadership, reduce inflation, and enhance his role as a tribune of the taxpayers' money against what he called a spendthrift Congress. It fit Ford well, taking into consideration his unique position as an unelected president who lacked an electoral mandate. Given the congressional feistiness of the time, it was perhaps a uniquely 1970s form of presidential leadership.

Ford and Compromise

Though he could be blunt with veto messages and harsh with rhetoric against government spending, Ford was amenable to political compromise. *Washington Post* economic writer Hobart Rowen described Ford's economic policies as "pragmatic economics" because of Ford's ability to lay ideology aside to achieve practical solutions. In his confirmation hearings for the vice presidency, he stated his standard refrain that "truth is the glue that holds government together" and added, "compromise is the oil that makes government go."[91] He may have mixed metaphors, but Ford recognized that the Democrats had a formidable majority in Congress, and he gave ground in order to gain ground. After spending almost all of his House career in the minority, he emerged well schooled in the art of compromise. Melvin Laird remarked that "Gerald Ford was more willing to compromise with Congress than any recent President that I can remember. He had perfected the art of compromise during his congressional career. Compromise is the way to get things done if you're used to operating in the minority."[92] Philip Buchen also thought that Ford's experience influenced his tendency toward compromise: "As a minority leader, he had to keep a rather disparate set of Republicans together. He had the conservative and liberal Republicans to satisfy. And I'm sure in developing positions that the minority party was able to stick by, he had to accommodate conflicting interests and had to compromise."[93]

The veto strategy often paved the way for compromise. "I would compromise, but [only] after I had vetoed something and gotten a better version," Ford said.[94] He was wary of being rigid and inflexible. Because America comprised a wealth of different interests, he believed that conciliation was essential for national progress.[95] And while he espoused conservatism, as president he embraced the country's more moderate needs; Paul O'Neill called Ford "philosophically flexible" and "willing to learn, and to listen. . . . I think he was always open to ideas."[96]

James Lynn recalled a meeting at which Ford outlined his philosophy for dealing with Capitol Hill. Ford explained that in Congress, even political adversaries could find areas where their interests met. The president then drew overlapping circles, noting that the points where the circles met represented coinciding interests. "If . . . these circles intersect each other—even if it's only [a little bit]," Lynn recalled Ford's saying, "work with them on that one, and you can get something done in there." As Lynn observed, Ford skillfully adhered to this philosophy: "He'd find places up on the Hill where he could put together enough of those little patches to get things done. He was a master of the Hill."[97]

The partisan split between the executive and legislative branches made compromise critical. Divided government was a relatively novel predicament in twentieth-century politics. For the first half of the century, from 1900 to 1952, one party controlled both the presidency and Congress simultaneously for forty-four years. But since 1953, divided control had been the rule in Washington for all but ten years, with legislative stalemate often resulting. During the 1970s, voters felt more inclined to engage in "ticket splitting" and ensure divided government as they grew more distrustful of politics and preferred to see the evil forces battle one another rather than let one party gain the upper hand. To Ford, compromise was the only solution to the deadlock.[98]

Not all Republicans welcomed Ford's tendency toward accommodation. Hard-line conservatives grumbled over his willingness to accept legislation that they believed conceded too much to the Democrats. Their discontent helped explain the widening rift between GOP moderates and conservatives, as well as Reagan's appeal in the 1976 primaries. Goldwin observed that Ford "couldn't follow a course in the presidency that would be satisfying to doctrinaire conservatives, because the realities of the situation were that he had to deal with an opposition Congress, he hadn't been elected, there was very little discretionary power, anyhow. And so it was easy for Reagan . . . to spout orthodox, pure Republican positions and make it seem that this president was a false Republican, not true to the real principles."[99]

Ford's friends worried. Barber Conable despaired of Ford's behavior, writing in his journal, "It seems to me that his legislative background and training is [sic] constantly pushing him toward compromise, when his image would be much better enhanced by the appearance of willingness to stand up and fight for what he believes in." Conable later recalled, "I worried about Ford compromising too much. That was part of my feeling that he must radiate strong leadership if he were to be elected president."[100] Ford was stuck in an untenable political situation. His conservative, free-market rhetoric infuriated liberals, while his compromises irritated his party's right wing. As a result, Ford sometimes found himself occupying a gray area, which handicapped him in attracting a loyal and well-defined national following. Still, he was comfortable with compromise and believed that the moderate approach was correct. In 1976, shortly before the New Hampshire primary, Ford declared himself "a moderate, middle-of-the-road Republican." He stated that his record as president "conforms with the moderate Republican philosophy that is necessary to win." In a dig at Reagan, he added, "Anything to the extreme right of that philosophy can't win a national election. So, I think my philosophy, my record, is what is good for the Republican Party, and I think it is good for the country as a whole."[101]

Most legislation results from compromise. Ford knew that, in the words of John Kennedy, "every President must endure a gap between what he would like and what is possible."[102] One of Ford's challenges was to compromise while preserving essential elements of his proposals. Ultimately, compromise was often his only alternative. As Conable reflected, "There's a limit to the amount of hard-lining you can do when the cards are stacked against you."[103] Ford's conciliatory leadership, while producing legislation, also prevented an exacerbation of the executive-legislative tension inherent in divided government. After Watergate, his moderate politics served a functional purpose, preventing the further polarization of an electorate that had grown anxious and divided over war, scandal, and economic hardship.

Part Two
The Economic Challenge

Chapter 5

The Great Inflation of the 1970s

In many ways, the Fords were like the typical American family after World War II. While still single, Gerald Ford fought in the war, returned home, and resumed his career. After marrying, he moved to Washington, D.C., to embark on a new profession—politics. Then Ford and his wife, Betty, began a family that included four baby boomers: Mike, born in 1950; Jack, 1952; Steve, 1955; and Susan, 1957. The Fords moved from the city to the suburbs, leaving a Georgetown apartment for one in Alexandria, Virginia. They needed more space as their family grew, and in 1955 they bought a four-bedroom home in Alexandria, added a heated swimming pool, and enjoyed the amenities of suburban life.[1]

But like many American families, the Fords felt the pinch of inflation once the 1970s arrived. Now living in the White House, Gerald Ford—a dedicated swimmer—wanted to continue his twice-daily swim routine there but hesitated to install a new pool, fearing it would look wrong in a time of austerity (although in 1975, a pool was built using private donations).[2] Betty Ford recognized that she had to set a good example in the fight against rising prices. She urged the mansion's housekeeping staff to limit purchases and reviewed expenses herself. "There are certain things we will have to do to cut down," she believed. "There are lots of things we can do which are glamorous and elegant, without being very expensive." She pledged to set a clothes budget for herself, saying, "I know certain things are expected of the wife of the President, but I can do without buying expensive designer clothes." The First Lady economized by sharing clothes with her teenage daughter and using scarves to make the same outfits look different.[3] Because the president objected so much to the high cost of sugar—its price rose 400 percent in just one year—the First Family banned it from their dining table. (Nationwide, some consumers began calling sugar "white gold," while others organized boycotts.)[4]

The heady postwar years were over. During the 1970s, millions of American families found themselves scrimping or saving, as even the First Family did. The heart of the problem was the Great Inflation.

The Postwar Economic Miracle

For two decades after World War II, American economic progress was impressive. Physically unscathed by the war—while the lands of many allies and enemies were ruined—the country emerged with no great economic competitors. In a twist of fate, the war that destroyed other countries represented a huge leap forward for the United States, which entered an era of prosperity, optimism, even hubris. Those years, magazine magnate Henry Luce confidently declared, would be the "American Century," with the country dominating world events through its affluence and influence.

There seemed no reason to doubt it. The United States was the world's military giant and industrial titan, and its economic engine ran at almost full steam. In 1948, the United States produced about 45 percent of the world's total industrial output, and demand for American exports ran high, as rebuilding countries turned to the lone industrial power that could meet their needs.[5] The GNP jumped (in real prices) from $212 billion in 1945 to $688 billion in 1965. By 1971, the United States had become the world's first trillion-dollar economy.[6] No nation ever emerged from a war as such a clear victor or enjoyed such prosperity. The United States was the land of plenty. Americans owned 75 percent of the world's automobiles and came to expect a gamut of goods at department stores and supermarkets.[7] Technological breakthroughs in countless industries and fields—medicine, computers, electronics, chemicals, plastics—paced the breathtaking gains in the economy, resulting in even more new products for consumers, plus a burgeoning job market. On a more personal level, Americans happily reaped the benefits of the country's treasure. In most families, only one working parent could support the household and enable family members to live comfortably. By the mid-1950s, the postwar economic boom had allowed 60 percent of all Americans to climb into the middle class.

Within the span of one generation, Americans went from the shriveled expectations of the Great Depression to economic exhilaration. They knew no limits to their expectations. Economist Kenneth Boulding said America had a "cowboy economy" that, like the frontier of western legend, stretched on and on. In 1952, Illinois governor Adlai Stevenson declared, "Our people have had more happiness and prosperity . . . than men have ever had since they began to live in ordered societies four thousand years ago. Since we have come so far, who shall be rash enough to set limits on our future progress?"[8]

Population growth during the baby boom years reflected this attitude, and the country grew physically, too. Middle-class families broke free from the confines of city apartments and built homes in the suburbs. The housing industry boomed, the educational system expanded at all levels, and millions of new miles of highways sprouted up to accommodate more commuters and increased traffic. In 1959, America added two new states, Alaska and Hawaii, breaking free from its confines as a nation of contiguous states.[9]

There was an overweening pride palpable in America in the immediate postwar decades. In 1954, after returning from a trip to Japan, Secretary of State John Foster Dulles condescendingly declared the Asian nation incapable of producing products sophisticated enough to market in the United States.[10] Three years later, when the Soviets launched *Sputnik*, the world's first satellite, Americans reacted with a sense of wounded pride, disbelieving that any other nation, especially one that they considered technologically inferior, could trump the United States. As if to win the rubber match, John Kennedy galvanized the nation to land a man on the moon during the 1960s, a tremendous technological undertaking requiring billions of dollars in federal money.

The nation even achieved Kennedy's goal. But by the 1970s America had lost its heady confidence, and all signs pointed to an end to the American Century. It had lasted less than thirty years.

The Vietnam War had something to do with the crashing halt to American confidence, gouging a deep wound in national will and destroying the idea of American invincibility. The war showed that a small nation could oppugn American hegemony. Later in the decade, the Iranian hostage crisis once again made Americans feel that they were being kicked and mocked by a smaller nation. Larger nations, too, challenged American strength. By 1971 the Union of Soviet Socialist Republics (USSR) passed the United States in military spending and achieved nuclear parity. America's cohesion with its European allies began to fray, partly because the country's weaknesses were on view, partly because these nations found that they could compete with the United States economically. Many European countries adopted protectionist trade policies against the United States, and Americans saw Western Europe and Japan not as partners but as rivals. In 1969, West German chancellor Willy Brandt inaugurated a policy of Ostpolitik, in which his country independently pursued improved relations with the Soviet Union and East Germany.[11]

Domestic stalkers were at work, too: inflation, unemployment, and general stagnation. By 1970, the American economy entered middle age, losing the energy and vitality that marked the incredible gains of the earlier postwar years. Key industries like automobiles suffered slumps and appeared unlikely to regain their vitality. Few new industries emerged during the 1970s, and few existing ones grew. Corporations were reluctant to expand or build new plants because of the pessimistic economic climate, the high cost of construction materials, and the uncertainty about energy costs.[12] America's lagging growth in GNP told a tale of economic stagnation. Between 1948 and 1966, real GNP growth averaged 3.8 percent a year; between 1966 and 1973 it fell to 3.1 percent, and it fell still further during the rest of the 1970s (to 2.5 percent from 1973 to 1979). The growth of American productivity started to slide, from 2.6 percent in 1948–66 to 1.8 percent in 1966–73 (and slipping further to a scant 0.6 percent increase in 1973–79). Moreover, unemployment inched upward. The jobless rate, below 4 percent during 1966–69, averaged almost 7 percent from 1973 to 1979.[13]

Relative to other world economies, America's no longer seemed so impressive. Japan, the Soviet Union, and Western Europe caught up in productivity and economic strength, while America's industrial infrastructure became comparatively obsolete. As other countries produced inexpensive, high-quality goods, the demand for American products declined. By the 1970s, Americans admitted that some domestically produced goods were of shoddy quality. They pointed to the "built-in obsolescence" of Detroit cars, which were deliberately manufactured to break down over time and force consumers to purchase new ones. They relied increasingly on foreign-made electronic goods such as cameras and radios. America's share of world trade plummeted from 25 percent in 1948 to just over 10 percent at the end of the 1960s—still the largest share, but by a greatly diminished margin. Between 1965 and 1970, output per man-hour in manufacturing, the key index of productivity, rose an average of 14 percent per year in Japan, over 6 percent in France, and 3.6 percent in industrially beleaguered Great Britain. In the United States, the figure was just 2.1 percent.[14]

Pundits joked that during the 1970s, the incurable American optimism was cured.[15] The nation's self-confidence sputtered, and its economic performance betrayed clear symptoms of decline. The decade represented America's worst economic performance since the Great Depression.[16] Columnist Russell Baker lamented, "It appears that the 1970s' claim to distinction will be that it was the time when the United States became poorer." Disturbingly, economic events suggested a trend rather than a mere cycle. Speaking to media executives in 1971, Nixon observed the nation's flagging economic competitiveness and commented, "I think of what happened to Greece and Rome and, as you see, what is left—only the pillars."[17]

Causes of the Great Inflation

During only two decades in the twentieth century did Americans end the decade poorer than when they began it. One was the 1930s; the other, the 1970s. But the two decades were economic calamities for different reasons, the 1930s for depression and the 1970s for inflation. The Great Inflation of the 1970s hit Americans hard and defied usual inflationary behavior. For much of American history, inflationary periods were spasms—short outbursts in which prices spiked upward but quickly settled down again, as during and after a war. During the economic cooling off that followed such a period, living costs frequently declined to a point equal to or even lower than the level before the inflation. In this way, prices stayed stable for much of the nineteenth century, so that items cost about the same in 1900 as they did in 1800.[18]

What made the economic situation of the 1970s unprecedented was that while deflation usually followed previous wars, the opposite happened after the Vietnam War. Moreover, since 1913 (when the consumer price index [CPI] was established), the country had never experienced a string of monthly cost-of-living increases exceeding six months. But at the time Ford took office, the CPI had registered consecutive monthly increases since January 1967—by far the longest streak in the CPI's history, with no end in sight.[19] Industrialist David Packard, cofounder of Hewlett-Packard and a close Ford friend, wrote to the new president and soberly observed that the country was "in a transition from a lower price level economy to a higher price level economy." During the 1970s, inflation raged at an average 8.8 percent rate.[20]

By and large, Americans who grew up in the 1950s and early 1960s were strangers to inflation. The country enjoyed price stability and only experienced "creeping inflation," where prices increased at an annual rate of 1 or 2 percent. That was easy to tolerate, even a healthy thing. At the time, many economists considered creeping inflation necessary to maintain full employment, and a little inflation stimulated growth and benefited the economy.[21] From 1953 to 1964, inflation averaged only 1.9 percent a year, a rate that many economists considered equivalent to no inflation at all.[22]

During the 1960s, inflation picked up speed. Between 1961 and 1971, the CPI inched up at an annual rate of 3.1 percent. In 1972, the CPI rose at a still low rate of 3.3 percent, but the 1973 rate was 6.2 percent. Then came 1974, when inflation hit an average 12.2 percent—a dreaded "double-digit" rate and the highest annual average rate of price increase since 1946. At this pace, prices in the United States would double within six years.[23] As inflation accelerated, the growth rate of the economy slowed. This linkage between inflation and slower growth reflected the economic uncertainty that inflation created, discouraging business investment.

While Americans felt these doleful effects, most were puzzled why their generation was so victimized by inflation. "What I don't understand is why the horrible, tremendous increases in prices," despaired a Seattle woman in 1974. "Things went up not just a few cents, or gradually, but whole dollars and seemingly all at once."[24]

In Ford's view, high federal spending was a root cause of inflation.[25] He believed that in the 1960s, the government had lived outside the rules that apply to individuals and institutions, namely, that spending more money requires collecting more money, either through higher taxes or higher prices. Unconcerned with the long-term effect on the economy, the Johnson administration had dispensed billions of dollars to fight two wars simultaneously, overseas against Vietnam and at home against poverty.[26] For too long Johnson refused to raise taxes, fearing that it would weaken support for the war (he finally relented in 1968, asking Congress for a tax increase). Without a tax increase, taxpayers continued to spend, while government spending for the Great Society and the Vietnam War increased. As government and civilians bid against each other for goods and services in the free market, the economy overheated, resulting in steep inflation. Excessively strong demand also produced shortages of critical materials such as copper, chemicals, and paper, which drove up prices.[27] This scenario constituted what economists called "demand-pull inflation" (too much money chasing around too few goods), where the economy was trying to operate beyond its capacity to produce goods and services.

A basic problem was that fiscal planners overextended Keynesian economic policy, which had gained credence during the Great Depression and aimed to counteract deflation. The premise was that the government could stabilize the economy over the swings of the business cycle by increasing spending and running a budget deficit during hard times and lowering spending and building a surplus during boom times. By applying Keynesianism correctly, the government could use fiscal policy to stimulate the economy out of a recession. But Keynesianism proved too much of a good thing, as government policy tried to promote perennial economic growth. Fiscal planners juiced up the economy and ran deficits during slack times and ignored the complementary idea of running budget surpluses during prosperity. The result was a chronic inflationary bias in the economy, where prices tended to be flexible upward but inflexible or "sticky" downward.[28]

In a way, the Great Inflation of the 1970s was a sequel to the Great Depression of the 1930s, an outcome of the government's shifting fiscal policy toward pumping up the economy to achieve lower unemployment without ever shifting back toward a less stimulative policy. This pendulum swing toward expansive government economic policy helped to explain why no deflationary period followed World War II, as had been the case after other wars. Instead, a mild undercurrent of inflation ran throughout the postwar period and flooded to the surface in the 1970s. By then, some economists argued that they needed to modify or even replace the Keynesian formula with a new doctrine. Yet while old economic assumptions and political prescriptions seemed bankrupt, no new solutions arose to take their place.[29]

In addition to the demand-pull inflation racking the 1970s economy, "cost-push" inflation was at work. As inflation rose, labor unions demanded wage increases so that workers could keep up with inflation; they often won escalator clauses in contracts that linked cost-of-living increases to workers' pay and fought for larger pensions and benefits. Acceding to labor's demands, companies felt justified in pushing the cost of increased wages on to consumers in the form of higher product prices. (The Nixon administration regarded cost-push inflation as the major factor behind early 1970s inflation and implemented wage and price controls in 1971 largely to induce labor to restrain wages and halt the spiral. By contrast, the Ford White House downplayed cost-push inflation and rejected wage and price controls.)[30]

Demand-pull and cost-push factors alone did not account for the Great Inflation. The Federal Reserve's monetary policy often reinforced the inflationary bias of expansive fiscal policy. From 1962 to 1972, the Fed allowed a bulge in the money supply to finance the Vietnam War, fund new domestic spending programs, and facilitate American multinational corporations to acquire overseas assets. During that decade alone, the United States created more money than it had accumulated in the entire 186-year history of the nation up to 1962. Easy money was the politically easy row to hoe; neither the president nor Congress relished the idea of supporting tight money. Low interest rates created an economic environment conducive to investment and strong growth, which in turn helped the political fortunes of the incumbents. Milton Friedman, the University of Chicago economist and 1976 Nobel Prize laureate, was the most influential advocate of the monetarist school, which posited a close and direct relationship between money supply and inflation. He calculated that to keep prices steady, the money supply should increase annually by more than 3 but no more than 5 percent. During 1970, the money supply grew at 5.1 percent; in 1971, at 6.3 percent; then, in 1972, it rose by 8.5 percent, and Fed chairman Arthur Burns later conceded that the expansion had been too rapid. Speculation was that Nixon's political operatives pressured Burns into endorsing expansive monetary policy, or even that Burns, a Nixon appointee and longtime friend, wanted to boost the president's reelection prospects.[31]

Nixon's economic thunderbolts contributed to inflation. In August 1971, he upset orthodox Republican free-market tenets when he ordered a wage and price freeze, the first time the country ever had to suffer such austerity during peacetime. The move marked "Phase I" of a series of wage and price controls, and the country remained under controls for most of the remaining years in the Nixon presidency (economist Paul Samuelson called the welter of phases "schizoid economics"). But the measures gradually grew less effective, and by the time "Phase III" ended in June 1973, even Treasury Secretary George Shultz called it "a failure." The administration phased out controls piecemeal by industry, with the last controls of "Phase IV" lifted at midnight on April 30, 1974 (except for those on health care and oil). With each phaseout, prices exploded—sometimes increasing by 50 percent—as businesses tried to recoup lost profits with immediate price hikes. Some estimates were that businesses spent up to $2 billion complying with controls, costs that they passed on to consumers. Worse, the controls had only aggravated shortages of materials by decreasing output.[32] While Nixon had once proclaimed that his administration had been elected to fight inflation, in the summer of 1973 *Time* concluded, "By all available measures, Nixon has thoroughly botched the job he said he was elected to do."[33]

Another component of Nixon's so-called New Economic Policy that aggravated inflation was the devaluation of the dollar. This move was another thunderbolt that dismantled the international money system that had existed since World War II. As a result of the 1944 Bretton Woods Agreement, all currencies of the world were pegged to the dollar, which in turn was fixed to an international gold standard. But under this system, the dollar became overvalued relative to other world currencies, which encouraged the United States to import cheap foreign goods and increased the trade deficit. In 1971, a sobering result of this deficit appeared. Nervous about the dollar's stability, foreign countries demanded U.S. gold instead, and the stash at Fort Knox shrunk from a postwar high of $25 billion to $10.5 billion. To boost American exports and decrease the trade deficit, Nixon acted boldly, taking the dollar off the gold standard and thus severing that relationship. The dollar's value fell, and as imports became more expensive, inflation grew.[34] (For example, between 1971 and 1974 the price of Volkswagens increased by almost 40 percent.) Meanwhile, American exports, now cheaper to foreigners, increased by one-third in 1973, which exacerbated domestic shortages, especially of food.[35]

These shortages—"shocks" to the economy—fueled inflation. The food shock was born of not only excessive world dependence on U.S. food exports but also of bad weather and the energy crisis. Aid programs heavily subsidized agricultural exports, making it cheap for foreigners to buy American food. With plentiful, low-cost U.S. exports, developing and Third World countries found little incentive to invest in their own agriculture, even as their populations grew rapidly. They bought extensively from the United States, running down its grain reserves. In affluent countries, people were eating better, creating an even greater demand for U.S. food supplies. Yet the problem was that American food was no longer so plentiful, because during the 1960s the U.S. Department of Agriculture had encouraged a policy of deliberate scarcity to increase crop prices, supporting farmers who let some of their land lie fallow. One-sixth of America's farmland went out of cultivation, and food production fell. Nixon's agriculture secretary, Earl Butz, said that in 1972 the administration was "spending money like a drunken sailor" to win the farm vote, granting the largest agricultural subsidies in history, which boosted farm incomes but encouraged a 2 percent drop in production.[36]

As luck would have it, during 1972–74 the world food supply suffered terrible blows. In 1972, the Soviet Union experienced a massive crop failure and, as a result, purchased huge amounts of grain from the United States. While in the 1971–72 crop year the Soviet Union bought 1.2 million metric tons of grain, in 1972–73 it purchased 19.1 million metric tons. U.S. grain sales to the Soviet Union, partly a desperate attempt to overcome the American trade deficit and partly a reflection of détente, drained domestic stocks and pushed up food prices. In just one month in 1973, the cost of farm food in the United States rocketed 23 percent.[37] In a comment that reflected the decreased trust in government that the weak economy engendered, one California worker remarked, "The wheat deal with Russia really ticked me off, and since then I've lost faith in everything the government says." (In October 1974, Ford jawboned two U.S. companies into scrapping a planned grain sale to the Soviet Union; he feared that the sale would cut stockpiles to risky levels and fuel inflation.)[38]

Compounding the unprecedented foreign demand for grain were bad harvests. During 1973, summer fuel shortages prevented farmers from harvesting large portions of their crops. In 1974, capricious weather parched the lands of the Midwest—with a drought that reduced wheat, corn, and soybean harvests—and then chilled these same areas with an early frost. The resulting agricultural shortfalls increased the cost of everything from human food to livestock feed. During the first month of the Ford presidency, the wholesale price of farm and food products jumped 7.6 percent.[39]

Most economists pointed to the oil shock as the major cause of the Great Inflation. It additionally demonstrated that America no longer stood immune to international stresses or controlled its economic destiny.[40] America was built on cheap and abundant energy. But the country's extravagant energy consumption, along with its declining oil production, set the stage for a rude awakening.

The Organization of Petroleum Exporting Countries (OPEC) was formed in 1960 but for over a decade wielded little power. During the 1960s, it quietly nursed grudges against the United States. One was economic: that American inflation eroded the value of the dollar. Because OPEC's oil contracts were denominated in dollars, a weak, devalued dollar robbed OPEC of revenues.[41] Another grievance, more political in nature, was that America supported the Israeli army during the 1973 Yom Kippur War, an action that antagonized the Arab nations of OPEC.

In October 1973, in response to America's help to Israel, the Arab nations of OPEC slapped an embargo on oil to the United States. By the time they ended their embargo in March 1974, Arab nations had increased the price of their oil to $12 a barrel, up from $3 a barrel—a 400 percent increase. As a result of the embargo and government interference with oil prices, during the winter of 1973–74 the price of gasoline and heating oil in the United States shot up by as much as 33 percent. A California couple complained that it took $11 to fill the tank of their family station wagon; just a few months earlier it cost only $6. The Arab oil embargo and the "energy crisis" seemed the final act in a decade-long drama of economic, political, and social unrest.[42] Some Third World leaders proudly proclaimed 1973 as a year whose historical importance equaled that of 1905 (when for the first time a non-European power—Japan—defeated a major European power, Russia). In 1973, the developing countries, represented by OPEC, scored their first significant victory over the advanced countries of the West.[43]

Nixon tried to assure the nation that the energy crisis was "a temporary problem" and soon the United States would enjoy plentiful supplies of inexpensive energy. Speaking words that Americans wanted so badly to believe, he declared, "Scare stories that the American people will soon be paying a dollar for a gallon of gas are just as ridiculous as the stories that say that we will be paying a dollar for a loaf of bread. The American people cannot afford to pay such prices, and I can assure you that we will not have to pay them." But with the country's wheat reserves at their lowest level in a quarter century, baking industry leaders predicted that bread might indeed soon cost a dollar a loaf.[44] The idea of a dollar for a gallon of gas was not so far-fetched.

The monumental increases in oil prices had serious repercussions. High oil prices aggravated inflation through a ripple effect, pushing up the prices of the innumerable items derived directly or indirectly from petroleum: gasoline, heating oil, chemicals, roofing shingles, plastics, and synthetic textiles. Although Americans never thought of it, many everyday essentials contained petroleum: glue, garbage can liners, record albums, nylon stockings, lipstick, even hockey pucks. Their prices all increased. For example, in 1974 the price of plastic filler used in auto body repair shops tripled in just nine months. Hoarding of chemicals like automobile antifreeze was common.[45] One Indiana man reported, "I've heard of many dealers, etc. holding back cases [of antifreeze] waiting for the price to go up. I paid $1.99 a year ago. It is now selling for $6 on up here."[46] The cost of paving and repairing streets and highways soared, since liquid asphalt was petroleum based, and all road construction machinery depended on gasoline or diesel.[47] Heavy industries such as steel, aluminum, and wood relied on petroleum-based fuels to run their factories, so the prices of their products increased. Transportation services like airlines and trains also hiked ticket prices to reflect higher fuel costs.[48]

The rising costs of fuel and food were vivid examples of what economists labeled "supply-shock inflation," where the high price of scarce raw materials forced up production costs and resulted in higher product prices. Supply-shock inflation was the supreme agent behind the Great Inflation, and it seemed to signal that America was entering a new phase as a civilization: a postpetroleum, limited-resource era.[49]

Americans and the Great Inflation

By 1974, inflation was the whale in the bathtub, crowding out everything else to become the huge concern. Americans almost obsessed over it; surveys showed that by a margin of almost two-to-one they regarded inflation as a greater hardship than unemployment. On the day Ford took office, the *Washington Post* editorialized that his "first and most urgent concern, as President, will necessarily be inflation. . . . The current surge of inflation, which has been running for nearly two years now, is affecting every family and diminishing the nation's general standard of living."[50] The paper's priorities spoke volumes; it did not even want Watergate and the resulting constitutional crisis to detract from the national focus on inflation.

As inflation eroded the value of their money, Americans' confidence and spending decisions crumbled. Less secure about their financial future, they postponed purchases. Because personal income could not keep up with the rise in prices, real buying power fell. Ford thought that inflation "hit consumer confidence and put the brakes on consumer spending harder than at any time since World War II." Storekeepers proved unable to induce reluctant shoppers to buy goods.[51] Reluctance sometimes turned to anger, as many consumers flung charges of price gouging or price fixing at merchants.

The anger over rising prices led to an epidemic of strikes. In 1974, 6,074 work stoppages took place, more than during any previous year in the postwar era, and the average duration of each strike was 27.1 days, also a postwar record. (By comparison, ten years earlier there were 3,655 work stoppages.)[52] Especially troubling were walkouts in the public-service sector. In Baltimore, trash piled up in the streets as striking sanitation crews fought for pay increases, and the city's police officers also walked off their jobs. Ohio and Rhode Island prison guards went on strike. A transit strike crippled public transportation in San Francisco. Greyhound bus lines was hit with its first nationwide strike in late 1974, lasting almost a week and stranding travelers in various cities.[53]

Striking workers were hardly alone in their discontent; inflation affected everyone. Hardest hit were minorities, the underprivileged, and those on fixed incomes. Economist John Kenneth Galbraith described inflation as taking from "the old, weak and small."[54] It shattered black Americans' dreams of having an income that kept pace with those of whites. The elderly were easy prey, because they relied primarily on savings, the real value of which eroded. President Ford talked about meeting a woman whose husband was retired. The couple relied on Social Security and a small pension and lived frugally. The woman handed Ford a receipt from the supermarket, bemoaning that "the total each week of this little grocery slip kept going up and up and up," as Ford recalled. Appalling stories of privation among the elderly spread, such as an old woman in Milwaukee who ate cat food to survive or Miami retirees who searched in garbage dumps for food scraps.[55]

Nor were the young immune to inflation. A twelve-year-old boy from Indianapolis, Indiana, addressed a letter to President Ford: "I am writing to you about this country. I think it is getting pretty bad." The youngster described a movie he had recently seen, *Soylent Green*, set in a future where food costs thousands of dollars, inciting riots.[56] A ten-year-old boy from Tennessee wrote to Ford, "I didn't buy as many baseball cards this year because they went up from 5 cents to 15 cents. So did football cards. I hope you stop inflation soon!"[57] Galbraith warned that unless Ford stopped inflation he would become "another in our extending list of presidential basket cases."[58]

Middle-class Americans felt the squeeze of inflation when high tuition costs made college too expensive. One electrical worker in Arkansas dropped out of college due to its high cost and lamented his generation's plight: "I guess we were spoiled. We were brought up to believe that if you went to college and then went out and worked you could make a decent living and get what you want. It's not so. Prices are too high." Colleges and universities, looking for ways to cut costs, targeted athletic programs, especially football, a sport that devoured money. Following the 1974 season, the University of Vermont canceled its football program, and the president of California's Long Beach State University even predicted that there "may be only four college football teams left by the 1980s."[59]

The staple dream of owning a home slipped beyond the reach of many Americans. During the Nixon presidency, the price of the average home jumped almost 40 percent. In 1974, despite a surplus of unsold homes, home prices still rose. At least one member of the Ford administration felt the shock of high home prices. William Seidman recalled, "I had to buy a house in Washington and I couldn't believe it. The prices were going up so fast. I thought the house [that I wanted to buy] was worth about $60,000. It turned out that I had to pay $200,000! So I had a real good look at what inflation does."[60] Democratic senator Alan Cranston of California said that one resident of his state wryly told him "that inflation is not all bad, that it has enabled every American to live in a more expensive neighborhood without moving."[61]

Inflation was the killer of dreams; its most lugubrious effect was to destroy the traditional hopes of Americans. In the past, they expected almost as a birthright that conditions would improve during their lifetimes and that their children would have it better. For the first time in recent memory, public opinion research found declining expectations of what the future promised. A comprehensive 1975 *New York Times* survey revealed that Americans despaired of the widening gap between what they could afford and what they wanted; they feared this chasm would grow. A college professor in New Orleans said, "America is not over the hill as a people. But tomorrow is not going to get any better in the way that people in 1955 would say that tomorrow would be better. That's gone." The feelings of helplessness and disillusionment were understandable. Over the past decade, Americans had witnessed a series of crises that their government was powerless to control—and even seemed to have contributed to: riots, student uprisings, the Vietnam War, a disgraced presidency. The economic crisis added yet another to this string of traumas. In many ways, this crisis eclipsed the earlier ones, for it affected everybody.[62]

The country needed strong economic leadership, a revamping of Keynesian principles, perhaps radical new policies. Two of Ford's advisers warned, "We can scarcely underestimate [inflation's] impact. A prolonged period of unchecked, double-digit inflation poses a severe threat to the economic and social structure of the United States."[63] An Ohio couple wrote to Ford in his first weeks in office, "We consider the national economy in a critical state!!" Urging him to declare a national emergency, they closed their letter by imploring, "Act now, or it will be too late."[64]

The warnings were not exaggerated. Once an unwelcome guest, inflation threatened to become a permanent boarder. Years of persistent high prices embedded rising prices in the national consciousness, and inflation became part psychological; the mere expectation of more inflation was enough to perpetuate it.[65] Worse, people were losing faith in the ability of their leaders to find solutions.

Americans blamed their government for inflation partly because the presidency failed to stop it. Nixon proclaimed on one Oval Office tape that he did not "give a [expletive deleted] about the economy."[66] Ford recalled that during the last months of his administration, Nixon "was doing two things. One, he was concentrating on foreign policy, which he enjoyed and where he was truly an expert. But also, he was concentrating on how to handle the Watergate problem. And the consequence was the White House was not really involved in domestic economic problems during that period of three months before he resigned."[67] After this eclipse, Ford wanted to reestablish activist presidential leadership in economic policy making.

But a mid-1975 poll showed that only a slim majority—54 percent—of Americans expressed confidence in the American economic system, while 42 percent voiced only little or no confidence. When such doubt casts a pall over a people, they lose loyalty to their government as an instrument that can adequately serve them. As Ford commented, "The worst inflationary toll of all is . . . the erosion of confidence in the future, the loss of faith in the American society and our government."[68] Thus the Great Inflation was not just an economic problem. It threatened America and its political institutions. Gary Seevers, a Ford CEA member, recalled "a crisis environment" at the time Ford took office. The president had to "get the economy back to some sort of normal path."[69] Americans had come to expect "normal" during previous postwar decades. The 1970s economy was anything but normal.

The Great Inflation and an Age of Limits

With a faltering economy, America in the 1970s seemed to enter a new phase in its history, one that augured ill. The economy showed signs of entering maturity, a postindustrial phase, one indication being that America was the only nation in which the service sector accounted for more than half its total jobs and GDP. During the 1970s, the service and retail trades composed 70 percent of all new private-sector jobs. A sad but popular perception was that

America would someday become a nation of "fast-food servers."[70] The transition to a service economy in itself fueled inflation, as labor costs in service industries added to a product's cost, with unions demanding high wages to keep pace with inflation. The shift to a service economy seemed to symbolize America's decline, since services represented less productive jobs than those in industry or agriculture, offering shorter hours, lower wages, and fewer opportunities for advancement.[71]

During the 1970s, Americans began to fear that the country's complex problems could not be solved. Had the 1960s economy suffered such maladies, U.S. policy makers would have thought twice about embarking on the Great Society, the Vietnam War, or the Apollo space program. Americans no longer wanted such grand projects; they rejected liberalism and the idea that government could solve the country's ills and simultaneously contain communism abroad. The Great Society and the Vietnam War had an unhappy economic synergism, leading to inflation, which came to be associated with liberal ideas and projects and accelerated a conservative upsurge in the country. Milton Friedman thought that Ford's conservative philosophy fit the temper of the times by addressing the public's disenchantment, noting that in trying to decrease federal spending, "President Ford is responding to a widespread public sentiment that we have not been getting our money's worth, that throwing increasing amounts of the taxpayer's money at very real social and economic problems has made them worse, not better."[72]

The idea of limiting government spending mirrored a 1970s ethic, thinking small, which replaced the postwar concept of limitless growth. Squeezed by international competition, slim profits, and tough times, American corporations went on a binge of downsizing and retrenchment. A popular 1973 book, E. F. Schumacher's *Small Is Beautiful*, expressed concern over industrial society's obsession with growth and large-scale production.[73] Reinforcing the emphasis on downsizing was *The Limits of Growth*, a seminal 1973 report by the "Club of Rome," an informal organization that began meeting in 1968 in the Italian capital to discuss the future of humankind. The group, which included scientists, economists, and civil servants from different countries, warned that the world's population was depleting the earth's resources and that within the next century the planet would no longer be able to support further growth.[74]

Many Americans believed it. The country had lived beyond its means, ignoring the future or the possibility that its resources were finite. Now the land of plenty seemed the land of scarcity. One writer to the *Washington Post* lamented that "we are consuming the earth's resources, benefiting from the labors of less developed regions, and mortgaging our environment, all in an effort to sustain a standard of living which is somewhat above our ability to support by our ingenuity and productivity: The strains show in the guise of uncontrolled inflation." Ford recognized that Americans would have to live more frugally but hoped that it would be beneficial: "We just have to tighten our belts and get rid of the fat and excesses, and we will be a lot better off as a country and as individuals."[75]

The Great Inflation coincided with the increasing awareness of the fragility and finitude of planet earth. The idea of an "age of limits" hit Americans especially hard because the postwar era had previously emphasized limitless growth and resources.[76] The pessimistic outlook for the country represented a prevailing 1970s theme. The greatest challenge for presidential leadership was to find a suitable economic policy to guide the nation through the troubled times and win acceptance for it.

Chapter 6

Taking Aim at Inflation

Saturday, September 28, 1974, was a gray and rainy day in Washington, D.C. As Gerald Ford stepped out of the presidential limousine and walked inside the Hilton International Hotel, his thoughts were racing. He was about to spend a second day hosting an enormous summit conference that assembled the nation's top economists and government officials. The president needed to absorb their analyses and recommendations and distill his own perspective in a speech that he and Robert Hartmann had prepared that morning.

But Ford's thoughts were preoccupied by an urgent personal matter. That morning, while Ford and Hartmann worked on the speech in the Oval Office, his personal physician, Dr. William Lukash, called to tell Ford that a lump found on First Lady Betty Ford's breast during a routine exam was malignant. The doctor was about to perform a full mastectomy, and subsequent tests would determine whether the cancer had spread. After hearing the news, Ford could not concentrate. He tried to focus on the speech, but soon he and Hartmann both broke down and cried. He decided to rush by helicopter to visit Betty in the hospital before attending the conference. (Pathology reports later showed that the cancer had been confined.)

As Ford walked into the hotel after the emotionally wrenching morning, his thoughts were jolted back to the economic suffering of Americans. Noisy demonstrators carried signs protesting inflation and chanted, "Milk up. Meat up. Bread up. We're fed up." Addressing the conference, Ford thanked well-wishers and reported on the healthy recovery of his wife. He then pledged, "I will roll up my sleeves and work every bit as hard as you do, starting this weekend, until every American is enlisted as an inflation fighter and as an energy saver until this job is done."[1] Ford now had to digest the economists' wildly diverse recommendations and organize his White House to battle inflation.

Domestic Enemy #1 and the "Old-Time Religion"

From the outset of his administration, Ford called inflation the nation's number one domestic enemy. At his first press conference, he declared, "If we take care of inflation and get our economy back on the road to a healthy future, I think most of our other domestic programs or problems will be solved."[2] This theme was to be often repeated, even during the harsh recession that deepened in late 1974. A year after leaving office, Ford reflected, "The fight against inflation provided the basic theme of my administration."[3]

Ford's advisers reinforced this focus. Four days after Ford took office, he received a memorandum from outgoing CEA chairman Herbert Stein that cobbled together the thinking of the administration's top economic advisers: new CEA chairman Alan Greenspan, Budget Director Roy Ash, Treasury Secretary William Simon, Stein, plus Fed Chair Arthur Burns. "We all start from the proposition that inflation is the great problem," Stein wrote.[4]

Ford and his advisers were more preoccupied with inflation than unemployment because the former aggravated the latter, promoting a general economic malaise. Inflation battered two key sectors of the economy, housing and retail sales, into prostration. The tight monetary policy that the Federal Reserve used to combat inflation left little money for banks and savings and loan institutions to make home loans, thus shriveling the supply of mortgage money. Inflation hurt retail sales by exacerbating consumer uncertainty, robbing shoppers of purchasing power and making them less willing to spend.[5] The resulting economic contraction increased unemployment.

Ford recalled that Greenspan, whom he praised as a master at reading public opinion, "was convinced that inflation was of far more concern than unemployment to the vast majority of Americans, and he was sure that people in the heartland weren't buying all that Capitol Hill propaganda about the need for more federal programs for which they'd have to pay." The economist surveyed politics with the eyes of Argus; Ford remembered, "Whenever I was under pressure to add funds to a program and he thought I might be influenced by the political aspects of the decision, he would caution me to hold the line."[6] Quiet and scholarly, Greenspan was the economic adviser Ford listened to most closely. As Ford later commented, "I think he's not only highly knowledgeable — technically a real expert — but he's got a lot of common sense. And the combination of expertise and common sense made me very supportive of his recommendations."[7] Ford and Greenspan — both low-key, thoughtful men with an intense anti-inflation focus — had the best relationship of any president and CEA chairman, and the economist also enhanced the CEA's reputation and made it less partisan, earning it greater respect from the political and business worlds.[8]

Next to Greenspan, Ford considered Fed chairman Burns his most helpful and influential economic adviser.[9] After injudiciously following a loose monetary policy in the early 1970s, Burns tightened the money supply in the belief that a restrictive supply would drive up interest rates. Such a forbidding environment discouraged borrowing, and overall demand in the economy decreased, thus reducing the upward pressure on prices. But critics screamed at the policy, charging that tight money was strangling the economy. Liberals excoriated Burns. Otto Eckstein, a member of Johnson's CEA, called him "one of the four major wholly unforeseen shocks that upset all our economic forecasts in the last couple of years. We've had the food shock, the oil shock, Watergate and its malaise—and Arthur Burns."[10]

Ford supported a tight money policy, but he knew that the Fed alone could not bear the burden of fighting inflation. To demonstrate his own initiative, the president wanted to trim the federal budget, believing that fiscal prudence would reduce inflationary pressures. He charged that during the previous twenty years, the Democrats who controlled Congress had engaged in reckless spending. A lower budget would have an anti-inflationary effect in itself, lead to less federal borrowing and crowding out of private sector spending, and ease reliance on monetary policy as the sole instrument of fiscal restraint. Moreover, it would mark the first step in slowing federal spending, a signal that the government was ready to put its fiscal house in order.[11]

Nixon had bequeathed to Ford a record $305 billion budget for the 1975 fiscal year. (By contrast, federal expenditures for the 1974 fiscal year were $270 billion.) David Packard recommended holding spending to $300 billion, a cut of $5 billion, or a 2 percent reduction.[12] Burns and Simon offered similar advice, Ford recalled; the two "thought I could slash between $5 and $10 billion from the [$305 billion Nixon budget], and although I wasn't so optimistic, I was determined to try. A cut of $5 billion wouldn't have any real effect on the inflation rate, but its impact would be beneficial psychologically."[13] While conceding that a $5 billion budget cut was "trivial," Greenspan nonetheless argued that it would signal a new government determination to hold down spending.

Ford expected benefits from even a small budget cut. Deficits increase federal borrowing, and when the government borrows a dollar, it is then unavailable to home buyers and businesspeople.[14] As he pointed out at a press conference, a $5 billion cut would make money "more easily available in the money markets of the U.S. so that home purchasers will have more money at a better rate of interest to borrow so they can build homes. This will stimulate the homebuilding industry and, I think, provide jobs."[15] The combination of decreased federal spending and a tight monetary policy constituted the conservative "old-time religion" central to Ford's fight against inflation. But the cure required patience and pain, both delicate commodities in politics. To garner support, Ford began by reaching out to politicians, businesspeople, and ordinary Americans.

The Economic Summits

One of Ford's most visible actions in his battle against inflation was to engage the nation in a series of ambitious economic summit meetings. Senate majority leader Mike Mansfield originally suggested the idea of an economic summit to Nixon because "neither Congress nor the Administration is doing a damn thing [about inflation]."[16] Nixon accepted Mansfield's idea, which several other senators enthusiastically backed, just two days before resigning, and Ford enlarged the process by sponsoring several smaller summits around the country, in which Americans from all walks of life expressed their economic concerns and suggestions.[17]

The series of economic summits was a grand undertaking, all the more impressive because the Ford administration carried it out with just one month of planning. On September 5, 1974, the summitry kicked off with a special conference at the White House. William Seidman wanted the preliminary meetings to give the president the nation's "best thinking" on how to combat inflation. Twenty-five of the country's most eminent economists gathered in the East Room to give prescriptions for improving the nation's economic performance. Noting the congenial atmosphere of the new administration, Democratic economist Walter Heller remarked that "it is refreshing to be in a White House that once again is open to a little laughter, a little dissent and willing to face the unvarnished, and at the moment, rather dismal economic facts of life."[18]

The atmosphere may have been bright, but the news was bleak. Most economists predicted that inflation would worsen. Nobel Laureate Paul Samuelson—who had been on Nixon's "Enemies List"—said, "This inflation has been building for ten years, and it can't be stopped in a year. . . . I don't think we are going to get down to three percent inflation in a year or so if we bite every bullet in sight." The news on unemployment was just as bad. The jobless rate had hit 5.4 percent in August, and some economists predicted that it would rise to more than 6 percent, which could signal the onset of a recession.[19]

Harry Truman once remarked that he wanted a "one-handed economist," because practitioners of this dismal science too often offered contradictory advice, saying "on the one hand" and then "on the other hand." Ford may have felt like Truman; he heard economists zigzag and contradict one another at the White House meeting. Seidman found that "many of the recommendations [at the summit] were diametrically opposed to each other. For example, one group claimed that prices were being forced up by rising wages, and that of course was attributed to unions. . . . Unions, for their part, accused greedy industrialists of raising prices well beyond the level they needed to cover their labor contracts."[20] Proposed solutions at this White House meeting varied as widely as the philosophical stripes of the economists. Yale's Richard Cooper suggested a tax cut of up to $15 billion for lower- and middle-income groups to help them cope with rising prices and quell labor's demands for wage hikes. Harvard's John Kenneth Galbraith suggested the opposite, a tax increase on income earners of $15,000 and above to reduce demand-pull inflation pressures and help balance the budget.[21] The new administration seemed whipsawed between the tenets of fiscal conservatism and liberalism, underscoring the difficulty of guiding an economy plagued simultaneously by inflation and rising unemployment.

Inflation, a problem with multiple causes, demanded multiple cures. Cutting the budget would not be enough. The attack on inflation would have to be a coordinated effort involving all branches of the federal government as well as business, labor, and individual Americans. But Ford would have to walk a tightrope. Anti-inflationary policy risked cooling off the economy too much, which could prompt a recession. Economists at the conference stressed that Ford must dampen inflation while simultaneously maintaining high employment.[22]

During the next three weeks, the Ford administration embarked on what *Time* called "an unprecedented experiment in economic summitry." At fourteen meetings in major cities, administration officials, senators, representatives, and governors heard Americans speak their minds on economic issues. After three weeks, the summitry culminated with a two-day Conference on Inflation at the Washington Hilton, which began on September 27. On what was a turbulent autumn day for Ford because of Betty's health crisis, he received a torrent of conflicting opinions, diagnoses, and prescriptions. Ford's concluding remarks, adopting a suggestion from columnist Sylvia Porter, asked Americans to make a list of ten ways to fight inflation and save energy and send their lists to the White House. Ford promised more substantive help as well, saying that within ten days he would announce a program to combat inflation.[23]

The summits aired the issues, in keeping with Ford's drive to maintain an open administration. As a bipartisan effort, they gave the new administration an opportunity to build alliances. At the summits, Ford noted, "We had a wide spectrum of people—business, labor, finance, et cetera. I thought that their participation representing their part of their economic sphere was very helpful to [the anti-inflation effort]."[24] Economist Paul McCracken, a participant, considered them a success for encouraging the discussion and debate so critical to public policy in a democratic society. "It is very important to have arenas where the president gets feedback from people," McCracken explained. Ford heard views from many different Americans, McCracken recalled, "and if he got a little different slant on the way the [economy] looked as a result of listening to all these people speaking—it was worthwhile."[25]

The well-publicized summitry was politically useful, too. Ford emphasized his activist approach to economic policy making. For many Americans, the summits afforded their first glimpses of their new president in action. Robert Hartmann recalled that they were important "for a president who had never campaigned nationally and was a very little known figure in human terms and suddenly became president. [They were a way] of getting him around the country and establishing himself as a person who had the people's confidence."[26] Ford's first task as president was simply to lead, and the summits allowed him to be seen as the country's new leader. They also provided a menu of options for tackling inflation, and Ford noted, "I utilized some of the material that came from [the economic summits] in my subsequent [anti-inflation] program."[27]

But the summit initiative was riddled with criticism. Detractors scored the summits' failure to produce concrete results. Democratic senator Robert Byrd dismissed them as "meaningless." Joseph Alsop of the *Washington Post* called them "an inherently silly idea from the outset."[28] Some sniping came from within the administration. William Simon feared that they would aggravate the perception that Washington only talks about problems and does nothing about them.[29]

Ford disagreed with Simon about the summits; he considered them "very helpful" and "a rather bold approach . . . [that] had never been done before."[30] Later in the year, when the country slipped into a recession, critics charged that the summits focused on the wrong subject—inflation—when the real problem was recession. Such criticism became easy to levy with the wisdom of hindsight, but through most of 1974 inflation was a pressing issue that demanded public attention. Some economists emphasized that inflation was still the number one problem even while conceding an approaching recession.[31] While some voices at the summits did warn of an economic downturn, no one predicted its severity; it fell harder and faster than anyone anticipated. It was easy, months later, to charge that the summits focused on the wrong issue. "What was bugging people at the time? It was inflation," McCracken remembered.[32] (Even in mid-October, a newsletter from the Democratic National Committee [DNC] reported that 75 percent of contributors to the DNC felt that the party should stress inflation as the most important issue in the 1974 campaign.)[33]

The summits also edified the public, bringing the nation's economic concerns under sharper media focus and riveting public attention on the problem and possible solutions. Hartmann remarked afterward, "For the first time since I can remember, at least since I was a small boy in the Great Depression, people are really interested in economics." *Time* magazine concluded, "For conducting a national town meeting on a subject normally regarded as too abstruse for public consumption, Ford deserves only praise."[34]

In allowing economists to air discordant views, the summits painted in sharp relief the contrast between conservatives and liberals. One issue was money supply. At the first White House conference on inflation, speaker after speaker blasted Burns's tight money policy and demanded a relaxation of the money supply.[35] Democratic senator Alan Cranston of California warned, "We need monetary restraint, but when restraint becomes a noose, it's time to ease up and let the patient breathe." AFL-CIO president George Meany was a principal archer of arrows fired at Burns, saying, "If unemployment is to rise, then let Dr. Arthur Burns be the first to volunteer."[36] But Burns stood firm, insisting that loosening the money supply would hike inflation and interest rates.

Some economists and politicians urged a resumption of controls. A majority of Americans liked the idea, and *Time* predicted that Ford would soon be forced to adopt selective wage and price controls.[37] That was unlikely; the president found the idea philosophically repulsive. He recalled, "I have always been opposed to price and wage controls. When I was in Congress the first term, we imposed wage and price controls during the Korean War. They were a mistake. And we suffered until we got rid of them."[38] At his first press conference, Ford told reporters that "wage and price controls are out, period."[39] This decision showed economic wisdom. Controls, while lulling people into a false sense that the government was taking effective action, were just palliatives that temporarily eased inflation's symptoms rather than attacking its causes. McCracken thought that Ford's decision to reject them was correct in part because "empirical evidence makes it very clear that they never had any effect on the rate of inflation."[40] More seriously, Ford believed controls required a cumbersome bureaucracy to enforce and distorted the economy by preventing market forces from naturally dictating an efficient allocation of resources. Because controls restricted profits, industries would scale back expansion plans. Investment would sag, shortages would occur, and the result would be higher inflation.[41] Worse, before the government slapped on controls, businesses would engage in a frenzy of price hikes in worried anticipation, exacerbating inflation.

In rejecting controls, Ford also practiced the politics of conciliation. Trying to get Congress to pass controls could have touched off an acrimonious struggle that would have ruined his reputation as a healer. The *Washington Post*, though admitting that it found controls attractive, praised the president for his "olive-branch politics" in rejecting them. Ford informed one reporter, "I have been told by the Democratic leaders that there is no prospect of the Democratic Congress enacting wage and price controls" because they were so controversial.[42] To have sought them would have been an act of executive heavy-handedness as well as economic imprudence. Instead, Ford sought more effective solutions to inflation.

The Economic Policy Board

Concluding the Conference on Inflation, Ford announced that he was consolidating his administration's economic efforts under a new Economic Policy Board (EPB). This organ was an innovation that stemmed from a late-August meeting at which Ford and Seidman discussed organizing economic policy making. Noting that many interdepartmental committees acted without coordination, Seidman sought to consolidate economic policy making within one group outside the White House. Ford designated Simon as chairman of the new agency and Seidman as executive director. On September 30, he signed an executive order to create the EPB.[43] The EPB's modus operandi was, for minor economic issues, to reach decisions itself and, for major ones, to develop an array of policy options for Ford and allow him to make the final decision.

By rejecting wage and price controls and establishing the EPB, Ford visibly broke from the Nixon administration, demonstrating the importance of economic policy and his involvement in it.[44] Whereas Nixon had preferred to leave the details of the economy to his advisers, Ford enjoyed the nuts and bolts of economic tinkering.[45] McCracken commented that in contrast to Nixon, "Ford found economic policy intellectually interesting" and recalled that Ford had once told him that if he had had more confidence that he could have made a living as an economist, he might have pursued that profession instead of law.[46] The inclusion of high-ranking administration members in the EPB indicated that, unlike Nixon, Ford wanted to restore authority to top-level administration members, making them true advisers. Their inclusion in presidential decision making would help remedy the problem of low morale among senior advisers, who felt that Nixon often shut them out of policy making.[47]

For the remainder of Ford's presidency, the EPB met three to four times a week, and Ford was present during at least one meeting each week, where he and the committee made virtually all of the administration's important economic decisions. These meetings reflected Ford's leadership style. Oral discussions, supplemented by written reports, allowed advisers to express their views with fewer inhibitions, since they sometimes feared that written words might leak or become available in the future. Simon recalled that the EPB, which he thought more effective in setting economic policy than any group that Nixon employed, gave everyone a chance to be heard. Ford's ability to elicit opinions and enjoy frank, spirited discussions contributed to this success. He never disparaged or belittled those who disagreed with him, whether they belonged to Congress or his administration. One EPB member noted that he felt comfortable disagreeing with Ford because the president welcomed dissenting views.[48]

Ford considered the EPB "the most important institutional innovation of my administration." In 1992, it received a belated accolade when the Carnegie Endowment for International Peace and the Institute for International Economics, two Washington think tanks, presented recommendations to President-elect Bill Clinton for organizing his White House. Their study concluded that of all recent administrations, the Ford White House had been the best organized in its ability to lay out policy options before the president and then execute his decisions.[49]

With the aid of the economic summit conferences and open discussion among his economic advisers, Ford hoped to set the right course for the economy. In the fall of 1974, that meant stopping the Great Inflation.

Chapter 7

Teetering on a Knife's Edge

Almost every American has seen pictures of this stunning day. On August 9, 1974, Gerald and Betty Ford somberly accompanied Richard and Pat Nixon down the White House lawn, where the thirty-seventh president boarded a helicopter, flashed an incongruous victory sign, turned, and retreated to private life. Earlier that morning, Gary Seevers, a member of the CEA, listened to Nixon's farewell speech in the East Room and then joined the crowd assembled on the lawn to say good-bye to Nixon. After the helicopter took off, Seevers returned to the West Wing and, as he walked down a narrow hallway, he suddenly saw the new president. At that moment, Seevers remembered, Ford "was the saddest-looking man I've ever seen. Sad for Nixon, and I think he knew the burden he was [inheriting]."

Seevers said that "the first priority was economic policy when Ford took office," and the president and his team had a heap of worries. The economy was sending mixed signals of both high inflation and sluggishness, even an impending recession. But after studying the data, Ford's economists reached a consensus that the outlook was "basically steady." "The economy might tilt up a little; it might turn down a little," Seevers said. While unemployment edged up, "there was quite a high level of employment." As a result, the Ford administration decided to maintain its focus on inflation rather than a possible downturn. Seevers recalled that the White House felt "we have to deal with inflation before we can get back to solid economic growth."[1] Soon that decision needed sharp revision.

Ford's Anti-inflation Proposals

Few recent presidents have had to act as urgently as Ford did upon assuming office. At the final day of the Conference on Inflation, he promised that within ten days he would present an economic program to the nation for waging war on inflation. Robert Hartmann recommended the ten-day promise, even urging Ford to give himself a one-week deadline. Hartmann, whose keen political instincts Ford valued highly, feared that if Ford set no deadline, an economic program might develop too slowly, and he would lose momentum and public confidence, crippling his presidency and letting the nation drift.[2]

On October 8, just twelve days later, Ford addressed a joint session of Congress. The EPB had arrived at a ten-section, thirty-one-point economic program that was a mélange of initiatives. Ford addressed the problem of high food prices by imploring farmers to produce as much as possible and asked Congress to remove acreage limitations on rice, peanuts, and cotton. He called upon his newly created Council on Wage and Price Stability (CWPS) to monitor all wage and price increases throughout the economy. While avoiding wage and price controls, Ford pledged that his administration would enforce laws against price fixing and require that all major legislative proposals and regulations from the executive branch be accompanied by an "inflation impact statement," which would assess their potential effect on prices. His program also proposed aid to the housing industry and savings and loans institutions.[3]

"During the meetings on inflation, I listened carefully to many valuable suggestions," Ford explained. "Since the summit, I have evaluated literally hundreds of ideas, day and night. My conclusions are very simply stated. There is only one point on which all advisors have agreed: We must whip inflation right now." As what he termed "the acid test of our joint determination to whip inflation in America," Ford pronounced the cornerstone of his new economic program, a one-year, 5 percent surcharge on corporate and personal incomes. The surtax was directed at individuals with yearly earnings of $15,000 or more for married taxpayers and $7,500 for the unmarried. (Taxpayers would have to figure out what they normally owed the government, then add the 5 percent surtax to it.) The advantages of the surtax were that it would be mildly progressive, since the rich would pay more, and temporary, lasting only the calendar year 1975. Nor was it onerous. For example, a single person earning $15,000 would pay a federal income tax of $2,549; the surcharge would add $78.[4]

Ford also reaffirmed his commitment to a $300 billion spending limit for the 1975 fiscal year. "It is my judgment that fiscal discipline is a necessary weapon in any fight against inflation," Ford declared. "I do not think that any of us in this Chamber today can ask the American people to tighten their belts if Uncle Sam is unwilling to tighten his belt first."[5] But wary of alienating voters before the upcoming congressional elections, he refrained from divulging exactly where he would make the cuts.

To encourage production, Ford proposed increasing the 7 percent business investment tax credit to 10 percent, to apply to new purchases of machinery and equipment. The investment tax credit for public utilities would rise from 4 to 10 percent. Estimates were that the proposals would save corporations $2.7 billion in taxes for 1975, offsetting the $2.1 billion in higher taxes that they would have to pay with the surcharge.[6] Most important for the nation, Ford believed that the new investment tax credit would encourage plants to buy equipment and thus boost the country's productive capacity.

To aid the casualties of economic woes, Ford introduced two major initiatives. First, for those who had exhausted their unemployment benefits, Ford called for thirteen weeks of special payments. Second, Ford asked Congress to create a Community Improvement Corps (CIC) to provide $500 million in public service for the unemployed, to be triggered when the unemployment rate hit 6 percent for three consecutive months or where local labor markets suffered unemployment of over 6.5 percent. Ford believed that the CIC would be an improvement over traditional public-service employment because it would be deactivated when unemployment abated. As he observed, "They're short-range, short-term projects, so that you don't have government programs that carry on and on."[7]

Reaction to Ford's program was lukewarm. Most pundits noted its mild character. Ford avoided draconian measures such as wage and price controls or a gasoline tax. He gave the CWPS no real powers, nor did he ask business and labor to hold prices or wages. The president had vowed to "bite the bullet," but *Time* called his proposals "more balm than bite" and "small weapons for the two-front war" against inflation and unemployment. The *New York Times* dismissed Ford's speech as "weak, flaccid, and generally disappointing." Some members of Congress expressed outrage at the final package, which seemed an anticlimax after weeks of economic summitry and White House brainstorming. Democratic senator James Abourezk of South Dakota said, "The nation needed a strong, specific program. It got an uncoordinated mishmash of public relations gimmickry and precious few concrete ideas." (One economist's skepticism about the surtax generated what later became a mainstay of Ronald Reagan's "supply-side" economics. Arthur Laffer doubted that the 5 percent surtax would generate much revenue, and while dining at a restaurant with Ford administration members Don Rumsfeld and Dick Cheney, he drew a graph on a napkin to illustrate his belief that tax cuts— rather than increases—would raise more revenue because of increased business activity. His illustration became known as the "Laffer Curve.")[8]

At a Rose Garden press conference the day after Ford's speech, Peter Lisagor of the *Chicago Daily News* told the president that "a great many people" considered his proposals "not tough enough."[9] Cries for a stronger elixir formed a theme among Ford's critics, and the comments indicated that during the mid-1970s, citizens still looked to the federal government for programs or "tough" measures to solve the nation's economic and energy challenges. But Ford knew that schemes like wage and price controls and fuel allocations, which the government had instituted under Nixon, had exacerbated inflation and fuel shortages. Relying more on fiscal restraint and market forces made Ford seem to bite marshmallows instead of bullets, yet he was wise to do so, and not just for the sake of his teeth.

Democrats also criticized the program's pro-business slant. Most of the money the surtax raised would eventually be returned to business through the new investment tax credit, reflecting Ford's belief that in the long run, the country needed a more favorable climate for capital investment so that business could create more jobs. Not surprisingly, business reacted favorably to Ford's proposal, but some congressmen condemned it as an attack on the average American. The surtax seemed to crucify middle America, they insisted, threatening to diminish consumer purchasing power. Democratic congressman Henry Reuss of Wisconsin called the surcharge "a rip-off of the middle class." House majority leader Tip O'Neill charged that Ford's "extremely unfair" proposals would force not corporations but taxpaying Americans to shoulder the burden.[10]

The criticism frustrated Ford. After all, he maintained, the program incorporated the advice from the economic summit and reflected the consensus of the attendees. He emphasized that the surtax was mild (in fact, the administration even considered proposing a surtax of 10 percent to dampen inflation) and would affect only 26 percent of all personal income taxpayers.[11] While critics charged that the surtax was cruel, Ford believed that crueler still was the hidden tax on all incomes that inflation imposed. Above all, he stressed that his program was carefully balanced. He tried to offset the cost of the new policy initiatives with new tax revenue, thereby avoiding high deficits, which he saw as a major cause of inflation.[12]

That balance said something about the summits. Had there been no summits, Ford might have focused exclusively on inflation and left unemployment untreated. But participants in the summits underscored the importance of some mechanism to cushion groups such as the poor, elderly, and minorities, who were victimized most severely by belt tightening. Republican representative Albert Quie of Minnesota pleaded at one minisummit that "those who suffered most from inflation should not be asked to suffer more in order to solve inflation." Taking a page from the summits,

Ford tried to balance belt-tightening measures with unemployment benefits, the CIC, and aid to the housing industry.[13]

Still, Ford took a political risk by proposing a surtax less than a month before congressional elections. Unveiling a tax increase at such a time was like unleashing a skunk at a picnic; representatives and senators ran in the opposite direction, refusing to embrace or even come close to it. Officeholders facing difficult reelection battles, such as GOP senators Bob Dole of Kansas and Marlow Cook of Kentucky, deserted their president rather than support the proposal. Ford's call for austerity was a blandishment that few leaders had made in peacetime. William Seidman recalled, "The President announced he would oppose spending on any new programs until the budget deficit was under control, which was an entirely new approach to government by any president."[14]

But Ford's program was troubled from the start. Seidman had written the speech and, with self-effacing humor, scorched his own efforts: "It was a terrible speech—not in substance, but rhetorically. It was a stinker!"[15] Seidman said that he wrote what may have been "one of the most boring speeches ever delivered to any joint session." The address contained too many ingredients for Congress and the public to digest. It had thirty-one proposals. "On a good day Congress can usually absorb about three," Seidman believed. "It was not a speech, it was a treatise. The effort ended my career as a speech writer for President Ford."[16]

The program itself was a political bomb. The jumble of proposals gave the whole thing an eclectic feel, and the centerpiece—a tax increase—fell flat. One poll showed that Americans opposed the surtax, 58 to 34 percent.[17] Members of Congress resisted it. Just two days after the speech, William Baroody warned Ford that it was "in serious trouble on the Hill and very unpopular politically" and that Congress was in no mood to reduce spending. Two weeks before the midterm elections, Seidman publicly acknowledged that the surtax faced an uphill struggle on Capitol Hill and called its prospects "uncertain."[18] The overwhelming Republican repudiation in the ensuing elections turned "uncertain" to "doomed." Ford's policy making was off to a rocky start. Most important, economic events soon overtook Ford and the nation.

The Looming Recession

The 1970s economy was especially unsettling because its high inflation, traditionally an index of boom times, often coincided with sluggishness. Fighting one problem or the other was almost mutually exclusive, and nobody knew the right path to take. Max Friedersdorf recalled that some advisers "were saying we've got to stimulate the economy. Others were saying we've got to de-stimulate it to fight inflation. There was a lot of uncertainty about which policy to follow."[19]

Many Democrats threw cold water on Ford's anti-inflation surtax because they argued that it targeted the wrong enemy. The economy was entering a recession, they maintained, and cooling it off was the incorrect policy. In an address in Illinois several days after Ford's speech, Carl Albert remarked, "I believe that one of the problems with the president's economic program is that it fails to consider recession as great a threat as inflation." The House Speaker continued: "The fact is that we now face recession—as well as inflation—at the same time, and that any economy recovery program should deal with both of these problems."[20]

Albert was prescient. Just days after the November elections, the EPB conceded that the October economic indicators might reveal that the country was entering a recession.[21] Rumors of recession had circulated for some time. Key economic indicators had crested in November 1973, making the current downturn—or recession—a year old, threatening to become the longest of the five previous post–World War II recessions (beating the old record of thirteen months set in 1953–54). As early as January 1974, the *New York Times* believed that the economy was "entering the second recession of the Nixon years." By the time Ford took office in August, the economy was soft enough to prompt George Meany to declare, "We are in a recession now, and there is every indication we are going into a depression."[22]

As summer turned to autumn, the word "recession" was uttered with growing force. At the Conference on Inflation in late September, some Democrats and labor leaders argued that recession and growing unemployment were dangers tantamount to inflation. Senator Hubert Humphrey commented that the conference's most important finding was that recession was an enemy as much as inflation. The *Washington Post* editorialized, "The long succession of speakers left no doubt that, for all the talk about the overriding importance of controlling inflation, it is still the specter of high unemployment that this country fears more."[23]

The traditional definition of a recession was two consecutive quarters of decline in economic output, and output had declined in each of the first three quarters of 1974 (7 percent in the first, 1.6 in the second, and 2.9 in the quarter ending in September).[24] As further confirmation, unemployment increased from 5.4 percent in August to 5.8 in September and then 6 percent in October, the highest jobless level since September 1972, when the United States was still shaking off the 1969–70 recession. Presidents are seldom eager to admit a recession, especially before elections. At an October 9 press conference, Ford flatly stated, "I do not think the United States is in a recession," although he conceded that the economy was in a "very mixed situation." For this reason, Ford explained, he introduced a mild anti-inflation program that would not "tighten the screws too tightly and precipitate us into some economic difficulty." (The EPB spent much of one October meeting discussing whether to use the "r" word. The committee decided that the economic data, although not a cause for happiness, did not indicate a recession. Moreover, committee members thought that the very term "recession" could kindle fears and anxieties.)[25] Ford did not think the "recession" label fit. These were new, unprecedented economic circumstances, he argued, "when you've got double-digit inflation and yet a certain softness in the economy. And to use the same labels for unique circumstances is inaccurate." Viewing the current economic softness as fleeting, "I didn't think it would be wise for me as President to stand up and say, 'Yes, we're in a recession.'"[26]

To some Americans, that was shilly-shallying. A vice president of a Georgia fiber sales company complained to Senator Herman Talmadge, "According to President Ford this country is not in a recession. I am in the textile business and call on carpet manufacturers, [who] supply a lot of carpet to the housing and automotive industry . . . most of my customers are in a depression not a recession."[27] The *Washington Post* deprecated Ford's verbal legerdemain, saying that it would be better for the country and for him to be more forthright: "To keep dodging around the word 'recession' gives an impression of comically inept evasiveness."[28] Supporters and critics alike expected more from an administration that sought a reputation for candor and openness.

When the October economic figures came out, the evasiveness ended. Ford instructed Ron Nessen to acknowledge at a November 12 press briefing that the country was entering a recession. Nessen later noted that the timing of the announcement was conveniently after the elections, to avoid political damage.[29] Prospects for economic improvement looked poor. Ford recalled, "Alan Greenspan was the one who alerted me first [to the onset of a recession]. He was concerned about the inventory build-up, which became obvious with the statistical data that he and his people at the [CEA] would be getting. He worried about that; he warned me that that was an ominous sign."[30] In late November, Greenspan soberly told Ford, "The economy is now in the midst of a marked contraction in production, employment and incomes. . . . Real GNP should be expected to decline in both the current quarter and in the first quarter of next year." The CEA chair told Ford to expect "pronounced increases in unemployment over the next few months."[31]

The EPB's December review of the economic outlook echoed Greenspan's cheerless forecast. Noting that the economy "has deteriorated more rapidly than expected," the EPB predicted that "this recession is likely to be the most severe since at least 1958, and probably the worst since the 1930's," with an unemployment rate of 8 percent. Added to this unhappy assessment were such ingredients as high inflation, plummeting consumer and business confidence, and high budget deficits. Noting "widespread expectations among the American people that we are having not just a recession but a depression," the EPB predicted a deep economic trough, with sluggishness continuing well into 1975.[32] The rapidly deteriorating economy represented a dramatically different challenge from the situation facing Ford when he took office, when inflation seemed the big threat. The new circumstances also constituted a serious political challenge.

"A 179-Degree Turn"

Critics assailed Ford for not acting quickly enough to combat the growing recession. The criticism highlighted a nagging public image problem. Throughout his presidency, Ford was hampered by the perception common of Republicans: that he lacked sympathy for the economically disadvantaged and favored business interests and the wealthy. His alleged delay in reacting to the recession aggravated this problem. Infelicitous remarks by administration members also damaged the president's image. In September 1974, at a White House economic minisummit for representatives of the poor, the elderly, the medically ill, and people with disabilities, Greenspan maintained that Wall Street brokers were the group hardest hit by inflation. Boos and catcalls rained down on the CEA chairman, drowning out anything more he had to say.[33] Such a statement, in an incongruous setting, strengthened suspicions that the Ford administration cared little about the underprivileged. Critics charged that Ford, reluctant to recognize the crisis and make policy adjustments, let the country drift helplessly into the recession. Columnist Joseph Kraft wrote that Ford engaged his attention "too long and too hard on inflation while the avalanche of recession" crushed the country.[34]

Ford's political problem was a genuine economic one. The economy teetered on a knife's edge between inflation and recession, and Ford struggled to maintain a delicate balance in policy. While the emphasis at the Conference on Inflation was ostensibly on inflation, many speakers warned about a recession. September's unemployment rate stood more than a full percentage point above the postwar average. Labor leaders at the summit worried openly about unemployment; so did many economists, congressional Democrats, and reporters. In his concluding remarks, economist Paul Samuelson stated, "The number one thing that is wrong about most discussions is the statement that our number one problem is inflation. A correct emendation is that our number one problem is stagflation, and stagflation has two parts to it [inflation and recession]." As the London *Economist* noted, Ford had "the worst of all possible worlds."[35] Even public perceptions echoed the contradictory mix between inflation and recession. While 52 percent of those polled believed that Ford's proposals had not gone "far enough" to combat inflation, 57 percent of respondents in another survey believed that the U.S. economy was heading toward a depression.[36]

Economists are notoriously poor at forecasting recessions. Ford's advisers believed that the economic outlook "was flat, which was okay, under the circumstances," recalled CEA economist Gary Seevers. Even those economists who warned of a recession failed to foresee its severity and quickness. Otto Eckstein had predicted only a "middling recession."[37] Just days after the Conference on Inflation, Paul McCracken warned the EPB, "There is now a rising probability of a 'v-type' recession." But a "v-type" recession would be short and the recovery quick (in contrast to a more protracted "u-type" recession), so McCracken maintained that the main focus should remain on inflation. But in November and December, the auto industry foundered fast. Ohio, which seemed economically robust early in the fall, was riddled by layoffs and plant closings by January 1975.[38] Associate Budget Director Paul O'Neill and others were surprised at how fast the recession seized the country, recalling that "it was as though the whole blood system of society kind of shut down at the same time. It was a really unusual kind of cliff-effect in economic affairs. I don't ever recall a period quite like that in my period of time in looking at economic affairs. It was really a sharp change. And I think for practical purposes, everybody missed [predicting] it."[39] Ford also blamed economists for not warning him sufficiently about how bad the recession might be, saying that "nobody at [the economic] summit told us that automobile sales were going to drop off as suddenly as they did in November and December. . . . Nobody who testified or spoke indicated that the unemployment would go up as rapidly as it did."[40]

While the speed and severity of the recession caught everyone off guard, the Ford administration chose to emphasize inflation well into December, when evidence of a recession was incontrovertible. Speechwriter John Casserly described the president even in January 1975 as "on the fence—one day emphasizing inflation, the next day stressing the recession."[41] Ford recalled that the recession constituted "changed circumstances that nobody foresaw," and given these circumstances, "we had to adjust and find some other answers."

But he was unwilling to experiment with short-term, politically expedient solutions to unemployment. Ford still saw inflation as the principal enemy. "We could turn on the spigot tomorrow and spend a lot of money and . . . in a relatively short period of time, I presume we could substantially lower the unemployment rate," Ford said. "But we would be right back up there with 12 to 14 or higher percent inflation, and then the next dip would be infinitely more severe." Moreover, whereas unemployment was a temporary problem affecting less than 10 percent of workers, Ford saw inflation as more tenacious and widespread, "the universal enemy of 100 percent of our people."[42]

Polls continued to show that Americans' greatest concern was inflation. As late as January 1975, a Gallup survey revealed that 46 percent of Americans still wanted the government to pay more attention to fighting inflation, while 44 percent wanted it to concentrate on reducing unemployment. Inflation, after all, was a prime cause of recession, and the more pernicious evil. Budget Director Roy Ash even said publicly that, over the long term, slightly higher unemployment might be the best way to lower inflation and strengthen the economy.[43]

That strategy was uniform throughout the Ford administration. William Seidman and Kenneth Rush even entertained the idea of a second conference on inflation for late November.[44] When the EPB executive committee met in early November and concluded that the economy might be entering a recession, it stressed that even so, the administration should maintain its economic policy and mentioned that the president's anti-inflation program was formulated with the possibility of a recession in mind.[45] Alan Greenspan and William Simon were especially focused on inflation. At a November 21 EPB meeting, Greenspan told the president that "we have not yet broken the back of inflation." As late as December 1974, Simon refused to abandon the surtax or change course publicly, saying it was too soon to say whether the administration would reverse policy and stimulate the economy, and adding, "The main thrust of our policy remains unchanged." Thus Ford's advisers reinforced his determination to continue to focus on inflation.[46]

Given the precarious economic situation—with double-digit inflation a certainty and a recession a possibility—the temporary surtax was a responsible policy to pursue. Employment was still rising, and the dip in GNP during the second quarter was small. A slight rise in unemployment would have been a small price to pay for a reduction in inflation.[47] At the time, a tax cut would have generated little support because many members of Congress and businesses viewed it as inflationary. Although in the spring of 1974 some liberal Democrats and economists called for tax cuts for low- and middle-income groups, many Republicans opposed the idea, as did Nixon, who said in July, "We are not going to respond to the short-term slack in the economy . . . with tax cuts that would only make inflation worse." At the time, Vice President Ford warned that a tax cut would "add to the fuel of inflation." In the fall, he felt the same way.[48] The alternative to proposing a surtax or a tax cut would have been to propose nothing and simply watch the economy, a supine posture that would have crippled faith in Ford's leadership.

By November, many economists, realizing that Ford had miscalculated, urged him to drop the surtax proposal and switch his focus to fighting the recession. The president stuck by the surtax and still urged budget cuts. On December 11, at a speech before the Business Council, an organization made up of the chiefs of more than one hundred of the country's largest corporations, Ford said that "if there are any among you who want me to take a 180 degree turn from inflation fighting to recessionary pump priming, they will be disappointed." The administration's economic mission was to reduce inflation, and it would require a reorientation of philosophy and a massive swing of the whole executive branch to change.[49]

But the rapidly changing conditions forced Ford to perform a volte-face. At a December 5 meeting of the EPB, which Roger Porter recalled as "one of the most heated in weeks," the administration's bulwark against inflation began to crack. Warning of a major recession with high unemployment, Seidman argued that it was time for a policy shift. While counseling against moving "aggressively on [a] Rooseveltian scale to seize economic initiative," the EPB recognized that "the present decline in consumer (public) confidence is so massive . . . that it may suggest the need for government action to arrest what would otherwise prove to be a . . . deep recession—if not worse." Over the next week, after reviewing the economic data, Ford concurred.[50] He could no longer afford to fight inflation exclusively. He made no apologies, as he had crafted the plan based on his own instincts and the information that he had early in the fall. In early December, he reflected, "I think we have a plan that we submitted in October that fitted the circumstances as we saw them and as we envisaged them over the horizon. I must confess that there has been a more rapid deterioration in the economy since October 8. . . . So, the plan we submitted in light of this deterioration may have to be modified some."[51]

"Some" was an understatement. As Ford later wrote, his new task would be to "reverse completely the economic strategy developed from the economic summit meeting and adopted during the first three months of my presidency." Once again, he had to act fast. In his speech before the Business Council, Ford promised a new economic program and vowed to work during the Christmas holidays and deliver it to Congress "in mid-January, if not sooner."

Yet he resolved not to make a "180-degree turn" on his anti-inflation policy. One reporter asked Nessen if Ford was doing just that. No, Nessen retorted, the president was making a "179-degree turn."[52]

The surtax was dead. Even during flush times, a tax increase would have been unpopular; during a slump, it had no chance. Seidman looked back ruefully on the surtax proposal, saying half-jokingly that he viewed it "with horror." He commented, "I think [the surtax proposal] was a bad idea. I wish we hadn't done it."[53] By the end of 1974, little of Ford's thirty-one-point program survived, and what remained were those parts aimed at fighting recession. In late December, Ford signed two bills to aid the unemployed: an emergency assistance bill to provide 100,000 public-service jobs and an emergency unemployment compensation bill to give thirteen additional weeks of benefits to the jobless. The two measures eventually enabled two-thirds of unemployed persons to receive benefits, a 50 percent increase compared to one year earlier. They were also the only components of Ford's October 8 anti-inflation program that Congress accepted.[54]

A political science axiom says that "the president proposes, Congress disposes." Congress certainly disposed of Ford's surtax, and quickly. Although he developed a fiscally balanced program incorporating many recommendations from the economic summit conferences, it was also like a multipronged barb that Congress could not swallow. And it soon became incongruous. The deteriorating economy, coupled with the inherent unpopularity of a tax increase, doomed Ford's first major economic initiative. But that failure was fortunate; as events played out, a surtax would have aggravated the downturn. Ford had to develop a new program, taking aim at a different enemy, recession.

Chapter 8

Rallying the Nation to Fight Inflation

The Gerald R. Ford Presidential Museum is a sprawling, 51,000-square-foot building that overlooks Michigan's Grand River, which flows from the rapids that give Ford's home city its name. The museum tells the story of Ford's life, emphasizing his presidency and the 1970s, and includes full-scale mock-ups of the Oval Office and the Cabinet Room, looking much as they did during the Ford years. Like many large museums, the Ford facility holds most of its collections in storage, including items that the public has never seen. Deep within the museum's bowels, carefully preserved in a large metal cabinet, is an array of memorabilia bearing the inscription "WIN" (Whip Inflation Now): key fobs, hot plates, mugs, paperweights, pens, watches, playing cards, even a garden kit. WIN clothing also lies in cabinets, including a colorful, hand-knitted sweater that Ford wore during Christmas of 1974. These items bear silent testimony to Ford's effort to enlist Americans in a crusade to fight inflation and conserve energy. But what began as an idealistic effort grew mired in controversy, criticism, and powerful economic forces.

The Genesis of the Voluntary Anti-inflation Campaign

While the surtax was the pillar of Ford's October 8 anti-inflation program, public involvement and voluntary effort were supporting elements. The weeks of economic summitry led to a conclusion that American citizens needed to play an active role in the fight against inflation. Paul McCracken stressed the role of increased consumer education on all issues and policies: "While experts may talk about overly expansive fiscal and monetary policies as basic causes, the relationship of these to changes in the price of flour seems far from evident to the citizens." McCracken recommended that Ford actively encourage consumers to engage in anti-inflationary behavior such as conservation and informed shopping. (During the post–World War II era, the idea was not far-fetched. In 1947, one of Harry Truman's anti-inflation initiatives depended on voluntary participation, while in 1973, Fight Inflation Together, a women's consumer group, organized a nationwide meat boycott to protest its high cost.)[1]

Given his aversion to big government, Ford found an appeal to the people attractive. William Seidman considered him "absolutely determined to have citizen participation." Compared to government fiat, Ford thought voluntary cooperation "far preferable and more in the tradition of the American system." He considered the economic conditions of the 1970s so severe as to be comparable to wartime, and he hoped the American people would answer the call to sacrifice and accept voluntary stringency measures, as they had during World War II.[2]

Ford's voluntary anti-inflation campaign had two principal roots, leading Robert Hartmann to describe the program as being like Siamese twins. One seed was planted during a Washington dinner attended by Paul Theis, executive editor of the president's speech writing office. Theis listened to a friend, Bill Meyer, president of the Central Automatic Sprinkler Company in Pennsylvania, talk about the need for voluntary business and labor involvement in the anti-inflation effort, in which the former would pledge to contain costs and the latter would promise to keep wages stable.[3] Columnist Sylvia Porter, who wrote about economic matters and had a talent for putting this abstruse science into layman's terms, constituted the second prime force behind the voluntary anti-inflation campaign, with her focus more on consumers than business.[4] Porter thought that a missing ingredient in the battle against inflation was the consumer, who had been "lectured, exhorted, patronized—but not enlisted. . . . This, I believe, is an extraordinary oversight. I also believe that consumers now are as eager to help combat inflation as we were eager to help fight Nazism." Porter noted "an unspoken cry of 'what can I do?' in the hearts of millions of Americans which the President can and should answer."[5] During the September 28 Conference on Inflation, she urged the president to get consumers involved. Ford agreed, appointing Porter to lead a voluntary citizens program, the Citizens Action Committee to Fight Inflation (CAC).[6]

Other participants at the economic summits implored Ford to launch a voluntary anti-inflation campaign. One of the most cogent voices, Gaylord Nelson of Wisconsin, was the Democratic senator who developed the idea for Earth Day 1970, during which Americans held environmental rallies and cleaned up parks, rivers, and streams. Nelson suggested that Ford "speak to the country with a message which says that uncontrolled inflation is a great threat to the security of the country—as great as World War II—and that the same kind of national cooperation will be required to meet the threat."[7]

Inflation, though an enemy, also represented an opportunity for the president to launch a national crusade.

Theis was motivated by his conversation with Bill Meyer and memories of the National Recovery Administration's (NRA) Blue Eagle effort during the New Deal, when the government launched a massive public relations campaign that used a Blue Eagle as a patriotic symbol of compliance with NRA regulations. He mentioned the idea of a voluntary campaign against inflation to Hartmann, and the two men broached the idea to Ford during an August 1974 meeting in the Oval Office. The president liked it. "Once you had 213 million Americans recognizing that inflation was a problem and joining in the effort to do something about it, positive results have to follow," Ford reasoned. "If both the government and the people tightened their belts voluntarily and spent less than they had before, that would reduce demand, and the inflation rate would start going down." Ford suggested that the program include an exhortation to save energy and asked the two men to write a memorandum detailing a plan.[8]

Theis suggested a program called "Inflation Fighters," or "IF," in which the federal government would actively encourage voluntary price freezes in business. IF would cover not only manufacturing plants but also a broad spectrum of businesses. Retail stores, supermarkets, gas stations, and many other companies offering goods and services to consumers could receive an IF decal if they pledged to hold prices stable for six months. The stores could display the IF symbol in their windows, along with a motto urging consumers to shop there, such as "IF you want a better America, patronize stores which display this emblem." The president would urge consumers to buy from stores that partook in the IF program, and participating companies would receive tax breaks.[9]

Journalists and historians have wrongly interpreted the voluntary anti-inflation effort as the heart of Ford's anti-inflation policy, but he never meant for this campaign to be his economic program's centerpiece. He recalled that "it was a supplement [to a much broader anti-inflation program]. . . . But it was an integral part of the effort to get the public to participate by producing more, saving more, doing anything they could individually to help in the battle against inflation. It was a part of an overall program."[10] The president wanted to stimulate public awareness of the discipline needed in the battle against inflation, and he wanted to furnish a rallying cry. He thought that a well-orchestrated voluntary campaign could generate support for his more concrete anti-inflation proposals, such as the 5 percent surtax and fiscal and monetary restraint.

Behind the voluntary anti-inflation campaign was the country's condition in the 1970s: America also needed something to cheer about. A voluntary program provided a way for the new president to dispel the miasma of Watergate, reassure Americans about the economy, and involve them in a national crusade. As Hartmann remembered, the anti-inflation fight needed "some [marching] bands and some excitement," and the voluntary effort was a missing piece that could generate such fanfare. Unlike the Vietnam and Watergate crises, which engendered raging controversy, no one argued whether the country needed to fight inflation, and the new crusade was to be nonpartisan.[11] Americans, feeling demoralized and powerless over recent crises as well as high prices, might finally feel that it was within their power to do something.

Not everyone in the administration liked the idea. At the White House meeting introducing the IF program, Theis recalled that Alan Greenspan, who felt uncomfortable with government jawboning, demurred: "Alan said he didn't like it [and] didn't think it would work. He was very negative on it from the beginning."[12] Greenspan, William Simon, and Roy Ash told Ford that the burden he would ask business to assume was unreasonable; staving off price increases for six months was no small task for companies. Yet if they raised prices merely to keep pace with rising costs, they would be tagged as unpatriotic. An even greater risk was that the program's effect would be similar to that of Nixon's wage and price controls. After six months of adhering to their pledges, businesses would stampede to raise prices.[13]

The voluntary anti-inflation campaign underwent several mutations, so that by the time Ford formally unveiled it, it deviated from the original concept, eroding support from its creators. Some administration members expressed reservations about the name "IF," believing that it sounded tentative. A New York City advertising agency, Benton and Bowles, developed a new name that both Hartmann and Theis liked: "WIN," for "Whip Inflation Now." Upbeat and positive, the name suggested the idea of conquering inflation in battle, and Theis asked the ad agency to develop a WIN button that the president could wear when he announced the program to Congress.[14] The program also emphasized the consumer aspect of voluntary cooperation but virtually ignored the activities of business and labor.

Hartmann asked journalist Russell Freeburg to serve as executive director of the CAC. Freeburg, the former Washington bureau chief for the *Chicago Tribune*, had covered Ford as minority leader and met Hartmann in Washington when both men worked as journalists. When Jerald terHorst abruptly resigned as press secretary, Freeburg drove from his Michigan cottage to Washington to see if he could be appointed to the job. When Freeburg arrived, he learned that Ron Nessen had already been hired, but Hartmann mentioned the CAC position to him. Freeburg agreed to serve for just two to three months, because the position paid only $100 a day (without providing an expense account). Because the vice presidency was vacant, for one week Freeburg had the privilege of working in the vice president's office, then established his own headquarters in the Executive Office Building. Although Freeburg had only two full-time staffers to assist him and the program's specifics had barely been developed, Ford was about to introduce WIN to a national television audience.

Response to WIN

Ford announced the WIN program during his October 8 address. He also unveiled the WIN button, a hand-painted prototype, pulling it out of his jacket pocket in the middle of his speech and pinning it conspicuously to his lapel. He praised Americans for the thousands of suggestions that they had sent to the White House after the economic summits. He introduced a short list of actions that Americans could follow to fight inflation and save energy. Urging Americans to "grow more and waste less," he advised, "If you cannot spare a penny from your food budget . . . surely you can cut the food that you waste by five percent." He announced plans for a massive citizens' mobilization effort, with a White House coordinator and staff. But he added that there will be "no big federal bureaucracy set up for this crash program."[15] It would rely solely on the volunteer spirit of the American people.

One week later, in a speech to the Future Farmers of America in Kansas City, Missouri, he expanded on his call for voluntary effort. Nessen convinced the television networks to cover the speech live; they were reluctant to do so, but Nessen stressed that the speech would be important. It turned out to be rich in folk wisdom but poor in concrete policy ideas. Many of the suggestions were familiar homilies, although Ford mentioned specific Americans to inject a dose of realism. He urged Americans to balance their family budgets, use credit wisely, economize, recycle, and reuse. He exhorted his listeners, "Shop wisely, look for bargains, go for the low-cost item, and most importantly, brag about the fact that you are a bargain hunter. You should be proud of it." In a recommendation reminiscent of the Victory Gardens of World War II, Ford advised Americans to plant WIN Gardens, mentioning a fifth-grader from Michigan who wrote to the White House to say that "we planted our own garden so we could save on vegetables." Chiding Americans for their "international reputation as the world's worst wasters," the president suggested that families make trash inventories to reduce waste. He rounded out his list of twelve suggestions by telling Americans to guard their health, as days lost through illness constituted a terrible waste.[16]

Despite the anticlimactic follow-up speech, the early response to WIN was generally enthusiastic. More than 200,000 Americans wrote to the White House, signing pledge forms, in return for which the CAC promised a free WIN button. Freeburg recalled that immediately "we were just inundated with telephone calls. . . . It was just really sort of overwhelming, the calls that started coming in."[17] WIN symbols and programs sprouted up in stores, banks, offices, and factories. Rite-Way drugstores used the WIN slogan in its advertisements.[18] Southern Airways used WIN bags to serve lunches to passengers.[19] The nation's largest food chain, A&P, froze prices on its store-brand Ann Page products, and food chains like Kroger and Giant took similar actions. The Ford Motor Company, U.S. Steel, and Bethlehem Steel all rescinded previously announced price increases.[20] The Ringling Brothers and Barnum and Bailey circus team tried to get into the act.[21] Representatives from the circus, whose headquarters were close to the CAC office in Washington, met with Freeburg and told him that they wanted to develop their entire 1975 season around the WIN concept. Meredith Willson, composer of *The Music Man*, drafted a short marching song, which the Navy Sea Chanters and the U.S. Marine Band recorded. McDonald's asked if Ford could endorse its new Egg McMuffin as an inexpensive breakfast that would fight inflation, but Freeburg turned them down. "I just thought it was too commercial," he explained. "You didn't want the president of the United States shilling for any particular company."[22]

Meanwhile, suggestions poured into the White House. Most were predictable and conventional: do home repairs yourself, shop for bakery bargains like day-old bread, use coupons, give children haircuts at home, rotate automobile tires for longevity. Some ideas were more thoughtful. A housewife reported that her family "decided we would eat fish twice a week in order to save grain to feed to [cattle]. We decided to eat regular cereal instead of sugar-sweetened varieties, and cut down on pop and candy to save sugar."[23] Schoolteachers, inspired by the WIN concept, instructed their students to write to the president with suggestions for fighting inflation. An Orlando, Florida, teacher wrote that his elementary school plowed up part of its playground and turned it into a WIN vegetable garden: "The rows may not be straight," the teacher reported, but he felt that "the values learned, helping one another, responsibility, and working together, did drive home a point straight and narrow that even the youngest school-child is aware of the situation at hand and is willing to go all out for help."[24]

Companies immediately capitalized on WIN by mass-producing merchandise of every kind (samples of which are now carefully preserved at the Gerald R. Ford Museum). A WIN Gardeners Club Starter Seed Kit, which one company marketed for $10, promised to produce an array of vegetables worth $290.[25] Ford visited the CAC office and found a room that was, as Freeburg recalled, "absolutely loaded. . . . There was just WIN paraphernalia everywhere."[26] Of all the WIN products, the button became the trendiest. Within a month after Ford introduced it to a national audience, orders for the button soared to fifteen million. Robert Slater, sales manager for a company that manufactured WIN buttons and designer of the "Smile" button inseparably associated with the 1970s, reported receiving more than eight million orders.[27] Golfer Arnold Palmer donned a WIN button and proclaimed, "This button, it's not a joke. I put it on because I believe in it."[28] Democratic governor George Wallace of Alabama, poised to make another run for the White House in 1976, appeared at a banquet wearing a WIN button. Asked why he sported a Republican administration's slogan, he quipped, "I don't see anything wrong with it. It does stand for 'Wallace in November,' doesn't it?" During Penn State's 1975 New Year's Day bowl game against Baylor University, the Nittany Lions wore WIN buttons on their parkas as they sat on the sidelines. Press Secretary Ron Nessen had fun with the button by wearing it upside down, explaining to reporters that "NIM" meant "No Instant Miracles" for inflation.[29]

The CAC also received numerous calls from local Republican committees asking for WIN buttons to use in the 1974 campaign. Since the program was intended to be an effort to rally Americans across party lines, Freeburg declined the requests. But the volume of Republican blandishments was so heavy that he went to Hartmann to express his concern. "You've got to stop this," Freeburg implored. "You can't let them use the WIN button in campaigns for local Republican workers to wear and hand out. You can't do it. We set this up as non-partisan. I'm running it as non-partisan. And you've got to call these people off."[30] Still, some Republicans used the WIN symbol in their campaigns, and it became something the Democrats would not touch. As the weeks passed, however, WIN ran into more serious trouble.

A No-Win Situation

Beneath the bubbly surface enthusiasm lay deeper problems with WIN. One of WIN's inherent weaknesses reflected the nature of Ford's sudden entry into the presidency and his new administration's inexperience at making policy. He proposed WIN just two months after taking office, leaving scant time to organize the national effort. Built on rickety foundations, WIN had an ad hoc feel to it, and it would have benefited from a longer incubation period for planning, staffing, and funding. Freeburg later lamented, "They announced the program and then said, 'Develop it.' From day one, it was just me and two [staff members], who were there every day, all day. And we could just barely keep our heads above water in handling daily things." To give WIN a better chance to succeed, Freeburg believed, administration planners "should have laid out a program first, before they ever announced it, because they announced it and we could never catch up." Freeburg compared the CAC's task to "building the airplane as you're flying." The administration should have developed a detailed program that had the commitment of business, labor, and consumers, along with supporting paraphernalia such as WIN flags and a rousing theme song, and should have had everything ready for the presidential address.[31]

WIN also created controversy in the administration. Hartmann believed that the original conception of a voluntary anti-inflation program that he and Theis discussed was "on a little more sophisticated level of getting both business and labor under sufficient pressure from the public, with the aid of all the media twisters, spin doctors, public relations [staff], to accept voluntary restraints on prices and wage increases and so forth."[32] Although the CAC had representatives from business and labor, these sectors had little active role in WIN, which instead focused on consumer support and thus left out part of CAC's original mechanisms for controlling inflation.

Other administration members disliked the WIN concept. Ford was chagrined to hear that some members of his staff derisively called his Kansas City address the "lick-your-plate-clean speech."[33] Some top-level administration members, left in the dark, were unpleasantly surprised to find out about WIN after it was too late to change or stop it. HUD Secretary James Lynn remembered, "I was shocked. I learned about it while sitting in an audience [during a presidential speech]. . . . I knew nothing about it. Absolutely nothing at all."[34] Paul O'Neill had no opportunity to express his reservations because the program "didn't go through the regular staffing process, which was a problem early in the Ford administration. . . . The speechwriters had an ability to put things into presidential speeches which they would discuss with him and he would agree to, and doing it that way, other people didn't have an opportunity to have an opinion."[35]

Key economic advisers judged WIN a bad idea. Greenspan later called it "an unfortunate program from the beginning, precisely what Gerald Ford did not need, and probably the low point in economic policymaking in the administration."[36] Roy Ash recalled, "I saw [WIN] as a rallying cry rather than *doing* anything. I didn't even take it seriously."[37] William Simon was characteristically acerbic. Calling WIN "ludicrous," he wrote, "Every time the 'WIN' issue came up we at the Economic Policy Board would hide our heads in embarrassment." Hartmann maintained that Simon led a cabal of Nixon administration holdovers who tried to torpedo the WIN program using "every dirty trick in their considerable bag to make it fail." One such tactic, Hartmann learned after WIN's demise, was to ignore consumer responses to WIN: cabinet secretary Jerry Jones, a Nixon veteran, failed to mail out 25,000 presidential form letters to WIN volunteers.[38] Hartmann thought that many of the Nixon holdovers, who were generally younger than Ford's own staff, were too young to remember the NRA's Blue Eagle program and the enthusiasm it had generated and scoffed at the whole WIN concept.[39] But even Ford himself eventually lost interest in the crusade; he later conceded that the WIN idea was "too gimmicky." WIN was hardly a salutary program for an administration plagued by internal squabbling, and Hartmann's adversaries within the administration were not sorry to let the episode cast a shadow on the wordsmith's reputation.[40]

When critics dismissed Ford's overall anti-inflation program as weak tea, they focused on WIN. A writer from Texas sent a letter to the White House crackling with sarcasm: "I gave up my gas-guzzling Rolls-Royce for a bike, and my wife and I are now using caviar-helper in our hors d'œuvres."[41] Ray Stroud, president of Continental Plastics of Oklahoma, berated the president: "Your appeal to the American public with the juvenile 'WIN' promotion was more fitting for a high school pep club than a leader of one of the world's great countries."[42]

No sooner had the WIN program been proposed than the EPB registered misgivings, the minutes of its October 23, 1974, meeting reporting that "serious reservations were expressed regarding start-up difficulties and a lack of private funds for WIN." Indeed, inadequate funding doomed WIN. Ford's firm desire to keep the program free of federal manipulation inherently limited its funding. Private contributions, the main source of money, were sparse.[43] The ambitious WIN advertising campaign fell victim to insufficient funding. In November 1974, one White House staff member warned Baroody and Seidman, "The WIN program will certainly fail to fulfill its potential, and may flounder, if it does not receive certain assistance in the way of staff, office space, postage, etc."[44] Baroody characterized the CAC as "woefully ill-equipped to lead a citizens' mobilization."[45]

A shoestring budget led to insufficient staffing. CAC headquarters consisted of two full-time volunteers and two part-time workers. A weary Freeburg complained that the avalanche of telephone calls—sometimes a thousand a day, plus almost a quarter-million letters—buried his staff. A vicious cycle was at work. As calls and letters went unanswered, the callers and correspondents could not participate in WIN, robbing the program of money and potential volunteers. One of the best examples of how the CAC's lack of personnel hurt it came late in 1974, when the WIN program was fading. Trying to dig out of the mail, Freeburg opened one letter and found a $10,000 donation inside, but by then it was too late to use it.[46] Frustrated, Freeburg complained in late November of "a complete lack of follow through by the White House. I've been unable to get any help or funding. I don't think [the administration] had any idea of the staff such an undertaking should have right at the start. Most days I've been juggling a dozen balls at one time."[47] By December, Freeburg left, replaced by Edward Block, an AT&T executive from New York who readily acknowledged that expectations for WIN had been too high. In fact, Block's main task, which he knew upon his hiring, was to shut down the program.[48]

By early 1975, WIN was on its deathbed. A deep recession replaced inflation as America's primary economic worry, and inflation became yesterday's enemy.[49] Frugality and decreased consumer spending would have only further hamstrung the economy. Before leaving his position, Freeburg observed that "the economic situation is changing rapidly. . . . My fingers are crossed we will not have a depression. The President is going to have to reappraise his position of October 8th."[50]

The volatile economic conditions put Ford in the embarrassing spot of having to change course in midstream. Although he liked Meredith Willson's WIN marching song and even carried the lyrics in his pocket, Ford never released it to the public.[51] By early 1975, administration members no longer wore WIN buttons, and Nessen recommended, "I suggest the WIN program be allowed to die a quiet, and unlamented death. It was a good idea at the time but was overtaken by [the recession]." He recognized that WIN "has been used to poke fun at the President and will continue to be the butt of jokes," marring Ford's image.[52] As was true for the entire Ford presidency, lack of congressional support stymied his efforts. Max Friedersdorf thought that Congress regarded WIN as "a commercial program, like selling a product, rather than serious legislation." He recalled, "My impression from the start was that it was perceived on the Hill more as a gimmick. I never felt we got . . . traction on it. It just seemed to me that congressmen were making fun of it."[53]

On March 8, 1975, the CAC voted to scrap the WIN slogan and concentrate more on energy conservation and much less on inflation. Hobart Taylor, a Washington lawyer and CAC member, called the whole thing a mistake, and Porter declared, "As an acronym, [WIN] is dead and God bless it." Ford seemed publicly to support WIN almost until its end. In late January 1975, at a briefing for economic writers, he was asked if it would be wise to dismantle WIN. No, he replied, governmental and nongovernmental actions to help the economy were complementary. "I think the American people are basically oriented toward voluntary action, and they have done some good things," Ford stated. "I don't think it is helpful to disparage what people do in a voluntary way."[54] After leaving office, Ford stood by WIN, maintaining that there was "lots of evidence that despite the press ridicule, there was a lot [more] good in it than bad. Maybe I didn't articulate it too well, but the truth is there were some excellent recommendations. And I always resented the sharpshooting, which I felt was unfair. . . . The program was helpful."[55]

Ford had proposed the most ambitious crusade based entirely on unpaid participation that any president had supported since World War II. "By initiating the WIN program," Ford believed, "I at least convinced a lot of Americans that they had to do something about inflation, or the government had to do something."[56] The early cascade of responses showed that WIN briefly inspired and edified some Americans. In his Kansas City speech, Ford cited examples of people who had responded to his anti-inflation clarion, including the Stevens family of Hillsboro, Oregon, who said they were using bicycles to run errands and cutting back on appliance use. Later, in a television interview, Mrs. Stevens explained, "I think the greatest thing that a leader can do—and I think [Ford] is trying to do—is to remind us who we are as a people, because there's no end to what we can do if we remember who we are and what's possible for us working together."[57] The campaign to boost public awareness, especially continued exhortations to conserve energy, outlived WIN itself. In early 1975, the American Automobile Association (AAA) unveiled a "Gas Watchers" program, which called upon drivers to reduce their gasoline consumption to make "five gallons of gas do the work of six" and thereby lower oil imports by a million barrels a day.[58] In the late 1970s and early 1980s, the Alliance to Save Energy sponsored commercials with celebrities like actor Gregory Peck giving the same kinds of tips that Ford did, urging every family to save one gallon of gas a week, cut down on heating and air conditioning, and use appliances sparingly.[59]

Occasionally, the campaign to save energy showed positive results. In 1975, the *New York Times* quoted a San Francisco computer programmer as saying that he turned off unneeded lights, drove his car at fifty-five miles per hour, and took public transportation whenever possible. "I do it to save energy, being as they ask you to do it," he said. "The money savings are not that big." In 1975, oil consumption fell, although the decrease was due in large part to a mild winter and an economic downturn.[60] While many Americans continued their spendthrift energy habits, conservation was important to any national energy policy and needed public blandishments to generate support. In that respect, Nessen believed that WIN "was worthwhile because it engaged people. It involved the public."[61]

But against inflation, WIN was ineffective. The hackneyed suggestions in Ford's Kansas City speech were small weapons against competitive marketplace forces. (Freeburg recalled the speech as "a terrible dud.") Thousands of letters streamed into the White House, but that represented only a small fraction of the country's more than 200 million citizens.[62] After several weeks, even that enthusiasm was gone. The initially promising response from the business world also sputtered, and political support never materialized. Toward the end of his tenure, Freeburg complained that "business has not responded in any important way to the program and neither have the governors or big city mayors."[63] Ford overestimated people's resolve and their willingness to sacrifice; voluntary action was just too weak against a muscular inflation.

Sadly, WIN handed Ford's detractors a weapon by making him and his economic team look like amateurs. Roger Porter considered WIN well intentioned but conceded, "In retrospect, it looks somewhat naïve. And it was interpreted that way at the time."[64] While a catchy slogan, WIN became a solid handle for critics to grip whenever they wished to batter the president's image. The button bore the brunt of attacks, as critics created the impression that Ford's anti-inflation policy boiled down to wearing buttons (CEA economist Gary Seevers even speculated that WIN might have been better received if not for the buttons).[65] The Democratic National Convention (DNC) gave a stinging appraisal: "The American public is not going to settle for a WIN button in place of programs to halt our recession and reduce inflation. Homey suggestions about clearing our plates and turning off the lights might be humorous if they weren't offered as the serious efforts of this Administration to change the economic situation."[66] WIN never received the bipartisan support that Ford hoped for, and in November Freeburg observed, "From talking to Democrats on the Hill, I must conclude they will work to gut the Win program because they see it as a Ford program and not a nonpartisan program."[67] Ironically, a program designed as a nonpartisan, patriotic effort ended up a political battering ram against the administration. Ford learned his lesson; after this episode, he more carefully vetted proposals, especially by using administration organs such as the EPB.[68]

In the end, the economic marketplace won and WIN lost. Inflation was a powerful force, as WIN's critics pointed out. The economy was not an athletic contest where an enthusiastic crowd could wave banners and use goodwill to propel their team to victory. Arch Booth, president of the U.S. Chamber of Commerce, was so upset by the simplistic approach that he walked out of the first CAC meeting. "Inflation can be controlled by sound fiscal and monetary policy at the federal level," he later wrote. "But inflation is too grave and too complex a problem to be treated like showbiz."[69] "Market forces are really strong," Paul O'Neill commented, and "the idea that you could get people to do the right thing by jawboning seems to me to be contrary to the facts we have in front of us. If we could, then we could solve an awful lot of society's problems pretty easily."[70] Like the surtax, the Ford administration quietly put WIN to rest after less than half a year, a short life for a major public relations campaign.

Chapter 9

The Great Recession of the 1970s

In the spring of 1936, Gerald Ford finished his first year on the Yale University athletic staff. The young Michigan alumnus served as an assistant to legendary football coach Ducky Pond, and he also coached the freshman boxing team (a funny role for Ford, who had never boxed before; he prepared by taking a course at the Grand Rapids YMCA). Ford had been cash-strapped throughout college, but his work enabled him to pay off loans and save money for the first time in his life.

That summer, Ford tried something new. He headed out to Yellowstone National Park to work as a ranger. (Although Ford later traveled extensively as president, he had never been west of the Mississippi until this journey.) One of his duties there was to feed the bears. Every afternoon, he helped unload food into a pit for grizzly and black bears. While the animals fed—and sometimes fought—Ford kept a rifle trained on them to protect the tourists who gathered to watch.[1] In the fall, Ford returned to Yale, and while his job was secure, the next year the economy collapsed into the "Roosevelt recession," precipitated when FDR reduced federal spending to balance the budget.

In the fall of 1974, President Ford found himself again concerned with bears—but those on Wall Street. Two years earlier, in November 1972, the Dow Jones industrial average broke the 1,000-point barrier. But during the first month of Ford's presidency, it sagged below 630, a twelve-year low. The drop portended tough economic times. Like Roosevelt, Ford restrained spending to balance the budget, and some critics labeled the steep downturn that came the "Ford recession."[2]

Planning an Antirecession Program

In late 1974, with the surtax and WIN all but dead, the Ford administration began to consider an antirecession program. Fearing renewed inflation, Alan

Greenspan and William Simon wanted to delay action as long as possible. William Seidman recalled that when the EPB debated an antirecession program, "By and large Ford's advisers, including Simon and Greenspan, advised us to do nothing. They argued that the economy was resilient and would recover." Blunter in his recollections, Robert Hartmann wrote that the antirecession philosophy of Greenspan and Simon "boiled down to 'let 'em eat cake.'"[3]

At an EPB meeting in mid-December, Greenspan advised Ford that unemployment might exceed 6.5 percent; public pressure, he warned, would urge him to increase federal spending. Indeed, Ford recalled that labor leaders and liberal Democrats in Congress all called for massive spending, which they defended as ultimately less costly than a deep recession. Ford feared that a quick-fix remedy to the recession would cause "a catastrophe down the road that would make the present recession look like a brush fire." A federal spending spree would increase the deficit. This situation would force the government to borrow money, pushing up interest rates and "crowding out" consumers and businesses, thus discouraging them from borrowing. The crowding-out effect would impede private investment as well as interest-sensitive consumer spending. While massive federal spending seemed a popular remedy for the recession, Ford feared that higher inflation would result. Greenspan characterized Ford's resolve to resist spending pressures as prudent and politically courageous.[4]

A tax cut emerged as the best policy alternative. It would avoid government pump priming, give consumers more money to spend, and provide a quicker jolt to the economy than government spending. Philosophically, a tax cut was compatible with Ford's belief in returning money to the people. He was also concerned with "tax drag." Inflation not only took money from Americans through higher prices but also acted as a tax increase. Price rises outstripped the pace of salary and wage increases, so that while real income dropped, inflation nonetheless pushed wage earners into higher tax brackets, forcing them to pay a double penalty of higher prices and higher taxes.

A tax cut also had political appeal. In late December, the Joint Economic Committee of Congress unanimously recommended an immediate tax cut of $10–12 billion, supplemented by actions Ford refused to touch—increased government spending on public jobs programs and selective wage and price controls.[5] Two of Ford's Michigan friends urged him to consider a tax cut. Paul McCracken, who had returned to his teaching position at the University of Michigan after acting as an adviser during Ford's first months in office, recommended a tax reduction of around $15 billion, or 1 percent of the GNP, which would increase take-home pay without reigniting inflation.[6] Representative Donald Riegle described the woes in Ford's home state, where the jobless rate topped 9 percent. (Ironically, Ford's was the state hardest-hit by the recession. In 1975, Michigan had the nation's highest unemployment rate, 12.5 percent, and Detroit had the highest unemployment rate of all major cities, 13.1 percent.) Riegle suggested a program with tax cuts and budget cuts, the latter to continue the fight against inflation, and stressed, *"The time to begin this effort is now."*[7]

Seidman played a behind-the-scenes role in building administration support for the tax cut. "I was for it, but I was supposed to be in the background [as an economic adviser], so I couldn't lead the charge for it," he recalled. Because Greenspan and Simon argued against a tax cut, in mid-December Seidman helped to arrange a bipartisan White House meeting of economists, at least half of whom advised a tax cut.[8]

At a December 21, 1974, EPB meeting, Ford and his senior advisers discussed the worsening recession. The room was quiet as death. Nessen described the mood as "somber, almost frightened." When the president asked Roy Ash for the good news, Ash replied, "That will take about four seconds." The EPB concluded that the economy needed stimulus through tax cuts rather than more spending. Ford approved but quickly added that "we can forget any new programs."[9]

Ford was taking risks. Cutting taxes as a short-term method to jolt the economy was still relatively new dogma, and it came with controversy. A tax cut, Ford feared, might "raise the budget deficit so high that instead of restoring the public's confidence in the economy, it might frighten people out of their wits. That deficit could spur a new round of inflation. Government borrowing to finance the deficit might drive up interest rates and worsen the recession."[10] The EPB shaped the tax cut to minimize these dangers. A moratorium on new spending programs would accompany the cut, which would be temporary, lasting for only one year.

The question was how big a tax cut to propose. Seidman and James Lynn wanted $30 billion or more, to match the new energy taxes the administration contemplated and give a shot of at least $10 billion more in spending power for consumers. But Greenspan and Simon wanted no more than $20 billion.[11] The EPB favored a $15 billion cut, with three-quarters going to individuals and one-quarter to corporations.[12] The EPB also recommended that the temporary tax refund include an increase in the investment tax credit to 12 percent, which would mean a tax break of $4.1 billion for corporations and a 10 percent individual income tax refund worth $11.8 billion. The total for the entire tax refund would thus be $15.9 billion.[13]

Since the economy deteriorated so rapidly, Ford had no time to waste. He summoned his top advisers to Vail, Colorado, during the Christmas holidays for a special meeting. These were cruel times for the nation as well as for administration members, as they had to spend holiday time away from family, sharing rented chalets like college roommates and meeting with the president to iron out details of the economic and energy program. The Vail meeting dragged on for four hours, complicated by some advisers who now argued against a tax cut, worried that the deficit would mushroom. After the long debate, Ford—anxious to take a respite and go skiing—decided to resume work once back in Washington.[14]

During White House meetings on January 10 and 11, Ford finalized the details. He agreed to include a $1,000 cap for the tax cut, partly in response to advice from his friend David Packard. With an unlimited rebate, high-income earners—like Packard, as he himself conceded—could receive an embarrassingly large sum, which would provide little economic stimulation, since wealthy recipients would likely save the money. Such large windfalls for millionaires also would have been a political black eye for the administration. Ford's willingness to listen to outsiders' views helped to develop a better program and prevent embarrassment. "Once again," Seidman wrote, "advice from individuals outside the economic inner circle saved us from what could have been a political disaster."[15] These details resolved, the tax cut proposal was ready to be unveiled.

Americans and the Great Recession

In the 1970s, the foundations of economic security shook and crumbled. It was a time of transition, as the nation underwent shifts that were partly created by the magnificent advances of the previous decades. Lynn Townsend, chairman of Chrysler, the auto company hardest hit by the recession, observed, "I think to some extent we will see a shrinking of desire for some of the things we always wanted—those two cars per family, two color television sets and lots of other things. We certainly as a people cannot continue piling luxury upon luxury. There has to be an end."[16]

Until 1974, the highest postwar unemployment recorded was 6.8 percent, during a recession in 1958. As the politically and economically tumultuous year of 1974 drew to a close, unemployment stood at 7.1 percent and was rising; real growth was at a negative rate of more than 5 percent; and American productivity fell 2.7 percent for the year, the first time productivity had registered a decline since 1947. And, of course, there was inflation.[17]

To be sure, America was not on its economic deathbed. The country was still the world's leading economic power. Its 1974 GNP was $1.4 trillion, far ahead of its nearest rival, the USSR. But this recession was especially painful, for it was the first in which unemployment and inflation simultaneously ran high. This stagflation made American workers face the double agony of losing a job and losing purchasing power. The situation was unprecedented. The traditional economic model described a trade-off between joblessness, on the one hand, and price levels, on the other, meaning that the economy might experience high unemployment or high inflation but not both simultaneously, a relationship defined on graphs by the "Phillips curve." For much of the postwar period, the Phillips curve fit inflation-unemployment data almost perfectly. The 1970s economy defied this model, as inflation raged while unemployment rose.[18]

Stagflation presented a perplexing new dilemma, because the policy prescriptions for high inflation and high unemployment were contradictory; the former involved slowing down the economy, the latter meant stimulating it. But with stagflation, as CEA member Paul MacAvoy remarked, "there is no clear path in monetary or fiscal policy to ameliorating that condition." Ford's economic advisers counseled him to adhere "to what was basically a hold-fast policy," MacAvoy recalled, "to hold fast until money supply excess growth had been absorbed in the economy and we started up on the natural business cycle inventory recovery." The administration wanted to reabsorb unemployed workers gradually, because to push them back in the workforce before the natural business cycle was ready to accommodate them risked aggravating inflation.[19] Administration critics lambasted the "hold-fast" policy as a "do-nothing" one that tolerated high joblessness.

Higher unemployment, while distressing, was no reason to panic. Ford believed that he could tolerate higher levels of unemployment than previous presidents. In the early 1960s, Kennedy's CEA defined "full employment" as a jobless rate of 4 percent. (Six percent unemployment was generally the flashpoint at which the president and Congress began to consider antirecession measures.) But by the 1970s, because of social and demographic factors, economists thought that the target unemployment figure should be revised to between 5 and 6 percent. Many women, teenagers, and minorities had entered the job market, groups that traditionally had trouble finding jobs. *Newsweek* worried, "Has unemployment in the U.S. become a new and chronic social problem?"[20]

If it seemed that way, it was ironic. Because the higher unemployment rates of the 1970s included so many of these new entrants, the figures reflected America's progress as a society, yet the felicitous achievement wore a doleful face. As Ford pointed out, the nation was also at peace, and the number of persons in the armed forces fell from 3.5 million to 2.1 million, which increased the ranks of the unemployed.[21] The country was better educated, too, but in a twisted way the new brainpower contributed to joblessness. As baby boomers graduated from high school, many chose a path that the preceding generation had not: they went to college. During the 1950s and 1960s, college graduates found work with relative ease, as industry, government, and education all expanded. But a contraction began in the 1970s, and the economy could not adjust to accommodate them. Thus a glut of college graduates faced a shrinking job market and could not find work (a mismatch that Harvard economist Richard Freedman examined in his 1976 book, *The Overeducated American*). To subsist, many college graduates—especially those with humanities degrees—accepted jobs far below their qualifications. The stories that came out of the 1970s were depressing: a University of Kansas Ph.D. in medieval history travailed as an office worker at a Kansas real estate firm; a magna cum laude Radcliffe grad cleaned houses in Boston; a University of California at Los Angeles alumnus worked as a pesticide sprayer. Other college grads refused to stoop to such menial jobs and continued to look for work, adding to the ranks of the unemployed.[22]

In addition to social and demographic factors, economic maladies lay behind the sudden downturn. Rising prices preceded almost every recession during the postwar era, and indeed, the Great Inflation contributed to the Great Recession. Part of the explanation was found in the normal pattern of business cycles. During high inflation, the Federal Reserve raised interest rates to slow the rise of prices and assuage lenders' demands to recoup losses on an eroding currency. Higher interest rates discouraged business investment and also choked off demand. The latter caused inventories to build, and businesses responded by curtailing production and laying off workers. Moreover, the particularly pernicious inflation of the 1970s—with high prices of food, fuel, and other necessities—rattled consumer confidence, leaving Americans with little money to buy big-ticket items whose sales help drive the economy. Inflation also created an uncertainty that made businesses reluctant to make new investments.[23]

The Great Inflation, the Great Recession, and the energy crisis operated in a cruel synergism. The economy is intimately connected to the oil markets—far more than the average consumer realized; in fact, since the 1970s, each time the world suffered a spike in oil prices (in 1973–74, 1979, 1990, and 1999–2000), a recession followed.[24] One reason for this relationship was simple: higher energy prices robbed consumers of purchasing power. As a consequence, consumers curtailed their spending, which accounted for two-thirds of all economic activity. Items related to oil especially took a nosedive; for example, consumers cut back on buying clothes because the prices of petroleum-based synthetic fabrics sharply increased. Shoppers shunned larger discretionary items, too. Purchases of energy-using home appliances fell by 5.3 percent in 1974 and by 10 percent in 1975. Hardest hit was the auto industry; the energy crisis raised the cost of operating a car, and consumers steered away from the huge, gas-guzzling American chariots.[25] Higher energy prices, by increasing the cost of business, also forced companies to stop hiring or even to lay off workers.

Jobless Americans wondered whether their president, in the rarefied atmosphere of the White House, felt their pain. Ford did, especially since the recession paralyzed his home state. In particular, Ford empathized with the auto industry's ills. One Republican congressional leader said that Ford's "whole ethos is bound up in the motorcar syndrome of the state of Michigan." By early 1975, the American auto industry, according to Ford Motor Company president Lee Iacocca, was in a depression.[26] The industry wallowed in its worst slump in the postwar era, signifying America's entry into an age of new economic constraints and consumer tastes. The convergence of these forces threatened to debilitate the industry.

Until the 1970s, auto manufacturing had been the big gem in America's industrial jewel box. One of the country's largest industries, it was responsible either directly or indirectly for one in every six jobs in the economy. In 1973, Detroit sold a record 9.7 million cars. The recession prompted questions about the industry's ability to sustain its preeminence in the world economy and prefigured the fierce competition the industry would face from Japanese, German, and Korean competitors. In 1974, sales of American-made cars slid to 7.5 million. Automakers were stuck with a glut of 1.6 million unsold cars, and production fell to its lowest levels since 1962. Many economists pointed to the auto industry's slump as the chief reason that the recession became so severe, so suddenly; cars were a postponable purchase, and in the frightening economic environment of late 1974, consumers stayed away from auto showrooms and tried to save their money, bracing for worse times ahead.[27]

By the end of 1974, the automakers had laid off 285,000 workers, almost half of their total workforce. After posting record profits of $2.4 billion in 1973, General Motors' profits plunged 60 percent in 1974 to $950 million, knocking General Motors off its spot as the nation's number one industrial corporation. Meanwhile, as Japanese manufacturers established a solid foothold in the domestic market, American automakers had barely a toehold in Japan (in 1970, General Motors claimed just 0.1 percent of the Japanese market). As Detroit faltered, shock waves rippled throughout the economy. Layoffs hit the tire and rubber industries, as well as plate glass producers. The fear was that the auto industry would never emerge from its depression, the jobs lost would never be retrieved.[28]

Another bedrock industry, housing, was in trouble, too. The industry was acutely vulnerable to inflation, not just because the cost of land, labor, and materials increased with inflation. The Federal Reserve's medicine of tight money had painful side effects on construction, as a tight credit supply hobbled builders and buyers who depended on borrowing. In 1974, housing starts fell to their lowest levels in five years. *Time* called it "the year the building stopped." "This is far and away the worst [slump] since the Depression days," commented the executive vice president of the National Association of Home Builders. Like the auto industry, the housing industry suffered from a surplus of unsold homes and worker layoffs. New, unsold condominium apartments littered the shores of California and Florida; in the Miami–Fort Lauderdale area alone, 18,000 units waited for buyers. Some large architectural firms cut their staffs by 70 percent. Senator William Proxmire, a Wisconsin Democrat, declared that the housing industry was "in a serious, all-out, 17-karat depression" and criticized the Ford administration for not doing enough to help it. Many Americans felt trapped, unable to buy their dream home and move from cities to suburbs. Geographic mobility, relatively easy in the postwar era, was no longer a birthright.[29]

The malaise of the 1970s hit a key pressure point in the economy, the city. After World War II, suburbanization changed the American landscape, usually at the expense of cities. Suburbs offered families an opportunity to own their own homes and raise children in a more quiet, clean, and safe environment. A mass exodus began, and by 1970 almost eighty million people had abandoned the city for the suburbs. Although at first suburbs functioned as bedroom communities, where wage earners came home at night after a day's work in the city, by the 1970s suburbs were much more than that. Businesses, factories, restaurants, and entertainment all developed there, so that suburbs rivaled and even surpassed core cities as centers of economic activity and population.

When the affluent left, cities had a smaller tax base. Their infrastructure crumbled, crime increased, and even more residents fled. Bad conditions in New Orleans prompted Mayor Moon Landrieu to warn, "It is appalling to believe this country would let a city like New Orleans go down the pipe, but if you're going to save it, you'd better save it now, because two or three years from now it may be too late," he declared. "We are a city of 600,000. In the last decade we have lost 125,000 people—mostly white and affluent—moving out to the suburbs, and in their place, 90,000, mostly poor and black, moved in."[30]

During the Great Recession, the crisis of urban America reached critical mass. Cities nationwide reported high unemployment rates, such as 15 percent in Buffalo.[31] They confronted huge deficits and spending cutbacks. Minneapolis, for example, had a 1975 budget deficit of $2 million. Double-digit inflation had made outlays rise faster than revenues, and the recession aggravated matters, as businesses brought in less revenue; meanwhile, demand for municipal services remained high. Cities tried various schemes to stay afloat. Miami instituted a gas-rationing program for the city's 3,000 cars. Chicago doubled fines for parking offenses. Detroit and Las Vegas implemented hiring freezes.[32]

The most celebrated case of urban blight was New York. By the 1970s, white flight, physical deterioration, and crime riddled the city. Many corporate giants pulled their headquarters out of Manhattan, including Pepsico, Shell Oil, and Eastern Airlines. By late 1974, the city faced a $330 million budget deficit, prompting a wave of job cuts. One Department of Public Works maintenance man, informed of his dismissal, immolated himself on a Queens sidewalk. In May 1975, Mayor Abraham Beame made the stunning announcement that 51,097 city workers would lose their jobs.[33] Soon the Big Apple risked defaulting on its debts and applied for a federal bail-out, which Ford at first refused. The *New York Daily News* splashed an angry headline across its front page: "FORD TO CITY: DROP DEAD." That famous line recast the president in the image of a callous, tightfisted man. Democratic New York congressman Edward Koch blasted Ford's decision as "immoral." The colorful future New York City mayor continued, "We are a city surrounded by Mongol hordes, and I look out the window and the faces aren't those of barbarians; they are those of the White House."[34]

Ford thought that tough action was necessary. He blamed New York City's plight on years of irresponsible spending and urged municipal authorities to rein in expenditures. As Ford saw it, "The problem was New York had a bad policy of paying too much in pensions, paying too much in salaries to New York City employees. And the City was going bankrupt because of this irresponsible fiscal policy. And I was not, as president, going to bail them out unless they took corrective action."[35] Eventually, Ford agreed to a funding plan to help New York, partly in response to the blandishments of West German chancellor Helmut Schmidt and Arthur Burns (who, like Ford, at first opposed federal assistance), both of whom warned Ford about the adverse economic and international effects of a New York default.[36] Additionally, Beame agreed to stern cost-cutting measures. He released over 60,000 workers from the city payroll, shut down firehouses, hiked subway fares, and ended the long tradition of free tuition at the City University of New York. Ford thought that he made his point. In 1976, he wrote, "No person can live beyond their [sic] means for very long without incurring a heavy penalty. The people of New York City learned this lesson last year, and they have shown admirable courage in finally putting their financial house in order."[37]

Ford's stance toward the Big Apple—his antirecession policy in general—seemed like "tough love."[38] Harshly condemned, the policy put the administration under tremendous political pressure and psychological stress. Alan Greenspan was "deeply troubled by the recession," according to William Seidman, and during a meeting with Chancellor Schmidt, at which Schmidt urged the Ford administration to stimulate the economy with government spending, Greenspan vehemently disagreed with Schmidt's exhortations but kept his cool. While walking back to his office, Greenspan collapsed. Seidman recalled that "as horns honked and passersby gawked, I hoisted him over my shoulder, fireman style, and carried him to his office in the Old Executive Office Building." Greenspan's bad back, which sometimes hurt so much that he conducted late-night meetings while lying on the floor, finally gave out due to mental and physical exhaustion.[39] The Great Recession had taken another toll, this time on Ford's top economist.

At the beginning of 1975, a *Newsweek* cover story capsulized the country's plight with the terse title, "Out of Work." During just one week in January, dozens of the country's mainstay industrial giants (including Goodyear, Firestone, Westinghouse, and General Electric) instituted layoffs, with the combined total reaching over 18,000 workers. That month, industrial production slumped 3.6 percent, the largest drop since the "Roosevelt recession."[40]

The 1974–75 recession was the longest and deepest since the Great Depression. Unemployment peaked at 8.9 percent in April and May. More than eight million Americans were out of work. While testifying before Congress, economist Arthur Okun declared that "the history books will record this episode as a depression rather than a recession." Senator Jacob Javits of New York warned that the discontent among jobless Americans could "threaten the social fabric of our nation."[41]

Indeed, some Americans reacted desperately. In Atlanta, a crowd of more than 3,000 lined up in a drizzle for 225 public-service jobs and broke a glass door in a mad rush to apply. Arson became the fastest-growing crime in the country, as business owners driven to financial ruin saw insurance money as a way out of their bind. In one sense, the most celebrated kidnapping of the decade, the 1974 abduction of newspaper heiress Patty Hearst, reflected the troubled economy. During the Great Depression of the 1930s, a rash of kidnappings broke out, some notorious, such as those of Charles Lindbergh's infant son and the eight-year-old son of Phil Weyerhaeuser, executive vice president of the Weyerhaeuser Timber Company. Ransom money provided an easy way for criminals to get ahead during economic privation. The Hearst kidnapping resembled this paradigm, as her abductors, a small band of California radicals who dubbed themselves the Symbionese Liberation Army (SLA), initially demanded that her wealthy parents underwrite a $2 million food giveaway program for San Francisco's poor. (The Hearsts complied, but the SLA reneged on its promise and kept their daughter.) Hearst was finally captured in September 1975, and the entire episode reflected how anachronistic 1960s-style radicalism was by the mid-1970s, when a gloomy economy dominated the concerns of most Americans, quieting the nation's campuses and all but snuffing out violent protest.[42]

As the country slipped deeper into recession, comparisons between the 1970s and the 1930s—between Gerald Ford and Herbert Hoover—cropped up. *New York Times* columnist C. L. Sulzberger scored Ford for his "Hoover-like incapacity" to find innovative solutions to the economic crisis. Sneering at Ford's WIN buttons, economist Robert Nathan distributed buttons emblazoned "BATH"—Back Again To Hoover.[43] Critics arraigned Ford's policies for excessively deflating the economy to dampen inflation, thus contributing to the deep recession. Speaking in Utica, New York, a city whose vacant factories stood as stark symbols of the nation's industrial decline, Democratic senator Birch Bayh of Indiana charged, "High unemployment was deliberately brought about by both President Nixon and President Ford as their short-sighted, callous and ultimately unproductive response to the problems of inflation."[44]

Approval ratings for Ford took a toboggan slide as the recession deepened. A January 1975 poll found that 86 percent of its sampling disliked Ford's handling of the economy, and in February his overall approval rating slid to 36 percent. The flinty problem of stagflation kept Ford's approval ratings low for most of 1975. Congressman Henry Reuss suggested that the Republicans not even field a candidate in 1976. Ford insisted that he would run, but the sobering truth was that never in the past quarter of a century had inflation and unemployment been simultaneously as high during a presidential election year.[45]

The recession fanned a feeling of helplessness that dated back months. Watergate made the recession all the more difficult to accept. In his 1974 State of the Union address, Nixon painted a rosy economic picture, extolling the past five years of his administration. "Despite this record of achievement," he said, "as we turn to the year ahead we hear once again the familiar voice of the perennial prophets of gloom telling us now that because of the need to fight inflation, because of the energy shortage, America may be headed for a recession. Let me speak to that issue head on. There will be no recession in the United States of America."[46] By late 1974, Nixon's assurances tasted like ashes; Americans felt they had been lied to again.[47] The feelings of deception and discouragement made them look anxiously to Gerald Ford for an answer.

Chapter 10

Ford's 1975 State of the Union Program

On June 20, 1975, *Jaws* opened. People who had worked on the film were nervous about its premiere. The film's production had been riddled with problems and complications, most notably involving "Bruce," the twenty-five-foot-long, quarter-million-dollar mechanical shark. Shooting the film was supposed to take 55 days; instead, it took 159, and the crew nicknamed the project "Flaws." The film's $4 million budget inflated to $12 million, prompting rumors that the twenty-seven-year-old director, Steven Spielberg, would be fired. There were worries that audiences would laugh at the preposterous ending; Frank Mundis, the Long Island shark fisherman who was the model for the character Quint, said that when he first saw the film, "it was so funny that I rolled in the aisles screaming." But *Jaws* was a smashing success. It set a record for an opening weekend, grossing $7 million over three days, and became the first film to earn more than $100 million at the box office. Eventually, it took in $260 million. (Although normally not an enthusiastic movie-goer, even President Ford decided to see *Jaws*, viewing it at Camp David in mid-July.)

The movie industry was a bright spot in the dull 1970s economy. After experiencing declining box office receipts in the 1960s, the industry scored spectacular successes. *Jaws* began an important trend: Hollywood invented the summer "blockbuster" during the decade, and the term even entered the American lexicon. Before the 1970s, the summer was a wasteland for films. Nobody wanted to spend a gorgeous day sitting in a hot, stuffy theater, so filmmakers released their refuse during the summer and unveiled marquee films during other seasons. But in the 1970s, air conditioning, multiplexes, product tie-ins, and films laden with special effects reeled in summer crowds. Filmmakers also began to use saturation advertising and widespread releases to hook audiences; *Jaws*, for example, opened in a record 455 theaters, and a $700,000 advertising blitz hyped up the film before it premiered.[1]

As they deluged theaters to watch *Jaws*, Americans had reason to relax. After feeling the bite of the Great Recession, they might have found a great white shark on the screen to be small stuff. By summer, the real beast was behind them, as a brutal recession faded and the economy took tentative steps toward recovery. Art practically imitated real life. In *Jaws*, a bickering team comprising a sheriff, an ichthyologist, and a shark hunter banded together to help the seaside town of Amity. In Washington, the quarreling executive and legislative branches composed their differences to aid the nation. For President Ford, the work involved employing his executive and legislative skills to make Capitol Hill move quickly.

A Vital Speech, an Unusual Preview

As 1975 began, despondent Americans thought that Ford was not leading. His administration apparently lacked a purpose or plan. *U.S. News and World Report* commented that Ford had yet "to convince the public and Congress that he can indeed be an effective leader. Throughout the government, there is a sense of drift, of tough decisions being put off, of policies being announced and then being abandoned."[2]

The State of the Union address represented an opportunity to answer these charges. It was not only a time to acquaint the country with Ford's new economic and energy program, which included his plans for battling the recession. It was to set the tone for his presidency. William Baroody reminded the president, "Your speech will mark a formal end to the transition period and the beginning of what will be seen by the public and by history as the Ford Administration. An important part of your message should be devoted to giving identity and direction to your Administration for the next two years."[3]

An apprehensive mood among Ford's advisers mirrored the feelings of most Americans. They, too, were uncertain of his leadership image and still adjusting to the fast-moving machinery of a presidential administration, as well as to the fickle economic conditions. Ron Nessen worried that unless Ford hit a home run with the speech, "the Ford presidency is never going to get off the ground and he is going to be a President for 2 1/2 years and that is all." Ford thought that if he came across as a president in command, he could persuade the public and Congress to support his program.[4] Moreover, a speedy economic recovery with limited government action would reaffirm Americans' faith in the free-market system and make them less receptive to draconian measures such as wage and price controls.[5]

Confidentiality was critical. If details of Ford's program leaked out, its impact would be blunted. On January 4, Nessen, William Seidman, and

Federal Energy Administration (FEA) head Frank Zarb advised the president that, because numerous leaks were leeching away the program's potential impact, "we feel that you should reevaluate your plans to announce the economic and energy proposals in the State of the Union speech and consider making at least some announcement before then in order to prevent a complete loss of impact." Their unusual proposal indicated how seriously they regarded the speech. With the Democratic leadership of Congress formulating their own economic program, the possibility of being upstaged presented a real danger. A House Democratic Steering and Policy Committee task force planned to unfurl a plan on the morning of January 13, calling for a "substantial" tax cut for low- and middle-income families, plus more public-service jobs and spending on public works, which Ford wanted to avoid.[6] Not to be upstaged, Ford decided to give Americans an early peek at his State of the Union address. On January 13, he would make a prime-time pitch on national television to give advance word of his program. In addition, he moved the date of his State of the Union address from January 20 to January 15.

Never before had a president given a "preview" of his State of the Union speech. The preview was designed to pressure the Democrats and even set a tone of intimidation that would be less fitting in the State of the Union message. As Zarb recalled, "He wanted to get the mood right. He wanted to get the Congress to understand that when they received the State of the Union [program], that if they didn't act there was going to be a penalty."[7] Above all, Ford wanted the preview to be for the people, who could help him persuade Congress to act fast. In his public appearances, Ford had spoken mostly to Congress, reporters, and the party faithful but not directly to the people, who badly needed reassurance and economic straight talk.[8]

Ford gave the speech from the White House library, a small, informal room rarely seen by the public. A fireplace and book-lined shelves furnished a warm, comfortable atmosphere; Robert Hartmann wanted to emulate the aura of Franklin D. Roosevelt's fireside chats.[9] Ford and his staff left nothing to chance. They used logs made of compressed sawdust so that the fire would not crackle or pop while the president was speaking. The week before the speech, the White House rented television equipment for rehearsals, and Nessen and former CBS producer Robert Mead gave Ford pointers. For the first time, Ford practiced using a teleprompter, which allowed him to look into the camera and appear to speak directly to the people. He coordinated his hand gestures to match the speech and rehearsed it half a dozen times, watching replays of his performance with a critical eye. Mead inserted cues into the teleprompter for Ford to follow—"Stand up. . . . Start sit. . . . Change camera"—instructed Ford not to eat for a few hours prior to the speech so as not to hiccup air, and even suggested that the president relax before the speech by taking a swim and downing a shot of bourbon.[10]

Just before Ford faced his national audience, Zarb noticed an inauspicious sign. "I walked in there right before he was about to give the speech," Zarb recalled, and noticed Ford fiddling with his sleeves. "He had forgotten his cufflinks, and he was putting paper clips to hold his sleeves together."[11] As it turned out, though, that might have been the only glitch. Ford's speech showed a polish and gleam that marked a pleasant departure from his normal speaking style. He began the speech while standing, then sat at a desk, and concluded the speech by standing again. He looked at different cameras and gestured throughout the speech. One reporter joked, "After tonight's performance on television President Ford may have to take out an AFTRA card [American Federation of Television and Radio Artists]."[12] While the speech won praise, it was terse and somber, with admissions that "the going is rough, and it may get rougher" and that "we are in trouble," although Ford reassured Americans that "we are not on the brink of another Great Depression." Ford first detailed his new energy program, then explained his plan to fight unemployment. He described a $16 billion tax cut proposal and promised to return quickly to the economy the new revenues from energy conservation taxes, totaling $30 billion, to bring the total of returned taxes to $46 billion. Ford's focus on the future was still steady, as he described inflation and energy as "long-range" problems. But he conceded that temporarily, "we must shift our emphasis from inflation to recession." In explaining his about-face since October, Ford observed that "the situation has changed. You know it, and I know it. What we need most urgently today is more spending money in your pockets rather than in the Treasury in Washington."[13]

"The State of the Union Is Not Good"

Two days later, Ford delivered his State of the Union address. Despite the overarching importance of this speech and the careful planning behind it, serious problems tainted it. Ford had assigned the speech to Hartmann, directing the speechwriting team to fashion the address in unadorned, easily understood language. Hartmann's draft was a pedestrian piece that left Ford severely disappointed. "It was short on specifics and long on rhetoric; worse, it didn't have a clear and central theme," Ford lamented. With the speech date so near, he was angered that his speechwriting staff risked political embarrassment.[14] During a meeting to discuss the speech, Robert Goldwin witnessed a flash of anger that he rarely saw in Ford, as the president broke a pencil and snapped, "This speech isn't ready, and it should have been ready." He then got up and walked out.[15]

Unknown to Ford, another group of aides, led by Chief of Staff Don Rumsfeld, had produced a rival draft. Ford sat down and compared the two drafts at 9 P.M. on January 14; he was scheduled to deliver the speech at 1 P.M. the next day. He forged an amalgam of the two versions that had to be speedily edited and assembled. The president approved the final version at 4 A.M. and delivered the speech on just three hours of sleep.[16]

The mess over the final draft reflected the dissension and backbiting that plagued the Ford administration. Most presidents forge their staff during the crucible of a long campaign, when they can observe aides' work habits and blend the right chemistry of staff members. Ford never had this opportunity, and his staff was an uneasy mix of his own aides and Nixon appointees.[17] With the exception of Phil Buchen, Hartmann had known Ford the longest. Unerringly loyal to the president but protective of his turf, he complained bitterly about the Nixon holdovers. He described them as dedicated not to Ford's presidency but to their own power within the White House. They constituted a cabal that he labeled the "Praetorian Guard," after the elite soldiers of late classical Rome who assumed formidable influence and privilege, overshadowing even the emperor in power. Hartmann criticized Ford's reluctance to demand obedience and purge his staff of the self-serving Nixon leftovers.

While many administration members believed that Hartmann's assessment of the Praetorian Guard was exaggerated, Nessen, appalled by the constant infighting, wrote that the disorganized and contentious manner in which the State of the Union address was assembled was "a wasteful and divisive process. It exposed a serious weakness in the Ford White House organization. More distressingly, it exposed Ford's unwillingness to get tough with his staff, to demand a better speechwriting operation and less infighting." Nessen thought that Ford was simply "too much Mr. Nice Guy" to squelch the internal dissension.[18]

Yet the episode also revealed some of Ford's qualities as a leader and in some ways stood as a metaphor for his steady style amid economic turmoil. With a potential public relations disaster brewing, Ford disciplined his staff, assigning individuals to reorganize and rewrite parts of the speech, setting firm deadlines, and working into the early morning hours. The resulting speech, while somber, was earnest and straightforward, and when Ford appeared before Congress and the American people, he showed no signs of the chaos during the previous twenty-four hours. Seidman recalled that Ford "took charge, got it done and came up with a great speech. It was a good example of his ability to handle pressure."[19]

Given the problems he had to defuse, Ford was pleased with the final speech draft and satisfied with his performance. He felt that "with less than three hours' sleep, I didn't do too badly." Devoted almost exclusively to domestic issues, the speech frankly acknowledged the crises facing the nation. Its somber tone was unusual for a State of the Union address, when a president normally speaks in honeyed words about his administration. At the beginning of the speech, Ford—who had an excellent memory—recalled when he was a freshman congressman, he sat at the back of the chamber and listened to Harry Truman, recently elected to lead the world's most powerful nation for a full term, pronounce the State of the Union "good." But these were the 1970s, and in a memorable line Ford declared, "The State of the Union is not good."[20] He enumerated the country's ills: "Millions of Americans are out of work. Recession and inflation are eroding the money of millions more. Prices are too high, and sales are too slow. This year's federal deficit will be about $30 billion; next year's probably $45 billion. The national debt will rise to over $500 billion. Our plant capacity and productivity are not increasing fast enough. We depend on others for essential energy." After this catalog of the country's conditions, Ford admitted, "I've got bad news, and I don't expect much, if any, applause." Indeed, applause interrupted his speech only nine times.[21]

The speech represented the official change in Ford economic policy from fighting inflation to fighting the recession. The president proclaimed, "The moment has come to move in a new direction. . . . The emphasis of our economic efforts must now shift from inflation to jobs." The one-year, temporary tax reduction of $16 billion that Ford proposed was designed to create jobs, because it would stimulate more consumer spending and business investment. Consumers were to get $12 billion in tax relief on their 1974 taxes, which represented a 12 percent rebate on 1974 taxes, paid out in two installments, in May and September. Businesses and farmers, getting $4 billion in the form of an investment tax credit of 12 percent, would also be expected to spend more (the investment tax credit was 7 percent for corporations and 4 percent for utilities). To underscore his desire for quick action from Capitol Hill, Ford asked Congress to act on the tax cuts by April 1. Since the tax cut was temporary, a second, more permanent step in pumping up the economy involved returning the $30 billion raised by Ford's new energy taxes on domestic oil, tariffs on imported oil, and a windfall profits tax.[22]

Since the new energy conservation taxes would bring $30 billion in revenue, Ford wanted to restore an equal amount to the economy. A total of

$7 billion was to be countercyclical federal spending in the form of payments to low-income individuals and to state and local governments; permanent tax reductions to individuals and businesses represented the balance, $23 billion. As with the temporary cuts, three-quarters of this tax reduction was allocated to individuals and the remaining quarter to businesses.[23]

Ford was temporarily subordinating fiscal austerity and the fight against inflation to the need for economic stimulation. But he was still concerned about the inflationary impact of a tax cut, which would also increase the deficit. This potential increase strengthened his determination to control the growth of federal expenditures. To restrain the deficit and inflationary pressures that could result from his program, Ford proposed a one-year moratorium on all new federal spending except for energy. He recommended a 5 percent limit on increases in federal pay and programs (including Social Security, food stamps, and civil service) and vowed to veto new congressional spending programs. Ford wanted to have a balanced budget in three years.[24]

The speech hit the right tone, and some observers welcomed Ford's honest appraisal of the country's dilemma. DNC chairman Robert Strauss said, "It's obvious and for the better that the President has changed course." The *Washington Post* liked the president's "honest and straightforward" tone, commenting, "After the [Vietnam] war and disorders of the 1960s and the scandals and constitutional stresses of the early '70s, what this country may be in need of is straight talk and realistic ambitions. And that is basically what it got."[25]

But Ford's plan came under fire. The temporary, one-year tax cut should have been the most appealing feature of his program, yet it drew a drumbeat of criticism. Many Democrats liked the idea but objected to Ford's formula. Democrat Russell Long of Louisiana, the powerful chairman of the Senate Finance Committee, commented, "It doesn't make sense to give a $1,000 rebate to someone who makes $50,000 or $100,000 a year."[26] One woman from New York State wrote to the White House to complain of the program's slant toward the upper class, asking the president, "And while we're pulling in our belts, after your speech will you continue to eat caviar?"[27]

Upper-income earners would benefit most from the tax cut. Families earning $50,000 or more would receive the maximum rebate of $1,000. By contrast, a family of four with an adjusted gross income of $5,000 would get a refund of only $12.[28] Ford reasoned that upper-income taxpayers deserved a tax break, too, and in keeping with his stress on long-term capital investment, he wanted to give them relief because they would make new investments and purchase durable goods, resuscitating the economy's softest sectors. If aimed at lower-income earners, the tax cut would do little to stimulate sales of big-ticket items that power the economy. Nessen explained that the president wanted people to use their tax cut rebate to "go out and buy TVs and cars and other items."[29]

Some economists deemed the $16 billion temporary tax insufficient to jump-start the economy. Since the rebate for many consumers would not be large, they might pigeonhole the rebate instead of spending it. Former budget director Charles Schultze estimated that a stimulative tax cut would have to be around $26 billion. A source of worry, especially for conservatives, was the budget deficits that might result from Ford's program, around $30 billion in the current fiscal year by Ford's estimate. Members of both parties faulted him for failing sufficiently to slash government spending. Republican senator James Buckley of New York called the potential deficits "ruinous," while Democrat Robert Byrd called them a "surrender to inflation."[30]

The deficits troubled Alan Greenspan and William Simon. But while Greenspan swallowed his misgivings, Simon vented his. Simon had been a reluctant convert to a tax cut, and he confided to a reporter that if the deficit exceeded $40 billion, he would bolt from the Ford camp and join forces with conservatives like Ronald Reagan. While conceding a tax cut was necessary, he threatened to warn Congress and the people about the deficit that could result. Ford called Simon and told him to support administration policy or face certain consequences, which no doubt involved a vacancy at the top job in the Treasury Department. Simon fell in line, but rumors circulated that his days in the administration were numbered. The United Press International (UPI) carried a story that opened, "Treasury Secretary William Simon is expected to leave the Cabinet soon."[31]

Ford publicly dismissed the reports. Despite Simon's outspokenness, Ford wanted him to stay but was worried "that his spirits were down because of all the newspaper hints that he was on his way out. I assured him that I retained full confidence in him. . . . Simon's spirits soared, and he said he would stay on the team." Yet Ford's concern for Simon illustrated his failure to be tougher on his staff. The mercurial treasury secretary was not only insubordinate, but he tainted the administration with the stain of scandal. A prominent Nixon holdover, he landed in trouble for retaining expensive gifts from foreign statesmen, violating federal law. In what became for Simon an embarrassing confrontation, Shirley Temple Black, the former child actress serving as the State Department's chief of protocol, forced him to relinquish the gifts. Moreover, Simon had already shown disregard for administration policy. When the president was promoting the WIN program, Simon riddled it with invective. Hartmann believed that "the scorn and ridicule he assiduously relayed to the media . . . severely embarrassed and undercut the President of the United States."[32] By failing once again to support an administration program, Simon jeopardized a critical initiative in the Ford presidency.

Ford had reversed course and developed a program designed to meet the challenge of recession. He had shown flexibility and reacted quickly to changing economic circumstances; he had gotten his administration to plan a comprehensive economic and energy package. Yet it was off to a shaky start. Despite his two candid speeches, Capitol Hill was not embracing it. The reactions of members of Congress, Ford recalled, "frustrated me. What I had proposed were reasonable recommendations for the improvement of our economy and the solution of our energy problem. What they were engaging in was partisan politics."[33] In general, Democrats saw a need for greater economic stimulus than he proposed and were less concerned with inflation. Ford faced an uphill struggle.

"I Just Want Them to Act"

The House split Ford's program into two separate packages, the tax cut legislation and the energy plan, a division that the White House found agreeable because it allowed the House to work faster on the tax cut. Two weeks after Ford introduced his tax cut, House Ways and Means chairman Al Ullman of Oregon submitted his own plan, with a tax cut of $22 billion, $18 billion for individuals and $4 billion for businesses. This division meant that while businesses would get the same tax break as under the president's plan, individuals would get an additional $6 billion. In addition, 94 percent of the tax cut for individuals would go to persons and families with adjusted gross incomes of under $20,000, in contrast to 54 percent under Ford's plan. The cap on Ullman's plan would be $300 (instead of the administration's $1,000), and the payment would be made in one lump sum in May, not two.[34] Congress was determined to give more tax relief to lower-income groups. By slanting the tax cut more toward lower-income groups and concentrating the stimulus in May, Congress improved the proposal, making it not only more equitable but also more sensible, since these groups were more likely to spend than save, thus stimulating the economy in a quick jolt.

Ford detected "some room for flexibility" between the two versions. What mattered most to him was that Congress act speedily. In February, he noted that weeks had passed, yet members of Congress had failed to act decisively on their versions of the tax cut. "I just want them to act, and [their delay] does bother me," he complained. He thought that his administration had moved quickly, and he tried to encourage similar speed from Congress. As the weeks passed, Ford's criticism grew more strident. At a press conference in late

February, a reporter raised the possibility that Congress might not act on a tax cut until June. Ford found the prospect "ill-advised and extremely serious." He stressed that "our proposal was very simple, and hopefully it would result in Congress acting very quickly. It is almost five weeks now, and the House of Representatives has not yet acted."[35]

On February 27, the House finally passed a tax cut of $21.3 billion, with $16.2 billion for individuals and a maximum refund of $200 and a minimum of $100. Eighty-five percent of the rebate was for families with yearly incomes below $20,000. The bill proposed $5.2 billion in tax relief to business through a higher investment tax credit of 10 percent, up from 7 percent. Repeal of the oil depletion allowance made its way into the bill, much to the chagrin of Ullman, who begged his House colleagues not to include the measure, fearing it would provoke debate and delay in the Senate.

Repealing the oil depletion allowance would bring in more revenue for the government, compensating for revenue lost due to the tax cut. The allowance was a fifty-year-old provision that saved the industry an estimated $2 billion a year by exempting the first 22 percent of an oil producer's income from taxation.[36] Originally conceived as an incentive for the industry to explore for oil, the allowance was based on the argument that oil is capital; by taking it out of the ground, an oil producer loses some of his property. But President Truman had deemed it "inequitable" and "excessive," and many Democrats charged that the oil industry made enough profits without it. In the 1960s, the allowance came under sharper attack because it allowed wealthy oil producers to avoid paying taxes.[37]

Yet petroleum producers argued that the incentive was necessary. When the allowance fell from 27.5 percent to 22 percent as part of the Tax Reform Act of 1969, exploratory oil drilling in the United States dropped by 21 percent, the biggest one-year decline in the industry's history.[38] C. M. McLean, a Louisiana petroleum geologist, wrote to Ford to urge him to keep the oil depletion allowance, describing it as critical to the smaller domestic independent oil companies, which had drilled more than 80 percent of the exploratory oil wells in the United States during the past few years. For the independent oil man, McLean maintained, the allowance "is his *only* means of attracting the vast amounts of risk capital necessary to drill wells. Without it he is dead, out of business, and will be forced to sell his holdings."[39] The thorny issue threatened to add to the congressional delays that so vexed Ford.

In March, Ford's frustrations continued, this time with the Senate. Economists forecast that unemployment might hit 9 percent, and Ford signaled his amenability to a larger tax cut. "The big problem is not the size of the tax reduction," he said, "but the slowness with which the Congress is acting on it." Quoting Ralph Waldo Emerson, the president said, "In skating over thin ice our safety is our speed," and he observed that "the spring thaw is coming, and the Congress must pick up its speed." At a March 17 press conference, he noted, "It is now two months and two days" since his State of the Union speech, "and the Congress has not completed action on that tax reduction bill." Ford hoped that lawmakers would finish their work on the legislation before the Easter recess, and he pressured them by threatening to cancel his own vacation plans (he was to go golfing in Palm Springs, California) and to bring Congress immediately back into session to speed things up.[40]

Some Democrats took umbrage. Robert Byrd said, "The manner in which the President has initiated this confrontation, I think, does not bode well." The senator charged that Ford launched into his strictures without giving Congress an opportunity to scrutinize his programs. "We were not consulted," Byrd protested. "He sprung [the tax cut] out of the blue . . . and then immediately lays it on the Congress's back, goes around the country and says that Congress is dragging its feet, that we're not passing his programs." Ford thought that the time period during which he and his staff formulated the program—the Christmas holidays—as well as the urgency they felt had militated against congressional consultation. "We did most of the decision-making while Congress was in recess, both when they adjourned and before they came back," Ford explained. "And I felt it was of maximum importance to have something on the desk of Congress as soon as they reconvened."[41]

The Senate passed a bill on March 21—the final vote coming in at 1:52 A.M.—but it was hardly what Ford wanted, a $29.2 billion tax cut, nearly twice his original request. The president found the expensive special interest amendments especially objectionable: costly provisions like a $100 bonus for all recipients of Social Security, railroad retirement and federal welfare benefits, and child-care deductions for working parents. Even Al Ullman conceded that the bill emerging from his senatorial counterparts had gotten "out of hand."[42]

Like the House version, the Senate bill contained an amendment repealing the oil depletion allowance. Ford, who opposed the action as long as domestic oil prices were artificially controlled, wanted a "clean" bill, free of pork; he objected to the "unfortunate piecemeal additions."[43] A House-Senate conference committee was set to reconcile the two versions of the tax cut and present a final version. Alarmed by the Senate bill, Ford asked House Speaker Carl Albert and Senate president pro tempore James Eastland to tell the conference committee "that I will be unable to accept a bill so encumbered with extraneous amendments and of such deficit-increasing magnitude as to nullify the intended effect of a one-time stimulant." Coupled with other congressional actions on spending, the Senate's tax cut could increase the deficit by $50 billion, which "jeopardizes the prospect of economic recovery and makes us hostage to future inflation." Ford much preferred the House bill—with minor revisions—and urged the conferees to accept it.[44]

Following difficult negotiations between House and Senate conferees, Congress on March 26 approved a $22.8 billion tax cut, which would give a 10 percent rebate on 1974 taxes. The bill favored lower- and middle-income taxpayers, giving only 14.8 percent of the individual tax benefits to persons with incomes above $20,000 a year. Those falling in the $10,000–$20,000 range would get 41.6 percent of the benefits, with 43.5 percent of the benefits going to those making less than $10,000.[45] The rebate would have a cap of $200 for taxpayers with an adjusted gross annual income of $30,000, phased down to $100 progressively as income decreased to $20,000 per year. The bill contained many of the extraneous amendments, which some Ford staffers called "garbage," including the earned income credit (designed to help low-income taxpayers by proposing a temporary, refundable credit on earned income), the housing provision (which gave tax breaks to people buying a new home), a $50 bonus payment to Social Security recipients, and a partial repeal of the oil depletion allowance.[46]

Ford's advisers reviewed fifteen major daily newspapers and found that only three favored a veto.[47] Newspapers that wanted the president to reject the bill, such as the *Wall Street Journal*, were especially displeased with its numerous amendments. Labeling it "a collection of flotsam and jetsam," the *St. Louis Globe-Democrat* said the bill was "like a magnet in attracting junk provisions that belong in the trash heap," and stated, "President Ford definitely should veto this mish-mash bill." But most newspapers, while attacking the bill's flaws, urged Ford to sign it. The *Los Angeles Times* called provisions like the housing credit "outrageously shabby" and the $50 bonus payment "utterly cynical" but echoed Ford's emphasis on quick action by warning that "a veto could delay a tax bill as long as a month."[48]

"Time Was of the Essence"

The *New York Times* reported that, to the last moment, Ford was undecided about whether to sign the bill. Uncharacteristically secretive about his leanings, he asked his advisers for written recommendations and later sought additional oral consultations. The day before he announced his decision, some of his closest aides still did not know what he would do. Ford's speechwriting team developed both a veto speech and an approval speech.[49] In his memoirs, Ford described the tortuous thought process over this bill and used this incident to illustrate the difficulty of presidential decision making. The problems that reached his desk were the most agonizing, he reflected, because the easy ones were resolved at lower levels of the federal bureaucracy.[50]

Even Ford's advisers recognized the difficulty of this decision. Simon scrawled a sympathetic postscript to his recommendation: "I don't envy you on this one Mr. President!" while Burns wrote that "my heart goes out to you as you move towards a decision."[51] Both men urged a veto. They feared that the bill would overstimulate the economy and swell the deficit. Burns opined, "I do think that a line must be drawn and that anything in excess of [a tax cut of] $20 billion should be resisted." Simon argued that the resulting deficit would defeat the purpose of the tax cut by killing off a recovery and causing "substantial unnecessary unemployment in future years."[52]

The veto message prepared for Ford struck out against the most objectionable amendments, "hasty and ill-considered additions" that warped the bill's fundamental purpose. Opponents of the oil depletion allowance, for example, were using the bill to achieve its repeal. "This precipitate action," the veto speech declared, "cannot but help to discourage exploring and drilling for oil for the near term at a time when we should instead use every tool at our disposal to encourage such risk-taking."[53] Worst of all, the bill was inflationary.

But the majority of Ford's advisers recommended that he sign the bill. Many expressed concern about its effect on the already massive federal deficit. But if Ford vetoed the bill, James Lynn pointed out, an irritated Congress might claim that more spending would be in order.[54] Lynn urged Ford to make the bill part of a broader program of fiscal restraint, linking it with reasonable spending. Richard Dunham, deputy director of the Domestic Council, reasoned similarly: "Since a tax cut is, in terms of your position, a better way to stimulate the economy than governmental expenditures, your approval of this bill may put you in a better position to resist further expenditure increases while still maintaining your original position of tax cut stimulus vs. governmental expenditure stimulus." Republican senator Paul Fannin of Arizona seemed to confirm future congressional support, telling the White House that two senators, Bob Dole and J. Glenn Beall, indicated that if Ford signed the bill, they would support his future efforts to hold down spending.[55]

Many advisers urged Ford to accompany his signature with a strong statement against fiscal excesses. Greenspan's advice consisted of only one sentence: "I recommend that the tax bill be signed but that you simultaneously come down very hard on expenditure increases."[56] As for the extraneous amendments, Nessen recommended that Ford tell Congress that he swallowed them only on the condition that it now "act in a responsible way and not load any more stimulation onto the budget."[57]

Political considerations were critical. Nessen wanted the president to "take full credit for initiating and pushing [a tax cut] through a foot-dragging Congress." Hartmann wrote, "I am of course concerned about your election in 1976. But I am even more concerned about your ability to lead the country between now and November 1976." Here was a first big victory, Hartmann exhorted. Congress would seize upon a veto as an example of presidential intransigence, and irritated lawmakers might send him another bill even less to his liking. Russell Long bluntly predicted that if Ford vetoed this bill, "he'll get a chance to veto a bigger one next time." Hartmann warned that a veto might be so vexing to key figures in Congress, like Ullman, that hopes for Ford's energy program and future tax legislation might be dashed.[58] William Kendall, the administration's legislative liaison with the Senate, warned that "there is no doubt that we would have problems with Senator Long on future tax bills and possibly the energy bills should the President veto the bill and it is sustained."[59]

Ford had exhorted Congress to pass a tax cut measure by April 1, which it did. After all the fuss over speed, if Ford vetoed the bill, he would appear fickle and obstructive. "This is exactly the idea the Democrats are striving to promote," Hartmann observed. The president could not turn his back on the momentum that his own words had created. Hartmann reminded him, "You have gone up and down the country, scarcely missing a day without chiding Congress for not acting faster against the recession and unemployment, saying every day counts, and demanding a tax cut bill on your desk before April 1." He beseeched the president to make a decision "consistent with your past utterances."[60]

Indeed, Ford found the amount of the tax cut less important than quick action. "Time was of the essence. The precise dollar amount was not as critical," he recalled. "We wanted action so the public could get the benefit of whatever the figure was. And from my long experience in Congress, I anticipated that when a president recommends 'X' figure, the Congress has to show its figure and get some independence by adding to it. . . . What I was anxious to get was action—prompt."[61]

Tip O'Neill boasted, "We shoved the tax cut down [Ford's] throat."[62] Yet Ford orchestrated events shrewdly and expected that Congress would raise the ante. Lynn recalled that there were always some "rules of the game" in dealing with Congress. When the administration wanted to propose a tax cut or a spending level to Congress, one rule was that "you always come in 20 percent—at least—less, maybe sometimes 50 percent less, than you really want to get, because you've got to leave room for the Congress to add to it." Ford thus made the initial proposal of $16 billion, a reasonable figure that was high enough for Congress to take seriously and low enough that even a 50 percent addition to it would not create an excessive tax cut.[63] Max Friedersdorf commented that Congress often adds to a tax cut because "Congress wants to get credit for it, and if they come out with the exact figure that the president has asked it will be his tax cut. If they add to it, it's their tax cut. . . . That usually is the way it goes."[64]

Knowing that Congress would add to his original amount, Ford found $22.8 billion acceptable. He recalled, "Having been in the Congress for 25 and a half years, I knew the Congress better than anybody in the White House. And although we proposed a $16 billion reduction, I knew from experience— practical experience especially on Capitol Hill—that Congress wasn't going to reduce my $16 billion in tax cuts. If anything, they were going to increase it. So we . . . were pleased with the way it turned out."[65]

But Ford kept everyone guessing what he would do. As he explained, "I never thought it was a good policy for a president to make a public announcement when the issue was very controversial and very substantive. My policy in general was to wait and get the pros and cons and then make a decision. I don't think a president should signal what he's going to do in most cases." Ford had actually made up his mind early. He knew that he would sign the bill because the economy needed stimulation. "I never really thought about vetoing it, although I respected the people who recommended [a veto]," he recalled.[66] Nonetheless, he canvassed his advisers for their recommendations. As Seidman explained, Ford "wanted to assure everybody that he was going to take their views into consideration. He always did that." After all, Seidman added, Ford "might decide, for some reason, that he wanted to veto it. He was a genius at keeping that option open. But did he have a gut feeling about what he was going to do? He almost always did. He was a guy that was very, very seldom at sea about what he was going to do."[67]

Ultimately, Ford believed that the bill would not wreck his drive for fiscal integrity. Vetoing it might have even hurt his long-term strategy of restraining inflation. Recovery might be delayed, and Greenspan foresaw the possibility that "there would have been tremendous pressure from the Congress—not only the Democrats, but I suspect the Republicans as well—for a massive cut in taxes beyond anything we had calculated or decided upon."[68] That situation would have been a setback in Ford's battle against inflation.

On March 29, Ford announced on national television his decision to sign the Tax Reduction Act. He made clear that he approved it reluctantly because of the "many extraneous changes in our tax laws" that Congress hurriedly tacked onto the bill before leaving for Easter recess. "This is no way to legislate fundamental tax reforms, and every member of the Congress knows it," the president chided his former colleagues. Despite the bill's drawbacks, he accepted it because of the nation's "urgent necessity of an antirecession tax cut right now."[69]

Then he threw down the gauntlet. Criticizing Congress for ignoring or rejecting his proposals to restrain spending, Ford turned to a series of charts to show how the deficit might swell to $100 billion. "Deficits of this magnitude are far too dangerous to permit," he said. "They threaten another vicious spiral of runaway, double-digit inflation that could well choke off any economic recovery." He marked off the $60 billion point on the chart and said, "I am drawing the line right here. This is as far as we dare go. I will resist every attempt by the Congress to add another dollar to this deficit by new spending programs." Ford later admitted that "if I were still in the House of Representatives, I would have opposed extraneous amendments and would have voted to send this bill back to [conference] committee for further cleaning up."[70] But as president, he was concerned with the weak economy and the more than seven million people without jobs. He was willing temporarily to abandon his intense anti-inflation focus and advocate a tax cut to break the slump.

Although the veto was one of his favorite executive weapons, his chances of getting a better bill were marginal, and delay would have been harmful. A veto might have not only postponed recovery but damaged Ford's image by making him seem uncaring toward the unemployed. By accepting the bill, Ford promoted economic recovery. Just as important, he hoped that his willingness to compromise might translate into increased congressional cooperation on his energy proposals and his struggle to reduce spending.

Perhaps the most noteworthy aspect of the tax cut was its speed. Congressional sluggishness is legendary. The slow pace makes antirecession fiscal policy like the doctor who arrives after the patient recovers; by the time Congress finishes debating and passing a tax cut, the recession has usually ended (or "self-corrected," as economists say). At that point, the belated stimulus becomes dangerous, threatening to increase inflation. But by employing a mix of coercion, cajolery, and compromise, Ford got Congress to act quickly. The two months it took legislators to pass his tax cut represented blinding speed by Washington standards. By contrast, when John Kennedy proposed a tax cut in late 1962 to stimulate a weak economy, Congress finally passed a bill in January 1964 and would have taken even longer if not for the president's assassination, which turned the bill into a tribute to a slain leader.

Similarly, in August 1971 Nixon proposed a tax cut, which Congress did not approve until December; by then, the economy was expanding, and the stimulus only contributed to inflation.[71]

Because Ford's tax cut was so speedy, it took effect in May. The next month—as Americans began to enjoy the summer, flocking to theaters to see *Jaws*—unemployment edged down from 8.9 percent to 8.6 percent, prompting Greenspan to suggest to Ford that the recession had "bottomed-out."[72] The stock market climbed (by midsummer the Dow Jones industrial average stood at 881, up from 632 in early 1975), and when third-quarter figures showed the GNP rising at a robust annual rate of 11.2 percent—the highest in twenty years—Assistant Commerce Secretary James Pale declared the recession over.[73] The tax cut encouraged the nation to shake off the Great Recession and avert a more serious downturn. One movie reviewer even compared Ford to Sheriff Martin Brody in *Jaws*. Initially, townspeople expressed angry disenchantment with Brody's leadership, arguing that he dealt with a big problem ineffectively. But in the end, Brody found a solution, and his leadership was vindicated.[74]

Yet real life was not quite so easy. By summer's end, many Americans were still out of work, the economy weak. Ford would have to address the issue of stagflation and tax cuts again in the fall.

Chapter 11

Economic Initiatives, 1975–76

G erald Ford "was very concerned about the crime problem, which was becoming severe" in the mid-1970s, recalled presidential adviser Robert Goldwin. Between 1973 and 1974, serious crimes—murder, rape, robbery, and assault—jumped 17 percent, the largest increase since the FBI began recording national crime statistics in 1930. While some observers blamed the crime wave on moral decay or a permissive justice system, New York City mayor Abraham Beame attributed it to the "acute inflation-recession" that afflicted the country and made lower-income Americans desperate.[1]

On September 5, 1975, Ford was in Sacramento to deliver an address on crime to the California state legislature. Before entering the capitol building, he worked the crowd gathered nearby. At one point he noticed a woman in a bright red dress, standing just two feet away from him. He reached out to shake her hand, then noticed she had a gun. She pulled the trigger. Nothing happened. The firing chamber contained no bullet—although the gun had four in its magazine. Secret Service agents quickly tackled the woman, twenty-eight-year-old Lynnette "Squeaky" Fromme. She was later sentenced to life in prison.

On September 22, Ford was back in California, visiting San Francisco. Just before entering his limousine, he waved to a crowd across the street. *Bang!* A gunshot rang out. Secret Service agents threw Ford into the car and sped off. The assailant, forty-five-year-old housewife Sara Jane Moore, had aimed a gun at the president and fired, but a bystander lunged at her and deflected the shot. The bullet missed Ford by five feet. Moore, too, received a life term.[2]

Two assassination attempts within three weeks made September 1975 a bad enough month for Ford. Back in Washington, he faced more grim news. The economy was still wobbly, trying to shake off the Great Recession, and the *New York Times* labeled Ford's economic policies a failure: "The economic recovery is sluggish and sputtering, unemployment remains high, and inflation is again surging forward."[3] Ford had to do something about the lingering recession. In October, he also planned to unveil dramatic deregulation proposals; beyond that, he would have to manage the economy during an election year.

The Dollar-for-Dollar Proposal

Because unemployment remained high in September, Ford considered recommending that Congress extend the tax cut that he signed in March, since the expiration of that temporary tax cut was equivalent to a tax increase. In January 1975, planning the antirecession program, Ford's economic team anticipated the possibility of proposing an extension of the tax cut at the end of the year.[4] By that fall, Ford began to weigh this option more actively. The temporary cuts were scheduled to expire on December 31. If the economy remained depressed, the danger was that consumers, hit by higher taxes once the new year began (in the form of greater withholding rates), would reduce spending. The recovery could stall as an election year began.[5] That prospect was unpalatable for a president with soft national support. Possible Democratic challengers Henry Jackson, Hubert Humphrey, and Edmund Muskie drew close to Ford in the polls. The president expected trouble from his own party, too, because Ronald Reagan was positioning himself to vie for the nomination.

But extending the tax cut could agitate inflation, which had dropped slightly during the recession. Ford's advisers wanted to be safe, building a recovery around gradual tax cuts; they believed that since inflation was a cause of recession, too much tax stimulation could land the economy back in a downturn. While most postwar recoveries from recession experienced GNP growths of over 8 percent in the first four quarters, William Simon said that a 6 percent growth rate was fast enough, even if it meant that unemployment would remain "distressingly high" for a long period.[6] This was the Ford White House's "go-slow" approach.

The administration's caution led to an innovative idea: linking a tax cut with a commensurate cut in spending, an idea that the *Economist* called "a bold new departure in fiscal policy." Concerned that a tax cut might swell the deficit, administration members considered this concept at the December 1974 meetings in Vail, Colorado. Although the idea never found its way into the State of the Union program, by the fall of 1975 the time was ripe.[7]

On the evening of October 6, 1975, Ford spoke to the nation from the Oval Office to unveil a new proposal, a $28 billion tax cut. But it was to be matched by a $28 billion cut in federal spending, imposing a $395 billion ceiling on the fiscal 1977 federal budget. For businesses, Ford proposed a number of measures, including lowering the corporate tax rate from 48 percent to 46 percent and making permanent the increase in the investment tax credit, keeping it at 10 percent for businesses and utilities. Just as with his State of the Union proposal, the tax cut was allotted in the ratio of three-quarters for individuals ($20.7 billion) and one-quarter for businesses ($7.0 billion).[8]

Ford explained that a tax cut was only half the answer to improving the economy. The other half was curbing the growth of government spending, which he said was crowding out the private sector from borrowing. Ford concluded his speech with an acid indictment of wasteful spending: "Sometimes when fancy new spending programs reach this desk, promising something for almost nothing and carrying appealing labels, I wonder who the supporters think they are kidding." The country was at a crossroads, where Americans "must decide whether we shall continue in the direction of recent years—the path toward bigger government, higher taxes, and higher inflation—or whether we shall now take a new direction, bringing to a halt the momentous growth of government, restoring our prosperity, and allowing each of you a greater voice in government."[9]

James Lynn later described how the OMB formulated the budget cuts. "We set out in a very methodical way to look at everything the federal government does, and to make cuts wherever we legitimately could. We worked in secret," Lynn said. "I was very proud that there were no leaks out of OMB on the work we were doing." Lynn estimated that at least sixty-five people in OMB worked on the proposal, yet they never disclosed details to the media. One of the reasons for the tight secrecy, Lynn explained, was that a program "can be killed aborning before people see what you've got in its entirety, the whole package. The press—if details come out in little trickles—can demolish it before it ever arrives."[10] The administration had been developing the proposal with a feverish urgency since the summer of 1975, and Paul O'Neill recalled that he had OMB planners working on it on a "forced draft basis," meaning that all other work was put aside to concentrate exclusively on the proposal and finish it fast.[11]

The secrecy was almost too good. When Ford unveiled the package, it caught Congress and the media off guard, and critics alleged that he was playing politics. Members of Congress and newspaper reporters pointed out that the tax cuts would take place in January 1976, while the spending cuts would come at the end of the fiscal year (September 30). Thus, at the time of the elections, voters would not have yet felt the effects of the spending cuts, yet they would have already enjoyed the benefits of the tax cut. Senator Walter Mondale accused Ford of stooping to a Nixonian trick. "Nixon hyped up the economy in 1971 and 1972," Mondale maintained, "and then right after the election we went cold turkey." Even some Republicans considered his scheme transparent. Senator Henry Bellmon commented, "If I had an evil political mind—and I have—I might think that there was some political motive in this timing. I would say that it would be very convenient to have a tax cut early in the year and an expenditure cut later in the year."[12]

The media were openly skeptical. *Newsweek* asked, "A Plan or a Ploy?" NBC and CBS refused to broadcast Ford's address on the grounds that it was a political statement and therefore subject to the "equal time" rule for other declared political candidates. That left only ABC to carry the address.[13] Lynn, who had hoped that the program would receive good press coverage, was "really appalled" that only ABC covered the president's speech. "We had put [the proposal] together in good faith. We were proud of what we had been able to come up with. I was madder than hell that only one network would cover it," he remembered. In retrospect, Lynn felt that the secrecy surrounding the proposal inadvertently hurt it because it shocked the media, which famously dislike being surprised. The media refused to take it seriously, interpreting it as a political gimmick cooked up at the last minute. "I guess it's just the pundits were so surprised by it," Lynn surmised. "They couldn't believe that anybody in Washington could do anything that well without leaking. . . . And as a consequence they thought it was just a political ploy and wouldn't put it on [the air]. It was a very, very sincere proposal."[14]

To Congress, Ford's proposal upset normal budgetary procedures. The president wanted his budget cuts approved before he had submitted a budget and specified where he would make the cuts. Maine's Edmund Muskie, chairman of the Senate Budget Committee, said that approving budget cuts without knowing where they would take place was "hogwash."[15] Tip O'Neill did not want Congress to be straitjacketed by agreeing to budget cuts in advance. Contingencies could arise to make such a move unwise. "We'd love to have a $395 billion ceiling. But how do we know about the economy? How do we know about defense? A million things could happen," O'Neill protested.[16]

Just as annoying to Congress, new congressional budget procedures, approved in 1974, stipulated that a committee in each house of Congress, along with the Congressional Budget Office, would establish overall spending, revenue, and deficit targets. Congress took pride in the new process to discipline federal spending, and Ford's proposal threatened to upset the apple cart. The 1974 Budget Impoundment and Control Act, the creation of the Congressional Budget Office, and all the new budget procedures were intended to limit presidential control over the budget process, a power that

Nixon had used heavy-handedly to deny money to programs he opposed. Members of Congress viewed Ford's proposal as an encroachment on their new prerogatives as well as a bad precedent. Many congressional Democrats accepted a spending ceiling per se but wanted to wait until May, the time prescribed by the new budgetary procedures. By then Ford would have submitted his budget, due in late January, and Congress would know which programs he wanted to cut.[17]

Adding to congressional ire were reports describing how the program allegedly came about. The *Washington Post* and the *Wall Street Journal* claimed that the tax cut was orchestrated not around how much stimulus the economy needed but how much the budget could be cut. These newspapers reported that Lynn determined where spending cuts could be made and then matched a tax cut with the spending cuts. The reports, although erroneous, added to the impression that the package was hastily thrown together.[18]

Challenging Congress and the Big Apple

During the twentieth century, the federal budget had grown inexorably. In 1929, federal spending represented just 5 percent of GNP; by 1976 it was approaching 25 percent. The trend troubled Ford because of inflation and the burden of debt on future generations. In the past, when budget deficits occurred, they usually resulted from exceptional economic circumstances, such as war or recession. During the 1920s, the federal budget was in balance every year, a norm that the Great Depression and World War II upset.[19] Budget surpluses almost never returned. There had been only four balanced budgets in the 1950s, one in the 1960s, and none in the 1970s.[20] The budget's growth and size were dizzying. In fiscal year 1962, the federal budget crossed the $100 billion mark; in 1971, $200 billion; in 1975, $300 billion. Ford warned that "without some serious trimming, [the budget] will go over $400 billion in the next fiscal year. That is a 300-percent increase in the short span of 13 years."[21]

The prospect of a budget exceeding $400 billion was a terrible irony for a politician devoted to fiscal austerity. Ford said that his proposal had two objectives. "Number one . . . if you look at the curve [of federal spending] for the last 14 years, and if we focus specifically on the growth from 1970 on, you will find that there has been a tremendous acceleration in federal spending that this country cannot tolerate and we must change," he explained. "Number two, it is my belief that the American people want a fair, sizable, substantial tax reduction."[22] "I basically thought that it was a fair proposal, a fair recommendation," Ford later reflected. "We wanted to give a tax cut to stimulate the economy. On the other hand, I wasn't going to give [Congress] tax cuts and let spending go free. It seemed to me like a balanced economic approach and good, sound, fiscal policy."[23] Ford thought that "unless Congress recognized this link [between the tax cuts and the spending cuts] we would risk a new round of double-digit inflation and a recession worse than anything we had seen before."[24]

Ford believed that he was tapping a rich vein of public indignation. Many Americans were disillusioned with the costly Great Society programs and concluded that the government should limit its tinkering with the nation's social and economic structure. Writing to Speaker Carl Albert in late 1975, a Missouri resident implored, "Our wonderful country is going down the drain because of excess federal spending. Please help our President bring spending under control *now*! No tax cut without a corresponding cut in spending!"[25]

While politicians loved to promise tax cuts and increased spending, few of them acknowledged the fiscal dangers. Lynn noted that "the difference between Ford and [other politicians] is that he had the responsibility to say, 'I want very, very much to cut taxes, but if I do that, I'm going to have to do things that aren't very popular with anybody.' . . . In other words, he looked upon the spending cuts as the sine qua non to be able to justify the tax cut." Ford's approach distinguished him not only from most politicians but also from conservative economists who focused almost exclusively on the stimulative effects of tax cuts while failing to mention the importance of simultaneously reducing spending.[26] As David Gergen explained, "In effect, [Ford] was saying no dessert until you eat your spinach." Ford vowed publicly to veto any bill without a restraint on spending.[27] In private, he was even more vehement. At a White House meeting with GOP congressional leaders, Ford declared, "I will do my damndest to sell this program," adding that he would "veto a hundred bills if necessary" to keep congressional spending down.[28]

Democrats feared that a budget cut, even when accompanied by a tax cut, would harm the sluggish economy. Albert remarked, "It seems very unwise for the President to offer tax reductions and lowered expenditures at a time when the economy may well again be sliding downward."[29] Congressional critics charged that Ford would receive the political windfall of a tax cut in the spring of 1976 while spared the blow of spending cuts until after the fall election. This charge reflected a Keynesian economic assumption that the two cuts would cancel each other out, with no net increase in economic stimulus. The administration rejected this view, believing that the spending cuts would actually stimulate the economy by avoiding "crowding out."[30]

Ford's tough approach showed his frustration with legislators. They had been slower than he had wanted in passing the Tax Reduction Act and even slower in considering his energy program, still languishing on Capitol Hill.

He began to refer to the Ninety-fourth Congress as the "Can't Do Congress" and explained, "After I announced the $28 billion tax reduction and the $28 billion cutback in the growth of federal spending, all I heard from Congress was, 'We can't do it. The rules of the Congress won't permit us to do it.'" Ford said that Congress was obligated "to find a way in the parliamentary situation to respond to the desires of the American people." "Instead of whining and whimpering," he urged, "they ought to get out there and do the job."[31]

But the budget ceiling would force congressmen to oppose popular entitlement programs. "How dumb can you get?" Republican Robert Griffin of Michigan snapped. The president targeted food stamps for cuts and criticized Congress for allowing this program to run amok. "This Democratic Congress knows as well as I do," he said, "that approximately one — unbelievable — out of every five Americans has now become eligible for food stamps." Ford thought that the program could be cut by $1 billion without harming those truly in need. He also wanted to cut medical benefits. Nor was the Pentagon a sacred cow. "I think we can cut some of the frills in the military. . . . I think the Defense Department can run a tighter ship, and they will have to," Ford vowed.[32]

The administration was concerned that in the public eye, Ford would look like a reaper slashing federal programs, especially those designed to aid the disadvantaged. Ford explained at a press conference, "I just hope everybody understands it is not that we want to be penurious, because virtually every program this year got as much or slightly more than they got last year as required by the law."[33] Ford emphasized that his $28 billion plan represented a cut in the *growth* of federal spending, not just a straight cut.

The autumn of 1975 offered an opportunity for Ford to demonstrate his belief in fiscal austerity. He tried to win passage of his proposal against the backdrop of New York City's struggle to stay solvent. In Ford's opinion, the crisis served as a lesson to the nation that unchecked spending could lead to bankruptcy.[34] Some Americans drew a powerful conclusion from the Big Apple's troubles and wanted to apply the lesson to federal spending. "There is the certainty our federal government has to revise its fiscal policies or the country will go down the drain financially as it appears New York City will," a Tulsa man wrote to Carl Albert. "This government has got to live within its income. It cannot endure on deficit spending."[35]

Stalemate and Showdown

Once again, Ford's proposal faced rough sledding. Even his supporters offered only lukewarm backing. When administration economic advisers met with fifty Republican members of Congress to brief them on the plan, many laughed outright when Alan Greenspan stated that Congress would reject the tax cut if it were not accompanied by a spending cut.[36] At a White House meeting with Ford, some congressional Republicans raised the likelihood that Congress would give the president his tax cut but ignore the spending ceiling.[37]

Congress did just that. On December 17, lawmakers passed a bill with a temporary, six-month tax cut of $17 billion and no spending ceiling. Members of Congress felt confident that they could override a veto. Senator Russell Long predicted that "either someone will have to back down or the nation will suffer. It's sort of like playing that game of chicken."[38]

Ford vetoed the bill. Apparently Congress "didn't think I was serious." The tax cut was too small and, more seriously, since it was not tied to a spending ceiling, a "half-way measure," and he blamed Capitol Hill. "The Congress offers only to keep a temporary lid on taxes while leaving the federal cash register wide open for whatever spending Congress wants to take out in an election year," he complained. "That I cannot and will not accept." The quick veto caught Democrats off guard, and as Democratic representative Richard Bolling of Missouri conceded, "The President was more contentious than we expected he would be."[39]

Ford was pleasantly surprised when the House upheld his veto. Then, just as he had done in the spring, he made Congress move faster by threatening to infringe on their holiday vacation. He instructed his congressional relations office to inquire into the rules for calling Congress back for a special session during Christmas recess. To ensure the tactic worked, he wryly told aides to keep his inquiry "an absolute secret. That will get word around the Hill faster than Western Union." Predictably, word of the president's unusual query spread through Capitol Hill, pressuring Congress to develop a revised bill.[40]

Russell Long suggested that the Democrats in Congress break the impasse by simply sending the vetoed bill back to the White House with nonbinding language—a face-saving measure for both Congress and the president— promising to limit future spending as much as possible. Long met with fellow Republicans William Roth of Delaware, another member of the Senate Finance Committee; Congressman Barber Conable, a member of the House Ways and Means Committee and an expert on tax legislation; and Joe Waggoner of Louisiana, a leading conservative Democrat in the House. Worried that the battle lines between the White House and Capitol Hill were hardening, the four drafted a loophole and grafted it onto the bill.[41] While Ford had insisted on explicit and binding language, the addition was a vague escape clause that did not commit Congress to a spending ceiling. The fuzzy language indicated that if Congress extended the tax cut, due to expire in June, beyond that month and into fiscal year 1977, it would make dollar-for-dollar cuts in "the level of spending which would otherwise occur" in that fiscal year. Congress also reserved its right to adopt a higher or lower spending total for fiscal year 1977 if warranted by "changing economic conditions or other unforeseen circumstances." When Conable met with White House political aides, they balked, calling the new language unacceptable, but Conable reminded them that House Republicans had supported the president's veto, and now it was Ford's turn to give ground. Max Friedersdorf called the four men the next day to inform them that the president would sign the measure.[42]

Congress passed the bill by lopsided margins and adjourned for Christmas. It was the same bill Ford had just vetoed, except for the new nonspecific budget control language. Ron Nessen reported that Ford was "very pleased" with the revised bill.[43] Not everyone was; Simon urged a veto. But Lynn believed that "there is virtually no chance of Congress adopting [the] $395 billion ceiling now, either directly or indirectly."[44] Lynn advised the president that the bill was as good as the White House could expect, and Ford could later ask Congress for an additional $10 billion tax cut. On December 23, Ford signed the Revenue Adjustment Act aboard Air Force One, on his way to Vail for Christmas.[45]

Democrats crowed that Ford caved in. Al Ullman called the nonbinding resolution "a far cry" from the $395 billion spending ceiling "which the President told us for three months was the only thing he would take." The Democrats did not give a solid commitment to anything, avoiding a tax hike while successfully protecting their budgetary prerogative of setting tax and spending targets. Nessen later wrote, "It was not a victory [for Ford] at all, except perhaps for some public-relations benefit with voters who appreciated the president's efforts to limit government spending."[46]

In public, Ford put his best foot forward. "I think the compromise which was achieved was a good tax bill for six months," he observed, "but I under no circumstances believe that I backed off a very fundamental principle which was, if you are going to have a tax reduction, you have to have a corresponding limitation on the growth of federal spending. I think I won on that issue 100 percent."[47] Ford could claim that he held firm, used the veto once, and did all he could to contain federal spending while avoiding a tax increase. The timing of the veto demonstrated Ford's political determination. A stalemate could have forced Congress to stay in session into the Christmas holidays, which would have been extremely unpopular on Capitol Hill.[48] Ford explained, "I had lived in Congress long enough to know that sometimes the tougher you are, the better off you are." After showing resolve, Ford was ready to compromise. Long's compromise language represented "a good approach," Ford maintained, adding, "I was happy with the end result, or I wouldn't have signed it. I think I had to be firm with the first veto, and as a result I think we made some progress or improvement."[49]

William Seidman observed that while the administration was not entirely satisfied with the bill and the compromise language, "we really thought that the tax cut had to go through to help with the recovery." Therefore, Ford thought it important to accept the compromise language to gain the tax cut.[50] But Ford's decision to sign the Revenue Adjustment Act was not based solely on economic grounds. Carl Albert blamed Ford's stubborn behavior leading up to the final compromise on his "efforts to appeal to the right-wing Republicans and rescue his failing campaign for the presidential nomination." Ronald Reagan, who had already kicked off his run for the nomination, publicly urged Ford to veto the second version of the tax bill. Reagan led Ford among Republicans in the polls by eight points; no president in the postwar era had ever trailed a challenger within his own party by such a margin. The bad news made the prospect of a tax increase an even greater risk for Ford.[51]

The showdown again evinced Ford's precarious position with the post-Watergate Congress, as he accepted language that fell short of a $395 billion budget ceiling. Still, Ford did not emerge from the struggle empty-handed. He showed his resolve to limit government spending, and the compromise clause was a symbolic victory. For the first time, Congress accepted the principle that federal spending must have a ceiling.[52] Lynn said that "the president was able to say that [he] got [Congress] to move in a direction that they've not done before in the memory of current man."[53] The compromise language would be Ford's weapon to use if congressional spending grew excessive.

The importance of Ford's actions and the compromise language that he gained became clearer fifteen years later, when President George H. W. Bush signed the 1990 Omnibus Budget Reconciliation Act (OBRA), which shifted the emphasis in federal budgeting away from deficit reduction—the approach taken by the Gramm-Rudman-Hollings Act of 1985—to spending reduction, which Ford had sought. OBRA set spending limits to be deducted from a baseline budget—the spending and revenue levels that would otherwise occur if programs and policies were continued unchanged.[54] Lynn, who considered spending caps more effective than deficit caps in controlling spending, observed that "the whole concept of working from 'the level of spending which would otherwise occur' is a concept that has been used extensively by Congress later." The Revenue Adjustment Act of 1975 was a fair achievement for a proposal that had caught the Democratic Congress off guard and had been scorned by the media. It was also a harbinger of future budget policy, as Lynn remarked that Ford "got [a spending limitation] in a way that after many years became the adopted norm of the way [federal budget making] is done today."[55] It was not a 100 percent victory, as Ford had claimed. But by incorporating a symbolic pledge, the tax cut represented a political achievement for the deficit hawk in the White House.

The Drive to Deregulate

In his October 8, 1974, anti-inflation program, Ford unveiled one of his little-known but lasting legacies in government retrenchment: deregulation. At the Conference on Inflation, some economists had urged the president to reduce onerous regulations to control inflation, so early in his administration Ford set out on this mission.[56]

The mushrooming federal bureaucracy horrified Ford. Worse, it drove up prices. Ford estimated that government regulations cost each American $300 a year, observing, "They were increasing the cost of doing business—a cost that's always passed along to consumers—and thus contributing to inflation." Watching his stepfather operate the Ford Paint and Varnish Company allowed Ford to understand the difficulties of business ownership and the onus of overregulation. In his memoirs, Ford mentioned egregious examples of 1970s red tape: to renew licenses for three television stations, one company had to complete forty-five pounds of Federal Communications Commission (FCC) paperwork; to comply with Interstate Commerce Commission (ICC) regulations that prevented competition with established trucking firms, some trucks had to return (or "backhaul") empty on journeys up to 1,000 miles long.[57] Ford mentioned one of the most preposterous examples of overregulation to French president Valéry Giscard d'Estaing. The Occupational Safety and Health Administration (OSHA) required Basque sheepherders working in Montana to have lodging in "migratory workers' standard housing." To comply with this rule, a rancher obtained a small house that migrants had used in California fruit orchards, bringing it to Montana. But sheep—unlike fruit—move around, so the rancher had to mount the house on a flatbed truck that followed the sheep. Ford and Giscard d'Estaing enjoyed a good laugh over the episode, but the conclusion was clear.[58] Excessive regulations forced companies and workers into Promethean positions, costing money and reducing productivity. Overregulation also stifled competition and robbed consumers of choice in the economic marketplace. Ford believed the time had come to deregulate certain industries.

But deregulation alarmed some liberals. Ralph Nader called Ford's view "careless," while the *New York Times* warned against Ford's "rhetorical assault" on federal safeguards that ensured the safety of consumers and the environment. But Ford's proposals drew support from across the aisle; Senator Edward Kennedy backed Ford's efforts to circumscribe the power of the Civil Aviation Board (CAB), citing benefits to consumers. Many Democrats conceded that Ford was on to something. They worried that some regulatory agencies acted favorably toward industries—not consumers—and realized that Ford capitalized on a perception that developed after the Great Society and Watergate, that government tends to foul things up. Speaking about deregulation to the National Federation of Independent Business, Ford pledged, "We must free the business community from regulatory bondage so that it can produce." The audience applauded him at a rate of more than once a minute; it was one of the most enthusiastic receptions he received as president.[59]

In 1975, trying to encourage competition and remove government red tape, Ford initiated studies into regulatory reform. For the rest of his presidency, the CEA devoted more attention to deregulation than perhaps to any other topic next to inflation. While previous administrations had explored deregulation, Ford "capitalized on it, to his credit, and made that a plank" in his overall economic program, observed CEA member Gary Seevers. "[Deregulation] had never been something that presidents had talked much about before Ford."[60] Ford made it a theme of his administration, and when Seevers left the CEA in early 1975, Ford appointed Paul MacAvoy, a strong advocate of deregulation, to replace him. MacAvoy headed a task force that investigated the deregulation of various industries, including airlines, trucking, cable television, and insurance. In this instance, paradoxically, Ford benefited from his status as an unelected president, because he could initiate investigations without fear of violating earlier campaign pledges. As MacAvoy noted, "The kind of things that I was involved in could grow out of the fresh earth."[61] Ford especially focused on the transportation industry, which he believed was most smothered by regulation, targeting the CAB and the ICC for streamlining.

By the 1970s, many federal regulations had become dinosaurs that lumbered along, antiquated and cumbersome. Ford's task force on airline deregulation concluded that the Civil Aeronautics Act of 1938, established to oversee an infant industry, was anachronistic; the airline industry was developed enough that it no longer needed protection from market forces. The act had become detrimental to consumer interests. The CAB had the power to forbid competitive pricing; airlines could not lower fares without CAB approval. The CAB protected established airlines and restricted the entry of new firms into airline markets; no new airlines had entered the transportation industry since 1950, and for five years the CAB blocked major airlines' attempts to establish new routes. Ultimately, federal regulations denied consumers an array of price and service options. The absence of price competition induced airlines to use business practices that ultimately increased ticket prices. The Ford administration found that they competed using services—offering passengers meals, drinks, and movies—or offered more flights, forcing planes to fly with empty seats.

In October, the Ford administration proposed the Aviation Act of 1975 to promote better service and lower passenger fares. It spelled out a five-year timetable to reverse federal protection of the airline industry and emphasize free-market competition instead. The act encouraged new airlines, markets, and routes to develop, and it fostered price competition among airlines by allowing them to lower fares without CAB approval. By outlawing anticompetitive activities, the act also limited the CAB's ability to grant antitrust immunity to the airlines.[62]

The major airlines felt threatened by the Aviation Act. Over three decades, they had developed a close relationship with the CAB, which had protected them from competitors invading their markets or offering lower ticket prices. They had few worries about financial mismanagement or bankruptcies because the CAB protected them with higher prices, new routes, or mergers (in fact, no major airline suffered bankruptcy). The major airlines prepared to fight the bill, and the airline industry's trade group, the Air Transport Association (ATA), warned that the act meant chaos. It would "tear apart a national air transportation system recognized as the finest in the world." The ATA charged that Ford's proposal would disrupt service to small communities, push huge price increases on to consumers, and force airlines into bankruptcy.

Yet most industries functioned, even thrived, with far fewer regulations than the airline industry. Newspapers nationwide applauded Ford's initiative. The *Washington Post* called Ford's proposal "a big step in the right direction." The *Dallas Morning News* looked forward to "economical tickets instead of 2-olive martinis and high-fashion stewardess costumes," and the *Baltimore Sun* predicted that millions of consumers unable to afford airline tickets would now fly. Ford believed that the bill would reduce airline fares by up to 20 percent during a full Ford term and that airline passengers would increase by nearly the same amount. With increased competition, less viable airlines also faced the prospect of bankruptcy.[63]

In November, the administration tried to tackle regulation in trucking with the Motor Carrier Reform Act of 1975. Like those in aviation, trucking industry regulations dated back to the 1930s and limited service (for example, directing what commodities a company carried or routes it used), controlled rates (in ways that were complex and inflated), and suppressed competition by restricting new companies from entering the industry. Truckers had sometimes to take circuitous routes to abide by federal regulations, which also worked to the detriment of rural areas.[64] The proposed act aimed to open trucking to more competition and liberalize rate setting.

The Teamsters union lashed out, almost violently, against Ford's proposal. The president of the Teamsters union told MacAvoy that trucking deregulation would spell "the end of Western civilization." Secretary of Transportation William Coleman recalled that the Teamsters head "almost threw me out of the building" when the two met to discuss deregulation.[65]

Although the House and Senate held hearings on airline and trucking deregulation in 1976, the controversy over the issue, combined with industry opposition and the constraints of an election year, prevented legislative progress, despite Ford's campaign complaints that Congress tarried on this important issue. The one transportation area where Ford realized deregulation success was railroads. In February 1976, he signed a bill that gave railroads more freedom to set the rates they charged for carrying freight, thus reducing ICC regulations.[66]

Ford's task force developed ambitious plans for deregulation, covering almost every conceivable industry: chemicals, automobiles, food processing, communication, finance, and more. Many of his plans were implemented after he left office, many by Democratic administrations, which showed the bipartisan support for his ideas: the airlines were deregulated in 1978; trucking in 1980; cable television in 1996. This was one of the unsung successes of the Ford presidency; he envisioned an economic environment with more freedom and laid the groundwork for later deregulation.[67]

"Steady and Stable"

In January 1976, Ford delivered the second State of the Union address of his presidency. He devoted most of the speech to domestic concerns and called for a "new realism." The Vietnam War and the Great Society showed that Americans had become "overconfident of our abilities. We tried to be a policeman abroad and the indulgent parent here at home." Government planners dreamed that they could "transform the country through massive national programs, but often the programs did not work," Ford observed. "In our rush to accomplish great deeds quickly, we trampled on sound principles of restraint and endangered the rights of individuals. We unbalanced our economic system by the huge and unprecedented growth of federal expenditures and borrowing."

Now, Ford declared, "the way to a healthy, non-inflationary economy has become increasingly apparent. The government must stop spending so much and stop borrowing so much of our money. More money must remain in private hands where it will do the most good. To hold down the cost of living we must hold down the cost of government." Stating that his first objective was "sound economic growth without inflation," he proposed a new tax cut for July but reiterated the principle that for every dollar cut in taxes, there should be a matching dollar saved in the federal budget. With spending restraints, Ford hoped to balance the budget by 1979.[68]

Newsweek called Ford's budget for fiscal year 1977 a "Go-Slow Budget," because it proposed "cuts in practically everything cuttable" and a modest $394 billion in spending, which liberal economists argued was not enough to produce the 5.7 percent growth that Ford projected. To achieve those numbers, they believed, Ford would need a budget of $420 billion or more. But fearing renewed inflation, Ford wanted to avoid excessive fiscal stimulus; inflation would choke off the recovery (especially because consumer spending was sensitive to even slight upticks in prices).[69] Thus Ford's budget also contained two key proposals (which Ronald Reagan later advocated as president): budget cuts ($20 billion in areas like medical care for the elderly and subsidized school lunches) and a greater emphasis on block grants (as opposed to grants for specific purposes) to state and local governments. (Total outlays for fiscal year 1977 ended up at $409 billion. The year's deficit, $56.9 billion, was greater than the $43 billion Ford predicted but $13 billion less than for fiscal year 1976. Even with tax cuts, deficits decreased during Ford's final two years in office.)[70]

Ford had reason for both optimism and caution. The economic recovery proceeded, and the nation was calm; he had steadied the ship in a storm. But in a way, the ship was still at sea. The recovery could stall, keeping unemployment high. Ford's cutbacks and frugality were not exciting political ideas and, in bad economic times, were hard to defend. Ford's approach to the recovery seemed "unduly timorous—and unfair" to jobless Americans, the *New York Times* charged.[71] The Democrats ached to regain the White House and aimed to use this attack against Ford.

Still, the new year offered hope. While Ford had estimated that the budget deficit for fiscal year 1976 would be $76 billion, it turned out to be less, $69.6 billion. Inflation eased its iron grip (and for 1975 was 5.7 percent, even lower than the 6.3 percent that Ford predicted in his budget).[72] In 1976, the economy shook off the Great Recession, partly through Ford's tax cuts. Otto Eckstein believed that without the Tax Reduction Act of 1975, the economy would have stuck to its downward course much longer, and unemployment would have peaked at close to 10 percent in late 1975. Instead, the tax cuts helped to reduce unemployment much earlier, so that the jobless rate crested in May 1975, and most economists thought the economy was in recovery the next month. Moreover, Eckstein believed that the spending power that consumers received from the temporary tax cuts generated an additional 400,000 new car sales, stimulating this sagging industry and sending beneficial ripples throughout the economy. Additionally, a tight monetary policy and the recession had exerted downward pressure on prices, lowering inflation despite the stimulus of the tax cuts.[73] Ford's signing of the tax cut was one of the most judicious acts of his presidency.

Ford promised that his top priority in a full term was a healthy economy with low inflation and plentiful jobs, especially in the private sector. It seemed possible. In March, the Dow Jones industrial average closed above the 1,000 mark for the first time in three years. Wall Street considered the 1,000-point mark "magical," and the breaking of that psychological barrier reflected shareholders' confidence in the economy. By September 1976, eighty-eight million Americans were working, an increase of almost four million since the recession hit bottom and the most in the country's history.[74] One of the last economic figures that Americans saw before the election was in the Labor Department's report on consumer prices, which had edged up by the lowest amount since April and ran at just a 5 percent for the year, dramatically less than when Ford took office. The United States had one of the lowest inflation rates in the industrialized world. Even the *New York Times*, no fan of Ford's, judged that his economic record "after two years seems much more positive than negative," although it cited his greatest failing as the lack of any program to reduce unemployment.[75]

Indeed, unemployment was the bad news. Ford called his economic policies "steady and stable" for a reason. Until he tamed inflation, he dared not risk overstimulating the economy. Unfortunately, a consequence of Ford's caution was his prediction that unemployment would remain "distressingly high" during 1976, averaging 7.7 percent. In February, when the political primaries began, although the unemployment rate registered its fourth consecutive month of decline, it was still at 7.6 percent. By contrast, during the 1950s and 1960s, unemployment never rose above 4 percent during a peacetime year. But if Ford pumped up the economy, Greenspan said in mid-1976, "the level of economic activity wouldn't have been any better than it is now, but you . . . would have significantly increased the risk of inflation."[76]

That became a bone of contention between Ford and the Democrats. Many Democrats argued that the economy needed more fiscal stimulation. One emerging congressional bill that distinguished Ford from the Democrats was the Humphrey-Hawkins full employment bill, sponsored by Hubert Humphrey and Augustus Hawkins, a representative from California, which was designed to add teeth to the Full Employment Act of 1946. The bill would have required the president to coordinate fiscal and monetary policies to reduce unemployment to 3 percent within the next four years. If conventional fiscal and monetary policies could not achieve this goal, then the Labor Department would establish federally funded jobs programs. Jimmy Carter endorsed the Humphrey-Hawkins bill, as did all the Democrats who entered the primaries. But Ford called it "an election year boondoggle," warning that it would fuel inflation and add $10–$30 billion to the federal budget.[77] (In 1978, Congress finally passed Humphrey-Hawkins, but its terms became so infeasible that the federal government largely ignored it.)

Carter wanted to manipulate macroeconomic levers to speed the recovery. He favored a looser monetary policy and said that he would even try to force Arthur Burns to resign before his term expired in 1978. Carter supported public works programs, and to reduce unemployment in inner cities, he favored creating an agency similar to the New Deal's Civilian Conservation Corps. These beliefs contrasted with Ford's. "The best way to get jobs is to expand the private sector where five out of six jobs exist in our economy. We can do that by reducing federal taxes," Ford explained in his first debate with Carter. "The private sector," he said, "where you have permanent jobs, with the opportunity for advancement, is a better place than make-work jobs under the program recommended by Congress."[78]

A critical component of Ford's strategy was the veto. In February, he rejected a $6 billion public works program that would have provided federal money for public works projects (such as government buildings and recreational facilities) and various municipal departments. Ford called it "an election year pork barrel." Congress scaled it down to $4 billion and returned it to him, but in July Ford again vetoed it. He believed that the bill would have given no aid to unskilled workers, who needed benefits the most, and its construction projects would get under way in 1977, too late to aid in the recovery; the added stimulus would be inflationary. When questioned about this veto during his first debate against Carter, Ford pointed out that even its supporters estimated that it would create only 400,000 jobs; the administration pegged the number as low as 150,000, with each job costing the taxpayer $25,000. Ford charged that the bill would lead to "larger deficits, higher taxes, higher inflation and, ultimately, higher unemployment."[79] Even liberal economists conceded that the bill was bad policy, because "make-work" public jobs were often wasteful and crowded out more meaningful work in the private sector.[80] But Congress, feeling election year political heat, overrode Ford's veto.

Ford was undeterred. In July, he vetoed a $3.3 billion bill that would have prevented military base closings. Although supporters argued that base closings devastated entire communities, Ford believed that maintaining unnecessary bases wasted taxpayers' money; his veto was sustained. In late September, he vetoed a massive $56 billion appropriations bill for social services, fearing its effect on inflation, but Congress overrode him. Despite the two overrides, the *Wall Street Journal* called Ford's vetoes "politically courageous." Normally, the paper noted, a president would have liked the idea of "opening the spending floodgates in the months before an election."[81]

Throughout the 1976 campaign, Ford touted his vetoes as savings to taxpayers. He recalled that in the intensive barnstorming blitz just before Election Day, "at every stop I told [crowds] how my sixty-six vetoes had saved taxpayers at least $9 billion."[82] But he needed something more, since the vetoes came across as essentially negative in nature; Carter attacked them as obstructionist. Tax cuts were Ford's strength. He had already signed two during 1975. In October 1976, he signed a tax revision bill that extended the 1975 personal and corporate tax cuts and overhauled the nation's tax system by preventing abuses in tax shelter investments and higher taxes on the wealthy.[83] Ford promised that if elected, he would recommend another tax cut of around $10 billion and would again ask Congress for a concomitant spending reduction. He vowed to put a tax cut "at the top of the legislative agenda for 1977" and said that it would be directed especially toward "hard-hit" and "short-changed" middle-class Americans. That would be a big difference between him and Carter, Ford pointed out, charging that Carter would use budget surplus money for federal programs, whereas he would return it to taxpayers and call for matching spending cuts to keep the deficit in check. While Carter boasted of his "compassion," Ford retorted, "How about some 'compassion' for the American taxpayer?"[84]

But Ford did not play this issue much in the campaign because he feared that talk of more stimulus might alarm consumers, who were hypersensitive to anything that might trigger more inflation. Yet he should have; he was a proven tax cutter, and the image distinguished him from his challenger, who planned more social programs. Carter shied away from promising tax cuts.

Instead, the most he offered was that he "would never seek an increase" in taxes if elected—and even that statement surprised his aides, forcing him later to hedge by saying that no increase would occur "barring some unforeseen development." By failing to emphasize tax relief throughout his campaign, Ford committed a costly tactical error.[85]

The costliest economic news of 1976 was no fault of Ford's. As the election drew near, he recalled, "my advisers warned me that there would be a pause in the recovery. They didn't know when it would happen, they just knew it would occur and that it would be a 'perfectly natural' phenomenon."[86] (A "pause" meant a slower rate of recovery.) Economic recoveries always fluctuate; Greenspan advised that the normal pattern was "spurt, pause, spurt." Businesses, their inventories low, faced the increased demand of an improving economy and tended to buy and restock, only to decrease buying to work off their inventories, causing the spurt-pause cycle. By late August 1976, Greenspan conceded that the economy had hit a "pause."[87] The GNP, which had leaped forward by a torrid 9.2 percent in the first quarter of 1976, grew at a 4.5 percent rate in the second quarter, and 3.8 percent in the third. It was normal for a recovery to post strong gains initially and then taper off, but a 3.8 percent growth rate was slightly below the 4.8 percent average during other postwar expansions and was not fast enough to reduce unemployment. Unemployment, which had dropped to 7.3 percent in May, edged up to 7.9 percent in August. The final jobless report that Americans saw before the election was 7.8 percent for September. (These statistics were more grim than the true economic picture. The economy had added four million jobs since the recession hit bottom in the spring of 1975. The unemployment rate seemed unduly high because employment figures lagged behind the general recovery rate, as employers preferred to wait until the economy was flush before hiring new workers. Moreover, jobless statistics factored in many women and minorities, who were just entering the labor force and experienced greater difficulty in finding jobs. For example, for African American adults, the jobless rate was stuck at more than 12 percent; for black teenagers, it was more than 30 percent.)[88]

Although most widely known for his economic thought, Greenspan also had a sharp political mind, and a year and a half before the election he told CEA member Gary Seevers that the unemployment rate itself would not determine Ford's fate. "It only matters whether [unemployment] is going up or going down," Greenspan observed.[89] The economic pause came at a bad time for Ford. As Election Day approached, the pause made unemployment figures edge upward. Moreover, the downturn was worse than Ford's economic advisers had expected. Burton Malkiel, a CEA economist, remembered that government spending for the second quarter (ending June 30) was "a great deal less than we had anticipated, and it was really a mystery; we didn't know what the heck was going on."[90] While some administration insiders, including Nelson Rockefeller, urged Ford to pump up the economy and boost his election prospects, the president refused. He doubted the beneficial effects in the short term, and in the long term such actions might unleash inflation. Ford was determined not to repeat Nixon's 1972 tactics, when he boosted federal spending to assure his reelection, disregarding the inflationary consequences. Forced to pick his poison, Nixon preferred inflation because, as he liked to point out, he had never heard of an election being lost over inflation, but many had been lost because of unemployment.[91]

Ford avoided tampering with the economy so that it would be healthier over the long term. In 1976, that boiled down to choosing between his political fortunes and the nation's economy. "To forestall [the economic pause], I could have accelerated federal spending, pushed for an increase in the money supply and then tried to reduce interest rates," he reasoned. Ford conceded that these actions would have postponed the pause past the election, but bad conditions would have come back to bite the country in the spring of 1977, first with higher inflation, then another recession. "So I told my advisers, 'I'm not going to gun the economy for short-term political benefits—it just isn't right.'"[92] *Time* praised Ford's actions as "a refreshing departure from the usual tendency of Presidents to pump up the economy during an election year." The irony was that Ford's politically unselfish action hurt him. He had portrayed economic policy as a top priority, but despite lower inflation, the recovery still had not produced enough jobs. Meanwhile, the Democrats, united for the first time in a decade, rallied around what they deemed the centerpiece of their party platform, a pledge to reduce unemployment to just 3 percent.[93]

The 1970s economy was unforgiving to incumbent presidents. Stagflation led voters to blame their president and seek a new economic steward. As a fiscal conservative, Ford was especially vulnerable; high unemployment reinforced the old image of him as insensitive to economic hardship. The *New York Daily News* headline came back to haunt him and cost votes, perhaps the election. Big Apple subways were plastered with posters of Carter saying, "If I am elected president I guarantee that I will never tell the greatest city on earth to drop dead." Carter also mentioned the headline in his third debate with Ford. (Ironically, the *Daily News* endorsed Ford.) Ford had hoped to eke out a victory in New York State with votes from Republican areas upstate and on Long Island, which he visited just before Election Day, but polls revealed that Long Islanders disliked his handling of the New York City fiscal crisis, and Ford lost the state—and with it, enough votes to slip behind Carter in the electoral college.[94]

An irony of Ford's presidency was that despite the public's concern over inflation and his apparent success in reducing it, he still lost the presidency. When Ford left office, inflation stood at just 4.8 percent; it had been more than sliced in half. In the Western world, only Switzerland had a lower rate.[95] Unemployment, although still high, headed down. In Ford's last month as president, the jobless rate stood at 7.3 percent. Public confidence in the economy was rebounding.[96] Before he left office, the *Wall Street Journal* declared that despite signs of sluggishness earlier in the fall, "the economic recovery is on track after all" and termed it "a vindication of the general thrust of Gerald Ford's economic policies."[97] Not all presidents can leave office saying that their fundamental goals were intact, especially during the 1970s. Ford, who all along had promoted long-term growth without rising prices, could. He seemed to have ended another long national nightmare, the Great Inflation.

Part Three
The Energy Challenge

Chapter 12

The Energy Crisis of the 1970s

"You got First Mama," Betty Ford said into her citizens band (CB) radio. In 1976, the First Lady used the device to campaign for her husband, communicating with motorists as she traveled the country. Her use of a CB was so endearing that President Ford's advertising team even considered playing a song called "First Mama Reggae" as a campaign commercial. CB radio, the most promising communications gadget since the telephone, was a hot 1970s fad. In 1976, CB sales jumped to eleven million, up from four million the year before, and Americans owned an estimated twenty-five million sets.[1] Popular culture embraced the contraption. CB lingo (such as "10–4" for okay and "smokey" for state police) became everyday slang. In 1975, the song "Convoy," with a trucker jabbering on his CB, hit number one on record charts and inspired a motion picture of the same name. Truckers Sonny and Will used CBs in the 1975–76 *Movin' On* television series, as did Burt Reynolds in *Smokey and the Bandit*, the second most popular film of 1977. (Gerald Ford enjoyed watching *Movin' On* and once met Claude Akins, the beefy-faced actor who portrayed trucker Sonny Pruitt, when they stayed at the same Atlanta, Georgia, hotel. After talking with Akins, the president declared, "Now I can tell Betty I know more about *Movin' On* than she does.")[2]

The CB's popularity sprang from one of the 1970s most important events: the energy crisis, a time when fuel became scarce and expensive, and gas station lines snaked for miles. In January 1974, as one emergency response, President Nixon made the fuel-saving fifty-five-miles-per-hour speed limit national law. Truckers were furious. To protest the lower speed limit and diesel shortages, they staged massive, sometimes violent demonstrations, blocking highways and tying up traffic.[3] Throughout the crisis, the CB helped truckers evade speed traps, form convoys, and find stations with fuel. Soon, regular motorists adopted the radio sets, finding them useful and fun.

Drivers railed against the fifty-five-miles-per-hour speed limit on their CBs, but it stuck. The new law also illustrated a devastating truth about the energy crisis. The federal government's reactions affected certain groups and regions severely and often proved counterproductive. The "double nickel" vexed truckers, slowed transportation, and annoyed motorists in sprawling midwestern states, yet it remained the law for two decades. Even more seriously, the government adopted a disastrous policy of price controls and allocations that exacerbated—and really caused—the energy crisis. Gerald Ford found this policy, once entrenched, devilishly hard to remove.

"A Crisis of Government"

Americans might think that the energy crisis began with the Arab oil embargo. In reality, the problem manifested itself months, even years, before the embargo. A convergence of factors caused it, including an unfortunate system of price controls that the Nixon administration imposed during the early 1970s that played hob with the normal equilibrium of supply and demand. Energy experts Douglas Bohi and Joel Darmstadter later wrote, "It took several years to realize that earlier government regulation was responsible for much of the crisis itself."[4]

Once it came, the crisis stunned Americans. Until the 1970s, they experienced no scarcity in energy resources, which had always been abundant, making postwar prosperity possible. From 1945 to the early 1970s, even recessions and political unrest in the Middle East (including two closings of the Suez Canal) did not upset energy prices or supply. During the postwar decades, the world's peoples consumed more energy than during all of history before 1940.[5] Domestic petroleum consumption jumped 50 percent between 1950 and 1960 (from 6.5 million to 9.8 million barrels a day) and another 50 percent from 1960 to 1970 (to 14.7 million barrels a day).[6] By 1970, transportation consumed one-fourth of the country's energy: Americans moved to suburbs, relied much less on public transportation (by the 1970s, train ridership had plummeted 83 percent from 1945 levels), and built a massive interstate highway system to facilitate travel.[7] Yet increased energy use posed no problem before the 1970s. Americans thought that the only problem was surplus, not shortage. In 1960, *Time* even encouraged motorists to drive four minutes more every day to reduce glutted gasoline supplies.[8]

Oil was the country's most important energy resource. America ran on oil; it met 42 percent of the nation's energy needs (versus 31 percent for natural gas, 18 percent for coal, and 9 percent for nuclear).[9] Its versatility was astounding. Oil did things no other fuel could: it ran cars, trucks, trains, boats, and jets; heated homes and buildings; powered generators to create electricity; and made by-products such as plastics. In addition, unlike other sources of power (such as nuclear, solar, or wind), oil was easy to transport. Until the 1970s, the federal government pursued policies favoring the oil industry. In 1959, President Eisenhower imposed quotas to limit oil imports and keep domestic oil prices high to protect the industry, although he explained that the quotas were for national security, which he maintained an influx of imports would threaten. Congressional giants hailing from oil states like Texas, such as Senate majority leader Lyndon Johnson and House Speaker Sam Rayburn, also helped the oil industry; Rayburn, for example, required that all prospective members of the Ways and Means Committee support the oil depletion allowance.[10]

But by the 1970s, various factors put pressure on oil as an energy source while decreasing its supply. The political oil giants were gone, and the supportive relationship between Washington and the oil industry crumbled. Environmentalists, galvanized in part by a disastrous 1969 oil spill off Santa Barbara, California, began to catch politicians' ears. Although supertankers carried up to 500,000 tons of oil, no American port could accommodate tankers with more than 80,000 tons, in part because environmentalists fought deepwater ports.[11] They opposed offshore oil drilling and temporarily halted construction of the Alaskan pipeline and refineries on the East and West coasts. The Clean Air Act of 1965 and its 1970 amendments fundamentally changed U.S. environmental regulation. The laws mandated stringent automobile emissions standards; manufacturers had to modify engines, which as a result burned 10 percent more fuel.[12]

The Clean Air Act also made coal, a dirty fuel with a high sulfur content, fall out of favor, increasing reliance on oil. "The ambient air quality standards for sulfur dioxide and particulate matter were very difficult for the then existing coal-fire power plants to meet," explained Robert Nordhaus, a counsel to the House Commerce Committee. "And, as a result, a number of [companies and utilities] took the strategy of simply switching those plants from coal to oil." In 1950, coal accounted for 38 percent of the nation's energy consumption, but by 1972, just 17 percent.[13] Although one substitute for oil, natural gas, was a clean fuel, its price was under controls, which discouraged companies from producing more of it.

As energy consumption rose, domestic oil production peaked in 1970 and then declined, increasing the country's dependence on imports.[14] Then came price controls. In August 1971, Nixon controlled oil prices as part of his general wage and price freeze, planting the seeds of the 1970s energy crisis. Creating artificially low prices discouraged oil exploration and production yet encouraged consumption. Concerned about profits, environmental objections, and the availability of crude, oil companies decided not to build refineries, which left the United States with inadequate refinery capacity. To complicate matters, oil fields in the lower forty-eight states matured and yielded less oil, yet the industry had yet to develop the technology to explore for oil in remote areas, such as the deep ocean.[15]

Controls distorted the oil market. The federal government defied a basic economic principle: suppliers feel less incentive to produce a commodity when its price decreases, while consumers use more of it. Controls reflected the Nixon administration's preoccupation with inflation; the White House was "much more focused on trying to limit prices" than ensuring oil supplies, recalled Charles DiBona, who served as Nixon's special assistant on energy and later headed the American Petroleum Institute for two decades. Another Nixon administration member, William A. Johnson, a senior economist for the CEA, commented that administration members who were implementing price controls refused to change their program, even when he pointed out to them that their policies were causing severe heating oil shortages.[16]

During the winter of 1971–72, consumers began to feel the pinch of an energy crisis. Shortages caused brownouts in South Florida and other localities. By May 1972, the *New York Times* declared, "The energy crisis is already here, and the shortage of fossil fuels is already noticed by consumers across the nation." During the winter of 1972–73, more serious shortages surfaced, especially in the Midwest, which had fewer oil refineries than other areas. Some companies shut down production lines.[17] The lack of fuel forced Denver, Colorado, and Des Moines, Iowa, to close public schools for a few days. Connecticut senator Abraham Ribicoff reported that throughout the Northeast, fuel oil supplies were "at alarmingly low levels."[18] By April 1973, more than one hundred independent gasoline stations had shut down in Minnesota.[19]

The oil industry protested controls. In February 1973, the president of the Kansas Independent Oil and Gas Association declared that "it would be the catastrophe of the century for the United States to become so dependent on foreign oil to the extent that exploration in this country becomes apathetic to the vast resource of undiscovered reserves, simply because of an inadequate price for crude." He argued that the "controlled price of crude and crude products will continue to be the key to depressed exploration and development." Yet the next month, the administration reimposed mandatory price controls on the petroleum industry. In June, the administration imposed a sixty-day price freeze, and in September "Phase IV" of its price controls took effect, setting ceiling prices for crude oil and various fuels. That month,

CEA member Gary Seevers wrote that "the current controls are no doubt compounding the Nation's basic energy shortage."[20]

Another element in the Nixon system of controls worsened oil shortages: allocations. The administration believed "that price controls weren't enough unless you had some kind of allocation system" to ensure that petroleum was evenly distributed, Nordhaus recalled.[21] In a free-market environment, prices send the signals that decide how much of a product is used and by whom. Since price controls had disrupted this mechanism, some individuals argued that government guidance had to allocate fuel among users. In February 1973, William Simon, who had no experience in energy or the oil industry, began chairing the administration's Oil Policy Committee. A bond trader, Simon struggled to understand the complexities of fuel supply chains, and he introduced a plan for voluntary oil allocation to divide up crude oil and its refined products according to industries and regions. But allocation failed to address the problem that had created shortages in the first place, the price controls. The scheme alarmed DiBona, who warned Treasury Secretary George Shultz that the voluntary allocation was "going to become the mandatory scheme, because you've given up the principle. You can't then argue that it's a bad idea." Moreover, unless the system were mandatory, no company would comply with it. Only a law would compel oil companies to break existing contracts, DiBona predicted. At one meeting, Simon exploded at DiBona, arguing that his voluntary plan would be better than any mandatory legislation that Congress might impose. Shultz felt uncomfortable with Simon's plan, but with Simon insisting, the administration went ahead.[22]

In May 1973, the White House announced a voluntary program to allocate crude oil and refinery products to independent refiners and marketers, which major oil companies would have to supply with amounts of crude oil and oil products based on their 1971–72 sales. The Office of Oil and Gas could also increase allotments for "priority activities" (such as medical care, police and fire duties, and airline and bus transportation) that were unable to secure sufficient supplies.[23]

Throughout the summer of 1973, the Federal Energy Office (FEO) received complaints that voluntary allocation was insufficient. Baltimore mayor William Donald Schaefer told Simon that his city's transit authority "has been cut in its allocation of diesel fuel. As a result, it has been forced to reduce its scheduled service and to cut out air-conditioning in its buses." The New England Congressional Caucus reported, "Many gasoline stations in New England are working short hours or are actually closed" and warned that "in the heating fuel area, another crisis is possible this winter." The caucus unanimously supported mandatory allocation.[24] Democratic senator George

McGovern informed Simon, "The fuel supply situation in South Dakota has reached the point where it can only be described as critical." Representatives, senators, governors, state legislatures, and city councils demanded that the federal government allocate fuels on a compulsory basis.[25]

Pressure also came from the "independents," smaller corporations that competed with the two-dozen major, vertically integrated corporations. Rather than produce their own crude oil, independent refiners bought it from the big oil companies and sold their refined products, such as gasoline, to independent distributors, who sold to independent gasoline stations. These retailers, such as those at convenience stores, sold unbranded gas at cut-rate prices, much lower than at brand-name stations such as Mobil or Gulf. The independents, who were major political contributors, charged that the leading oil companies were trying to drive them out of business. Members of Congress believed it. In the spring of 1973, independent service station owners warned lawmakers that they would shut down because their suppliers no longer furnished them with gasoline.[26] The major oil companies argued that they had only enough fuel to supply their own customers; they had no surplus gasoline for independents.[27] Some independent concerns limped along at reduced capacity, while others closed. After learning that his supplier might not give him gasoline, the owner of a small service station in Newton, Georgia, complained to his congressman, "I have been in the Service Station business for 15 years and have never faced a situation like this. It seems that the major oil companies have their supply and are forcing out small independent dealers like myself. If something is not done to help the little man like myself, then we can look for more soup lines like we had in the 30's."[28]

As the independents suffered, they argued for mandatory allocation, believing it would force the big companies to share their crude oil and finished products with independent refiners and marketers.[29] The independents, DiBona recalled, "wanted a scheme where they would guarantee a supply" to themselves.[30] They also wanted access to domestic crude oil, the price of which was controlled; what oil the major companies did sell them, independents complained, was imported, which had higher, uncontrolled prices. Senator James Abourezk of South Dakota told Nixon that the voluntary allocation program was "a charade" and said that the energy crisis was "deliberately contrived by the major oil companies" to drive the independents out of business. Abourezk and others in Congress demanded that the administration make the allocation system mandatory.[31]

Most of Nixon's advisers had little faith in mandatory allocation, believing it would add to the bureaucracy and aggravate shortages. John Love, head of the FEO, opposed compulsory allocation, but Simon, who drafted a mandatory program in June, urged him to change his mind.[32] Americans wanted the federal government to "do something," and the administration wanted to appear proactive. A big problem was public perception: only when the government adopted allocations did it appear to fight the energy crisis; the public thought an "energy policy" meant controls and regulations.[33] Duke Ligon, director of the Office of Oil and Gas, admitted that a major reason for mandatory allocation was "political, to show that the administration is doing everything possible to keep people supplied with fuel."[34]

Branding voluntary allocation a failure, Simon wanted stronger medicine. Thus came a fateful decision: In October 1973, the administration announced a mandatory allocation program for propane, home heating oil, jet fuel, and other middle-distillate fuels. According to the new program, suppliers and wholesalers were to sell fuel to customers based on monthly sales figures from 1972.[35] That was only the beginning; the administration planned to announce more allocations for other fuels, such as gasoline, based on the Emergency Petroleum Allocation Act (EPAA), a bill making its way through Congress.

Controls and allocation, coupled with greater reliance on imports, meant that an oil disruption could bring energy chaos. That came in October 1973. After the fourth Arab-Israeli war, the Arab nations of OPEC brandished oil as a political and economic weapon, announcing that they would cut off oil supplies to any nation aiding Israel. When the United States supplied Israel with military weapons and parts, the Arabs retaliated with a total oil embargo against America, reducing its oil supply by two million barrels daily. Although the war ended later that month, the Arabs sustained the embargo. By the end of 1973, the price of OPEC oil had increased by 400 percent, from $3 to $12 a barrel (one barrel contains forty-two gallons).[36] Controls, allocations, increased demand coupled with decreased supply — "all of these factors came together," Nordhaus recalled, "to give the Mideast oil producers increasing power and leverage in the world oil markets, which they were able to exploit very successfully following the Yom Kippur War."[37] The Arab oil embargo shocked an America already wounded by Vietnam; now, a previously impotent cartel held the country at its mercy.

Washington reacted to the embargo by imposing more controls on domestic crude prices. After the embargo began, Congress passed the EPAA to ensure that oil products would be fairly distributed throughout the nation. The EPAA, drafted much earlier that year, was a reaction not to the embargo but to the oil shortages during the winter of 1972–73. Before the embargo, it was controversial. In May, when the Senate Interior and Insular Affairs Committee considered the bill, all six committee Republicans opposed it, arguing that it "could cause a worsening of, rather than relief from, the nation's current fuel shortage."[38] With the urgency of the Arab oil embargo, such warnings were forgotten. While the embargo did not cause the 1970s energy crisis, the emergency atmosphere it created—of the nation under economic attack—prompted Congress to pass one of the worst acts of modern economic history. On November 27, bowing to the crush of events, Nixon signed the EPAA.

The EPAA price controls comprised two tiers, distinguishing between "old" and "new" oil. "Old" oil, produced before 1973, had a ceiling of $5.25 per barrel. "New" oil was defined as coming from wells that started operating in 1973 or after or from old wells operating above their 1972 (or earlier) production levels. New oil was uncontrolled and floated up to $11 per barrel, slightly below the world oil price of $12. (The idea was to cap prices on old oil from existing wells while encouraging exploration for new reserves by allowing new oil prices to rise.) During the 1970s, the United States produced 60 percent of its oil, of which old oil constituted 60 percent, while the remaining 40 percent was new.[39] Thus the EPAA put most domestically produced oil under price controls.

Because the act also aimed to "share the shortages as fairly as possible," as Senator Henry Jackson said, the EPAA instituted a mandatory, nationwide allocation system for crude oil and petroleum products. On the surface, the idea appeared logical: shift oil around from areas with surpluses to those with shortages. By mid-January, every major fuel produced from a barrel of crude oil—including gasoline—was under allocations. The regulations used each month of 1972 as a base period to set allocations for the corresponding month of 1974 and assigned levels of priority to industries. Examples were endless: Police, fire, medical and sanitation services, and telecommunications were allotted 100 percent of their 1972 propane levels. Schools received 90 percent. For middle-distillate fuels, agricultural production and industry were allotted 110 percent of their 1972 levels. Commercial aviation got 95 percent of its 1972 levels of jet fuel, while personal and instructional flyers got 70 percent.[40] Although the program did not ration gasoline to individual motorists, it was, as Nordhaus recalled, "an indirect form of rationing to make sure that essential uses of petroleum were covered and that there was a fair allocation within regions and within different segments of the petroleum industry."[41]

Mandatory allocation was a regulatory nightmare. The *New York Times* poked fun at the convoluted rules by asking, "Is That All Clear Now?" After quoting the first three paragraphs from the FEO's directives, the paper proved its point: the jumble of words made no sense. Worse, almost weekly, Simon's office revised allocations. Each revision created more complications, which demanded new rules.[42] Roy Ash, who had predicted that the scheme would be disastrous, commiserated with John A. Hill, a member of OMB's Natural Resource, Energy, and Science group, who had to help devise the allocation rules. Ash told Hill that the system was like a big pillow that was squeezed in various areas, creating bulges and distortions all around. Hill agreed, saying, "There are just too many variables, too many different actors in the system to ever control everything."[43]

Simon enlarged precisely the kind of bureaucracy that he professed to hate, as his FEO staff grew from 12 to 1,800.[44] To monitor the allocations, the FEO established a new Office of Petroleum Allocation (OPA), with ten regional offices. The FEO and OPA tracked the movement of petroleum throughout the country, investigated compliance with the program, and imposed penalties for violations. Oil companies had to report their activities to the government. One propane marketing manager grumbled that the allocation program "has created a lot of paperwork for us, but it hasn't created another gallon of propane." Conditions at the OPA were chaotic, with staffers—who often had no experience with oil—pulled from other agencies and feeling ambushed once they arrived. By December, a backlog of 15,000 letters inundated the OPA.[45]

At first, the FEO made its calculations with incomplete data, which shortchanged some regions. Using a base year of 1972 had inherent problems, because 1974 conditions were different. Industries and regions that had grown over the past two years needed more fuel; farmers needed more fuel due to a larger crop; even sweater makers wanted a larger allocation to meet the higher demand for warmer clothes that accompanied lower thermostats. In Vermont, despite poor ski conditions during 1973–74, allocations based on a great 1972–73 season meant plentiful fuel. But in neighboring New Hampshire, twenty-five towns stricken with shortages had no police and fire protection, garbage pickups, and other essential services.[46]

One month into the program, administrators realized that they had created a monster. William A. Johnson wrote to Simon, "The crude oil allocation program is causing serious dislocations and disruptions in the oil industry." The program hurt many of those it was designed to help. Independent refiners received inadequate oil supplies.[47] Big oil refineries sometimes had no crude to sell them, because they were selling their oil abroad at uncontrolled prices.[48] Other segments of the economy suffered, too. The president of the International Taxicab Association, protesting that his industry was excluded from priority allocations, predicted "the impending destruction of the taxicab industry in the United States." The government failed to grant oil drilling top priority in allocations, and many drilling rigs operating on diesel ran out of fuel. Ironically, the very devices that could have helped to alleviate the fuel shortage had insufficient fuel.[49]

Complaints flooded Simon's office. In February, Senator Clifford Case of New Jersey dashed off an urgent telegram reporting "cases of extreme personal inconvenience and real hardship" in his state. Some doctors had no gasoline to travel to patients; fights erupted at gas stations. Noting that other areas of the country were receiving adequate gasoline supplies, Case pleaded for "an immediate emergency allocation" to his region or even "immediate imposition of nationwide gasoline rationing." Florida governor Reuben Askew reported "extremely chaotic conditions" in his state and asked for an increase in fuel allocations.[50]

The most memorable inconvenience of the energy crisis was the lines at gas stations, sometimes so long that motorists waited three hours to get to the pump, burning gasoline—even running out of it—while waiting. In at least one state, queues stretched for four miles. In New Jersey and Connecticut, trains destroyed cars in lines that extended over railroad tracks. As drivers waited, tempers flared. In Indiana, an enraged customer shot a service station attendant. One beleaguered station owner complained, "The women are sullen and the men want to punch you out." A Connecticut station limited gasoline purchases to just $2, and when it ran out, employees barricaded the station with their own cars. Responding to a Nixon request, many gas stations closed on Sundays, and eight states received federal authority to institute "odd/even" rationing, whereby the last numeral on motorists' license plates determined the alternate days that they could buy gas.[51]

The energy crisis fed on itself. Lines and apparent shortages created a panic psychology that begat more panic. Some Americans urged the federal government to go a step beyond allocations and ration gasoline at the consumer level. The clamor for rationing was so loud that Nixon—who hated the idea—ordered rationing stamps printed, just in case.[52] The crisis atmosphere made drivers feel that they had to stop for gasoline whenever they could. John Hill recalled one study that concluded the average motorist drove with the gas gauge reading one-third full and opted to fill up when the tank went down to one-quarter. "But during this fear period," Hill said, "drivers were trying to keep their tanks topped off." Skittish motorists stopped for just $.50 worth of gas or stooped to strange behavior. One Pennsylvania woman wanted gasoline so badly on an "odd" day that she argued that "8" was an odd number. Others hoarded gasoline. An Ohio man stored sixty-five gallons at his home, saying, "I'm afraid the rationing they're talking about probably won't be enough for me." A Pennsylvania man died when the gas he was storing in his car trunk ignited and burned his vehicle.[53]

By late February 1974, 20 percent of service stations had no gas; others deliberately shut down to protest the allocation policy. When gas stations closed, consumer panic intensified. Allocations also messed up fuel delivery, forcing stations to wait days at a time for their monthly quota. Once they received it, many stations soon ran out of gas and had to wait until the new month's shipment. The end of the month was the worst time to look for gas; by then, many service stations had exhausted their allocation, while others operated on restricted hours. By late January 1974, for example, 95 percent of Connecticut's stations had run dry. Distributions were also unequal; one station might have no gas, while another a block away had plenty.[54] Regional variations were tremendous. New Jersey congressman Joseph Maraziti observed that in nearby Easton, Pennsylvania, consumers easily purchased gasoline, while New Jersey suffered a "crisis and 'near riot' situation."[55]

Other areas managed fine; the South and the Midwest had fuel aplenty. Even on the East Coast, most areas escaped shortages. During the 1973 Christmas holidays, one man spurned warnings about shortages and drove his car and trailer from Cortland, New York, to Florida's Disney World. "We had apprehensions—but no problems," he reported. Yet in an illustration of how the crisis hurt the economy, Disney laid off hundreds of employees because tourists were afraid to travel there.[56]

Simon's despotic rule at the FEO worsened matters. In early December 1973, John Love quit his post, refusing to continue as part of the Nixon energy team when Simon became head of the proposed FEA. Love's departure left Simon fully in charge of energy policy. He regarded it almost like a personal fiefdom and brooked little interference, despite misbegotten policies. When Budget Director Roy Ash commented on these policies, Simon lashed out against him on national television, saying that Ash should "keep his cotton picking hands out of energy."[57] One administration insider said of Simon, "When the President appointed an energy czar, he didn't know he was getting Ivan the Terrible." Brash and arrogant, Simon boasted of having "a temper like a thunderstorm" and broke pencils to show his rage.[58]

A prickly personality was problem enough, but Simon's policies were the height of hypocrisy. He supported them, in part, for political ambition. When he was appointed to head the FEO, "far from rejoicing, Simon was appalled by this development," recalled William Johnson. "He came to Washington to be the eventual Treasury Secretary and not the nation's energy czar." Energy was an explosive issue, and Simon worried that a misstep could ruin his career goal. Acutely aware that his appointment at Treasury needed congressional approval, he supported intrusive government actions in energy to accommodate congressional concerns, telling aides, "First take care of senators, then representatives."[59]

Simon's subsequent actions contradicted the philosophy he preached. "For a person who later talked as if he were only interested in the free enterprise system," DiBona recalled, "he was willing to give it up pretty quickly in the early stages."[60] Simon clung to price controls despite their obvious ill effects on oil production, warning that their removal "could result in very substantial price increases." His allocations only aggravated matters. In a devastating editorial entitled "William Simon Is Incompetent," the *Wall Street Journal* condemned the allocation scheme and said that the energy czar had a staff of young lawyers "who gather at 7:30 every morning to order supplies of oil products hither and yon. But before the ink is dry on the regulations they have to write, someone discovers something they haven't thought of," forcing regulations anew. Staff members found themselves constantly fixing yesterday's problems and making exceptions to their rules. Simon later admitted that the allocation program was "a disaster."[61]

Indeed it was. Within just a few months, allocations tried to revise a vast, complex system of oil refining and distributing that had taken decades to build. As Simon later conceded, "All we were actually doing with our so-called bureaucratic efficiency was damaging the existent distribution system."[62] Government allocation represented a drastic intrusion into the free market. Natural price mechanisms would have been the best way to allocate fuel; the new policies created a crisis. "At no time was the shortage of gasoline—the shortage of energy in the United States—more than two or three percent," DiBona said. "The scarcity was caused by price and allocation controls." To counteract the small shortage, gasoline prices needed to rise approximately 10 percent—just pennies. The market would have then "cleared," or reached the equilibrium where quantity demanded equaled quantity supplied. Instead, "the whole pricing system—the whole market allocations—were destroyed, and we had these horrible lines," DiBona recalled, "when for a few cents a gallon more, the market would have cleared and there would be nobody in line."[63]

As FEA director Frank Zarb recalled, "The whole idea of allocation and two-tiered pricing was a nightmare."[64] Controls and allocations created not one drop of fuel. By limiting profits, price controls discouraged oil producers from exploring for more oil. Price controls also encouraged oil companies to sell their oil abroad. Faced with the choice of sending tankers to the United States, where they would have to sell at low prices, or to other countries with uncontrolled prices and more profit, companies naturally chose the latter.

During the Arab oil embargo, when this practice hurt consumers, Alan Greenspan found evidence of "fairly large diversions" of oil to other countries.[65] Then there was the burden of regulation itself. One Ford administration study concluded that the petroleum industry annually paid $500 million and compiled 600,000 forms to comply with government regulations.[66]

Although economically deleterious, controls made political sense. They were designed to keep consumers happy by holding down the cost of oil and minimizing profits of the oil industry, which many Americans saw as powerful and venal. Most people did not blame government policy for fuel shortages. "Rather, the petroleum companies," the *Wall Street Journal* noted, "on the front line and visible, are absorbing public frustration and bitterness."[67] An Oregon woman complained to her congressman, "Do the gas companies want more money? Do they want the Alaska pipeline bad enough to make everyone miserable by forcing people to stop fighting it? Are they wanting to force the independent dealers out of business?"[68] A ringing phrase that emerged was "obscene profits," which Henry Jackson popularized to describe oil companies' alleged greed.[69]

Public suspicion of the oil industry, especially the belief that it artificially created the energy crisis, prompted many politicians to support controls.[70] They portrayed themselves as inflation-fighting consumer champions and foes of the oil industry. Campaign literature for Indiana senator Birch Bayh's successful 1974 reelection bid explained that he "has been doing his best to help fight the increased cost of living. For example, he has consistently voted to roll back the price of petroleum products. He believes it is wrong for the large multi-national oil companies to make record profits while we consumers pay ever higher prices for gasoline, heating oil, plastic, synthetics, and other petroleum-based products."[71] In this way, politicians portrayed detrimental actions as measures benefiting consumers, whose cries proved too loud to ignore.

While controls were popular in the United States, America's industrial competitors shied away from them and adjusted more easily to Arab oil reductions. The gas station lines shocked foreign visitors to the United States; Canada imposed no controls and suffered no lines.[72] Japan, although dependent on petroleum for 71 percent of its energy needs in 1973 (much more than the United States's 46 percent), refused to regulate oil prices, encouraging conservation and reducing its dependence on oil to just 25 percent during the next fifteen years.[73] West Germany also rejected controls. Economist Paul McCracken recalled that at the height of the oil embargo, while irate American motorists suffered in gas lines, the German economic minister asked rhetorically at a press conference whether his country would face the same fate. The minister smiled and said, "No, we're going to recognize that if we want oil, we're going to pay the world price."[74] Countries that refused to impose oil price controls reduced usage because the high world price discouraged domestic consumption.[75]

The energy crisis, DiBona said, was "a crisis of government. There was mismanagement by government."[76] Gerald Ford had to develop better policies. Government price controls and allocations proved inimical to free-market principles and the nation's oil production. In Ford's view, any solution to the country's energy challenge would have to eliminate controls. He recalled that "although I had no particular plans for decontrol of oil prices when I became president, in the back of my mind I knew [controls] were wrong, and we just had to find the right time to get rid of them."[77]

Americans and the Energy Crisis

Budget Director Roy Ash deprecated the panic and ill-advised government policies during the Arab oil embargo. He said that the energy crisis "is manageable, it's one time and it's short term." He believed that it would last months, not years, without fundamentally damaging the economy. The mess finally eased in the spring of 1974, after Nixon, persuaded by officials like Ash, ordered Simon to increase gasoline allocations for states suffering shortages, an action that Simon had resisted. Gas station queues dissolved, the sense of urgency faded, and as if to underscore the point, on March 18, 1974, the Arab oil embargo ended.[78]

But the feeling that shortages were real and another oil cutoff could aggravate them troubled Americans. Until the 1970s, they thought that their country supplied all of its own energy needs. The Arab oil embargo proved otherwise; shortages seemed to reveal that resources were limited. Discerning citizens expressed shock. In 1975, one man counted automobiles on Washington's streets and reported that three out of every four had only one occupant. "When are we going to realize that our land of plenty is not that plentiful anymore?" he asked. "When are we going to get serious over conservation of our energy resources?"[79]

By late 1975, a Library of Congress study warned, "Energy may well become the 'Achilles heel' of United States foreign policy in the same way as agricultural shocks are for the U.S.S.R."[80] "Dangerous dependence" described the relationship between America and oil. The energy crisis had two components. One was the perceived scarcity of resources, especially nonrenewable sources such as petroleum, and the other was America's vulnerability to future disruptions in its oil supply, along with the economic and national security effects concomitant with oil deprivation.[81]

Just as inflation imposed profound changes, the energy crisis forced Americans to alter lifestyles, partly in response to presidential blandishment. Two weeks after the oil embargo began, Nixon addressed the nation and asked Congress for emergency legislation to institute year-round daylight savings time and a lower national speed limit, both of which Congress quickly granted. During the winter of 1973–74, the nation remained on daylight savings time to have more natural light in the evening and thus reduce energy usage.[82] For the first time in postwar America, energy conservation was in vogue. Responding to another Nixon request, homeowners turned down their thermostats and installed additional insulation and storm windows, and commuters took to carpooling.[83]

Public officials tried to set good examples. On December 26, 1973, as a United Airlines jet prepared to take off for a post-Christmas Washington-to-Los Angeles flight, travelers in the first-class section were startled when an unusual passenger joined them: Richard Nixon. "All of a sudden he was just there," one passenger said. "He was standing there in the aisle shaking hands with everybody." In an extraordinary move designed to show Nixon's effort to conserve energy, the White House secretly arranged to fly him aboard a commercial airline instead of Air Force One; the decision reportedly saved 60,000 gallons of fuel. Although the Secret Service was miffed, the White House dismissed security concerns and viewed the trip as a public relations victory.[84]

Cities and states joined the battle. A Milwaukee city committee worked by candlelight to save electricity. The capitol domes in Connecticut, New Hampshire, Rhode Island, and Vermont fell dark at night, unlit for the first time since World War II, when skylines were kept black as safety against German attacks. Christmas was unusually dark in 1973. Pittsburgh and Detroit canceled their holiday light displays. In New York, the Rockefeller Center Christmas tree had 25 percent fewer lights than usual, and nearby stores like Saks Fifth Avenue and Lord and Taylor cut back on holiday illuminations.[85]

Some public school systems shut down during the 1973–74 winter. Colleges, especially in New England, extended winter breaks; Bowdoin College in Maine shut down for most of January, while Tufts University began its new term in late February. At the New England School of Art, where room temperatures were set at 65 degrees, a nude model stayed within a transparent plastic canopy that insulated her without obstructing the view.[86] Small crises also turned up. Frank Zarb recalled that "we had problems with hospitals going low on fuel, and so we'd have to actually direct tankers on the high seas to change their port-of-call, which was extraordinary."[87] Whether they were trying to be funny or scary, some children dressed as Arab sheiks at Halloween.

Many Americans traveled less or traded in their big Detroit cars for small, fuel-stingy imports. Some Americans, for the first time, began to flirt with Japanese brands. Datsun (later Nissan) lured them with slogans such as "Datsun Saves," boasting that one of their models averaged 37.9 miles per gallon in a coast-to-coast drive; by contrast, Datsun pointed out, the average American car's fuel economy was just 13.5 miles per gallon. (For many motorists, the courtship of Japanese cars that began in the 1970s blossomed into a long marriage.) Detroit's "Yank Tanks" (as the British dubbed large American cars) seemed headed the way of the dinosaur. Frank Ikard, president of the American Petroleum Institute, predicted that the oil shortage would last "as long as most of us will live. We will have to adopt a whole new way of life. The love affair of the American with the large automobile has come to an end." Most auto industry executives agreed.[88]

Many Americans had slumbered until the Arab oil embargo jerked them awake. One facet of the crisis seemed clear. The United States was addicted to foreign oil, almost like a drug. In 1974, the country imported 37 percent of the total oil it consumed. By contrast, in 1960 only 18 percent of its oil was imported, mostly from Canada and Venezuela. These friendly nations steadily decreased oil exports, so that by the 1970s the United States depended on politically unstable sources such as the Middle East. "The Saudis," President Ford confided to a reporter with uncharacteristic bluntness, "have us by the balls."[89] By 1975, the United States imported 6 million barrels of oil daily, and the Ford administration predicted that by 1977, the total would reach 7.2 million barrels of oil a day, 3 million of that from politically insecure sources. Nelson Rockefeller described America's energy vulnerability by recounting that a state governor badgered him about the so-called energy crisis, refusing to believe that a crisis could exist when motorists still found gas at stations. "That's just it," the vice president exclaimed. "There is gas at the pump because we are importing nearly 40% of it from abroad—and *that* is the energy crisis."[90]

That was only part of the crisis. The other aspect was domestic production, which had slipped since 1970. By 1974, for the first time, the United States was no longer the world's greatest oil-producing nation; the Soviet Union now held that distinction. While these ominous changes silently took place, domestic demand grew, and with it America's dependence on foreign oil sources and vulnerability to another embargo.[91]

The energy crisis also exemplified a new era in which Americans realized that the planet and its resources were smaller than they had once seemed. The *New York Times* called the 1970s "An Age of Scarcity." Academic reports warned that a day of reckoning was near. In early 1975, the National Academy of Sciences warned that most of the world's oil reserves would run dry within fifty years, and the United States likely would never enjoy large annual increases in its oil and natural gas production. Noting that new oil wells yielded relatively little crude in 1975, *Time* speculated, "It may well be that there is just not much oil left in the continental U.S."[92] Economists agreed when Ford conceded that the era of low-cost energy "has now come to an end."[93] Americans interpreted—incorrectly, as it turned out—fuel disruptions as evidence that the earth was running out of oil.

The energy crisis induced a self-flagellation. One statistic that frequently appeared was that that United States, with just 6 percent of the world's population, consumed more than 30 percent of the world's energy; yet, in reality, the United States used energy to make food and industrial products for the rest of the world, a fact that critics overlooked.[94] The recriminations persisted. Simon denounced Americans as "energy wastrels" and warned that shortages would continue even after the Arab oil embargo ended. The crisis prompted reassessments of the nation's growth rates, forcing Americans to content themselves with slower development. They sensed that their "good life" was over.[95]

Doomsday movies provided allegories for the energy crisis. In late 1974, a popular box-office draw, *The Towering Inferno*, depicted valiant attempts to rescue people trapped in a skyscraper engulfed in flames. The burning building was a metaphor for the waste and extravagance that caught up with America. The massive structure cost a fortune to build, gulped huge amounts of energy, and symbolized overindulgence. Now the skyscraper, like wasteful energy habits, threatened to destroy those within.[96] Many of the popular disaster films of the 1970s, such as *Airport 1975* and *The Poseidon Adventure* (1973), expressed the idea that the prodigal creations of humans (a jumbo airliner in the former, a luxury cruise ship in the latter) had spun out of control and threatened doom.

Just as frustrating, the proud nation, which had recently landed men on the moon, was hard-pressed for solutions. Americans explored energy avenues but each seemed a dead end. Petroleum-based fuels seemed to be running out. Coal was plentiful, but mining and burning this dirty fuel threatened to upset the fragile ecological balance. New energy sources, in addition to being technically complex, had problems. Nuclear energy harbored the ghastly danger of toxic waste and meltdown. Solar devices, although safe, were expensive, bulky, or primitive.[97]

As the energy crisis deepened, confidence waned. Because their trust in government plummeted after Vietnam and Watergate, many Americans had no faith even in its reports on oil levels. An Indiana man despaired, "Why? Why is the U.S. Government conspiring against the public?" The man said that the government was "lying . . . by saying that there is an oil shortage when there really isn't any."[98]

While the government was not lying, it had developed bad policy. By the time Ford took office, the nation needed "a president's ability to articulate a comprehensible and cohesive set of steps to address the energy circumstance . . . that we found ourselves in," recalled Charles Curtis, counsel to the House Interstate and Foreign Commerce Committee. "That required the president to lay out a program."[99] It was another challenge facing Ford and the nation.

Chapter 13

A New Energy Program

Frank Zarb was Gerald Ford's new energy czar. During his first day on the job, he decided to test the efficiency of the FEA. He ordered two items, specifying that they had to be on his desk by afternoon: a rubber stamp with his name and a *Roget's Thesaurus*. When he returned from lunch, a brown paper bag sat on his desk. He looked inside and pulled out a rubber stamp reading "Frank Zarb." But there was no thesaurus. He noticed another stamp inside the bag and tried it out: "Roget's Thesaurus."

Someone at the FEA could secure rubber stamps quickly, but overall Zarb found conditions there "pretty chaotic." The agency lacked the authority it needed to spearhead the drive for effective ideas and legislation. "Energy policy was kind of being driven out of the White House, so that we [at the FEA] didn't really stand for anything," Zarb recalled. Moreover, after a high turnover of energy czars, he found that "the agency was demoralized . . . [and] really needed some firming up in terms of leadership and spirit." These conditions translated into poor prospects for a national energy policy. "On balance, [the FEA] was not in good shape, nor was energy policy in good shape," Zarb remembered. "The initiative had been lost, the momentum was on the side of Congress and consumer groups. So the country was somewhat leaderless [in energy policy] at that stage."[1] Ford's first contribution was installing a promising new administrator to head the struggle.

The Problem of Policy

Formidable obstacles blocked Ford's efforts to develop an energy program. One was that the nation had never had a comprehensive energy policy. Until the 1970s, few presidents could have imagined fuel scarcity. After shortages appeared in 1972, the Nixon administration developed initiatives but no energy policy, leaving Ford a small foundation on which to build. William Simon felt that the first director of the FEO, former Colorado governor John Love, lacked commitment to the job. Simon recounted that shortly after the Arab oil embargo began, he overheard Love and Interior Secretary Rogers Morton cavalierly planning to spend a weekend quail hunting. Simon wrote, "Quail hunting—when the United States was in the middle of a catastrophic oil embargo? I knew then that Love never fully grasped the magnitude of the emergency, and I was not alone in that opinion." Nixon soon removed Love from his post, replacing him with Simon, who promptly demonstrated his incompetence. Simon complained, "I don't believe I slept more than four hours in any single night, including weekends, from the end of November until the embargo was lifted." Sadly, this overwork was unnecessary, for Simon's work in allocating oil products prevented the market from clearing gasoline lines; he might have been better off quail hunting.[2]

Many of Nixon's responses to the crisis emphasized conservation. He asked Americans to reduce their energy consumption by 5 percent and the federal government's by 7 percent. Private citizens, he urged, should use car pools or public transportation. He called on federal agencies to reduce air conditioning and heating, switch to smaller automobiles, and take fewer business trips. He ordered that the indoor winter temperatures of federal buildings be set between 65 and 68 degrees, adding, "Incidentally, my doctor tells me that in a temperature of 66 to 68 degrees you're really more healthy than when it's 75 to 78, if that's any comfort." At the White House, Nixon had exterior illumination shut off at 10:00 P.M., the thermostats set at 68 degrees, and every other lightbulb in long corridors removed.[3] Other Nixon moves were more substantive. He urged more leasing of offshore areas for oil and gas exploration and created an Energy Research and Development Administration to explore new energy resources. But he also announced a Project Independence, aimed to reduce oil imports to zero by 1980. That goal sounded nice but made no sense.[4] Melvin Conant, an assistant administrator at the FEA, had strong words about Project Independence: "One has to make up his mind as to whether it was ignorance, fraud, or a kind of deception to raise everyone's spirits. But it was utterly ridiculous." Frank Zarb called Project Independence a public relations ploy that was neither feasible nor realistic.[5] He thought that the "whole idea of energy independence was a political slogan, not a substantive policy. . . . As a result, it subtracted credibility from the overall public policy initiative."[6]

Though Nixon's response to the energy crisis was wanting, Ford partly blamed Congress for the failure to formulate a national energy policy. "Even after the Arab oil embargo of 1973, Congress refused to believe that a crisis was at hand," he wrote. "The lawmakers failed to see the need for a comprehensive energy policy, and the results of their neglect were painfully obvious not long after I became President. Domestic production of coal was below the level of the 1940s. Oil production had been declining every year since 1970. . . . Natural gas production was starting to decline." When Zarb became FEA director (the FEA was created in May 1974 to supercede the FEO), he expressed to Ford the two major deficiencies that he noted: "First, there never has been a clearly defined and believable [energy policy] goal; and secondly, such goals were never backed up with strong, pragmatic programs to achieve them."[7] Nor had any government official been clearly in charge of energy policy. Two weeks after Ford's inauguration, Undersecretary of the Treasury Gerald Parsky wrote to Simon, "There is a mounting concern among industry, Congress, and the Nation that in the midst of bureaucratic shuffling no one is in charge of energy policy. This must be corrected immediately by the President making clear who is in charge."[8]

Because the administration devoted its first hectic months to planning and consensus gathering, nothing concrete emerged. Ford's first enunciation of an energy plan, in his October 8 anti-inflation speech, included exhortations for natural gas deregulation and, additionally, energy conservation as part of the WIN program. He called on Americans to "drive less, heat less." As he explained, "If we all drive at least 5 percent fewer miles, we can save, almost unbelievably, 250,000 barrels of foreign oil per day. By the end of 1975, most of us can do better than 5 percent by carpooling, taking the bus, riding bikes, or just plain walking." Ford set a national goal of reducing oil consumption by one million barrels a day, mostly by cutting oil imports, believing that Americans could rise to the challenge without onerous regulations.[9]

Many of the enthusiastic public responses to Ford's call to "Whip Inflation Now" included tips on saving energy: join car pools, observe speed limits, lower thermostats, and use home lighting and appliances sparingly. More unconventional suggestions included a Pennsylvania woman's idea to raise the minimum driving age to eighteen to force teenagers to take the bus and an Oklahoma City man's proposal to outlaw auto racing. Many Americans used the opportunity to express opposition to crosstown busing of children to desegregate schools, arguing that it wasted gasoline.[10] In his Kansas City speech exhorting voluntarism, Ford mentioned homespun suggestions from Americans: "Margaret and Bill Dalton of High Falls, New York, write me on recycled paper that 1 ton of recycled fibers saves 17 live trees and a ton of waste." Some tips came from children. A seventh-grader suggested that people eat by candlelight and take showers in the rain, and a Connecticut girl wrote to President Ford, "You should shut off most of the lights around the White House."[11]

The advice, while amusing, was thin gruel. Just as the voluntary fight against inflation failed to check price increases, the voluntary fight to solve the energy crisis sputtered. Critics wanted Ford to take sterner measures, such as gas rationing or a gas tax. But Ford opposed such government measures, especially because they failed to remedy the real problem, oil price controls. The issue of the gas tax, in particular, caused a shake-up at the FEA.

Many administration members, most prominently Simon, liked the idea of a higher gas tax. He recommended that the administration seek a $.20 increase in the federal gas tax to $.24 per gallon. Besides his hope that the higher price would encourage conservation, Simon reasoned that the current $.04-per-gallon tax had stood untouched since 1959, while many states had increased their gas taxes. The United States, moreover, lagged far behind the rest of the industrialized world in imposing gas taxes, as Japan and European nations had fees that equaled $.75 to $1.25 per gallon.[12]

FEA administrator John Sawhill, who emphasized conservation, publicly favored a higher gas tax. Members of Congress vehemently opposed the idea. Riling them even more was Sawhill's outspokenness and the timing of his remarks. Republican congressman Tim Lee Carter of Kentucky wrote to Sawhill to plead, "Please, for godsake, don't mention any more tax on gasoline! This adversely affects every congressional candidate in the United States. . . . I have travelled from one end of this district to the other and I found only one man who supported the 10¢/gallon tax on gasoline and he was a kook."[13] Others in Congress complained that the tax would aggravate inflation and hurt those least able to afford it. Those representing remote districts feared that their constituents would be unfairly victimized by the tax. A retired woman living in the California desert wrote to Ford saying that she had a twenty-two-mile trip just to get groceries and was "greatly disturbed by the discussion of a gas tax."[14]

Even after the president stated his opposition to a higher gas tax, Sawhill continued openly to recommend it. Such behavior left Ford little choice; he asked Sawhill to resign. One reporter saw Sawhill's dismissal as "another episode in the country's uncomfortable transition from an era of cheap, abundant energy to one in which unpleasant choices must be made."[15]

To replace Sawhill, Ford turned to Frank Zarb, then the associate director of the OMB for science, energy, and natural resources. Initially, Zarb hesitated. "I wasn't particularly pursuing the post," he recalled, "and I wasn't sure if I wanted it or not, because I was in OMB, where the power really was, and I didn't know if the FEA was going to turn into something that had a real presence in public policy making."[16]

Zarb enjoyed a reputation as a problem solver in both business and government. Before joining the government in 1971, he worked as an executive vice president of Hayden Stone, Inc., a Manhattan investment banking firm, and he engineered the takeover of the large Hayden Stone concern by a smaller firm. Awed at the takeover, one of Zarb's associates remarked, "Frank made it possible for a minnow to swallow a whale." If Zarb joined the energy team, Ford would have a capable administrator in charge of a key corner of national policy. But before accepting Ford's nomination, Zarb wanted the president's assurance of direct Oval Office access. Zarb felt that Sawhill "had no influence at all," and he "wanted to make sure that if I did take [the job], I would have an important place at the table. . . . President Ford assured me that I would." Zarb's nomination sailed through Congress, and Ford had his new energy czar.[17] Witty and candid, Frank Zarb was well liked in the media and on Capitol Hill. After a spinning turnstile of energy czars that left no reliable spokesman for policy, Ford installed a new FEA administrator who stayed for the rest of his presidency.

Planning a Program

Ford wanted an energy policy that held fast to his ideological moorings by promoting free-market principles. Ford's October 8 anti-inflation program emphasized energy conservation partly because it required no extensive government planning and was a safe measure that was easy to explain and implement. As Glenn Schleede, the associate director for energy and science in Ford's Domestic Council, commented, "In the short term, conservation is about the only thing you can do."[18] But conservation was like a tourniquet to staunch the bleeding; it was just a temporary step that needed to be replaced by more comprehensive measures.

By late 1974, Ford wanted sterner stuff. The planning for a new energy program began with weekend meetings at Camp David in the late fall, with finishing touches added during Christmas vacation meetings at Vail.[19] While there, Ford told an interviewer, "The public cooperation effort (to save oil) has not achieved all we feel is necessary. So there will be stronger measures." Ford's goal was to increase supply through greater domestic oil production, and he hoped to achieve this by eliminating price controls, which consumers would hate in the short term because prices would rise. But over time, decontrol would reduce their energy vulnerability. Eliminating controls would encourage the economic marketplace to increase energy supply and simultaneously decrease energy demand. Ford looked at the long term. His energy measures might draw cries of pain and protest in the interim, but he hoped that, over time, the country would increase its domestic oil production and thus reduce its energy vulnerability.

As Ford's advisers mapped out a new policy, they tossed around several options. Although critics shot down Sawhill's gas tax proposal, it still had numerous administration supporters.[20] Advocates of a higher gas tax argued that it would discourage wasteful overconsumption of gasoline, penalize gas-guzzling cars, and raise federal revenue. Simon and Interior Secretary Rogers Morton urged Ford to reconsider a higher gas tax.[21] Some representatives and senators liked the idea. Democratic congressman William Green of Pennsylvania supported a ten-cent-a-gallon gas tax. Like many gas tax advocates, he thought that by keeping prices artificially low, the government encouraged Americans to drive whenever they wished and to waste gasoline, "subsidizing people to drain America dry." The automobile, Green regretted, had became "a floating living room," a transportable luxury that Americans relied on excessively.[22]

But Ford viewed a gas tax as unfair. The American auto industry, already blindsided by a high demand for small cars that it could not meet overnight, would suffer more dislocations, while the tax would help Japanese and European automakers who made smaller cars. Of the myriad petroleum products, it affected only gasoline, thus placing undue conservation demands and tax burdens on those who depended heavily on it—rural residents, commuters, farmers with heavy machinery, and the travel and tourism business. Ford preferred to spread price hikes and demand reductions over the full spectrum of petroleum products, not just gasoline, which accounted for only 40 percent of petroleum consumption. Zarb implored, "We've got to save 100 percent of the crude barrel," not just 40 percent. Ford also viewed a higher gas tax as a short-term solution that would aggravate inflation while doing nothing to increase production of new resources. Besides, he knew that Congress would reject the idea.[23] Zarb also opposed the gasoline tax increase, but his reasoning differed from Ford's. He believed that legislators could be persuaded to pass a gas tax, but "it would give Congress an easy way out. They'd put a nickel on a gallon of gas and then go home, saying we don't need any more energy policy."[24]

Ford also rejected rationing. Whereas a gas tax proposed to use higher prices to dampen demand, rationing would limit the amount of gasoline that consumers could use. But, like allocations, it would provide no incentives for energy producers to seek and develop more energy resources. Just like a gas tax, it would be inequitable, penalizing individuals who depended on travel by car. Ford also feared that a massive new government bureaucracy would have to administer gasoline rationing. The administration estimated that an army of full-time bureaucrats, perhaps up to 25,000, would run the program. Costs would be considerable, ranging from printing coupons to policing the entire process. Rationing would hurt business and depress economic activity. Companies wishing to start or expand facilities would need special fuel permits from the government, and some businesses would have to curtail or end operations.[25] Rationing also would invite a black market for coupons and gasoline.

Yet rationing had many proponents. Supporters touted it as an effective way to cut oil consumption. A 1975 poll showed, surprisingly, that 55 percent of respondents favored a nationwide program. In Congress, Senators Mike Mansfield and Robert Byrd and Representatives Al Ullman and Henry Reuss were vocal advocates. But Ford had little confidence that the federal government could accurately determine how much gas each motorist in the country needed. To achieve his 1975 goal of cutting oil imports by one million barrels a day, Ford estimated that rationing would limit each driver to fewer than nine gallons a week—too little for many Americans. "Inequities would be everywhere," Ford warned. "How would people in remote areas of the country get enough gas to drive into town? How would farmers get enough gas to harvest their crops? What would happen to people who must drive a long way to work each day? And who would make those decisions?"[26] Ford saw rationing as a bureaucratic nightmare that would hit some Americans hard and touch others lightly. Inevitably, too, Americans would devise ruses to beat the system.[27]

Rationing also cut against the grain of Ford's long-term focus. Recalling that the United States successfully endured gasoline rationing during World War II, Ford said, "I have no doubt that this nation is capable of sustaining a rationing program during a short emergency. However, to really curb demand, we would have to embark on a long-range rationing program of more than five years. Those favoring rationing must be thinking of a short-term program, not a serious, long-term effort to end energy dependency." Moreover, the country had changed significantly since World War II; millions of Americans had moved to the suburbs and depended more on the automobile. Rationing could be disastrous, and were Congress to pass such a program over his protests, Ford promised a veto.[28]

The administration also considered imposing a dollar limit on oil imports. Senator Henry Jackson, who muscled to the forefront of Congress on energy issues, supported this move, which would stop the hemorrhaging of dollars and pressure OPEC to lower its prices. But Ford worried that quotas, by limiting the amount of oil entering the country, would replicate the shortages and high prices that the country experienced during the Arab oil embargo. The shortages could encourage rationing and other schemes.[29] Quotas could also lead industries to wrangle over which ones deserved more oil. Less oil for industries meant slower economic growth, a painful prospect for a recession-plagued nation.

Thus Ford wisely eliminated several energy options. What emerged as the best option, and the one philosophically most to his liking, was the decontrol of oil, which meant market—rather than government—allocation. The only way to foster energy independence, Ford believed, "would be to allow the prices of oil and gas to move higher—high enough to discourage wasteful consumption and encourage the development of new energy sources." In December 1974, the Energy Resources Council (ERC), a cabinet-level group that oversaw the FEA, recommended that Ford decontrol oil, either in phased steps or cold turkey, by simply letting price controls expire as scheduled in August 1975. The ERC wanted the new legislation for decontrol from Congress fast—in ninety days—and predicted that while decontrol would cause price increases of about $2.30 a barrel, such an increase would reduce demand by 850,000 barrels a day by 1977. The ERC also recommended an excise tax and an import tariff of $2, which would discourage consumption enough to realize an additional savings of 600,000 barrels a day by the end of 1977.[30]

The decontrol of domestic crude oil would let the price of old oil—held at $5.25 per barrel—rise to the market level of about $11, forcing consumers to conserve. But over the long term, prices would stabilize. By allowing private industry to work without price caps and earn greater profits, decontrol would stimulate domestic oil production. The FEA estimated that with decontrol, by 1985 annual domestic oil production would be 1.4 million barrels more than in 1975.[31]

Controls and lower profits had discouraged domestic producers from exploring for more oil. A White House memorandum spelled out a guiding principle of Ford's energy policy: "Additional energy supplies can be best obtained through the stimulus of free prices and a minimum of federal regulations. We should remember that we are suffering from the energy crisis of today largely because of government regulation of the past."[32] The critical flaw in the other energy options was that they provided no incentives for producers to extract a drop more of oil from the earth. Ford considered such incentives critical. At a speech in Houston, he made a pointed reference to congressional Democrats: "Now, some people in Washington do not seem to recognize the need for incentives in the marketplace, but we must, in my judgment, have sufficient incentives in the marketplace to increase production. Unless we create incentives, we will be settling for dependence on other nations."[33]

Ford's advisers also favored an excise tax of $2 per barrel to go with a $2-per-barrel oil import fee. The two fees would work together. At the time, the import fee on oil was a mere $.18 per barrel, not enough to encourage conservation. Hiking this fee to $2 would have more effect. Meanwhile, the excise tax would be added to domestic oil to prevent producers from raising the price of their own oil to keep up with the new import price and thus realizing a windfall profit; with the new excise tax added on, if they hiked the price, they would price themselves out of the market.[34] The excise tax would raise revenue while discouraging consumption and equalize the burden that the new oil import fee would create: Since the East and West coasts and the upper Midwest received most of the imported crude oil, the excise tax would help to prevent these regions from suffering higher costs than the rest of the country, making the domestic oil that other regions used more expensive as well.[35]

Reducing oil imports was also a critical goal. The Ford White House considered that the United States was vulnerable to another oil embargo, and this view constituted the driving force behind administration energy policy.[36] Ford believed that the oil shortages and price increases after the Arab oil embargo proved that "we were more and more dependent on the Middle East supply of oil. We were being held hostage by the Middle East oil barons."[37] At the time the administration planned the State of the Union program, the country imported six of the sixteen million barrels of oil it consumed daily, costing $24 billion a year—a staggering ten times more than it had spent on imported oil just four years earlier.[38]

Oil vulnerability was also a matter of international importance. State Department officials believed that if the United States did not reduce its oil dependence, allies already implementing conservation programs would lose faith in America. Especially after Vietnam, the country's reputation as a superpower took a beating, and allies as well as Americans doubted the country's ability to meet the challenges of a changing world. Arthur Burns warned that if the nation continued to drift without an energy policy, the result would be a "permanent decline in our nation's economic and political power in a very troubled world." The energy crisis was thus more than a crisis of limited resources. It involved a shift in power from the Western world to OPEC, inflation prompted by higher oil prices, and perceptions that America could not respond fluidly to a world in transition.[39]

At a White House meeting with Republican congressional leaders, Alan Greenspan spoke anxiously about these concerns, saying that oil vulnerability imperiled the United States. The price that the Arabs charged for their oil would rise inexorably, he warned. "Our society is based on low-cost energy but the cost of that energy is changing," and the country was "playing Russian roulette," cautioned the CEA chair. "This dependence on Arab oil makes our society susceptible to blackmail . . . a severe embargo now could bring unbelievable devastation," such as a 25 percent unemployment rate and the paralysis of car-dependent Los Angeles County.[40]

Because its dependence on imported oil was increasing, America would suffer more from a future embargo. As Zarb recalled, "We were doing everything we could to get us on a path to reduce the amount of dependence on foreign oil, and not increase it. Everything we did—coal, natural gas, nuclear power, oil, conservation—the five pieces [of energy policy] were all designed around that strategy."[41] Ford wanted to diminish the chance of foreign nations holding the United States hostage. If the United States protected itself against another embargo, that in itself would reduce OPEC's inclination to use oil as an economic weapon.[42] Ford's energy program was, in a sense, a national security program.

Unveiling the Program

As he planned the State of the Union address, William Baroody noted among Americans "an anxiety about the ability of our government institutions to manage serious domestic and international problems, such as energy and food."[43] The Ford administration regarded the 1975 State of the Union address as critical not only to unveil its antirecession proposals but also to demonstrate its determination to reduce the country's energy vulnerability. As he spoke to Congress and the nation, Ford laid out three energy goals. "First, we must reduce oil imports by one million barrels per day by the end of this year and by two million barrels per day by the end of 1977. Second, we must end vulnerability to economic disruption by foreign supplies by 1985. Third, we must develop our energy technology and resources so that the United States has the ability to supply a significant share of energy needs of the free world by the end of this century."[44] Freedom from economic blackmail meant reducing imports, stockpiling oil for an emergency, and relying on alternative energy sources.

Ford's goals sounded ambitious. Reducing oil imports by one million barrels a day within one year was an unrealistic objective that, even if attained, would have caused severe economic dislocations. In fact, Ford and his advisers knew that this goal was unreasonable.[45] The president nevertheless insisted on including it because he "wanted a very tough 'stretch goal,'" Zarb explained.

In setting a national policy objective, Ford believed that the public had to grasp it. Zarb said that the goal "had to be understandable. It had to be a number that the people could comprehend and that would mean something, that would be material . . . because in the political world, if you put in a lesser number, then people would start playing with it."

Just as important, the goal had to be ambitious. Ford thought that if the American people set their sights high, while they might fall short, they would still achieve something significant in striving to attain the goal. Moreover, the sheer magnitude of a lofty goal would force the public to realize the gravity of the crisis. "[Ford] felt the nation needed to perceive the urgency of the [crisis]," Zarb remembered. "And more than that, he wanted to keep the Congress's feet to the fire. It was he who really wanted the tough stand," Zarb recalled. "Because if he would have said '650,000 barrels,' in the world of politics in Washington, that would have been lost. . . . He said, 'A million barrels, a million barrels, a million barrels.' That had some impact."[46]

Another ambitious goal Ford unveiled in his address was decontrol. To promote a greater oil supply, he announced that he wanted to decontrol the price of domestic crude oil on April 1 — in less than three months. "I urge the Congress to enact a windfall profits tax by that date to ensure that oil producers do not profit unduly," he added. Many members of Congress were especially concerned about oil companies' reaping windfall profits from decontrol; namely, they would gain additional money from oil already under production, decontrol not having acted as an incentive to obtain this oil. To forestall this problem, Ford asked Congress to enact a windfall profits tax by April 1.

With this proposal, the EPAA's two-tiered price-control system would be washed away, letting free-market forces dictate the price of oil. Ford also requested that within three months, Congress should act on the energy taxes he desired: the excise tax and import fee of $2 per barrel of oil and an excise tax of $.37 per thousand cubic feet of natural gas. In addition, he proposed deregulation of new natural gas. If Ford's plans were passed, Americans would soon get hit with higher energy prices.

As with his proposal for an antirecession tax cut, an urgency marked the president's energy program. But he feared Congress would move with frustrating slowness, especially with any measure involving price increases to consumers. Thus he imposed deadlines. He announced that he would use his presidential authority to raise the fee on all imported crude oil and petroleum products by $3 per barrel — a $1 increase on February 1, another $1 on March 1, and a final $1 on April 1. These increases would be replaced by the $2-per-barrel import fee as soon as the latter became law.[47] The $3-per-barrel fee would raise $5 billion in federal revenue. Its effect on deterring consumption, however, would be negligible, causing a price rise at the pump of $.03 a gallon.[48] It was directed not at the consumer but at Congress, encouraging lawmakers to act speedily. As the administration planned the president's energy program, Dick Cheney stressed to Ford, "We need to find some way to force Congress to act" fast by imposing an import tax on oil, using it as a fillip to make Congress pass energy legislation. "It is important that we not simply follow our October [1974] posture of submitting a long list of proposals and then sitting back and waiting for Congress to act," Cheney believed.[49]

Ford's plan contained other measures to increase domestic energy production and meet energy emergencies. He asked Congress to authorize oil production from reserves owned by the U.S. Navy. He wanted Congress to permit the conversion of power plants from oil to coal; coal was the country's most abundant energy resource, and Ford wanted to encourage its development and reverse the trend for utilities to switch from coal to oil. He announced steps to stimulate production of other alternative energy sources, such as synthetic fuels, nuclear fission, and solar and geothermal power. To boost conservation, his program included plans to improve the corporate fleet gas efficiencies of American automakers by 40 percent by 1980, which would demand quick and radical engineering changes from Detroit. Ford wanted manufacturers to raise the efficiency of electrical appliances and label them with energy standards to allow consumers to select energy-efficient appliances. As a cushion against future energy emergencies, Ford asked Congress to authorize development of a strategic petroleum reserve (SPR), a storage system of 1 billion barrels of petroleum for domestic uses and 300 million barrels for military use.[50]

Ford's proposed new energy taxes meant that consumers would pay higher prices for petroleum-based energy of all forms, not just gasoline. But with the nation in a recession, withdrawing so much money from the economy through the energy taxes was dangerous. So Ford planned to redistribute the revenue from the energy taxes to consumers to restore their purchasing power. The new energy taxes were expected to raise $30 billion ($18 billion from the excise taxes and oil import fees plus $12 billion from the windfall profits tax on the oil industry). Because he wanted to lower taxes, Ford planned to return the $30 billion to Americans in permanent tax reductions, including a tax cut of $16.5 billion for individuals on 1975 income taxes (not to be confused with the temporary, antirecession tax cut of $16 billion he proposed for 1974 taxes), a corporate tax cut of $6 billion, $2 billion in federal benefits, and other measures.[51]

Ford also hoped that an attack on the country's energy problems would restore business and consumer confidence and help to end the recession. All in all, Ford's was a thoughtful program that proposed many different measures to meet the energy challenge; half a year after taking office, he had proposed a more comprehensive plan than Nixon had during his last two years in office. Once again, it was up to Congress to act on his proposals.

Chapter 14

The Energy Stalemate

The passions were reminiscent of the Civil War, only it was the 1970s. Members of the Texas legislature were fiercely debating the nation's energy crisis. One lawmaker, exasperated that the South had to endure the fifty-five-mile-per-hour speed limit due to alleged northeastern wastefulness, shouted, "To hell with the Yankees and their speed limit!" In other parts of the South, a popular bumper sticker read, "Let the bastards freeze in the dark." The sentiments were mutual. Northeasterners resented the oil prosperity of the Gulf Coast states, and they began calling visitors from the Lone Star State "Texas Arabs."

Energy was a bitter issue that pitted one section of the country against another. Gulf Coast residents angrily charged that northeasterners wasted oil. Because they relied much more on natural gas and enjoyed mild winters, they lacked sympathy for the Northeast's problems. Residents of the Northeast wanted more sympathy; above all, they wanted more oil. Yet they depended heavily on imports either from abroad or from other areas of the country.[1]

The regional battles were just one of many factors that tied up the energy issue on Capitol Hill. Conflicts between the president and Congress often stem from the president's need to represent the entire nation versus representatives' and senators' solicitude for their constituencies. On energy, Gerald Ford observed, parochial interests often prevailed; people in one sector of the country tended to share a similar philosophy on energy, one that "doesn't bear a Democratic or Republican label."[2] For Ford, the situation made 1975 a difficult year on energy.

Reaction to the Program

The response to Ford's State of the Union energy proposals was generally negative. Business leaders voiced objections, while utility and petrochemical

1. The new look: to convey the feeling of a more open, relaxed White House, Ford replaced the bulky, bulletproof lectern with a slender one and rearranged seats so that he stood before an open doorway. All presidents since Ford have followed this seating arrangement.

2. For his first two weeks as president, Ford (pictured here with his wife, Betty) continued commuting to Washington, D.C., from his Alexandria, Virginia, home. He declined to move into the White House immediately so as to give the Nixon family time to move.

3. August 1974. Ford met with Republican congressman Barber Conable of New York, one of his closest House colleagues, to solicit advice on possible vice presidential choices. Shocked to learn that Conable, a strong Nixon supporter, had never been in the Oval Office, Ford reaffirmed his desire to restore sound relations with Congress, which became a hallmark of his presidency.

4. Trying to allay suspicions surrounding Nixon's pardon, Ford testified before a House subcommittee chaired by Democratic representative William Hungate of Missouri. It is one of the few times a president has appeared before a congressional committee.

5. Before the 1974 midterm elections, Ford campaigned extensively for Republican candidates, including Senator Bob Dole of Kansas, whom he picked as a running-mate two years later. (Although sponsors designed the "WIN" program to be non-partisan, some Republicans appropriated it as a campaign symbol.) Riding an anti-Watergate backlash, the Democrats won landslide victories.

6. Ford meets with economic advisors during the fall of 1974. The economy took a dramatic tumble, forcing Ford to concentrate on recession rather than inflation. Clockwise, from left: James Lynn, William Simon, L. William Seidman, William Eberle, Paul McCracken, Alan Greenspan, Ford, Arthur Burns, Roy Ash.

7. December 1974. During the Christmas holidays, Ford summoned his advisers to Vail, Colorado, to work on his 1975 State of the Union economic and energy program. Clockwise, left to right: William Simon, Ron Nessen, Ford, unidentified, Don Rumsfeld, Alan Greenspan, Arthur Burns, Roy Ash, Frank Zarb, unidentified, James Lynn, L. William Seidman, William Eberle.

8. Ford rehearses his 1975 State of the Union "preview," which he delivered from the White House Library. The president made meticulous preparations for this speech and used a teleprompter for the first time. Sitting on the floor: unidentified (back facing camera), and Dick Cheney. Left to right: unidentified, Alan Greenspan (standing), Donald Rumsfeld, Ron Nessen, Ford, unidentified, Robert Mead (standing).

9. May 1975. Ford rehearses for the angriest speech of his presidency, in which he ripped pages from a calendar to show how Congress had squandered time in formulating an energy program.

10. In 1976, Ford signed new energy legislation to increase oil production from the Naval Petroleum Reserves. Here he is shown visiting the largest of these reserves in Elks Hills, California.

11. In June 1976, Ford hosted leaders of America's industrial allies in Puerto Rico. It was the second such meeting, and the economic summits marked the beginning of the annual G-7 talks. From left to right: Japanese prime minister Takeo Miki, West German chancellor Helmut Schmidt, French president Valéry Giscard d'Estaing, American president Gerald Ford, Canadian prime minister Pierre Trudeau, Italian prime minister Aldo Moro, British prime minister James Callaghan.

12. August 1976. At around 2:00 A.M., with strain evident on their faces, Ford and Ronald Reagan emerged from their reconciliation meeting in Reagan's hotel room at the Republican National Convention. Ford had finally clinched the nomination after months of bitter primaries, and he recalled, "The tension of our long contest permeated that room."

13. Ford often disdained presidential pomposity and believed he should continue to travel and mingle with Americans despite two 1975 assassination attempts. Here he braved a drenching rain during a 1976 campaign swing through New Jersey. One woman who saw Ford that day praised him in the *New York Times*, writing that "the little things we do are the things that really count."

14. The active president. One of the most athletic chief executives ever, Ford enjoyed golf, swimming, tennis, and skiing while in his sixties. Yet the media often chose to ignore his athleticism—including his being the first president to ski regularly while in office—and instead focused on occasional pratfalls.

15. Although Ford lost the 1976 presidential election, by the time he left office many observers felt that he had restored integrity to the White House. Courtesy of the Gerald R. Ford Museum.

executives rushed telegrams to the White House protesting that the oil import fee would hurt their industries. Edward Carlson, head of America's largest airline, United, warned Ford that higher energy taxes would raise fuel costs and force airlines to increase fares and freight rates.[3] Curiously, FEA director Frank Zarb found that environmentalists linked arms with consumer advocates to oppose decontrol and the higher prices that would result. Zarb said, "I remember saying to them, 'You're environmentalists! Higher-priced gasoline is going to lower consumption. So why aren't you campaigning with me rather than against me?'" The reason, Zarb found, was that consumer groups had supported environmental issues, so environmentalists wanted to reciprocate the help.[4]

Many economists found the proposals puzzling. Hendrick Houthakker of Harvard, a member of Nixon's CEA, called Ford's program "foolishness," commenting, "Our principal problem is that the price of imported oil is already too high . . . so on the face of it, it appears strange to put another duty on . . . or to impose additional excise taxes." While some economists conceded that price increases would discourage oil consumption, they worried about Ford's timing, because the decrease in fuel use would depress economic output and worsen the recession. Other critics contended that Ford mistook the demand for oil and oil products to be more elastic than it really was. When the price of oil products rose, consumption would fall far less than Ford hoped, they predicted. One amusing incident revealed the shallow support for Ford's program among economists. Defending the oil fees before the Senate Finance Committee, William Simon downplayed their effects on inflation, arguing that the price increases would add only two percentage points to the inflation rate. A skeptical Senator Walter Mondale asked Simon whether any economists outside the administration supported Ford's program. Simon rambled on without naming any, and Mondale repeated the question twice. Finally came Simon's strange reply: "Alan Greenspan." Senators broke into laughter as Mondale sarcastically shot back, "He's no longer with the government?"[5]

In the marble hallways of Capitol Hill, Ford's energy proposals met their greatest resistance. Many congressmen thought that Ford was trying to pull dollars out of Americans' pockets with the new energy taxes and then stuff them back with his tax breaks, or as Robert Byrd scoffed, "just swapping money." Worse, the added taxes would hit hardest those Americans least able to afford them. With no progressivity built into the taxes, everyone would have to pay them, regardless of income.[6]

The inflationary effects of Ford's proposals were a concern. "Inflation was such a big part of the backdrop here," FEA Deputy Administrator John Hill recalled. "It really did shape people's views as to whether we should have immediate decontrol or not."[7] Decontrol, taxes, and fees would send ripples throughout the economy, increasing the price not only of essential commodities like gasoline and heating oil but also of products made using oil, such as plastics and chemicals, not to mention all goods that had to be transported—essentially, everything. The FEA estimated that energy taxes would increase the average American family's cost of living by as much as $345 in 1975. Senator Alan Cranston remarked that Ford "had abandoned his fight against inflation to fight recession and was now proposing more inflation."[8]

Traditionally, the public greeted presidential proposals, especially those promulgated in a nationally broadcast address, with enthusiasm. But after Watergate and Vietnam, public resistance to presidential authority was more rigid; moreover, Ford proposed higher prices on essential commodities when the nation already suffered from inflation. In its first count of public reaction to the president's proposals, the White House found, for one of the first times in recent memory, that critical responses ran even with favorable ones, 259 negative to 258 positive.[9] While he expected some resistance, Ford said that the public disapproval of his program caught him off guard, "because I thought that people would understand that it was the kind of thing that was important for national security. But the public doesn't always react that way."[10]

In planning his energy program, Ford repeatedly told aides that he wanted to do what he felt was right for the country, and if the resulting program was unpopular, he would risk the political consequences.[11] Michael Duval, a special counsel to the president, noted that the greatest fear of some presidents is not being reelected. But Ford's greatest fear, Duval observed, "was that he'd do something really bad for the country." Polls and popularity, he said, mattered less to Ford than the quality of his policy.[12] As Ford liked to say, "Presidents shouldn't make major decisions based on what the polls showed. A president should do what he thinks is right based on the substance." Ford also dared to propose an unpopular program because he believed in the separation of powers. The chief executive should be willing to strike out on a path different from Congress, he believed, especially if the two sides are far apart on an issue. Ford believed that if members of Congress "don't like what the White House recommends—under our coequal, coordinate branch concept—they have an obligation to come up with something they say is better." Ford was pressuring Congress to act. After an initial period of uncertainty and hesitation in office and the failure of his October 8 anti-inflation plan, he wanted members of Congress to develop alternatives to his program—if they had the political will.[13]

Challenges to the Program

One of the most innovative but controversial components of Ford's energy program was his proposed $3, three-stage oil import fee. The fee constituted an ingenious strategy that was largely Ford's brainchild. Energy advisers laid a number of options before the president, and he seized on the idea of an oil import fee. He decided to apply the fee in three monthly stages, rather than all at once, "to turn the heat up gradually" on Congress, Zarb explained.[14] Ford regarded the fee as the most formidable weapon in his arsenal for prodding Congress to act.

Strictly speaking, the fee was never a substantive part of Ford's energy policy. "It was always just a tool to get the Congress moving," Zarb said. It was also a way to act quickly and unilaterally, Ford believed, explaining that "when that was imposed, we didn't call it a 'tax.' If it had been a tax, we would have had to get authority from Congress [for it]." Instead, Ford called it a "fee" that involved national security, bypassing Congress, which probably would have refused to grant him the necessary authority to impose a tax—or if it had, would have been slow to do so. The president found legal authority to impose the oil import fee in the 1955 Trade Expansion Agreements Extension Act and the 1962 Trade Expansion Act, which allowed the president to adjust imports in the name of national security. Ford believed that imposing the fee was "a very strategic move, and . . . by predicating it on the basis of national security, [it was] a justifiable action by the president."[15]

Members of Congress were "apoplectic" about the fee, Robert Nordhaus recalled. It riveted congressional attention to Ford's proposals. Democratic congressman John McFall of California admitted, "If the goal of the import tariff was to get the mule's attention, you've got the mule's attention."[16] Congress feared the fee's inflationary impact and resented the pressure tactic. Senator Henry Jackson believed that the tariff showed the arrogance of "unbridled discretionary authority," and Democrats predicted that it would drain money from the economy and impede the recovery. The adverse reaction on Capitol Hill reflected concerns over abuses of presidential authority. To Congress, the fee smacked of executive high-handedness. In this respect, the oil import fee got Ford's program off to a bad start and ran counter to one of Ford's major goals, restoring good relations between the branches. Bruce Pasternack, the FEA's associate administrator for policy, admitted that the fee "probably more than anything else became the downfall of a lot of what we wanted to do because it created such an overwhelming response."[17] Ford found no other way to get Congress's attention quickly and effectively.[18] Yet to many members of Congress, it was an arbitrary use of presidential power.

From the outset, administration advisers recognized that Ford's energy plan swam against the tide. In late January, Robert Goldwin wrote to him to warn that "the chances of the energy program getting through Congress in its present form are doubtful."[19] New England's response was particularly blunt. While other areas drew from a diverse spectrum of energy sources—natural gas, coal, running water, or the sun—New England could not. Supplying only 9 percent of its own energy needs, it depended almost completely on imported oil, especially to keep warm during winter. By contrast, the other regions of the country depended on oil for just 46 percent of their energy needs.[20]

Ford modified his program to accommodate the Northeast. He offered a special rebate to the northeastern states on the oil import fees, exempting the region from the $1 increase set for February 1 and imposing fees of $.60 and $1.20 on March 1 and April 1, respectively.[21] While aware that his proposals would elicit howls of protest from the region, Ford stood by them. "Of course New England objected, because they depend on imported oil and crude products more than any other part of the United States," Ford reasoned. "And we understood that. Tip O'Neill [from Massachusetts] used to give me hell, but the truth was it was the way to do it. We got a lot of criticism. But it was the right policy."[22]

The Northeast disagreed. On January 23, 1975, ten governors from the Northeast stormed into Washington to meet with Ford. Pennsylvania's Milton Shapp, who had told the president that his program was "a blueprint for economic disaster," reported after the session, "None of the governors agreed with the President's position, none of them." Massachusetts governor Michael Dukakis, whose state was most dependent on oil, said the meeting had "no jokes and very little laughter." He told the president that "he was holding the Northeast hostage to his program." But Ford's perspective was more national than regional. To ensure the country's energy security, Americans would all have to suffer, and the suffering could not be distributed perfectly. After the tense meeting with the governors, Ford went into the Oval Office and signed the proclamation instituting the first $1 oil import fee, to take effect on February 1. Aides and reporters watched in silence as he signed the controversial act. Noting the anxiety, Ford quipped, "I don't see anybody clamoring for extra pens."[23]

The northeastern governors did not think it was funny, nor would they let the matter rest. In late January, eight took legal action, filing suit to invalidate Ford's oil import fee on the grounds that it infringed on Congress's power to tax. Meanwhile, five days after the State of the Union address, Senators Henry Jackson and Edward Kennedy introduced a resolution to delay the oil import fees for ninety days, hoping to gain breathing room for Congress to develop alternatives to Ford's plan.[24] The obstructive congressional tactics were just the beginning of Ford's frustrations.

Struggling to Sell the Program

To Ford, the effort to beat back the Kennedy-Jackson resolution was not just between the president and Congress or Republicans and Democrats. It was a test of national will. A nation unwilling to discipline itself to endure a $3-per-barrel oil import fee could never be seen as strong. OPEC nations would raise oil prices with little fear of reprisal. Ford explained, "The United States will not bring about lower world oil prices without some evidence of the seriousness of our intentions. . . . Removing the power of the President to force Congress to act isn't very good evidence of the seriousness of our intentions."[25] While he could postpone the second and third fees, he had to get Capitol Hill to accept the first $1 fee to display national will. Then, "if we can win on this first big test," he could discuss compromise.[26]

But on February 5, after Ford had imposed his February 1 fee, the House voted to suspend Ford's power to impose his oil import fees for ninety days. The 309–114 vote was far more than the two-thirds needed to override a veto and came despite Ford's efforts to swing House members to his side. The night before the vote, he met with almost a hundred Republicans in Congress, and the morning of the vote with eighty-five Democrats, asking them to defeat the resolution.[27] Since the vote was a first real test of Ford's political strength in the new Ninety-fourth Congress, the results revealed not just legislators' determination to resist energy price increases but the president's weakness as he made a stand on a critical corner of national policy.[28]

Yet Ford's plan was the only game in town. Instead of offering an alternative to his 167-page program, he complained, Congress simply drafted a 4-page piece of legislation to suspend his authority to implement the oil import fees. "Now, it seems to me that the American people want something that is a plan for forward-moving action rather than a four-page bill to move backward," Ford remarked. As with his antirecession tax cut, he had stolen a march on Congress. Ford "liked the idea of taking the high ground fast," Zarb recalled.[29] His plan was to throw the legislators off balance and keep Capitol Hill in the posture of reacting.[30] Many Americans agreed that he had gotten the jump on Congress, which seemed stuck in the starting blocks. A North Carolinian wrote to Ron Nessen, "Our President Gerald Ford has tried to chart us in the right direction with his tariff on imported oil. Right or wrong, he has done SOMETHING, while the Congress has done nothing toward solving our energy crisis."[31] Congress was vulnerable to charges of drift and disorganization because it offered no viable alternatives. "I welcome any suggestions that are constructive," Ford said. "I welcome an alternative program or plan if one can be put together by the Congress. But I will not tolerate delay; I will not tolerate inaction." Calling continued dependence on foreign oil "a reckless gamble," Ford said, "Those who propose no action now hope there will be no future embargoes. . . . This is a little like saying a man with a very large family needs no insurance."[32]

But Ford met resistance outside Washington as well. During trips to Texas and Kansas, he met with fifteen state governors, all but two of whom opposed his energy program, although they appreciated Ford's sincerity. David Pryor, the Democratic governor of Arkansas, epitomized the dichotomy of feeling when he praised and damned Ford in one sentence: "First, I basically would support the moratorium on the imposition of the tax [on imported oil], and two, I would personally like to thank President Ford for coming [here] tonight."[33]

The Senate also registered its opposition. On February 19, it approved the ninety-day delay in the oil import fee, 66–28, as in the House, with more than the two-thirds needed for a veto override. On March 4, Ford vetoed the bill, but fearing that Congress would override his veto, he made an important concession.[34] He agreed to delay his next two scheduled increases in the oil import fee for sixty days and postpone the decontrol of domestic oil for sixty days. While the $1 levy of February 1 would remain in effect, the March 1 and the April 1 fees would be postponed. The delay was meant to give Congress a chance to develop a compromise energy program by May 1 and, even more important, complete work on the antirecession tax cut. Representatives had complained that wrangling over the energy plan interfered with work on the tax cut, especially since the same committee, Ways and Means, was saddled with most of the work on both. Calling Ford's move "quite a concession," Democratic senator John Pastore of Rhode Island remarked, "I think it behooves Congress to respond in kind. If we can't resolve this in 30 days, we can't resolve it at all."[35]

Ford's political maneuvering enabled Congress to act speedily on his antirecession tax cut. His energy proposals also galvanized Congress into action. The Senate passed an energy bill in early April, representing Congress's first concrete step toward creating its own energy policy. But the bill relied on government intervention and contradicted Ford's long-term desire for decontrol, retaining most controls on old oil while clamping down a lid of $11.25 a barrel on the price of new oil. Instead of relying on market forces, the bill called for federal and state governments to implement conservation programs, set thermal standards for buildings, and create regulations for lighting and car use.[36] The story was similar in the House. The Ways and Means Committee worked slowly on an energy bill whose centerpiece was a plan for a stiff gasoline tax, taxes on inefficient automobiles, and quotas on oil imports that a proposed new bureaucratic agency, the Office of Petroleum Purchasing and Reserve, would administer. The House Commerce Committee's energy subcommittee labored on its own bill—with more, not fewer, controls—and tinkered with lowering the price cap on old oil to $4 a barrel, from $5.25.[37]

Ford's deadline of May 1 approached. With Congress moving slowly, some members of Congress urged Ford to impose the second $1 oil import fee.[38] Instead, he made another concession. On April 30, the White House announced that he would again defer the scheduled increase in the oil import fee, giving Congress another reprieve. Ford risked losing momentum for his program, but he wanted to give the House Ways and Means Committee and John Dingell's energy subcommittee more time to develop alternatives. Ford also recalled that "by the time spring came, the urgency wasn't quite as evident" for him to impose the import fees because the winter months and the threat of oil shortages had passed.[39] Zarb also worried that if Ford imposed the second $1 fee, Congress would revive the Kennedy-Jackson resolution and try to override his veto. If that happened, Zarb warned, "our strength for the rest of the program could be eroded."[40]

Thus the administration took some related steps. While holding the threat of the oil import fee in reserve, Zarb insisted that Ford set administrative gears turning to end all price controls on domestic oil in two years, instead of immediately, gradually reducing the volume of price-controlled oil by about 4 percent a month. Ford also warned Carl Albert that if the House and Senate failed to move more quickly on energy legislation, he would impose the next import fee in thirty days or less.[41]

The Angriest Speech of Ford's Presidency

During May 1975, Congress squandered Ford's grace period, putting the House Ways and Means Committee bill aside. By month's end, dissatisfied with Congress's slow progress, Ford took forceful action. On May 27, he made a televised, prime-time nationwide address from the Oval Office. He announced that he would add a second $1 oil import fee on June 1. Later that month, he would begin to phase out price controls on domestic oil supplies. He would also ask Congress to pass a windfall profits tax.[42]

It was the angriest speech of Ford's presidency. He expressed grave disappointment with Congress and included some dramatic gestures. As

Robert Hartmann recalled, "We were always conscious of the need for something that was telegenic in a presidential speech—something [the public] could zoom in on, and wake people up a little in the middle of these speeches, because they get to be terribly dull." A large calendar stood next to Ford's desk, and he recounted the sequence of events since January. "Now, what did the Congress do in February about energy?" he asked, ripping the page for that month off the calendar. "Congress did nothing—nothing, that is, except rush through legislation suspending for 90 days my authority to impose any import fees on foreign oil. Congress needed time, they said." He explained that he delayed his next oil import fee, giving Congress a sixty-day cushion to generate its own program. "What did the Congress do in March? What did the Congress do in April about energy? Congress did nothing," Ford declared, as he ripped the pages for those months off the calendar. Finally, May came: "So, what has the Congress done in May about energy?" Pulling this page off, Ford reported, "Congress did nothing and went home for a ten-day recess." He ticked off the months on his fingers: "February, March, April, May—as of now, the Congress has done nothing positive to end our energy dependence."[43]

Ford said the word "nothing" seven times, a choice of words and tone pointedly reminiscent of Harry Truman's attacks on the "do-nothing" Eightieth Congress that stymied many of his programs. The speech convinced some viewers of Ford's earnestness; one North Dakota man commented, "Tearing off the calendar pages was useful and called attention to the do nothing legislators that in six months have achieved zero."[44] But Congress liked neither the tone of Ford's presentation nor its substance. Carl Albert called the speech "a childish act," and Tip O'Neill remarked, "I'm surprised that Jerry would demagogue like that."[45] Even some Republicans felt dismayed. Senator Charles Percy of Illinois, a close friend whom Ford respected so much that, while vice president, he had encouraged Percy to seek the 1976 Republican nomination, called the speech "as amateurish a presentation to the nation as I've ever seen."[46] The dramatic speech allowed Ford to express his frustration with Congress but bruised his amiable relationship with legislators.

The spring of 1975 was ending in frustration over energy policy. Ford had proposed a forceful program. But as the New York Times observed, "Clearly, many Democrats fail to share President Ford's sense of urgency about an energy program." Nixon, too, had been frustrated by Congress's slow pace on energy. In April 1973, he proposed seven initiatives to address the crisis; half a year later, the Arab oil embargo took place, yet Nixon complained that "thus far, not one major energy bill that I have asked for has been enacted." Less than two years after the embargo, another energy crisis seemed a distant concern to Congress and consumers. Americans barreled along with energy-wasting lifestyles, and Congress mirrored their nonchalance. A program that demanded sacrifice stood little chance of passage. John Zuckerman, deputy director of the University of Houston's Energy Institute, noted, "In terms of actual behavior [among Americans], I'd say nothing has happened. Until outside pressure comes on, it is the American temperament not to do anything." Some Democrats in Congress were unwilling to accept Ford's premise that the nation needed to reduce its oil imports. To them, buying oil from abroad was not so bad. After all, Europe and Japan depended far more on oil imports than did the United States yet enjoyed economic vitality. While Ford and Henry Kissinger warned that heavy reliance on oil imports limited America's world leadership, many Americans did not want to hear such talk. After the tragedy of Vietnam, they felt comfortable with less active international involvement. Just as unappealing were the alternatives to imports, such as massive government spending to develop alternative fuels, dirty sources like coal, or toxic ones like plutonium. Many in Congress preferred to stick with oil, even if imported.[47]

One problem was that Ford and his administration formed an unconvincing sales team. While believing that the country verged on great changes in its resource availability and usage, Ford was unable to portray this watershed to Americans. Congressman John B. Anderson remarked that Ford "didn't go far enough, in my opinion, to try to turn around public indifference to the necessity of really embracing a new conservation ethic that we drastically change our habit patterns, our lifestyles, and do it in the interests of being good stewards of the earth."[48] Zarb admitted that the administration and Congress failed to rally Americans behind stringent energy measures, in part because neither Congress nor "we in the executive branch have done a good job" of conveying the magnitude of the problem to the people. The administration groped for a way to define the problem to Americans in clear, cogent terms; it considered holding a White House conference on energy in the summer of 1975, similar to the Conference on Inflation, to generate public awareness of the need for voluntary energy conservation.[49] It never happened, which was a lost opportunity, for it might have generated badly needed media and public attention on the issue.

To compound the difficulty in attracting public attention, Ford's program was difficult to sell. Prescribing higher prices was like offering pain; no one wanted it. Republican congressman Albert Johnson of Pennsylvania said that his mail ran 90 percent against Ford's proposals. "If it's not popular here, it's not popular anywhere," Johnson concluded. "This is Ford country."[50] Americans would endure sacrifice only for a tangible goal with a convincing rationale. Memories were still raw of how a national goal, containing communism worldwide, dragged the country into Vietnam. For the president to convince the public to strive for a public objective that enhanced national security, he would have to convey a sense of "crisis." But without skyrocketing prices or long gas station lines, nobody felt an energy crisis, and Ford found trouble trumpeting his program's rationale.

The recession further blunted the force of Ford's message. Americans feared that slashing imports to meet Ford's import reduction goals would decrease economic output and worsen the downturn. The price increases that he prescribed would also take money from consumers and hurt business sales, devastating sectors such as used-car dealerships, where old gas guzzlers sat idly in lots. Higher prices would thus reinforce the inflationary-recessionary cycle that plagued the economy.

Few representatives or senators wanted to stick their necks out to back a program that lacked national support. While Ford's energy plan could not be easily explained to or understood by the public, it was actually simple: increase prices and supply, decrease demand. Where members of Congress and the public saw high oil prices as the problem, Ford viewed them as the solution, which made his proposals seem curious, even cruel, and put him at odds with Capitol Hill. And while some congressmen favored higher prices to reduce consumption, they called Ford's techniques unjust. Democrats much preferred a gradual, government-regulated mechanism, such as a higher gas tax or rationing, to free-market forces.[51] In early March, Zarb reported to Ford that after meeting with Al Ullman and John Dingell, he found that "their main concern centers around exclusive reliance on market forces to obtain a 2 million barrels a day reduction by 1977. Both stated they felt serious economic disruption would result if we relied on immediate price increases to obtain this goal, and that politically Congress would have to reject such a proposal."[52]

Ford not only believed in market forces but trusted the oil industry. Many Democrats blamed Ford for accepting the industry's view that fewer taxes, controls, and environmental restrictions would ease the nation's energy problems. Columnist Joseph Kraft described the president's energy program as "just a cozy arrangement for lining the pockets of the big oil companies," while Birch Bayh commented that "Ford and the big oil companies are made for each other. They own the wells and he gushes all over them."[53]

These were misleading characterizations, but they created the image of a president in the oil industry's hip pocket. "Anytime you propose price increases for oil," Glenn Schleede observed, "the public and the people who are heavy users of the oil are going to suspect that this is a cabal arranged by the oil companies in cooperation with the administration."[54] Indeed, Nixon faced the same charges, especially after revelations that oil companies generously contributed to his 1972 reelection campaign. "Impeach Nixxon" was a bumper sticker that addressed both his involvement in Watergate and his alleged complicity with oil companies such as Exxon.[55] Nor did Ford escape. "There was always the charge that we were in bed with the oil industry," Zarb said. John Hill found that one reporter confessed to him an almost knee-jerk distrust of the Ford administration's business motives after the Nixon years; eventually, though, the journalist supported deregulation.[56]

Every generation has its corporate villains. Since the 1970s, consumer animus has focused on Big Tobacco, Microsoft, and pharmaceutical giants. While Ford was president, it was Big Oil. Yet Ford believed that the oil industry, unhindered by regulations, could provide energy supplies at fair prices, and he wanted to provide a better business environment. As Schleede recalled, "Most people [in the Ford administration] didn't start with the assumption that the oil industry was in some conspiracy to push up prices." By contrast, Democrats believed that federal regulations were essential to prevent Big Oil from driving out competitors and hiking prices. Suspicion of the industry dated back to the late nineteenth century, when John D. Rockefeller built the huge, vertically integrated Standard Oil empire and ruthlessly eliminated competitors. The industry's ancestry made it perennially suspect and was one reason that Congress agreed to oil price controls in the early 1970s. In early 1974, Congress even tried to roll back the price of new oil, but Nixon vetoed the measure. These struggles reflected the divide that made energy policy so contentious. Congress wanted to protect the consumer, who stressed the avaricious or conspiratorial nature of oil price increases. But oil producers believed that prices should rise to natural market levels, and Ford supported this view.[57]

Mike Mansfield noted that Ford was "not an obdurate man. He's flexible." The president was willing to compromise to avoid delay, but many members of Congress were less concerned with the speedy action that he valued; economic recovery interested them more. Democratic senator Frank Church of Idaho wrote, "With the American economy sliding into deep recession, the Congress has concentrated on blocking the Ford domestic energy program in order to better help the American people get jobs."[58] Like Ford's economic and budgetary policies, his energy program focused on the long term. As Michael Duval observed, "The basic solution is geared to last over the long haul and we should seek to avoid mixing into the energy solution other short-term issues such as fighting the business recession. Most of the energy decisions we will make now, especially on the supply side, will not have their impact on our economy until many years into the future."[59] But for recession-weary consumers and politicians, the long term was difficult to see.

Public apathy made Ford's task even harder. Energy was an abstract issue that lacked drama or excitement, and the solutions were complex. Even the term "decontrol" was nebulous to the average American, who heard the word in the news but did not understand it. Hartmann once wrote to the president, "Frankly I think the public has been aroused by your leadership to recognition of the long-range energy problem but continues to be completely bored by complicated and generally unpleasant detailed solutions." Reporters also failed to grant serious coverage to energy issues. Nessen recalled his disappointment at the media's response to Ford's fireside State of the Union preview. "On this complicated, complex subject [of energy] they could only think of two questions," he wrote. "One reporter wanted to know why he gave the speech from the [White House] library, and Helen Thomas [of UPI] wanted to know how he liked using the teleprompter. There wasn't enough expertise on this complex subject to even ask the right questions."[60]

Americans did not see the energy picture in profound terms that involved the "survival of freedom" in the world, as Vice President Rockefeller complained at one White House meeting, where he stressed that Arab nations and the Soviet Union could imperil the United States by cutting off oil delivery.[61] Incredibly, a majority of Americans did not even realize that the United States imported oil. Al Ullman called energy "the invisible crisis," because by 1975 energy supplies once again seemed bountiful. Many Americans suspected that greedy oil companies, aided by the government, manufactured a "crisis." Surveys in 1974 and 1975 revealed that one of every three Americans believed the energy crisis was a hoax. Later in the 1970s, Jimmy Carter found that when he visited areas that had been plagued by gas shortages, "people had asked me, 'Mr. President, is there really a shortage? Aren't the gas companies just holding back supplies to squeeze more money out of us?' The skepticism about oil and gas companies was pervasive, leading many people to doubt the need for any sacrifice or new legislation."[62]

A year after the Arab oil embargo, the average price of gasoline in the United States was a tolerable $.53 per gallon, and it was business as usual for American motorists and energy users. By October 1975, one California woman observed, "At the time of the gasoline crisis when people were forced to cut down and threatened that gasoline rations would be given, they did cut down. Yet now that all is back to normal, people drive around freely again, when often not necessary."[63]

Americans demanded low gasoline prices almost as a birthright. To counter this thinking and elevate public consciousness on energy issues, the FEA developed a public relations campaign to promote conservation, admonishing Americans, "Don't Be Fuelish." Celebrities such as actor George C. Scott and Miami Dolphins football coach Don Shula pitched conservation in FEA spots.[64] Some Americans took the message to heart; many more did not. As a consequence, Ford's ability to get his energy program through Congress suffered.

Congress and the Energy Stalemate

While disappointed at the public apathy, Ford added, "I had more frustration trying to convince some of the leaders in Congress that we needed a different, stronger approach."[65] Members of Congress tended to fall back on noncontroversial policies such as conservation, which carried a small price tag and was environmentally friendly and easy to propose. Ford was more farsighted; to him, conservation just lowered energy consumption. He wanted more fundamental solutions that increased energy production. But that was like a third rail to many representatives and senators, something they dared not touch because of environmental issues, widespread distrust of the oil industry, and costs to consumers.

Some congressmen appeared not to understand basic economic principles. They argued that the oil industry needed no additional incentive to explore for petroleum, denying that higher prices spurred greater production. Democratic congressman Bob Eckhardt of Texas said, "A person can pay me to jump 2 1/2 feet for $5, but he cannot get me to jump 6 feet for $15. I just cannot do it. Such is analogous to the theory that you can bring in new oil quickly by merely raising the prices."[66] As John Hill regretted, "That was the level of [Eckhardt's] economic thinking." When the congressman used that argument against him, Hill—an economist by training—countered by telling him that "your position is saying that there should only be one price for gas and one price for oil; one size fits all." Hill continued, "It's sort of like if you were in the army, and you wear a size 11 shoe, but the army says to save money, we only have size 9. Everybody has to wear the same shoe. Would that have worked?" Hill's analogy drew laughter in the hearing room, but still, the Democrats' greatest fear was that even gradual decontrol would hurt consumers, discriminate against certain industries, and harm the economy with higher prices. Lobbyists for organized labor and the airline industry, two groups that higher fuel prices would have adversely affected, also exerted fierce pressure on congressional Democrats.[67]

Other members of Congress discounted the energy crisis. Douglas Bennett told Max Friedersdorf that some Ways and Means Committee members felt that "there is *no* energy problem. This is somewhat a reflection of public opinion resulting from the availability of gasoline." Bennett concluded, "This, obviously, makes it very difficult for those members who recognize the problem to try to convince other members on the Committee as well as the full House that something 'tough' must be done."[68]

By 1975, Congress was ill-disposed to take stern or quick measures on energy. Many in Congress were mystified that Ford established a national goal to reduce oil imports by two million barrels a day in two years. To them, it was unnecessary.[69] Zarb felt that "Congress moved from a mood of concern, terror, willing to give us whatever we wanted, to a very political, business-as-usual mood right after the embargo was over." He remembered going to Henry Jackson to complain about oil controls, urging the senator to help the administration to find a way to reinvigorate public interest in energy issues and get controls removed. Jackson laughed and replied, "Do you know how to make another embargo?" As Zarb recalled, "The implication was that in the absence of a crisis, we weren't going to get public policy moving."[70]

That was unfortunate. Although controlling domestic prices was politically popular, it increased American vulnerability and impaired the country's ability to endure another oil embargo. The energy impasse painted Ford's long-term focus in sharp relief against Congress's tendency to prescribe short-term solutions. Pasternack commented that "it's hard to convince Congress to do anything that's long-term, to do anything that has long-term strategic value and short-term pain."[71]

As a former congressman, Ford was not surprised. Congressional procrastination "was in line with past performances. It had taken the Congress a full four years to pass the Alaska pipeline bill," considered one of the most important energy bills ever undertaken. Ford also pointed to Nixon's April 1973 request to deregulate new natural gas supplies, which Congress had yet to act on when Ford became president more than a year later. Ford's complaints reflected a classic source of conflict between a president with a limited tenure and members of Congress who spend decades in office, immunized against pressure to act rapidly. John Lichtblau, head of the Petroleum Industry Research Foundation and a critic of Ford's energy program, conceded that the president "is right about one thing—Congress has been playing with oil policy for 18 months and not one thing has been done about solving the energy crisis." Even some congressional Democrats agreed. Henry Reuss of Wisconsin said of his fellow Democrats, "We're saying nuts to the Ford [energy] program, and we should, but we don't have anything of our own."[72] Ford's was still the only game in town, and Congress was strewing obstacles in his path while blazing no trail of its own. A Florida woman commented, "After the non-performance of Congress in regard to energy concerns, I am ashamed to be a Democrat."[73]

The energy impasse reflected Congress's lack of discipline. The situation arose in part because its leaders, notably Albert and Mansfield, were weaker than those of decades past. Other factors hindered its progress. Unlike other national concerns, such as defense or social welfare, energy was relatively new, and legislators had not had decades to explore the issue, hear from constituents, and develop a policy. As a result, Congress spent much of 1975 just flailing about, trying to forge a consensus. The whirlwind turnover in energy czars in the mid-1970s indicated that the executive branch of government was also groping for someone to give energy policy some direction.

Moreover, energy divided the country and Congress by region. The Northeast had different fuel priorities from the West; the former was more concerned with oil for heating and industry, the latter more anxious about gasoline for its driving-dependent residents. Tip O'Neill labeled energy "the most parochial issue ever to hit the [House] floor," and his colleagues referred to oil as a "party splitter."[74] New Englanders repined bitterly against Ford's oil import fee, and representatives and senators from this region took up cudgels against it. Douglas Bennett commented that few New Englanders in Congress supported the oil import fee because if they did, "they probably wouldn't be returning to Congress next year."[75]

Geographical divisions and power considerations made consensus on energy almost impossible. The Northeast produced little of its own energy, and Zarb recalled that "a lot of guys in Middle America didn't care, and would just as soon have seen the Northeast take it on the chin, [which would] take the heat off the rest of the country."[76] Northeasterners resented the newfound power and wealth of the oil-producing states. Politicians from that region were a force to be reckoned with, including Oklahoma's Carl Albert and Louisiana's Russell Long; not only was Texas's John Tower a Senate power, but the state's rich lode of electoral votes made it an important consideration in presidential elections.

The new structure of Congress also discouraged speedy action. This was a young, callow Congress. Almost half of all House members had been elected since 1970, while more than a third of all senators were serving their first term. During the first weeks of the new Congress, members regrouped and formed new committees. Max Friedersdorf commented that "when you have a new Congress like [the Ninety-fourth], and they have to reorganize and get their ducks in a row, they're not going to do much for the first six months."[77]

The intractability of first-term Democrats made reaching agreements even more arduous. It was Ford's bad luck that the energy subcommittee of the House Commerce Committee, which took much responsibility for energy legislation, had many first-term members. Robert Nordhaus, the counsel to the subcommittee, remembered that "they were all a bright and aggressive crew" that leaned politically left.[78] Subcommittee chairman John Dingell of Michigan admitted that the new members on his subcommittee were difficult to control, slowing progress. In some cases, senior House Democrats and lobbying groups brought tremendous pressure on malleable freshmen. Colorado's Timothy Wirth was one freshman Democrat who caved in to such pressure, abandoning his support of Ford's program to argue against decontrol.[79]

With political experience comes political wisdom, but many members of the Ninety-fourth Congress had neither. As a result, they often lacked the ability to frame a national issue in light of its true importance, rather than against their desire for reelection. Energy became a victim of the visceral desire to stay in office. Columnist David Broder noted that while members of Congress instinctively followed their constituents' sentiments on many mundane issues, "there are a few large issues—e.g., energy—where the conscientious members know they have to lead their districts, even if it entails a degree of political risk." In mid-1975, Broder noted, "So far, there is little sign the juniors in Congress recognize that distinction."[80]

Another structural problem in Congress was the proliferation of committees and subcommittees, which blurred jurisdiction over energy. Congress chopped up Ford's energy package and meted it out to various committees. John Rhodes commented, "It has been patently obvious for some time that Congress will never successfully meet the energy challenge until the jurisdictional confusion on energy committees is eliminated. We have too many cooks in the kitchen and nothing is getting done." Ruing that his coherent package had splintered as soon as it entered Congress, Ford once said, only half-jokingly, that there were "535 energy programs up on Capitol Hill."[81] He continued, "With a problem as broad-based and diverse as energy, with many things that have to be done on taxation, conservation and a wide variety of things . . . when you send the package up, it goes to six or eight committees there on each side of the Hill." Each committee had its turf and special interests to look after, further fracturing and slowing the original bill. Ford tried to streamline the process by asking Mansfield and Albert to form an ad hoc committee to consider his comprehensive energy package as a whole. Both declined (although the episode became a lesson for Tip O'Neill, who as speaker set up such a committee for Jimmy Carter's energy package). It was no wonder that Albert once remarked that "the so-called energy crisis is the most difficult, controversial and emotion-laden problem I've faced since I've been in Congress."[82]

In May 1975, the London *Economist* observed that on energy, "Congress has indeed not done much."[83] So at the end of that month, Ford felt compelled to act, venting his frustrations with his angry speech and imposing another import fee. He had offered a three-month truce on the import fees and said that "by not putting on the second and the third increment, I think we were trying to indicate that we were willing to work with the opponents."[84] But the truce yielded little. Congress delivered no energy program of its own. Meanwhile, OPEC could dangle a sword of Damocles above the nation's head. Thus Ford served notice of renewed executive action. Motivating him was the firm belief that his solutions were right for the country. Right or wrong, they were better than no solution and better than the international embarrassment of no national energy policy.

Chapter 15

Breaking the Energy Logjam

Dale Bumpers was a member of the Ninety-fourth Congress's large Democratic freshman class. After serving four years as Arkansas governor, he decided to run for the U.S. Senate in 1974. He won easily and moved to Washington, but as he drove through the city's streets during the energy crisis, something bothered him. "It occurred to me," he said, "as I sat at stop lights without a car in sight in any direction, idling, that I was sitting there using precious fuel at a time when we were trying to become energy independent." Bumpers knew that since 1937, California had permitted motorists to make a right turn at red lights. He recalled, "I got to thinking if you did that nationwide, it would obviously save quite a bit of fuel."

Congress was developing a bill in response to Gerald Ford's energy program, and Bumpers proposed to include a "right-on-red" provision, citing statistics that a national law would save 12,000 barrels of oil daily. Initially, the Ford administration balked, citing safety concerns for pedestrians. But Democratic congressman John Moss of California reminded legislators that his state had safely practiced the law for almost three decades. Convinced of its merits, Congress included right-on-red in the bill. The White House ultimately agreed that in the struggle to make Americans more conscious of energy issues, right-on-red was "something that was visible and that the American people could touch," Frank Zarb recalled.[1]

Right-on-red was one of the new energy bill's sensible components. But Ford administration members disliked the bill's central feature, the crude oil pricing provisions, and with good reason. One member was bent on getting Ford to veto the bill. On December 21, 1975, just before midnight, Ford received an unusual telephone call upstairs in the White House residence. It was from William Simon. For half an hour, Simon engaged in a vigorous verbal arm-twisting, finally giving up when he realized that Ford had made up his mind.[2] But the president knew that the controversial bill would have serious political and economic implications.

Phased Decontrol

After Ford's angry television performance and actions, Congress temporized. In June 1975, it gutted what was supposed to be forceful energy legislation. The House Ways and Means Committee had approved a bill with rigorous measures to enforce gasoline conservation and reduce dependence on foreign oil. But the full House removed key provisions. It approved quotas on imported oil but left them higher than the Ways and Means Committee had proposed, then drove a stake through the heart of the committee's package by rejecting a $.23-a-gallon increase in the gas tax. Pleading for at least a $.03 increase, Tip O'Neill said, "Have we got the guts to stand up and vote for the future of America?" Democratic congressman Joseph Karth of Minnesota told his colleagues that if they "can't vote to raise [gas] taxes we don't deserve to sit here as leaders of the nation."[3] No amount of impassioned oratory could save the measure. Zarb recalled that Ford's "political instincts were right. [The gas tax] was a non-starter. Actually, when [Ways and Means Committee chair] Al Ullman constructed that bill, he asked for our help. I talked to the president, and the president said, 'Give him all the technical help he needs, as a friend, but don't support the bill.' The thing fell of its own weight, as [Ford] knew it would."[4]

On June 13, the House doled out more bad news for the Ways and Means bill, eliminating its proposed tax on gas-guzzling cars. On June 19, the House passed a weak bill. Republicans claimed it would neither encourage production nor discourage consumption. Its provisions included quotas on oil imports, tax credits for homeowners for energy-saving measures such as installing solar heating and cooling devices, an excise tax on businesses that used oil and natural gas as fuels, and a $50-per-car penalty against automakers for each mile per gallon below federally prescribed standards.[5] Now that the House finally passed a bill, Ford faced new pressures. The EPAA was scheduled to expire on August 31, removing controls on domestic oil prices. Democrats raised a hue and cry over the prospect.

Since the State of the Union address, Zarb and other FEA officials had met daily with energy advisers to the House and Senate to negotiate a compromise. During these negotiations, the idea of phased decontrol emerged, and according to Bruce Pasternack, "it seemed like that might be the only way we'd break this logjam, from the Democrats not wanting any decontrol and the Republicans wanting immediate decontrol. So the idea of compromising over a phased period made some sense." As early as March, the administration began considering decontrolling old oil gradually, over a period of two years.[6] Zarb favored the idea, and a number of congressmen told him that they opposed immediate decontrol but would support gradual decontrol.[7] Phased decontrol offered a buffer period before the jolt of price hikes, plus economic, political, and psychological preparation. As Zarb commented, "[Phased decontrol] gave the Congress a political way out. It gave the economy a soft landing. It gave the system a chance to adjust. For some of us, it was not the best answer, but it was as good an answer as any."[8]

On July 14, Ford announced a new proposal. He would dismantle price controls on domestic oil over a thirty-month period. Starting on August 1, the amount of old oil under price controls would be reduced slowly, by 3.3 percent per month, until at the end of the thirty-month period no old oil would be left under controls, reaching equilibrium with the higher world price. To offset price increases resulting from the plan, Ford proposed to fix a temporary ceiling on new oil, namely, the $11.50-per-barrel price of new oil as it stood in January 1975, plus the $2 oil import fee he had added, for a total of $13.50 a barrel.[9]

Congress faced two alternatives and found neither palatable. It could pass Ford's new compromise or reject it and let controls expire at the end of August. But as Ford warned, if Congress refused to accept "this reasonable compromise," he would consider vetoing a congressional bill to extend controls beyond August 31. Some Democrats maintained that Ford was bluffing.[10] On July 22, the House rejected his compromise plan.

Ford was disappointed, but on July 25 he offered another compromise. The new plan essentially stretched out the thirty-month plan to thirty-nine months, with a rollback of prices on all domestically produced oil to $11.50 a barrel, followed by an increase of 5 percent per month. The plan also called for a windfall profits tax and a three-month extension of the EPAA, to give Congress time to work on the new plan.[11]

Ten Democratic governors stated their support for the new plan, and newspapers across the country, including the *New York Times*, *Chicago Tribune*, and *Los Angeles Times*, applauded Ford's efforts to seek compromise and urged Congress to accept his latest proposal, while criticizing its dilatory behavior.[12] But Congress voted down the plan. Zarb recalled, "I was astounded that Congress rejected the thirty-month and thirty-nine-month decontrol [proposals]. It was so logical that they [vote for] it. It was shocking that they didn't do it."[13]

On August 11, Ford received more bad news. The U.S. Court of Appeals for the District of Columbia denied his authority to levy the $2 of oil import fees that he had so far imposed. The court maintained that Congress granted authority to limit imports by quota, not through such fees. The plaintiffs— eight northeastern states, utilities, and Democratic congressman Robert Drinan of Massachusetts—were elated. Massachusetts governor Michael Dukakis praised it as "a great victory for consumers, homeowners, and factory owners throughout [the] Northeast and the nation."[14] The administration decided to appeal the case to the Supreme Court, keeping the fees in effect but suspending collection of the revenue.

The court's decision was yet another standoff between Ford's administration and the forces arrayed against its program. Now those forces seemed to include not only the legislative branch but the judicial. More than a year since Ford had assumed office, neither he nor Congress had anything concrete to show in energy policy. His biggest disappointment in his first thirteen months as president, Ford admitted, was "the failure of Congress to move with me in solving the energy problem." The heart of the problem was that Congress "wants a cheap solution to the problem and there is none."[15]

The Energy Policy and Conservation Act

At the end of August 1975, oil controls expired. On Ford's desk sat the bill to extend controls for six months, but the president promised to veto it, as Zarb recommended. For the first time in four years, the nation would be without price lids on oil. Jittery consumers feared that oil companies were poised to hike prices.[16] Predictions were dire: the ripple effect from decontrol would force prices up across the whole spectrum of goods and services, including gasoline, air transportation, home heating oil, food, clothing, and more. Higher prices would drain consumer spending and threaten the economic recovery.[17]

On September 9, Ford vetoed the six-month EPAA extension. The Senate's attempt to override Ford's veto fell short by six votes. Democrat John Pastore of Rhode Island complained after the vote, "This has become a government by veto. We've got the minority dragging the majority by the nose." But Ford offered Congress a way out. Before vetoing the bill, Ford met with Mike Mansfield and Carl Albert to inform them that he was amenable to a extending controls for thirty to forty-five days, an offer he repeated in his veto message.[18] Zarb recalled that privately, Mansfield and Albert respected Ford's pressure tactics on Congress such as his $1-a-barrel fee "because they were frustrated that the Congress couldn't come together on anything." The two leaders "would personally be supportive, but they couldn't corral their Indians, especially on the House side."[19] But since they enjoyed a good working relationship with the president, they produced what seemed like a promising arrangement. Ford, Mansfield, Albert, and Zarb agreed on a thirty-nine-month compromise phaseout plan.

But neither Mansfield nor Albert could get his chamber to accept the proposal. "We had an agreement between the Speaker and the Majority Leader of the Senate," Zarb recalled. "I sat in the Oval Office and we all shook hands, Carl Albert and Mike Mansfield. And they went back and they could not deliver. The most astounding public policy lesson I have ever learned. The leadership went back and couldn't control their own people."[20] While the incident displayed the Ninety-fourth Congress's intractability, it also illustrated "the forces that were at bay in the Congress, these great regional differences" over energy, recalled Charles Curtis. Individual leaders could not negotiate deals on energy; "you had to have much broader involvement of the parties to succeed," Curtis said. Despite the disappointment, Ford honored his commitment to the two congressional leaders by signing an extension of the EPAA on September 29, restoring price controls until November 15 and making the restoration retroactive to September 1.[21]

While Ford wanted to give Congress time to work on phased decontrol, the extension was the liminal point. Nessen said that after November 15, Ford would take a harder line against Congress, telling reporters, "The President wants you to know that this is the last extension."[22] Another extension would continue controls into an election year, when getting Congress to remove them would be impossible.

Ford kept his word by extending the EPAA, but the wisest course would have been to let the disastrous act expire. By August, one survey showed that a majority of Americans supported decontrol, and the *Wall Street Journal*, arguing that Ford had tried too hard to compromise with Congress on a control phaseout, urged him simply to let controls end.[23] But Democrats predicted doomsday scenarios if that were to happen. Congressman John Dingell of Michigan, chair of the Subcommittee on Energy and Power, warned of "an unconscionable price in the game of economic brinksmanship" if controls on old oil expired. Accusing the Ford administration of "flirting with possible economic disaster," he predicted substantial increases in both unemployment and inflation and an end to the economic recovery if controls lapsed. Although many observers took these gloom-and-doom forecasts seriously, as crude oil was decontrolled in the late 1970s and early 1980s, they proved inaccurate. (Even Dingell later rued his dire predictions and regretted supporting controls.) Decontrol proved a boon to the economy, yet in the mid-1970s most members of Congress believed the contrary. This thought governed lawmakers' actions as they finally tried to iron out an energy bill.[24]

After the House and Senate passed energy bills in September, conferees from the two houses met to reconcile the versions and send a bill to the president before the November 15 deadline. On November 12, after a month of work, congressional conferees finally agreed on a comprehensive bill. The Energy Policy and Conservation Act (EPCA) represented the first attempt in American history to legislate a national energy policy. But the bill took an entirely different tack toward oil than Ford wanted. It called for a rollback of oil prices to take effect on February 1—initially, more controls, not fewer—followed by phased decontrol. All domestic oil would be under controls. Old oil would be kept at $5.25 a barrel, while new oil would be rolled back from the world market price of $12.50 a barrel to $11.28 a barrel. Over forty months, oil prices would be allowed to rise gradually (but without exceeding 10 percent per year), and controls would expire when the period ended, in May 1979. Observers cynically noted that the bill kept prices down until well after the 1976 election. Yet the bill granted the president some significant powers. If he recommended so, these increases could exceed 10 percent. Moreover, after EPCA was in effect for one year, the president could adjust the 10 percent increase limitation upward, subject to disapproval by either house.[25] The new price controls would force down the average price of domestic crude oil by $1 per barrel, cutting gasoline prices $.01 per gallon. (Gasoline prices in late 1975 were around $.60 a gallon.)[26]

The bill also had provisions to induce energy conservation. To be eligible for federal grants, states had to submit plans to the FEA for reducing energy consumption. At a minimum, a state's plan had to include some sensible and needed guidelines: (1) limitations on public buildings' lighting and thermal efficiency standards for new or renovated federal buildings; (2) promotion of car pools and public transportation; and (3) right-on-red laws.[27]

The bill included several measures that Ford had requested in January, or at least derivatives of them. One of the most important (and universally popular in a fractious Congress) was to establish within three years a strategic petroleum reserve of up to 150 million barrels of oil, and ultimately one billion barrels. Another was an extension of his authority to convert the power sources of electrical plants from oil and natural gas to coal. The bill contained Ford's proposal to label home appliances with their energy efficiency and set mandatory fuel economy standards for new cars and small trucks after the 1977 model year, with cash penalties for carmakers who failed to comply.

(These standards were an 18-miles-per-gallon average fuel economy for the 1978 model year, with gradual increases leading up to a 27.5-miles-per-gallon average in 1985, more than 50 percent over the current average.)[28]

The rollback provision disappointed Ford. The bill also failed to include many of his original tax proposals (such as a $150 tax credit for homeowners for installing insulation; an excise tax of $2 barrel on domestic crude production as well as a $2 import fee; and an excise tax of $.37 per thousand cubic feet on natural gas). The bill omitted several other Ford initiatives: natural gas deregulation, amendments to the Clean Air Act, and oil production from the Naval Petroleum Reserves (NPR). While the bill called for appliance labeling, it wanted government efficiency standards, which would affect the design of televisions, washing machines, dishwashers, refrigerators, and other major electrical appliances by requiring them to use 20 percent less energy by 1980. The administration worried that the standards might prove burdensome and costly for home appliance makers. It also considered the auto efficiency standards, although a good principle, unreasonably high. Automakers protested that they would need a major technological breakthrough to meet the new rules, and they might be forced to produce lighter cars, which could compromise passenger safety and which American drivers found unappealing anyway.[29] But after Congress passed the bill, it was up to Ford.

When Politics and Economics Collide

As so often during the 1970s, the demon looming large was inflation. Many Democrats in Congress genuinely believed that controlling oil prices would fight inflation and cushion consumers against OPEC price increases.[30] EPCA tilted toward consumers' short-term comfort. The continuation of controls on old oil and the rollback of new oil prices would keep domestic oil prices artificially low, and consumers would feel no compulsion to conserve. With domestic producers deprived of price incentives and demand for oil artificially less responsive to OPEC price hikes, America's vulnerability to imports might increase. And with more American money spent on imports came all the concomitant detrimental effects: a greater trade imbalance, loss of jobs, and compromised national security. In an eight-page letter excoriating the bill and urging the president to veto it, William Simon conceded that decontrol would increase unemployment and inflation but stressed that "on balance the short-run adverse economic effects of immediate decontrol are less of a danger to the nation than the long-term economic and national security risks inherent in the increased imports of petroleum from insecure sources."[31]

Even though he urged Ford to sign the bill, Zarb conceded that it would mean "a major reduction in incentives for investment in new, high-cost oil production." Estimates were that the bill would cost the petroleum industry $3 billion in revenue during its first year alone.[32] Alan Greenspan warned Ford that continued control of the oil industry would hinder deregulation of natural gas and encourage controls over the coal industry — "regulation begets regulation," as industry insiders warned. In the end, Greenspan told him that "total control of energy will be difficult to avoid."[33] Oil producers had special reasons to worry. Because oil prices were subject to political maneuvering, after forty months decontrol might again be postponed. By keeping domestic oil prices artificially low, EPCA would create a gap between these prices and world oil prices that could grow even wider at the end of forty months. With so large a chasm, Congress might decide to extend price controls. Zarb warned the president that even if he were to veto the bill, Congress might repeatedly try to legislate price rollbacks.[34] All the while, they could argue that they protected consumers while the president favored higher prices.

Many Republicans opposed EPCA. The danger of alienating his party supporters worried Ford. Senator Lowell Weicker of Connecticut called possible White House support of it "just plain screwy." Barber Conable urged Ford to veto the bill, explaining, "It is one thing to be reasonable and to try to achieve a compromise, and another to appear to capitulate."[35] Ford also learned that many Republican state governors thought that he should veto the bill, and Glenn Schleede reported that the mail count on the bill ran 10,381 advocating a veto, just 70 for signing.[36]

The upcoming presidential primaries raised the stakes. Ronald Reagan spoke against the bill, and the possibility of a powerful senator like Texas's John Tower declaring for Reagan worried the Ford White House. The Independent Petroleum Association of America, an organization representing small oil producers, considered the bill so anti-industry that it threatened that each of its members would give $1,000 to the Reagan campaign if Ford signed it. Indeed, the bill could be lethal to Ford's prospects in primaries in oil states.[37]

Yet the political consequences of a veto could be just as damaging. Oil prices would rise in New Hampshire and Massachusetts, sites of early primaries. With higher gas and heating oil prices during winter, voters could take out their frustrations on Ford at the polls. Even if he won the nomination, Democrats could blame Ford for leaving America without an energy policy and stalk him on the issue throughout the campaign. Forging an energy bill had involved "a huge amount of time," long hours since January, and had been a demanding process, John Hill recalled, and if Ford vetoed the bill, "it would have looked like [Ford] had gotten nothing for his first year in office, and that wouldn't have looked good going into his election."[38]

Shifting political currents produced fortuitous changes. As the weeks went by, it appeared that signing the bill might alienate fewer Republicans than the White House had feared. During the second week of December, Zarb reported to the president that even though Tower remained disenchanted, "his rhetoric has substantially subsided." Zarb wrote that the Texas senator was "going to fight for a veto, but I don't think his fight is as highly pitched as previously." Congressman Clarence Brown of Ohio, the president's point man for energy policy in the House, reversed his position and favored the bill. Zarb thought that Brown had "come a long way in understanding why signature could be in the best interest of the country, as well as industry." Perhaps members of Congress, like the public, were tiring of the pitched battle over energy.[39] Hill told Zarb, "[EPCA] will not only build a firm relationship between the Administration and the Congress on the energy issue, but it will also end the confrontation of the last 9 months with which the public has tired."[40] "This war with Congress was tense, and it was hot, it was nasty," Hill recalled. "Zarb really believed we had to end this fight. It was not healthy. And I think Ford, being a [former] member of Congress, really appreciated that argument."[41]

Ford worried about the damage a veto might do to national perceptions of his presidency. He could not view EPCA in isolation. Two other important bills sat on his desk, the Revenue Adjustment Act and the common situs picketing bill, which proposed to give labor unions more power to shut down construction projects during strikes. Republican conservatives wanted Ford to veto all three. But such sweeping negative action would have had serious ramifications. Hartmann told him that if he vetoed all three, "it will be said that you lack the ability to move the country forward and contribute to the Reagan and Democratic theme that yours is merely a caretaker Presidency." Although Hartmann disliked the energy bill, he recommended that if Ford vetoed the common situs picketing bill, "hold your nose and proclaim you have finally persuaded Congress to adopt an imperfect national energy program which can be further perfected next year."[42]

In fact, some of Ford's trusted advisers recommended that he sign EPCA.[43] Zarb's word mattered the most. After months of stalemate, he was convinced that the bill was the best Congress could produce, even though he later admitted, "My own view was that, on balance, it was flawed."[44] Ford respected Zarb's work and acknowledged that "his influence was significant" in deciding whether to sign the bill.[45] Zarb recalled that he said to the president, "If you sign it, we've got enough tools to work with to get you re-elected, and we can still get our objectives done, and there was enough in [EPCA] to do it with. If you don't sign it, we have immediate chaos in the country. And we're getting ready for the primary in New Hampshire, who knows what's going to happen." Moreover, as Zarb remembered, both of Ford's chief legislative aides told the president "that it was reasonably likely that he was going to have his veto overturned . . . and we'd be back to square one."[46]

Rumors were afoot in the press that a veto would force Zarb's resignation. Zarb publicly denied the reports, insisting that he would stay regardless.[47] He recalled that the rumors about his resignation started to fly because Secretary of Labor John Dunlop vowed to resign if Ford vetoed the common situs picketing bill. The media erroneously inferred that Dunlop's situation also applied to Zarb. While Zarb was determined to stay, a veto would have undermined his influence.

William Seidman commented that the Ford energy team had come a long way in the face of difficult odds. Hill told Zarb that if Ford approved the bill, "we will have achieved 60–70% of a national energy program—not a bad record for the Administration or for a Congress as deeply divided as this one." The bill contained several items that Ford had originally asked for, and Bruce Pasternack recalled, "We had a lot of stuff in [EPCA], and some of it we fought really hard to get through, and really wanted—and it was all going to get thrown aside" if Ford vetoed it. "There was more good than bad in there," Pasternack believed.[48]

Ultimately, Ford felt that "half a loaf was better than none." He was not going to get the decontrol, but by late 1975, he had weaned himself so far away from the goal of total decontrol that he viewed it as "not the best alternative."[49] With an election year approaching, immediate decontrol and the ensuing rise in fuel prices would be a political liability. In hindsight, most economists now believe that immediate deregulation would have caused only a marginal rise in oil prices. "But that wasn't the conventional wisdom at the time," John Hill recalled. "I think the thing that drove most of the policy makers, ultimately, towards signing this bill was fear of inflation, or what . . . immediate deregulation might do to inflation."[50]

EPCA could be a building block for better policy. As Seidman advised, "It sets a national energy policy that, while delayed, is a sound step in the right direction."[51] Some administration members were concerned that Congress would take umbrage at a veto; next time, the delay might be even longer, and legislators might legislate more controls. Zarb used impassioned oratory, describing "mad dogs loose" on Capitol Hill who would respond to a veto with even more damaging price controls.[52]

On December 22, 1975, Ford signed EPCA. He also announced that he was rescinding the $2 import fee on crude oil. (On the same day, Ford vetoed the common situs picketing bill; as a result, Secretary of Labor Dunlop resigned.) Ford cited three primary reasons for approving EPCA. First, it would allow the United States to achieve some of the goals contained in his State of the Union address. Second, it provided for gradual decontrol. Finally, he said, "I am also persuaded that this legislation represents the most constructive bill we are likely to work out at this time. If I were to veto this bill, the debates of the past year would almost surely continue throughout the election year and beyond. The temptation to politicize the debate would be powerful, and the Nation could become further divided."[53]

Ford later recounted weighing the bill's pros and cons, indicating how much Zarb's position influenced him. The decision to approve EPCA "was a very close call. I signed it primarily after listening to the arguments of Frank Zarb. . . . Zarb convinced me that we had a timetable for decontrol [in the bill], we ought to accept it; there was no way we could get decontrol [immediately]. So I thought it was the best package we could get."[54]

The administration member most chagrined was Simon. Calling EPCA "the worst error of the Ford Administration," he asserted that Ford wanted "a quick political fix just before the New Hampshire and Florida primaries" and for this reason had "caved in." Simon's construction of events emphasized election considerations: "'We'd better sign this [bill] or we'll lose the New Hampshire primary,' argued the political 'realists' at the White House. So principled were these advisers that I am convinced, if Texas had been the nation's first primary, these men would have been urging a veto."[55]

Ford downplayed the role of the imminent primaries in his decision to sign EPCA. But EPCA fueled conservative discontent. Reagan lambasted Ford for it, and in May Ford lost the Texas primary; Reagan drubbed him in all congressional districts there and walked away with all of the state's convention delegates. Ford conceded that EPCA hurt him there but believed that he would have lost the state anyway.[56] Besides, political considerations tended to cancel each other out. Vetoing the bill could have hurt Ford as much as signing it, because he would have had no energy policy to show for his efforts. As Zarb said, if Ford were inflexible, he would have found himself "back to where we started—with nothing."[57] As politically courageous as his veto strategy was, it did not strike a responsive chord among voters, who were more inspired by new legislation and action that seemed positive in nature and many of whom thought that controls actually benefited them.

The Oval Office is the spot where economic and political imperatives often collide. EPCA ran contrary to Ford's free-market instincts and threatened to hurt oil exploration and production. Critics of Zarb within the administration found his warnings of "mad dogs loose" exaggerated, and his prediction of "immediate chaos" overstated the impact of a veto.[58] Advisers frequently embroider their arguments to win over the president, who ultimately has to be sensitive to political arguments. Politicians, not economists, draft legislation (although the economy might benefit more if the latter did), and Ford worried that a veto would fail to stimulate Congress to draft an improved bill. Charles Curtis believed that a new bill in 1976 "wouldn't have been that much different."[59] In the mid-1970s, decontrol of crude oil, although economically sensible, was politically impossible.

In retrospect, of course, after decontrol in the early 1980s stimulated impressive crude oil production, observers recognized that from an economic standpoint, Ford would have been better off rejecting EPCA and continuing his fight for complete decontrol. Indeed, one economist later concluded that the EPAA and EPCA restricted domestic crude oil output by as much as 1.4 million barrels a day.[60] Hill commented that "knowing now what we know, it would have been better . . . to veto it and let the controls [lapse]. We would have had short-term hysteria, both in prices and [gas station] lines. It would have been gone in a few months."[61] Ford felt the same way, although he worried more about the staunch opposition on Capitol Hill. If not for that, he would have implemented decontrol at once, and the nation would have avoided the energy pinch of the late 1970s. "If I could [have acted] unilaterally, on my own, I probably would have decontrolled period, immediately," Ford reflected. "There would have been a little turmoil for a short period of time. But we would have opened the markets and the markets would have corrected things rather quickly. But that was not the real world. The real world was that I had to deal with the Congress." If he had acted unilaterally, Ford speculated, lawmakers "probably would have rammed through something that, if I had vetoed [it], I probably would have been overridden."[62]

Signing a bill like EPCA, which was "half-good and half-bad" and only "marginally signable," as Ford said, was one of his more difficult presidential decisions. But compared to other 1970s energy acts—especially ill-advised price controls and allocation—EPCA was "probably the most successful and longest-lasting of the initiatives that actually came along," said Robert Nordhaus.[63] Decades later, many of its provisions—the strategic petroleum reserve, corporate average fuel economy (CAFE) standards, appliance labeling, and conservation measures such as right-on-red—constitute the backbone of what little national energy policy the country has.

Ford's energy proposals illustrated the problems of trying to lead Congress on a divisive issue. Democratic congressman Jim Wright of Texas, chair of the House Task Force on Energy, scolded his colleagues for their sluggishness and partisanship. "Too often the Congress has been simply unwilling to make the hard decisions and take the difficult steps necessary to achieve energy self-sufficiency for the United States," he fumed. "Too frequently the majority of our Members has appeared so preoccupied with the next election as to forget about the next generation. We have frittered away much of the year in quibbling and petty bickering about little things." Ford shared Wright's exasperation. At an August 1975 press conference, just after Congress rejected his two phased decontrol proposals, Ford was asked, "What is the toughest thing that you are doing in Washington?" He immediately mentioned getting Congress "to pass an energy program—either my program or one of their own."[64]

In this respect, EPCA cleared the air. It allowed Ford to continue detoxifying Washington's post-Watergate political environment, especially on a contentious issue. "Signing the bill took so much heat out of the partisan debate," Hill recalled, "and that enabled Ford to calm Washington down for the first time since Nixon had left." (Hill was so exhausted and dispirited by the bitter struggles over energy policy that he decided to leave government service in 1976.)[65] Here Ford's political moderation aided the healing process, at least until he earned his own mandate at the polls, as he hoped to do in 1976.

Decontrol gave legislators political indigestion. Zarb reflected that it was too much for Congress; he believed that a better strategy would have been to propose gradual decontrol in the State of the Union message: "If I had to do it over again, knowing everything I know, I think I would have backed off sooner and gone incremental," Zarb mused. "That would have had a better chance of getting [the program] in place from the start." But in planning the program, Ford and his advisers believed that gradual decontrol would have set their sights too low and immediately allow Congress an opportunity to water down the president's proposals by expanding the time frame for gradual decontrol.[66]

EPCA was the bitter fruit of months of debate. Congressional leaders proved "a major frustration," Ford reflected, "and so in order to get something that was a step forward, I accepted a cutback or reduction [in my energy program] simply because that was the best we could get."[67] Conservatives wanted Ford to take a harder line. Realistically, Ford expected a compromise. By 1975, oil prices had stabilized, and Americans felt complacent. Zarb sensed that "by and large, the people lost the need to drive down oil imports after the embargo ended. The sense of urgency started to dissipate. . . . They understood the issue, they understood getting the Arabs under better control. But when it got down to the nutcrack, forcing their congressmen to act to raise the price of gasoline, the will wasn't there."[68]

As the sense of a crisis waned and an election year approached, political considerations palsied Congress against unpopular actions. As with the Revenue Adjustment Act, Ford believed that EPCA could serve as a foundation for more constructive energy policy during a full term. Zarb said that a major rationale for signing the bill was their expectation that Ford would win the election, and "we go back next year and get improvements. . . . Every time we did that, the Congress budged, because they never had an idea of their own."[69]

Energy in 1976

In early 1976, Paul Gerald Jr., a Social Security Administration worker from Detroit, bought a monstrous, twenty-two-foot-long motor home. It got just seven miles to the gallon, but that mattered little to him. "To tell you the truth we didn't think too much about mileage," Gerald admitted.[70]

Gerald's attitude typified that of many Americans in 1976. In their minds, the energy crisis was over. They started buying large, luxurious cars again and paid less attention to fuel economy. Enthusiasm for carpooling waned, and state troopers reported that more motorists were ignoring the fifty-five-miles-per-hour speed limit. During the bicentennial summer, tourists took to the roads for vacations, and predicted fuel shortages never materialized. In 1976, oil drilling hit a fourteen-year high; while domestic production continued to slide, the rate of decline decreased. There was a world glut of oil, and as a result, fuel prices leveled off. While gasoline had peaked at $.60-a-gallon the year before, in 1976 it sometimes dipped below $.40. Independent service stations, which had been starving for oil a few years earlier, came back so strong that some owners of major-brand stations worried that they would be forced out of business. In early 1976, Republican congressman Charles Grassley of Iowa reported, "Talk about energy has pretty much faded away. There is even an occasional gas war." Americans reverted to their old lifestyles and seemed indifferent to the concept of energy vulnerability.[71]

Despite public apathy and the distraction of an election year, the Ford administration continued to focus on energy issues, fighting for decontrol and pieces of his State of the Union proposals. As was true throughout his presidency, Ford blocked bad legislation, especially costly federal energy schemes. In September 1976, he vetoed the Electric and Hybrid Vehicle Research Development and Demonstration Act of 1976. The bill proposed $160 million for developing electric automobiles and required the federal government to purchase 7,500 of the new vehicles. Ford felt that electric battery technology was too primitive to justify such expenditures and wanted the private sector to take the initiative.[72] One problem with government-funded research into new technologies was that Washington "throws millions and millions of dollar at R&D projects that never find their way into the private, competitive economy," Glenn Schleede said. "What tends to happen is the government funds a second-class project; the stuff that is more likely to work is developed in the private sector."[73] Although Congress overrode Ford's veto, he persisted, just two weeks later vetoing a $100 million bill to develop alternatives to the internal combustion engine.[74] This time Congress sustained his veto, and the wisdom of Ford's action became clearer over time, as electric cars never proved technologically or economically viable (except as gasoline-electric hybrids, which appeared almost thirty years later), and alternative engines remain to emerge.

One of the most spectacular controversies over government funding of new energy technologies erupted on September 22, 1975—only it was Ford, ironically, who supported the venture. He announced an initiative called the Energy Independence Authority (EIA), a brainchild of Nelson Rockefeller's Domestic Council. Ford once wrote of Rockefeller that "nothing was too grandiose for him to propose," and the vice president thought big on energy, too. Rockefeller wanted something big and dramatic, recalling that one American told him, "If the United States had responded to the attack on Pearl Harbor the way we have responded to the energy crisis, we would all be speaking Japanese in the United States today."[75]

The EIA was meant to be a federal emergency response to the crisis. The proposed agency would offer up to $100 million in federal loans and loan guarantees to companies that would develop energy sources, especially those companies using new technologies. It would also build energy facilities that would be sold or leased to private industry. The premise was that to ensure America's "energy independence" within the next decade, massive amounts of private investment would be needed, and the EIA would act as a catalyst to spur investment needing government help. Rockefeller thought that America had all the resources it needed to be energy independent, but government needed to give private firms some incentives and encouragement to take high-risk energy ventures. Ford described the EIA as the 1970s equivalent of the Manhattan Project or the Apollo space program. In name as well as in function, the EIA was meant to invoke memories of the Tennessee Valley Authority, the successful New Deal program that revitalized a region by building dams that furnished hydroelectric power and reduced flooding.

Designed to be a crossbreed of a federal concern and a private corporation, the EIA was frequently described as a "quasi-public corporation." On the one hand, it would obtain funding from the Treasury Department and be run by a five-person board of directors, appointed by the president and approved by the Senate. Yet its operations would not be included in the federal budget; it was to be autonomous, exempt from annual congressional review and taxes, and would fold after ten years.[76]

But the EIA contradicted Ford's emphasis on decreased government, and almost all administration members opposed the scheme. "We all hated the idea," Hill recalled. "I remember [Rockefeller] couldn't get anybody to do the staff work on it"; the vice president had to hire an economist from New York to build the case for the proposal.[77] Despite the internal opposition, Zarb remembered that Rockefeller remained "very fierce" in promoting it. "When Nelson wanted something, he really wanted it," Zarb recalled. At one point, while quarreling with Zarb, the vice president telephoned Ford and requested a meeting. Ford, who was running a high fever, agreed, and the two men went to the White House residence and argued their respective views before the president as he lay in bed, too ill to get up (the only workday of his presidency that he failed to arrive at the Oval Office). Rockefeller plugged for the EIA; Zarb protested that the spending would be astronomical and the choice of projects arbitrary, and he maintained that the private sector—not government—should undertake energy research and development. But Ford decided to support the EIA, partly to keep the nation focused on energy issues but also because, as he admitted, "I wanted to show my loyalty and sympathy to the vice president." Paul MacAvoy said, "It was [Ford] being courteous again" to a member of his administration.[78]

But the EIA got nowhere. It was riddled with contradictions, and the very concept of "energy independence" was flawed. (Rockefeller believed that America could achieve energy independence by the end of the century.)[79] Whereas the vice president claimed that the EIA would eventually make a profit for the government, an OMB study showed that it would actually lose money. MacAvoy recalled, "The rationalists (i.e., economists) worked together to constrain the V.P.'s exuberance for ideas without analysis."[80] Greenspan and Simon especially believed that the EIA would violate principles of free-market enterprise and allow the government to intrude deeply in the field of energy. The potential for fraud and misappropriation of federal money was great, especially since the organization would be exempt from taxation and the normal review process. Zarb later said, "To have the government give out those grants was a recipe for scandal."[81]

Then there was the concern, as Schleede said, that "almost by definition, the kind of stuff that is brought to the government for subsidies is second-class stuff," while the private sector worked on more promising, cutting-edge technologies.[82] Many emerging energy sources that the EIA might have supported—solar, geothermal, and synthetic fuels—were new and untested.

Administration critics said that the EIA's potential waste would be as deleterious as another oil embargo and used the term "self-embargo" to describe Rockefeller's scheme.[83] (James Lynn even symbolically bet the vice president one dollar that the stock market would decline on the day that Ford unveiled the EIA. It did—whether because of the announcement or other factors—and a week later Rockefeller appeared at Lynn's office and surrendered a dollar bill.)[84]

Congress was also unenthusiastic. Zarb recalled that the EIA "was dead on arrival on the Hill. It had no real support from anybody inside the government." Ultimately, Ford conceded, "with the opposition that developed not only within the White House staff but in Congress, it was obvious that the program was not going to materialize." Ford knew it would not. His understanding of Capitol Hill allowed him to support the program as a gesture of courtesy to his vice president while feeling safe that Congress would never pass it. When Ford called John Hill to inform him that he would support the EIA, he said, "I know you're upset," but he added that "this thing's never going to fly" in Congress. Hill protested that he might have to testify before Congress to support the proposal, and Ford replied cheerfully but sympathetically, "Well, do your best."[85] The entire EIA fiasco reflected the uncomfortable position that Rockefeller had in the administration, as exponents of more doctrinaire conservatism looked askance at many of his ideas. The episode further diminished his influence in the administration. It also showed how attitudes toward large-scale government projects had changed by the 1970s. In arguing for the idea, Rockefeller mentioned examples of successful collaboration between the government and the private sector, including federal land grants that helped railroads open the western frontier in the late 1800s. But during troubled economic times, even a Democratic Congress no longer wanted to entertain projects involving federal initiatives of such scale.[86]

But other federal measures in energy encountered a warmer reception than the EIA. Work began on EPCA's strategic petroleum reserve, which many observers embraced as a much-needed safeguard against another oil embargo. In Texas and Louisiana, huge underground salt formations were hollowed out to form massive caverns, where the government prepared to store millions of barrels' worth of crude oil, which it would draw out during a future oil emergency. One of EPCA's most popular provisions became right-on-red, although initially some officials did not like it. New York City's traffic commissioner called the new law "asinine," and the city eventually decided to forbid it. But the law proved a tremendous convenience to motorists without endangering pedestrians.[87]

EPCA contained five of Ford's original State of the Union energy proposals, and in April 1976 a sixth proposal became law when Ford approved the Naval Petroleum Reserves Production Act. Early in the twentieth century, the federal government had established the NPR as an emergency source of oil for use during war. The strategic petroleum reserve made the NPR obsolete, as the government could draw oil more quickly from the former. The new law authorized increased oil production from the NPR located in Elks Hill, California (one of the richest oil fields remaining in the continental United States, containing more than one billion barrels of known reserves and capable of producing 250,000 barrels a day), and one in Teapot Dome, Wyoming (promising 20,000 barrels daily), and transferred another NPR in Alaska from the navy to the Department of Interior, which would explore and develop it.[88] Capitol Hill was enthusiastic about the measure (the House vote was 390–5), and many in Congress echoed the praise of Republican representative Joe Skutitz of Kansas, who called it the first congressional step "to directly increase the supply of domestic crude oil."[89]

The Ford administration took other steps to increase oil supplies. Because the lack of deepwater ports proved a liability in an era of supertankers, Secretary of Transportation William Coleman approved licenses for two deepwater ports that would together handle 7.4 million barrels of oil a day. Deepwater ports, situated away from America's coastline, allowed supertankers to dock far from inshore harbors, preventing environmental hazards and expensive dredging to create deep harbor ports, instead delivering oil through underwater pipelines to shore.[90]

In August 1976, Ford signed the Energy Conservation and Production Act (ECPA), which extended the life of the FEA until December 31, 1977 (the FEA folded that year when Carter established a cabinet-level Department of Energy) and, more important, provided measures for both energy production and conservation. ECPA freed "stripper" wells, which produced fewer than 10 barrels per day, from price controls. Their low output made many oil producers view stripper wells as too unprofitable to operate; decontrol gave incentive to keep them running. That was important: Stripper wells accounted for 12 percent of domestic oil production, and the administration estimated that decontrol would increase their oil production by 450,000 barrels a day within three years, while costing consumers less than a penny a gallon more for gasoline. Moreover, because thousands of stripper wells were in existence—some just producing a barrel a day—regulating them was a nightmare. "There's not enough people in the world to do that," Hill commented. (Even with the new dialogue on decontrol, Congress was slow. The bill was stalled for almost two months in a House-Senate conference committee, with legislators balking at the possibility of price increases.)[91] ECPA also allowed a 10 percent increase in the average price of domestic crude (under the terms of EPCA) and included two conservation measures that Ford had proposed in his January 1975 State of the Union program. It authorized HUD to develop mandatory energy performance standards for new residential and commercial buildings and established a $200 million, three-year program to give federal grants to states that supported free installation of storm windows and insulation in the homes of low-income and elderly residents. Congress also added conservation programs to the bill, which chagrined the Ford administration because of bureaucratic growth; for example, the federal government would guarantee $2 billion in loans to hospitals, universities, city governments, and small businesses for conservation measures. But what was most important to Ford was that the bill continued his drive toward decontrol. Moreover, with ECPA containing additional proposals from Ford's original energy program, he had gotten Congress to accept seven of the thirteen components of his original program.[92]

That was a notable achievement. Even though Zarb conceded that in 1976, "we made really little progress because it was an election year, and [energy] became a political issue," one of the administration's greatest energy accomplishments came in 1976, quietly and with little fanfare. "I continued to try to get prices deregulated," Zarb said. "That was our main effort."[93] His principal focus was on a regulatory bugbear that remained from the Nixon era: price controls and allocations on individual fuels.

EPCA contained a provision that allowed the administration to free finished petroleum products (such as various fuels) from price and allocation controls. If the administration proposed decontrol of the products, Congress could block the move within fifteen days with a one-house majority vote. Otherwise, decontrol would proceed. While price controls remained on crude oil, with petroleum products decontrolled, dealers could secure lower prices on products from suppliers, and retailers would have more latitude to lower prices to consumers.[94]

Once again, the Ford administration took the initiative on energy and caught Congress flat-footed. Throughout 1976, it submitted proposals to remove price controls and allocations from products, awaited Congress's approval, and then proceeded with decontrol. Having presented Ford with EPCA in late 1975, members of Congress "thought they put energy behind them, and all of a sudden we were consuming their time on these deregulation issues," Hill recalled.[95] In February, the FEA proposed to exempt residual fuel oil (a critical energy source along the East Coast, residuals were the heavy, least refined products of crude oil and were used to heat large buildings, apartments, industries, and utilities) from controls and allocation; on June 1, residual fuel was freed from controls. In July, the FEA ended price controls on the distillate oils, which included kerosene and home heating and diesel fuels (all chemically similar). Finally, in September, the administration lifted controls on a host of specialty oils (including naptha, benzene, lubricants, greases, and so-called carbon black feedstocks, which were used to make tires and plastics).[96]

The piecemeal decontrol of finished petroleum products was one of the underrated achievements of Ford's presidency. It "helped get rid of a lot of the regulatory mess," Hill commented.[97] The feat was all the more remarkable because it took place during an election year. Ultimately, the administration decontrolled about 50 percent of the products refined from a barrel of crude oil.[98] (What remained under control were gasoline, commercial jet fuel, and natural gas liquids, including propane and butane.) By proposing decontrol of crude oil—almost heretical to Congress—more than a year earlier, Ford began a process that gradually wiped away the price controls and allocations that had both caused and exacerbated the energy crisis. Zarb noted in 1976 that the "working environment on energy has changed. A year ago, if the President sent me up to the Hill to talk about deregulating the price of home heating oil, I would have been tarred and feathered."[99] Decontrol was no longer unthinkable.

A final petroleum product—the most visible and important—remained to be decontrolled. On his last day in office, Ford proposed that controls and allocations be lifted on gasoline. The move was to take effect on March 1, 1977, and would have helped to relegate long gas station queues to the past. But five days after taking office, Jimmy Carter rescinded Ford's order.[100] Allocations and price controls on gasoline remained. Two years later, when revolution in Iran disrupted oil supplies from that nation, American motorists again waited in line for gasoline.

Alternative Fuels

A founding member of OPEC once called petroleum "the devil's excrement." During the 1970s, many Americans probably used even stronger epithets. Hoping to reduce national dependence on this black bile, Ford looked at alternative fuels. Natural gas was the number two fuel in America and offered much promise. Companies found exploring for gas easier than for oil, and the United States supplied almost all of its own gas, importing only a small amount from Canada. Gas furnished a third of the nation's energy, heating half its homes and powering many industrial processes; it was also clean and cheap.[101]

But, like oil, natural gas was controlled; its prices were capped at levels that were comparatively even lower than those of oil. Prices had been controlled since 1954, when the Supreme Court gave the Federal Power Commission (FPC) authority to set natural gas prices in interstate commerce. Throughout the 1960s, gas producers fought the controls, complaining that the FPC pegged rates that were far too low to make them produce more natural gas. The FPC capped the price of interstate "new" gas (produced after January 1973) at $.52 per thousand cubic feet (Mcf)—an extraordinarily low price—while the price of intrastate gas was free to rise, hitting up to $2 per Mcf in some states. (The FPC capped "old" gas, produced before January 1973, even lower, at just 29.5¢ per Mcf—the equivalent of pricing a barrel of oil at less than $1.)[102] As a result, Robert Nordhaus explained, natural gas producers "preferred to sell their gas into the unregulated intrastate market, which was Texas, Louisiana, Oklahoma, and some other producing states. And the result was that the interstate pipelines, which supplied the big consuming markets in the West Coast, the Midwest, and the East Coast, were unable to meet their supply commitments."[103] Gulf Coast states suffered no shortage of natural gas, which was produced and used within the same state, without price controls. But delivering natural gas across state lines posed a problem, and states dependent on interstate transportation of gas suffered shortages. The controlled price discouraged producers from searching for new sources and encouraged consumer waste. By 1973, after slowing down for five years, natural gas production peaked and began to decline. As with oil, prophets of shortage issued warnings. Value Line, a leading business publisher, warned, "At current rates of consumption and discovery, the nation could run out of gas in less than 25 years."[104] (Unlike oil, natural gas could not be physically allocated because of pressure and delivery complications.)

Nixon urged an end to what he called the "ill-conceived regulation" of natural gas prices, but Congress was reluctant to decontrol natural gas because it feared adverse consumer reactions. Industrialists and farmers supported decontrol, because natural gas shortages had forced them to use more expensive fuels such as propane.[105] But opponents, like the *New York Times*, argued that higher prices would not lead to more gas production but instead "would mean much higher prices for the consumer and fatter profits for the gas industry." Democratic congressman John Moss of California charged that the gas industry deliberately lowered production to bolster its argument for deregulation, while actor Paul Newman tried to raise $600,000 for a new Energy Action Committee that opposed natural gas deregulation.[106]

In his October 8, 1974, economic program, Ford called for natural gas deregulation, and he repeated this proposal in his 1975 State of the Union program. While the measure was not in EPCA, in his 1976 Economic Message to Congress Ford said that "natural gas deregulation is now the most pressing of the issues on energy before the Congress," and he signaled a firm reluctance to sign any compromise measure.[107]

In October 1975, the Senate voted to approve a bill to deregulate natural gas (abolishing price controls for onshore gas fields immediately and for offshore wells in 1981). In the House, Democratic congressman Robert Krueger of Texas sponsored a decontrol bill that proposed immediate decontrol for new interstate gas and gradual decontrol for old gas. But opposition to natural gas decontrol was particularly severe in the House, and in early February representatives defeated the Krueger bill.[108] In August 1976, the FPC raised natural gas prices. Once again, there was a byzantine system of tiers. The FPC allowed the price of "new" gas to rise from $.52 per Mcf to $1.42. ("New" gas was from discovered after January 1, 1975.) Gas discovered after January 1, 1973, would increase from $.52 per Mcf to $1.01, and gas produced before then, which composed 87 percent of the nation's gas supply, could rise from $.295 per Mcf to $.52. Although this action would have little effect on consumers' gas prices initially, as "new" gas increased its share of the nation's gas supply (it was only 7.5 percent in 1976), they would feel higher prices.[109] The FPC's summer price increase on natural gas vitiated the argument that prices should be deregulated, and for the rest of 1976 Congress was unable to send a natural gas bill to the president's desk.

Ford's hopes for another fuel, nuclear power, also fell short. During the 1970s, nuclear plants supplied 9 percent of the nation's energy needs, equivalent to one million barrels of oil per day. Although Ford supported developing more nuclear plants (his goal was for nuclear to supply 20 percent of the nation's power), a number of obstacles stood in the way, including concerns over location, availability of uranium, and disputes over environmental safety and waste disposal. The controversy over nuclear power prevented any progress during Ford's term.[110]

Ford achieved more with another fuel, coal. He urged the nation to double its coal production by 1985, calling coal "America's ace in the hole" in meeting the energy challenge. Even though the United States had a third of the world's known coal reserves, environmental concerns restricted it to supplying just one-fifth of the country's energy. Coal-fired plants belched thick, black smoke into the air; coal mining damaged the lungs of many workers; and strip mining scarred the earth.[111]

Environmentalists particularly focused on strip mining (also called surface mining), which involved removing massive areas of ground cover to dig out coal beds lying near the earth's surface. In late 1974, Congress approved a bill that forbade coal companies from strip mining if they could not restore the lands; Ford pocket vetoed it while Congress was on Christmas break. In the spring of 1975, Congress passed a similar bill, by a veto-proof margin in the House, 293–115 (21 votes more than the two-thirds needed for a veto override), and by a voice vote in the Senate, where support was overwhelming. The bill proposed to impose federal environmental restrictions on strip mining, introduce measures to restore strip-mined areas, and restrict so-called steep slope strip mining by requiring companies to fill in mountainside areas that were excavated for coal.

Ford again vetoed the strip-mining bill. His strip-mining vetoes received more criticism than perhaps any action other than the Nixon pardon. With an election year approaching, the issue generated intense partisan acrimony. Congressman Morris Udall of Arizona, who was running for the 1976 Democratic nomination, called Ford's veto "a discredit to the Presidency." Udall described strip mining as "raping the landscape" and angrily charged that Ford supported the "greed" and "avarice" of the strip-mining industry. The *New York Times* scored Ford for showing "a remarkable indifference to the harm that such mining inflicts upon the nation's land and water."[112] Yet Ford thought that restricting strip mining represented a grave setback in reducing dependence on foreign oil. Strip mining accounted for half of all the coal mined in the United States, and the method promised to extract billions of tons of coal in midwestern areas and the Rocky Mountain states. The bill, he feared, could reduce coal production by 20 percent and leave 40,000 coal workers unemployed. Moreover, the Ford administration felt that existing state environmental safeguards adequately regulated the industry. "I think that two of the best things that Ford ever did for energy," Hill recalled, "was to veto those [strip-mining] bills. Because we already had enough laws on the books to deal with strip [mining]. It was not that we were saying don't regulate it; we were saying don't shut it down," which was the goal of some environmentalists. Ultimately, the House upheld Ford's veto, failing in an override attempt by three votes.[113]

After using his veto power to settle the controversy over strip mining, Ford promoted coal production with subsequent legislation. EPCA and ECPA provided $750 million in loan guarantees to encourage coal producers to open new mines, and in 1976 coal production increased to a record 670 million tons.[114] In 1976, the FEA also ordered that thirty power plants under construction use coal instead of oil or natural gas and served noticed to forty-eight planned power plants that they, too, would have to burn coal. Ford's efforts to promote coal production and use started a small revolution. By the early 1980s, domestic coal produced more energy than oil; by the end of the century, almost twice as much. The Ford administration began a process that dramatically increased use of America's most abundant energy source, allowing it to overtake oil—for good—within just a few years.[115]

During Ford's term, America's dependence on imported oil grew, and it has continued to grow since the 1970s. But thanks in part to Ford's actions in decontrolling oil from stripper wells as well as residual fuels, by the end of his term domestic oil production, while still declining, did so at a slower rate, which represented a small victory.[116]

Ford's energy proposals also marked the beginning of a vociferous national discussion, and he had the satisfaction of knowing that he had acted as a catalyst. His program's controversial nature got opposing sides talking and wrangling and ultimately involved all three branches of the federal government. In June 1976, the Supreme Court unanimously upheld the legality of Ford's oil import fee, which Congress and the states had protested against vigorously. (The Court's decision overturned the August 1975 ruling by the U.S. Court of Appeals.) Ford had already ended the $2-a-barrel fee that he had imposed, but the high court buttressed the president's power in shaping national energy policy.

Ford kept energy at the forefront of the national policy debate. He was relentless in prodding Congress toward decontrol, forcing legislators to devise their own counterproposals. In mid-1975, Mike Mansfield gave him credit for making lawmakers act. "I am frank to say that it has been your effort that has provided the primary impetus to the energy issue and to the need to develop a comprehensive energy policy for the Nation," the Senate majority leader wrote to Ford. "Because of your effort, much has been done to shape and implement such a policy; more, in fact, in the past 6 months than ever before in the Nation's history."[117] That a Democrat could praise a Republican president in such terms was significant. The energy issue bitterly divided the nation's political parties, yet Ford's fight was intense but civil. Hill commented, "I think that he really thought he was taking as many steps as he could in the direction of his philosophy without creating further antagonism toward the Congress."[118]

Most scholars have viewed Ford's energy policy efforts charitably. Arabinda Ghosh, an expert in oil and energy economics, wrote, "No one can accuse President Ford of not trying. He was a victim of the time when the economy was recovering slowly and Congress was reluctant to stifle that growth." Once again, the stagflationary economy stacked the political odds against Ford. Oil decontrol was an uphill sell because it would have stimulated inflation and choked off the recovery. Ford could not achieve decontrol, but his energy program, as Ron Nessen wrote, "was one of the outstanding—and underrated—accomplishments of his presidency." While Nessen conceded that Ford had not convinced the public of the sacrifices and discomfort needed to wean themselves from foreign oil, "at least he began the public discussion of the hard choices which eventually will have to be faced."[119] Ford had confronted another challenge of the 1970s and pointed the country toward the right solution.

Part Three
Diplomatic and
Political Challenges

Chapter 16

Gerald Ford's Internationalism

On December 18, 1944, in World War II's Pacific theater, a raging typhoon struck the light aircraft carrier USS *Monterey* sailing in the Philippine Sea. Hundred-knot winds battered the ship, and it struggled to stay afloat. At one point during the storm, the *Monterey*'s assistant navigator and athletic director, Lieutenant Gerald Ford, climbed to the flight deck. Just as he set foot there, the ship rolled violently, throwing him on his back. Ford slid across the deck, as if riding down a water chute, all the way to the port side, and he almost fell into the churning seas. Two inches of metal saved his life. His feet struck a two-inch-high steel ridge at the deck's edge, preventing him from plunging overboard and allowing him to clamber safely onto the catwalk below. (The typhoon hurtled planes below deck, rupturing their gas tanks and causing a devastating fire that almost paralyzed the *Monterey*. Ford liked to draw a parallel between the crippled ship and America's condition when he took the helm as president; he even prepared to use the analogy during a 1976 campaign debate with Jimmy Carter.)[1]

Ford's typhoon experience was one of his many frightening brushes with death during the war, but the conflict that almost claimed his life also changed his view of the world. Before the war, the young midwesterner espoused isolationism; in college and at Yale Law School, he wanted the United States to eschew "entangling alliances" abroad.[2] Ford recalled that "my experience in the Navy and World War II really had a big impact on my political thinking." For the rest of his career, Ford said, "Whether I was in Congress, vice president, or president, I was an internationalist in foreign policy."[3]

Ironically, Ford, who emerged from his World War II service convinced that the United States should play an active world role, became president at a time when Americans began once again to question the country's internationalism. Many Americans, traumatized by Vietnam and absorbed by economic woes, preferred to withdraw from the world and concentrate on domestic challenges. In 1975, *U.S. News and World Report* noted, "Looking inward, [Americans] see—and President Ford warns against—a trend toward a new isolationism because of the immensity of domestic problems."[4] One Henry Kissinger aide explained, "This is a time of inflation and recession, which limits your resources for carrying out foreign policy."[5] The world, and America's role in it, differed greatly from earlier postwar decades. By the 1970s, for example, the Marshall Plan of a quarter century earlier would have been unthinkable. That aid program to Western Europe, so successful and indicative of U.S. might, would have strained the 1970s economy. Nor would Americans have stood for it. They were preoccupied by domestic concerns, and while their country still led the world, it no longer dominated it or controlled its events. Many Americans preferred it that way.

Ford wanted to reinvigorate American internationalism, but he felt bound by the same constraints that affected his handling of economic and energy policies. The Ninety-fourth Congress resisted presidential authority and was eager to shape the country's diplomacy itself, and the people were weary of bleak international news and reluctant to rally behind the White House. Their dismay was understandable. Both Vietnam and the energy crisis portended a new era when Third World nations could demoralize or defeat a superpower. Ford faced plenty of obstacles. As Kissinger recalled, "No new President since Harry S Truman inherited quite the same gamut of foreign policy challenges in his first few weeks in office, and none since Lincoln in so uncongenial a domestic environment."[6]

Foreign policy is seldom the forte of members of the House, who are more concerned with the issues of their district, and it had not been Ford's. But for a midwestern representative, he had received an unusually extensive exposure to diplomacy. Foreign policy helped bring him to national attention and, in some ways, even the vice presidency. Advocating containment as a congressman, Ford generally supported Kennedy and Johnson on Vietnam. But after becoming minority leader in 1965, he criticized Johnson's gradual escalation of the war, gaining more national exposure. He opposed the deployment of U.S. ground troops (but favored more air and sea power to aid South Vietnam), and as the conflict grew, Ford charged that Johnson's leadership had "become a runaway locomotive with a wild-eyed engineer at the throttle." But with Nixon in the White House, the minority leader loyally supported the president's wartime leadership, even as congressional criticism increased. Nixon picked Ford as vice president in part to reward him for his unfailing support of the president's Vietnam policy.[7] And were Ford to become president, Nixon trusted him to continue his cherished foreign policy initiatives.

Upon entering the White House, Ford felt that he had more experience in foreign policy than his critics thought. Two decades on the House defense appropriations subcommittee allowed him to hear presidential advisers testify on diplomatic relations. During the Korean War, he traveled overseas to report on the American effort there; he also visited Vietnam, where France struggled to retain its former colony, and grimly noted that the French were losing their war. (During his congressional career, Ford visited nineteen nations.) As minority leader, Ford was privy to foreign policy briefings in the Nixon White House, and observing the president and Kissinger at work furnished valuable diplomatic training, enhanced by his tenure as vice president, when he received more intensive diplomatic and national security briefings.[8]

Yet Ford was not the foreign policy mogul that Nixon was. In truth, his strength was domestic policy, particularly the economy. He invoked no new diplomatic doctrines or grand visions, even as many previous cold war verities collapsed around him. Still, certain themes ran through Ford's foreign policy that reflected his political situation in Washington and the mood of Americans in the 1970s.

Ford and Congress

"Our forefathers," Ford declared during the bicentennial year, "knew you could not have 535 commanders in chief and secretaries of state, it just would not work."[9] The struggle between the White House and Capitol Hill over foreign policy became a theme of Ford's presidency. The two defining events of the early 1970s, the Vietnam War and Watergate, galvanized Congress to challenge executive authority in numerous areas. Foreign policy was a vexing one. Kissinger accused Congress of "micromanagement" and commented on "the irony that the Congress [Ford] genuinely loved and respected had harassed his presidency unmercifully from the beginning and encumbered it with unprecedented restrictions, crippling many aspects of his foreign policy."[10]

One of the first foreign crises on which Ford clashed with Congress came just after he took office: Turkey's invasion of Cyprus. Cyprus was an island in the Mediterranean at a strategically critical site near the Middle East and Eastern Europe. The ethnic composition of Cyprus's 650,000 inhabitants, roughly four Greeks for each Turk, was a combustible mix that embodied the historic antagonism between Greece and Turkey. Archbishop Makarios, a Greek Cypriot priest, was the island's leader, but Greece wanted to remove him to gain full control of Cyprus. On July 15, 1974, the Cyprus National Guard mounted a coup, forcing Makarios to flee the island. Since Greek officers led the coup, Turkey retaliated five days later by invading Cyprus, pouring in 40,000 troops and occupying 40 percent of the island. In August, holding the United States responsible for supporting Turkey, Greek Cypriots raided the American embassy in Cyprus and killed Ambassador Roger Davis. The island quickly became the focus of international attention, but some observers wanted the United States to keep out. *New York Times* columnist William Shannon argued, "Cyprus ought not to be an American responsibility. The crisis there is no direct concern of the American President or the American people." Shannon believed that "the real problems confronting America are here at home." The White House disagreed, especially given the island's geographic importance and the administration's concerns that the Soviet Union would use the crisis to embarrass the North Atlantic Treaty Organization (NATO) and perhaps even gain a foothold in the Mediterranean.[11]

Angered that the United States seemed to favor Turkey, Athens accused the United States of doing nothing to prevent Turkey's invasion. In Washington, Greek Americans protested outside the White House, one carrying a sign that read, "Kissinger is a Turkish lover."[12] On Capitol Hill, members of Congress vowed to punish Turkey. They pointed out that Turkey had used American-made weapons in the invasion, violating the U.S. Foreign Military Sales Act, which specified that they be used for defensive needs. By mid-October, led by a powerful Greek lobby, Congress passed legislation to cut off military aid to Turkey (embodied as an amendment to the Foreign Assistance Act of 1974) to pressure it to withdraw from Cyprus. During a reception, Ford smiled and gently chided Democratic congressman John Brademas of Indiana, who vigorously supported Greece and pushed for the amendment, telling him, "John, you're giving me a very difficult time." Brademas responded, "Mr. President, I'm just trying to help you obey the law." Brademas was so concerned over the violation of the military sales act that he told a reporter that if a president "doesn't enforce the laws, then . . . the only remedy may be impeachment."[13]

The congressional retaliation against Turkey dismayed Ford. Turkey was the NATO alliance's anchor in the east Mediterranean, a critical cold war ally that permitted U-2 flights over its airspace during the 1950s and stationed American missiles on its soil. Turkey had twenty-five American bases and intelligence posts where 7,000 U.S. servicemen were deployed, and those posts near its border with the Soviet Union allowed the United States to monitor Soviet military activities and verify Soviet compliance with arms control treaties. Ford pointed out that to retaliate for the aid cutoff, Turkey might close its American radar and listening installations. It could withdraw from NATO, which would leave the United States without allies in the eastern Mediterranean and permit what the Free World had feared for decades, the entry of "Reds into the Med." (There were even rumors that Turkey might buy arms from or sign a nonaggression pact with the Soviets.) U.S. sanctions against Turkey could also complicate the Cyprus crisis because Turkey might refuse to grant concessions while negotiating with the Greeks.[14]

Congress rejected Ford's remonstrations. After he twice vetoed congressional embargo measures, he agreed to a compromise in which legislators agreed to delay the ban, which finally took effect in February 1975. In July, the House voted against a partial lifting of the embargo, which Ford called "the single most irresponsible, short-sighted foreign policy decision Congress had made in all the years I'd been in Washington."[15] The Turks resented the linkage between the Cyprus crisis and arms shipments, and—as Ford feared— retaliated by shutting down all American military facilities except one. (Congress finally lifted the embargo during the Carter administration.) Republican congressman William Broomfield of Michigan said that some of his colleagues who voted to uphold the embargo regretted their actions, and most editorial comments around the country criticized Congress. Howard K. Smith of ABC News observed, "It seems an odd self-defeating way to run foreign policy in a time when our power is in retreat all over the world and Russia's is on the move that we have a Congressional democracy and Congress has decided." The *Wall Street Journal* believed that "Congress seems intent on proving what a disaster a congressionally-run foreign policy would be," and the *Atlanta Constitution* called the congressional vote "one of the stupidest and most gutless moves in living memory."[16]

In one sense, the Ford administration contained the crisis: both Greece and Turkey remained in NATO, and the Soviet Union stayed out of the Mediterranean. Yet the lessons were clear. Until the 1970s, the Free World enjoyed a remarkable consensus in fighting the cold war. America's allies, frequently scared of the Soviet Union, sought security in close ties with Washington. Turkey and Greece were special beneficiaries of the Truman Doctrine in the late 1940s; the Greeks even erected a statue of Truman in downtown Athens. But by the 1970s, they had become more independent and willing to defy the United States.[17]

These strains showed throughout NATO. A closely knit alliance in the 1950s and 1960s, it was now fraying, with member nations threatening to withdraw and the United States reexamining the value of defending its allies, since Western Europe was strong and wealthy enough to defend itself. At home, the cold war consensus had broken down after Vietnam. In previous decades, the president barely needed persuading to make Capitol Hill acquiesce in his foreign policy initiatives. Now Congress was willing to oppose the president. So great a gulf developed between the president and Congress that in 1975, as Congress debated aid to the foundering South Vietnamese government, Senate majority leader Mike Mansfield stated that the differences "are not so much between the parties as they are differences between the branches" of government.[18]

In late 1974, Congress asserted itself in another foreign policy area, U.S.-Soviet relations, contributing to the decline of détente. The administration wanted to grant the USSR most favored nation (MFN) status as a trading partner and grant benefits such as lower tariffs on vodka and other imports from the Soviet Union—a quid pro quo for the Soviets' finally repaying $722 million in Lend-Lease debts dating back to World War II. In addition to providing the Soviets the psychological satisfaction of becoming more an American equal on the world stage, MFN status would produce mutual economic benefits. MFN status was to be a dividend of détente, and a greater influx of American goods into the Soviet Union could help to incubate democratic thought and policies there. The United States had already bestowed MFN status on two countries behind the iron curtain, Poland and Czechoslovakia, and granting similar status to the Soviet Union represented the next logical step.[19]

Yet Congress attached a condition to granting the Soviets MFN status. The Jackson-Vanik Amendment to the Trade Reform Act of 1972 linked MFN status with Jewish emigration, stipulating that it would come only if the Soviet Union eased restrictions on Jewish emigration. The amendment's Senate sponsor, Henry Jackson, planned to seek the 1976 Democratic nomination and heavily courted the Jewish vote (the House sponsor was Democrat Charles Vanik of Ohio, who had many Jews in his Cleveland district). Jackson, a harsh détente critic also looking for political opportunities, jumped on the issue of Jewish emigration. Over the preceding two years, it had dropped from 34,000 to 20,000, after the Soviets, vexed at the large talent pool leaving their country, began to charge an "exit tax" on Jewish émigrés in 1972. From the Kremlin's perspective, the tax would compensate the Soviet Union for the money it had spent on the émigrés' education. The tax also discouraged many Jews from leaving.[20]

Jackson wanted the Soviet Union to allow 50,000 Jews to exit the country, and if he extracted this concession, the senator planned to hold a news conference proclaiming that his unyielding stance had won the day. Besides its obvious political benefits, the issue of Jewish emigration reflected the 1970s concern over human rights (later a linchpin of Jimmy Carter's foreign policy). Members of Congress found it attractive because it expressed American moral force without military intervention, which a Vietnam-weary nation wanted to avoid. Yet it was a touchy issue to exploit, and it complicated power relationships because the United States applied it selectively and it provoked resentment in countries the United States targeted.[21]

So it did with the USSR. The Soviets took umbrage at the American demand and the tie to MFN status. The Americans, they charged, were interfering with their domestic policy, and Congress was adding a stipulation ex post facto to a 1972 agreement. Kissinger noted that the USSR "found itself in the humiliating position of being the only country in the world to have conditions attached to its MFN status." To the Soviets, Jackson-Vanik represented a form of diplomatic and economic blackmail. When Ford met with Soviet premier Leonid Brezhnev in November 1974, the Russian leader complained specifically about congressional interference in American diplomacy, which also hampered the president's attempts to promote free trade.[22]

Nixon used to rage at "Scoop Jackson's demagoguery," and now Ford, too, deprecated Jackson's approach, which was colored with political ambition.[23] Ford noted that quiet diplomacy during the Nixon administration had resulted in an increase in Jewish emigration, from 400 in 1968 to an unprecedented high of 35,000 in 1973. Nevertheless, at an August 1974 meeting Ford persuaded Soviet ambassador Anatoly Dobrynin to give an oral assurance that the Kremlin would allow 50,000 Jews to leave the Soviet Union. It would be oral only, Dobrynin specified, because he wanted to deny Jackson the political victory of a written agreement. Ford presented Dobrynin's guarantee to Jackson and found the senator "adamant. He kept saying that we were being too soft on the Russians. . . . He was about to launch his Presidential campaign, and he was playing politics to the hilt."[24] (Once, when meeting with Kissinger, Jackson even demanded a written pledge from the Soviets to let 100,000 Jewish émigrés leave annually.) Jackson then publicized a letter Kissinger had written to him implying that the Soviet Union would permit 50,000 émigrés to leave annually, the very assurance that the Kremlin wanted to keep confidential. Moscow was furious with Kissinger and Jackson and soon abandoned its oral agreement. In private, Ford angrily commented that Jackson had "behaved like a swine."[25]

Under Jackson's leadership, the Senate passed the amendment, 88–0. Ford felt he had no choice. He signed Jackson-Vanik after "a realistic appraisal of what the circumstances were." He recalled that "there was so much domestic political pressure. It would have been a sign of weakness to have vetoed and then been overridden."[26] The same month, Congress also voted to restrict Export-Import Bank credits to the Soviet Union to $300 million over four years, shattering Moscow's hopes of gaining American credit to upgrade its economy. Ultimately, the effects of the congressional actions were inestimable.

Brezhnev dashed off an angry letter to Ford that said, "Grave damage has thus been inflicted to our trade and economic relations, which by no means encourages Soviet-American relations in other spheres." The Soviets tightened the lid on Jewish emigration, abandoned attempts to seek MFN status, and refused to repay its Lend-Lease debts. By dashing the imminent MFN status, Congress impeded the influx of American goods and ideas that helped to diversify the Soviet economy and dissolve the bonds of communism. Soviet ambassador Anatoly Dobrynin believed that the tussle over Jewish emigration damaged détente more than any other issue, and Kissinger even wondered whether the amendment prompted the Soviet Union to increase aid to North Vietnam and begin supplying Communist forces in Angola.[27]

The congressional rebuffs not only made Soviet-American relations grow frostier but also showed that Kissinger's luster had worn off. In 1973, he won the Nobel Peace Prize for negotiating a cease-fire in Vietnam. Early in 1974, as he engaged in "shuttle diplomacy" among Israel, Egypt, and Syria, he appeared untouchable. *Newsweek* pictured him on its cover as "Super K," flying in comic hero garb; *Time* dubbed him a "Miracle Worker." His 85 percent Gallup poll approval rating was a record for a public official.[28] But during the 1970s, public figures often went from hero to zero. By the fall of 1974, Congress and the media had soured on Kissinger's ego, secrecy, and reputation for deviousness. Although he remained a global celebrity, his Nixon-era triumphs belonged to the past, and his methods—personal diplomacy that relied heavily on secrecy—disturbed members of Congress after Watergate. Still suspicious of his Vietnam War role, lawmakers criticized his part in the CIA's overthrow of Salvadore Allende's Marxist regime in Chile. Kissinger also resisted Capitol Hill's quest for a stronger voice in diplomacy, further inciting congressional tempers. Complained Democratic representative Les Aspin of Wisconsin, "Mr. Kissinger appears to be either unable or unwilling to allow a group like Congress to have a substantive role in foreign policy." In 1976, the Washington, D.C.–based research firm Potomac Associates concluded, "To the extent that Congress has recently sought a role in foreign affairs it is congenitally incapable of playing, this may in part be seen as a reaction to the tactics employed by the Secretary of State . . . [who] has been either unable or unwilling to entertain a reasonably forthright relationship with the legislature."[29]

The controversy over Kissinger, the cabinet's most visible personality, made him a distraction. Rumors of his possible resignation made constant headlines, and he aggravated the whisperings by talking about quitting. At press conferences, Ron Nessen had to scotch rumors of Kissinger's imminent departure, and Ford did likewise. "I would not under any circumstances want

Henry Kissinger to quit," he vowed at one 1976 campaign stop.[30] But many Ford loyalists felt differently. Joseph Sisco, an undersecretary of state, recalled that Ford insiders "saw Henry as a self-serving man. They also saw him as a political liability and a residue of Richard Nixon."[31] During the Republican primaries, Ronald Reagan turned Kissinger into one of Ford's greatest liabilities, blaming the secretary of state for weakness in diplomacy. In the fall campaign, Jimmy Carter charged that American foreign policy "is primarily comprised of [sic] Mr. Kissinger's own ideas, his own goals, most often derived and maintained in secrecy. I don't think the President plays any substantial role in the evolution of our foreign policy." Carter pledged that as president, he "would quit conducting the decision-making process in secret, as has been characteristic of Mr. Kissinger and Mr. Ford." His penchant for secrecy left Kissinger vulnerable to such criticism, and Carter capitalized on post-Watergate concerns by calling for greater forthrightness in diplomacy.[32]

Ford showed tremendous loyalty toward his administration members, and he did toward Kissinger, with whom he enjoyed a good working relationship. "Our personalities meshed," Ford wrote, and the White House tried to spin a positive image by comparing their partnership to other presidents and their secretaries of state, such as Dwight D. Eisenhower and John Foster Dulles.[33] Ford "resented these unfair attacks" on Kissinger. "Henry was a staunch U.S. advocate," he maintained. "And the attacks, trying to make him out as a weakling and anti-U.S., were very wrong."[34]

Yet Kissinger's high profile incubated the very doubts in Ford's leadership that he tried to dispel. To some observers, Kissinger ran foreign policy. (One poll, taken after Ford's first trip abroad, showed that 57 percent of respondents felt that he was "relying on advisers" in foreign policy, while only 24 percent thought that he was acting on his own.) Robert Hartmann commented, "We did not like [Kissinger] publicly putting the President of the United States in a pupil's role. Perhaps he didn't really mean to, and Ford may be faulted for permitting it."[35] While Ford formulated his own foreign policy, Kissinger's continued presence detracted from Ford's need to appear presidential.

But for Ford, the greatest obstacle to implementing his foreign policy was Capitol Hill. "There was, I thought, an unfortunate encroachment by the Congress on foreign power action by the United States." He believed that "Congress was trying to claw its way into the foreign policy arena, and that inevitably was a potential encroachment on presidential power."[36] Congress could neither form a consensus nor act quickly in foreign crises, and it could disseminate sensitive information. Some congressmen even felt uncomfortable with their branch's behavior. Democratic representative Samuel Stratton of New York believed that foreign policy "is an area in which we in Congress clearly cannot provide the lead, and where we can't even come up with a coherent point of view on many occasions . . . because we're a body of 535 prima donnas."[37]

Détente Deteriorates

The Jackson-Vanik Amendment evinced not just congressional assertiveness but also the reality that, as Ford recalled, "relations with the Soviet Union were strained; we had moved from the more glamorous phase of détente into a time of testing."[38] In dealing with Moscow, he felt constrained by détente's opponents in Congress and the Republican Party. Yet Ford, whom Soviet ambassador to the United States Anatoly Dobrynin regarded as "openly hostile" and "highly negative" toward the Soviet Union while a congressman, wanted to maintain a dialogue with the country as president.[39]

Nixon, who launched his political career as a hard-line anti-Communist, was an unlikely champion of détente, but the impetus for détente reflected the changes in the world since he and Ford entered politics in the 1940s. By the early 1970s, the United States remained mired in Vietnam. Improved relations with the Soviet Union and China, Nixon hoped, might encourage those countries to reduce aid to North Vietnam and hasten the war's end. The cold war had dragged on for more than two decades, and both superpowers wanted to reduce the nuclear threat by negotiating. With the Soviets achieving parity in nuclear strength, détente appealed to the United States as a good alternative when economic problems forced it to limit defense spending, while these economic maladies made the prospect of increased trade with the Soviet Union and China attractive. Politically, Nixon also hoped to attract moderates and liberals through détente.

Thus détente seemed reasonable during the early 1970s. But in just a few short years, the situation changed dramatically, and the initial jubilation that accompanied détente had disappeared. By late 1974, Nixon was a disgraced ex-president, and his policies—including détente—were subject to bitter attacks. Moderates and liberals felt that détente failed to slow the arms race and promised more than it delivered. (Kissinger initially pledged it would usher in "a generation of peace.")[40] To Ford, even more vexing was conservative opposition within his own party. Admittedly, détente was an inherently tricky concept, involving an easing of tensions while at the same time requiring continued toughness with the Soviet Union. But the latter, conservatives charged, had suffered. The Soviets engaged in audacious moves around the globe—such as supplying aid to North Vietnam, thereby violating the 1973 cease-fire agreement—and threatened to overtake the United States in military strength. Conservatives also felt that détente ignored human rights and other moral principles. In November 1974, Ford felt this pressure from the Republican right when he traveled to the Soviet Union to open new Strategic Arms Limitation Talks (SALT) with Soviet premier Leonid Brezhnev.

More symbolic than substantive, the 1972 SALT treaty left a gaping hole by omitting multiple independently targeted reentry vehicles (MIRVs) from consideration; MIRVs allowed each missile to have up to sixteen independent warheads, each of which could reach its own target. MIRVs represented a tremendous leap in technology but also accelerated the arms race. Ford faced two avenues in pursuing arms control with the Soviets. Secretary of Defense James Schlesinger, the Joint Chiefs of Staff, and conservatives wanted him to seek equality in numbers, so that the United States and the Soviet Union would have the same amount of land- and sea-based missiles. Kissinger supported a more moderate approach of symmetry, arguing that equality was misleading and inflexible, since both countries had different kinds of weapons that strict numbers did not take into account. For example, the United States relied more on MIRVs, which could let the Soviets have greater numbers of intercontinental ballistic missiles (ICBMs), leaving the two sides equal in strength. But due partly to conservative pressure, Ford wanted to reach an agreement on equality. Recognizing the realities of domestic politics, Kissinger abandoned his push for symmetry.[41]

The Soviets had concerns about détente, too, and some stemmed from the American economic and political situation. With the president hampered by a Democratic Congress and the nation's attention absorbed by domestic problems, the Soviets questioned America's commitment to détente. Indeed, Ford fought brewing isolationist sentiment just to take his first trip overseas. "I don't think this trip is necessary," said Senator Robert Byrd, as the economy slipped into recession.[42] But Ford, viewing arms control a priority, was determined to go. After visits to Japan and South Korea, he landed in Vladivostok, a port city on the Pacific. Even though historians dubbed the event the "Vladivostok summit," the talks actually took place in Okeanskaya, a sanitarium an hour inland where Soviet military personnel vacationed. (Although Ford's hosts spent more than ten days refurbishing the resort, the president thought that the place "still looked like an abandoned YMCA camp in the Catskills." It was also bitterly cold there, and some of the only photographs of Ford wearing a hat—which he normally avoided—came from this summit. As Ford was leaving Washington, Dobrynin warned him about the harsh climate and gave him a warm Russian fur hat.)[43]

The negotiations produced a framework for a new, ten-year SALT treaty. The heart of the framework was the numerical ceilings. Each side agreed to limit its missiles and bombers to 2,400 each; of the missiles, no more than 1,320 could be MIRVed. By including a limit on MIRVs—even though the Soviets had yet to deploy any—the talks had proposed to make up for the largest omission in the 1972 SALT treaty.

Ford felt that the diplomatic junket "exceeded my expectations."[44] He believed that "the negotiations at Vladivostok made an honest effort to put a limit on warhead capability and missile range."[45] Ford's act of continuing SALT negotiations and forging a foundation for a new treaty added a solidity to the process after Nixon's resignation had threatened to disrupt it. Ford also took measure of his Soviet counterpart. He held firm when Brezhnev demanded that the United States scrap its planned Trident submarine and B-1 bomber programs. Kissinger remarked that Ford proved a superior negotiator to Nixon, due largely to his personality. Ford liked the give-and-take of bargaining and looked Brezhnev in the eyes, which Nixon avoided.[46]

The evening before he began talks with Ford at Vladivostok, the sixty-eight-year-old Brezhnev suffered a seizure. The Soviet premier insisted to his aides that he continue and demanded that his condition remain a secret. Although the Americans had no idea what had happened, the incident was an inauspicious sign, not for the talks themselves but for the process of détente. Brezhnev's declining health coincided with the beginning of détente's death throes.[47]

Congressional and conservative opposition, Soviet foot-dragging, plus Ford's short tenure in office unraveled his work at Vladivostok. Conservatives thought that the Soviet Union bested the United States in the first SALT treaty and were determined to avoid a repeat. Jackson, a hawk on defense issues, criticized the treaty framework and fomented opposition on Capitol Hill by charging that the proposals put the United States at a weaker position in land-based missiles.[48] Inside the administration, Secretary of Defense Donald Rumsfeld, whom Ford appointed in November 1975, was unenthusiastic about a new SALT treaty. The treaty also foundered on the issues of the Soviet Backfire bomber and the American cruise missile. Jackson and other critics insisted that any treaty include the Backfire, a new supersonic bomber that they argued was long range—not medium range, as the Soviets claimed—and could strike the United States because it could be refueled in flight. The Soviets objected and demanded that the new cruise missile, once deployed, should fall within the Vladivostok limits for strategic nuclear weapons. Even though Ford once stressed to Anatoly Dobrynin the importance of some positive signals from Brezhnev on arms control, Dobrynin recalled that "Moscow was in no mood to oblige. The Soviet leadership was under strong pressure from our own military, which sought restrictions on America's cruise missiles. . . . So, instead of attempting some goodwill gesture toward the president, we fell into our habit of stubbornly prolonging the argument."[49]

In early 1976, Ford sent Kissinger to the Soviet Union to continue negotiations on these issues, even proposing that they ratify the Vladivostok agreements and consider the Backfire and cruise missiles separately. The Soviets rejected these proposals. Détente also came under fire from Ronald Reagan during the 1976 primaries, making continued negotiations politically risky. Ford recalled, "The criticism of détente, by both Jackson and Reagan, was done for political reasons. And that upset me. It meant we couldn't do what we should have done on arms control."[50] Given Ford's political predicament in 1976, he reluctantly abandoned hope of concluding a new SALT treaty. He later cited the lost opportunity as his greatest foreign policy regret, saying, "The negotiations with Brezhnev—although they were productive—were not as productive as I would have hoped. I think if I had been elected in '76, we could have made significant progress with Brezhnev in '77, '78."[51]

Continued Soviet expansion also undermined détente. After the humiliating withdrawal from Vietnam, the Ford administration looked elsewhere to assert American power against communism. It found the spot in a new Third World battleground, Africa. Angola, rich in oil and mineral reserves, won its independence in 1974 after 500 years as a Portuguese colony. Three factions vied for control of the country. The Soviet-backed Popular Movement for the Liberation of Angola (MPLA) was the most powerful, and its strength fostered fears in the Ford administration that the USSR would use Angola to establish a foothold in Africa. In April 1975, President Kenneth Kauanda of Zambia visited Ford at the White House and urged him to intervene to prevent the Angolan Marxists from winning control of the country. Kauanda's blandishments provided the catalyst for American involvement in an African civil war.[52]

Once again, Ford found himself "run over by history," a victim of the oversights of previous presidencies. The Johnson and Nixon administrations paid little attention to Africa and Latin America, especially as they grew preoccupied with Vietnam. Journalist Walter Lippmann criticized Johnson's secretary of state, Dean Rusk, for being "so preoccupied with south-east Asia that he has neglected Europe, Africa, and Latin America." As a result, the executive branch failed to anticipate the end of Portuguese rule and the resulting civil war.[53] By the 1970s, the untoward events in Angola came as a surprise, and Ford had to make up for lost time.

Few Americans had heard of Angola before the 1970s, and fewer still could visualize it. Sitting on Africa's Atlantic coast, just below the bend in the continent's upside-down "L" shape, Angola was a faraway land that assumed a political and ideological importance far outleaping its value as a potential ally. But during the cold war, the Soviets were eager to expand their sphere of influence, while American presidents wanted to defend themselves against the charge of "losing" a country to communism, which was the political kiss of death. Truman "lost" Korea, and the Democrats relinquished the White House in 1952, while Eisenhower "lost" Cuba, and the Republicans gave up the presidency in 1960. These high stakes helped to explain why Angola became the cockpit of another confrontation between the cold war superpowers.

Ford was determined to check Soviet expansionism and take a strong stand in Angola. The administration provided covert CIA support to the two factions opposing the MPLA, the National Front for the Liberation of Angola (FNLA) and the National Union for the Total Independence of Angola (UNITA). In an illustration of the new cold war dynamics of the 1970s, China joined the United States in supporting these factions, fearing increased Soviet world strength.[54]

Brezhnev, who firmly believed that socialism would one day triumph over capitalism, declared that "our cause is just" in Angola. The Kremlin was anxious to increase Communist power worldwide and show China the Soviet Union's strength in aiding Communist movements. In Angola, those ambitions meant helping both the MPLA and Cuba, where Fidel Castro eagerly deployed 15,000 troops to Angola to assist the group. Meanwhile, threatened by the Soviet-backed group's opposition to apartheid, South Africa sent troops to back the FNLA and UNITA. Kissinger wanted the United States to send the Kremlin a strong signal. "If the Soviet Union could prevail so far from its borders in the face of such logistic difficulties and our command of the seas," he wrote, "to what measures might it be tempted in areas closer to Russian historical national interest—such as the Middle East?"[55] Angola, a proxy war between the United States and the Soviet Union, showed how much détente was withering.

After spending $32 million to support the FNLA and UNITA, the Ford administration planned to dispense an additional $25 million, hoping that this aid would help all sides accept a coalition government under the auspices of the Organization of African Unity. Congress, aware of the CIA's Angola activities, grew alarmed. Nineteen seventy-five was the "Year of Intelligence," when reports of CIA abuses dominated news headlines. Three separate investigations—by the White House, Senate, and House—into covert CIA operations over the past two decades uncovered plots to assassinate foreign leaders such as Fidel Castro. The agency had overstepped its original mission, which was to gather foreign intelligence, by engaging in domestic espionage and coups against foreign governments. Many members of Congress, already leery of presidential abuses, wanted to rein in the CIA as well, and Congress formed intelligence subcommittees to oversee CIA operations, requiring the agency to keep them informed of its doings. Kissinger described Congress as "violently opposed to intervention abroad, especially in the developing world, ever suspicious of the CIA, deeply hostile to covert operations, and distrustful of the veracity of the executive branch."[56] Moreover, Vietnam remained on everyone's minds.

Thus, in December 1975, Congress voted to cut off all funds for CIA activities in Angola. Democratic senator John Tunney of California, who sponsored the amendment to a defense appropriations bill, declared, "I don't want to see any more money go down this rathole."[57] Because the bill funded defense programs that Ford deemed critical, such as the B-1 bomber and the Trident and cruise missiles, he felt he had to sign the bill. But he was, again, severely disappointed in Congress. "I was absolutely convinced that a favorable vote would have given us the tools to nip Castro's adventure on this crucial continent," he wrote. "But Congress had lost its nerve and, as a result, we were bound to see further Cuban involvement in Africa."[58] The congressional actions marked a bitter defeat for Ford. His policy involved a delicate balance between détente and resistance to Soviet encroachment, and congressional resurgence upset the balance. It marked the first time during the cold war that the United States had to stand aside before Soviet proxies. The administration also feared that the congressional rebuff publicly undermined America's bargaining position in SALT negotiations. Kissinger found the defeat even more difficult to accept because congressional conservatives were strangely silent. Throughout the year, they vocally denounced purported signs of Ford administration weakness before Soviet threats, but now, when the administration took a firm stance yet faced congressional defeat, Kissinger found conservatives "very restrained."[59] In private, Kissinger blamed Ford for the defeat, suggesting that he should have persisted in securing aid for Angola, even if it meant ignoring the congressional ban (as Nixon might have done).[60] Ford, however, respected the integrity of constitutional checks and balances and abided by Capitol Hill's action.

With the FNLA and UNITA bereft of American support and Cuban troops helping it, the MPLA won the Angolan civil war in 1976. Cuba's deep involvement in the war ended talk of détente between America and its island neighbor (rumors of a rapprochement had circulated since early 1973, when the two countries reached an agreement to cooperate on preventing airline hijackings). In March 1976, Ford blasted Castro as an "international outlaw" and vowed to respond forcefully if the Cuban dictator created trouble in the Western Hemisphere, a pledge that appeared to constitute a new "Ford Doctrine."[61] To critics, Angola offered more proof that the United States was getting short-changed in détente. Ford observed, "The public quite understandably found it hard to comprehend why we should have any dealings with the Russians when they were stealing a march on us in Africa."[62] By late 1975, Harvard diplomatic historian Richard Pipes declared, "I think détente is finished. . . . It was supposed to keep the two superpowers out of confrontation, but instead we have allowed the Russians to expand all over the world."[63]

During the 1976 primaries, the coffin lid slammed down hard on détente. Reagan stung Ford with charges that détente allowed the United States to fall behind the Soviet Union militarily. In defending himself against the accusations, Ford dropped the word "détente" from his speeches, replacing it with "peace through strength," a slogan that Reagan later adopted as president. "I never backed away from détente as a means for achieving a more stable relationship with our Communist adversaries," Ford said. "But the situation that developed in connection with the presidential primaries and the fight at the convention made it necessary to de-emphasize détente."[64] Détente became unpopular enough that both a Democrat (Carter, criticizing its weakness on human rights) and a Republican (Reagan, claiming that it relegated the United States to military inferiority) won the White House while flailing away at it.[65] Yet had Ford won the 1976 election, détente might have made a comeback. "I thought détente was constructive," he reflected. "I was not embarrassed that we were negotiating, despite the criticism from the hard right. I probably would have continued negotiating under détente." Détente reflected Ford's brand of moderate Republicanism, which contrasted with what he viewed as the "more hard-line, inflexible" views of détente's foes. "In conjunction with Kissinger, we were more anxious to negotiate than Nixon," Ford said, and he had hoped to do so during a full term.[66]

"The Fading of America"

Besides resistance to détente, Ford struggled against another growing sentiment. Americans, their confidence rattled by the bitter Vietnam experience, had little appetite for overseas intervention, and a reflexive neo-isolationist sentiment set in. After carrying the burden of Free World defense for a generation, they became weary and cautious. Their impulse was to forswear foreign engagements and any temptation to act alone in faraway regions, and half of Americans believed that the country's power would decline.[67] In 1972, while campaigning for president, George McGovern advocated a lesser international role. By 1974, one-quarter of Americans described themselves as "isolationist." Concern for allies vastly diminished: a 1975 Harris poll showed that only 39 percent of Americans favored military intervention to defend Western Europe, and the only country that most Americans would support with troops if it were invaded was Canada.[68] The new attitude was an antidote to any tendency to act as a "world policeman" and seemed true to America's past.

Isolationism had a long tradition in the United States. Safely cloistered by two oceans, the nation could afford to shut itself away from the rest of the world. In his farewell address, George Washington warned against the "insidious wiles of foreign influence" and urged Americans to "steer clear of permanent alliance" with foreign nations. For generations, they did. After World War I, the United States rejected participation in the League of Nations. During the Great Depression, Americans wanted to avoid another world war and were absorbed by the domestic economic crisis. The troubled economy of the 1970s offered a replay of these sentiments.

Economic problems, Vietnam, creeping isolationism, and the crumbling of the cold war consensus led to perceptions of U.S. decline throughout the world. A U.S. Information Agency survey found that Western European perceptions of U.S. prestige dropped to their lowest levels in the twenty-two-year history of the agency. Ford recalled that in the spring of 1975, *Frankfurter Allgemeine Zeitung* ran a front-page editorial, "America—A Helpless Giant."[69] In April 1975, the London *Economist* entitled a cover story, "The Fading of America." The venerable magazine, noting "the pulling in of burned American fingers," thought "the question of American credibility a genuine one" and observed that Americans were reevaluating whether to defend valuable allies militarily or even to react to Communist political victories in Western Europe.[70]

Ford fought this emerging worldview. He pointed out, "We still had excellent relations with the European community. We had continuing good relations with the Japanese. I think that's a misconception that we were a fading power." He added, "Maybe we weren't a giant power, throwing our [weight] around, trying to tell everybody to do what we wanted. But that's not evidence that we were without power."[71]

Ford bolstered America's foreign standing early in his term by fostering an economic dialogue with allies and encouraging their support to fight rising prices worldwide. Immediately after he unveiled his October 8, 1974, anti-inflation program, he dispatched a cabinet-level group that flew to Canada, Belgium, France, Italy, West Germany, and Japan to introduce his proposals to foreign economic leaders. The Ford team included not only officials from the State and Treasury departments, with whom foreign governments routinely conferred, but also Trade Representative William Eberle, CEA member Gary Seevers, and lower-level administration staff. The initiative "was billed as the first time that the U.S. president had done such a thing," Seevers recalled. "So I think that's very much to Ford's credit."[72]

Still, the notion of a "fading America" persisted, and perhaps the greatest legacy that Ford counteracted was from Vietnam. The sad conflict made many Americans want to throw their internationalism into reverse. In the spring of 1975, the tragedy returned to haunt Ford. South Vietnam's collapse illustrated themes dominating 1970s diplomacy: a neo-isolationist mood, a worldwide perception of American decline, and congressional resistance to presidential initiatives.

Ford was saddled with the burden of a failed "Vietnamization" policy. Nixon began his presidency pledging to shift the burden of fighting to South Vietnam, yet the country proved utterly incapable of defending itself against North Vietnamese advances. The government of Nguyen Van Thieu was impotent. In early 1975, North Vietnam, violating the 1973 Paris Peace Accords, went for the kill. In January 1975, its forces advanced into the South and captured a province, marking the first time during the entire war that Hanoi gained control of a South Vietnamese province. In response, Ford requested $522 million in emergency aid for South Vietnam and Cambodia, which was also in danger of surrendering to Communist rebel forces. Determined to support an American ally, viewing it—like Nixon had—as a test of American credibility, he said, "It cannot be in our interest to cause our friends all over the world to wonder whether we will support them." The House rejected Ford's request by a lopsided margin. In early March, a group of thirty-seven members of Congress made their beliefs clear to Ford, telling him, "For many of us, this war has been a constant backdrop, a permanent policy of our government, for most of our adult lives. We watched this war maim and kill our friends, and then maim and kill the trust of American people in their leaders." Informing Ford that they opposed any more aid to South Vietnam, they concluded, "We face our own war here at home against crippling economic developments, the crisis in energy and other public resources and other serious problems. . . . We cannot confront and resolve these crises while the United States continues involvement in Southeast Asia."[73]

On March 10, 1975, North Vietnam—boasting the world's fifth-largest army—launched a massive offensive to gain control of South Vietnam. The army easily overran any South Vietnamese soldiers it encountered; in fact, many of Thieu's troops simply ran off, leaving cities and military bases defenseless. One American military analyst compared the South Vietnamese army to a suit of armor in a museum: it looked impressive, but a swift kick could knock it to the floor.[74] In late March, army chief of staff Frederick Weyand, accompanied by White House photographer David Kennerly, went to Vietnam to assess the situation. (Kennerly, just twenty-eight, won the Pulitzer Prize while working as a *Time* photographer covering the Vietnam War.) Weyand grimly reported to the president that, just to hold Saigon and hope for a political solution, the South Vietnamese would need $722 million in aid. Conferring separately with the president, Kennerly was blunter and less optimistic. The military was "bullshitting you if they say that Vietnam has got more than three or four weeks left," Kennerly told Ford. "There's no question about it. It's just not gonna last."[75]

Under great stress, Ford received a flurry of negative press in early April when, against the advice of several aides, he flew to California for an Easter golf vacation instead of monitoring the precarious South Vietnamese situation from the White House. Television news broadcasts showed the president golfing as North Vietnamese troops overran the South. At one point, hounded by reporters' questions about Vietnam at the Bakersfield airport, Ford broke away from the reporters and ran, chiding them to keep up with him. Ford recalled that at that moment, "I just had the feeling that I had answered their questions. Why in the heck do I have to answer them again and again?" Looking back at his sprint, though, Ford smiled and said, "I probably shouldn't have," and believed that the press distorted the incident.[76] One reporter later joked that Ford ran as fast as the South Vietnamese army.[77]

When he returned to Washington, Ford decided to ask Congress for additional aid to South Vietnam. "I firmly believed," he later recalled, "that if we got the money for the economic aid and the military aid, there was a chance the South Vietnamese were strong enough to negotiate a final settlement with the North Vietnamese. Without that money, there was no hope."[78] On April 10, Ford addressed a joint session of Congress and gave a "State of the World" address in which he asked for almost $1 billion in aid to South Vietnam, $722 million in emergency military assistance and $250 million in economic and humanitarian help. To protest the president's request, half of all representatives and senators refused to attend the session. Those present gave him a chilly reception, listening in a demurring silence. They offered no applause, and some Democrats hissed when he mentioned the $722 million. Ford also observed two first-term Democratic congressmen get up and walk out of the chamber. "As best I could recall," Ford reflected, "this had never happened before, and I thought it an appallingly rude display."[79]

In an unusual move, the Senate Foreign Relations Committee requested an audience with the president and on April 14 met with him in the Cabinet Room. After an hour, the two sides remained deadlocked. Republican senator Jacob Javits of New York told Ford, "I will give you large sums for evacuation, but not one nickel for military aid." Members of Congress were ill-inclined to help a South Vietnamese army that, in retreating, left millions of dollars' worth of American military hardware for the enemy. Moreover, Americans were sick of the war. One poll showed that 78 percent opposed more aid. Democratic senator Sam Nunn of Georgia reported that people in his state felt "isolation, anger, frustration" regarding Southeast Asia. Missouri senator Stuart Symington wrote, "With our increasingly limited resources, it would seem more wise to use any available money for such problems in this country as schools, highways, mass transit, aid to the sick and aged, etc." Democratic congressman Robert Leggett of California was more blunt: "We're going bankrupt and the Ford Administration wants to send millions to Southeast Asia. It's crazy. Turning down aid would be a reflection of economic responsibility."[80]

Although Thieu lashed out against American credibility in resigning ("Are U.S. statements worthy? Are U.S. commitments still valid?" he asked), Ford's argument about credibility was tenuous. The country demonstrated its credibility in other, less costly ways, through economic strength, international trade, and arms control negotiations. By spurning more aid, Congress saved the country more heartache and expense. North Vietnam's quick, easy invasion exposed South Vietnam's futility. Whereas the North Vietnamese originally estimated that conquest would require two years, it took just fifty-five days. No amount of aid could have helped such a weak ally, and many of Ford's advisers argued against any further help. Nessen recalled, "I felt conquest by the Communist forces was inevitable and saw no sense in prolonging the agony."[81] Just days after his address, in a dramatic speech, Ford seemed to concede that the South Vietnamese cause was hopeless.

Although Ford rarely uttered diplomatic pronouncements without consulting Kissinger, he asked his speechwriters to prepare an address in secret. He explained that "I had come to the conclusion, even though I wanted Congress to give us the money for weapons and economic aid . . . that the American public was not going to tolerate a never-ending Vietnam War. . . . I said to myself, 'That's a realistic approach of the American people, and I have to be accountable.'"[82] On April 23, he addressed students at Tulane University and declared, "Today, America can regain a sense of pride that existed before Vietnam. But it cannot be achieved by refighting a war that is finished as far as the American people are concerned." The audience roared its approval. Students jumped up and down; Robert Hartmann recalled seeing one group linking arms and gleefully chorusing, "It's over, it's over."[83] The speech's setting was symbolic, because the war polarized and deeply scarred the nation's youth, having such a divisive effect that Presidents Johnson and Nixon avoided appearances at colleges and universities. (Nixon could not even attend his daughter Julie's college graduation because his advisers feared student protests.) Ford brought the presidency back to the nation's campuses, and words such as these acted as a balm to students.[84] Even more important, as Nessen wrote, "The speech was a milestone in contemporary American history. Ford did something no American president had been able to do for thirty years: He spoke of the Indochina war in the past tense."[85]

Yet the war was not quite finished. The North Vietnamese began an offensive to capture Saigon, and Americans remaining in the besieged city had to be evacuated. About 5,000 Americans were trapped there, mostly military personnel, government officials, businesspeople, and journalists. They could not be evacuated by airplane because the North Vietnamese had shelled the Saigon airport so heavily that its airstrip, pockmarked with craters, was unusable. Although in early April Ford rejected Secretary of Defense Schlesinger's request to begin an evacuation, by April 28 he had no choice. He ordered the helicopter evacuation of all Americans and some South Vietnamese from Saigon.[86] In a massive airlift, more than eighty U.S. helicopters ferried thousands of evacuees to U.S. Navy ships offshore.

On April 30, Communists overran Saigon. The Vietnam War was finally finished. America had failed to keep South Vietnam out of Communist hands, despite an effort that stretched back a generation and cost 57,000 American lives. As Ford later reflected, "To sit in the Oval Office in April of 1975, and to see American military and civilian personnel being literally kicked out of Saigon—and I mean kicked out, driven out, beaten out—was not a happy experience for a president."[87]

South Vietnam's collapse brought refugees to the United States. In early April, Ford ordered a special $2 million fund to allow 2,000 South Vietnamese orphans to be flown to the United States. "Everyone suffers in a war," Ford explained, "but no one suffers more than the children, and the airlift was the least that we could do." Yet many Americans protested the arrival of South Vietnamese citizens. Racism, concern over job competition, and revulsion at visible reminders of a painful war prompted some citizens to object. At a refugee camp near Fort Chafee, Arkansas, demonstrators carried signs reading, "Go Home" and "Gookville." Clare Boothe Luce, the former ambassador to Italy and widow of magazine magnate Henry Luce, openly advocated giving sanctuary to the Vietnamese but received ugly letters of protest. "They are lazy, corrupt, and cowardly. Who needs their kind?" wrote one person. Another objected, "We have too many Orientals now. We are losing our national character." A Gallup poll showed that Americans opposed admitting the refugees by 54 to 36 percent. Congress reflected these sentiments, much to Ford's chagrin. Two days after the evacuation, the House rejected a $327 million bill to aid the Vietnamese refugees.[88]

Ford was furious. Ron Nessen recalled taking the Associated Press (AP) report of the House vote to the Oval Office to show the president, who read it and said, "Those sons of bitches." It was the first time Nessen had heard Ford curse.[89] Earlier, Ford had been irritated that the WPA hampered his ability to carry out the evacuation. The act required him to inform Congress of his use of military forces to aid in the operation, yet in early April many members of Congress were spending their Easter vacation overseas. "Although we went to incredible lengths to reach them and explain the situation, we did not succeed. . . . Yet when Congress reconvened after its recess, several members accused me of violating the law," Ford recalled.

Now Ford tried to convince lawmakers and the public of their duty to welcome the Vietnamese refugees into the country. "To ignore the refugees in their hour of need would be to repudiate the values we cherish as a nation of immigrants, and I was not about to let Congress do that," Ford said. He campaigned hard to win acceptance for the Vietnamese refugees. On April 5, he made an unscheduled trip to San Francisco to welcome a plane carrying 325 South Vietnamese children and twice entered the plane to carry off babies in his arms. "I thought he had tears in his eyes," observed one doctor.[90] Ford gave speeches around the country to emphasize the American tradition of charity and compassion toward newcomers. The initial resistance began to fade. Nessen recalled that the president "turned public opinion around; he turned congressional opinion around. And I thought that was one of the best examples of moral leadership by Ford. . . . [He] felt that we had a responsibility to these people who had worked for us or counted on us."[91] Ultimately, 120,000 Vietnamese refugees settled in America and started new lives.[92]

After the humiliating fall of South Vietnam, Ford worried that allies doubted the nation's strength to carry out its commitments. At a press conference one week after Saigon fell, Ford tried to reassure them by saying, "The United States is strong economically, despite our current problems . . . and we want our friends to know that we will stand by them, and we want any potential adversaries to know that we will stand up to them."[93] Just two weeks after the fall of South Vietnam, Ford saw an opportunity to demonstrate that the United States was not fading. On May 12, 1975, the new Communist

Khmer Rouge forces in Cambodia, which had just gained control of the country weeks earlier, captured an unarmed American merchant vessel, the *Mayaguez*, as it sailed in international waters off the Cambodian coast. The ship carried a crew of thirty-nine and was taking a cargo of food, paints, and chemicals to Thailand. Intelligence reports about the captive crew's whereabouts were sketchy: Some may have remained aboard the ship, others may have been taken to the mainland, and still others may have been led to a nearby island, Koh Tang. Ford said resolutely, "I can assure you that, irrespective of the Congress, we will move." At a special National Security Council (NSC) meeting that Ford assembled to discuss the crisis, Kissinger stressed that American prestige was at stake and that doing nothing would make the country look weak. Kissinger and Rockefeller advocated B-52 bomber strikes on mainland Cambodia. That would be overkill, Schlesinger argued; he wanted simply to rescue the crew and forgo punitive bombings. Ford decided to let navy carrier-based jets attack Cambodian patrol boats in the area and perform four surgical bombing raids against the mainland to prevent mainland reinforcements from going to Koh Tang and to punish Cambodia for an act of piracy. Meanwhile, a force of marines landed on Koh Tang, attempting to rescue the ship and any crew on the island.

On the third day of the crisis, the Cambodians released the *Mayaguez* crew (which had been held at nearby Rong Sam Lem Island, twenty miles from Koh Tang), and a U.S. Navy battleship recovered them aboard a Cambodian fishing vessel. The rescued crew believed that the American military action had pressured the Cambodians enough to release them. Charles Miller, captain of the *Mayaguez*, said, "Without our Air Force, without our marines, I don't think this crew would be standing before you today." In appreciation, they presented Ford with the tiller to the *Mayaguez* when they visited the White House.[94]

But the operation had been messy. Bad intelligence had prompted Ford to order the marine assault on Koh Tang, where no *Mayaguez* crew members were located and which was much more heavily defended than expected, resulting in numerous American casualties. Ford's military advisers had predicted that military operations would result in twenty to forty casualties.[95] Instead, casualties numbered more than ninety, including forty-one dead. Initially, the administration dissembled, withholding true casualty figures to make the rescue operation appear more successful. Some Democrats in Congress charged that Ford violated the WPA by failing to consult Congress fully before undertaking the military reprisals, and a partisan General Accounting Office report maintained that Chinese negotiators secured the release of the hostages, rather than the military action.[96] Recent investigations have revealed that three marines, originally reported as missing in action, were left behind on Koh Tang Island and later were captured and executed by the Khmer Rouge.[97]

But Americans rallied around the president during the crisis, and his public approval ratings spiked eleven points. Representative Carroll Hubbard of Kentucky exulted, "It's good to win one for a change." Ford's primary objective was the speedy recovery of the *Mayaguez* crew. He was haunted by the 1968 capture of the USS *Pueblo*, when North Korea took the ship's eighty-three crew members hostage and, in the absence of U.S. military retaliation, held them for eleven months. Indeed, had the United States waited to show force against the Khmer Rouge, the delay would have defused the urgency of the crisis and made future military action more subject to international criticism.[98] (In the Carter presidency, Iranians held fifty-two American embassy workers hostage for 444 days, crippling the administration and draining the country's morale; Carter attempted a failed rescue mission six months after the crisis began, which by then seemed an act of desperation.) Ford believed that "decisive action would reassure our allies and bluntly warn our adversaries that the U.S. was not a helpless giant."[99] The *Mayaguez* crisis had done so, although its toll in human life was costly. But by acting forcefully during both the South Vietnam and *Mayaguez* crises, Ford exercised American power when many Americans found isolationism attractive. The use of military force enabled Ford to maintain a vigorous international profile.

An Agreement before Its Time

One of Ford's greatest — and, at the time, most maligned — efforts to enhance American internationalism was his participation in the Conference on Security and Cooperation in Europe (CSCE). Since 1954, the Soviets had wanted Western nations to take part in such a conference to ratify boundaries established after World War II. The West resisted, fearing that the Soviet Union would turn any such conclave into a propaganda tool. Détente brought a more conciliatory attitude, and in 1973 the Nixon administration began planning for a U.S. delegation to attend a European security conference. Once president, Ford agreed to go in person.[100]

Conservatives were infuriated. They drew a parallel with the 1945 Yalta Conference, where they believed that Franklin Roosevelt and Winston Churchill betrayed Eastern European countries by giving Josef Stalin the impression that he could pull them into the Soviet orbit. Over the years, Yalta had become synonymous with selling Eastern Europe down the river.

"Jerry, Don't Go," the *Wall Street Journal* implored, while Henry Jackson openly urged Ford to boycott the conference.[101]

But Ford had to go. It was one of the largest summits in history, attended by leaders of thirty-five nations (even a representative of the Vatican came), and marked the culmination of three years of intensive negotiations. An American absence would have antagonized European allies, since the conference was intended to benefit them, and signaled a reluctance to participate in European affairs, an impression of isolationism that Ford distinctly wanted to avoid.[102] Kissinger stressed to domestic critics that "the President is going to Helsinki as a result of consultation and very close coordination with every one of our allies."[103]

Still, the results were controversial. The Helsinki Conference produced four categories, called "baskets" in diplomatic parlance, of agreement, and participating nations signed an act comprising the baskets. (Since the Helsinki accords were a declaration rather than a treaty, it was not legally binding on signatories and did not require U.S. Senate approval.) In the first basket, "Security in Europe," the countries pledged to observe human rights, respect (specifically avoiding the verb "recognize") the post–World War II boundaries in Europe, and "refrain . . . from assaulting them." The second concerned improved cooperation in business, technology, tourism, and trade. The third, "Humanitarian and Other Fields," supported human rights, travel privileges, access to media information, the free movement of people and ideas, and improvement in family reunification. Because Moscow had been historically reluctant to relent on these issues, this represented an unprecedented cold war concession. While the first two baskets were most important to the Soviet Union for their economic and propaganda value, the West considered the third critical. Under great pressure from American and European diplomats, the Soviets would now accept items and events that it considered dangerous, such as newspapers and family visits. The fourth basket established procedures to monitor compliance with the Helsinki accords and hold follow-up conferences.[104] During Ford's address at the conference, he looked straight at Brezhnev and said, "To my country, [these agreements] are not clichés or empty phrases. We take this work and these words very seriously. It is important that you recognize the deep devotion of the American people and their government to human rights and fundamental freedoms."[105]

Ford was concerned with the conference's implications and the reactions of ethnic groups. As early as March 1975, he wrote to National Security Advisor Brent Scowcroft, "What will [the] European Security Agreement do to our relations with the Baltic groups—Latvia, Estonia and Lithuania—who are so friendly and dedicated?" The president continued, "These groups seem to imply it will confirm USSR permanent control. . . . Does our [signature] confirm this in writing?"[106] In the end, the president convinced himself, "If the nations attending the conference failed to live up to their agreements, Europe would be no worse off than it had been previously, but if they made good on their promises, the cause of freedom behind the Iron Curtain would advance."[107]

For Americans of East European descent, Helsinki was a bitter pill. The Polish-American Congress told the president that it strongly opposed the accords, warning that the Soviet Union rarely, if ever, honored treaties, and the Helsinki accords implied that Western democracies accepted Soviet domination of East Central Europe and of Lithuania, Latvia, and Estonia.[108] Aleksandr Solzhenitsyn, the exiled dissident Soviet writer, blasted the accords as a "betrayal of Eastern Europe," and conservative Republicans agreed. Senator James Buckley of New York wrote to Ford that he was "deeply concerned" about the treaty, "which would have the effect of consolidating and sanctifying the Soviet sphere of influence in eastern Europe."[109]

A flood of letters into the White House ran heavily against the accords, and Ford's public opinion standing dropped. To his frustration, members of his own administration seemed to excuse the Helsinki accords rather than praise them, explaining them as "another Kissinger deal that was forced down the President's throat." A painful jab at Helsinki came during the Republican National Convention, when conservative pressure resulted in a party plank implicitly criticizing the accords. The fallout, Ford believed, reflected "a failure in public relations, and I will have to accept a large share of the blame."[110] Part of the blame, too, rested with Kissinger. Robert Hartmann believed that Kissinger, chronically obsessed with secrecy, failed to brief White House staff members about the meaning and importance of Helsinki, which left them unable to disseminate advance word and inoculate the White House against future criticism. Helsinki became an issue during the 1976 campaign, as Jimmy Carter charged, "I think we lost in Helsinki. We ratified the takeover of Eastern Europe. We got practically nothing in return."[111] Ford's overeagerness to defend himself against this criticism contributed to his infamous gaffe during the 1976 debates, in which he maintained that "there is no Soviet domination of Eastern Europe."

But the Helsinki accords, and Ford's trip to Europe itself, were watershed events in the Soviet Union's relationship with its satellites. On the way to Helsinki, Ford became the first leader of a democratic country to visit Eastern Europe, stopping in Poland, Romania, and Yugoslavia, the most independent of the Eastern European countries. The junket was Ford's not-so-subtle way of encouraging these countries along an independent course.[112] Although basket one recognized the inviolability of frontiers, Western nations emphasized that they were not formally recognizing European borders or conceding that these borders would remain. In fact, at the conference, West Germany won a provision, with U.S. backing, for the peaceful change of frontiers, which paved the way for the eventual reunification of Germany.[113] (Unfortunately, critics of the accords interpreted the references to "inviolability of frontiers" to mean an acceptance of Soviet hegemony in Eastern Europe.)[114] The accords also forced the Soviets to renounce the "Brezhnev Doctrine" of 1968, which the Soviet Union had proclaimed after invading Czechoslovakia that year, declaring the Soviet Union's right to intervene militarily in any of its satellites to preserve a socialist government. By inducing the Russians to renounce the doctrine, the Helsinki accords weakened the Soviet domination of Eastern Europe.[115] As one foreign affairs correspondent predicted before the conference, "Though the Iron Curtain won't collapse, the assembled grand personages will promise to punch a few (small) holes in it."[116]

The 1970s was the right time to encourage freedom within the Soviet satellites. Protests and independent thought had become so common that a popular joke circulated that the Soviet Union was the only country surrounded by hostile Communist nations.[117] Ford saw what critics could not, that the Helsinki accords, instead of endorsing Soviet domination of Eastern Europe, could serve as a vehicle to help Eastern Europeans bring change to their economies and political systems, without violence or outside interference.[118] Over time, his predictions were realized. The Communist Party newspaper *Pravda* published the Helsinki accords in the Soviet Union, giving it official heft and inspiring a new generation to clamor for reform. Dissident movements sprouted up in the wake of Helsinki, among them the Polish labor union Solidarnošc. As Kissinger recalled, "At Helsinki, all the East European countries increased their maneuvering room and felt encouraged by Ford's demonstrative visit to the most independent of them." The first cracks in the Soviet monolith came as a result of the Helsinki accords.[119] Ford believed that the Helsinki accords constituted his greatest foreign policy achievement. "There were many people who disagreed with my willingness to sit down with thirty-four other heads of state [at Helsinki]," he recalled. "But it was the right thing to do, and I think in retrospect now, most objective critics will agree that the Helsinki accords was the spark . . . that brought about the demise of the Soviet Union."[120]

Like many of Ford's achievements, the Helsinki accords were controversial at the time and underappreciated. By the late 1980s, Ronald Reagan also grew convinced that negotiation rather than confrontation was the sensible approach toward the Soviet Union. Helsinki was an agreement before its time, and by participating in the CSCE, Ford showed that, just as in domestic economics, in foreign policy he took a farsighted approach.

Personal Diplomacy

"When I became president," Ford remembered, "I found that our friends were apprehensive about the reliability of the United States as a partner. I set out to reassure them, through both bilateral and multilateral meetings."[121] Ford practiced personal diplomacy; as president, he used his gregarious nature as an instrument of diplomacy, holding talks with foreign leaders to cement alliances and ease tensions. As a young boy, Ford seldom journeyed beyond Grand Rapids. As president, during just two years he became one of the most widely traveled chief executives ever, meeting with more foreign heads of state (124) than any previous president (the runner-up was LBJ, who met with 122 during 1966–68).[122]

Personality, Ford believed, was "a point often overlooked in discussions of foreign policy." He commented, "I had excellent relations with Jim Callaghan, Helmut Schmidt, and Valéry Giscard d'Estaing [leaders of Britain, West Germany, and France, respectively]. Those three were good friends and good allies."[123] He remembered that when Schmidt visited the White House in December 1974, he invited the West German chancellor to join him upstairs in the family quarters after dinner, and the two men talked until 2 A.M. Ford believed that "relations between the U.S. and West Germany were excellent throughout my Administration, primarily because Schmidt and I got along so well."[124] (After leaving office, Ford continued his friendships with Callaghan, Schmidt, and Giscard d'Estaing, hosting them every summer at his Colorado home for the World Forum Conference.)[125]

Ford wanted to improve relations with Asia, too. His November 1974 trip to the Soviet Union originally had been planned only as a trip to Japan, and he became the first American president to visit this critical ally. The trip was long overdue. The Japanese had been unpleasantly caught off guard by what they dubbed the "Nixon shokkus [shocks]," the devaluation of the dollar and rapprochement with China, Japan's traditional enemy. By making a visit to Japan his first overseas trip, Ford—who had once fought the Japanese in the Pacific—flattered them, and his visit helped to salve the slights that they received during Nixon's presidency. He also visited South Korea, and his presence helped to reassure both nations that, despite America's withdrawal from Vietnam the year before, the United States remained committed to defending Asia. (In February 1976, Ford showed his sensitivity to Japanese

Americans by officially nullifying Franklin Roosevelt's Executive Order 9066, which authorized the World War II detainment of Americans of Japanese ancestry and grossly violated their civil liberties.) When he debated Carter in the campaign, Ford was able to proclaim, "Japan and the U.S. are working more closely together now than at any time in the history of our relationship."[126]

Ford also took advantage of a good personal chemistry with Giscard d'Estaing to warm relations between the United States and France, which had been tense since the presidency of Charles de Gaulle. The camaraderie between Ford and Giscard d'Estaing was good therapy for the countries. In December 1974, Ford met with Giscard d'Estaing on the French West Indian island of Martinique in a relaxed atmosphere that included talks in a resort swimming pool. The two leaders concentrated especially on cooperation to meet the worldwide energy crisis and agreed to establish meetings among economic advisers of the major industrial democracies.[127]

Thus emerged one of the most significant diplomatic traditions of the late twentieth century. The first meeting between Ford and Giscard d'Estaing and the resulting meetings of their economic advisers gave rise to the annual summit meetings of the industrialized democracies. At the 1975 CSCE, Giscard d'Estaing proposed that the leaders of five major industrialized countries (the United States, Britain, France, Japan, and West Germany) convene for an economic summit in France. (Ford also convinced Giscard d'Estaing to invite Italy, and the next year, when Ford hosted the summit in Puerto Rico, he included Canada, making it the Group of Seven, or "G-7.") The meetings represented an opportunity for the United States to practice internationalism on economic and trade issues, particularly important since its foreign trade during the 1970s jumped to 7 percent of its GDP (compared to previous estimates of around 4 percent) and the Arab oil embargo illustrated the interconnectedness of the world's economies.[128]

In November, the six leaders met at Rambouillet castle, a retreat thirty-three miles outside Paris where French leaders spent weekends; in essence, it was their Camp David. The leaders discussed the energy crisis, trade, and the world economic situation. Kissinger believed that the summit "launched a new era of institutionalized economic and political cooperation among the democracies." Although it produced no substantive agreements on OPEC or an international antirecession policy, the summit did yield an agreement on flexibility in currency exchange rates, which facilitated trade. Ford touted the principle of economic deregulation, an idea that he believed he needed to stress to his European counterparts, who were more used to the concept of activist government and expansionist fiscal policy.[129] When the meetings concluded, there was talk of a "Spirit of Rambouillet": Ford said that the summit created "a political will and spirit of cooperation."

In June 1976, Ford hosted the G-7 nations in San Juan, Puerto Rico. Because he worried that the worldwide economic recovery (especially in countries such as Germany and France, which were well into an expansion phase) could touch off more inflation, he wanted to synchronize policies to encourage a slow, steady expansion without rising prices. In this crusade, he enlisted the support of Schmidt, a former finance minister who also viewed inflation as the principal economic threat, even if that meant tolerating higher jobless rates. The leaders discussed the energy crisis, free trade (which Ford firmly advocated, even refusing to grant special protection to the domestic shoe industry despite intense election-year pressure from Congress), and relations with Third World countries. Ford urged his fellow leaders to set "realistic" economic goals and practice the conservative "old-time religion," although some European leaders grumbled that unemployment was more severe than inflation in their countries. Nonetheless, at the summit's conclusion, the leaders issued a joint statement pledging themselves to an "orderly and sustained expansion," demonstrating international support for Ford's policies.[130] (At the end of his presidency, Ford even suggested that Puerto Rico become the fifty-first state, partly a result of his being impressed during his visit there.)

The summit conferences helped to cement worldwide economic ties and dispel some of the acrimony and suspicion that dogged relations among the industrialized nations (accusations, for example, that Japan deliberately depressed the value of its yen to boost exports). When Jimmy Carter visited the White House as president-elect, he expressed interest in continuing Ford's practice of economic summits with foreign leaders, saying that it would provide an opportunity for him to meet other heads of state.[131] Ford's White House successors have all continued the annual meetings, and the site has rotated among participating countries, allowing different leaders to serve as hosts.

Through his travels abroad and personal diplomacy, Ford resisted what Democratic congressman Samuel Stratton of New York called "a very definite trend toward isolationism" in America. The president swore that "as long as I am in this job, our policy will be one of a global policy. . . . We are not going back to the old 'Fortress America' concept." He made no attempt to introduce bold new doctrines in foreign policy, saying, "I don't like to label what we are doing a 'doctrine.' I would rather have this Administration known as a problem-solving Administration in the pages of history."[132] Major foreign policy initiatives require years of negotiating with an administration that other countries know will be well ensconced, an assurance that Ford could never give. But what he lacked in sweeping diplomatic visions, Ford made up for with sensible policies that kept the fundamental premises of American foreign policy intact: containment, a strong defense budget, a commitment to arms control, and an active international role. By 1976, he proudly proclaimed that he was the first president since Eisenhower to preside over a nation at peace.[133] Evaluating the Ford presidency before the election, *U.S. News and World Report* noted, "Abroad, the U.S. not only is at peace for the first time in a decade but finds itself in a much stronger position that anyone predicted two years ago."[134] Events at home may have derailed some of his efforts, but Ford demonstrated that the United States could maintain its strength during political and international tumult.

Chapter 17

Thunder from the Right

A year and a half before the Republican primaries, the president already anticipated a challenge from his popular, charismatic party rival. It was September 1910, and William Howard Taft detected rumblings from ex-president Theodore Roosevelt, who had just returned from a long stay in Europe. Would Roosevelt begin angling for the presidency in 1912? Taft privately remarked, "If you were to remove Roosevelt's skull now, you would find written on his brain '1912.'"[1] Less than two years later, Taft's premonitions rang true when Roosevelt declared, "My hat is in the ring." Although Taft won the GOP nomination, Roosevelt formed a third party to continue his White House bid, and the general election degenerated into a bitter one. The contest cleaved the Republican Party and eroded the incumbent's authority; on Election Day, Taft and Roosevelt both went down to defeat. Forty years later, during the 1952 Republican primaries, Taft's son, Robert, a prominent U.S. senator (whose son played football at Yale under assistant coach Gerald Ford), was at the center of another fierce intraparty fight that pitted him, representing the GOP's conservative, isolationist wing, against the moderate, internationalist Dwight Eisenhower. When the general won the nomination, Taft's supporters were so infuriated that some of them spat on Eisenhower delegates at the Republican National Convention.[2]

Throughout the twentieth century, GOP moderates and conservatives fought like scorpions in a bottle. In a sense, their battle helped to make Ford vice president. When Nixon asked him for recommendations on Spiro Agnew's successor, Ford listed three possibilities, in order: John Connally, Ronald Reagan, and Nelson Rockefeller. Although Connally was Nixon's favorite, Republicans looked askance at him because he had only recently switched from the Democratic to the Republican Party, while Democrats saw him as a turncoat. The other two reflected the GOP divide. Ford recalled, "You had Reagan, who was a conservative. He would not have been approved by the liberal Republicans. And you had Rockefeller, who would not have been approved by the conservative Republicans."[3] A moderate alternative — Ford — became the wisest choice. But once president, he found himself caught in the divide.

The Resurgent Right

For decades, intraparty bickering ripped away at the GOP, and the wounds never healed. Shifts in fortunes and power during the 1960s portended turmoil in the 1970s. When Vice President Richard Nixon, who represented the moderate wing, lost the 1960 election, conservatives wanted the GOP take a more ideological stance. They prevailed at the party's 1964 convention, nominating Barry Goldwater (booing Rockefeller off the podium and even slipping nausea-producing agents into his supporters' drinks at a cocktail party), but were discredited when LBJ drubbed him at the polls.[4] Instead of sounding a death knell for conservatism, Goldwater's disastrous defeat sparked the movement's rebirth. From Goldwater's effort, conservatives learned the techniques of going door-to-door, soliciting donations, winning primaries, using the media, and mounting a national race.[5] By the mid-1970s, they were ready to make a comeback.

In the 1970s, Americans were surprisingly conservative, according to the findings of Robert Teeter, the pollster for Ford's election campaign, which officially kicked off in July 1975. "I didn't believe those numbers either," he said when he reported his poll results to a colleague. "I've run them through the computer hundreds of times. I can't make 'em come out any other way. America seems to be considerably to the right of Barry Goldwater."[6] The conservative upsurge Teeter recorded was not so shocking; it drew strength from many sources. The social ferment of the 1960s caused massive moral and ideological indigestion among middle-class Americans, whom Nixon targeted as a "silent majority." They were repulsed by the protests and movements of the 1960s, which they feared would endanger traditional family values. Civil rights, feminism, gay rights, and affirmative action empowered minority groups, and conservative middle America felt disenfranchised and threatened. The 1973 Supreme Court decision in *Roe v. Wade* that legalized abortion further galvanized social conservatives into opposition, and the right-to-life movement generated passionate support.

Prominent spokespersons emerged to spearhead the right. Phyllis Schlafly led an antifeminist movement. Former beauty queen Anita Bryant fought a gay-rights statute in Miami. From electronic pulpits, preachers such as Pat Robertson, Oral Roberts, and Jerry Falwell cultivated national followings that funneled fortunes into their coffers and created virtual religious empires. Blurring the church-state boundary, the religious right invaded the political arena, mobilizing its troops to oppose abortion and support school prayer, pouring money into political campaigns and targeting liberal candidates for defeat. Conservatives also drew strength from high-profile writers, like William Buckley and George Will, and from think tanks that began to rival the influence of liberal organizations such as the Brookings Institution. In 1973, the Heritage Foundation was founded, followed five years later by the Manhattan Institute, and the American Enterprise Institute's budget grew tremendously during the 1970s. These think tanks allowed conservatives to ruminate over issues and generate new policies, functioning almost as a shadow government.

The troubled economy of the 1970s played a large role in the conservative upsurge. The 1974–75 recession made Ford politically vulnerable by casting doubts on his economic stewardship; had unemployment and inflation been low in 1975, conservatives would have been less tempted to oppugn his leadership (unemployment was still above 8 percent when Ronald Reagan announced that he would challenge the president). More fundamentally, during the 1970s the political pendulum began an inevitable swing back to center. The nation's previous economic crisis, the Great Depression, pushed American government and political opinion to the left. The apogee of this movement came in the 1960s, with the liberal programs of LBJ's Great Society. But the Great Society generated socially controversial results and helped to create large budget deficits, higher taxes, and inflation. Inflation thrust wage earners into higher tax brackets, forcing them to surrender more money to Uncle Sam; the government benefited from inflation, and taxpayers resented it. A groundswell against social engineering and high taxes built up, along with an antigovernment feeling that Watergate only accelerated.

Thus the nation's worst economic crisis since the 1930s, the Great Inflation, helped swing the pendulum to the right. The movement was visible in both political parties and helped explain why, surprisingly, so many of Ford's vetoes stuck in the Ninety-fourth Congress, as conservative Democrats joined Republicans to uphold them. While more government seemed the solution to the Great Depression, less government appeared the answer to the Great Inflation. Conservatives wanted to reduce taxes and the size of government, and the fastest-growing areas of the country, the South and the West, were hotbeds for such sentiments, especially the South, with its strong states' rights tradition and social and religious conservatism.

The resurgent right created a rough political terrain for GOP moderates. Long considered solidly conservative himself, Ford wound up at ground zero for the most bitter intraparty fight since the Tafts had done battle earlier in the century. During his quarter century in the House, Ford had tirelessly promoted Republican policies and candidates and did so again in the 1974 elections. "Ford fits the Republican party like a glove," commented GOP National Committee counsel Harry Dent. Yet after his long and loyal service to the GOP, Ford found the right abandoning him. Conservative congressman Philip Crane of Illinois dismissed him as just "a caretaker president." New Hampshire's right-wing and often vituperative *Manchester-Union Leader* labeled him "Jerry the Jerk."[7] Ford's political moderation and attempts to appeal to a broad national constituency thrust him into an awkward position within the GOP, caught between Scylla and Charybdis.[8] While his moderation vexed right-wingers, moderate Republicans were upset with his fiscal conservatism and concessions to the right, so much so that they murmured about fielding a candidate to run against him in the Republican primaries, perhaps Senator Howard Baker of Tennessee or Senator Charles Mathias of Maryland.[9] "The right wing was pushing [Ford] pretty hard," Mathias recalled. "And there were some of us who felt that he was going to far to the right." Although both Baker and Mathias declined to challenge the president, Mathias admitted that the idea "had a certain utility" in that it could provide a counterbalance to right-wing pressure on Ford.[10] Seldom had the GOP been so divided, and the split yanked Ford in two directions.

A conservative politician by most measures, Ford maintained that he "very definitely" sought to move the nation to the right. But he explained, "I didn't want to go overboard," taking a moderate approach in his policies and showing flexibility on social issues while practicing fiscal conservatism.[11] Ford described his policies as "middle of the road" and added, "I believe that being in the middle of the road, as far as the Republicans are concerned, on a nationwide basis, is the right policy." He wanted the GOP to be an "umbrella of many colors," welcoming independent and moderate Democrats. Given the Republican Party's anemic condition, Ford additionally worried that a conservative GOP nominee would frighten mainstream and independent voters. Two recent elections offered proof. When the Republicans in 1964 and the Democrats in 1972 embraced ideological extremes in their presidential nominees, they lost badly. Mid-1976 polls supported Ford's contentions about his electability versus Ronald Reagan's, as they showed the president enjoyed more support among independents than Reagan and was a stronger candidate than Reagan against Carter everywhere except California.[12]

But by the mid-1970s, Ford led a party that was more conservative than just four years earlier. Right-wing Republicans disdained his middle-of-the-road approach. Whereas Ford was a more traditional Republican who espoused free-market principles and a reduced governmental role in the economy, many of the new conservatives raised social issues in which they, paradoxically, advocated a more active role for the federal government, such as banning abortion or supporting school prayer with constitutional amendments. The new conservatives, Mathias believed, "really look for a good deal of government action that we don't need." (By contrast, Ford believed that many social issues should be left to the states.) Although their social philosophy made for an uncomfortable fit in the GOP, the new conservatives' cries were louder within the party because moderates muted their voices after Watergate, when their leader had been disgraced.[13] Other moderates declared themselves independent, thereby accentuating the strength of conservatives who remained with the party. Still other high-profile moderates left elective office, such as John Sherman Cooper of Kentucky, who concluded a lengthy Senate service in 1973. By 1980, other Republican Senate moderates (including Edward Brooke of Massachusetts, Clifford Case of New Jersey, and Jacob Javits of New York) lost efforts to retain their seats.

In addition to taking positions to the right of Ford on many social issues, the new conservatives also rallied around hawkish foreign policy issues. They had been unpleasantly jolted by Nixon's diplomatic earthquakes, détente with the Soviet Union and peaceful overtures to the People's Republic of China (Nixon's wage and price controls piqued their disaffection as well). Some of Ford's actions further alienated the right. His appointment of Rockefeller as vice president, an anathema to the right, angered conservatives. Rockefeller's views were so liberal that Hubert Humphrey twice contacted him about being a running mate in 1968, and right-wing leader Richard Viguerie commented, "I could hardly have been more upset if Ford had selected Teddy Kennedy," even positing the beginning of the New Right as the Rockefeller appointment. At Ford's first presidential press conference, one reporter mentioned the Rockefeller nomination and noted, "Mr. President, you have been in office 19 days now, and already some of your natural, conservative allies are grumbling that you are moving too far to the left."[14]

Further affronts, however inadvertent, followed. As part of his effort to salve wounds left from Vietnam, Ford offered an amnesty program to draft dodgers, which upset conservative groups such as the American Legion. Conservatives bemoaned Betty Ford's outspoken support for the Equal Rights Amendment. That was bad enough; but they were infuriated with a 1975 interview on CBS's 60 Minutes in which the First Lady praised Roe v. Wade (calling it "a great, great decision"), compared marijuana experimentation to a first beer or cigarette, and said that she would accept her teenage daughter Susan's having an affair.[15] Ford's November 1975 dismissal of Secretary of

Defense James Schlesinger also nettled conservatives, who additionally saw the president as too willing to compromise with Congress on litmus-test issues. Some conservatives expressed disappointment when Ford accepted the two 1975 tax cuts as well as EPCA, which they believed conceded too much to the Democrats. Right-wingers presented a potential problem for Ford in the primaries, where party voters traditionally tended to be more conservative than most GOP members.

Conservative affection centered on Ronald Reagan, the former California governor, and speculation brewed that he would challenge Ford for the nomination. The former actor was also a former Democrat, having changed parties relatively recently, in 1962; Ford, by contrast, was a lifelong Republican. William Seidman recalled that as the election year approached, "Ford had the view that the Republicans would not dump a Republican president, particularly one who had been as long-standing and loyal a Republican as Ford." But Reagan had cultivated a national following through weekly newspaper columns, a radio program, and the lecture circuit. Hartmann warned the president that Reagan might take him on, and other advisers were concerned. In April 1975, noting that Reagan's radio broadcasts aired in key primary states, presidential aide John Hoornstra worried that the California governor would indeed run in 1976. But other Ford administration insiders joked about Reagan and dismissed him as a nuisance; to them, he was little more than an ex-actor, and a bad one at that. Ford himself admitted, "I didn't take Reagan seriously."[16]

But the president did take Reagan seriously enough to try various ways to keep him at bay. In late 1974, he invited Reagan to join his cabinet, offering a choice of positions, but Reagan declined. He tried again the following year, offering the post of commerce secretary, but again Reagan refused.[17] He appointed Reagan to Rockefeller's blue-ribbon panel to investigate the CIA. During his 1975 Easter vacation in California, he hosted the Reagans for dinner. He also read Reagan's weekly newspaper column, and on one essay that repined against the growth of federal bureaucracy, the president scrawled, "He's *behind* us," as if to convince himself and his staff that it were true.[18] Subsequently, Ford may have lulled himself into the false security that Reagan would not run.

Ford only went so far to ward Reagan off, and the Californian only got so close to the Ford White House. Part of the problem was poor personal chemistry. Reagan's memoirs barely mention Ford; Ford's memoirs contain cool references to Reagan, including the observation, "I have always been able to get to know people pretty easily. I tried to get to know Reagan, but I failed. He was pleasant and congenial, yet at the same time formal and reserved with me. I never knew what he was really thinking behind that winning smile." Hartmann, observing the almost tangible awkwardness between the two when they were together, concluded, "The fact of the matter is that they just don't like each other." Reagan envied Ford's job; Ford envied Reagan's ability to command high lecture fees and his natural feel for the spoken word. Neither man thought much of the other's ability to govern, and Reagan viewed Ford as merely an "appointed" president. This mutual mixture of envy and disdain added a personal element to the brewing political drama.[19]

On November 19, 1975, the rumblings from the right turned to thunder. While at the White House, Ford received a phone call from the former California governor. "I am going to run for President," Reagan told Ford. He was to announce his candidacy tomorrow and wanted to inform Ford first, saying, "I trust we can have a good contest, and I hope that it won't be divisive."[20] Ford knew that it would be. The rancorous fight that followed reflected not only the strength of the conservative resurgence but also Ford's precarious political position and the post-Watergate backlash among voters.

The next day, Reagan publicly announced his candidacy. In December, Ford administration members drew up a list of Reagan's strengths and weaknesses, and Ford's, and they found that the challenger's strengths outnumbered his weaknesses, where the converse was true for the president. Worse, a Gallup poll showed that Reagan led Ford by 40 to 32 percent among Republicans.[21]

The Reagan Challenge

Although the Reagan challenge caught Ford off guard, he expected to win the nomination "in a breeze." Reagan's solutions to the country's problems, Ford believed, were simplistic, and his nine-to-five work ethic would prove inadequate for a rigorous campaign. Like many of Reagan's adversaries, Ford underestimated the genial Californian, a mistake that proved almost politically fatal.

Still, Ford had taken precautions against Reagan. In the summer of 1975, he selected army secretary Howard "Bo" Callaway to run his campaign. Ford hoped the former Georgia congressman would help him in the South and among conservatives. But Callaway had never managed a national campaign and demonstrated his gift for the indiscreet remark almost immediately. In July 1975, in a moment of excess candor, he told reporters that Vice President Rockefeller was Ford's "number-one problem." He continued, "You and I both know that if Rockefeller took himself out, it would help with the nomination." For a campaign manager to criticize a vice president so openly was unprecedented, and Callaway's characterizations came even after Ford had warned him about previous slights against Rockefeller. Ford recalled, "I was furious."[22]

Yet Ford apparently realized that Rockefeller presented problems. In May 1975, he had given Rockefeller a vote of confidence, calling him "a good partner" and expressing a desire to keep him as vice president.[23] But by September, he noted a poll indicating that 55 percent of respondents gave Rockefeller a negative job approval rating. The resentment Rockefeller generated especially among the Republican right led to a highly controversial action that Ford dissembled about for years afterward before conceding that it was "one of the few cowardly things I did in my life." On October 28, 1975, he met the vice president in the Oval Office. As a result of the meeting, Rockefeller agreed to draft a letter requesting that Ford remove him from the 1976 ticket. As Ford recalled it, the two men "discussed the growing strength of the GOP's right wing. Perhaps, he said, the best thing he could do would be to withdraw from consideration as my running mate."[24]

Ford's recollection clashed with those of Rockefeller and other administration members. Hurt by his removal, Rockefeller remarked, "I didn't take myself off the ticket, you know—he asked me to do it." He recalled Ford explaining that "it's very important that I get this nomination. And I have been talking with my political advisers and I think it would be—as much as personally I feel badly about it—it would be better if you were not on the ticket and if you would withdraw." Hartmann reluctantly concluded that in presenting Rockefeller's withdrawal as voluntary, Ford "fudged his pledge of openness and candor with the American people."[25]

The whole episode was surprising, not just because Ford's version of the event contradicted others' recollections. Some modern presidents have contemplated changing running mates as they prepared to run for a new term; that was not unusual. In 1956, Eisenhower considered abandoning Nixon, ostensibly so that the vice president could gain experience in other executive branch positions; additionally, Eisenhower felt uncomfortable with Nixon, complaining that he could never figure out Nixon's "personal equation" (an expression that the general used to denote someone's essence).[26] In 1992, many insiders urged George Bush to drop Dan Quayle for a running mate with more stature; in early 2004, rumors circulated that George W. Bush might replace Dick Cheney, whose negative poll ratings acted as a drag on their ticket. Yet each president decided to keep his vice president. Ford dropped Rockefeller, and his action indicated some of the drawbacks in appointing him. Although the former New York governor lent gravitas to the new administration at a time when Americans needed confidence in the executive branch, he failed to promise future leadership for the GOP. Most presidents select younger vice presidents who later become party leaders in their own right, often running for president. Ford felt psychologically secure enough to pick an older vice president with a well-established reputation, but the disadvantage was that by 1976, Rockefeller was sixty-eight years old and in the twilight of his political career. Moreover, his liberal political philosophy clashed with Ford's fiscal discipline, and his presence in the administration made the president vulnerable to conservative attacks, which Ford hoped to avert by letting him go.

Yet the Rockefeller dismissal failed to appease the right. The new conservatives had the energy of an angry teenager and were just as rebellious. It was a young movement, comprising many persons in their thirties and forties who were flexing their political muscles for the first time.[27] It was decades before they had to reckon with opponents like Bill Clinton, who chastened conservatives by co-opting the political center and winning the White House for two terms. In 1976, the conservative rebels subordinated party to ideology, hurting Ford's chances.

Ironically, the youthful neoconservative movement put its hopes in an older warrior, the sixty-five-year-old Reagan, who decided to challenge Ford partly because he felt this might be his last chance to run for president. Although he said he was "astounded" at Rockefeller's dismissal, Reagan immediately added that he had no interest in becoming Ford's vice president.[28] Instead, he entered the lists, and Ford braced himself for a showdown in snowy New Hampshire.

While Reagan had time to organize his campaign in New Hampshire, enlisting the help of former governor Hugh Gregg and compiling computerized lists of registered voters, Ford found his campaign there "in disarray." He faced serious obstacles. Under the new campaign finance laws, he could make only two trips to the Granite State, since the cost of his White House entourage pushed his campaign toward the spending limit; Reagan, by contrast, spent twenty-one days there campaigning. (Money was so tight in New Hampshire that Ford's campaign abandoned the idea of printing $.80 photos of Ford for press kits.) Nixon's name popped into the news again, reminding voters of Ford's controversial pardon. Even though he had promised Ford that he would travel to China only after the 1976 election, Nixon accepted an invitation to visit the country, which he did just before the primary. Nixon not only reneged on his promise but inflicted political injury on the president who, by pardoning him, made possible his freedom to travel. When he heard the news, National Security Advisor Brent Scowcroft, who usually never cursed, exclaimed, "Nixon's a shit!" Ford's aides were so concerned about the prospect of bad publicity that they briefly considered schemes to prevent the trip, such as refusing to let a Chinese plane land in the United States to pick up the former president, even seizing the plane to demand that China pay debts to the United States.[29]

Despite all the ominous signs for his New Hampshire effort, Ford suspected that Reagan would fall victim to his skimpy understanding of complex issues. "I thought his knowledge of the way the federal government worked was superficial at best," Ford commented. "Inevitably he would slip, and once he made a mistake, we could pounce on that."

Ford soon found it. In September 1975, before he had kicked off his campaign, Reagan gave a speech in which he suggested that $90 billion in federal programs could be transferred to the states. Reagan's plan lay quietly for months but exploded in New Hampshire. Ford's campaign publicized Reagan's remarks, creating a stench among tax-averse New Hampshire voters. Callaway slammed the plan as "a $90-billion boondoggle," and Ford called it "totally impractical." Such a massive transfer of programs could force the Granite State to adopt its first-ever income or sales tax to raise money for the programs that Reagan targeted, many of them critical services in education, transportation, and urban renewal. Worse, they might cease to exist altogether. The ill-advised scheme put Reagan on the defensive and heightened fears that many voters, deep down, harbored: he appeared too conservative to be president.[30]

New Hampshire governor Meldrin Thomson boldly predicted a Reagan victory, raising expectations and making Ford almost an underdog. The president even tried to brace himself for a possible defeat by saying that a loss would not be too harmful, and he would concentrate on other primaries.[31] When Ford won the primary, though it was by a sliver—1,317 votes out of more than 100,000 cast—the prediction of a Reagan triumph only magnified the challenger's defeat. Ford's victory was uncomfortably narrow, but he proved that he could win a political contest outside of Grand Rapids. He gained momentum; he also saved his campaign. A loss in New Hampshire would have been humiliating for a sitting president, perhaps fatal against so popular a campaigner as Reagan. As Ford admitted, "We'd be in real bad shape if we hadn't won in New Hampshire."[32] But the thin victory was a harbinger of trouble ahead.

Ford beat Reagan in the next two primaries, Florida and Illinois (the latter, Reagan's native state). After the Florida victory, the *Wall Street Journal* ran a headline, "Ford's Florida Victory Seems to Assure Him of GOP Nomination." Ford's strategy had been to go for an early knockout, beating Reagan convincingly in the early primaries and forcing him to give up.[33] The strategy seemed to be working, and after notching three consecutive victories, the Ford camp pressured Reagan to drop out. Such talk only made the former actor dig in his heels. "Tell *him* to quit," Reagan angrily retorted. His campaign manager, John Sears, explained, "You have to recognize he made some pretty bad movies. It must have been pretty embarrassing. But he knows that if you make a bad movie, you don't stop making movies." Ford's campaign grew confident of a victory in North Carolina, the next primary, and even cut back on advertising there. Bob Teeter recalled, "We just didn't take North Carolina seriously enough. . . . The feeling was Reagan was beaten and there was no sense mauling him."[34] By contrast, Reagan—whom North Carolina senator Jesse Helms openly endorsed—turned to the medium on which he performed best, television. His campaign sent half-hour spots to almost all of the state's television stations, and they aired in prime time.

Reagan stunned Ford in North Carolina, winning 52 percent of the vote and more than half of the state's delegates. The aura of presidential invincibility, and along with it the inevitability of Ford's nomination, was punctured. It was only the third time a sitting president had lost a primary and the first time in Ford's political career that he tasted defeat at the polls.[35] Reagan's upset victory breathed life into his campaign and gave him all the incentive he needed to stay in the race, which was tight from there on.

Reagan took the gloves off. Earlier, he vowed to adhere to Marquis of Queensberry rules by professing an "Eleventh Commandment," namely, "Thou shalt not speak ill of any fellow Republican." The loss in New Hampshire changed that, and Reagan broke his own commandment. He taped television "infomercials" and refined his target. He found that the Ford campaign had a soft underbelly on foreign policy, and there he cut deeply. One theme that he carved away at was the perceived decline in U.S. military strength. He equated détente with a Munich-like appeasement, and charged that by pursuing détente, Ford had given away the store to the Soviet Union, allowing the United States to slip to the status of "a second-rate power." "Under Messrs. Kissinger and Ford," he contended, "this nation has become Number Two in military power in a world where it is dangerous—if not fatal—to be second best."[36] Reagan adopted the campaign slogan "Make America No. 1 Again" and vowed that as president, he would send Kissinger packing and install a new secretary of state.[37]

Frequent, direct jabs at the president would have been unseemly, so Reagan found the perfect punching bag in Kissinger, capitalizing on conservative disaffection with the secretary of state. Although in mid-1976 a plurality of Americans (49 percent) approved of Kissinger's performance, his popularity was eroding, and a growing chorus of Republicans expressed displeasure with him, especially in the South.[38] A Texas woman wrote to the White House, "I simply WILL NOT, CANNOT vote for Mr. Ford, if Kissinger is to continue making foreign policy decisions. . . . He has grown stale, ineffective, and MUCH TOO controversial." An Alabama neurosurgeon reported, "The single biggest problem I have in selling physicians on the President, is Henry Kissinger. It seems to me to be imperative that he be replaced." By declaring that he wanted to retain Kissinger's services for a full term, Ford needlessly inflamed a powerful segment of his own party. As one California man wrote, "That declaration by Mr. Ford puts us in a position by which, if we vote for Ford, we are also voting for Kissinger. Nothing doing!"[39]

Many Republicans apparently believed Reagan's accusations that through détente, Kissinger had conceded too much to the Soviet Union, and he implied that Ford was soft on defense. The charges infuriated Ford, a naval veteran who advocated a strong military. "Reagan's statements," Ford wrote, "were inflammatory and irresponsible." Indeed, in light of the president's Pentagon budgets, the largest ever in peacetime, the *Economist* wrote, "The accusation that Mr. Ford neglects defence is absurd. . . . Nor can Mr. Ford be accused of 'softness' to the Russians." As a congressman, Ford had advocated military muscle despite détente, returning from a 1972 trip to China convinced that the United States had to maintain a tough defense posture. As president, Ford supported the B-1 bomber to supercede the air force's aging fleet of B-52s, and in March 1976, dismayed at stalled arms talks with the Soviet Union, he asked Congress for a $322 million supplemental appropriation to produce more Minuteman III missiles. Yet Reagan's allegations were believable because of the widespread perception that America was in decline, and he charged that the fault rested with Ford and Kissinger. Moreover, conservatives were so strong that Ford hesitated to strike back too forcefully against Reagan. Whereas Kissinger urged Ford to lash out against Reagan's accusations, Dick Cheney and Rogers Morton warned Ford that hard-hitting counterpunches would alienate conservatives, whose support he needed for the general election.[40]

Reagan stalked Ford on another foreign policy issue that addressed the frustrations and uncertainties of the 1970s: the Panama Canal. The Panamanian government had long disputed American rights to the canal, and the Ford administration continued decade-old talks to renegotiate the 1903 treaty rights over the canal. Reagan seized on the issue, charging that Ford planned to give up U.S. sovereignty over the canal. Realizing that the issue evoked a patriotic response from crowds, Reagan drove at it full bore, declaring, "When it comes to the canal, we built it, we paid for it, it's ours, and . . . we are going to keep it." Reagan's statements were misleading, and even Senator Barry Goldwater accused him of speaking "in an irresponsible manner on an issue that could affect the nation's security."[41] Still, some Americans believed that relinquishing the canal signaled a cold war setback. A Pennsylvania man wrote to the Ford campaign committee to warn that Panamanian ruler Omar Torijos "is a Commie, and if we give the canal to him we'll be giving it to Russia." The canal became a focal point for post-Vietnam concerns that communism was making gains around the world. Reagan aide David Keene commented, "The Panama Canal issue had nothing to do with the canal. It said more about the American people's feelings about where the country was, and what it was powerless to do."[42]

By seizing on issues where Ford appeared vulnerable, Reagan jump-started his campaign and mounted a serious challenge. The attacks fed the fiction that Ford's foreign policy was weak on communism; at one point, Reagan even charged that the Ford administration was set to give diplomatic recognition to North Vietnam. Charges so chimerical caught Ford off guard and kept him on the defensive for much of the primary season. Ford backed away from pursuing a new SALT agreement, which deprived him of a potential diplomatic achievement to tout during the general campaign. (Soviet ambassador Anatoly Dobrynin even believed that Ford's decision to placate the right "probably cost him the presidency.") After Reagan won the Nebraska primary, Ford postponed by two weeks the signing of an agreement on the peaceful use of nuclear explosions, fearing that conservatives would point to it as another sign of Ford "weakness" against the Russian bear.[43] Reagan also attacked Ford for the high federal deficit, promising a balanced budget during a Reagan presidency. Instead of focusing attention on the improving economy or arms control progress, Ford had to defend himself against Reagan's onslaught.

The sight of an incumbent president in such political trouble was unusual. Part of the problem was that Ford had put ineffective hands in charge of his campaign. After Bo Callaway stepped aside amid financial investigations, Rogers Morton took his place. Morton lacked a sense of political strategy and committed embarrassing gaffes. On one occasion, he was photographed sitting before a desk crammed with alcohol bottles and beer cans (although they belonged to others); after a primary loss, he made the unfortunate remark that he would not "rearrange the furniture on the deck of the *Titanic*."[44] The error-prone managers, coupled with Ford's slight gifts as a campaigner, put Ford in political jeopardy.

But a principal explanation for Ford's trouble was his opponent's formidable strengths. Reagan was an inherently attractive candidate. An outsider to the federal government at a time when voters distrusted it, he referred to Washington as a "foreign power" and lambasted the "buddy system" that reigned there. To voters, his tough talk on foreign policy reflected real leadership qualities. Reagan was also a celebrity. Ford remembered enviously, "I wasn't even in the same league with him when it came to movie star quality; he was a born showman and all he had to do was smile to turn on a crowd."[45] Where Ford could be soporific, Reagan was a superb stump speaker who could devote himself full-time to campaigning. As a spokesman for General Electric in the 1960s, he began jotting down key ideas, statistics, and anecdotes on index cards, and he had assembled a stack of cards that he transformed into a campaign presentation. Reagan's campaign called it "The Speech," and by shuffling the index cards and making small changes, Reagan added variety that kept it fresh for each delivery. One Ford supporter listened in admiration and commented, "He gives a hell of a speech. Don't you wish Ford could talk like that?"[46]

Even Reagan's adversaries admitted that when it came to spinning a yarn, he was the best. At one press conference, Rockefeller testily avoided answering questions about differences between him and Reagan. When pressed, he finally offered, "He can tell better stories than I can."[47] But Reagan's ideas were important, too. His message was an indictment of big government, and he often opened with the line, "A government bureau is the nearest thing to eternal life that we'll ever see on this earth." He then launched his attack, dragging out examples of excess government that engaged and enraged crowds. A New Jersey man's veterans benefits suddenly ceased because the government declared him dead. A "welfare queen" used eighty aliases, held a dozen Social Security cards, and collected veterans benefits on four deceased husbands. The trouble with these stories was that they were untrue. Reporters found that Reagan had exaggerated the facts, yet he continued to use the same stories to capitalize on the feelings of estrangement from Washington and disgust with big government. Journalist Walter Mears, who won the Pulitzer Prize for his coverage of the 1976 presidential race, called Reagan "the master of the unassailable statistic." The California governor cited astounding figures about the yearly volume of paperwork that Washington produced, joking that "it would make a great annual bonfire." When Mears questioned him about the source of his statistics, Reagan replied that he recalled reading or hearing them, a response that was impossible to verify or refute.[48]

Reports also surfaced that Reagan paid no federal or state income taxes in 1970 and that in 1972 and 1974 he paid federal taxes substantially lower than others in his income group. Although Ford tried to pressure Reagan to release a full financial disclosure, Reagan only provided a summary of his income tax returns, and the press did not pursue the story. Ford was mystified, because the press had aggressively pursued Nixon's financial irregularities. Reagan's "lack of full disclosure never became the issue I expected it would," Ford recalled.[49] Reagan's ability to withstand media scrutiny after embellishing stories and withholding financial information was indeed striking, given the atmosphere of 1976, when integrity in public officials was a hot issue. His apparent invulnerability testified to his popularity and effectiveness as a campaigner, qualities that earned him the sobriquet of the "Teflon president" once elected; it also showed that the media liked a telegenic candidate. Partly, Reagan railed against the very sentiments that would have generated criticism of his stories, the distrust of politicians, and by championing this theme he inoculated himself against it. The silky-voiced former radio announcer also had a gift for using words to create a reality in his audience, making listeners believe that his embroidered stories were true. One of the most skillful politicians of the twentieth century, he slipped effortlessly through potential minefields.

After North Carolina, Reagan reeled off four primary wins in a row—Texas, Alabama, Georgia, and Indiana—and pulled ahead of Ford in the delegate count. The Ford campaign appeared to be in crisis. Top aides described Ford as "bewildered." The president seemed out of his league. Ford later admitted, "All of a sudden I found myself in a different ballpark. I just didn't comprehend the vast difference between running in my district and running for President." Nessen feared that Ford would lose the nomination and wondered whether he would mount a third-party campaign in the general election.[50]

By late spring, after thirty primaries, neither Ford nor Reagan had enough delegates to clinch the nomination. The president had to endure the humiliating ordeal of courting uncommitted delegates. State conventions followed the primaries, and Ford invited entire delegations to the White House to wine and dine them, attempting to shake loose uncommitted delegates. He also telephoned them to ask for their support, sometimes after his staff had tracked them down to obscure places. One delegate was shocked to receive a phone call from the president while she was at a beauty parlor in Oakville, Missouri. But the efforts, both tiresome and demeaning, yielded few new delegates. As the two bruised warriors limped toward the Republican National Convention in Kansas City, Missouri, both eyed the magic number of 1,130 delegates, and although Ford had a fragile lead, he was short by about 130.[51]

Reagan had to court delegates, too, and in an attempt to win some from Pennsylvania and neighboring states, he blundered. Bucking tradition, on June 26 he announced his vice-presidential running mate before the convention: Senator Richard Schweicker of Pennsylvania. White House chief of staff Dick Cheney wore a Cheshire cat grin as he strolled into the Oval

Office to tell Ford of Reagan's pick, saying, "We just got the best news we've had in months." Ford was flabbergasted. Schweicker was a liberal Republican who had supported him and was far apart from Reagan on major issues. The move was designed to win Reagan support from moderate and liberal Republicans, especially in the Northeast, but he stunned his supporters, especially since he had earlier dismissed the idea of picking a liberal running mate to give ideological balance to his ticket. The conservative backlash was immediate. Congressman John Ashbrook, an Ohio conservative, called the Schweicker choice "the dumbest thing I ever heard of." Illinois congressman Henry Hyde compared Reagan's move to "a farmer selling his last cow to buy a milking machine." Drew Lewis, the leader of the Pennsylvania delegation, refused to support Reagan, despite entreaties from the challenger's camp, and instead declared for Ford. Southern conservatives began to drift toward Ford. Texan John Connally finally decided to endorse the president at a special White House news conference. "It is quite clear now," Connally declared, "that the president is the better choice, not only for the party but for the country."[52]

After the Schweicker gamble backfired, John Sears, Reagan's campaign manager, introduced a proposal that became known as "Rule 16-C," which would have required all candidates to name their vice-presidential selection before the nomination. The ploy was transparent, designed to force Ford into naming his running mate and potentially suffering the same damage Reagan had. Critics mocked Rule 16-C as the "misery loves company" proposal. Losing a vote on procedure would have weakened the president's authority and jeopardized his ability to win the nomination, so Ford forces fought Rule 16-C tooth and nail, and the Republican National Convention voted against it. But the convention approved a foreign policy plank designed by Reagan's forces. Called "Morality in Foreign Policy," the plank criticized détente and the Helsinki accords and forbade "secret agreements," an obvious reference to the Panama Canal negotiations. "When I read the plank," Ford recalled, "I was furious. It added up to nothing less than a slick denunciation of Administration foreign policy." While Kissinger, Rockefeller, and Scowcroft urged Ford to fight the plank, Cheney, Nessen, and campaign aide Stuart Spencer warned him that losing a fight on the plank could cost him the nomination. Reluctantly, Ford agreed, and the convention adopted the plank.[53]

Ford clinched the GOP nomination on the first ballot, but the vote was close. Ford had 1,187 delegates to Reagan's 1,070. In addition to stomaching the foreign policy plank, Ford also had to pay studious attention to conservatives in selecting a running mate. Mississippi's state chairman and Maine's delegates threatened to drop their support if Ford selected a running mate they disliked.

Such an audacious warning to the president contrasted vividly with the tight control and discipline that Johnson and Nixon wielded at their conventions.[54] Speculation seesawed between two men, Senator Howard Baker of Tennessee and William Ruckelshaus, Nixon's deputy attorney general. Both had reached almost folk-hero status during Watergate, Ruckelshaus for resigning rather than carrying out Nixon's order to fire Special Prosecutor Archibald Cox, Baker for repeatedly asking during the Watergate hearings, "What did the president know, and when did he know it?" But both had handicaps. They were moderates, and their selection would have rankled conservatives. Ruckelshaus was little known among voters. Baker was no fiery orator (he gave an insipid keynote address at the convention), and even though from Tennessee, offered little help in the South against Jimmy Carter's strength there. Baker's wife was also a recovering alcoholic, which might have looked bad in the character-sensitive times. Ford admitted that had Rule 16-C been adopted, forcing him to name his running mate, he would have picked Ruckelshaus.[55]

Although many delegates would have loved a Ford-Reagan ticket, Reagan insisted that Ford not ask him to join the ticket and made it a condition of their conciliation meeting following Ford's nomination. The meeting took place close to midnight, with Ford finally leaving at 2:00 A.M. He was exhausted but assembled aides for a brainstorming session at 3:15 in the morning to discuss a vice-presidential choice. After tussling with four names, Ford narrowed it down to Baker and another senator who had escaped media speculation, Bob Dole of Kansas. Just after 5:00 A.M., Ford adjourned the meeting so that everyone could get a few hours of sleep. When the group reconvened at 10:15 A.M., Ford announced that he was telephoning Dole.[56]

Since the beginning of the year, reporters had speculated on whom Ford might pick as his running mate. No attention focused on Dole, and in January even Ford, after reporters incessantly prodded him to name potential picks, mentioned eight men whom he considered "fully qualified" to be his running mate; Dole was not on the list.[57] At the Republican convention, the press barely mentioned Dole as a contender. Thus Ford's choice came as a surprise. Ford recalled that "the major factor [behind selecting Dole] was we knew we had to carry the western states unanimously to win, and someone like Bob Dole was by far the better candidate for that purpose."[58] Even though the addition of Dole made a geographically unbalanced ticket of two midwesterners, Ford hoped that Dole would help in the farm states. Support from farmers had been important to Ford throughout his political career; at his wedding, which took place while he first ran for Congress, he showed up with shoes that he had muddied from campaigning at a farm earlier in the day. In 1976, he had special reasons to court the agricultural vote. The year before, he temporarily suspended grain sales to the Soviet Union to give the United States time to reach a long-term agreement. Pressure for the embargo came from consumer groups worried about the availability of food for the domestic market and from longshoremen, who demanded that more grain be carried aboard American ships. The suspension infuriated farmers, especially because they had reaped a record harvest, and Dole, the ranking Republican on the Senate Agriculture Committee, lambasted the White House (an attack that now, viewed through a political rearview mirror, endeared Dole to Ford as a running mate). Carter posed a threat in farm states; he attacked the grain embargo and vowed never to impose an embargo as president.[59] (Ironically, Carter instituted a grain embargo against the Soviet Union in 1980 to protest its invasion of Afghanistan.) Additionally, Carter was a former peanut farmer who appealed to his agricultural brethren, even naming his campaign plane *Peanut One*.

The right also played a role in Ford's surprise selection. Dole was acceptable to conservatives, and if Ford were to unite his party, he had to pick someone whom the right would accept. Importantly, the choice had Reagan's blessing. Before Ford's conciliation meeting with Reagan, his campaign sent a delegation to meet with the defeated challenger to sound him out about possible running mates, hoping that Reagan himself would express interest in joining the ticket. He did not, but he mentioned Dole (Dole had earlier asked Reagan aide Lyn Nofziger to have Reagan put in a good word for him). Later, during their tense meeting, the president mentioned six names to Reagan: Bill Simon, John Connally, Bob Dole, Howard Baker, Elliot Richardson, and Bill Ruckelshaus. Reagan again singled out Dole.[60] Last-minute pressure from conservative southern delegates may have pushed Ford further toward picking Dole.[61] Dole knew why Ford had picked him; when asked what assets he brought to the ticket, Dole immediately responded that he would be "a bridge with the Reagan forces."

Ford felt comfortable with Dole, whom he knew would be a feisty campaigner, attacking Carter while Ford remained presidential (Baker and Ruckelshaus lacked Dole's slashing style). Ford liked Dole's sometimes vitriolic sense of humor, and he may have also felt a sense of political noblesse oblige toward the Kansas senator. In 1965, while Dole was a congressman, he helped elect Ford minority leader. The contest between Ford and Charles Halleck was tight, and a few Kansas representatives were undecided. Ford recalled, "In the end, Bob Dole persuaded three other Kansas Republicans to vote with him, and those four votes probably saved the day."[62]

In a reflection of 1970s power politics, the resurgent Democratic Congress also affected Ford's running mate selection by eliminating one of his favorites from contention. When he had become president, Ford narrowed his choices of prospective vice presidents to two men, Nelson Rockefeller and a GOP rising star, fifty-year-old George H. W. Bush, a former Texas congressman who was serving as Republican National Committee chair. Ultimately, Ford picked the more experienced Rockefeller, a decision that the ambitious Bush privately called "an enormous personal disappointment." But Ford still employed Bush's political talents, naming him ambassador to China and then, in November 1975, appointing him as the new CIA director. Senate Democrats, sensing that the nominee had a bright political future, demanded that Bush forswear vice-presidential ambitions in 1976 as a condition of heading the CIA. While Ford was angry at the senators' stipulation, viewing it as "blatant partisanship," Bush convinced the president to relent. At the 1976 convention, though, the quid pro quo constrained Ford. As he mulled over possible running mates, he regretted being unable to pick Bush, as his presence on the ticket would have helped to unify the party. If not for the feisty Ninety-fourth Congress, Ford might have chosen Bush for the number two spot, four years before Reagan did.[63]

Nonetheless, Ford had his team, and he had to weld the GOP back together, beginning with the traditional show of unity. But his effort was endangered by Reagan supporters who would not accept defeat. On the evening of Ford's acceptance speech, Reagan's followers demonstrated noisily for their candidate, delaying the president's appearance. From his hotel suite, a furious Ford ordered events to move forward. The show of disrespect stoked his anger, and he recalled that he "used four-letter words that I almost never use." He could not begin his speech until 10:40 P.M. That was a shame for the president and the party, because it was one of his finest speeches. He showed a rare passion and fire, hurling challenges at the Democrats almost as Jove threw thunderbolts, and the convention interrupted Ford's speech sixty-five times with applause. Repeatedly urging his audience, "Let's look at the record," Ford extolled the achievements of his presidency and predicted that on Election Day, voters would conclude, "Jerry, you've done a good job — keep right on doing it!" After watching Ford's rousing address and the apparent Republican harmony, Carter campaign manager Hamilton Jordan said, "It scares the shit out of me."[64]

In a surprise move, Ford also invited his Democratic challenger to a televised forensics match, declaring, "I am ready, I am eager to go before the American people and debate the real issues face-to-face with Jimmy Carter." He had discussed the idea with Betty and then Bob Hartmann, both of whom liked the idea, and just two hours before he was scheduled to appear before the convention, he incorporated the lines in his speech. It was a daring move.

No incumbent president had ever debated a challenger, and the prospect risked giving free national television exposure to Carter. Still, Ford was far behind in the polls, and he needed a dramatic gambit to close the gap.

Winning the nomination and hearing the acclamation of his supporters was one of the highlights of Ford's presidency. Max Friedersdorf said that he had never seen Ford happier: "He was very euphoric. He gave a great speech that night." Still, bitterness remained. Many Reagan supporters wept when their candidate was defeated, and during Ford's address, television cameras caught one woman covering her face with a Reagan book in protest. After he finished speaking, Ford graciously invited Reagan to give the final address of the convention, a speech that, while moving, barely mentioned the nominee. Yet as Ford stared out over the enthusiastic, appreciative crowd, he thought hopefully, "Maybe party unity wasn't so ephemeral a vision after all."[65]

Ford had beaten back the Reagan challenge, but barely. He was the first president since Taft in 1912 to have faced so serious a threat for the nomination.[66] Nothing in Ford's term upset him more than the conservative revolt against his leadership: "I was angriest [during my presidency] with some of the tactics of the challenges to me in the Republican convention," he once said. "I thought it was a mistake from their point of view, a mistake from the point of view of the party, because it diverted a lot of my time and attention, and I should have been campaigning against Jimmy Carter."[67] The Reagan challenge undermined Ford. Divided parties leave the nominee wounded, and journalist Lou Cannon said that when he interviewed Ford a year after the election, the former president blamed Reagan for his defeat.[68]

Ford felt deeply hurt, both personally and politically. "The Reagan attack on me in '76 was not a healthy attack," he later said. "It was a demagogic attack. And I resented it."[69] The grueling intraparty challenge took Ford away from his real joy, tending to the operations of government. It also drained his energy and resources and prevented him from rallying Republicans solidly behind him. Ford had agreed to a convention relatively late in August partly because he anticipated no challenge for the nomination; instead, he worried whether he would even be the nominee until August 18.[70] Only then could Ford concentrate on mending breaches and building alliances, a task that Carter began before the Democratic National Convention in July (he had sewn up the nomination by June). Moreover, Reagan's ability almost to wrest the nomination from a sitting president made Ford look vulnerable and planted doubts even among Republicans about whether he could run a strong race against Carter.

Reagan seemed eager to forget his challenge to Ford, devoting just three pages of his memoirs to the 1976 race.[71] Although Reagan lost the battle for the 1976 nomination, he in effect won the presidency. The primaries gave Reagan tremendous national exposure, and he honed a message that gained popularity: "Government is the problem, not the solution." His political feat was remarkable, bouncing back from a string of early primary losses and almost winning the nomination. A bona fide contender, he became the instant front-runner for the 1980 nomination, which he easily clinched and then scored a resounding election victory in the fall. At the Republican National Convention in Detroit, he did something curious. When Ford visited him at his hotel suite, Reagan asked his former foe to be his running mate. The offer came out of the blue and caught Ford off guard. "It was a big surprise," Ford recalled, and at first he was tempted to accept.[72] Reagan wanted so much for Ford to join him that he offered to grant Ford unprecedented authority over areas such as the federal budget and National Security Council. For a moment, the two men looked close to sealing a deal, and the *Chicago Sun-Times* headlined its morning edition, "It's Reagan and Ford." But Ford decided that the arrangement would be impractical; it would involve significant sharing of power, amounting almost to a "co-presidency," and he worried about the uneasy mix of staffs that would result, a problem that had plagued his own presidency, with his staff sometimes clashing with Nixon holdovers and Rockefeller loyalists.[73] Ultimately, Ford declined the offer. But Reagan's unexpected invitation showed that, despite his criticisms of Ford in the 1976 primaries, he thought well enough of Ford's leadership to want him to be his vice president.

After their bitter 1976 face-off, Ford reconciled with Reagan, campaigning for him in 1980. He developed great respect for Reagan's administration, calling him a "first-class president," and Ford, who retired to California, visited Reagan when Reagan battled Alzheimer's. The disease had advanced so far that the fortieth president had difficulty recognizing Ford, who mentioned some anecdotes that seemed to revive Reagan's memory. "We became good friends despite that [1976] contest," Ford reflected, commenting that "in politics, you have to give and take and respect the views of others, and I certainly felt that way toward Reagan."[74]

But in 1976, the conservative challenge represented another mountain of adversity that Ford had to climb. After the Republican convention, moreover, he was still stuck with a public approval rating below 50 percent. That benchmark represented a dividing line in elections. Since 1948, presidents with ratings above 50 percent on Election Day have always triumphed; few presidents with numbers below 50 percent have won. Ford's greatest political challenge lay ahead.

Chapter 18

Back from the Brink

*Ford, the 1976 Election,
and the Republican Party*

During a campaign stop in 1976, when a hotel assigned President Ford its "Emperor Suite," he told his staff that he disliked the snooty title on the door. A staff member covered it with a handwritten cardboard sign reading "Jerry Ford's Room."[1] At another campaign swing through Paterson, New Jersey, Matilda Durget, a resident of nearby Franklin, came out to see the president despite the steady rain the day he visited. As Ford's limousine motored down the street, he requested that the Secret Service open the vehicle's roof. When the driver told him that it was raining, Ford replied, "It's raining on all these people, too." As Durget recounted, "The top opened, and the President stood waving in the pouring rain to all. I admire this humility in our leader and feel that the little things we do are the things that really count."[2]

Such stories were legion. Throughout his presidency, Ford acted unpretentiously, and that came as a welcome sight to Americans disgusted with the imperial presidency. But as Ford prepared to face Jimmy Carter in the 1976 election, the question was whether his decency and warmth would be enough to help him win a full term. Or were the challenges of the 1970s so daunting that—despite the incumbent's solid performance—Americans would want another leader to tackle them?

Closing the Gap

The summer of 1976 belonged to Carter. In early August, before the Republican National Convention, polls showed Carter ahead of Ford, 62 to 29 percent, a better than two-to-one margin. Even after the convention, which usually gave a lift to the GOP candidate, a Gallup poll showed that Carter enjoyed a 52 to 37 percent lead.[3] Ford was determined to make the fall campaign belong to him. He had less than eighty days to do it and win the election.

After the exhausting convention, Ford left for a working vacation in Vail, where he and aides gathered to plan a strategy. In June, White House aides had presented Ford with a road map for turning his campaign around. They referred to it as the "Planning Document," and it included an assessment candid enough to make any reader wince: "If past is indeed prologue," the document informed Ford, "you will lose on November 2nd—because to win you must do what has never been done: close a gap of about 20 points in 73 days from the base of a minority party while spending approximately the same amount of money as your opponent." But the document concluded, "We firmly believe you can win."[4]

The Ford camp ironed out a strategy to enable him to overcome his huge deficit in the polls. The campaign decided to build on a base in the heartland, in the industrial Midwest and farm states, and concentrate on swing states with a large number of electoral votes (California, Illinois, Michigan, New York, New Jersey, Ohio, Pennsylvania, and Texas). Ford needed to win five of them.[5] His campaign was to depend heavily on television, since only through the mass media could he convert millions of voters by Election Day. As Ford and his advisers huddled and talked tactics, he made one thing clear. He would not engage in fiscal pump priming, saying adamantly, "I'm not going to bankrupt the country to get reelected."[6]

A controversial element of the campaign strategy concerned Ford's role. Almost a year earlier, Robert Teeter suggested that Ford "remain as non-political and as far above the battle as possible."[7] In the "Planning Document," presidential aides Michael Duval and Foster Chanock outlined a "high-risk" plan that Ford could adopt to gain an edge on Carter, especially if he were trailing Carter by more than fifteen points in the polls, which he was. The Ford camp settled on a Rose Garden strategy—which Duval called the "no-campaign campaign"—where Ford would spend considerable time at the White House instead of on the campaign trail.[8]

For several reasons, this unconventional approach made sense. Emphasizing incumbency might help, since voters were averse to throwing out a sitting president, not having done so since 1932. Ford could concentrate on executive work and appear presidential, and the media would be forced to concentrate on his actions and campaign issues rather than on symbols and images. Ford's real love was, after all, the business of government, and "he wanted to protect the operation of government against the campaign," William Seidman recalled. "So he really wanted to stay in the White House. . . . His first priority was to make sure the government was running." Nineteen seventy-six was also the first year that both campaigns labored under federal spending limits, a reaction to the Watergate-related campaign abuses of 1972, and they wiped out the traditional Republican advantage in fund-raising. Presidential trips were expensive; one Ford strategist in Ohio, lamenting that Ford had to limit visits to the crucial swing state, complained, "One of the real problems is that it costs so bloody much to move the man around."[9] Ford wanted to husband financial resources to prepare for a barrage of advertisements and appearances during the last ten days of the campaign.

Perhaps most important, there was something peculiar about Ford as a campaigner. In an individual setting, he was impressive; anyone who met Ford came away feeling that he was genuine—a kind, thoughtful, and gentle man. Yet on the campaign trail, this personal magic disappeared. The primaries showed that Ford's national support slipped when he appeared in certain regions. Scrabbling for votes, he seemed less human and less statesmanlike. The Rose Garden strategy would allow voters to judge Ford more on his presidential performance, which the White House felt good about, rather than his abilities as a campaigner, which it did not. Nestled in the cocoon of the White House, Ford could avoid verbal or physical gaffes and play to his strength—running the government. The heavy campaigning and attacks on Carter were left to Dole, who hit the stump almost immediately.[10]

The Carter campaign and the media criticized the Rose Garden strategy as using the presidency for political ends, and the accusation clouded the open, accessible image the White House had tried to project since Ford took office. Carter said, "Gerald Ford has hidden himself from the public even more than Richard Nixon at the depths of Watergate." But the strategy played to Ford's strengths. Carter press secretary Jody Powell conceded that "we completely misfigured Ford's ability to pull off his 'Rose Garden campaign.' That was really a surprise to us. They've worked that to perfection."[11]

Crucial changes in Ford's campaign staff infused new blood into his effort. Jim Baker, a Houston lawyer and former undersecretary of commerce, had done yeoman work in securing delegates; he replaced campaign chief Rogers Morton, who lacked the political savvy and dynamism needed for a presidential campaign (he was also ill with cancer). The team of Doug Bailey and John Deardourff took charge of advertising to design new television and radio spots that would emphasize Ford's achievements and his outstanding personal qualities.

The 1976 campaign featured the first presidential debates since 1960. Winning these contests was a linchpin of Ford's strategy. As Ron Nessen noted, "All the eggs are being placed in one basket with the debates." Since Ford was a much better president than campaigner, the face-offs represented a chance to demonstrate his knowledge of the federal government and his leadership qualities. As Ford began to prepare for the debates, he received unsolicited advice from his predecessor, who knew more than anyone else the pain of "losing" a presidential debate. When the White House barber, Milton Pitts, returned from visiting Richard Nixon in California, the former president transmitted these words to Ford: "Prepare, prepare, prepare. Take the amount of time you plan for preparation and double it." Ford trained hard. He studied a tape of the first 1960 Kennedy-Nixon debate that was so damaging to Nixon. The campaign staff transformed the White House theater into a stage where Ford practiced mock debates for four days. They videotaped and studied the practice sessions to examine areas for improvement.[12] Carter was less conscientious. He, too, watched the 1960 Kennedy-Nixon debates and studied his campaign briefing books, but he refused dress rehearsals. Once, Jody Powell found Carter sitting with his daughter, Amy, reading comic books instead of studying for the debate.[13]

An estimated eighty-four million viewers watched the first debate, held on September 23 in Philadelphia and devoted to domestic policy. Ford was clearly the more physically impressive of the two. At six feet one, he still had the broad, muscular torso of a football player; Carter was five feet ten and slightly built. (In negotiating for the debate, one of Carter's advisers had even requested that Carter stand on a riser or Ford in a pit, so that they would look of equal height, but his request was ridiculed.) Ford dressed in a three-piece suit, meant to suggest an executive officer in command; when he strode onto the stage, the word "vest" wafted up from the audience, as those present were immediately impressed with his appearance. Carter wore a tie that was slightly skewed and a shade too red. Ford "looked like a President," journalist Kandy Stroud wrote. "Carter seemed to sense it. He tensed." Ford appeared more relaxed and even cracked a joke before the forensics began. When a comely assistant asked him to test his microphone, he intoned, "I'm glad to be here. I'm looking forward to it. You're a very attractive stage manager." The good-natured compliment brought laughter from the audience.[14]

Television debates often help the underdog, who enjoys equal terms with the favored candidate, sharing a dais and facing the same questions. Usually, expectations are low enough that, barring major mistakes, he or she conveys an unexpectedly favorable impression. Ford was the underdog, but his experience in the executive and legislative branches gave him a special advantage. During the debate, Ford mentioned his plans to cut taxes, in contrast to Carter, who projected a $60 billion budget surplus by 1981 but wanted to spend it on federal programs. Ford looked directly at his challenger when Carter spoke, while Carter looked down at his lectern during many of

Ford's answers. Especially at the beginning, Carter appeared nervous and tentative, and he later regretted his "excessive deference" to Ford. Both the Gallup and Harris polls judged Ford the winner, although by slim margins; even more encouraging, he sliced into Carter's lead in the polls. An AP survey revealed that he trailed by just two points.[15]

Ford gained momentum partly because he capitalized on Carter's vagueness and tendency to embrace contradictory positions to attract votes — the impression that Carter "doesn't stand for anything," as one dismayed Democrat charged. Ford's first line in the debate was, "I don't believe that Mr. Carter has been any more specific in this case than he has been in many other instances." On other occasions during the campaign, Carter promised to overhaul the nation's tax code but failed to offer details. When prodded, he protested, "I don't know how to write the tax code in specific terms."[16] Depending on his audience, Carter spoke out for fiscal discipline or more liberal spending. One of Ford's favorite campaign lines was, "Jimmy Carter will say anything anywhere to be President of the United States. He wavers, he wanders, he wiggles and he waffles, and he shouldn't be President of the United States."[17]

An unusual development also contributed to the rise in Ford's fortunes and Carter's swoon. Carter, a born-again Christian, prayed as many as twenty-five times a day, and his deep piety was a political plus. It appealed to an electorate hungering for moral regeneration after Watergate and won adherents among the growing corps of evangelicals in the country (one 1976 poll showed that 39 percent of those surveyed claimed to have had a personal experience with Christ).[18] In late September, *Playboy* magazine published an interview with Carter that delved into his faith. That a deeply devout man and presidential candidate would grant an interview to *Playboy* raised eyebrows. What Carter said generated even more controversy. Responding fervently to a question about his religious beliefs, he used verbs like "shack up" and "screw" to describe sexual acts. After describing his deep love for his wife earlier in the interview, he confessed, "I've looked on a lot of women with lust. I've committed adultery in my heart many times." He went on to lump Lyndon Johnson with Richard Nixon, condemning both for "lying, cheating and distorting the truth." Johnson's widow, Lady Bird, said that Carter's remark "distressed, hurt and perplexed" her, and he telephoned her to apologize.[19] But the sexual references, unprecedented for a presidential nominee, were even more damaging. His words sullied his stock-in-trade, the image of the pious candidate. Religious figures were aghast at the earthy language and frank admissions. Cartoonists had a field day (one showed Carter mentally ogling a naked Statue of Liberty), and reporters composed parodies.

Moreover, Carter's comments aggravated uneasy feelings that many voters felt toward him. He was an unknown quantity, and no one really knew what thoughts lurked behind his toothy grin (something that Hamilton Jordan, Carter's chief of staff, referred to as the "weirdo factor"). Carter pollster Pat Caddell reported that he dropped as much as ten points in the polls and temporarily fell behind Ford. As Ford would later in the campaign, Carter lost ground when the wrong words slipped out of his mouth, a simple mistake that a skeptical media ambushed.[20]

Although Ford's campaign initially benefited from Carter's troubles, it, too, soon soaked up bad news like a sponge. The UPI ran a story that Ford had been a guest of U.S. Steel executive William Whyte at a golf resort. The news suggested a potential conflict of interest because members of Congress were forbidden to accept gifts "of substantial value" from anyone representing groups that had legislation associated with their interests. Although Whyte was Ford's close personal friend and the golf games may not have been of "substantial value," Ford admitted to having been his guest in New Jersey and also twice in Orlando, Florida.[21] The controversy was inconclusive; the post-Watergate hypervigilance over ethics simply hovered over Ford.

Then came more bad news. On September 21, the *Wall Street Journal* broke a story that Charles Ruff, a special prosecutor appointed by Attorney General Edward Levi, was investigating charges that Ford had used congressional campaign donations from the Marine Engineers Beneficial Association, a maritime union, for personal use. Ruff, who taught law part-time at Georgetown University Law School, dragged out the investigation before finally clearing Ford on October 14. In the intervening period, reports on the allegations called Ford's probity into question. Ford felt helpless: "No one ever said specifically what it was that I was alleged to have done . . . and I had no way to defend myself" until the investigation was completed.[22] Another blow to the Ford campaign came when John Dean published a story in *Rolling Stone* magazine that described a Ford cabinet officer telling a crude joke about African Americans. When another newspaper identified the jokester as Secretary of Agriculture Earl Butz, an uproar followed and persisted even after the president publicly reprimanded Butz. On October 4, in a tearful press conference, Butz announced his resignation, becoming another victim of the post-Watergate vigilance over character.

The troubles were bad omens that distracted Ford as he prepared for the second debate, scheduled for October 6 in San Francisco. Carter, promising to be more assertive, rehearsed assiduously. One Carter aide reported, "Carter was determined to bust his ass to beat Ford this time. He put in twice the amount of time preparing." The White House and most observers were confident that Ford would handily win this match, on foreign policy, where the president had a clear advantage.

In political debates, nothing succeeds like pounding away at nerve-touching themes. In this face-off, Carter capitalized on the gnawing fear of a fading America by using the words "strong" or "strength" thirty times, and he tarred Ford with the anti-Kissinger brush by criticizing "secrecy" or "secret" diplomacy eleven times, emphasizing Kissinger's role in foreign policy and even opening the debate by charging that "as far as foreign policy goes, Mr. Kissinger has been the President of this country." But Ford was supposed to have a trump card. Since the primaries, Republican congressional leaders had urged the president to emphasize his great achievement in foreign policy, peace plus a diminished threat of war. During the debate, Ford planned to stress two themes, peace and experience, using them to answer virtually every Carter charge. Yet not until midway into the debate did he mention these ideas, touching on them only lightly. And these themes were overshadowed by one explosive sentence.[23]

In Eastern European diplomacy, controversy over the Helsinki accords kept Ford on the defensive. During the debate, Ford tried to explain the accords to Max Frankel, an associate editor of the *New York Times*, who inquired about U.S.-Soviet relations. The very nature of Frankel's question put Ford on the defensive. The reporter gave a litany of purported Soviet global gains: "Our allies in France and Italy are now flirting with communism; we've recognized a permanent Communist regime in East Germany; we virtually signed, in Helsinki, an agreement that the Russians have dominance in Eastern Europe." Is this "a two-way street," Frankel wondered. The Russians bragged that they'd "get the better of us." "Is it possible they've proved their point?"

These were sensitive charges that Ford had parried since the primaries. He launched into a defense of Helsinki, vehemently denying that the thirty-five signatories of the accords "have turned over to the Warsaw Pact nations the domination of Eastern Europe. It just isn't true." He continued, "There is no Soviet domination of Eastern Europe, and there never will be under a Ford administration." With a look of amused bewilderment, Frankel immediately probed the curious remark, gesturing with his hands to indicate borders, asking if the Soviets "are not using Eastern Europe as their own sphere of influence and occupying most of their countries there and making sure with their troops that it's a Communist zone?" Ford waded into deeper trouble with his answer, stating, "I don't believe, Mr. Frankel, that the Yugoslavians consider themselves dominated by the Soviet Union. I don't believe that the Romanians consider themselves dominated by the Soviet Union. I don't believe that the Poles consider themselves dominated by the Soviet Union."[24]

Ford meant to convey what he had observed in Eastern Europe during his visit the previous year, that the people there were not spiritually or culturally dominated by the Soviet Union. "My real feeling was that the Polish people would never accept, over the long haul, Soviet domination," he later explained. After the iron curtain fell, Ford joked that his remark was correct, just years too early. He said that "the facts are, as soon as the Poles had a chance to get their freedom, whom did they throw out? The Soviet Union, which was a clear indication that, fundamentally, my comment in the debate was accurate."[25] Unfortunately, the words came out wrong.

Ford's mistake originated with debate rehearsals, during which he practiced denying the "Sonnenfeldt Doctrine." In March 1976, columnists Roland Evans and Robert Novak reported that a few months earlier Assistant Secretary of State Helmut Sonnenfeldt, an expert on East-West relations and a Kissinger confidant, told a group of American diplomats in London that a "permanent 'organic' union" existed between the Soviet Union and its satellite countries. On a semantic level, these words implied a geopolitical bond between the Soviet Union and its neighbors and suggested that the United States accepted Soviet control over them. Actually, Sonnenfeldt meant almost the contrary, that the Soviet relationship with Eastern Europe should be more "natural" and involve less military domination, more tolerance, and less violent political protest by the satellites. Violence could compel the United States to use force in the region; by discouraging Soviet military domination, the United States could encourage political moves toward independence in Eastern Europe without worrying about triggering World War III. But Sonnenfeldt's remarks appalled conservatives and Americans of East European descent, and he later regretted using the word "organic." Throughout 1976, the White House practiced damage control, denying that a Sonnenfeldt Doctrine existed. On April 3, speaking to ethnic groups in Milwaukee, Ford stated that his administration did not accept Soviet "dominion of Eastern Europe or any kind of organic union."[26]

In preparing for the debate, Ford practiced denying the existence of a Sonnenfeldt Doctrine (writing, "*There is none*") and planned to stress that he visited Poland, Romania, and Yugoslavia to symbolize their independence and autonomy.[27] Aides wrote out suggested response lines such as, "To say that my policies accept Soviet domination over Eastern Europe is patent nonsense," and "Our relations with and support for the countries of Eastern Europe have never been stronger. I don't see how you can talk about conceding

Soviet domination in light of this record."[28] Another proposed line was, "I am totally opposed to so-called spheres of influence—or 'dominion' of Eastern Europe—by any power."[29]

If Ford meant to say "dominion" rather than "domination," his response was a simple semantic mistake. Under the intense pressure of a debate before seventy-five million television viewers, he may have confused the two similar words. More likely, he meant to say that his administration "does not accept" or "does not concede" Soviet domination. Ford's error was understandable; the semantic difference was slight. If not for his follow-up response to Frankel's questions, his initial answer might have even escaped controversy. Most of Ford's advisers, although watching intensely, detected nothing unusual about the remark.[30] Assessing the debate immediately after it ended, one hundred George Washington University law students scored the contest close, with a slight edge to Carter, and thought that Ford's greatest mistake was being too defensive; they mentioned nothing about the East Europe statement. Five college forensics coaches, asked by the AP to score the affair, declared that Carter won narrowly, 110 to 108.[31]

But a media fallout began. There were calls for Ford to apologize and retract his statement. Aboard Air Force One, Chief of Staff Dick Cheney asked Robert Hartmann to talk to the president. "He won't budge. He virtually threw us out of the cabin. See if you can do anything with him," Cheney implored. When Hartmann entered the cabin, Ford insisted, "I am not going to change what I said. I've been fighting for twenty-five years for those captive nations and everyone in the country knows it."[32]

Ford had a stubborn streak, and he might have recovered more quickly had he issued an immediate clarification, as some aides urged. Instead, he dug himself deeper into the hole. Two days after the debate, in California, he spoke to a group of San Fernando businesspeople, and although Nessen recommended that he confess to misspeaking during the debate, Ford said, "I was in Poland a year ago, and I had the opportunity to talk with a number of citizens, and believe me, they are a courageous, strong people. They don't believe that they are going to be forever dominated—if they are—by the Soviet Union."[33] Aides were horrified by words like "if they are."

Ford's remark snowballed when he refused to recant fully. Carter charged that Ford lacked "common sense and knowledge" in foreign affairs. Mondale said that Ford's answer would have kept him from being passed to third grade and later even attributed the election outcome to the gaffe.[34] The comment reawakened Ford's image problem, the perception that he was prone to slips, even that he lacked the wits for the job. In the days after the debate, polls showed that viewers felt that Carter had crushed the president; one survey indicated that the Georgian had won, 60–18 (a Gallup poll had Carter the winner by 48–42). Four days after the debate, Ford met with a group of Americans of East European ancestry at the White House, where he clarified his remarks and apologized. Afterward, Cheney bitterly sighed that the media had finally gotten their "pound of flesh."[35]

Ford fell victim to an unfortunate media tendency to magnify mistakes. The media focused relentlessly on Ford's remark, beating down public perceptions of an otherwise solid debate performance. Ford was angered that the media had concentrated on just one sentence, ignoring everything else and defeating the purpose of the whole exercise.[36] Historian Leo Ribuffo criticized the media for distorting the significance of Ford's remarks. "Where they should have seen a slip of the tongue and stubbornness," Ribuffo observed, "most reporters, in search of a lively story, claimed to find evidence of ignorance or immorality."[37] The most damaging effect of the incident was that it stalled Ford's momentum. Until this point, he had been gaining ground on Carter in the polls. After the debate, Carter was solidly ahead again. (After the election, Ford jested that he might accept a teaching job at the University of Michigan in a field other than European history. Strangely, reporters failed to catch the joke and filed serious reports about Ford returning to his alma mater as a professor.)[38]

The wind out of his sails, Ford was not helped by the next contest—only it did not directly involve him. On October 15, the first-ever debate between vice-presidential candidates took place. When he picked Dole, Ford worried about the senator's acid tongue, cautioning him, "You'll have to be careful with what you say." Reporters in Washington, the president observed, often paid more attention to Dole's stinging remarks than his political record. In his convention speech, Dole already unleashed a lacerating one-liner, calling Carter a "Southern-fried McGovern," which made Ford campaign advisers wince.[39] On the stump, Dole continued to let loose with attacks, and the press began to call him a "hatchet man" and "Doberman Dole." This campaign was Dole's first exposure to the national media, and he was far from the polished performer he became two decades later as Senate majority leader, presidential nominee, and even Viagra pitchman. He had a rough edge and tended toward a caustic sense of humor. Ford aides were understandably concerned about what Dole might say in the upcoming debate.

Dole resented the idea of a vice-presidential debate, viewing it as an intrusion on his campaigning. His preparations were peremptory. He could be wickedly funny, though, and his wit was on display when he sparred with Mondale. He opened with the line, "[Mondale and I have] been friends and we'll be friends when this debate is over. And we'll be friends when this election is over—and he'll still be in the Senate."[40] But for most of the debate, Dole looked too casual, leaning against the lectern with his left arm and twice referring to viewers "who may still be tuned in." Toward the end of the debate, he dropped a bombshell. Advisers and colleagues, including Jacob Javits, had suggested that Dole stress tranquility and peace in a closing statement.[41] Dole found a curious way to do it. He mentioned World Wars I and II, the Korean War, and the Vietnam War, and observed, "All Democrat wars. All in this century. I figured up the other day, if we added up all the killed and wounded in Democrat wars in this century, it would be about 1.6 million Americans, enough to fill the city of Detroit." Mondale counterattacked: "Does he really mean to suggest to the American people that there was a partisan difference over our involvement in the war to fight Nazi Germany?" Dole's remark infuriated many Americans. Nessen observed, "Our apprehensions before the vice-presidential debate, that the possible benefits did not justify the possible risks of a mistake, appeared to be well founded."[42]

After the debate, Dole labored in Mondale's shadow; opinion polls showed Mondale drawing more favorable marks than Dole, and he also attracted larger audiences.[43] Because the Carter campaign found that Dole's negative ratings were higher than Mondale's, it made Dole an issue as the race got tighter. Carter reminded listeners, "Remember, you're voting for a ticket. . . . Carter-Mondale, that's our ticket. Ford-Dole, that's the other ticket." In the third and final debate, from Williamsburg, Virginia, Carter spoke proudly of Mondale, saying he had full confidence that his running mate could perform as president should something untoward happen to him. Pausing for a moment to measure his words carefully, Carter said, "I don't want to say anything critical of Senator Dole. But I've never heard Mr. Ford say that was his primary consideration" in selecting Dole.[44] Ford defended Dole's Senate record, but after his running mate's vituperation during the campaign, many Americans agreed with Carter.

In the last debate between Ford and Carter, the sharpest exchanges were over the economy. One journalist asked about the "pause," and Ford, showing a command of economic statistics, explained that the blistering 9.2 percent growth of the second quarter was unsustainably high and the 4 percent growth rate of the third quarter better than the average rate for the past ten years. Moreover, the country's economy was recovering more quickly than those of major industrial allies. "The United States is leading the Free World out of the recession that was serious a year and a half ago," Ford declared. "I think this is a record that the American people will understand and appreciate." Carter, smiling and laughing slightly to soften what he was about to say, retorted, "With all due respect to President Ford, he ought to be ashamed of making that statement." The challenger reminded viewers of "the highest unemployment rate since the Great Depression" and then rattled off the effects of inflation: "People can't plan anymore. Savings accounts are losing money." Carter concluded that "this shows a callous indifference to the families that have suffered so much."[45] The exchanges left no doubt that the troubled economy cast a huge shadow over the election.

The last debate over, only ten days remained in the campaign. The Ford campaign engaged in an intensive speaking and $10 million advertising blitz that Cheney called "the ten-day orgasm." Continuing its heavy reliance on media, the Ford camp produced six half-hour programs, broadcast in crucial swing states, featuring sportscaster and former St. Louis Cardinals catcher Joe Garagiola interviewing the president. Garagiola's genial, disarming manner led to easy banter with Ford. He asked softball questions like, "What do you feel have been your major accomplishments in office?" The occasional presence of former Democratic congresswoman Edith Green of Oregon bolstered their efforts with a grandmotherly touch. The advertisements redirected attention to issues after the various distractions.[46] The Ford team also developed eight five-minute morning radio spots and produced a masterful television commercial, "Feelin' Good about America," with catchy, upbeat lyrics:

> I'm feelin' good about America
> I feel it everywhere I go.
> I'm feeling good about America
> I thought you ought to know
> That I'm feelin' good about America
> It's something great to see
> I'm feeling good about America
> I'm feeling good about me!

The commercial featured slices of America, including marching bands and Americans vouching for Ford's leadership, and was unabashedly patriotic, capitalizing on bicentennial fervor. Advertising executive Malcolm MacDougall remembered, "I thought it had to be one of the finest political commercials ever produced"; certainly, it made viewers feel warm. As a grand finale, Ford barnstormed through the swing states. The strain of speaking reduced his voice to a hoarse whisper, but as the campaign wound down, he narrowed the gap in the polls. Ford felt confident enough to invite crowds to come to Washington in January and witness the swearing-in of a Ford-Dole administration. Ford staged one of the greatest comebacks in history. By Election Day, the polls showed an even race. Gallup even reported that Ford led Carter, 47 to 46 percent, while a Harris poll showed Carter ahead, 46 to 45 percent.[47]

On November 2, Ford was back in Grand Rapids. After voting, he had a breakfast of blueberry pancakes, a good-luck ritual that he developed during years of winning congressional elections. Before flying back to Washington, at the Kent County Airport (later renamed the Gerald R. Ford International Airport), the city unveiled a large mural depicting scenes from his life, such as his high school football days, first car, and wedding. Memories flooded back to him, reminding him of his parents, and Ford wept. He spoke from the heart, saying that the mural "means so much to me because of . . . my mother and father. I owe everything to them." Once back at the White House, Ford, his family, and friends watched the returns during the evening. Trailing Carter but with the outcome still undecided, an exhausted Ford went to bed at 3:20 A.M., hoping that he won.

When Ford awoke that morning, he learned that had lost the popular vote by just two percentage points, 50 to 48 percent. The contest was close in the electoral college, where Carter won, 297–240. Ford telephoned Carter to offer congratulations and, his voice shot, asked Cheney to read his concession statement to the president-elect. In the early afternoon, the Ford family gathered in the Oval Office and went on national television. Ford said, "It is perfectly obvious that my voice isn't up to par and I shouldn't be making very many comments, and I won't." He thanked his supporters, urged Americans to unite behind Carter, and then asked Betty to read his concession statement. While she had stumbled over words while rehearsing it, she now read it flawlessly. After the television cameras went off, despite his personal and vocal anguish, Ford stayed to mingle with the media who were now covering the twilight of his presidency. "Many of the reporters were moved to tears," Ron Nessen recalled. "Ford's gracious gesture explains as well as anything why relations between the White House and the press improved so much while he was president."[48]

Over the next two and a half months, Ford did everything possible to prepare the president-elect to assume the reins of government. "I wanted the new president to have an easier start than I had," he remarked. Ford's courtesies led Carter to comment that no outgoing president had ever done as much as Ford to insure a smooth transition of power.[49]

The Challenges of the 1970s

Before Election Day, cautiously favorable assessments of Ford appeared. Calling him "a good president," the *Economist* said he "reminds [Republicans] of President Eisenhower," and the *National Journal* judged, "By most standards, the Ford Administration has been at least modestly successful in its over-all objectives." *U.S. News and World Report* commented, "Taken as a whole, the record of the last two years would probably guarantee another term for most Presidents."[50] But the 1970s was a dramatically different decade and 1976 no ordinary election year. For the first time since the Great Depression, domestic issues dominated a presidential contest. Two of the era's great challenges, the issue of "trust" after Watergate and the troubled economy, especially influenced voters. Both worked to Ford's disadvantage.

Newsweek called 1976 the "Year of the Outsider" because, as Reagan and Carter demonstrated, the candidate who boasted a past profession outside politics and a provenance outside Washington enjoyed an advantage.[51] An incumbent and career politician, Ford was hurt by the dark anti-Washington mood carpeting the country. The ethos allowed Carter to succeed using a campaign theme, populism, that has seldom worked in American politics. An anti-elitist appeal to ordinary people, populism evoked anger and pessimism, which frightened voters. Its most memorable moment came in the 1896 election, when the Populist Party fused with Democrats to support William Jennings Bryan, who spoke with a silver tongue, rallied agricultural support but lost to William McKinley. (As recently as the 2000 election, Democrat Al Gore invoked populist strains, railing against corporate elites and high prescription drug prices for the elderly, but fell short of the White House—even though he won the popular vote.) Carter's embrace of populism had roots dating back to his grandfather, who supported populism during the 1890s. Accepting the Democratic nomination—in a speech that he described as "populist"—Carter lashed out against the "political and economic elite" and the "self-perpetuating alliance between money and politics."[52] (Ironically, Carter—who repeatedly promised voters, "I'll never lie to you"—embellished the truth in trying to burnish his populist credentials. The Georgian claimed that he grew up without electricity and running water, an assertion that both his mother and sister denied.) On the campaign stump, Carter intoned in his southern drawl, "This is the ye-uh of the people."[53]

In post-Watergate America, populism pulled heavy oar. Part of its appeal was its contempt for dishonest politicians. Ford believed that voters "didn't care that much about my position on this specific issue or that. What they wanted was someone in the White House who would be honest with them."[54] As never before during a presidential campaign, the single word "trust" stood out. Carter remarked, "Trust of people in Government is the No. 1 issue. It transcends unemployment and inflation."[55] Trust was a simple, vague, nonideological issue, yet it was a winner. Carter appealed to Americans' yearning for a trustworthy Washington outsider to occupy the White House and scrub dishonesty from the capital. He used the simple phrase, "Trust me," which captured the essence of his campaign, allowing him to avoid policy specifics. Carter promised, "I intend to take a new broom to Washington and do everything possible to sweep the house of government clean," and he took advantage of Ford's quarter-century identification with Washington by declaring, "Anything you don't like about Washington, I suggest you blame it on Jerry Ford." Ford rued the irony that Carter's slim political experience could be an advantage.[56] He countered Carter's catch phrase by saying, "It is not enough for someone to say, 'Trust me.' Trust must be earned."[57] Ford hoped that voters would recognize that his administration marked a clean break from Nixon's. "The record is very clear that I had nothing to do with Watergate, and this Administration had nothing to do with Watergate," he declared. "It has been the most open, candid, and straightforward Administration in recent years—certainly in the memory of most people."[58]

Still, Watergate made Ford vulnerable. In a Manichaean world, many voters saw Republicans as evil and wanted to punish them, just as in the 1974 midterm elections. House minority leader John Rhodes said in exasperation, "For those of us who thought all along that our battle on behalf of fiscal responsibility and smaller government would eventually be rewarded, the realization that many Americans regard Republicans as the bad guys has come as quite a shock." Because Watergate had tarnished the presidency, incumbency failed to bestow its usual advantages.[59] Moreover, Ford's pardon of Nixon had ripped open the scandal's wounds. Americans had not forgiven Ford; in 1976 they viewed the pardon unfavorably by two-to-one. As he campaigned, hecklers sometimes greeted him with signs reading, "Does Nixon Drive a Ford?" and "Beg Your Pardon?" Carter flailed away at Ford's contention that he had restored trust in the presidency, alluding to high government officials who committed crimes and were "then condoned."[60] Simply because he was Nixon's Republican successor, Ford bore an ethical millstone around his neck that constituted a liability greater than any president suffered since the Great Depression bogged down Herbert Hoover's reelection bid.

The question of trust impinged on pocketbook issues more strongly than during any election in the postwar era. Middle- and working-class Americans felt that they had obeyed the law and worked hard, yet they were angered that government and business elites (such as Nixon and oil companies) prospered while inflation ate away at their paychecks. Poor economic conditions even jeopardized Ford's political standing in his home state, as his lead over Carter in Michigan shrunk to just one percentage point. Decrying a "lackluster" recovery, Carter hammered away at his theme that Ford's mind was curtained to the jobless and the need to stimulate growth. Ford vetoed bills that would have increased federal funding to fight unemployment, Carter charged, preferring instead a slow, steady economic recovery with low inflation. "These vetoes haven't helped our economy. They have only contributed to needless human suffering," he said.[61] The Democratic challenger promised to reduce both inflation and unemployment to 4 percent, and creating new jobs was his priority. He vowed that, given the choice, "I'd put my emphasis on employment and take my chances with inflation."[62]

The grim unemployment picture reinforced party images that existed since the Great Depression. Voters viewed Democrats as the party of labor, willing to use government to aid the unemployed and more effective at solving economic problems or social issues. By contrast, they saw the Republicans as beholden to business and indifferent to workers, especially those without jobs, and successful in foreign policy and national defense, which were less relevant in 1976.[63] One Gallup poll showed that, on economic issues, voters trusted Democrats over Republicans by a two-to-one margin.[64]

Appearances loom large inside the voting booth, and expectations that conditions might get worse can produce a vote against the incumbent. Near Election Day, twice as many voters thought the economy would deteriorate as believed it would improve. Paul MacAvoy believed that in view of Carter's narrow margin of victory, the economic pause may have been the deciding factor in the close contest, a view that Ford shared.[65] Improving poll numbers lag behind improving economic numbers, which frustrated Ford throughout 1976. But with Ford gaining ground every month and the recovery proceeding naturally, had the election been held two months later, he might have won. The Carter camp noted a steady decline in its support in key states and a shift toward Ford, even in the South.[66] But as it was, MacAvoy regretted that "the economy was lagging two or three months from the ideal growth pattern that would cause voters to be able to say the current administration should be returned."[67] Although an improving economic picture supported Ford's argument of successful leadership, the fall 1976 "pause" contributed to political failure. Many Americans must have agreed with Birch Bayh, who quipped that a Ford was fine in the garage but not in the White House, urging, "We must get the American economy off a Republican roller-coaster that has sent prices to dizzying heights and then sent employment plummeting downward with a sickening drop."[68]

The economic jolts paralleled the era's political volatility. In consecutive decades, both parties suffered stunning reversals of fortune. After the greatest triumph ever in 1964 (Johnson with 61 percent of the popular vote), the Democrats lost the White House just four years later. Then, after the most resounding victory in their party's history in 1972 (Nixon with 60.7 percent), the Republicans were ousted in 1976. The vicissitudes reflected the raw power of the issues troubling the nation, Vietnam and domestic turmoil in 1968 and Watergate and the economy in 1976. They turned once-popular incumbents into damaged goods not to be retained.

Denied the presidency for a full term, Ford lost the chance to implement his fiscal philosophy, which he felt would have improved the nation's economic health. He had hoped to achieve a balanced budget by 1979. "Had we won, I would have had the reduction of spending and the vetoes as part of my mandate; and that would make a significant impact on my relations with Congress," Ford reflected. "No longer could they say I was not an elected President. I would have had greater support for the same restrained fiscal policy that I could carry out in cooperation with Arthur Burns, who had the same philosophical view on monetary policy. I was really looking forward to the opportunity."[69]

Substance and Slogans

In 1976, the odds were stacked against Ford. Throughout the cycle of political elections since World War II, neither party has had much success in holding the White House for more than eight years; only once has this happened, when the GOP won all three elections during the 1980s. A political rhythm almost directs voters to turn the party in power out after two terms. In 1976, denied the White House since 1968, the Democrats were determined to get it back, and many Americans sympathized. CBS White House correspondent Bob Schieffer recalled that "after the years of Nixon, I always had the feeling that the electorate just wanted a change, and I never believed that there was really much that Ford could have done about it."[70] Riding this rhythm for change, Carter rallied the fraying Democratic coalition of urban voters, the elderly, farmers, labor, and especially African Americans, winning over 90 percent of the black vote. To this he added Baptists and born-again Christians, both usually inclined to vote Republican.

Ford needed these groups. To win a presidential election, a candidate needs defections from the other party. Republicans depended on two key swing blocs, conservative southern whites and, more generally, conservative Democrats, who had abandoned the party four years earlier because its nominee, George McGovern, was too liberal for their liking. But Carter was conservative enough to retain their allegiance.[71]

The South played a pivotal role in these dynamics. Carter had a lock on the region, and no candidate has won the presidency without help from the South. Beginning in the 1950s with Eisenhower, the GOP made steady inroads into the once solidly Democratic South. In 1968, Nixon deliberately appealed to white conservatives with a "Southern strategy" that capitalized on their discontent with Washington's encroachment on states' rights, especially manifested in federal support for civil rights and school busing. But Carter's hold on the South was so strong that Ford felt that the only southern state he could win was Virginia (which, indeed, was how it turned out). Carter solidified his grip on the South by appealing to regional pride, airing radio ads proclaiming, "On November 2, the South is being readmitted to the Union. . . . Are you going to let the Washington politicians keep one of our own out of the White House?" When speaking to southern audiences, Carter often asked with a sly grin, "Isn't it time we had a President without an accent?" After almost a century with only one southern president, Lyndon Johnson, the region hungered for one of its own in the White House. Carter won ten southern states with 118 electoral votes, almost half the 270 he needed to win.[72]

Carter had a strong geographical base; Ford lacked one, a serious handicap. In Ford's native Midwest, his support was surprisingly tepid, partly because unemployment hit this Rust Belt region hard. But the election was so close that he would have won with just one or two more states. Frank Zarb believed that that the devastating *New York Daily News* headline, "FORD TO CITY: DROP DEAD," might have cast the deciding vote in the election. Big Apple residents had bad blood for Ford, and Carter swamped him in New York City. Zarb believed that "if we had lost New York City less big, we would have taken New York State."[73] A victory in the Empire State would have given Ford more than 270 electoral votes.

Ford also might have won the election if he had concentrated more on Ohio, which every Republican has needed to win the presidency. The Buckeye State, along with Michigan, was to have been a centerpiece for an electoral base in the industrial Midwest. The area had been a swing region since the late 1800s and, deeply affected by the recession, was volatile in 1976. Midwesterners needed to hear the good news that Ford had to offer, that a record eighty-eight million Americans were working. In August, a senior White House strategist said, "I'd follow Ohio like a book. If we win in Ohio, we win the election." Ford lost Ohio. Had he won it plus one more midwestern state, such as Wisconsin or Missouri (both of which went Republican in the previous two elections), he would have stayed in the White House.[74]

One additional factor, overlooked but perhaps decisive, was that Ford's moderately conservative vision for America did not inspire voters. In a presidential campaign, ideas do matter; they often furnish a compelling reason for voters to pick a new leader. By eschewing bold, daring programs and even a name for his presidency, Ford failed to capture the public's imagination and contributed to an immanent perception that he was a "caretaker." As his presidency faced the deciding test at the polls, many Americans, failing to find a creative spirit in Ford, probably agreed with the assessment of reporter Howard K. Smith: Ford was decent and good of heart but did not bring imaginative leadership to a diverse nation that appeared caught in troubled times.[75]

Ford had solid legislative as well as spiritual accomplishments: the antirecession tax cut and economic recovery, EPCA, improved relations with Congress, and a more serene mood in the country. But the election did not just reward past achievements. It was a referendum on the future, and many Americans could not decipher where Ford wanted to take them. Ford won universal praise as a decent man, but the usefulness of this image was inherently limited; once its political capital was spent, he was left with a perception that he was a good man but a mediocre leader. A Ford campaign memorandum noted that Americans felt that he lacked "a clear view of where he is going and why; doesn't seem to understand our problems or have solutions to them."[76]

Carter accused Ford of letting the nation float aimlessly. He compared the president to Herbert Hoover, whom he called a "decent, well-intentioned man" who left America "drifting without inspiration, without vision and without a purpose." In the first debate, Carter charged that "Mr. Ford, so far as I know, except for avoiding another Watergate, has not accomplished one single major program for this country."[77] Ford contrasted himself with Carter by emphasizing their fiscal orientations. Carter endorsed "60-some new programs that will cost $100 billion a year at a minimum and $200 billion, probably, on an annual basis," he charged. "So there is a distinct difference between Governor Carter on the one hand and myself. He wants to spend more, and I want to hold the lid on federal spending."[78] But fiscal integrity did not light enthusiasm in the average voter and troubled those constituents who expected government largesse. James Lynn said that the idea of not offering new programs reminded him of humorist Robert Benchley's line, "Hark, I distinctly did not hear the clock strike twelve." Lynn explained, "There's no romance to it," and the principle was hard to tout during an election.[79] Before he became Ford's running mate, Dole commented, "I think Ford's been preoccupied with holding back, cutting back, reducing spending. I don't think we'll become a majority party doing that."[80]

Ford did promise specific changes in a full term. In addition to cutting taxes, eliminating regulations, and beefing up defense, Ford wanted to stiffen crime laws, limit school busing, and double the national parks system as a bicentennial gift to the nation. He pushed for Social Security reform and indexed income tax rates to keep wage earners in lower brackets. In foreign policy, he wanted to conclude a new SALT treaty with Moscow and establish diplomatic relations with China. Perhaps most important, during his final, intensive campaign blitz, Ford promised to ask Congress for another tax cut, making it a key pledge in his speeches.

In promoting these ideas, Ford's speaking skills hampered him. His wooden oratory did not generate enthusiasm as a polished performer like Reagan did. In June 1976, White House photographer David Kennerly wrote a confidential letter to Ford, saying, "Your speeches are usually long, boring, and filled with rhetoric that turns people off. I've seen advancemen literally cry when after 10 or 15 minutes after you started speaking the people would start leaving."[81] Ford never mastered the sound bite so critical on television and did not translate his philosophy into a short, stylish phrase. "There wasn't even a slogan, except for 'Whip Inflation Now.' If he could've had a few more slogans the people could've responded to . . ." Philip Buchen wondered.[82] Noting that a rule of politics is that proposals needed to be simplified and repeated often, in late 1975 Bob Teeter wrote that "we have reached the point where the President's program needs to have a specific name or slogan."[83] Throughout Ford's struggles against Reagan and then Carter, his campaign staff stressed the need for a "theme" and expressed frustration that they were unable to translate the president's commendable record in office into a rallying cry.[84] By August 1976, the Ford campaign still had no theme, and speechwriter David Gergen stressed that the president's speeches and statements needed "far better coordination in their preparation."[85]

William Seidman recalled that in the peroration of Ford's first State of the Union address, he spoke of a "new direction," which fittingly summed up the administration's fiscal plans. "We looked at all the trends and said, 'We've got a whole bunch of lines that are all going in the wrong direction. We've got to head this country in a new direction,'" Seidman explained.[86] Ford was no stranger to the phrase. In 1967, delivering the Republican State of the Union message, he called for a "new direction" in federal policy making. Three years later, declaring that the era of the New Deal had finally ended, Congressman Ford called for a "new direction" in the 1970s.[87]

As president, Ford never seized on this apposite phrase of a "new direction" or "new realism," although he mentioned the latter in his 1976 State of the Union address. The *Washington Post* picked up on it, headlining its front page story, "Ford calls for 'New Realism' on Defense, Welfare."[88] Henry Perritt Jr., a member of the Domestic Council, suggested afterward that "New Realism" would be an excellent campaign theme. The phrase was catchy, and the adjective "new" conveyed the idea that Ford was attempting a change in fiscal policy after years of deficit spending. But Ford may have been averse to a new slogan after the embarrassment of WIN. After decades as a legislator in the minority, he also may have been too accustomed—to use a sports metaphor—to playing defense, finding it difficult to switch to offense and promote programs. By nature, he also avoided catchy phrases. "These are nice for speeches, but I'm always one who believes in substance, not in labels," he said.[89]

Unfortunately, substance was not enough. As the Reagan challenge demonstrated, symbols like the Panama Canal carried a transcendent importance, swaying voters. A marketable theme or name for the Ford administration might have added some ginger to his campaign and promoted understanding of his economic goals. The science of economics is arcane to most Americans, and the age of modern communications favors a president who can tune the public ear to a coinable phrase that quickly and easily defines the president's agenda. Ford's twentieth-century predecessors capitalized on this technique. Theodore Roosevelt trumpeted a Square Deal, followed by a string of Democrats who adopted variants that helped to produce election victories: Franklin Roosevelt's New Deal, Truman's Fair Deal, Kennedy's New Frontier, and Johnson's Great Society. Recent presidential victors, while not promoting sweeping legislative programs, have generated voter and media enthusiasm through memorable catch phrases. In 1988, George H. W. Bush promised "a kinder, gentler nation" and "no new taxes"; four years later, Bill Clinton's strategy-making "war room" bore a famous sign that simply read, "The economy, stupid"; in 2000, George W. Bush touted "compassionate conservatism." While no guarantor of victory, the political slogan gives an almost talismanic charm to a campaign.

In 1976, Carter's promises of "trust" and "I'll never lie to you" became, in effect, his campaign shibboleths; moreover, he published an autobiography with the memorable title, *Why Not the Best?* Ford's need for comparable slogans was especially acute since his economic policy emphasized less government spending and fewer initiatives. Ford ruefully admitted that his administration had not "sold our accomplishments as well as we should have."[90] A smart, modish name for his economic vision (such as "New Realism" or his "3 percent, 3 percent, 3 percent" goals) might have helped. Had he embraced one, historians today might be analyzing "Gerald Ford and the New Realism" rather than writing of Ford as a nexus between Nixon and Carter.

Other presidents have failed to convey a vision for the country. George H. W. Bush famously failed, by his own admission, to articulate "the vision thing" and lost his 1992 reelection bid. Ultimately, Reagan succeeded where Ford and Bush failed. He won two full terms and enjoyed high public opinion ratings while hammering home a message remarkably similar to Ford's: the federal government was too big, taxes too onerous, and individual Americans and the private sector too constrained.

Events also played into Reagan's hands. During Carter's presidency, Americans suffered higher prices. Inflation accentuated the country's swing toward conservatism, stoking anger toward big government and high taxes that became starkly visible with the 1978 Proposition 13 tax revolt in California when state residents voted for a referendum that slashed property taxes by almost 60 percent. Reagan also won elections and remained popular despite, or perhaps because of, knowledge of the federal government that Ford considered "superficial at best."[91] Dick Cheney remarked that Ford's strength was "his enormous knowledge of government." He observed that Ford "was clearly oriented toward the substance of policy, the nitty gritty detail." Reagan, by contrast, dispensed with details and articulated broad themes such as tax cuts, deregulation, and a strong defense.[92] Although Reagan never adopted a slogan for his presidency, he never had to, because he was a master of political shorthand, reducing national issues to small, digestible sentences. Television, a medium often cruel to Ford with scenes of his stumbles, was a boon to the former actor Reagan.

The supply-side economics that Reagan preached rejected the gloomy 1970s talk of "limits to growth" and instead promised that the free market, untrammeled by high taxes and federal regulations, would promote growth.[93] One question in the 1980 Carter-Reagan presidential debate captured the essence of America in the 1970s, and the candidates' responses were vastly different. A reporter asked Carter what he would do during a second term to reduce inflation; would he "tell the American people they are going to have to sacrifice to adopt a leaner lifestyle for some time to come?" Whereas Carter acknowledged, "We have demanded that the American people sacrifice and they've done very well," Reagan rebuffed the notion of limits. Carter, he charged, had "accused the American people of living too well and that we must share in scarcity, we must sacrifice and get used to doing with less. We don't have inflation because we're living too well. We have inflation because the government is living too well."[94]

As Reagan did four years later, Ford challenged Carter's apparent pessimism, reminding listeners that America is "the greatest country in the history of mankind."[95] But Ford tempered his encomium with a sense of realism and did not promise the deep tax cuts that anchored Reagan's 1980 campaign. He warned that his economic policy does not "hold out the hollow promise that we can wipe out inflation and unemployment overnight. Instead, it is an honest, realistic policy—a policy that says we can steadily reduce inflation and unemployment if we maintain a prudent, balanced approach." Perhaps the best statement of Ford's philosophy were two sentences that he honed and delivered during the campaign's closing days, often in a hoarse whisper after he lost his voice: "You know where I stand. I stand for limited government, for fiscal responsibility, for rising prosperity, for lower taxes, for military strength and for peace in the world."[96]

Ultimately, Ford was stuck in the frustrating position of presiding over an improving economy yet being unable to make the public recognize his achievements. He could not induce Congress, the media, or the people to accept his political agenda. For Ford, adhering faithfully to principles returned no reward in the market of popular politics.

"The Polls and the Pundits Who Say Our Party Is Dead"

The day after Ford lost the election, people who caught glimpses of him noticed a deep sadness in his eyes. After seeing the palpable hurt in Ford, *New Republic* writer John Osborne said, "I was certain that Gerald Ford in defeat had suffered a wound that would never heal."[97] That was ironic, because observers have credited his presidency with healing the nation.

But he did more. Ford also healed the scars of fratricidal battle within the GOP and, in so doing, preserved the vitality of America's two-party system. After Watergate, numerous publications and pundits speculated on the Republican Party's demise. The scandal, combined with a dismal showing in 1974 and the crippling feud between moderates and conservatives, gave the GOP the look of death. Harvard political scientist Sidney Verba called Republicans "an endangered species." The *New York Times* reported in a front-page headline, "Some Republicans Fearful Party Is On Its Last Legs." *Newsweek* asked if the century-old party was "slowly and painfully dying." The *National Journal* wondered, "GOP: Is the Party Over?"[98]

While reports of the GOP's death were greatly exaggerated, some signs were ominous. Only thirteen state governors were Republican, and in many southern states, the party's infrastructure was as weak as it had been when Reconstruction ended. Demographic surveys showed that just 16 percent of voters under the age of thirty identified themselves as Republicans, which meant that the party might have even fewer members as the electorate aged. The 1974 elections marked the third and most pulverizing defeat of congressional Republicans in as many decades; those in 1958 and 1964 began a process of party degeneration that now looked complete. The setback of

1974 reached deeper than the previous two, down to state and local levels; nationwide, the Republicans controlled just four state legislatures. Even the GOP's strong suit, its rich coffers, seemed in jeopardy, as the Nixon campaign scandals deterred Republicans from contributing money.

Compared to Democrats, whose diversity and tolerance of internal differences radiated strength, Republicans appeared homogenous and intolerant of dissent. America was the most diverse nation in the world, and its minorities were growing, yet the GOP conveyed an impression of remaining mostly male and white. Moreover, as the feud between party moderates and conservatives illustrated, moderates felt increasingly marginalized. Some, like Michigan congressman Don Riegle, joined the Democrats. "We were like the tail of the dog; we couldn't wag the dog," complained Riegle of the moderates' lack of leverage. The GOP seemed so anemic that political scientist Nelson Polsby felt that America no longer had a two-party system but a "one and a half party system." Other pundits believed that by failing to embrace women and minorities, the Republicans would remain a permanent minority—at best.[99]

Had Spiro Agnew remained vice president, the GOP's situation would have been even worse. After Nixon's fall, America would have been saddled with President Agnew, a politician not known for harmonious leadership. Indeed, his pungent rhetoric might have added to GOP detractors. Had his improprieties been unearthed while he was in the White House, the GOP would have been devastated.

Instead, the nation had President Ford. Ford's contrast with the Nixon-Agnew administration reaffirmed Republican credibility. By fostering an atmosphere where the executive and legislative branches could cooperate as well as clash, Ford breathed life back into the two-party system. During the campaign year, he diverted Republicans from a fractious course. Accepting the party's nomination, he scoffed at "the polls and the pundits who say our party is dead" and vowed to prove them wrong.[100] He believed that the GOP's viability lay in a moderate course. "As long as we adhered to our fundamental moderate Republicanism, both domestically and internationally, I had no apprehension about the future of the Republican Party," he recalled. "It's only when we became isolationist in foreign policy, when we became hard right in domestic policy; under those circumstances, we were not going to be a viable political party in the future. We had to take the middle road in both foreign and domestic policy."[101]

The middle road almost worked for Ford, and it nursed the party back to health. His dramatic comeback and strong showing in the 1976 election surprised skeptics and showed that the patient was not "on its last legs" but competitive, even robust. Talk of a "dying party" stopped after the 1976 election. In the words of historian Thomas Bailey, Ford "restored respectability to a Republican party that was careening down the road to the Federalist-Whig cemetery."[102] Ford made possible a GOP rebound in 1980, as well as a more fundamental transformation a generation later.

Since the Civil War, major economic crises have been followed by a national shift in party alignment. Frequently, voters have abandoned a party after its economic leadership proved feckless and embraced the party that promised prosperity. After the Depression of 1893, as voters blamed Democratic president Grover Cleveland for their economic hardships, Republican William McKinley promised a "full dinner pail" and won the 1896 election, ushering in a generation of Republican ascendancy. During the Great Depression, left with a bitter aftertaste from Herbert Hoover's gloomy leadership, many Americans loved Franklin Roosevelt's promise of "Happy Days Are Here Again" and entered the New Deal coalition, making the Democratic Party the majority political force for more than a generation.

Then came the Great Inflation. In 1980, exasperated that prices rose even higher during Carter's presidency, Americans voted in Reagan, who optimistically promised, "A New Morning in America." The "Great Communicator" presided over a reduction in inflation, popularized Republican ideals, and drew more voters into GOP ranks. Reagan's presidency marked the beginning of a new shift. Inflation remained below 5 percent during the last six years of his administration, and by 1988, his last full year in office, 31 percent of voters identified themselves as Republicans (compared to 40 percent for Democrats), a sharp increase from 18 percent after Watergate.[103] During the 1990s, the GOP gained control of both houses of Congress, and party identification between Republicans and Democrats approached parity. Three decades after Watergate and the Republican carnage that followed, the two parties competed at equal strength: 45.5 percent of Americans identified themselves as Republicans and 45.2 percent as Democrats.[104]

Ford laid the groundwork for this post-1970s Republican resurgence. It was an accustomed role; his work in Republican rehabilitation began in the wake of the 1964 Goldwater election debacle, when he replaced autocratic, tired-looking Charles Halleck as minority leader and provided a more youthful and telegenic spokesman for the minority. In 1965, Ford published an article in *Fortune* magazine entitled "What Can Save the GOP?" While conceding that his party needed "strong medicine and major surgery," Ford argued that the GOP was still vibrant, boasting a "deep reserve of recuperative powers in its basic organization and philosophy." He spurned the notion of a Republican coalition with southern Democrats and instead prescribed the "high middle road of moderation" to nurse the party back to health. During the 1966 midterm elections, Republicans dispelled some of their gloom to gain 47 new House seats. Minority Leader Ford made 200 speeches a year to support his party, and his colleagues' gratefulness was one reason that GOP representatives and senators enthusiastically supported his nomination as vice president. As president, Ford's steady leadership restored credibility to the party, so that by 1976, GOP voter identification had edged up four points to 22 percent.[105]

As Ford left office, tributes poured in, and the GOP bathed in the reflected glow. (The New York Times, for example, editorialized, "Mr. Ford today enjoys the respect and affection of his fellow citizens. Moreover, he leaves the country in better shape than he found it.") Ford's economic stewardship, in retrospect, seemed particularly solid. During the Carter presidency, inflation increased (6 percent in 1977, 9 percent in 1978, and 13 percent in both 1979 and 1980), and the country even experienced a recession in 1980. The hobbled economy made Americans more appreciative of Ford's leadership; by September 1979, a Gallup poll showed that voters would elect Ford over Carter, 51 to 42 percent.[106] One of the most effective debate lines in history came when Reagan faced off against Carter in October 1980, and the challenger mentioned the "misery index," the sum of the inflation and unemployment rates, which had risen since Ford left office. As Reagan did this, he benefited from Ford's economic performance, which persuaded many voters that a Republican president could deal effectively with pocketbook issues, practically reversing a long-standing Democratic edge in this area. In 1974, just after Ford took office, only 17 percent of poll respondents viewed the GOP as the party best suited to keeping America prosperous (versus 47 percent for the Democrats). When Ford ran against Carter two years later, the number had risen to 23 percent; by 1980, it was at 35 percent, almost even with the Democrats' 36 percent.[107]

Unlike his immediate Oval Office predecessors, Ford left both the economy and his party in better shape than when he took office. His credible handling of the Great Inflation brought him close to election victory. More important, combined with his personal integrity, he gave the Republican Party a new lease on life. While his term was too short to transform the GOP, he stopped its slide and began its rebuilding.

Conclusion

The Long-term President

Presidential Leadership in Troubled Times

The task of leadership in the 1970s was trying. Speaker Carl Albert found his duties uniquely onerous compared to those of recent House leaders, because he had "a greater variety of difficult issues and situations to deal with than any past speaker. I mean Watergate, impeachment, two resignations [Agnew and Nixon], Vietnam, and now the economic and the energy crisis."[1] Gerald Ford confronted these challenges and thought the solutions lay in steady leadership and a conservative approach. He saw a brighter future for the country in the principles of its past: frugal government, greater reliance on private industry and initiative, tax relief, and economic growth marked by low inflation and low budget deficits.

Some presidents are wafflers. To remain popular or win an election, they expediently shift their stance according to which way the winds of public opinion blow. As a consequence, their actions are inconsistent, their core beliefs difficult to discern. Richard Nixon relinquished free-market tenets to adopt wage and price controls and oil allocations. George H. W. Bush abandoned his "no new taxes" pledge. Bill Clinton was notorious for measuring public opinion to decide what concerned voters, like health care in 1993, an issue that he dropped as quickly as he adopted it. Ford betrayed no such vicissitudes; while willing to compromise, he remained loyal to his ideology. A consistent thread ran throughout his policies and utterances, one of conservative economic principles. Paul O'Neill observed, "He was true to them every day of his presidency."[2] Ford's economic and energy programs provided a window through which to view the beliefs he espoused.

Throughout his presidency, Ford saw inflation as the greatest danger. His anti-inflation program began with an uneven gait; Congress immediately rejected his proposed surtax, and the WIN program embarrassed his administration. More important, a severe economic slump forced him to focus on battling recession, temporarily blurring his anti-inflation policy.

Nonetheless, Ford remained intent on achieving price stability. He believed the nation had to endure high unemployment while he first subdued inflation. High jobless rates were painful for him to see and politically damaging, but Ford preferred that to increased spending, which he believed would spur inflation. Central to Ford's fiscal restraint was his veto strategy, which marshaled presidential power against Congress.

But Ford was no rigid, doctrinaire ideologue. After a quarter century in the House minority, he was steeped in the art of compromise, and his legislative skills enabled him to reach agreements with Congress. If Ford had refused to compromise with Congress, he would have been left with nothing; by flowing with, rather than perennially fighting, the currents of the mainstream, he helped calm the turbulence left from the Nixon years. Political scientist Nelson Polsby observed, "Ford restored normal political relationships in Washington. Nixon was essentially a destroyer of normal political relationships. In restoring them, Ford performed a great service, really."[3]

Yet at the end of Ford's term, political skepticism still hung like a storm cloud over the nation. Some of Ford's shortcomings hardened the cynicism. He handled the Nixon pardon badly and could not prevent huge GOP losses in the 1974 elections. Nor did he project the image of a hero that Americans longed for in the mid-1970s. For those Americans aching for inspirational leadership, Ford disappointed.

But in some fundamental qualifications, Ford fit the times well. The president who succeeded Nixon needed impeccable moral character. The media would see to it, functioning as character cops after Watergate, questioning even the slightest moral tincture. This desire for integrity meant the absence of dalliances, drug use, dubious associates, officious or unruly family members—problems that have plagued recent presidents. A bland, even boring, character was both desirable and functional, for it would defuse the overwrought emotions of the time. The new president had to show an amicable disposition toward the press, which had suffered a turbulent relationship with Nixon. Nixon's successor also had to exercise power circumspectly, within constitutional bounds, and be self-effacing enough to deflate some of the presidency's pomp.

These were rigorous criteria, yet Ford possessed many of them. He was, in fact, so free of moral and psychological hang-ups that the press highlighted his only palpable though irrelevant flaw, an alleged proclivity to stumble. That media preoccupation was a backhanded compliment, indicating the absence of more serious character flaws. But the portrayals damaged Ford's public image and made him appear unpresidential. The media's caustic treatment reflected the cynicism of the era and a difficulty of 1970s presidential leadership. Decades passed before reporters began to appreciate fully Ford's stewardship. Moreover, Ford remained one of the few presidents since the 1960s who needed no psychohistory.

The Energy and Economic Challenges

Ford knew that the energy crisis was, in large part, a crisis of policy, that market mechanisms worked best. By proposing decontrol, Ford broached a goal that later proved a boon. When Reagan took office in 1981, one of his first executive orders was to end the remaining controls on domestic oil, which Carter had almost entirely phased out. The market responded as Ford predicted. Oil prices increased, and in response to this incentive U.S. oil drilling hit record levels in 1981. Domestic oil production rose rapidly, by 400 million barrels a day between 1979 and 1985, while domestic consumption fell. Consequently, oil imports fell by over 47 percent during that same six-year period (and as insurance, the SPR that EPCA had created grew from 91 million barrels in 1979 to 493 million barrels at the end of 1985 to 640 million barrels in 2004). By 1984, the United States was importing only 30 percent of its oil, down from 46 percent at the time Ford left office (although imports increased after world oil prices collapsed in 1986).[4]

Congressman John Dingell recalled that with a Republican president and a Democratic Congress approaching the decontrol issue with different philosophies, "working out a compromise out of that kind of a situation was a very hard thing to do." Under these adverse circumstances, Ford was satisfied with the administration's accomplishments. "I think we did focus the country [on energy] at a time of need," Zarb commented. "We got some things done, like the strategic stockpile, which today is a nice national security cushion. We gave a little bit of a push to some of the alternate forms of fuel. We got things in place like standards for appliances so that there were measurements of fuel efficiency. We got the parameters of an energy focus in place. With a two-and-a-half year presidency, right after Watergate—not too bad, given what we had to work with." Over the long term, Ford's efforts looked good. In 1994, Dingell, an ardent opponent of Ford's energy program, looked back charitably on the president's efforts. "At the time I would have given him a 'D.' Now I would give him a 'B' or a 'B+,'" he mused.[5]

Ford's difficulty in forming an energy policy was unsurprising. Decontrol meant dispelling concerns over inflation and persuading a reluctant Congress to follow him. An energy policy demanded a national consensus and executive-legislative agreements that have been impossible to forge over decades, let alone during one congressional session. When the Arab oil embargo ended and the crisis mentality faded, chances of a national policy dimmed. As Zarb succinctly explained, "In the absence of a crisis, no major public policy shift. Ever." He noted that a presidential program depends on public and congressional acceptance, and Congress decided that "there really was no crisis, and they weren't going to rewire the circuit board in the absence of a crisis."[6]

In retrospect, the energy scarcity of the 1970s was more apparent than real. In 1976, Jimmy Carter warned that the world had only thirty-five years worth of oil left. Such a prediction sounded plausible but was wrong. Moreover, the concept of energy vulnerability lost impact after the 1970s, and the United States began to live comfortably with the idea of importing oil. When Ford left office, the country was importing 46 percent of its oil.[7] Energy vulnerability, which the administration feared so much and tried to reduce, had increased.

But Ford was right about one thing. In energy, the free market provided the best solution. Charles DiBona remarked that while "there were no heroes" in the 1970s energy mess, Ford "was the closest thing to a hero in the whole business, because he was trying to do the right thing. And he found it impossible to do."[8] Price controls illustrated that energy was a sector where government interference disrupted market allocations. Decontrol was the answer, one that Congress refused to accept, although Ford achieved the gradual decontrol of petroleum products during his last year in office.

Ford had economic achievements, too. In April 1974, four months before he became president, the *New York Times* complained that "this country has no inflation policy," blaming both Nixon and Congress. Nixon oscillated among the tenets of monetarism, fiscalism, wage and price controls, and dollar devaluation. Ford had an anti-inflation policy, a remedy that he prescribed while still vice president, when he said that "the basic solution is fiscal and monetary restraint."[9] More skillfully than previous presidents, Ford used these two macroeconomic levers in tandem, sticking with the combination throughout his term.

Inflation, the economic terror of the 1970s, went down during every year of Ford's presidency, from 11.0 percent in 1974 to 9.2 in 1975 and 5.7 in 1976.[10] While federal spending and the deficit remained high, with budget cuts and vetoes Ford brought both down, and he directed attention to the federal debt. "I think [Ford] succeeded pretty well in setting out a program that got us on the way to getting our financial house in order," William Seidman believed. "When he left, if you took the trend lines and carried them out, we would have had a balanced budget within a short period of time. When he left, inflation was under control, or down below 6 percent, interest rates were down—almost everything that was going on, you would have to say the trend line was in the right direction."[11] Ford also beat back another demon, considering one of his great achievements to be "defeating the worst economic recession following World War II and turning the economy around."[12]

In a fortuitous twist, the recession bled life out of inflation. Ford continued this fight for the rest of his presidency. Critics charged that by focusing so intently on inflation, Ford neglected unemployment. Because of the recession, the average unemployment rate during Ford's term was the highest under any postwar president, 7.4 percent.[13] This high rate, a dark blotch on Ford's record, had adverse political consequences. But to achieve stable, sustainable growth, Ford understood that lowering inflation was peremptory. Economist Herbert Stein called Ford's policies "resolute and responsible." To fight the recession, Stein wrote, Ford "had to resist temptations and demands for strong action to pump up the economy. He had to be willing to accept, and to lead people to accept, sacrifices in the form of unemployment in order to avoid the continuation of double-digit inflation, or its revival after a short lull. He did what had to be done, directly through his support of the restrained policy of the Federal Reserve."[14]

If, as many congressional Democrats urged, Ford tried to reduce unemployment by artificially stimulating the economy, he would have created larger deficits and more inflation. His refusal to do so aggravated image problems. In reality, Ford felt deeply the plight of the jobless, repeatedly maintaining that the greatest regret of his presidency was his inability to reduce unemployment speedily. "The most frustrating problem—the one I felt saddest about not solving quickly—was the unemployment problem," he lamented. "A President cannot just turn a switch in the society in which we live and end unemployment—at least, not on a constructive basis."[15]

Ford was a long-term president. That thought might seem curious; his time in office was brief—only 895 days—the fifth-shortest presidency in history.[16] But Ford focused on the long term, believing that a true statesman should anticipate the concerns of later generations. He worried about the latent effects of quick fixes to the recession. His continued emphasis on inflation set a new foundation for the nation's future direction. For a quarter century after World War II, the federal government's main economic focus was ensuring full employment. The 1970s marked a watershed. Since then, the Federal Reserve and government economists have aimed to keep inflation low while sustaining steady growth, a policy bias that Ford shaped while president.

A linchpin of Ford's anti-inflation strategy was lower budget deficits. While the fiscal momentum of government is difficult to slow, especially in as short a period as Ford's term, he alerted the nation to the perils of deficits, provided leadership in making unpopular budget cuts, and pointed America toward a path of deficit reduction. Deficits under Ford's watch, which ran in the neighborhood of $60–$70 billion, were small by future standards. Later, as the federal debt grew to over $1 trillion, Ford's warnings took a prophetic tone. Roy Ash observed, "We rang the bells of warning."[17] Ford would have resisted the budget deficits of later years.[18] He affirmed that "if I had been elected, we would have continued to fight to reduce expenditures." He said that he would have persisted in using the veto against Congress as an instrument of budget reduction. "I would have been very firm," he said. "I would have continued a policy of submitting lower and lower deficits and fighting with the Congress, which still would have been Democratic, to get a better control of expenditures."[19]

Ford's other economic initiatives blazed trails for future presidents. Carter and Reagan continued his work in decontrolling oil prices and stimulating coal production, which eased the energy crisis. Carter deregulated the airline and trucking industries, and Reagan likewise emphasized government deregulation. During the 1990s, Democrat Bill Clinton even co-opted Ford's emphasis on a smaller federal government, declaring in 1996 that "the era of big government is over."

In many other areas, Ford anticipated long-term concerns. Some actions that sparked furious controversy in the 1970s have been vindicated over time. Longtime CBS Washington correspondent Bob Schieffer has written, "In those days, I didn't buy the Ford argument that the [Nixon] pardon was good for the country. I thought it was a terrible thing to do, but as the years have passed, I have concluded that Ford was right and I was wrong." Schieffer said that the pardon was "a break the country sorely needed," and it coincided with the Ford years' halcyon tone. Preceding and succeeding presidencies suffered either wars, scandals, or paralyzing crises, and Schieffer believed, "In the turbulent period that stretched from Johnson to Clinton, it may well be the impact of Gerald Ford that is remembered as most significant."[20]

At the time, no one knew that Ford's actions would set precedents or constructively shape future events. Only in the rearview mirror of history has this become clear. The Helsinki accords, which fomented conservative wrath, helped to drive a wedge between the Soviet Union and its satellites, a watershed event in bringing down the iron curtain and freeing millions enthralled under communism. Economic summits among industrialized nations continued to cement ties among America and its allies. When Republicans defected from their party after Watergate, bringing its share of the electorate to less than half that of Democrats, Ford stemmed the hemorrhaging; a generation later, the GOP made a remarkable comeback, standing at parity with its opposition. Ford remarked, "Historians generally rank Presidents by what they complete while in office. Another way of assessing them is by what they begin."[21] By this standard, Ford's compass settings passed the test of time, for they transcended the 1970s and set a new direction for the nation.

Returning Us to Normal

Ford's achievements were slow and steady, reflecting his leadership style. His successes passed unnoticed, as when the economy quietly slipped past its recession and as price increases gradually slowed. Ford's actions called into question the very definition of presidential achievement. Traditionally, Americans accepted such accomplishment in an activist sense, appreciating chief executives who introduced programs and persuaded Congress and the people to support them. To Ford, presidential success also meant blocking undesirable legislation. Presidential adviser Roger Porter commented that "if you take that two-fold definition of accomplishment, then it clearly raises the accomplishment level of the Ford administration, because he forced an overwhelmingly Democratic Congress . . . from doing certain things he felt were not in the country's best interest."[22] Yet Ford's solutions conveyed an image of insensitivity to suffering and inadequacy for the task of leadership. Unable to translate his accomplishments into a cogent platform, Ford lost the 1976 election.

In part, Ford was a victim of the era. Governing during the 1970s was enormously difficult. The abuses of previous presidents led Congress to circumscribe presidential power and resist presidential initiatives. The media openly investigated and assailed presidents, and the public mood was often grim. Immediately affected by the loss of power and prestige following Nixon's resignation, Ford governed when the presidency was weakened. After the 1974 elections, the loss of power was more pronounced. Thus, despite exemplary personal relations with Congress, Ford had more difficulty than most presidents in leading Capitol Hill. That he tackled domestic crises provided another obstacle, since domestic policy sparked heated debate, unlike diplomacy, which often seemed remote and where the president appeared to have special knowledge, encouraging Congress to defer.[23]

Nor could Ford arouse ardent admirers. James Cannon observed that Ford was not "as loved as other Presidents have been."[24] Ford was not as hated, either. This absence of love and hate was another factor in his election defeat.

Since the 1970s, only presidents who have created the powerful elixir of love and hatred—the polarizing presidents—have won two terms: Nixon, Reagan, Clinton, and George W. Bush. Paradoxically, they have triumphed despite harsh detractors. They electrified their party, and devoted partisans provided a base to which they added independent voters, forming a formidable coalition. Those presidents who inspired ambivalence or only mild emotions—Carter, George H. W. Bush, and Ford—failed on Election Day. Had Ford won, he would have come closer to emulating Eisenhower, his presidential idol, who twice won the presidency and remained well liked but little hated.

Although perhaps a political handicap, the absence of hatred made Ford the right man after Watergate. He had no enemies or record of presidential abuses. He detoxified the poisoned political atmosphere of Washington, through his personal relations with Congress and respect for adversaries. Like his economic achievements, the moral regeneration he fostered was undramatic. The calm that prevailed during the Ford years even seemed boring. But the *Washington Post*, which had once scored Ford as "pedestrian, partisan, dogged," praised him at the end of his presidency for having "brought to the White House an open, unsinister and—yes—decent style of doing things that altered the life of the city and ultimately of the country."[25] Rebuilding trust was Ford's goal, and he felt he succeeded. "In the relatively short period of time that I served," he reflected, "the major problem was to restore integrity and public confidence in the White House, which we did."[26]

The 1970s was no ordinary era. Ford led a country that trembled on the cusp of ominous changes. Cynicism and distrust permeated politics. The fell specters of inflation and recession threatened prosperity, while government controls and regulations created an energy crisis. The Republican Party grew so anemic that the future of the two-party system appeared doubtful. Abroad, allies nervously observed an American isolationism reemerge. By restoring vitality to America's institutions and policies, Ford brought a sense that everything was healthy and routine again. "If I had to describe [Ford] in one word it would be 'normal,'" said National Security Advisor Brent Scowcroft, "and that says a lot because I think his presidency will be known in future years as a presidency which returned us to normal."[27]

Ford ameliorated the decade's problems. Keeping a steady hand on the tiller, he led a country confronting perhaps its greatest challenges of the postwar era. Domestically, he restored economic stability; overseas, he projected power confidently; on a personal level, his White House radiated a civility and openness, replacing earlier attitudes. Some of Ford's ideas—the "old-time religion" in fighting inflation or a tax cut to cure the recession—proved effective. Others—oil decontrol, deregulation, and concern over deficits—attracted attention and led to action after he left office. The decade's challenges were daunting, and Ford struggled to bring them under control. In the end, he left a lighter burden for the country to bear.

Notes

Introduction

1. George Gallup, *The Gallup Poll: Public Opinion, 1972–1977*, (Wilmington, Del.: Scholarly Resources, 1978), 1:230; 2:656; *The Gallup Opinion Index*, September 1974, 27–28. See also *New York Times*, March 17, 1974 (hereafter cited as *NYT*), for a poll of Republican leaders who ranked inflation, the energy crisis, and Watergate and honesty in government as the most important issues in the fall 1974 congressional elections.

2. *NYT*, July 25, 1975.

3. *Wall Street Journal*, May 14, 1976 (hereafter cited as *WSJ*); *The Gallup Opinion Index*, June 1979, 7.

4. Post-Meeting Review (handwritten notes), Box 25, Folder: Debate Negotiations, Michael Duval Papers, Gerald R. Ford Presidential Library, Ann Arbor, Mich. (hereafter cited as GRFL).

5. Memorandum from Alan Greenspan, January 22, 1975, Record Group 26, Series 3, Vice Presidential Central Files, Subseries: Business Economics, Box 163, Folder BE5, Rockefeller Archive Center, Tarrytown, N.Y.

6. Gallup, *The Gallup Poll*, 2:656; Godfrey Hodgson, *America in Our Time* (New York: Simon and Schuster, 1976), 11; *Washington Post*, October 27, 1974 (hereafter cited as *WP*).

7. David Frum, *How We Got Here, The 70's: The Decade That Brought You Modern Life (For Better or Worse)* (New York: Basic Books, 2000), 317.

8. Louis Harris and Associates, "A Proposal for a Basic Study of the American Public and the Leadership Community to Determine the Parameters of Public Consent to Face Critical Alternatives in the Conduct of Foreign Policy (October 1974)," Box 182, Folder 6, Legislative Files, Carl Albert Congressional and Research Studies Center, University of Oklahoma at Norman (hereafter cited as CACRSC).

9. *WP*, July 7, 1975.

10. Simon Whitney, *Inflation since 1945: Facts and Theories* (New York: Praeger, 1982), 51.

11. Jeffrey Hart, "A Comparative Analysis of the Sources of America's Relative Economic Decline," in *Understanding American Economic Decline*, edited by Michael Bernstein and David Adler, 207 (New York: Cambridge Univ. Press, 1994); David Gordon,

"Chickens Home to Roost: From Prosperity to Stagnation in the Postwar U.S. Economy," in Bernstein and Adler, eds., *Understanding American Economic Decline*, 42.

12. Whitney, *Inflation*, 39.

13. Gerald Ford, interview by author, October 25, 1994.

14. *World Almanac and Book of Facts: 1977* (New York: Newspaper Enterprise Association, 1977), 135.

15. "Energy, the Economy, and Policy," by Walter Heller, statement before the Subcommittee on International Economics of the Joint Committee of Congress, December 12, 1973, Box 549, Folder: Economic Policy Memoranda-1974, Lilly Library, Indiana University at Bloomington (hereafter cited as IU).

16. Alan Pater and James Pater, eds., *What They Said in 1974: The Yearbook of Spoken Opinion* (Beverly Hills, Calif.: Monitor, 1975), 39.

17. "Happy Days," *A&E Biography*, produced by Kevin Bachar and Whiz Iiames-Damutz (2001), video.

18. *Guardian* (London), May 18, 1999.

19. David Broder, *Changing of the Guard: Power and Leadership in America* (New York: Simon and Schuster, 1980), 122.

20. *Miami Herald*, December 29, 1974; *Public Papers of the Presidents: Gerald R. Ford, 1974* (Washington, D.C.: Government Printing Office, 1975), 737.

21. David Adler, "Preface," in Bernstein and Adler, eds., *Understanding American Economic Decline*, xiii–xiv.

22. Ron Nessen, *It Sure Looks Different from the Inside* (New York: Playboy Books, 1978), xiv.

23. Richard Reeves, "I'm Sorry, Mr. President," *American Heritage*, no. 8 (December 1996): 53.

24. *Las Vegas Sun*, August 10, 2000.

25. Gerald R. Ford, *A Time to Heal: The Autobiography of Gerald R. Ford* (New York: Harper and Row, 1979), 105–6; *Time*, October 22, 1973, 16, 18.

26. Bud Vestal, *Jerry Ford, Up Close: An Investigative Biography* (New York: Coward, McCann, and Geoghegan, 1974), 178.

27. James Cannon, *Time and Chance: Gerald Ford's Appointment with History* (New York: HarperCollins, 1994), 411; Richard Reeves, *A Ford, Not a Lincoln* (New York: Harcourt Brace Jovanovich, 1975), ix.

28. *Time*, August 19, 1974, 27.

29. Ford, *A Time to Heal*, 56; Vestal, *Jerry Ford*, 64.

30. Cannon, *Time and Chance*, 44, 49.

31. Frederick Schapsmeier and Lewis Schapsmeier, *Gerald R. Ford's Date with Destiny: A Political Biography* (New York: Peter Lang, 1989), 40, 64.

32. Cannon, *Time and Chance*, 75–77; Vestal, *Jerry Ford*, 119–22.

33. *NYT*, March 2, 1975.

34. *Newsweek*, October 22, 1973, 38; Cannon, *Time and Chance*, 88.

35. *Time*, October 22, 1973, 18; Cannon, *Time and Chance*, 91–92, 94.

36. *NYT*, May 26, 1975; Schapsmeier and Schapsmeier, *Date with Destiny*, 94; *U.S. News and World Report*, December 17, 1973, 23 (hereafter cited as *U.S. News*).

37. *NYT*, October 13, 1973.

38. *President Ford: The Man and His Record* (Washington, D.C.: Congressional Quarterly Press, 1975), 27; *Time*, August 19, 1974,.

39. Vestal, *Jerry Ford*, 145.

40. The only other vice president to resign was John C. Calhoun, who left in 1832 to become a U.S. senator representing South Carolina.

41. Robert Hartmann, *Palace Politics: An Inside Account of the Ford Years* (New York: McGraw-Hill, 1980), 18.

42. Previously, a vacated vice presidency remained empty until the next election. Under the terms of the Twenty-fifth Amendment, a president selects a nominee, who is then subject to confirmation by a majority vote of both the House and Senate. See *Documents of American History*, vol. 2, *since 1868*, edited by Henry Steele Commager and Milton Cantor, 10th ed., 890 (Englewood Cliffs, N.J.: Prentice Hall, 1988); see also *U.S. News*, October 22, 1973, 17.

43. Cannon, *Time and Chance*, 209.

44. Ibid., 205; Schapsmeier and Schapsmeier, *Date with Destiny*, 137.

45. *U.S. News*, October 22, 1973, 17.

46. Ford, *A Time to Heal*, 111; *President Ford*, 46.

47. *Newsweek*, December 17, 1973, 25.

48. *Ithaca Journal*, July 14, 2000.

49. Cannon, *Time and Chance*, 273.

50. Schapsmeier and Schapsmeier, *Date with Destiny*, 148.

51. Cannon, *Time and Chance*, 274.

52. James Lynn, telephone interview by author, February 2, 1995; Thomas P. O'Neill, *Man of the House: The Life and Political Memoirs of Speaker Tip O'Neill* (New York: Random House, 1987), 261.

Chapter 1. Hungering for Heroes

1. Ace Collins, *Evel Knievel: An American Hero* (New York: St. Martin's Press, 1999), 147–94; Hartmann, *Palace Politics*, 240.

2. Ford, *A Time to Heal*, 28.

3. Hartmann, *Palace Politics*, 159.

4. *President Ford*, 2.

5. George Edwards III, *The Public Presidency: The Pursuit of Popular Support* (New York: St. Martin's Press, 1983), 51–61.

6. Richard Neustadt, *Presidential Power and the Modern Presidents: The Politics of Leadership from Roosevelt to Reagan* (New York: Free Press, 1990), 188; *Time*, July 15, 1974, 23.

7. Michael Doyle, ed., *Gerald R. Ford: Selected Speeches* (Arlington, Va.: R.W. Beatty, 1973)

8. Edwards, *The Public Presidency*, 221.

9. John R. Greene, *The Presidency of Gerald R. Ford* (Lawrence: Univ. Press of Kansas), 19.

10. Edwards, *The Public Presidency*, 79; Jules Witcover, "The Political Legacy: A

Climate of Cynicism, an Atmosphere of Mistrust," in *The Fall of a President*, by the *Washington Post* Staff, 109 (New York: Dell, 1974); *NYT*, January 3, 1974.

11. Stanley Kutler, *The Wars of Watergate: The Last Crisis of Richard Nixon* (New York: Alfred Knopf, 1990), 454.

12. Carl Bernstein and Bob Woodward, "A Passion for the Covert: The Response to the Threat of Discovery," in *The Fall of a President*, 37.

13. George Reedy, *The Twilight of the Presidency*, rev. ed. (New York: New American Library, 1987), 158, 179.

14. Kutler, *The Wars of Watergate*, 607.

15. Ron Nessen interview by author, January 29, 2002.

16. Shana Alexander, in *Crisis in Confidence: The Impact of Watergate*, edited by Donald Harward (Boston: Little, Brown, 1974), 46.

17. *Economist*, January 12, 2002, 23; *USA Today*, February 17, 1994. By 1994, the figure had fallen to just 19 percent.

18. *WP*, October 31, 1975.

19. Elliot Richardson, *The Creative Balance: Government, Politics, and the Individual in America's Third Century* (New York: Holt, Rinehart, and Winston, 1976), 96.

20. *WP*, March 1, 1975; Letter to Birch Bayh from Ruth Steward, March 20, 1974, Box 55, Birch Bayh Papers, Lilly Library, IU; *Time*, July 15, 1974, 23.

21. Memorandum from Doug Bailey, September 30, 1976, Papers of Gerald R. Ford, Staff Secretary, Special Files, Box 3, Folder: Second Debate: Suggestions from White House Staff, GRFL.

22. Peter Carroll, *It Seemed Like Nothing Happened: America in the 1970s* (New Brunswick, N.J.: Rutgers Univ. Press, 2000), 171; *Congressional Quarterly Almanac 1976* (Washington, D.C.: Congressional Quarterly Press, 1976), 3.

23. Cannon, *Time and Chance*, 414.

24. John B. Anderson, telephone interview by author, May 5, 1994.

25. Greene, *The Presidency of Gerald R. Ford*, 104–12; Bruce Schulman, *The Seventies: The Great Shift in American Culture, Society, and Politics* (New York: Free Press, 2001), 48.

26. Frum, *How We Got Here*, 34.

27. Mark Rozell, *The Press and the Ford Presidency* (Ann Arbor: Univ. of Michigan Press, 1993), 226.

28. Jerald terHorst, interview by Mark Rozell, GRFL; John Dumbress, *The Carter Presidency: A Re-evaluation* (Manchester: Manchester Univ. Press, 1993), 23.

29. Richardson, *The Creative Balance*, 94; *Newsweek*, November 4, 1974, 17.

30. "Departmental Plan-Issues" (a strategy paper for the 1974 campaign), Box 526, Folder: Campaign, Birch Bayh Papers, Lilly Library, IU.

31. *Newsweek*, November 4, 1974, 17; *NYT*, October 22, November 21, 1975; May 30, 1976.

32. *U.S. News*, July 21, 1975, 16, 18; *Time*, July 15, 1974, 21; September 9, 1974, 19.

33. *WP*, September 23, 1974.

34. Joan Blair and Clay Blair, *The Search for JFK* (New York: G.P. Putman's Sons, 1976), 209–70, 585–86; Benjamin Bradlee, *Conversations with Kennedy* (New York: W.W. Norton, 1976), 74–75, 157, 186, 227; see also Lewis Paper, *The Promise and*

the Performance: The Leadership of John F. Kennedy (New York: Crown, 1975), 377–78.

35. *Newsweek*, March 28, 1975, 28

36. Ibid.; *Time*, June 9, 1975, 45; *U.S. News*, September 29, 1975, 42; *NYT*, April 18, 1975; Robert Lamm, "Harry Truman," from the album *Chicago VIII* (Columbia Records, 1974).

37. *WP*, January 12, 1975; Ford, interview, October 25, 1994.

38. Robert Dallek, *Hail to the Chief: The Making and Unmaking of Presidents* (New York: Hyperion, 1996), 155; *Time*, January 9, 1975, 45; Speech before Michigan State College Young GOP, East Lansing, October 1948, Gerald R. Ford Congressional Papers, Press Secretary and Speech File, 1947–73, Box D13, GRFL.

39. Vestal, *Jerry Ford*, 196; American Enterprise Institute, *A Discussion with Gerald R. Ford: The American Presidency* (Washington, D.C.: American Enterprise Institute, 1977), 5.

40. Vestal, *Jerry Ford*, 44.

41. Robert Shogan, *The Riddle of Power: Presidential Leadership from Truman to Bush* (New York: Dutton Books, 1991); Schapsmeier and Schapsmeier, *Date with Destiny*, 98; Vestal, *Jerry Ford*, 44, 152.

42. Ford, *A Time to Heal*, 109–10; Vestal, *Jerry Ford*, 15.

43. Cannon, *Time and Chance*, 230; *Time*, August 19, 1974, 32.

44. Ford, *A Time to Heal*, 126.

45. Roy Ash, interview by author, August 21, 2001.

46. James Cavanaugh, interview by author, April 17, 2003.

47. Richard Cheney, "Forming and Managing an Administration," in *The Ford Presidency: Twenty-two Intimate Portraits of Gerald R. Ford*, edited by Kenneth Thompson, 85 (Lanham, Md.: University Press of America, 1988); Hartmann, *Palace Politics*, 164; Ford, *A Time to Heal*, 139.

48. Ibid., Ford, *A Time to Heal*, 140; Hugh Sidey, *Portrait of a President* (New York: Harper and Row, 1975), 35.

49. Arthur Dudden, "Not a Lincoln But a Ford," in *Gerald R. Ford and the Politics of Post-Watergate America*, edited by Bernard J. Firestone and Alexej Ugrinsky, 2:616 (Westport, Conn.: Greenwood Press, 1993).

50. Sidey, *Portrait*, 36; Ford, *A Time to Heal*, 141.

51. Paul O'Neill, telephone interview by author, August 17, 1994.

52. Edwards, *The Public Presidency*, 128–31; John Casserly, *The Ford White House: Diary of a Speechwriter* (Boulder: Colorado Associated Univ. Press, 1977), 12; Nessen, *It Sure Looks Different*, 350; Sidey, *Portrait*, 66.

53. Mark Rozell, interview by Jerald terHorst, GRFL.

54. Sarah McClendon, *My Eight Presidents* (New York: Wyden Books, 1978), 181; *Time*, September 9, 1974, 11.

55. *Time*, August 19, 1974, 13; *U.S. News*, August 26, 1974, 15; Jules Witcover, *Marathon: The Pursuit of the Presidency, 1972–1976* (New York: Viking, 1977), 41; *Newsweek*, August 26, 1974, 16.

56. *Time*, August 26, 1974, 14; Ford, *A Time to Heal*, 178.

57. Bob Schieffer, *This Just In: What I Couldn't Tell You on TV* (New York: G.P.

Putnam's Sons, 2003), 223; Bob Woodward, "Gerald R. Ford," in *Profiles in Courage for Our Time*, edited by Caroline Kennedy, 294 (New York: Hyperion, 2002).

58. Gerald Ford, interview on ABC's *Good Morning America*, April 22, 1994.

59. Kutler, *The Wars of Watergate*, 555; Nessen, *It Sure Looks Different*, 30.

60. David Gergen, *Eyewitness to Power: The Essence of Leadership, Nixon to Clinton* (New York: Simon and Schuster, 2000), 118.

61. Stephen E. Ambrose, *Nixon: Ruin and Recovery, 1972–1990* (New York: Touchstone, 1991), 461–62; *Time*, September 23, 1974, 11.

62. Telegrams to Carl Albert, Box 169, Folder 1, Legislative Files: Pardon, CACRSC.

63. Ford, *A Time to Heal*, 175–76; Nessen, *It Sure Looks Different*, 10.

64. Dallek, *Hail to the Chief*, 45, 143–44, 167.

65. Godfrey Hodgson, *All Things to All Men: The False Promise of the Modern American Presidency* (New York: Simon and Schuster, 1980), 43.

66. Rozell, *The Press*, 51.

67. Reeves, *A Ford, Not a Lincoln*, 97.

68. Clark Mollenhoff, *The Man Who Pardoned Nixon* (New York: St. Martin's Press, 1976), 94–95.

69. *Time*, September 23, 1974, 86; Rozell, *The Press*, 178; Reeves, *A Ford, Not a Lincoln*, 93

70. *Detroit News*, September 9, 2001; Cannon, *Time and Chance*, 386. The pardon—at least initially—had the exact opposite effect on the White House press corps that Ford intended. Instead of allaying interest in the former president, the pardon only stoked it. At Ford's first press conference as president at the end of August, seven of twenty-seven questions—approximately one-quarter—dealt directly or indirectly with Nixon or Watergate, with five different reporters asking specifically about the possibility of a pardon. During Ford's first press conference after the pardon, sixteen of twenty-one questions—approximately three-quarters—had to do with the Nixon pardon or Watergate. (By Ford's third press conference as president, one month after the pardon, things had settled down: Only three of twenty-seven questions were about Nixon or the pardon.) See *Public Papers, Gerald R. Ford, 1974*.

71. *Time*, September 23, 1974, 11.

72. Robert Shogan, *The Double-Edged Sword: How Character Makes and Ruins Presidents, from Washington to Clinton* (Boulder, Colo.: Westview Press, 1999), 143; Bob Woodward, *Shadow: Five Presidents and the Legacy of Watergate* (New York: Simon and Schuster, 1999), 5–11.

73. Woodward, *Shadow*, 28; Woodward, "Gerald R. Ford," 306.

74. For a more skeptical construction of the Nixon pardon, see Seymour Hersh's article, "The Pardon: Nixon, Ford, Haig, and the Orderly Transfer of Power" (*Atlantic*, August 1983, 55–78). Hersh maintains that Ford and his aides had frequent communication with Nixon chief of staff Alexander Haig about the possibility of a pardon before Nixon resigned and after Ford became president and that Ford even talked with Nixon by phone the night before issuing the pardon. Hersh also suggests that Ford dissimulates on certain points regarding when during August 1974 he began to consider the possibility of pardoning Nixon and when and how often he communicated with Haig about it.

75. Elford Cederburg, telephone interview by author, July 20, 2003.

76. Barber Conable, interview by author, February 9, 1994.

77. Jonathan Aitken, *Nixon: A Life* (Washington, D.C.: Regnery, 1993), 530; Woodward, "Gerald R. Ford," 310–11.

78. Woodward, "Gerald R. Ford," 310.

79. Ford, interview on *Good Morning America*, April 22, 1994.

80. Nessen, interview, January 29, 2002.

81. Gergen, *Eyewitness to Power*, 121.

82. Ibid., 122.

83. Ford, *A Time to Heal*, 175; Woodward, *Shadow*, 22.

84. Woodward, *Shadow*, 22; Hersh, "The Pardon," 76.

85. Dallek, *Hail to the Chief*.

86. *WSJ*, August 20, 1976.

87. *NYT*, October 6, 1974; Woodward, *Shadow*, 25.

88. Ford, *A Time to Heal*, 197–99; Sidey, *Portrait*, 73.

89. Woodward, *Shadow*, 26.

90. Rozell, *The Press*, 70–71.

91. Conable, interview, February 9, 1994.

Chapter 2. The Congenial Presidency

1. *Time*, February 2, 1976, 73; Doug Hill and Jeff Weingrad, *Saturday Night: A Backstage History of Saturday Night Live* (New York: Beech Tree Books, 1986), 132.

2. Cannon, *Time and Chance*, 100; Schapsmeier and Schapsmeier, *Date with Destiny*, 98–99.

3. Reedy, *The Twilight of the Presidency*, 100; Nessen, interview, January 29, 2002.

4. Dudden, "Not a Lincoln But a Ford," 2:617; Rozell, *The Press*, 180.

5. Nessen, interview, January 29, 2002.

6. Ron Nessen, "The Ford Presidency and the Press," in Thompson, *The Ford Presidency*, 183.

7. John Osborne, *White House Watch: The Ford Years* (Washington, D.C.: New Republic Books, 1977), 88–89; John Hersey, *The President* (New York: Alfred Knopf, 1975); Rozell, *The Press*, 230.

8. William Baroody, interview by William Syers, GRFL.

9. *Ann Arbor News*, November 21, 1974.

10. Baroody, interview by Syers, GRFL; McClendon, *My Eight Presidents*, 188; James Lynn, interview by author, October 27, 1994.

11. Stephen Wayne, "Running the White House: The Ford Experience," *Presidential Studies Quarterly* 7 (Spring/Summer 1977): 96–97; WP, May 20, 1975; *U.S. News*, November 25, 1974, 17.

12. Robert Orben, "Speeches, Humor, and the Public," in Thompson, *The Ford Presidency*, 235; *Time*, May 5, 1975, 31; *U.S. News*, December 1, 1975, 49.

13. Robert Goldwin, interview by Martin Nolan, Box 4, Folder: Goldwin—Interviews/Lectures, Robert Goldwin Papers, GRFL.

14. Robert Goldwin, interview by author, March 3, 1994.

15. Betty Ford with Chris Chase, *The Times of My Life* (New York: Harper and Row, 1978), 172.

16. Nessen, interview, January 29, 2002.

17. Ford, *A Time to Heal*, 53; Cheney, "Forming and Managing an Administration," 73.

18. Michael Duval, interview by author, March 8, 1994; WP, January 1, 1975.

19. Conable, interview, February 9, 1994.

20. WP, August 3, 1975; *Brill's Content*, November 1998, 131.

21. Douglas Bennett, interview by author, October 19, 1994.

22. James Cannon, interview by author, October 19, 1994.

23. *Brill's Content*, November 1998, 131.

24. Phil Buchen, "Reflections on a Politician's President," in Thompson, *The Ford Presidency*, 35.

25. Rozell, *The Press*, 7; *Time*, July 14, 1975, 7.

26. Sidey, *Portrait*, 64.

27. WP, January 1, 12, 1975.

28. *Public Papers, 1974*, 691; Gergen, *Eyewitness to Power*, 127; see also Orben, "Speeches, Humor, and the Public," 250.

29. WP, December 20, 1974.

30. Nessen, *It Sure Looks Different*, 119.

31. Dudden, "Not a Lincoln But a Ford," 2:619.

32. WP, January 12, 1975.

33. Pater and Pater, *What They Said*, 39.

34. *Newsweek*, August 25, 1975, 23; *Time*, September 1, 1975, 9.

35. NYT, July 20, 1975.

36. Bennett, interview, October 19, 1994.

37. Videotape of third campaign debate, GRFL.

38. Dallek, *Hail to the Chief*, 183–86.

39. O'Neill, *Man of the House*, 271.

40. WP, January 16, 1977.

41. James Hanley, telephone interview by author, June 14, 1994.

42. Rozell, *The Press*, 154, 155, 157.

43. Anderson, interview, May 5, 1994.

44. Henry Bellmon, interview by author, September 21, 1995.

45. Bennett, interview, October 19, 1994.

46. Paul McCracken, interview by author, February 8, 1994.

47. Alan Webber, "Gerald R. Ford: The Statesman as CEO," *Harvard Business Review*, no. 5 (Sept.–Oct. 1987): 77.

48. Anderson, interview, May 5, 1994.

49. Gallup, *The Gallup Poll*, 1:543; 2:945–46.

50. Conable, interview, February 9, 1994; Conable knew Johnson, Nixon, Ford, Carter, Reagan, and Bush (senior).

51. Nessen, *It Sure Looks Different*, 245.

52. *Time*, October 13, 1975, 17; Rozell, *The Press*, 81.

53. *Time*, August 23, 1976, 30.

54. George Edwards III, *Presidential Influence in Congress* (San Francisco: W.H. Freeman, 1980), 87.

55. Nessen, interview, January 29, 2002.

56. Greene, *The Presidency of Gerald R. Ford*, 34.

57. Nessen, *It Sure Looks Different*, xiv.

58. Ford, *A Time to Heal*, 289; Nessen, *It Sure Looks Different*, 165; Herbert Parmet, "Gerald R. Ford," in *The Presidents: A Reference History*, edited by H. Graff, 654 (New York: Charles Scribner's Sons, 1984), 654.

59. Witcover, *Marathon*, 86.

60. John R. Greene, "'A Nice Person Who Worked at the Job': The Dilemma of the Ford Image," in Firestone and Ugrinsky, *Gerald R. Ford*, 2:637.

61. Nessen, *It Sure Looks Different*, 167.

62. *Boston Globe*, February 14, 1976, in Box 17, Folder: President and the Press (3), Ron Nessen Files, GRFL; *Time*, January 5, 1976, 33; Hill and Weingrad, *Saturday Night*, 128, 132; Schapsmeier and Schapsmeier, *Date with Destiny*, 206.

63. *U.S. News*, April 14, 1975, 51; Gannett Center for Media Studies, *The Press, the Presidency, and the First Hundred Days* (New York: Gannett Center for Media Studies, 1989), 15.

64. *Sports Illustrated*, August 27, 2001, 55.

65. Nessen, interview, January 29, 2002.

66. Gerald Ford, telephone interview by author, January 24, 2002.

67. Gannett Center for Media Studies, *The Press, the Presidency*, 14; Gerald Ford, *Humor and the Presidency* (New York: Arbor House, 1987), 48; Nessen, *It Sure Looks Different*, 169.

68. J. William Roberts, interview by Mark Rozell, GRFL.

69. Martin Schram, "Discussant: Martin Schram," in Firestone and Ugrinsky, *Gerald R. Ford*, 2:656. For similar comments, see Schieffer, *This Just In*, 236–37.

70. "Strategy Specifics," National Surveys-Strategy Book Memorandum, August 1976, Robert Teeter Papers, 1967–77, GRFL.

71. Ford, *A Time to Heal*, 289.

72. Malcolm MacDougall, *We Almost Made It* (New York: Crown, 1977), 11.

73. Nessen, *It Sure Looks Different*, 163.

74. Witcover, *Marathon*, 89.

75. Nessen, *It Sure Looks Different*, 164.

76. Reeves, *A Ford, Not a Lincoln*, 25–26; *Newsweek*, October 22, 1973, 37; *Time*, October 22, 1973, 18. Johnson cribbed the "played football too long without a helmet" from former Detroit mayor Jerome Cavanagh.

77. Max Brodnick, *The Jerry Ford Joke Book* (New York: Leisure Books, 1976).

78. Witcover, *Marathon*, 45.

79. John Waugh, *Reelecting Lincoln: The Battle for the 1864 Presidency* (New York: Crown, 1997), 201, 262.

80. The first was Rutherford B. Hayes (nineteenth president, 1877–81), with a law degree from Harvard.

81. Gerald Ford, interview by author, January 24, 2002.

82. Nessen, *It Sure Looks Different*, 177.

83. Nessen, interview, January 29, 2002.

84. Gannett Center for Media Studies, *The Press, the Presidency*, 15.

85. Edwards, *The Public Presidency*, 151.

86. Ben Bradlee, *A Good Life: Newspapering and Other Adventures* (New York: Simon and Schuster, 1995), 408.

87. Philip Shabecoff, "Appraising Presidential Power: The Ford Presidency," in *The Presidency Appraised*, edited by Thomas Cronin and Rexford Tugwell, 2nd ed., 24 (New York: Praeger, 1977); *Time*, January 5, 1976, 33.

88. Hill and Weingrad, *Saturday Night*, 183; Nessen, *It Sure Looks Different*, 176.

89. Nessen, interview, January 29, 2002.

90. Rozell, *The Press*, 94.

91. Paul O'Neill, from comments in Thompson, *The Ford Presidency*, 121–22.

92. Peggy Noonan, "Ronald Reagan," in *American Legends* (New York: Time, 2001), 21.

93. Robert Hartmann, interview by author, September 17, 2003; MacDougall, *We Almost Made It*, 22; Martin Schram, *Running for President, 1976: The Carter Campaign* (New York: Stein and Day, 1977), 341.

94. *NYT*, August 19, 1976.

95. Michael Cader, ed., *Saturday Night Live: The First Twenty Years* (Boston: Houghton Mifflin, 1994), 14; Hartmann, *Palace Politics*, 30–31.

96. *WP*, January 6, 1976.

97. Gallup, *The Gallup Poll*, 2:649; *Facts on File*, February 28, 1976, 152; March 6, 1976, 168; June 5, 1976, 396.

Chapter 3. Gerald Ford and the Ninety-fourth Congress

1. Ford, *A Time to Heal*, 442.

2. *Esquire*, January 2003, 74; *Ann Arbor News*, September 28, 1999.

3. Stephen E. Ambrose, *Nixon: Triumph of a Politician, 1962–1972* (New York: Simon and Schuster, 1989), 406; *Florida Today*, May 27, 2004.

4. Robert Semple Jr., "Richard M. Nixon: A Tentative Evaluation," in *Power and the Presidency*, edited by Philip Dolce and George Skau (New York: Charles Scribner's Sons, 1976), 165–67; Max Friedersdorf, interview by author, August 14, 2001; Ambrose, *Nixon: Ruin and Recovery*, 179; Barry Goldwater with John Casserly, *Goldwater* (New York: Doubleday, 1988), 262.

5. Ford, *A Time to Heal*, 88; Edwards, *Presidential Influence*, 121, 162; Cannon, *Time and Chance*, 99; Hugh Scott, interview by James Reichley, GRFL.

6. Cannon, *Time and Chance*, 211; *U.S. News*, December 17, 1973, 25.

7. Sidey, *Portrait*, 12; *Public Papers, 1974*, 7.

8. Patrick O'Donnell, interview by William Syers, GRFL.

9. Vernon Loen, interview by James Hyde Jr. and Stephen Wayne, GRFL; O'Donnell, interview by Syers, GRFL; Stephen Wayne, *The Legislative Presidency* (New York: Harper and Row, 1978), 157.

10. Conable, interview, February 9, 1994.

11. Friedersdorf, interview, August 14, 2001.

12. Ford, *A Time to Heal*, 140; NYT, October 29, 1974; Austin Ranney, "The President and His Party," in *The American Presidency: Contemporary Historical Perspectives*, edited by Herry Bailey and Jay Shafritz, 284 (Pacific Grove, Calif.: Brooks/Cole, 1988); William Kendall, interview by William Syers, GRFL.

13. Hanley, interview, June 14, 1994.

14. Edwards, *Presidential Influence*, 122.

15. Ford, *A Time to Heal*, 89–90.

16. Ford, interview, January 24, 2002.

17. Commission on the Bicentennial of the U.S. Constitution, *We the People: The President and the Constitution. Part I: President Ford*, 1991, video (hereafter cited as *We the People*); see also WP, August 9, 1974; Hartmann, *Palace Politics*, 424.

18. WP, August 16, 1976; Sidey, *Portrait*, 40; NYT, March 10, 1976.

19. NYT, May 25, 1975; O'Neill, *Man of the House*, 266–67.

20. Friedersdorf, interview, August 14, 2001.

21. Greene, *The Presidency of Gerald R. Ford*, 55; U.S. National Survey, December 1974 (Analysis), Box 50, Teeter Papers, 1967–77, GRFL.

22. Sidey, *Portrait*, 86; Gergen, *Eyewitness to Power*, 119; John R. Greene, *The Limits of Power: The Nixon and Ford Administrations* (Bloomington: Indiana Univ. Press, 1993), 207; Witcover, *Marathon*, 44; *Economist*, November 9, 2002, 29; *Newsweek*, November 18, 1974, 24, 33; *U.S. News*, January 20, 1975, 27.

23. *U.S. News*, November 25, 1974, 20; Cheney, "Forming and Managing an Administration," 72.

24. Larry Speakes, interview by Mark Rozell, GRFL.

25. *Economist*, November 16, 1974, 63; *U.S. News*, January 20, 1975, 27.

26. Broder, *Changing of the Guard*, 34–35; *Economist*, December 7, 1974, 60.

27. Charles Leppert, interview by William Syers, GRFL; Broder, *Changing of the Guard*, 76.

28. *U.S. News*, March 10, 1975, 15; Hedrick Smith, *The Power Game: How Washington Works* (New York: Ballantine Books, 1989), 516.

29. "General Political Overview," by Jerry Jones, Box 11, Folder: Presidential-National Vision (1), Goldwin Papers, GRFL; James Sundquist, *The Decline and Resurgence of Congress* (Washington, D.C.: Brookings Institution, 1981), 369.

30. NYT, October 17, 1976; Anatoly Dobrynin, *In Confidence: Moscow's Ambassador to America's Six Cold War Presidents* (New York: Times Books, 1995), 337.

31. Sundquist, *The Decline and Resurgence of Congress*, 23, 25, 30; NYT, February 16, 1975.

32. Sundquist, *The Decline and Resurgence of Congress*, 147; Semple, "Richard M. Nixon: A Tentative Evaluation," in Dolce and Skau, 165–66.

33. WP, January 30, 1975.

34. William Watts and Lloyd Free, *State of the Nation* (Washington, D.C.: Potomac Associates, 1974), 33; Tom Korologos, interview by William Syers, GRFL; NYT, February 17, 1975; Dudden, "Not a Lincoln But a Ford," 2:616.

35. *Newsweek*, March 24, 1975, 23.

36. *WP*, December 30, 1973; Doyle, *Gerald R. Ford*, 31.

37. Ford, interview, October 25, 1994.

38. Bellmon, interview, September 21, 1995.

39. O'Donnell, interview by Syers, GRFL.

40. Friedersdorf, interview, August 14, 2001.

41. Shabecoff, "Appraising Presidential Power," 27; Ambrose, *Nixon: Ruin and Recovery*, 60–61.

42. Appendix IV: 1, Speaker's Materials Files, Box 5, Folder 11, Legislative Files, CACRSC; Greene, *The Limits of Power*, 206; Daniel Franklin, *Making Ends Meet: Congressional Budgeting in the Age of Deficits* (Washington, D.C.: Congressional Quarterly Press, 1993), 32–33; Smith, *The Power Game*, 23.

43. *Congressional Quarterly Almanac 1975* (Washington, D.C.: Congressional Quarterly Press, 1975), 28, 29.

44. *We the People*; John Bibby, Thomas Mann, and Norman Ornstein, *Vital Statistics of Congress, 1980* (Washington, D.C.: American Enterprise Institute, 1980), 58.

45. *NYT*, November 10, 1974; Smith, *The Power Game*, 25.

46. *Congressional Quarterly's Guide to the Congress of the United States: Origins, History, and Procedure* (Washington, D.C.: Congressional Quarterly Press, 1984), 158.

47. Broder, *Changing of the Guard*, 122; Edwards, *Presidential Influence*, 44.

48. *NYT*, November 10, 1974; Smith, *The Power Game*, 26.

49. Thomas Cronin, "An Imperiled Presidency," in *The Post-Imperial Presidency*, edited by Vincent Davis, 139 (New York: Praeger, 1980); James Pfiffner, "Divided Government and the Problem of Governance," in *Divided Democracy: Cooperation and Conflict between the President and Congress*, edited by James Thurber, 42 (Washington, D.C.: Congressional Quarterly Press, 1991); Broder, *Changing of the Guard*, 24.

50. Letter from Jeanne Igersheimer, September 15, 1974, 156:28, Legislative Files: 94th Congress, CACRSC.

51. Lawrence Dodd and Bruce Oppenheimer, eds., *Congress Reconsidered*, 4th ed. (Washington, D.C.: Congressional Quarterly Press, 1989), 23–24.

52. *WP*, June 17, 1975; Newspaper clippings from June 1975, 2:63, 94th Congress, CACRSC.

53. Smith, *The Power Game*, 335.

54. Ford, *A Time to Heal*, 355–56; *Time*, November 10, 1980, 30–31.

55. Ford, interview, October 25, 1994.

56. George Melloan and Joan Melloan, *The Carter Economy* (New York: John Wiley and Sons, 1978), 100; Jimmy Carter, *Keeping Faith: Memoirs of a President* (New York: Bantam Books, 1982), 73.

57. Edwards, *Presidential Influence*, 163; Gerald Ford, *The Presidential Campaign 1976* (Washington, D.C.: Government Printing Office, 1979), 3:86.

58. *NYT*, October 30, 1976; Greene, *The Presidency of Gerald R. Ford*, 54.

59. Lynn, interview, October 27, 1994.

60. Bennett, interview, October 19, 1994.

61. Minutes of Cabinet Meeting aboard *Sequoia*, Box 4, Folder: 5/7/75 Cabinet Meeting, James Connor Files, GRFL.

62. Ford, *A Time to Heal*, 150.

63. Cheney, "Forming and Managing an Administration," 65; *The Presidential Campaign 1976*, 2:695–96.

64. Bennett, interview, October 19, 1994.

65. A. James Reichley, *Conservatives in an Age of Change: The Nixon and Ford Administrations* (Washington, D.C.: Brookings Institution, 1981), 333; O'Donnell, interview by Syers, GRFL.

66. Edwards, *Presidential Influence*, 175; Ranney, "The President and His Party," 284.

67. Cronin, "An Imperiled Presidency," 140–42.

68. *NYT*, June 3, 1975; Reichley, *Conservatives*, 335–36.

Chapter 4. Ford's Vision for America

1. Ford, *A Time to Heal*, 49–50; *Michigan Alumnus*, March/April 1986, 39, Vertical File, GRFL.

2. Gerald Ford, interview by author, August 21, 2003.

3. *Detroit Free-Press*, October 14, 1973, Vertical File, GRFL.

4. Ford, interview, August 21, 2003.

5. Gerald R. Ford Museum, Grand Rapids, Mich.

6. *Time*, December 10, 1973, 22. The third senator, Democrat William Hathaway of Maine, objected because he believed that Nixon's impeachment should proceed before a vice presidential confirmation.

7. "(Goldwin) revised 7/23/76," Box 11, Folder: President-National Vision (2), Goldwin Papers, GRFL; Buchen, "Reflections on a Politician's President," 28.

8. Philip Buchen, interview by author, February 25, 1994.

9. Treasury Department Q and As, Box 87, Folder: Q&As, November 1975, William Seidman Files, GRFL.

10. *NYT*, August 8, 1975; William Seidman, interview by William Syers, GRFL; *President Ford*, 27; Sidey, *Portrait*, 51.

11. William Boyes and Michael Melvin, *Macroeconomics*, 2nd ed. (Boston: Houghton Mifflin, 1994), 119; Hersey, *The President*, 138.

12. (Goldwin) 8/9/75, Box 11, Folder: President-National Vision (1), Goldwin Papers, GRFL.

13. "Social Issues (An Overview)," by Jim Cavanaugh, Box 11, Folder: President-National Vision (2), Goldwin Papers, GRFL.

14. Jerald terHorst, *Gerald Ford and the Future of the Presidency* (New York: Third Press, 1974), 212–13.

15. American Enterprise Institute, *A Discussion with Gerald R. Ford*, 15.

16. Box 5, Folder: President's Economic Program: Background (January 11, 1975), Marvin Kosters Files, GRFL.

17. Ronald King, "The Supply-Side Reformation," in Firestone and Ugrinsky, *Gerald R. Ford*, 1:249, 266.

18. Goldwin, interview, March 3, 1994.

19. Roger Porter, telephone interview by author, May 8, 1995.

20. Ford, *A Time to Heal*, 263; *Time*, February 2, 1976, 11–12; *The Presidential Campaign 1976*, 2:304, 621.

21. William Seidman, interview by author, October 18, 1994.

22. *NYT*, October 22, 1976; Bellmon, interview, September 21, 1995.

23. *Newsweek*, December 9, 1974, 20.

24. Economic Philosophy, AG 11/7/75, Box 11, Folder: President-National Vision (1), Goldwin Papers, GRFL.

25. Gerald Ford, "My Definition of a Statesman as Opposed to a Politician," materials from the writing of *A Time to Heal*, GRFL.

26. *Public Papers*, 1975, 1:162, 443–44; Reichley, *Conservatives*, 383; *U.S. News*, August 11, 1975, 23.

27. Paul MacAvoy, interview by author, May 2, 2002.

28. *U.S. News*, March 10, 1975, 14; *NYT*, August 8, 1975.

29. Hersey, *The President*, 44.

30. *Newsweek*, October 18, 1976, 34, 36; Sidey, *Portrait*, 51, 54.

31. *Public Papers*, 1975, 1:77–78, 162.

32. Roger Davidson, "The President and Congress," in Bailey and Shafritz, *The American Presidency*, 162; *NYT*, August 8, 1975.

33. Rozell, *The Press*, 160; O'Neill, interview, August 17, 1994.

34. McCracken, interview, February 8, 1994.

35. Cannon, *Time and Chance*, 266. Burns served as Federal Reserve chairman from 1970 to 1978; Arthur Burns, "Ford and the Federal Reserve," in Thompson, *The Ford Presidency*, 136–37; *Time*, February 24, 1975, 14.

36. Lynn, interview, March 3, 1994.

37. *NYT*, February 2, 1975; Gergen, *Eyewitness to Power*, 127; O'Neill, "President Ford and the Budget," in Thompson, *The Ford Presidency*, 120.

38. Ford, *A Time to Heal*, 352.

39. Roy Ash, telephone interview by author, January 10, 1994.

40. Bennett, interview, October 19, 1994.

41. Goldwin, interview, March 3, 1994.

42. O'Neill, interview, August 17, 1994.

43. Nessen, *It Sure Looks Different*, 29.

44. James Lynn, interviews by author, March 3, October 27, 1994, and telephone interview by author, February 2, 1995.

45. Cannon, *Time and Chance*, 58; Reichley, *Conservatives*, 384; *Time*, February 2, 1976, 11.

46. Seidman, interview, October 18, 1994.

47. Webber, *Gerald R. Ford*, 78.

48. Seidman, interview, October 18, 1994.

49. Memorandum to the president from William Baroody, September 17, 1975, Box 4, Folder: FG 1, 8/29/75–11/4/75, White House Central File (hereafter cited as WHCF) FG 1, GRFL.

50. Goldwin, interview, March 3, 1994.

51. Seidman, interview, October 18, 1994.

52. Ford, interview, October 25, 1994; *The American Enterprise*, May/June 1999,

Vertical File, GRFL. A compelling comparison between Ford and Eisenhower can be found in a Douglas Watson essay, "Another Eisenhower" (*WP*, February 20, 1976), which compares the personalities, political and economic philosophies, and cabinets of the two men.

53. Hersey, *The President*, 138; Elmo Richardson, *The Presidency of Dwight D. Eisenhower* (Lawrence: Univ. of Kansas Press, 1979), 25, 41.

54. Stephen E. Ambrose, *Eisenhower: The President* (New York: Simon and Schuster, 1984), 488, 496; Richardson, *The Presidency of Dwight D. Eisenhower*, 142; Dwight D. Eisenhower, *The White House Years, vol. 1: Mandate for Change: 1953–1956* (Garden City, N.J.: Doubleday, 1963), 127.

55. Ambrose, *Eisenhower*, 496; Richardson, *The Presidency of Dwight D. Eisenhower*, 42, 43.

56. Yanek Mieczkowski, "Eisenhower's Reaction to *Sputnik*: Presidential Calm and National Panic" (master's thesis, Columbia University, 1989).

57. Ford, interview, October 25, 1994.

58. Richardson, *The Presidency of Dwight D. Eisenhower*, 27; *Economist*, December 21, 2002, 64.

59. Raymond Saulnier, *Constructive Years: The U.S. Economy under Eisenhower* (Lanham, Md.: Univ. Press of America, 1991), 24.

60. *Newsweek*, October 18, 1976, 36.

61. Ford, *A Time to Heal*, 293.

62. Ford, interview, October 25, 1994.

63. Buchen, interview, February 25, 1994.

64. William Simon, *A Time for Truth* (New York: Reader's Digest Press, 1978), 105, 110; *We the People*.

65. *NYT*, October 1, 1976; Lloyd Free to Stuart Spencer, December 1975, GRFL.

66. Ford, *A Time to Heal*, 293; *We the People*; Samuel Hoff, "Presidential Success in the Veto Process: The Legislative Record of Gerald R. Ford," in Firestone and Ugrinsky, *Gerald R. Ford*, 1:295; Cabinet Meeting Talking Points, May 6, 1975, Box 1, Folder: Cabinet Meeting, 5/7/75, Greener Notes, William Greener Papers, GRFL.

67. Gerald Ford, "Importance of Veto," materials from the writing of *A Time to Heal*, GRFL.

68. Lynn, interview, October 27, 1994.

69. Ford, *A Time to Heal*, 293; Minutes of cabinet meeting aboard *Sequoia*, Box 4, Folder: 5/7/75 Cabinet Meeting, Connor Files, GRFL.

70. *Time*, January 26, 1976, 12; *Public Papers*, 1975, 1:4; Schapsmeier and Schapsmeier, *Date with Destiny*, 185.

71. Ken Glozer, interview by author, April 22, 2004.

72. *Congressional Quarterly Almanac 1975*, 516, 40-A.

73. Friedersdorf, interview, August 14, 2001.

74. Seidman, interview, October 18, 1994; Robert Spitzer, *The Presidential Veto: Touchstone of the American Presidency* (Albany: State Univ. of New York Press, 1988), 88–89.

75. *Congressional Quarterly Almanac 1975*, 34-A, 421–22, 436–37.

76. Anderson, interview, May 5, 1994.

77. *NYT*, April 11, 1976; Memorandum to John Marsh from Vernon Loen, January 9, 1976, Box 2, Folder: Legislative Report for 1975, Robert Wolthius Files, GRFL.

78. Ford ranked ninth among presidents for vetoes issued during his administration. Franklin Roosevelt, with the longest presidency, had the most with 635; Grover Cleveland, during his first term, had 414. Edwards, *Presidential Influence*, 23; Louis Fisher, *The Politics of Shared Power: Congress and the Executive*, 2nd ed. (Washington, D.C.: Congressional Quarterly Press, 1987), 30; *Economist*, February 18, 1995, 23.

79. Reichley, *Conservatives*, 323–24; Fisher, *The Politics of Shared Power*, 30.

80. Davidson, "The President and Congress," 164.

81. Ford, interview, October 25, 1994.

82. Ronald Peters Jr., *The American Speakership: The Office in Historical Perspective* (Baltimore: Johns Hopkins Univ. Press, 1990), 197; *National Journal*, June 21, 1975, 926; *Time*, July 28, 1975, 9.

83. *U.S. News*, July 21, 1975, 34; Letter from W. Leslie Starnes, June 25, 1975, 85:1, 94th Congress, CACRSC.

84. Gerald Ford, interview by author, March 30, 1994.

85. Edwards, *Presidential Influence*, 23; Reichley, *Conservatives*, 324–25.

86. *Time*, January 20, 1975, 16.

87. Goldwin, interview, March 3, 1994.

88. Lynn, interview, October 27, 1994.

89. PFC Records, 1975–76, Box 8, Folder: Hughes Subject File, Reagan campaign (2), GRFL; Box 1026, 11/12/75 NYC, Birch Bayh Papers, Lilly Library, IU.

90. *The Presidential Campaign 1976*, 2:1,000, 1,007; Spitzer, *The Presidential Veto*, 93.

91. *WP*, May 2, 1976; David LeRoy, *Gerald Ford—Untold Story* (Arlington, Va.: R.W. Beatty, 1974), 105.

92. Melvin Laird, interview by William Syers, GRFL.

93. Buchen, interview, February 25, 1994.

94. Ford, interview, March 30, 1994.

95. Memorandum to the president from Robert Goldwin, January 22, 1975, Box 1, Folder: FG 1, 1/1/75–1/31/75, WHCF FG, GRFL.

96. O'Neill, interview, August 17, 1994.

97. Lynn, interview, October 27, 1994.

98. Smith, *The Power Game*, 684; Eric Uslaner, *The Decline of Comity in Congress* (Ann Arbor: Univ. of Michigan Press, 1993), 50–51.

99. Goldwin, interview, March 3, 1994.

100. Conable, interview, February 9, 1994.

101. *Public Papers, 1976–1977*, 1:273.

102. *National Journal*, April 26, 1975, 637.

103. Conable, interview, February 9, 1994.

Chapter 5. The Great Inflation of the 1970s

1. Cannon, *Time and Chance*, 55.

2. Various letters, Box 2, Folder: RE 3, 7/10/75, WHCF Subject File, GRFL; NYT, May 15, 1975.

3. *U.S. News*, December 23, 1974, 15; WP, November 14, 1974.

4. "Bee Hijacking a New Racket," Associated Press story 10/30/74, Box 4, Presidential Daily News Summaries, GRFL.

5. Gordon, "Chickens Home to Roost," 34.

6. Ibid.; U.S. Bureau of the Census, *Statistical Abstract of the United States: 1978*, 94th ed., Washington, D.C.: U.S. Government Printing Office, 470.

7. William Chafe, *The Unfinished Journey: America since World War II*, 2nd ed. (New York: Oxford Univ. Press, 1991), 114, 119; William Leuchtenburg, *A Troubled Feast: American Society since 1945* (Boston: Little, Brown, 1973), 56.

8. *1976 Report on National Growth and Development: The Changing Issues for National Growth*, February 1976, 5995-A, Oversized Attachments, Box 326, GRFL; NYT, December 9, 1973; *Great Speeches of the 20th Century*, vol. 1 (Rhino Records, compact disc, 1994).

9. Leuchtenburg, *A Troubled Feast*, 39–40, 42.

10. Howard K. Smith, *Events Leading Up to My Death: The Life of a Twentieth-Century Reporter* (New York: St. Martin's Press, 1996), 358.

11. WP, November 22, 1974; Allen Matusow, *Nixon's Economy: Booms, Busts, Dollars, and Votes* (Lawrence: Univ. Press of Kansas, 1998), 118, 131.

12. *1976 Report on National Growth and Development*, Oversized Attachments, Box 326, GRFL.

13. Gordon, "Chickens Home to Roost," 37, 39, 41.

14. Frum, *How We Got Here*, 25; Matusow, *Nixon's Economy*, 133; Hodgson, *America in Our Time*, 258–59.

15. Watts and Free, *State of the Nation*, 130.

16. David Calleo, *The Imperious Economy* (Cambridge, Mass.: Harvard Univ. Press, 1982), 41; Chafe, *The Unfinished Journey*, 445; Ezra Solomon, *Beyond the Turning Point: The U.S. Economy in the 1980s* (San Francisco: W.H. Freeman, 1982), 2.

17. Russell Baker, *So This Is Depravity* (New York: Washington Square Books, 1980), 317; Matusow, *Nixon's Economy*, 133.

18. Frum, *How We Got Here*, 291–92; Max Shapiro, *The Penniless Billionaires* (New York: Times Books, 1980), 225.

19. Whitney, *Inflation*, 39; Shapiro, *The Penniless Billionaires*, 226.

20. Memorandum to the president from David Packard (hereafter cited as Packard memo), Box 4, Folder: Business and Economics, National Economy, 8/74, Presidential Handwriting File (hereafter cited as PHF), GRFL; Michael Bernstein, "Understanding American Economic Decline: The Contours of the Late-Twentieth-Century Experience," in Bernstein and Adler, eds., *Understanding American Economic Decline*, 18.

21. Whitney, *Inflation*, 40; Arthur Burns, *Reflections of an Economic Policy Maker: Speeches and Congressional Statements: 1969–1978* (Washington, D.C.: American Enterprise Institute, 1978), 212.

22. Alan Blinder, *Economic Policy and the Great Stagflation* (New York: Academic Press, 1981), 1; Timothy Taylor, "The War against Inflation," *Classrooms and Lunchrooms: A Journal for Teachers of Economics* (Fall/Winter 1992–1993): 9; William Lovett, *Inflation and Politics: Fiscal, Monetary, and Wage-Price Discipline* (Lexington, Mass.: Lexington Books, 1982), 36.

23. WP, August 12, 1974; Memorandum from Paul McCracken to the EPB, September 21, 1974, "The Nature of the Current Economic Problem," Box 3, Folder: Economic Policy Board, Paul McCracken Files, GRFL (hereafter cited as McCracken memo to EPB); NYT, February 13, 1975; see also Campbell McConnell, *Economics: Principles, Problems, and Policies*, 9th ed. (New York: McGraw-Hill, 1984), 158–59. According to economists' "rule of 70," dividing the number 70 by the annual rate of inflation will yield the number of years it will take for prices to double.

24. NYT, July 14, 1974.

25. Ford believed that "big government spending is a basic cause of the inflation spiral that is plaguing us at this moment." *Public Papers, 1974*, 433, 442.

26. "Economic Philosophy" essay, Box 11, Folder: President-National Vision (1), Goldwin Papers, GRFL; Ford, *A Time to Heal*, 151.

27. Matusow, *Nixon's Economy*, 220.

28. Robert Fuller, *Inflation: The Rising Cost of Living on a Small Planet* (Washington, D.C.: WorldWatch Institute, 1980), 19; Don Paarlberg, *An Analysis and History of Inflation* (Westport, Conn.: Greenwood Press, 1993), 125.

29. Smith, *The Power Game*, 346.

30. NYT, March 31, April 14, July 24, 1974; Lovett, *Inflation and Politics*, 25, 100.

31. Shapiro, *The Penniless Billionaires*, 228; Calleo, *The Imperious Economy*, 34; Paarlberg, *An Analysis and History of Inflation*, 131; "Burns, Arthur," in *Profiles of an Era: The Nixon/Ford Years*, edited by Eleanora Schoenebaum, 97 (New York: Harcourt Brace Jovanovich, 1979); WSJ, August 18, 1976; Blinder, *Economic Policy*, 183–84.

32. *Time*, June 25, 1973; December 24, 1973; *U.S. News*, July 22, 1974, 21; NYT, August 15, 1976; WP, January 12, 1975; WSJ, February 7, 1974.

33. *Time*, August 27, 1973, 27.

34. McConnell, *Economics*, 789, 791; Theodore White, *America in Search of Itself: The Making of the President, 1956–1980* (New York: Warner Books, 1982), 142–43.

35. Watts and Free, *State of the Nation*, 120; Matusow, *Nixon's Economy*, 238.

36. Watts and Free, *State of the Nation*, 118; *Time*, August 27, 1973, 31; Matusow, *Nixon's Economy*, 222.

37. Calleo, *The Imperious Economy*, 112; Chafe, *The Unfinished Journey*, 446–47; Otto Eckstein, *The Great Recession* (New York: North Holland, 1978), 61–64.

38. Carroll, *It Seemed Like Nothing Happened*, 132; *U.S. News*, October 21, 1974, 24–25.

39. Ford, *A Time to Heal*, 151; *Time*, October 14, 1974, 28.

40. Chafe, *The Unfinished Journey*, 447.

41. Anthony Campagna, *The Economic Consequences of the Vietnam War* (New York: Praeger, 1991), 118.

42. Chafe, *The Unfinished Journey*, 447; Eckstein, *The Great Recession*, 112; *U.S. News*, September 9, 1974, 15; *Newsweek*, June 2, 1975, 55.

43. The *Business Week* Team, *The Decline of U.S. Power (and what we can do about it)* (Boston: Houghton Mifflin, 1980), 112.

44. Walter Heller, *The Economy: Old Myths and New Realities* (New York: W.W. Norton, 1976), 31; Ambrose, *Nixon: Ruin and Recovery*, 295; Vestal, *Jerry Ford*, 201.

45. *U.S. News*, September 9, 1974, 15; *NYT*, October 13, 1974.

46. Letter from Edmond Cobler, October 2, 1974, Box 568: Gas Tax, Birch Bayh Papers, Lilly Library, IU.

47. Alfred Marcus, *Controversial Issues in Energy Policy* (Newbury Park, Calif.: Sage Publications, 1992), 9; Margaret Blain Cervarich, National Asphalt and Paving Association, e-mail message to author, May 30, 2002.

48. Memorandum to Ash et al. from Simon, November 4, 1974, Box 118, Folder: Economic Briefing Books-changes, 10/30/74–11/5/74, Seidman Files, GRFL. Treasury Secretary William Simon estimated that the higher oil prices were responsible for half of the United States's inflation rate, which was an exaggeration (*NYT*, September 29, 1974).

49. Richard Barnet, *The Lean Years: Politics in the Age of Scarcity* (New York: Simon and Schuster, 1980), 19; Campbell McConnell, *Macroeconomics: Principles, Problems, and Policies*, 12th ed. (New York, 1993), 143. Supply-shock inflation was also known as "commodity inflation."

50. *WP*, August 9, 1974.

51. *Public Papers, 1974*, 546; *U.S. News*, August 12, 1974, 30–31.

52. *Statistical Abstract of the United States: 1957*, 234; *1964*, 234; *1966*, 247; *1977*, 420.

53. *U.S. News*, July 29, 1974, 61; *WP*, November 25, 1974; January 25, 1975.

54. Barbara Kellerman, *The Political Presidency: The Practice of Leadership* (New York: Oxford, 1984), 160.

55. *Public Papers, 1974*, 535–36; *Time*, August 27, 1973, 27; *U.S. News*, October 14, 1974, 43.

56. Letter from Norman Blunk, April 4, 1975, Box 27, Folder: BE 5, 4/4/75–4/14/75, WHCF BE 5, GRFL.

57. Letter from Jerrell Houston, January 22, 1975, Box 25, Folder: 2/21/75–2/25/75, WHCF BE 5, GRFL.

58. Kellerman, *The Political Presidency*, 160.

59. *WP*, September 22, 1974; January 3, 1975.

60. *U.S. News*, September 2, 1974, 33; October 14, 1974, 54; Seidman, interview, October 18, 1994.

61. *The Conference on Inflation: September 27–28, 1974, Washington, D.C.* (Washington, D.C.: U.S. Government Printing Office, 1974), 94.

62. Haynes Johnson, *In the Absence of Power: Governing America* (New York: Viking Press, 1980), 132–33; *NYT*, October 26, 1975; Fuller, *Inflation*, 16–17; *WP*, Jan 12, 1975.

63. Memorandum to the president from Rush and Seidman, August 20, 1974, Box 13, John Marsh Files, GRFL.

64. Letter from Sheila and Bill Kosler, Box 16, Folder: BE 5 9/1/74–9/20/74, WHCF BE, GRFL.

65. Irving Friedman, "Democracy and Persistent Inflation," in *Dilemmas Facing the Nation*, edited by Herbert Prochnow, 57–58, 73 (New York: Harper and Row, 1979).

66. *WP*, 2, 1975.

67. Ford, interview, October 25, 1994.

68. Gallup, *The Gallup Poll*, 528; *Public Papers, 1974*, 546.

69. Gary Seevers, interview by author, January 16, 2003.

70. Bernstein, "Understanding American Economic Decline," in Bernstein and Adler, 20; Lawrence R. Klein, "The Restructuring of the American Economy," in *Inflation and Income Distribution in Capitalist Crisis: Essays in Memory of Sidney Weintraub*, edited by J. A. Kregel, 37 (New York: NYU Press, 1989).

71. Daniel Bell, *The Coming of Post-Industrial Society: A Venture in Social Forecasting* (New York: Basic Books, Inc., 1973), 15, 124, 133, 156; Bernstein, "Understanding American Economic Decline," in Bernstein and Adler, 21.

72. Johnson, *In the Absence of Power*, 127; Broder, *Changing of the Guard*, 118–19; Campagna, *The Economic Consequences*, 67–68; Hodgson, *America in Our Time*, 272, 367; *Newsweek*, February 9, 1976, 64.

73. *Newsweek*, June 2, 1975, 54–56; E. F. Schumacher, *Small Is Beautiful: Economics as if People Mattered* (New York: Perennial Library, 1973).

74. Donella Meadows et al., *The Limits of Growth: A Report for the Club of Rome's Project on the Predicament of Mankind* (New York: Universe Books, 1974), 9, 24.

75. Lovett, *Inflation and Politics*, 25; WP, September 8, 1974; *Public Papers, 1974*, 607.

76. Fuller, *Inflation*, 5, 18.

Chapter 6. Taking Aim at Inflation

1. Ford, interview, March 30, 1994; Ford, *A Time to Heal*, 190–92; Hartmann, *Palace Politics*, 294; *Public Papers, 1974*, 206–10; *Economist*, October 5, 1974, 53; *Time*, October 7, 1974, 39.

2. Ford, *A Time to Heal*; *Public Papers, 1974*, 63, 87.

3. Reichley, *Conservatives*, 383–84.

4. Memorandum to the president from Herbert Stein, August 13, 1974, Box 1, Folder: Economic Policy Recommendations, Kenneth Rush Files, GRFL.

5. Memorandum to economic advisers from W. Simon, November 4, 1974, Box 118, Folder: Economic Briefing Books-Changes, 10/30/74–11/5/74, Seidman Files, GRFL.

6. Ford, *A Time to Heal*, 153.

7. Ford, interview, March 30, 1994.

8. Justin Martin, *Greenspan: The Man behind the Money* (Cambridge, Mass.,: Perseus, 2000), 125; NYT, August 22, 1976.

9. Ford, interview, March 30, 1994.

10. WP, September 28, 1974; *Newsweek*, February 24, 1975, 59.

11. "The Budget," October 6, 1974, Folder: Economic Program-General: 1974 (September–October), 21:13, William Simon Papers, David Bishop Skillman Library, Lafayette College, Easton, Pa. (hereafter cited as WS Papers, DBSL).

12. *Statistical Abstract of the United States: 1981*, 245; Packard memo, GRFL.

13. Ford, *A Time to Heal*, 154.

14. *Time*, October 7, 1974, 39.

15. *Public Papers, 1974*, 127; similar sentiments are expressed on page 59. At the Conference on Inflation (September 28, 1974), Budget Director Roy Ash commented, "Reducing federal spending by $5 to $6 billion in a $1.4 trillion economy may appear to

be something of a gesture but it is not. Slower growth in federal spending reduces significantly the government's demands upon the financial market not only making those funds available elsewhere in the economy [but also] contributing to a reduction in interest rates" (*The Conference on Inflation*, 6).

16. *U.S. News*, July 22, 1974, 19. Other senators who supported the idea included Republicans Dewey Bartlett and Peter Domenici and Democrats Lawson Childs, Walter Huddleston, and Sam Nunn; *NYT*, July 20, 1974.

17. Ford, *A Time to Heal*, 154; *New York Times Magazine*, August 3, 1975, 40.

18. *WP*, August 27, 1974; Economists, 9/5/74: Transcripts, Box 1, Seidman Files, GRFL (hereafter cited as Economists, 9/5/74); *Time*, September 16, 1974, 88.

19. *Newsweek*, September 16, 1974, 24–25; Martin, *Greenspan*, 83; Economists, 9/5/74.

20. Seidman, interview, October 18, 1994.

21. *Newsweek*, September 16, 1974, 25.

22. McCracken memo to EPB.

23. Ibid.; *Time*, October 7, 1974, 39; *Public Papers*, 1974, 206–10.

24. Ford, interview, March 30, 1994.

25. McCracken, interview, February 8, 1994.

26. Robert Hartmann, interview by author, October 17, 1994.

27. Ford, interview, March 30, 1994.

28. *NYT*, March 16, 1975; *WP*, September 9, December 7, 1974.

29. Memorandum to William Seidman from William Simon, August 14, 1974, Folder: Economic Program-Summit Conference: 1974 (August–September), 21:19, WS Papers, DBSL.

30. Ford, interview, March 30, 1994; *NYT*, July 25, 1975.

31. *NYT*, August 3, 1975; Economists 9/5/74: Transcript. These economists included Milton Friedman, John Kenneth Galbraith, and Andrew Brimmer.

32. McCracken, interview, February 8, 1994.

33. *Democratic Newsletter*, October 14, 1974, 182:1, Legislative Files, Carl Albert Papers, CACRSC.

34. *U.S. News*, September 23, 1974, 12; *Time*, October 7, 1974, 43.

35. *National Journal*, October 5, 1974, 1503; *WP*, September 6, 1974.

36. *The Conference on Inflation*, 96.

37. *Newsweek*, December 9, 1974, 23; *Time*, October 19, 1974, 27.

38. Ford, interview, March 30, 1994.

39. *Public Papers*, 1974, 60.

40. McCracken, interview, February 8, 1994.

41. Memorandum to EPB Executive Committee members from Roger B. Porter, September 8, 1976, "Statements on Economic Policy: Wage and Price Controls," Box 57, Folder: Economic Policy statements (2), Seidman Files, GRFL.

42. *WP*, August 29, 1974; *Public Papers*, 1974, 605.

43. Roger Porter, *Presidential Decision Making: The Economic Policy Board* (Cambridge: Cambridge Univ. Press, 1980), 40.

44. William Seidman, *Full Faith and Credit: The Great S&L Debacle and Other Washington Sagas* (New York: Times Books, 1993), 26–27, 34, 44.

45. Ford, *A Time to Heal*, 53; see also Reichley, *Conservatives*, 384.

46. McCracken, interview, February 8, 1994.

47. Porter, *Presidential Decision Making*, 44.

48. Seidman, interview by Syers, GRFL; Porter, *Presidential Decision Making*, 3, 65, 69; William Simon, interview by James Reichley, GRFL.

49. Porter, *Presidential Decision Making*, 3; Seidman, *Full Faith and Credit*, 27.

Chapter 7. Teetering on a Knife's Edge

1. Seevers, interview, January 16, 2003.

2. WP, October 3, 1974.

3. *Public Papers*, 1974, 228–38.

4. WP, October 3, 1974; *Time*, October 21, 1974, 42.

5. *Public Papers*, 1974, 236.

6. WP, October 9, 1974.

7. *Public Papers*, 1974, 234; *Time*, October 21, 1974, 47; *U.S. News*, November 25, 1974, 22.

8. Arthur Laffer, telephone interview, *Street Signs*, CNBC News Network, June 11, 2004.

9. *Gerald Ford's America*, Part 3, produced by TVTV and the Television Laboratory at WNET-13 (1975), video, GRFL.

10. WP, October 9, 1974; NYT, October 29, 1974.

11. Ford, *A Time to Heal*, 195; "Tax Proposal: Option A," October 3, 1974, Folder: Economic Program-General: 1974, 21:13, WS Papers, DBSL; *U.S. News*, November 25, 1974, 21–22.

12. WP, October 9, 1974.

13. WP, September 28, 1974; *Public Papers*, 1974, 233.

14. *Time*, October 21, 1974, 41; Seidman, *Full Faith and Credit*, 20.

15. Seidman, interview, October 18, 1994.

16. Seidman, *Full Faith and Credit*, 20–21.

17. "The Phillips-Sindlinger Survey," Box 6, Folder: Miscellaneous, Alan Greenspan Files, GRFL.

18. Kellerman, *The Political Presidency*, 161; WP, October 24, 1974.

19. Friedersdorf, interview, August 14, 2001.

20. Carl Albert address in Salem, Ill., October 18, 1974, Biographical Files, Economy, Fall 1974-Surtax, Carl Albert Papers, CACRSC.

21. "Minutes of the EPB Executive Committee Meeting," Box 20, Folder: EPB Meeting Minutes, November 8–10, 1974, Seidman Files, GRFL.

22. *Time*, December 9, 1974, 31; NYT, January 19, September 1, 1974.

23. WP, September 29, 1974.

24. *U.S. News*, October 28, 1974, 24; WP, October 11, 18, 1974.

25. *Economist*, September 14, 1974, 63; WP, October 5, 1974; *Public Papers*, 1974, 245–46; Porter, *Presidential Decision Making*, 104.

26. WP, October 27, 1974; Ford, *A Time to Heal*, 203.

27. Letter to Senator Herman Talmadge from William E. Smith, December 16, 1974, Box 96, Folder: BE 5–5, Recessions-Depressions, 8/9/74–1/20/77, WHCF BE, GRFL.

28. *WP*, November 3, 1974.

29. Ford, *A Time to Heal*, 204; *WP*, November 13, 1974; Nessen, *It Sure Looks Different*, 76.

30. Ford, interview, March 30, 1994.

31. Memorandum to the president from Alan Greenspan, November 26, 1974, Box 4, Folder: B&E NE 11/74–12/20/74, PHF, GRFL.

32. "Economic Policy Review and Initiatives," December 24, 1974, Box 57, Folder: EPB-December 1974 (2), Greenspan Files, GRFL.

33. *WP*, September 20, 1974.

34. *NYT*, March 16, 1975; *WP*, December 19, 1974; February 8, 1975.

35. *WP*, October 5, 1974; *The Conference on Inflation*, 87; *Economist*, August 31, 1974, 37.

36. *The Gallup Opinion Index*, November 1974, 24, 26.

37. *Economist*, February 24, 2001, 34; Seevers, interview, January 16, 2003; *Time*, December 9, 1974, 34.

38. McCracken memo to EPB; *NYT*, January 16, 1975.

39. O'Neill, interview, August 17, 1994; Reichley, *Conservatives*, 390; *WP*, February 8, 1975.

40. *Public Papers, 1975*, 1:95.

41. John Casserly, *The Ford White House: The Diary of a Speechwriter* (Boulder: Colorado Associated Univ. Press, 1977), 26.

42. *NYT*, July 25, 1975; *Newsweek*, February 17, 1975, 58.

43. Gallup, *The Gallup Poll*, 1:415; *NYT*, September 3, 1974.

44. Memorandum to the president from Kenneth Rush and William Seidman, August 16, 1974, Folder: Economic Program-Summit Conference: 1974 (August–September), 21:19, WS Papers, DBSL.

45. "Minutes of the EPB Executive Committee Meeting," Box 20, Folder: EPB Meeting Minutes, November 8–10, 1974, Seidman Files, GRFL.

46. Porter, *Presidential Decision Making*, 109; *WP*, December 5, 18, 1974; Herbert Stein, *Presidential Economics* (New York: Simon and Schuster, 1984), 212–13.

47. *Economist*, August 17, 1974, 70; August 31, 1974, 37–38.

48. *NYT*, April 1, 4, 22, 23, 1974. Senate Democrats supporting a tax cut included Hubert Humphrey, Edward Kennedy, Mike Mansfield, and Walter Mondale; economists included Arthur Okun and Walter Heller.

49. *Public Papers, 1974*, 737; Alan Greenspan, "The Council of Economic Advisers under Chairman Alan Greenspan, 1974–77," in *The President and the Council of Economic Advisors: Interviews with CEA Chairmen*, edited by Erwin Hargrove and Samuel Morley (Boulder, Colo.: Westview Press, 1984), 444.

50. Seidman, *Full Faith and Credit*, 31; "Economic Policy Issue Paper on Consumer Confidence," Folder: Economic Policy Board-Executive Committee: 1974 (December 18), 29:7, WS Papers, DBSL; Porter, *Presidential Decision Making*, 109.

51. *U.S. News*, December 9, 1974, 33; *WSJ*, April 21, 1976.

52. Ford, *A Time to Heal*, 204; *Public Papers, 1974,* 735; Nessen, *It Sure Looks Different,* 77.

53. Seidman, interview, October 18, 1994.

54. Economic Policy Initiatives, Box 29, Folder: EPB Memoranda, January 27, 1976, Seidman Files, GRFL; WP, January 1, 1975.

Chapter 8. Rallying the Nation to Fight Inflation

1. McCracken memo to EPB; *NYT,* January 30, 1974; Gary Donaldson, *Truman Defeats Dewey* (Lexington: University Press of Kentucky, 1999), 46.

2. *Newsweek,* October 18, 1976, 57; *Public Papers, 1974,* 247; WP, October 27, 1974.

3. Hartmann, *Palace Politics,* 296; Paul Theis, interview by author, October 20, 1994.

4. Hartmann, interview, October 17, 1994.

5. *Washington Star-News,* September 23, 1974, from the personal papers of Paul Theis.

6. *The Conference on Inflation,* 49–50; *Public Papers, 1974,* 209.

7. Conference on Inflation transcripts, 16:6, Seidman Papers, GRFL.

8. Hartmann, *Palace Politics,* 296; Ford, *A Time to Heal,* 194.

9. Memorandum to the president from Paul Theis, August 30, 1974, from the personal papers of Paul Theis. See also *Newsweek,* October 18, 1976, 57.

10. Ford, interview, October 25, 1994.

11. Hartmann, interview, October 17, 1994.

12. Theis, interview, October 20, 1994.

13. *Newsweek,* October 18, 1976, 57.

14. Theis, interview, October 20, 1994; Note from Neta (Hartmann's secretary) to Hartmann, October 1, 1974, Box 22, Folder: WIN campaign-General (3), Robert Hartmann Files, GRFL.

15. *Public Papers, 1974,* 237; Gergen, *Eyewitness to Power,* 125–26.

16. *Public Papers, 1974,* 309–11.

17. Russell W. Freeburg, interview by author, August 31, 2001.

18. Advertisement, *Chicago Tribune,* November 13, 1974, from the personal papers of Russell Freeburg.

19. Undated newspaper article, from the personal papers of Russell Freeburg.

20. Newspaper clipping, Box 4, Folder: Business and Economics, National Economy 2/21–28/75, PHF, GRFL; Osborne, *White House Watch,* 55.

21. Memorandum to the president from Russell Freeburg, October 18, 1974, Box 32, Folder: BE 5–3 10/17/74–10/23/74, WHCF BE 5–3, GRFL.

22. Freeburg, interview, August 31, 2001.

23. Vertical File, Folder: WIN Program, newspaper clippings, GRFL.

24. Memorandum to the president from Russell Freeburg, October 18, 1974, Box 27, Folder: BE 5 3/26/75–3/31/75, WHCF BE 5, GRFL.

25. Collection of the Gerald R. Ford Museum, Grand Rapids, Mich.

26. Freeburg, interview, August 31, 2001.

27. Memorandum to the president from Russell Freeburg, October 18, 1974, Box 32, Folder: BE 5–3 10/17/74–10/23/74, WHCF BE 5–3, GRFL.

28. "He's Arnie, Captain America," undated newspaper article, personal papers of Russell Freeburg.

29. Vertical File, Folder: WIN Program, newspaper clippings, GRFL; *NYT*, January 1, 1975; *National Journal*, November 16, 1974, 1741.

30. Freeburg, interview, August 31, 2001.

31. Ibid.

32. Hartmann, interview, October 17, 1994.

33. Ford, *A Time to Heal*, 195.

34. Lynn, interview, October 27, 1994.

35. O'Neill, interview, August 17, 1994.

36. Greenspan, 425.

37. Ash, interview, August 21, 2001.

38. Simon, *A Time for Truth*, 105; Hartmann, *Palace Politics*, 300.

39. Hartmann, interview, October 17, 1994.

40. Ford, *A Time to Heal*, 204; Reichley, *Conservatives*, 391.

41. Vertical File, Folder: WIN Program, newspaper clippings, GRFL.

42. Letter to Gerald Ford from Ray Stroud, October 11, 1974, Carl Albert Legislative Files 160:15, CACRSC.

43. Minutes of the EPB Executive Committee Meeting, October 23, 1974, Box 20, Folder: EPB Meeting Minutes, Seidman Files, GRFL; Hartmann, *Palace Politics*, 300.

44. Memorandum to Baroody and Weidman from Richard Krolick, November 4, 1974, Box 170, Folder: WIN (Whip Inflation Now) (3), Hartmann Papers, GRFL.

45. Memorandum to the president from William Baroody, February 21, 1975, Box 4, Folder: Business and Economics, National Economy 2/21–28/75, PHF, GRFL.

46. Freeburg, interview, August 31, 2001.

47. Letter to Frank Stanton from Russell Freeburg, November 24, 1974, personal papers of Russell Freeburg.

48. *WP*, December 20, 1974; Freeburg, interview, August 31, 2001.

49. Seidman, interview, October 18, 1994.

50. Letter to Stanton from Freeburg, November 24, 1974, personal papers of Russell Freeburg.

51. Tom Shales, "We Ain't Got a Barrel of Money," and Kathy Burke, "L.A. Composer Whips Up Inflation Fight Song," newspaper articles from the personal papers of Russell Freeburg.

52. Memorandum to the president re WIN, Box 4, Folder: Business and Economics, National Economy 2/21–28/75, February 28, 1975, PHF, GRFL.

53. Friedersdorf, interview, August 14, 2001.

54. *NYT*, March 9, 1975; *Public Papers*, 1975, 1:129.

55. Ford, interview, March 30, 1994.

56. Ford, interview, January 24, 2002.

57. *Gerald Ford's America*, Part 1, video, GRFL.

58. Energy Committee, Energy Conservation (January 3, 1975–February 4, 1975), Box L-142, Legislative Files: Energy, Carl Albert Papers, CACRSC.

59. Alliance to Save Energy commercial by the Ad Council (1980), personal collection of author.

60. NYT, October 29. 1975; WSJ, April 5, 1976.

61. Nessen, interview, January 29, 2002.

62. O'Neill, interview, August 17, 1994.

63. Letter to Stanton from Freeburg, November 24, 1974, personal papers of Russell Freeburg.

64. Porter, interview, May 8, 1995.

65. Seevers, interview, January 16, 2003.

66. Carl Albert Legislative Files 182:1, CACRSC.

67. Letter to Stanton from Freeburg, November 24, 1974, personal papers of Russell Freeburg.

68. Cannon, Time and Chance, 401.

69. WP, November 15, 1974; WSJ, November 8, 1974.

70. O'Neill, interview, August 17, 1994.

Chapter 9. The Great Recession of the 1970s

1. Ford, A Time to Heal, 55.

2. Hobart Rowen, Self-Inflicted Wounds: From LBJ's Guns and Butter to Reagan's Voodoo Economics (New York: Times Books, 1994), 109.

3. Newsweek, December 23, 1974, 16; Seidman, Full Faith and Credit, 30; Hartmann, Palace Politics, 176.

4. Ford, A Time to Heal, 204–5; "Minutes of EPB Executive Committee Meeting," October 18, 1974, Box 20, Folder: EPB Meeting Minutes, October 10–22, 1974, Seidman Files; Alan Greenspan, interview by James Reichley, GRFL.

5. WP, December 19, 26, 1974.

6. McCracken, interview, February 8, 1994; Letter to the president from Paul McCracken, December 24, 1974, Box 4, Folder: Business and Economics, National Economy, 12/21–31/1974, PHF, GRFL.

7. Letter to the president from Donald Riegle, December 14, 1974, Box 1, Folder: December 1974, Greenspan Files, GRFL; WP, May 13, 1976.

8. Seidman, interview, October 18. 1994; Seidman, Full Faith and Credit, 31; WP, December 20, 1974.

9. Nessen, It Sure Looks Different, 76–77; Memorandum to the president from Seidman, December 24, 1974, Box 4, Folder: Business and Economics, National Economy 12/21–31/1974, PHF, GRFL; Porter, Presidential Decision Making, 113; Time, January 27, 1975, 16; NYT, January 15, 1975.

10. Ford, A Time to Heal, 231.

11. "Economic Policy Review and Initiatives," December 24, 1974, Box 57, Folder: EPB-December 1974 (2), Greenspan Files, GRFL; National Journal, January 11, 1975, 40; Newsweek, January 13, 1975, 59.

12. *NYT*, January 15, 1975, 12.

13. "Meeting Minutes of the EPB Executive Committee," Box 20, Folder: Meeting Minutes of the EPB, January 9–12, 1975, Seidman Files, GRFL.

14. William Eberle, interview by author, March 29, 2002; Nessen, *It Sure Looks Different*, 78–79.

15. Porter, *Presidential Decision Making*, 117; Seidman, *Full Faith and Credit*, 32.

16. *NYT*, November 24, 1974; *Newsweek*, February 17, 1975, 71; *Time*, February 10, 1975, 72.

17. Melloan and Melloan, *The Carter Economy*, 20; *U.S. News*, February 10, 1975, 74; *NYT*, January 5, February 14, 1975. By contrast, economists in the 1970s estimated that if the economy were to create enough new jobs for all the new workers entering the job market, the GNP would have to grow 4 percent annually.

18. Howard Ellis, *Notes on Stagflation* (Washington, D.C.: American Enterprise Institute, 1978), 5; McConnell, *Economics*, 170. Stagflation was also called (although less commonly) "stumpflation" and "inflump."

19. MacAvoy, interview, May 2, 2002.

20. "National Growth and Development" (February 1976), Oversized Materials 5995-A, WE 6/1/75–1/20/77 (Executive), Box 2, WHCF Subject File, GRFL; Calleo, *The Imperious Economy*, 41, 97; *Business Week*, December 7, 1974, 84; *National Journal*, August 21, 1976, 1174–75; *Newsweek*, July 26, 1976, 62.

21. Videotape of third campaign debate, GRFL.

22. *Time*, March 29, 1976, 46–48.

23. *Economist*, March 10, 2001, 67; Wyatt Wells, *Economist in an Uncertain World: Arthur Burns and the Federal Reserve, 1970–1978* (New York: Columbia Univ. Press, 1994), 18.

24. *Economist*, April 13, 2002, 67.

25. Eckstein, *The Great Recession*, 116–20.

26. *Time*, January 27, 1975, 16; *NYT*, January 5, 1975.

27. *Time*, February 10, 1975, 68–69; *U.S. News*, December 9, 1974, 21; *WP*, January 4, 1975; *WSJ*, August 18, 1976.

28. *National Journal*, January 11, 1975, 40; *WP*, February 4, 21, 1975; Matusow, *Nixon's Economy*, 134; *NYT*, July 27, 1975.

29. *Time*, October 28, 1974, 88–90; *U.S. News*, September 2, 1974, 33; *The Conference on Inflation*, 121.

30. Robert Hargreaves, *Superpower: A Portrait of America in the 70s* (New York: St. Martin's Press, 1973), 13–16.

31. Letter to Carl Albert from Mayor Stanley Makowski, January 21, 1975, Energy Committee, Oil Tariffs, L-150, Legislative Files: Energy-Reaction to State of the Union speech, Carl Albert Papers, CACRSC.

32. *U.S. News*, December 30, 1974, 43–45; October 27, 1975, 15–16.

33. *NYT*, September 1, 1974; *New York Daily News*, September 20, 21, 2001.

34. Ford, *A Time to Heal*, 315.

35. Ford, interview, January 24, 2002.

36. "Proposed statement by the President," October 30, 1975, Box 54, Folder: Tax

Reduction (1), Greenspan Files, GRFL; Greene, *The Presidency of Gerald R. Ford*, 95; Wells, *Economist in an Uncertain World*, 175.

37. "Beame, NYC Mayor during Fiscal Crisis, Dies," http://www.usatoday.com/news/nation/2001-02-10-beame.htm; "Abraham Beame dies, first Jewish mayor of New York," http://www.cnn.com/2001/ALLPOLITICS/02/20/beame.obit/; *NYT*, October 29, 1976.

38. Exhibit video, Gerald R. Ford Museum, Grand Rapids, Mich.

39. Seidman, *Full Faith and Credit*, 33–34; Martin, *Greenspan*, 129.

40. *Newsweek*, January 20, 1975; *NYT*, January 16, March 9, 31, 1975; *Economist*, February 22, 1975, 61.

41. *NYT*, January 16, March 9, 31, June 7, 1975.

42. *Time*, January 27, 1975, 16; March 31, 1975, 68–69; *Newsweek*, December 2, 1974, 70; January 20, 1975, 56; *NYT*, April 13, 1975; *U.S. News*, January 27, 1975, 22; Carroll, *It Seemed Like Nothing Happened*, 133.

43. *WP*, December 8, 1974.

44. Speech in Utica, N.Y., January 8, 1976, Box 1027, Birch Bayh Papers, Lilly Library, IU.

45. *NYT*, February 5, 12, 1975; *Newsweek*, January 20, 1975, 16; February 10, 1975, 14; Gallup, *The Gallup Poll*, 1:441; *WP*, February 4, 1975.

46. Office of the Federal Register, *Weekly Compilation of Presidential Documents*, February 4, 1974, 114.

47. Vestal, *Jerry Ford*, 203.

Chapter 10. Ford's 1975 State of the Union Program

1. "Jaws: The E! True Hollywood Story," produced by E! Entertainment Television (2002); *NYT*, March 20, 1977; Nancy Mirshah, Gerald R. Ford Library archivist, e-mail message to author, June 1, 2004; Nancy Mirshah, Gerald R. Ford Library archivist, e-mail message to author, August 4, 2004.

2. *U.S. News*, December 9, 1974, 19.

3. Memorandum to the President, November 13, 1974, Box 22, Folder: SP 2-4/1975, State of the Union 8\9\74–11\27\74, WHCF SP 2, GRFL.

4. Nessen, *It Sure Looks Different*, 78, 80; see also Osborne, *White House Watch*, 91–92; Ford, *A Time to Heal*, 231.

5. "Note for EPB Executive Committee Members, " February 27, 1975, Folder: Economic Policy Board-Executive Committee-Meeting Summary Reports-John Harper: 1974–1975, 20:38, WS Papers, DBSL.

6. Kellerman, *The Political Presidency*, 165; *Newsweek*, January 20, 1975, 16; *NYT*, January 14, 1975; *National Journal*, January 18, 1975, 100; *WP*, January 14, 1975.

7. Frank Zarb, interview by author, September 26, 1994.

8. *WP*, January 14, 1975.

9. Hartmann, interview, October 17, 1994.

10. Nessen, *It Sure Looks Different*, 80, 82; *NYT*, January 14, 1975; *Newsweek*, January 27, 1975, 18.

11. Zarb, interview, September 26, 1994.

12. Videotape of speech, GRFL; *NYT*, January 14, 1975.

13. Nessen, *It Sure Looks Different*, 84; *Public Papers*, 1975, 1:32–33.

14. Nessen, *It Sure Looks Different*, 78; Ford, *A Time to Heal*, 232.

15. Goldwin, interview, March 3, 1994.

16. Ford, *A Time to Heal*, 232–33.

17. Nessen, interview, January 29, 2002.

18. Nessen, *It Sure Looks Different*, 85, 161; Hartmann, *Palace Politics*, 1–10, and passim.

19. William Seidman, interview by author, May 19, 2004.

20. Ford, *A Time to Heal*, 232; *Newsweek*, January 27, 1975, 16; Memorandum to Milton Friedman from Dick Cheney, December 30, 1974, Box 12, Folder: President-Speeches-State of the Union, 1975, Background (1), Goldwin Papers, GRFL.

21. *Public Papers*, 1975, 1:37; *Time*, January 27, 1975, 13.

22. *Public Papers*, 1975, 1:37; "The President's Program" and "The President's Economic Program: A Summary," January 14, 1975, Box 5, Folder: President's Economic Program, Kosters Files, GRFL; "A 5-Page Layman's Summary: Summary of the President's Program," Box 3, Folder: Economic and Energy Proposals-Spokesman's Briefing Book, 1/29/75, Cheney Files, GRFL.

23. "The Economic Program," January 11, 1975, Box 5, Folder: President's Economic Program, Kosters Files; "A Brief Factual Summary of the President's Economic and Energy Programs Outlined in His State of the Union Message" and "Summary of the President's Programs-New Directions," Box 3, Folder: Economic and Energy Proposals-Spokesman's Briefing Book, 1/29/75, Cheney Files, GRFL; *Time*, January 27, 1975, 17.

24. *Public Papers*, 1975, 1:38; "Summary of the President's Economic Policies," by L. William Seidman, Box 57, Folder: Economic Policy Statements (2), Seidman Files; also in Box 5, Folder: President's Economic Program, Kosters Files, GRFL.

25. *NYT*, January 16, 1975; *Time*, January 27, 1975, 14; *WP*, January 14, 16, 1975.

26. *NYT*, January 16, 1975.

27. Letter from Betty Behrns of Tonawanda, N.Y., Box 44, Folder: Speeches-1/13/75, Economy and Energy (2), PHF, GRFL.

28. "The President's Economic and Energy Proposals: Understanding the Economics," Box 13, Folder: Economic and Energy Program, 1/75 (1), Marsh Files, GRFL.

29. Q&A on wealthy taxpayers and tax breaks, Folder: Q&A-Taxes: 1975 (January 17), 34:5, WS Papers, DBSL; *WP*, March 25, 1975.

30. *Newsweek*, January 27, 1975, 17, 20; *WP*, January 9, 1975; *NYT*, January 15, 16, 1975.

31. Nessen, *It Sure Looks Different*, 152; *Newsweek*, January 27, 1975, 18, 26.

32. Ford, *A Time to Heal*, 238; Rowen, *Self-Inflicted Wounds*, 149–50; Hartmann, *Palace Politics*, 300.

33. *Newsweek*, January 27, 1975, 17; Ford, *A Time to Heal*, 234.

34. "Comparison of Plans," Box 16, Folder: Energy-Proposal by Rep. Al Ullman, 1/75–5/75, Marsh Files, GRFL; *NYT*, January 29, 1975.

35. *Public Papers*, 1975, 1:128, 193, 245, 292, 298–99.

36. *WP*, October 10, December 24, 1974.

37. *WP*, February 28, 1975; *Congressional Quarterly*, March 8, 1975, 470; Hargreaves, *Superpower*, 177.

38. Statement of C. John Miller, president of the Independent Petroleum Association of America, before the House Ways and Means Committee, March 6, 1975, Box 476, Birch Bayh Papers, Lilly Library, IU.

39. Letter to President Ford from C. M. McLean, October 14, 1975, Box 13, Folder: BE 4–29 Petroleum and coal products, 8/9/74–12/31/74, WHCF BE, GRFL.

40. *Public Papers*, 1975, 1:327, 352, 367; *Economist*, April 5, 1975, 49.

41. *NYT*, February 17, 1975; *Public Papers*, 1975, 1:125.

42. *WP*, March 22, 1975; *NYT*, March 23, 1975.

43. Kellerman, *The Political Presidency*, 172–73; *WP*, March 15, 1975.

44. Letter to Speaker of the House from Gerald R. Ford, March 25, 1975, Box 24, Folder: FI 11 1/11/75–3/26/75, WHCF FI, GRFL; *Public Papers*, 1975, 1:399–401.

45. *Time*, April 7, 1975, 49.

46. "Summary of the Conference Report on H.R. 2166: The Tax Reduction Act of 1975," Box 25, Folder: Taxes (2), Vern Loen and Charles Leppert Files, GRFL; *NYT*, March 27, 29, 1975; "A Brief Review of the Tax Reduction Act of 1975," August 26, 1975, Box B98, Folder: Taxes (2), Arthur Burns Papers, GRFL; *Time*, April 7, 1975, 45; *WP*, February 7, 1975; *Newsweek*, April 7, 1975, 30.

47. "Review of 15 metro daily editorials," Box 27, Folder: Tax Cut, FY '75 (1), Gerald Warren and Margarite White Files, GRFL.

48. *Editorials on File*, March 16–31, 1975, 292, 294, 297–98; "Editorial opinions," Box 25, Folder: FI 11 3/27/75–3/31/75, WHCF FI-11, GRFL.

49. *NYT*, April 3, 1975.

50. Ford, *A Time to Heal*, 259; see also "The President and Decision-Making (An Overview)," by Jim Connor, November 1975, Box 11, Folder: President-National Vision (2), Robert Goldwin Files, GRFL.

51. Memoranda to the president from William Simon and Arthur Burns, March 28, 1975, Box 20, Folder: Finances-Taxation (3), PHF, GRFL.

52. Ibid.

53. "To the House of Representatives," March 28, 1975, Box 54, Folder: SP 3–83, WHCF Subject Files, GRFL.

54. Memorandum to the president from James Lynn, March 28, 1975, Box 20, Folder: Finances-Taxation, PHF, GRFL.

55. Memorandum to the president from R.L. Dunham, March 27, 1975, Box 20, Folder: Finances-Taxation (3), PHF, GRFL; Memorandum to the president from John Marsh, March 28, 1975, Box 20, Folder: Finances-Taxation (3), PHF, GRFL.

56. Memorandum to the president from Alan Greenspan, March 28, 1975, Box 20, Folder: Finances-Taxation (3), PHF, GRFL.

57. Memorandum to the president from Ron Nessen, March 28, 1975, Box 20, Folder: Finances-Taxation (3), PHF, GRFL.

58. *Newsweek*, April 7, 1975, 31; Memorandum to the president from Robert Hartmann, March 27, 1975, Box 20, Folder: Finances-Taxation (3), PHF, GRFL; Memorandum to the president from Max Friedersdorf, March 27, 1975, Box 11, Folder: Economy, February 1975–March 1976, Max Friedersdorf Files, GRFL; *WSJ*, March 21, 1975.

59. Memorandum to John Marsh from William Kendall and Patrick O'Donnell, March 28, 1975, Box 20, Folder: Finances-Taxation (3), PHF, GRFL; see also

Memorandum to the president from Max Friedersdorf, March 27, 1975, Box 11, Folder: Economy, February 1975-March 1976, Friedersdorf Files, GRFL.

60. Hartmann memo, March 27, 1975.

61. Ford, interview, March 30, 1994.

62. *Time*, January 5, 1976, 37.

63. Lynn, interviews, March 3, October 27, 1994.

64. Friedersdorf, interview, August 14, 2001.

65. Ford, interview, October 25, 1994.

66. Ford, interview, March 30, 1994.

67. Seidman, interview, October 18, 1994.

68. Greenspan, "The Council of Economic Advisers Under Alan Greenspan, 1974–77," in Hargrove and Morley, 447.

69. *Public Papers*, 1975, 1:406–8.

70. Ibid., 1:408–9; Ford, *A Time to Heal*, 407.

71. *Economist*, February 3, 2001, 36; Edwards, *Presidential Influence*, 48; Matusow, *Nixon's Economy*, 165.

72. Memorandum to the president from Alan Greenspan, July 3, 1975, Box 1, Folder: July 1975, Greenspan Files, GRFL.

73. *Baltimore Sun* editorial (undated), Box 9, Folder: 5.181 Ford's Tax Program (2), Charles McCall Files, GRFL; *NYT*, January 1, 1976.

74. Nigel Andrews, *Nigel Andrews on Jaws* (New York: Bloomsbury, 1999), 148.

Chapter 11. Economic Initiatives, 1975–76

1. Goldwin, interview, March 3, 1994; *Time*, June 30, 1975, 10; *U.S. News*, April 7, 1975, 31–32.

2. Ford, *A Time to Heal*, 309–11; *Newsweek*, September 15, 1975, 16–18; *Time*, September 15, 1975, 9–11; October 6, 1975, 12–14.

3. *NYT*, September 15, 1975.

4. *Public Papers*, 1975, 1:872; Memorandum to the Executive Committee of the Economic Policy Board from Alan Greenspan, January 6, 1975, Box 20, Folder: EPB-Executive Committee-Meeting Summary Reports, WS Papers, DBSL.

5. *Editorials on File*, October 1–15, 1975, 1174.

6. Wells, *Economist in an Uncertain World*, 167; *NYT*, July 20, 1975.

7. *Economist*, October 11, 1975, 35; "A Radical Policy to bring energy consumption and federal spending under control," December 3, 1974, 22/1, WS Papers, DBSL; Porter, *Presidential Decision Making*, 114–15; *WP*, October 14, 1975.

8. Fact Sheet for Presidential Spokesmen, Folder: Taxes-Tax Cuts, 1975-Briefings (1), GRFL.

9. *Public Papers*, 1975, 2:1604, 1608.

10. Lynn, interviews, October 27, 1994, February 2, 1995.

11. O'Neill, interview, August 17, 1994.

12. *NYT*, October 22, 1975; *Baltimore Sun* editorial, McCall Files, GRFL.

13. *Newsweek*, October 20, 1975, 73; *Editorials on File*, October 1–15, 1975, 1175–76.

14. Lynn, interview, October 27, 1994.

15. *NYT*, October 22, 1975; William Seidman's notes of a meeting with Muskie, Long, Lynn, Greenspan, and the president, 12/11/75, Box 167, Folder: Taxes, 12/1–12/75, Seidman Files, GRFL (hereafter cited as Seidman meeting notes, 12/11/75).

16. *Newsweek*, December 22, 1975, 55.

17. *NYT*, December 18, 1975; WP, October 15, 30, December 20, 1975.

18. WP, October 15, 1975; *Newsweek*, October 20, 1975, 73.

19. *Newsweek*, February 9, 1976, 64; Whitney, *Inflation*, 61.

20. Richard Carroll, "An Economic Record of Presidential Performance: From Truman to Bush" (unpublished manuscript, author's copy, 1994), 182.

21. *Public Papers, 1975*, 2:1704.

22. *NYT*, October 12, 1975; *Public Papers, 1975*, 2:1619.

23. Ford, interview, March 30, 1994.

24. Ford, *A Time to Heal*, 338.

25. Letter from Don Lyon of Ellisville, Mo., December 11, 1975, Legislative Files: Revenue Adjustment Act, Carl Albert Papers, CACRSC.

26. Lynn, interview, February 2, 1995.

27. Gergen, *Eyewitness to Power*, 140; *Public Papers, 1975*, 2:1646.

28. GOP Leadership Meeting, October 7, 1975, Box 2, Folder: Congressional Leadership Meetings: GOP, 10/7/75, Wolthius Files, GRFL.

29. Speech before Retail Druggists' Convention, Miami, October 13, 1975, Congress and the Economy, Speeches and Press Releases, 18:2391, Legislative Files: Revenue Adjustment Act, CACRSC.

30. Lynn, interview, February 2, 1995.

31. *Public Papers, 1975*, 2:1666–67.

32. *Newsweek*, October 20, 1975, 19; *Public Papers, 1975*, 2:1659, 1673, 1744.

33. GOP Leadership Meeting, October 7, 1975, Wolthius Files, GRFL; *Public Papers, 1975*, 2:1577.

34. Proposed statement by the president, revised October 30, 1975, Box 54, Folder: Tax Reduction (1), Greenspan Files, GRFL.

35. 94th Budget Committee, General (May 8–December 15, 1975), Box B, Legislative Files: Budget, Carl Albert Papers, CACRSC.

36. *New York Daily News*, October 9, 1975, Box 26, Folder: Tax cuts and federal spending restraint-Editorial reaction to proposal: 1975 (October 7–9), WS Papers, DBSL.

37. Conable, interview, February 9, 1994; GOP Leadership Meeting, October 7, 1975, Box 9, Folder: Congress-Leadership Meetings: Republicans, 10/7/75, Marsh Files, GRFL.

38. *NYT*, December 18, 1975; WP, December 10, 1975.

39. Ford, *A Time to Heal*, 338; *Public Papers, 1975*, 2:1972–75; WP, December 21, 1975.

40. Ford, *A Time to Heal*, 339; U.S. News, December 29, 1975, 7; *NYT*, December 19, 1975; Ford, *Humor and the Presidency*, 125.

41. U.S. News, December 29, 1975, 9; WP, December 24, 1975.

42. *NYT*, December 19, 1975; WP, December 20, 1975.

43. *NYT*, December 19, 1975; WP, December 24, 1975.

44. Memorandum to the president from James Lynn, December 17, 1975, Box 179, Folder: 12/17/75-Veto Message on Tax Cut Bill, H.R. 5559 (2), Hartmann Papers, GRFL.

45. Ford, *A Time to Heal*, 339; Seidman meeting notes, 12/11/75; *WP*, December 24, 1975.

46. *NYT*, December 20, 1975; Nessen, *It Sure Looks Different*, 89.

47. *Public Papers, 1975*, 2:1988.

48. Lynn, interview, March 3, 1994.

49. Ford, interview, March 30, 1994.

50. Seidman, interview, October 18, 1994.

51. *WP*, December 19, 24, 1975; *Time*, December 22, 1975, 12.

52. Sundquist, *The Decline and Resurgence of Congress*, 221–22; The Tax Bill, A Spokesman's Guide, December 21, 1975, Q&A for spokesmen, Box 54, Folder: Tax Reduction (1), Greenspan Files, GRFL.

53. Lynn, interview, February 2, 1995.

54. Franklin, *Making Ends Meet*, 103.

55. Lynn, interview, October 27, 1994.

56. Seidman, *Full Faith and Credit*, 22.

57. Ford, *A Time to Heal*, 271–73.

58. Paul MacAvoy, e-mail message to author, June 23, 2004; MacAvoy, interview, May 2, 2004.

59. *NYT*, June 16, 18, 29, July 7, September 29, 1975; *Congressional Quarterly Almanac 1976*, 729.

60. Seevers, interview, January 16, 2003.

61. MacAvoy, interview, May 2, 2002.

62. Aviation Act of 1975, Box 6, Folder: Civil Aviation-Regulatory Reform, PHF, GRFL; Box 13, Folder: Aviation Act of 1975, January 1–19, 1976, Judith Hope Files, GRFL.

63. Editorials, Memorandum from Paul MacAvoy, October 13, 1975, Box 52, James Cannon Files, Folder: Regulatory Reform Meeting, 10/24/75, GRFL.

64. Paul MacAvoy and John Snow, eds., *Regulation of Entry and Pricing in Truck Transportation* (Washington, D.C.: American Enterprise Institute, 1977), 3–43.

65. MacAvoy, interview, May, 2, 2002; William Coleman, interview by author, September 16, 2003.

66. *Congressional Quarterly Almanac 1976*, 637–38; *WSJ*, January 29, February 6, 1976.

67. MacAvoy, interview, May 2, 2002; Paul MacAvoy, ed., *Federal Energy Administration Regulation: Report of the Presidential Task Force* (Washington, D.C.: American Enterprise Institute, 1977); Paul MacAvoy and John Snow, eds., *Regulation of Passenger Fares and Competition in the Airline Industry* (Washington, D.C.: American Enterprise Institute, 1977); MacAvoy and Snow, *Regulation of Entry and Pricing in Truck Transportation*; Paul MacAvoy and John Snow, eds., *Deregulation of Cable Television* (Washington, D.C.: American Enterprise Institute, 1977); *WSJ*, May 14, 1976.

68. Ford, *The Presidential Campaign 1976*, 2:62, 64–65.

69. *Newsweek*, January 26, 1976, 49; February 9, 1976, 55.

70. *Economist*, January 24, 1976, 52–53; *Public Papers 1976–1977*, 1:45–53; *Statistical Abstract of the United States: 1988*, 108th ed., 291.

71. *NYT*, February 8, 1976.

72. *Economist*, July 24, 1976, 39.

73. Eckstein, *The Great Recession*, 128–34.

74. Videotape of first campaign debate, GRFL; *NYT*, March 20, May 30, 1976; *U.S. News*, November 1, 1976, 84.

75. *NYT*, July 25, October 22, 1976.

76. *NYT*, March 6, April 3, August 22, 1976; *WSJ*, January 27, 1976; *Time*, January 14, 1974, 62.

77. *Congressional Quarterly Almanac 1976*, 371; Ford, *A Time to Heal*, 415; *Newsweek*, May 31, 1976, 57.

78. *Economist*, May 22, 1976, 38; Debate videos, GRFL.

79. Reasons for the President's Veto, February 13, 1976, Box 29, Folder: EPB Memoranda, February 6–16, 1976, Seidman Files, GRFL; Videotape of first campaign debate, GRFL; *Congressional Quarterly Almanac 1976*, 68; *NYT*, July 7, 1976; *Newsweek*, July 26, 1976, 62.

80. *NYT*, August 18, 1976.

81. *NYT*, July 23, October 1, 1976; *WSJ*, October 28, 1976.

82. Ford, *A Time to Heal*, 431.

83. Memorandum for the EPB Executive Committee, September 11, 1976, Box 43, Folder: Briefing Papers, September–November 1976, Seidman Files, GRFL; *Congressional Quarterly Almanac 1976*, 41.

84. *WSJ*, September 27, October 15, 29, 1976; *NYT*, October 15, 1976.

85. *NYT*, October 15, 1976; Greene, *The Presidency of Gerald Ford*, 188.

86. Ford, *A Time to Heal*, 428.

87. News Conference Transcript, August 30, 1976, Cabinet Meetings, Collected Items, Box 4, Folder: 8/30/76, GRFL; *NYT*, October 17, 1976; *WSJ*, August 31, 1976.

88. Economic Policy Initiatives, Box 29, Folder: EPB Memoranda, January 27, 1976, Seidman Files, GRFL; *Economist*, August 14, 1976, 36; *U.S. News*, November 1, 1976, 36; *WSJ*, August 13, September 20, November 19, 1976.

89. Seevers, interview, January 16, 2003.

90. Burton Malkiel, telephone interview by author, January 23, 2002.

91. Alan Greenspan, Jim Lynn, and John Marsh, interviews by James Reichley, GRFL; Matusow, *Nixon's Economy*, 55.

92. *NYT*, June 13, 1976; Ford, *A Time to Heal*, 428–29.

93. *Time*, November 1, 1976, 19; *NYT*, June 16, 1976.

94. MacDougall, *We Almost Made It*, 180, 221; Schram, *Running for President*, 364.

95. Hedley Donovan, *Roosevelt to Reagan: A Reporter's Encounters with Nine Presidents* (New York: Harper and Row, 1985), 138; Lovett, *Inflation and Politics*, 22; *Time*, August 23, 1976, 10.

96. *Facts on File*, January 22, 1977, 37; February 19, 1977, 110; Gallup, *The Gallup Poll*, 1:336, 2:769.

97. *WSJ*, December 31, 1976.

Chapter 12. The Energy Crisis of the 1970s

1. *Newsweek*, May 3, 1976, 17; MacDougall, *We Almost Made It*, 102–4; NYT, March 7, July 29, 1976; April 17, 1978.

2. Tim Brooks and Earle Marsh, *The Complete Directory to Prime Time Network TV Shows, 1946–Present* (New York: Ballantine Books, 1979), 420.

3. *Time*, December 17, 1973, 30; December 24, 1973, 20; NYT, December 9, 1973.

4. Douglas Bohi and Joel Darmstadter, "The Energy Upheavals of the 1970s: Socioeconomic Watershed or Aberration" (paper prepared for the symposium "Twenty Years after the Energy Shock—How Far Have We Come? Where Are We Headed?" University of Tennessee–Knoxville, April 19, 1994), 16.

5. *U.S. News*, August 25, 1975, 15; Thomas Lee et al., *Energy Aftermath* (Boston: Harvard Business School Press, 1990), 23, 25, 28, 29; NYT, April 17, 1973.

6. National Petroleum Council, *Factors Affecting U.S. Oil and Gas Outlook: A Report of the National Petroleum Council* (Washington, D.C.: National Petroleum Council, 1987), 15 (hereafter cited as NPC, *Factors*).

7. NYT, February 10, 1974.

8. Craufurd Goodwin et al., "Energy: 1945–1980," *Wilson Quarterly* 5 (Spring 1981): 69; Reichley, *Conservatives*, 359.

9. Reichley, *Conservatives*, 372, for 1973; Elliott Richardson and Frank Zarb, *Perspectives on Energy Policy*, December 14, 1976, 65 from the personal papers of Frank Zarb.

10. NYT, April 17, 1973; *Time*, February 18, 1974, 22.

11. NYT, April 17, 19, 1973.

12. NYT, April 19, 1973; February 10, 1974.

13. Robert Nordhaus, interview by author, September 18, 2003; Matusow, *Nixon's Economy*, 242, 244.

14. S. David Freeman, *Energy: The New Era* (New York: Walker, 1974); MacAvoy, *Federal Energy Administration Regulation*, 4–5; Memorandum from John Love and Roy Ash, September 21, 1973, 15:28, WS Papers, DBSL; *Time*, April 16, 1973, 88.

15. Charles Curtis, interview by author, January 22, 2003.

16. Charles DiBona, interview by author, January 23, 2003; William A. Johnson, interview by author, April 20, 2004.

17. White House Statement, August 6, 1970, WS Papers, DBSL; *Time*, December 25, 1972, 66; NYT, March 19, May 7, 1972; *Time*, December 25, 1972, 67.

18. Letter from Abraham Ribicoff, February 12, 1973, WS Papers, DBSL.

19. Telegram from Thomas Eagleton, April 25, 1973, WS Papers, DBSL; *Time*, April 16, 1973, 88.

20. Letter from Warren Tomlinson, February 28, 1973, WS Papers, DBSL; Memorandum from Gary Seevers, September 28, 1973, 15:39, WS Papers, DBSL; Summary of the Proposed Phase IV Price Program, July 16, 1973, 15:38, WS Papers, DBSL; *Time*, April 16, 1973, 88; November 12, 1973, 107.

21. Nordhaus, interview, September 18, 2003.

22. DiBona, interview, January 23, 2003.

23. "Allocation of Crude Oil and Refinery Products," May 4, 1973, 15:26, WS Papers,

DBSL; Letter from William Simon, July 17, 1973, 15:27, WS Papers, DBSL; *Time*, May 21, 1973, 86.

24. Letter from William Donald Schaefer, June 15, 1973, 15:27, WS Papers, DBSL; letters from the New England Congressional Caucus, June 11, 1973, and June 21, 1973, WS Papers, DBSL.

25. Letter from George McGovern, July 17, 1973, WS Papers, DBSL.

26. Les Aspin, Testimony before the Oil Policy Committee, June 14, 1973, and letter from Les Aspin and congressmen, June 6, 1973, 15:29, WS Papers, DBSL; Letter from Noah Neace, May 31, 1973, WS Papers, DBSL.

27. *Time*, December 25, 1972, 67.

28. Letter from Arthur Steffan, March 21, 1973; letter from L.W. Johnson, received June 4, 1973, WS Papers, DBSL.

29. Letter from Robert Nunn, June 14, 1973, 15:27, WS Papers; Statement by William Millikin, June 14, 1973, WS Papers, DBSL.

30. DiBona, interview, January 23, 2003.

31. Letter from James Abourezk, June 1, 1973, WS Papers, DBSL.

32. DiBona, interview, January 23, 2003; *Time*, October 22, 1973, 77; December 10, 1973, 37.

33. Memorandum from John Love and Roy Ash, September 21, 1973, 15:28, WS Papers, DBSL; *Time*, January 23, 1974, 23.

34. *Dallas Morning News*, July 3, 1973, WS Papers, DBSL.

35. *Congressional Quarterly Almanac 1973* (Washington, D.C.: Congressional Quarterly Press, 1973), 624; *WSJ*, October 3, 15, December 12, 1973.

36. NPC, *Factors*, 15; *NYT*, November 11, 1973.

37. Nordhaus, interview, September 18, 2003.

38. *National Journal*, April 26, 1975, 622; *Congressional Quarterly Almanac 1973*, 624.

39. MacAvoy, *Federal Energy Administration Regulation*, 7–8; *NYT*, April 11, July 4, 1975; *WP*, January 19, 1975.

40. *Congressional Quarterly Almanac 1973*, 623; "Emergency Petroleum Allocation Act," undated, 12:27; Memorandum from John Love and Roy Ash, September 21, 1973, 15:28, WS Papers, DBSL. The Economic Stabilization Act amendments of 1973 granted the president authority to establish mandatory allocation and priorities for petroleum use; *Time*, January 21, 1974; *WSJ*, December 12, 1973; January 16, 22, 1974.

41. Nordhaus, interview, September 18, 2003.

42. *NYT*, January 16, 1974; *Time*, March 18, 1974, 25.

43. John A. Hill, interview by author, May 11, 2004.

44. Memorandum from William A. Johnson, February 4, 1974, 13:4, WS Papers, DBSL.

45. *WSJ*, November 2, 1973; "A Proposal for Mandatory Allocation of Oil and Liquefied Petroleum Gases," July 16, 1973, 15:27, WS Papers, DBSL; *NYT*, January 11, 1974; *WSJ*, December 21, 1973; *Time*, January 23, 1974, 23.

46. W. Allen Wallis, *An Overgoverned Society* (New York: The Free Press, 1976), 23; *NYT*, January 16, 1974; *WSJ*, October 17, November 12, 1973; January 2, 11, 1974; *Time*, December 10, 1973.

47. Memorandum from William A. Jonson, February 4, 1974, 13:4, WS Papers, DBSL.

48. *WSJ*, January 22, February 4, February 14, 1974; *Time*, March 4, 1974, 22; *NYT*, November 4, December 18, 1973 .

49. Letter from Robert Samuels, October 26, 1973, 15:28, WS Papers, DBSL; Letter from the International Association of Drilling Contractors, June 5, 1973, 15:27, WS Papers, DBSL.

50. Letter from Clifford Case, January 30, 1974, WS Papers, DBSL; and Telegram from Clifford Case, February 4, 1974, 13:7, WS Papers, DBSL; Telegram from Reuben Askew, February 21, 1974, 13:52, WS Papers, DBSL.

51. Carroll, *Seems Like Nothing Happened*, 118; Frum, *How We Got Here*, 320; Alfred Marcus and Mark Jankus, "The Auto Emissions Debate during the Ford Administration: The Role of Scientific Knowledge," in Firestone and Ugrinsky, *Gerald R. Ford*, 2:323; Matusow, *Nixon's Economy*, 267; Simon, *A Time for Truth*, 53; *Newsweek*, March 4, 1974, 66; *Time*, February 18, 1974, 35; *NYT*, December 28, 1973; September 24, 1990; *WSJ*, February 4, 8, 1974. The eight states observing odd/even rationing were Hawaii, Maryland, Massachusetts, New York, New Jersey, Oregon, Pennsylvania, and Washington.

52. Simon, *A Time for Truth*, 53.

53. *Time*, February 25, 1974, 26; *WSJ*, December 10, 1973.

54. *Time*, March 4, 1974, 23; *NYT*, January 5, 25, February 1, 1974.

55. Telegram from Joseph Maraziti, February 14, 1974, 13:7, WS Papers, DBSL.

56. *NYT*, January 7, February 3, 1974; *WSJ*, January 2, 1974.

57. Roy Ash, telephone interview by author, February 8, 1994.

58. *Time*, March 18, 1974, 25; *WP*, January 24, 1976; Gergen, *Eyewitness to Power*, 113.

59. Johnson, interview, April 20, 2004; William A. Johnson, letter to author, June 4, 2004.

60. DiBona, interview, January 23, 2003.

61. *WSJ*, January 11, 25, 1974. In truth, most of Simon's assistants were economists, not lawyers. Hill, interview, May 11, 2004; Memorandum from William A. Johnson, February 4, 1974, 13:4, WS Papers, DBSL; Simon, *A Time for Truth*, 57.

62. *WSJ*, January 11, 1974; Simon, *A Time for Truth*, 57.

63. DiBona, interview, January 23, 2003.

64. Zarb, interview, September 26, 1994.

65. *Time*, March 4, 1974, 22; *WSJ*, February 14, 1974.

66. MacAvoy, *Federal Energy Administration Regulation*, preface, 47, 143.

67. *WSJ*, January 11, 22, 1974; Solomon, *Beyond the Turning Point*, 99.

68. Letter from Lowell Zentner, May 29, 1973, WS Papers, DBSL.

69. Daniel Yergin, *The Prize: The Epic Quest for Oil, Money and Power* (New York: Touchstone, 1992), 657.

70. NPC, *Factors*, 48.

71. Campaign Materials 1974, Box 1092, Folder 2, Birch Bayh Papers, Lilly Library, IU.

72. Matusow, *Nixon's Economy*, 266; *Time*, March 4, 1974, 22.

73. William Nester, *American Power, the New World Order and the Japanese Challenge*

(New York: St. Martin's Press, 1993), 114; Heizo Takenaka, *Contemporary Japanese Economy and Economic Policy* (Ann Arbor: Univ. of Michigan Press, 1991), 17.

74. McCracken, interview, February 8, 1994.

75. Between 1973 and 1976, oil consumption fell in Great Britain (17 percent), West Germany (7.6 percent), France (6.5 percent), and Japan (5 percent). But during the same period, U.S. oil consumption increased marginally (1 percent). George Shultz and Kenneth Dam, *Energy Policy behind the Headlines* (New York: W.W. Norton, 1977), 188.

76. DiBona, interview, January 23, 2003.

77. Ford, interview, March 30, 1994.

78. "New Petroleum Allocation Rules Proposed, December 12, 1973," 13:4, WS Papers, DBSL; *NYT*, February 13, 1974; Matusow, *Nixon's Economy*, 268–69, 273; Reichley, *Conservatives*, 362–65.

79. *WP*, January 2, 1975.

80. *Congressional Quarterly Almanac 1975*, 173.

81. James Griffin and Henry Steele, *Energy Economics and Policy* (New York: Academic Press, 1980), 19.

82. Melvin Small, *The Presidency of Richard Nixon* (Lawrence: Univ. Press of Kansas, 1999), 203.

83. "Specific Examples of Conservation," in "The Effects of Decontrol," Box 48, Folder: Oil Decontrol (2), Greenspan Files, GRFL.

84. *NYT*, December 27, 28, 1973; *Time*, December 31, 1973, 19.

85. *Time*, December 10, 1973; *WSJ*, November 12, 1973; *NYT*, November 13, 1973.

86. Goodwin et al., "Energy: 1945–1980," 70; *WSJ*, December 21, 1973; *Time*, November 26, 1973, 24.

87. Frank Zarb, interview by author, February 6, 2003.

88. Ed Cray, *Chrome Colossus: General Motors and Its Times* (New York: McGraw-Hill, 1980), 485; *NYT*, January 6, 1974.

89. Watts and Free, *State of the Nation*, 124; Nessen, *It Sure Looks Different*, 305.

90. "A Workable Plan for Energy Independence," attached to a May 21, 1976, memorandum, Nelson Rockefeller Vice Presidential, Series 15, Box 4, Folder: Energy Independence Authority, Rockefeller Archive Center.

91. "Domestic Vulnerability without New Action," in "The Effects of Decontrol" (FEA publication, August 18, 1975), Box 48, Folder: Oil Decontrol (2), Greenspan Files, GRFL; James Katz, *Congress and National Energy Policy* (New Brunswick, N.J.: Transaction Books, 1984), 34.

92. *NYT*, April 7, 1974; February 12, 1975; February 21, 1976; *Time*, August 11, 1975, 54.

93. Lester Sobel, ed., *Energy Crisis: 1974–75* (New York: Facts on File, 1975), 2:116; *Time*, December 31, 1973, 25.

94. Marcus and Jankus, "The Auto Emissions Debate," 2:323; *WP*, February 24, 1975; DiBona, interview, January 23, 2003.

95. *Time*, January 21, 1974, 22; *U.S. News*, October 6, 1975, 12.

96. *WP*, December 25, 1974.

97. Meadows et al., *The Limits of Growth*, 9, 24.

98. Letter from Mark Bradbury, March 4, 1974, Box 55: Energy Prices, Birch Bayh Papers, Lilly Library, IU.

99. Curtis, interview, January 22, 2003.

Chapter 13. A New Energy Program

1. Zarb, interview, September 26, 1994.

2. Simon, *A Time for Truth*, 50. For his part, Love complained about access to the president, saying he saw Nixon alone at most five times during as many months. Upon quitting, he complained that he could never "get the attention of the president"; *Time*, December 17, 1973, 30.

3. NYT, June 30, November 9, 1973; *Public Papers of the Presidents of the United States, Richard Nixon: Containing the Public Messages, Speeches, and Statements of the President, 1969 to August 9, 1974* (Washington, D.C.: Government Printing Office, 1971–75), November 7, 1973.

4. Bruce Pasternack, interview by author, March 21, 1994.

5. *National Journal*, June 12, 1976, 806; Frank Zarb, "Discussant: Frank G. Zarb," in Firestone and Ugrinsky, *Gerald R. Ford*, 2:354.

6. Zarb, interview, September 26, 1994.

7. Ford, *A Time to Heal*, 228; Memorandum to the president from Frank Zarb (ca. December 1974), Box 5, Folder: Energy Policy Options Papers, Cheney Files, GRFL.

8. Memorandum to William Simon from Gerald Parsky, 20 August 1974, Box 25, Folder: President-Memoranda re Meetings with William E. Simon: 1974–75, WS Papers, DBSL.

9. *Public Papers, 1975*, 1:237; Memorandum to William Simon from Gerald Parsky, Talking Points for Briefings on Economic Message, October 7, 1974, and Q&A, October 7, 1974, Box 21, Folder: Economic Program—A Program to Control Inflation in a Healthy and Growing Economy, 1974 (October 8), WS Papers, DBSL.

10. Various letters, February 4, 1975–August 28, 1975 and January 3, 1975–February 4, 1975, Energy Committee, Energy Conservation, L-142, Legislative Files: Energy, Carl Albert Papers, CACRSC.

11. *Public Papers, 1974*, 310; Letter from Susan Flanagan, December 2, 1974, Box 72, Folder: BE 5–3, WHCF, GRFL; Letter from Melissa Casadalaan, Box 72, Folder: BE 5–3, WHCF, GRFL.

12. Memorandum to the president from William Simon (filed October 7, 1974), Box 25, Folder: FI 11–1 10/1/74–10/9/74, WHCF, GRFL.

13. Letter from Tim Lee Carter, October 2, 1974, Box 25, Folder: FI 11–1, 10/1/74–10/9/74, WHCF, GRFL.

14. Letter from Mrs. Bruce Bowslaugh, September 30, 1974, Box 26, Folder: FI-1, 10/11/74–11/13/74 (general), WHCF, GRFL.

15. Ford, *A Time to Heal*, 229; NYT, October 31, 1974.

16. Ford's first choice to replace Sawhill, Andrew Gibson, ran into trouble. Gibson, a federal maritime administrator and an assistant commerce secretary in the Nixon administration, withdrew over an apparent conflict of interest. A company that leased

tankers to the oil industry had paid him a salary settlement totaling more than $800,000; *WP*, November 20, 1974; Zarb, interview, September 26, 1994.

17. Zarb, interview, September 26, 1994; *Business Week*, November 30, 1974, 29; *NYT*, November 26, 1974.

18. Glenn Schleede, interview by author, October 20, 1994.

19. Ford, interview, March 30, 1994.

20. *WP*, December 29, 1974.

21. Energy Policy Meeting, Camp David, December 14–15, 1974, Box 3, Folder: Camp David Meeting on Energy; December 1974, Michael Duval Files, GRFL; *U.S. News*, January 6, 1975, 13.

22. William J. Green, interview by author, February 28, 1994.

23. *Service Station Management*, April 1975, 22; "Crude Oil Tax and Tariff: Proposal," in "A Radical Policy to Bring Energy Consumption and Federal Spending Under Control," December 3, 1974, 22:1, WS Papers, DBSL; "The President's Economic and Energy Proposals: Equating the Burden: No Direct Gas Tax," Box 13, Folder: Economic and Energy Program, 1/75 (1), Marsh Files, GRFL; Ford, *A Time to Heal*, 229.

24. Zarb, interview, September 26, 1994.

25. "The President's Economic and Energy Proposals: Gasoline Rationing," Box 13, Folder: Economic and Energy Program, 1/75 (1), Marsh Files, GRFL; "Greenspan, Energy Crisis," Box 4, Folder: Greenspan, Alan, Duval Papers, GRFL; Summary of Economic Meeting, January 14, 1975, Box 30, Folder: EPB-Executive Committee-Meeting Summary Reports, WS Papers, DBSL.

26. *Time*, February 3, 1975, 15; *WP*, December 29, 1974; January 17, 21, 1975; *NYT*, February 2, 1975; *Public Papers*, 1975, 2:61.

27. Rationing, Q&A, Box 13, Folder: Economic and Energy Program, 1/75 (2), Marsh Files, GRFL.

28. *Public Papers*, 1975, 1:61, 62, 68.

29. "Options," Box 24, Folder 49, WS Papers, DBSL; Q&A, October 8, 1974, Box 21, Folder: Economic Program Q&A 1974 (September–October), WS Papers, DBSL.

30. Ford, *A Time to Heal*, 242; President's Energy Briefing Book, December 19, 1974: "Short-Term Energy Program Options and Recommendations," Box 50, Folder: Utilities-Energy: Energy Policy Briefing Book 2, PHF, GRFL.

31. Draft of Energy Section of Economic Report, Box 2, Folder: Economic Policy Address-Energy, McCracken Files, GRFL; *Federal Energy News*, July 1, 1975, Box 7, Folder: Press Releases, June 1975–August 1975, Frank Zarb Files, GRFL.

32. Memorandum to Jones from Michael Raoul-Duval, February 20, 1975, Box 50, Folder: Utilities: Energy-Legislation (1), PHF, GRFL.

33. *Public Papers*, 1975, 1:210.

34. *NYT*, January 3, 1975; Excise Tax and Import Fees on Crude Oil, January 13, 1975, Box 34, Folder: Qs & As-Taxes: 1975 (January 17), WS Papers, DBSL.

35. *NYT*, January 3, 1975.

36. Draft of Energy Section of Economic Report, GRFL; Schleede, interview, October 20, 1994.

37. Ford, interview, March 30, 1994.

38. *Newsweek*, January 27, 1975, 23; *WP*, January 12, 24, 1975.

39. "Proposed National Energy Goals and Principles," Box 50, Folder: Utilities-Energy: Energy Policy Board (2), in President's Energy Briefing Book, December 19, 1974, PHF, GRFL; *WP*, December 29, 1974; *NYT*, June 1, 1975.

40. Meeting Notes, Box 9, Folder: Congressional Leadership Meetings: Republicans, 1/21/75, Marsh Files, GRFL.

41. Zarb, interview, September 26, 1994.

42. "Greenspan, Energy Crisis," Box 4, Folder: Greenspan, Alan, Duval Papers, GRFL; Draft of Energy Section of Economic Report, GRFL.

43. Memorandum to the president from William Baroody Jr., November 13, 1974, Box 22, Folder: SP 2–4/1975 State of the Union, 8/9/74–11/27/74, WHCF SP 2, GRFL.

44. *Public Papers*, 1975, 1:40. Ford meant a reduction from those import levels the United States would otherwise be at without any countervailing government action.

45. Energy Policy Meeting, Camp David, December 14–15, 1974, Box 3, Folder: Camp David Meeting on Energy; December 1974, Duval Files, GRFL.

46. Zarb, interview, September 26, 1994.

47. A Brief Factual Summary of the President's Economic and Energy Programs Outlined in His State of the Union, January 28, 1975 (draft), Box 3, Folder: Economic and Energy Proposals-Spokesman's Briefing Book, 1/29/75, Cheney Files, GRFL; David Davis, *Energy Politics*, 4th ed. (New York: St. Martin's Press, 1993), 62.

48. *NYT*, January 3, 1975; *WP*, January 16, 25, 1975.

49. Memorandum to the president from Dick Cheney, December 21, 1974, Box 4, Cheney Files, GRFL.

50. A Brief Factual Summary of the President's Economic and Energy Programs Outlined in His State of the Union Message, January 28, 1975 (draft), Cheney Files, GRFL.

51. *NYT*, January 15, 1975; The President's Economic and Energy Proposals: A Factual Summary, Box 13, Folder: Economic and Energy Program, 1/75 (1), Marsh Files, GRFL.

Chapter 14. The Energy Stalemate

1. Memorandum to William Seidman from William Gorog, Subject: Second Subcabinet Briefing, Box 63, Folder: Economy and Energy: Meetings-Subcabinet briefing, June 11, 1975, Seidman Files, GRFL; *U.S. News*, August 25, 1975, 15.

2. *NYT*, July 25, 1975.

3. *NYT*, January 15, 1975; *WP*, January 16, 1975.

4. Zarb, interview, February 8, 2003.

5. *NYT*, February 11, 1975; *WP*, January 24, 1975.

6. *WP*, January 14, 1975; *NYT*, January 27, 1975.

7. John A. Hill, interview by author, September 19, 2002.

8. *Time*, January 27, 1975, 19; *NYT*, January 28, 1975; *WP*, January 16, 1975.

9. *WP*, January 15, 1975.

10. Ford, interview, March 30, 1994.

11. Pasternack, interview, March 21, 1994.

12. Duval, interview, March 8, 1994. Besides Ford, the other presidents Duval worked with were Nixon, Reagan, and George H. W. Bush.

13. Ford, interview, March 30. 1994.

14. Zarb, interview, September 26, 1994.

15. Ford, interviews, March 30, 1994, October 25, 1994; Zarb, interview, September 26, 1994; *Congressional Quarterly Almanac 1975*, 196; NYT, January 26, 1975.

16. Nordhaus, interview, September 18, 2003; Memorandum from Ron Nessen, May 27, 1975, Box 51, Folder: Utilities-Energy Legislation (6), PHF, GRFL.

17. WP, January 16, February 20, August 12, 1975; Pasternack, interview, March 21, 1994.

18. Conable, interview, February 9, 1994.

19. Memorandum to the president from Robert Goldwin, January 31, 1975, Box 3, Folder: FG, 1/1/75–1/31/75, WHCF, GRFL.

20. NYT, July 27, 1975; "Northeast," in The President's Economic and Energy Proposals: A Summary for the Layman, Box 13, Folder: Economic and Energy Program, 1/75 (1), Marsh Files, GRFL; NYT, January 17, 1975.

21. The President's Economic and Energy Proposals: A Factual Summary, Box 13, Folder: Economic and Energy Program, 1/75 (1), Marsh Files, GRFL.

22. Ford, interview, March 30, 1994.

23. WP, January 24, February 4, 1975; "Greenspan, Energy Crisis," Box 4, Folder: Greenspan, Alan, Duval Papers, GRFL; *Time*, February 3, 1975, 12.

24. NYT, January 16, 21, 28, 1975; The eight governors represented New York, Pennsylvania, Connecticut, Massachusetts, Maine, New Jersey, Rhode Island, and Vermont.

25. Memorandum to the president, January 31, 1975, Box 14, Marsh Files, GRFL; *Public Papers*, 1975, 1:213.

26. Memorandum to the president from Max Friedersdorf, February 17, 1975, Box 16, Folder: Energy-Oil Import Fees (2), Marsh Files, GRFL.

27. NYT, February 6, 1975.

28. Conable, interview, February 9, 1994.

29. *Public Papers*, 1975, 1:217; Zarb, interview, September 26, 1994.

30. Zarb, "Discussant: Frank Zarb," 354.

31. Letter to Ron Nessen from Gerald Drake of Raleigh, N.C., February 25, 1975, Box 27, Folder: BE 5, 4/1/75–11/8/75, WHCF BE 5, GRFL.

32. *Public Papers*, 1975, 1:209, 217, 222.

33. NYT, February 13, 21, 1975; *Time*, March 10, 1975, 11.

34. NYT, February 20, 1975; Republican Congressional Meeting, March 3, 1975, Box 5, Folder: Congressional Meetings with President, Nessen Files, GRFL.

35. *Public Papers*, 1975, 1:315; NYT, March 5, 1975; *Congressional Quarterly Almanac 1975*, 195.

36. NYT, April 11, 1975; WP, April 11, 1975.

37. *Congressional Quarterly Almanac 1975*, 208–11; WP, April 16, 21, 29, 1975.

38. Memorandum to Max Friedersdorf from Douglas Bennett, April 28, 1975, Box 12, Folder: Energy, April–May 1975, Friedersdorf Files, GRFL.

39. Ford, interview, March 30, 1994; WP, April 28, 1975.

40. Memorandum to the president from Frank Zarb, April 28, 1975, Box 1, Folder: Memorandum to the President, 4/18/75–5/30/75, Zarb Files, GRFL.

41. *Public Papers, 1975*, 1:611; *NYT*, May 1, 1975.

42. *NYT*, May 28, 1975.

43. Hartmann, interview, October 17, 1994; *NYT*, May 28, 1975; *Public Papers, 1975*, 1:730–31.

44. *WP*, May 28, 31, 1975; Letter to Carl Albert from Skulli Stefanson, June 20, 1975, Ways and Means Energy Conservation, June 10–October 9, 1975, Box L-151, Legislative Files: Energy, Spring 1975, Carl Albert Papers, CACRSC.

45. Energy Clippings, 88:32, General Files: Energy-Spring 1975, Carl Albert Papers, CACRSC.

46. Charles Percy, interview by author, March 1, 1994; *National Journal*, June 21, 1975, 924.

47. *Public Papers of the Presidents, Richard Nixon*, November 7, 1973; *NYT*, May 28, 29, June 15, October 29, 1975.

48. Anderson, interview, May 5, 1994. When Congressman Anderson ran for president in 1980 as an independent candidate, a cornerstone of his campaign platform was a $.50-per-gallon gasoline tax, which he believed would force conservation and raise revenue for the federal coffers. While he admitted that his proposal was a draconian measure, he felt that it was needed "to discipline ourselves so that we could slake our insatiable thirst for imported oil."

49. *NYT*, September 1, 1975; Memorandum to John Marsh from Frank Zarb, July 18, 1975, Box 3, Folder: Chronological Files, August 1–11, 1975, Paul O'Neill Papers; Memorandum to Jim Connor from Mike Duval, July 30, 1975, Box 5, Folder: Energy Conservation, Duval Files, GRFL.

50. *Newsweek*, February 24, 1975, 16.

51. *U.S. News*, March 3, 1975, 20; Franklin Tugwell, *The Energy Crisis and the American Political Economy: Politics and Markets in the Management of Natural Resources* (Stanford, Calif.: Stanford Univ. Press, 1988), 108; *NYT*, May 28, 1975.

52. Memorandum to the president from Frank Zarb, March 8, 1975, Box 50, Folder: Utilities-Energy-Legislation (2), PHF, GRFL.

53. *WP*, January 15, August 14, 1975; Speech text, Delaware City, Iowa (11/17/75) Box 1026, Birch Bayh Papers, Lilly Library, IU.

54. Schleede, interview, October 20, 1994.

55. Matusow, *Nixon's Economy*, 275.

56. Zarb, interview, September 26, 1994; Hill, interview, September 19, 2002.

57. Schleede, interview, October 20, 1994; *National Journal*, April 26, 1975, 619; Alfred Marcus, *Controversial Issues in Energy Policy* (Newbury Park, Calif: Sage Publications, 1992), 50.

58. *Time*, March 10, 1975, 11; *WP*, February 23, 1975.

59. Memorandum to Jerry Jones from Mike Duval, Box 50, Folder: Utilities: Energy-Legislation (1), PHF, GRFL.

60. Memorandum to the president from Robert Hartmann, December 18, 1975, Box 11, Folder: EPCA, Hartmann Files, GRFL.; Nessen, "The Ford Presidency and the Press," in Thompson, 189.

61. Meeting with Republican Congressional Leaders, January 21, 1975, Box 9, Folder: Congressional Leadership Meetings, Republicans 1/21/75, Marsh Files, GRFL.

62. James Katz, *Congress and National Energy Policy* (New Brunswick, N.J.: Transaction Books, 1984), 20–21; *National Journal*, June 7, 1975, 837; Opinion Research Corporation, *Highlight Report* 15 (October 1975): 8; Carter, *Keeping Faith*, 93.

63. WP, January 3, 1975; Letter to Carl Albert from Monique Hothuis, October 30, 1974, Interest and Foreign Commerce, October 2, 1975–November 24, 1975, L-161, Legislative Files: Energy, Albert Papers, CACRSC.

64. Pasternack, interview, March 21, 1994.

65. Ford, interview, March 30, 1994.

66. *Congressional Quarterly Almanac 1975*, 236.

67. Hill, interview, September 19, 2002; *NYT*, July 23, 31, 1975.

68. Memorandum from Douglas Bennett to Max Friedersdorf, March 19, 1975, Box 16, Folder: Energy-Proposal by Representative Al Ullman, 1/75–5/75, Marsh Files, GRFL.

69. Memorandum to the president from Frank Zarb, March 8, 1975, Box 50, Folder: Utilities-Energy-Legislation (2), PHF, GRFL.

70. Zarb, interview, September 26, 1994.

71. *Long Island Press*, July 20, 1975, in Box 6, Folder: Newspaper Clippings, Zarb Files, GRFL; Pasternack, interview, March 21, 1994.

72. Ford, *A Time to Heal*, 243; Edwards, *Presidential Influence*, 4, 47; *NYT*, May 29, 1975; WP, January 28, 30, 1975.

73. Letter to Carl Albert from Nadine Clark, June 17, 1975, Ways and Means Energy Conservation, June 10–October 9, 1975, Box L-151, Legislative Files: Energy-Spring 1975, Albert Papers, CACRSC.

74. *Congressional Quarterly Almanac 1975*, 175; Davis, *Energy Politics*, 63.

75. Bennett, interview, October 19, 1994.

76. Zarb, interview, September 26, 1994.

77. WP, January 30, 1975; Friedersdorf, interview, August 14, 2001.

78. Nordhaus, interview, September 18, 2003.

79. John Dingell, telephone interview by author, February 14, 1994; WP, April 16, 1975; *Baltimore Sun*, August 1, 1975.

80. WP, August 13, 1975.

81. Charles Leppert, interview by William Syers, GRFL; WP, May 23, 25, 1975; *Public Papers*, 1975, 1:801.

82. *NYT*, July 25, 1975; Ford, *A Time to Heal*, 243–44; News clipping, Box 2, Folder 57, Biographical Files: Energy, Albert Papers, CACRSC.

83. *Economist*, May 31, 1975, 53.

84. Ford, interview, March 30, 1994.

Chapter 15. Breaking the Energy Logjam

1. Dale Bumpers, interview by author, June 17, 2003; Zarb, interview, February 8, 2003.

2. Ford, *A Time to Heal*, 341.

3. The vote rejecting the gas tax was a resounding 345–72. *NYT*, June 13, 1975; WP, June 12, 1975.

4. Zarb, interview, September 26, 1994.

5. *NYT*, June 13, 20, 1975; *WP*, June 20, 1975.

6. Pasternack, interview, March 21, 1994; Oval Office meeting memorandum from Frank Zarb, March 18, 1975, Box 9, Folder: Legislative Alternatives to President's Energy Program-Congress (3), Duval Files, GRFL.

7. Zarb, interview, September 26, 1994; Memorandum to the president from Frank Zarb, March 8, 1975, Box 50, Folder: Utilities-Energy-Legislation (2), PHF, GRFL.

8. Zarb, interview, September 26, 1994.

9. *Public Papers, 1975*, 1:989–90; *NYT*, July 15, 1975.

10. *Public Papers, 1975*, 1:990; *NYT*, July 20, 27, 1975.

11. *Public Papers, 1975*, 1:1030; *WP*, July 26, 1975; Fact Sheet: Oil Price Decontrol, Box 8, Folder: Energy-Oil Decontrol (1), Loen and Leppert Files, GRFL.

12. *Federal Energy News*, July 30, 1975, Box 8, Folder: Energy-Oil Decontrol (2), Loen and Leppert Files, GRFL; *Washington Star*, July 28, 1975.

13. Zarb, interview, September 26, 1994.

14. *NYT*, August 12, 1975.

15. *Ann Arbor News*, August 22, 1975.

16. Memorandum to the president from Frank Zarb, August 6, 1975, Box 1, Folder: Memoranda to the President 8/1/75–8/6/75, Zarb Files, GRFL; *NYT*, September 1, 1975.

17. "The Energy Allocation Act Should Be Extended," Box 3, Folder: Business and Economics-Industry: Petroleum 8/23/75–9/75, PHF, GRFL; "The Impact of Decontrol of Oil Prices," Congressional Budget Office, Box 48, Folder: Oil Decontrol (1), Greenspan Files, GRFL.

18. *NYT*, September 11, 1975; Letter to Mike Mansfield and Carl Albert from Frank Zarb, August 29, 1975, Box 12, Folder: Energy, August–December 1975, Friedersdorf Files, GRFL.

19. Zarb, interview, February 8, 2003.

20. Zarb, interview, September 26, 1994.

21. Curtis, interview, January 22, 2003; *NYT*, September 26, 27, 1975.

22. *NYT*, September 27, 1975.

23. "Public Opinion on Decontrol," Box 44, Folder: August 29, 1975, Nessen Papers, GRFL; *WSJ* editorial, August 4, 1975, in Box 8, Folder: Energy Legislation-General (2), Loen and Leppert Files, GRFL.

24. Statement of Hon. John Dingell, July 2, 1975, Box, 8, Folder: EPCA (3), Loen and Leppert Files, GRFL; John A. Hill, interview, September 19, 2002.

25. "Summary of the Adverse Effects of the Energy Policy and Conservation Act of 1975," Box 44, Folder: Energy-Legislation (1), Greenspan Files, GRFL; "Conference Energy Bill," Memorandum to Jim Connor from Frank Zarb, Box 2, Folder: Memorandum to the President 11/1–12/75, Zarb Files, GRFL; Memorandum to the president from Frank Zarb, November 7, 1975, Box 2, Folder: Memorandum to the President 11/1–12/75, Zarb Files, GRFL.

26. "Summary," Box 12, Folder: Energy 1975: Omnibus Energy Bill (S.622), October–November (2), Glenn Schleede Files, GRFL; "Summary of the Adverse Effects of the Energy Policy and Conservation Act of 1975," Box 44, Folder: Energy-Legislation (1), Greenspan Files, GRFL; The White House Fact Sheet: Energy Policy and Conservation

Act (S. 622), December 22, Box 9, Folder: Energy-General (2), Nessen Papers, GRFL; *Time*, November 24, 1975, 91.

27. "Significant Problems with the Non-Pricing Provisions of Conference Bill," Box 12, Folder: Energy, 1975: Omnibus Energy Bill (S. 622), October–November (2), Schleede Files, GRFL; *WP*, January 16, 1976.

28. Summary of Conference Committee Omnibus Energy Bill, Box 44, Folder: Energy-Legislation (2), Greenspan Files, GRFL; "Significant Problems with the Non-Pricing Provisions of Conference Bill," Box 12, Folder: Energy, 1975: Omnibus Energy Bill (S. 622), October–November (2), Schleede Files, GRFL; Richardson and Zarb, *Perspectives on Energy Policy*, 31; *Time*, January 5, 1976, 34.

29. "Summary: Assessment of the Omnibus Energy Bill," Box 12, Folder: Energy, 1975: Omnibus Energy Bill (S. 622), October–November (2), Schleede Files, GRFL; *Time*, January 5, 1976, 34.

30. Letter from Henry Jackson, November 14, 1975, Box 12, Folder: Energy, 1975: Omnibus Energy Bill (S. 622), Oct–Nov (1) Schleede Files, GRFL; Letter from Harley Staggers et al., December 3, 1975, Box 12, Folder: Energy, 1975: Omnibus Energy Bill (S. 622), December (3), Schleede Files, GRFL.

31. Memorandum to the president from William Simon, December 8, 1975, Box 51, Folder: Utilities-Energy Legislation (1), PHF, GRFL.

32. Memorandum to the president from Frank Zarb, November 7, 1975, Box 2, Folder: 11/1–11/14/75, Zarb Files, GRFL; Memorandum to the president from William Simon, December 8, 1975, Box 51, Folder: Utilities-Energy Legislation (1), PHF, GRFL.

33. Draft memorandum to the president from Alan Greenspan, "The Long-Term Effects of the Conference Energy Bill," Box 44, Folder: Energy-Legislation (2), Greenspan Files, GRFL.

34. Comments on the pricing provision of the Energy Policy and Conservation Act (prepared by the American Petroleum Institute Staff), December 1, 1975, Box 12, Folder: Energy, 1975: Omnibus Energy Bill (S. 622), December (2), Schleede Files, GRFL; Memorandum from Frank Zarb (undated), Box 12, Folder: Energy, 1975: Omnibus Energy Bill (S. 622), Oct–Nov (1), Schleede Files, GRFL.

35. *NYT*, November 15, 1975; Letter to the president from Barber B. Conable Jr., November 17, 1975, Congressional Mail File: Conable, Barber B. (1), GRFL.

36. Memorandum to the president from Jim Cannon, November 26, 1975, Box 51, Folder: Utilities-Energy-Legislation (7), PHF, GRFL; Memorandum from Glenn Schleede, December 15, 1975, Box 12, Folder: Energy, 1975: Omnibus Energy Bill (S. 622), December (3), Schleede Files, GRFL.

37. *NYT*, December 2, 1975; *Newsweek*, January 5, 1976, 59; Memorandum to the president from William Seidman, December 6, 1975, Box 76, Folder: Memoranda to the President, 1975–May 1976 (1), Seidman Files, GRFL (hereafter cited as Seidman memo, December 6, 1975); *NYT*, December 2, 1975.

38. Hill, interview, September 19, 2002.

39. Letter to John Marsh and Max Friedersdorf from Frank Zarb, December 9, 1975, Box 2, Folder: Memoranda to the President, 11/25/75–12/12/75, Zarb Files, GRFL; Seidman memo, December 6, 1975.

40. Memorandum to Frank Zarb from John Hill, November 18, 1975, Box 44, Folder:

Energy-Legislation (2), Greenspan Files, GRFL (hereafter cited as Hill memo, November 18, 1975).

41. Hill, interview, September 19, 2002.

42. Memorandum to the president from Robert Hartmann, December 18, 1975, Box 11, Folder: Energy Policy and Conservation Act, Hartmann Files, GRFL.

43. These advisers included Phil Buchen, Max Friedersdorf, Brent Scowcroft, and William Seidman; Seidman memo, December 6, 1975; Memoranda to Jim Connor from Phil Buchen and Max Friedersdorf, both December 18, 1975; Memorandum to the president from Brent Scowcroft (undated); all found in Box 11, Folder: Energy Policy and Conservation Act, Hartmann Files, GRFL. Henry Kissinger and Arthur Burns also urged Ford to sign EPCA; Hill, interview, September 19, 2002.

44. Zarb, interview, February 8, 2003; Memorandum to Dick Cheney from Jerry Jones, November 21, 1975, Box 20, Folder: Subject File-Energy, Jerry Jones File, GRFL; Zarb, "Discussant: Frank G. Zarb," in Firestone and Ugrinsky, *Gerald R. Ford*, 2:354–55.

45. Ford, interview, March 30, 1994.

46. Zarb, interview, September 26, 1994.

47. *WP*, December 8, 1975.

48. Seidman memo, December 6, 1975; Hill memo, November 18, 1975; Pasternack, interview, March 21, 1994.

49. Ford, *A Time to Heal*, 341; *Public Papers, 1975*, 2:1516.

50. Hill, interview, September 19, 2002.

51. Seidman memo, December 6, 1975.

52. Pasternack, interview, March 21, 1994; Hill memo, November 18, 1975; *Time*, November 24, 1975, 91; MacAvoy, interview, May 2, 2002.

53. *Public Papers, 1975*, 1:741–42.

54. Ford, interview, March 30, 1994.

55. Simon, *A Time for Truth*, 79–80.

56. Ford, interview, March 30, 1994.

57. Zarb, interview, September 26, 1994.

58. MacAvoy, interview, May 2, 2002.

59. Curtis, interview, January 22, 2003.

60. Joseph Kalt, *The Economics and Politics of Oil Price Regulation: Federal Policy in the Post-Embargo Era* (Cambridge, Mass.: MIT Press, 1981), 91, 207.

61. Hill, interview, May 11, 2004.

62. Ford, interview, October 25, 1994.

63. *Public Papers of the President, 1976–1977*, 1:573, 2:1286; Nordhaus, interview, September 18, 2004.

64. *Congressional Record-House*, December 11, 1975, H 12342; *Public Papers, 1975*, 2:1332, 1666.

65. Hill, interview, May 11, 2004.

66. Zarb, interview, September 26, 1994.

67. Ford, interview, March 30, 1994.

68. Zarb, interview, September 26, 1994.

69. Zarb, interview, February 8, 2003.

70. *WSJ*, May 3, 1976.

71. Richardson and Zarb, *Perspectives on Energy Policy*, 2; *NYT*, October 18, 1976; *Time*, November 8, 1976, 92; *WSJ*, June 16, 1976; *U.S. News*, January 26, 1976, 20; Memorandum to Bo Calloway from Bob Teeter, December 5, 1975, Box 4, Folder: Teeter, Robert—Memoranda and Polling Data (3), Foster Chanock Files, GRFL.

72. Box 121, Folder: Vetoes, Memorandum from October 30, 1974, Nessen Papers, GRFL; Memorandum from James T. Lynn, September 8, 1976, WHCF: Legislation Case Files, 1974–76, Box 55, Folder: 9/13/76, HR 8800 (1), GRFL.

73. Glenn Schleede, interview by author, August 28, 2002.

74. *Congressional Quarterly Almanac 1976*, 146.

75. "An Answer to the Energy Crisis," Record Group 26, Nelson Rockefeller Vice Presidential, Series 15, Box 4, Folder: Energy Independence Authority, Rockefeller Archive Center; Ford, *A Time to Heal*, 327.

76. Memorandum to the president from the vice president, May 1975, Box 13, Folder: Energy Independence Authority, May 1, 1975, Domestic Council: Cannon Files, 1975–77, GRFL; Draft, Zarb EIA Testimony, April 1976, Box 12, Folder: Energy, 1976: Energy Independence Authority, Schleede Files, GRFL; Fact Sheet on the Energy Independence Authority, October 10, 1975, Box 11, Folder: Energy, 1975: Energy Independency Authority (2), Schleede Files, GRFL; Davis, *Energy Politics*, 51.

77. Hill, interview, September 19, 2002.

78. Zarb, interview, February 8, 2003; Ford, interview, January 24, 2002; MacAvoy, interview, May 2, 2002.

79. Statement of the vice president, April 12, 1976, Record Group 26, Series 13, Subseries: EIA, Box 25, Rockefeller Archive Center.

80. Glozer, interview, April 22, 2004; MacAvoy, e-mail message to author, June 23, 2004.

81. Davis, *Energy Politics*, 53–55; Zarb, interview, February 8, 2003.

82. Schleede, interview, August 28, 2002.

83. MacAvoy, interview, May 2, 2002.

84. James Lynn, telephone interview by author, February 14, 2002.

85. Zarb, interview, February 8, 2003; Ford, interview, January 24, 2002; Hill, interview, May 11, 2004.

86. Seidman, interview, May 19, 2004.

87. *WSJ*, January 28, February 3, 1976.

88. Signing of the Naval Petroleum Reserves Production Act of 1976, Box 18, Folder: Naval Petroleum Reserve, 1976: Signing Ceremony, April 5 (1), Schleede Files, GRFL; *NYT*, March 5, July 3, 1976; *WSJ*, April 1, 1976.

89. *Congressional Quarterly Almanac 1976*, 107.

90. Statement by the president, January 4, 1975, Box 8, Folder: Deepwater Ports, 1974 (1), Schleede Files, GRFL; *WSJ*, December 20, 1976.

91. Hill, interview, May 11, 2004; *NYT*, August 11, 15, 1976; *WP*, August 11, 1976.

92. Richardson and Zarb, *Perspectives on Energy Policy*, 26, 44; *NYT*, August 11, 1976; *WSJ*, August 11, 16, 1976; *Congressional Quarterly Almanac 1976*, 95–96.

93. Zarb, interview, February 8, 2003.

94. *NYT*, June 30, 1976.

95. Hill, interview, September 19, 2002.

96. *NYT*, February 14, March 30, April 23, 1976; *Congressional Quarterly Almanac 1976*, 180–81; *WSJ*, July 21, 1976.

97. Hill, interview, September 19, 2002.

98. "Rationale for Exempting Middle Distillates . . . ," Box 9, Folder: Federal Energy Adm-Middle Distillates, Loen and Leppert Files, GRFL; Memorandum from Jim Cannon, August 13, 1976, WHCF: Legislation Case Files, 1974–76, Box 53, Folder: 8/14/76 HR 12169 (1), GRFL; Memorandum from Frank Zarb, September 9, 1976, Box 18, Folder: FEA, 1976: General, July–November, Schleede Files, GRFL; Memorandum from Frank Zarb, August 5, 1976, Box 31, Folder: Oil Decontrol, 1976, Schleede Files, GRFL; Richardson and Zarb, *Perspectives on Energy Policy*, 26.

99. *NYT*, October 18, 1976.

100. *NYT*, January 20, 25, 1977.

101. *Economist*, May 24, 2003, 78; *NYT*, July 28, 1976; *Time*, January 7, 1974.

102. *NYT*, October 18, 1976; Reichley, *Conservatives*, 372; *Congressional Quarterly Almanac 1974* (Washington, D.C.: Congressional Quarterly Press, 1974), 801; *NYT*, November 11, 1973; *WSJ*, January 27, 1976; *Time*, January 7, 1974, 40.

103. Nordhaus, interview, September 18, 2003.

104. *WSJ*, January 27, May 19, 1976.

105. *NYT*, April 19, 1973; February 3, 1976.

106. *Congressional Quarterly Almanac 1974*, 802; *NYT*, September 11, 1973; January 30, 1976.

107. *NYT*, February 27, 1976.

108. Nordhaus, interview, September 18, 2003; *Congressional Quarterly Almanac 1976*, 171.

109. *Newsweek*, August 9, 1976, 55.

110. Draft of Zarb Testimony, Box 18, Folder: FEA, 1976: General, December, Schleede Files, GRFL; Richardson and Zarb, *Perspectives on Energy Policy*, 78.

111. *NYT*, March 22, April 8, 1975.

112. *Public Papers, 1974*, 780–81; *NYT*, April 8, 9, May 2, 21, 1975.

113. Hill, interview, May 11, 2004; *NYT*, May 8, 20, June 11, 1975.

114. Draft of Zarb Testimony, Schleede Files, GRFL; Richardson and Zarb, *Perspectives on Energy Policy*, 78; *Time*, December 3, 1973, 35; March 1, 1976, 45–47.

115. *NYT*, February 8, 1976; *WSJ*, July 2, 1976; *Statistical Abstract of the United States 2002*, 563.

116. Draft of Zarb Testimony, Schleede Files, GRFL.

117. Letter to the president from Mike Mansfield, August 29, 1975, Box 10, Folder: Energy-Oil Decontrol, Nessen Papers, GRFL.

118. Hill, interview, May 11, 2004.

119. Arabinda Ghosh, *OPEC, the Petroleum Industry, and United States Energy Policy* (Westport, Conn.: Quorum Books, 1983), 174; Nessen, *It Sure Looks Different*, 89.

Chapter 16. Ford's Internationalism

1. Papers of Gerald R. Ford, Staff Secretary, Special Files, Box 2, Folder: Second Debate: Ford Notes on Briefing Materials, GRFL; Ford, *A Time to Heal*, 58–61.

2. Ford, *A Time to Heal*, 61; *Michigan Alumnus*, March/April 1986, 30, 39, Vertical File, GRFL.

3. Ford, interview, August 21, 2003.

4. *U.S. News*, April 7, 1975, 11.

5. Elizabeth Drew, *American Journal: The Events of 1976* (New York: Random House, 1977), 83.

6. Henry Kissinger, *Years of Renewal* (New York: Simon and Schuster, 1999), 33, 93.

7. Jeffrey Charnley, "Power Apprenticeship: Congressman Gerald R. Ford and the Vietnam War, 1964–1973," in Firestone and Ugrinski, *Gerald R. Ford*, 2:505–21.

8. Cannon, *Time and Chance*, 62–64; Ford, *A Time to Heal*, 128–29; *NYT*, November 18, 1974.

9. *Economist*, March 6, 1976, 36.

10. Kissinger, *Years of Renewal*, 37, 1064.

11. Ford, *A Time to Heal*, 137; Greene, *The Presidency of Gerald R. Ford*, 118; *U.S. News*, July 21, 1975, 58; Kissinger, *Years of Renewal*, 196–97, 199; *NYT*, August 15, 20, 1974.

12. *NYT*, August 19, 1974.

13. *Gerald Ford's America*, Part 4, produced by TVTV and the Television Laboratory at WNET-13, video, GRFL.

14. Ford, *A Time to Heal*, 137–38; Kissinger, *Years of Renewal*, 236; Greene, *The Presidency of Gerald R. Ford*, 118; *Economist*, February 15, 1975, 11–12; August 2, 1975, 45; *U.S. News*, August 5, 1974, 25; *NYT*, August 6, 1974.

15. Ford, *A Time to Heal*, 302.

16. "Comments from Members contacted" and "House Vote On Turkey Produces High Cost," Box 26, Folder: Turkey-Military Aid (3) and Turkey-Military Aid (4), Loen and Leppert Files, GRFL.

17. Kissinger, *Years of Renewal*, 238; *Economist*, February 15, 1975, 12.

18. *Economist*, April 5, 1975, 13; April 19, 1975, 69; *NYT*, August 20, 1974.

19. Ford, *A Time to Heal*, 139; Kissinger, *Years of Renewal*, 129; *U.S. News*, January 27, 1975, 24.

20. Stephen Ambrose, *Rise to Globalism: American Foreign Policy since 1938*, 5th ed. (New York: Penguin Books, 1988), 280; Kissinger, *Years of Renewal*, 128.

21. Ford, *A Time to Heal*, 138; Schapsmeier and Schapsmeier, *Date with Destiny*, 188.

22. Ford, *A Time to Heal*, 216–17; Greene, *The Presidency of Gerald R. Ford*, 122; Kissinger, *Years of Renewal*, 131, 270.

23. Yergin, *The Prize*, 656.

24. Ford, *A Time to Heal*, 138–39.

25. Kissinger, *Years of Renewal*, 131; Dobrynin, *In Confidence*, 335.

26. Ford, interview, August 21, 2003.

27. Ford, *A Time to Heal*, 225; Walter Isaacson, *Kissinger: A Biography* (New York: Simon and Schuster, 1992), 620; *U.S. News*, January 27, 1974, 24; Kissinger, *Years of Renewal*, 304, 308; Dobrynin, *In Confidence*, 334, 337.

28. Isaacson, *Kissinger*, 549, 572.

29. *Economist*, April 26, 1975, 69–70; *U.S. News*, October 28, 1974; October 11, 1976, 33; *NYT*, September 20, 1974.

30. *Economist*, March 20, 1976, 48; April 26, 1975, 69.

31. Joseph Sisco, "Ford, Kissinger and the Nixon-Ford Foreign Policy," in Thompson, *The Ford Presidency*, 331.

32. Papers of Gerald R. Ford, Staff Secretary, Special Files, Box 2, Folder: Second Debate: Carter on Foreign Policy (1), GRFL; Henry Plotin, "Issues in the 1976 Presidential Campaign," in *The Election of 1976: Reports and Interpretations*, Gerald Pomper et al., 50 (New York: Longman, 1977).

33. Ford, *A Time to Heal*, 129.

34. Ford, interview, August 21, 2003.

35. *Newsweek*, December 9, 1974, 23; Hartmann, *Palace Politics*, 329.

36. Ford, interview, August 21, 2003.

37. *U.S. News*, June 30, 1975, 39.

38. Ford, *A Time to Heal*, 125.

39. Dobrynin, *In Confidence*, 321.

40. *U.S. News*, February 16, 1976, 12; Dobrynin, *In Confidence*, 334.

41. Greene, *The Presidency of Gerald R. Ford*, 124; Isaacson, *Kissinger*, 624, 626.

42. *NYT*, November 23, 1974; *Newsweek*, November 18, 1974, 35.

43. Ford, *A Time to Heal*, 214; Dobrynin, *In Confidence*, 328.

44. Ford, *A Time to Heal*, 216, 219.

45. Ford, interview, August 21, 2003.

46. Nessen, *It Sure Looks Different*, 48.

47. Dobrynin, *In Confidence*, 329.

48. Greene, *The Presidency of Gerald R. Ford*, 126; Robert Schulzinger, "The Decline of Detente," in Firestone and Ugrinsky, *Gerald R. Ford*, 2:409.

49. Dobrynin, *In Confidence*, 349–50.

50. Ford, *A Time to Heal*, 357–58; Isaacson, *Kissinger*, 628, 629.

51. Ford, interview, August 21, 2003.

52. Kissinger, *Years of Renewal*, 791.

53. *Economist*, March 6, 1976, 36; May 29, 1976, 33–34.

54. Schapsmeier and Schapsmeier, *Date with Destiny*, 197.

55. Ambrose, *Rise to Globalism*, 288; Dobrynin, *In Confidence*, 371; Kissinger, *Years of Renewal*, 810.

56. Kissinger, *Years of Renewal*, 823–35, 826.

57. *Newsweek*, December 29, 1975, 28.

58. Angola news stories, Box 19, Folder: 7.15 Angola (1), McCall Files, GRFL; Ford, *A Time to Heal*, 359.

59. Talking Points from Brent Scowcroft, Box 33, Folder: National Security, Wars-Angola, PHF, GRFL; Kissinger, *Years of Renewal*, 831.

60. Isaacson, *Kissinger*, 683.

61. *Time*, March 15, 1976, 12; Thomas Paterson and J. Garry Clifford, *America Ascendant: U.S. Foreign Relations since 1939* (Lexington, Mass.: D.C. Heath and Company, 1995), 203.

62. Ford, *A Time to Heal*, 346.

63. *Newsweek*, January 19, 1976, 20.

64. Reichley, *Conservatives*, 353–54.

65. Isaacson, *Kissinger*, 609.

66. Ford, interview, August 21, 2003.

67. NYT, April 13, 1975; *The Gallup Opinion Index*, February 1974, 9.

68. *National Journal*, March 20. 1976, 364–65; Jerald Combs, *The History of American Foreign Policy*, 2nd ed. (New York: McGraw-Hill, 1997), 410; *Economist*, April 5, 1975, 12–13.

69. NYT, October 17, 1976; Ford, *A Time to Heal*, 275.

70. *Economist*, April 5, 1975, 12–13.

71. Ford, interview, August 21, 2003.

72. Seevers, interview, January 16, 2003.

73. Reichley, *Conservatives*, 338; *Economist*, February 22, 1975, 54; Letter to President Ford, March 7, 1975, Box 5, Folder: Vietnam: General, Wolthius Files, GRFL.

74. *Vietnam: A Television History*, produced by WGHB, 1996 and *Vietnam: The 10,000-Day War*, BWE Video, 1980.

75. Ford, *A Time to Heal*, 253; Greene, *The Presidency of Gerald R. Ford*, 136–37.

76. Ford, interview, August 21, 2003.

77. Nessen, *It Sure Looks Different*, 94–96; Osborne, *White House Watch*, 102.

78. Ford, interview, August 21, 2003.

79. Ford, *A Time to Heal*, 254.

80. Ford, *A Time to Heal*, 254, 255; Memorandum to Max Friedersdorf from Bill Kendall, April 7, 1975, Box 33, Folder: National Security, Wars-Vietnam (1), PHF, GRFL; Series 4, Subseries 2, Box 135, Jacob Javits Papers, Stony Brook University, Stony Brook, N.Y.; "Comments of Select Members with Respect to RVN," Box 33, Folder: National Security, Wars-Vietnam (1), PHF, GRFL; *U.S. News*, March 17, 1975, 17–18.

81. Isaacson, *Kissinger*, 648; "Vietnam: A Television History"; Nessen, *It Sure Looks Different*, 101.

82. Ford, interview, August 21, 2003.

83. Hartmann, *Palace Politics*, 322.

84. Paul Theis, interview by author, September 17, 2003.

85. Nessen, *It Sure Looks Different*, 108.

86. Ford, *A Time to Heal*, 252–53.

87. *Inside the Cold War*, produced by David Paradine Television (1998).

88. Ford, *A Time to Heal*, 252; Nessen, *It Sure Looks Different*, 114–15; NYT, May 11, 1975.

89. Nessen, interview, January 29, 2004.

90. Ford, *A Time to Heal*, 252, 257; NYT, April 6, 7, 1975.

91. Nessen, interview, January 29, 2004.

92. Ford, *A Time to Heal*, 257.

93. *U.S. News*, May 19, 1975, 22.

94. Nessen, *It Sure Looks Different*, 130.

95. Hartmann, *Palace Politics*, 327.

96. Cannon, *Time and Chance*, 399; Greene, *The Presidency of Gerald R. Ford*, 150.

97. See Ralph Wetterhahn, *The Last Battle: The Mayaguez Incident and the End of the Vietnam War* (New York: Carroll and Graf, 2001), especially chs. 30–33.

98. Michael Hamm, "The Pueblo and Mayaguez Incidents: A Study of Flexible Response and Decision-Making," *Asian Survey* (June 1977): 550.

99. Ford, *A Time to Heal*, 282; *Newsweek*, May 26, 1975, 6–27.

100. Ford, *A Time to Heal*, 298; Michael O'Mara report on CSCE, Box 66, Folder: 7/26–8/4/75, Finland-CSCE (5), Nessen Papers, GRFL (hereafter cited as O'Mara report, GRFL).

101. Ford, *A Time to Heal*, 300; Greene, *The Presidency of Gerald R. Ford*, 153.

102. Hartmann, *Palace Politics*, 340; "Conference on Security and Cooperation in Europe," Box 65, Folder: 7/26/75–8/4/75, Finland-CSCE (1), Nessen Papers, GRFL.

103. Background Briefing, July 23, 1975, Box 40, Folder: Material Not Released to the Press, Nessen Files, GRFL.

104. O'Mara report, GRFL; "Conference on Security and Cooperation in Europe," GRFL; *WSJ*, July 9, 1975, 10; Isaacson, *Kissinger*, 660; Dobrynin, *In Confidence*, 345–46.

105. Hartmann, *Palace Politics*, 344.

106. Box 25, Folder: International Orgs. CSCE, PHF, GRFL.

107. Ford, *A Time to Heal*, 299.

108. Box 13, Folder IT 104, CSCE 8/9/74–7/31/75, WHCF SF, GRFL.

109. Leo Ribuffo, *Right Center Left: Essays in American History* (New Brunswick, N.J.: Rutgers University Press, 1992), 295; Box 13, Folder: IT 104 CSCE, 8/1/75–8/31/75, WHCF, GRFL.

110. Ford, *A Time to Heal*, 301, 306.

111. Hartmann, *Palace Politics*, 339, 340; Papers of Gerald R. Ford, Staff Secretary, Special Files, Box 2, Folder: Second Debate: Carter on Foreign Policy (1), GRFL.

112. Papers of Gerald R. Ford, Staff Secretary, Special Files, Box 2, Folder: Second Debate: Ford Notes on Briefing Materials, GRFL; Ford, *A Time to Heal*, 299.

113. O'Mara report, GRFL; Kissinger, *Years of Renewal*, 639.

114. Box 49, Folder: Trips-Foreign (2), PHF, GRFL.

115. Ford, *A Time to Heal*, 299; Osborne, *White House Watch*, 174, 175.

116. *WSJ*, July 9, 1975.

117. Kissinger, *Years of Renewal*, 100.

118. Essay by Robert Goldwin, Box 49, Folder: Trips-Foreign (2), PHF, GRFL.

119. Kissinger, *Years of Renewal*, 660; Cannon, *Time and Chance*, 400.

120. Ford, interview, January 24, 2002.

121. Reichley, *Conservatives*, 337.

122. Papers of Gerald R. Ford, Staff Secretary, Special Files, Box 2, Folder: Second Debate: Ford Meetings with Foreign Leaders, GRFL; *U.S. News*, August 11, 1975, 15.

123. Ford, interview, August 21, 2003.

124. Ford, *A Time to Heal*, 221.

125. Ford, interview, August 21, 2003.

126. Videotape of second campaign debate, GRFL.

127. Ford, *A Time to Heal*, 222; Kissinger, *Years of Renewal*, 687–89.

128. Rowen, *Self-Inflicted Wounds*, 139.

129. Kissinger, *Years of Renewal*, 692–96; Seidman, interview, May 19, 2004.

130. Economic Developments and Outlook, Box 43, Folder: Briefing Papers, June 16–30, 1976 (1), Seidman Files, GRFL; Rowen, *Self-Inflicted Wounds*, 155; *NYT*, June 26, 27, 28, 29, 1976; *WSJ*, June 29, 1976; *Time*, May 17, 1976, 10; July 12, 1976, 52.

131. *WSJ*, November 23, 1976.

132. *U.S. News*, April 7, 1975, 12; June 30, 1975, 40; *Economist*, July 26, 2003.

133. Papers of Gerald R. Ford, Staff Secretary, Special Files, Box 3, Second Debate: Suggestions from White House Staff, Memorandum from Doug Bailey, September 30, 1976, GRFL.

134. *U.S. News*, August 30, 1976, 29.

Chapter 17. Thunder from the Right

1. Judith Anderson, *William Howard Taft: An Intimate History* (New York: W.W. Norton, 1981), 223.

2. Stephen E. Ambrose, *Eisenhower: Soldier and Statesman* (New York: Simon and Schuster, 1991), 271; Cannon, *Time and Chance*, 23.

3. Ford, interview, August 21, 2003.

4. Yanek Mieczkowski, *The Routledge Historical Atlas of Presidential Elections* (New York: Routledge Press, 2001), 120; Dobrynin, *In Confidence*, 324.

5. Richard Viguerie, *The New Right: We're Ready to Lead* (Falls Church, Va.: Viguerie, 1980), 45.

6. MacDougall, *We Almost Made It*, 35–36.

7. *Newsweek*, October 22, 1973, 37; *Economist*, March 8, 1975, 14; Greene, *The Presidency of Gerald R. Ford*, 59.

8. Roger Brown and David Welborn, "Presidents and Their Parties: Performance and Prospects," in Bailey and Shafritz, *The American Presidency*, 293.

9. Witcover, *Marathon*, 85.

10. Charles Mathias, telephone interview by author, May 26, 2004

11. Ford, interview, October 25, 1994.

12. *Public Papers, 1976–1977*, 2:1301; Memorandum from Rob Quartel and Ralph Stanley, June 21, 1976, and Harris Survey, June 7, 1976, PFC Records, 1975–76, Box 8, Folder: Hughes Subject File-Research, GRFL; terHorst, *Gerald Ford*, 134.

13. Mathias, interview, May 26, 2004; Drew, *American Journal*, 367.

14. Hubert Humphrey, *The Education of a Public Man: My Life in Politics, Hubert H. Humphrey*, edited by Norman Sherman, (Garden City: Doubleday, 1976), 490–91; David Reinhard, *The Republican Right since 1945* (Lexington, Mass.: Lexington Books, 1983), 228; Viguerie, *The New Right*, 52; *Public Papers, 1974*, 57.

15. Transcript of "The First Lady" on *60 Minutes*, vol. 7, no. 30, as broadcast over the CBS television network, August 10, 1975, produced by CBS News.

16. Memorandum from John Hoornstra, Box 164, Folder: Reagan, Ronald (2), Hartmann Files, GRFL; Seidman, interview, May 19, 2004; Ford, *A Time to Heal*, 294; Hartmann, *Palace Politics*, 334; *Economist*, November 15, 1975, 69.

17. *NYT*, February 21, 1976.

18. Memo, April 28, 1975, Box 39, Folder: Political Affairs-Reagan (2), PHF, GRFL.

19. Ford, *A Time to Heal*, 294; Hartmann, *Palace Politics*, 336; Edmund Morris, *Dutch: A Memoir of Ronald Reagan* (New York: Random House, 1999), 391.

20. Ford, *A Time to Heal*, 333.

21. Notes on the Campaign, Box 5, Folder: 12/10/75, Cabinet Meeting, Connor Files, GRFL; *U.S. News*, December 29, 1975, 10.

22. Ford, *A Time to Heal*, 294–97; Witcover, *Marathon*, 54.

23. *New York Daily News* interview, May 19, 1975, Box 25, Folder: Rockefeller, Nelson-General, Nessen Papers, GRFL.

24. Cannon, *Time and Chance*, 407; Ford, *A Time to Heal*, 327–28.

25. Greene, *The Presidency of Gerald R. Ford*, 159–60; Hartmann, *Palace Politics*, 367, 369.

26. Andrew J. Goodpaster, interview by author, June 15, 2000.

27. Viguerie, *The New Right*, 1.

28. UPI report, November 3, 1975, Box 25, Folder: Rockefeller, Nelson-General, Nessen Papers, GRFL.

29. Ford, *A Time to Heal*, 360; Nessen, *It Sure Looks Different*, 198–99; Witcover, *Marathon*, 391.

30. Ford, *A Time to Heal*, 348–49; Nessen, *It Sure Looks Different*, 198; Witcover, *Marathon*, 376–97.

31. Public Papers, 1975, 1:370.

32. Nessen, *It Sure Looks Different*, 198–201; Witcover, *Marathon*, 396–97.

33. Martin Schram, *Running for President, 1976: The Carter Campaign* (New York: Stein and Day, 1977), 228; *WSJ*, March 11, 1976; Witcover, *Marathon*, 433.

34. Witcover, *Marathon*, 409–11.

35. Ford, *A Time to Heal*, 375. The other incumbents to lose primaries were Harry Truman in Tennessee (1952) and Lyndon Johnson in Wisconsin (1968), after he had already withdrawn from the race.

36. Schapsmeier and Schapsmeier, *Date with Destiny*, 209; Witcover, *Marathon*, 92, 402, 411; *WP*, March 7, 10, 1976.

37. *Newsweek*, May 17, 1976, 25.

38. *The Gallup Opinion Index*, June 1976, 28; *Time*, April 19, 1976, 13.

39. PFC Records, 1975–76, Box 81, Folder: Correspondence-Topics, Kissinger, Henry, GRFL.

40. Memorandum from Robert Teeter, November 12, 1975, Teeter Papers, Box 63, Folder: 11/12/75, GRFL; Ford, *A Time to Heal*, 374; *WP*, March 7, 10, 1976; *Economist*, May 8, 1976, 43; *WSJ*, April 26, 27, 1976; *Time*, October 22, 1973.

41. Lee Edwards, *Goldwater: The Man Who Made a Revolution* (Washington, D.C.: Regnery, 1995), 409.

42. Letter from R. H. Ankeny, PFC Records, 1975–76, Box 81, Folder: Correspondence-Topics-Panama Canal, GRFL; Witcover, *Marathon*, 402–3; *WP*, May 3, 5, 9, 1976.

43. Dobrynin, *In Confidence*, 367, 369, 373.

44. *Newsweek*, May 24, 1976, 18–19.

45. *Newsweek*, January 12, 1976, 17; Ford, *A Time to Heal*, 364.

46. *NYT*, June 27, 1976; *Time*, February 23, 1976, 8; Witcover, *Marathon*, 100–101.

47. Vice presidential press conference, October 3, 1975, Box 25, Folder: Rockefeller, Nelson-General, Nessen Papers, GRFL.

48. Witcover, *Marathon*, 388–89; Walter Mears, *Deadlines Past: Forty Years of Presidential Campaigning: A Reporter's Story* (Kansas City, Mo.: Andrews McMeel, 2003), 142.

49. Ford, *A Time to Heal*, 362–73; NYT, May 16, June 27, 1976.

50. Witcover, *Marathon*, 420; *Economist*, June 26, 1976, 37; Cannon, *Time and Chance*, 406; Nessen, *It Sure Looks Different*, 214.

51. *Time*, August 2, 1976, 10; Witcover, *Marathon*, 435–39, 482; Schapsmeier and Schapsmeier, *Date with Destiny*, 210–11.

52. NYT, July 28, 1976; Ford, *A Time to Heal*, 394–95; Nessen, *It Sure Looks Different*, 223.

53. Ford, *A Time to Heal*, 398.

54. Ibid., 399; Witcover, *Marathon*, 502; WP, August 14, 1976; WSJ, August 20, 1976.

55. Memorandum from Teeter, Teeter Papers, Box 63, Folder: 8/16/76, GRFL; Ford, *A Time to Heal*, 402; *Newsweek*, August 30, 1976, 26.

56. *Newsweek*, August 30, 1976, 35.

57. *Time*, February 2, 1976, 10.

58. Ford, interview, January 24, 2002.

59. Cannon, *Time and Chance*, 51; NYT, August 26, 1976; Witcover, *Marathon*, 526.

60. Seidman, interview, May 19, 2004; Ford, *A Time to Heal*, 400; Jake Thompson, *Bob Dole: The Republicans' Man for All Seasons* (New York: Donald Fine Books, 1994), 92–93.

61. Greene, *The Presidency of Gerald R. Ford*, 173; MacDougall, *We Almost Made It*, 82.

62. *Newsweek*, August 30, 1976, 36; Cannon, *Time and Chance*, 83, Witcover, *Marathon*, 509; WSJ, August 20, 1976.

63. Ford, *A Time to Heal*, 142–43, 337–38, 401; Peter Schweizer and Rochelle Schweizer, *The Bushes: Portrait of a Dynasty* (New York: Doubleday, 2004), 237, 248, 249.

64. Kandy Stroud, *How Jimmy Won* (New York: Morrow, 1977), 346.

65. Ford, *A Time to Heal*, 407; Kandy Stroud, *How Jimmy Won*, 346; Friedersdorf, interview, August 14, 2001; Videotape of Ford acceptance speech, GRFL.

66. Schapsmeier and Schapsmeier, *Date with Destiny*, 203.

67. Ford, interview, January 24, 2002.

68. Lou Cannon, *Reagan* (New York: G. P. Putnam's Sons, 1982), 223.

69. Ford, interview, August 21, 2003.

70. Coleman, interview, September 16, 2003.

71. Ronald Reagan, *An American Life* (New York: Simon and Schuster, 1990), 200–202.

72. Ford, interview, January 24, 2002.

73. NYT, July 17, 1980.

74. Ford, interview, October 25, 1994; Ford, interview on *Larry King Live*, CNN television network, June 8, 2004.

Chapter 18. Back from the Brink

1. Nessen, *It Sure Looks Different*, 305.

2. *NYT*, June 13, 1976.

3. *NYT*, September 3, 1976.

4. Campaign Strategy Book, Research Room Copy, GRFL; Schram, *Running for President*, 252; *Newsweek*, August 30, 1976, 24–25.

5. Campaign Strategy Book, GRFL; Nessen, *It Sure Looks Different*, 247; Schram, *Running for President*, 292.

6. Seidman, interview, May 19, 2004.

7. Memorandum from Robert Teeter, November 12, 1975, Teeter Papers, Box 63, Folder: 11/12/75, GRFL.

8. Greene, *The Presidency of Gerald R. Ford*, 176.

9. Seidman, interview, May 19, 2004; *NYT*, October 4, 1976.

10. Ford, *A Time to Heal*, 411; Greene, *The Presidency of Gerald R. Ford*, 176–77; Witcover, *Marathon*, 530.

11. Nessen, *It Sure Looks Different*, 257; *NYT*, October 2, 10, 1976.

12. Ford, *A Time to Heal*, 415; Nessen, *It Sure Looks Different*, 258, 263.

13. *Newsweek*, October 4, 1976, 26; Witcover, *Marathon*, 573.

14. Nessen, *It Sure Looks Different*, 259, 264; Stroud, *How Jimmy Won*, 364.

15. Gerald Pomper et al., *The Election of 1976: Reports and Interpretations* (New York: Longman, 1976), 68; Videotape of first campaign debate, GRFL; Ford, *A Time to Heal*, 416; *NYT*, September 29, October 1, 1976.

16. Witcover, *Marathon*, 557, Nessen, *It Sure Looks Different*, 255; Stroud, *How Jimmy Won*, 393.

17. Ford, *A Time to Heal*, 428.

18. MacDougall, *We Almost Made It*, 46.

19. *Playboy*, November 1976, 86; *U.S. News*, October 4, 1976, 13.

20. Nessen, *It Sure Looks Different*, 300; Schram, *Running for President*, 305, 334–36; Tom Wicker, *On Press* (New York: Viking Press, 1978), 63; Witcover, *Marathon*, 590.

21. Nessen, *It Sure Looks Different*, 286; Witcover, *Marathon*, 584.

22. Ford, *A Time to Heal*, 418.

23. Box 27, Folder: Debate Working Papers-Second Debate, Duval Papers, GRFL; Stroud, *How Jimmy Won*, 374; Ford, *The Presidential Campaign 1976*, 3:92–118; Dobrynin, *In Confidence*, 366.

24. Videotape of second campaign debate, 1976, GRFL.

25. Ford, interview, August 21, 2003.

26. Ribuffo, *Right Center Left*, 218–19, 302; Schram, *Running for President*, 318; *Time*, April 19, 1976, 12–13.

27. Papers of Gerald Ford, Staff Secretary, Special Files, Box 2, Folder: Second Debate, Ford Notes on Briefing Materials, GRFL.

28. Memorandum from Bud McFarlane, Box 27, Folder: Debate Working Papers, Second Debate, Issues, Duval Papers; Papers of Gerald R. Ford, Staff Secretary, Special Files, Box 2, Folder: Second Debate, NSC Briefing Book (2), GRFL.

29. Papers of Gerald R. Ford, Staff Secretary, Special Files, Box 2, Folder: Second Debate, NSC Briefing Book (1), GRFL.

30. Handwritten notes, Benton Becker Papers, Box 1, Folder: Ford/Carter Debates,

GRFL; Hartmann, *Palace Politics*, 412; Nessen, *It Sure Looks Different*, 269; NYT, October 7, 1976.

31. Memorandum from Milt Mitler, Box 27, Folder: Debate Working Papers, Second Debate, Comment and Analysis, Duval Papers, GRFL; WSJ, October 8, 1976.

32. Hartmann, *Palace Politics*, 413.

33. Ford, *A Time to Heal*, 425.

34. NYT, October 10, 1976; Ribuffo, *Right Center Left*, 309.

35. NYT, October 15, 1976; Nessen, *It Sure Looks Different*, 276.

36. Memorandum from Mike Duval, Box 25, Folder: Debate Preparations, Duval papers, GRFL; Nessen, *It Sure Looks Different*, 276; Schapsmeier and Schapsmeier, *Date with Destiny*, 222.

37. Ribuffo, *Right Center Left*, 312.

38. "Playboy Interview: Jimmy Carter," *Playboy*, July 1977, 191.

39. Thompson, *Bob Dole*, 94; Witcover, *Marathon*, 535.

40. Witcover, *Marathon*, 613.

41. Letter from Jacob Javits, October 13, 1976, Series 5, Subseries 2, Box 30, Folder: 1976 campaign, Jacob Javits Papers, Frank Melville Library, Stony Brook University.

42. Thompson, *Bob Dole*, 102; Nessen, *It Sure Looks Different*, 278.

43. Gallup, *The Gallup Poll*, 2:887–88.

44. Schram, *Running for President*, 330; Witcover, *Marathon*, 629; Videotape of third debate, GRFL.

45. Videotape of third debate, GRFL.

46. Ford, *A Time to Heal*, 430; Nessen, *It Sure Looks Different*, 307–8; Stroud, *How Jimmy Won*, 394.

47. MacDougall, *We Almost Made It*, 199; WSJ, October 26, 1976.

48. Mieczkowski, *The Routledge Historical Atlas*, 130; Nessen, *It Sure Looks Different*, 318–19; Mears, *Deadlines Past*, 160.

49. Ford, *A Time to Heal*, 433–34; Nessen, *It Sure Looks Different*, 310–11.

50. *Time*, November 10, 1980, 30; *U.S. News*, August 30, 1976, 28–29; *Economist*, July 24, 1976; *Economist*, August 14, 1976, 10; *National Journal*, August 28, 1976, 1199.

51. *Newsweek*, May 17, 1976, 22.

52. Stroud, *How Jimmy Won*, 83, 328–30; *Time*, August 2, 1976, 13–14.

53. Stroud, *How Jimmy Won*, 136, 425.

54. Ford, *A Time to Heal*, 410.

55. *Time*, August 2, 1976, 24.

56. Cannon, *Time and Chance*, 219–20; NYT, August 12, 1976; Ford, *A Time to Heal*, 414.

57. *Time*, November 8, 1976, 30; NYT, March 21, 1976.

58. *U.S. News*, September 13, 1976, 26.

59. *Newsweek*, August 23, 1976, 35; Gerald Pomper, "The Nominating Contests and Conventions," in Pomper et al., *The Election of 1976*, 18.

60. NYT, August 12, October 13, 1976; *Newsweek*, August 23, 1976, 34.

61. *Time*, November 1, 1976, 19; Schram, *Running for President*, 349–50; Melloan and Melloan, *The Carter Economy*, 29; NYT, March 31, August 10, 24, October 20, 1976.

62. "Carter's General Economic Goals," David Gergen Files, 1974–77, Box 16, Folder: Debate Background-National Economic Planning, GRFL; WP, May 2, 1976.

63. Wilson McWilliams, "The Meaning of the Election," in Pomper et al., *The Election of 1976*, 151.

64. U.S. National Survey, December 1974 Analysis (1), Box 50, Teeter Papers, 1967–77, GRFL; *Newsweek*, March 15, 1976, 77; Mieczkowski, *The Routledge Historical Atlas*, 133.

65. NYT, October 15, 1976; Melloan and Melloan, *The Carter Economy*, 48; *Michigan Alumnus*, September/October 1995, 27.

66. Schram, *Running for President*, 329–30.

67. MacAvoy, interview, May 2, 2002.

68. *Economist*, May 27, 1995, 25; Speeches in New York City (11/12/75) and Delaware City, Iowa (11/17/75), Box 1026, Birch Bayh Papers, Lilly Library, IU.

69. Cannon, *Time and Chance*, 410.

70. Schieffer, *This Just In*, 240.

71. Mieczkowski, *The Routledge Historical Atlas*, 129–30.

72. Schram, *Running for President*, 332; Stroud, *How Jimmy Won*, 420. Woodrow Wilson was born in Georgia but spent his adult life in the North.

73. Zarb, interview, February 8, 2003; Memorandum to Don Rumsfeld, April 29, 1975, Box 7, Folder: Campaign-Ford Constituency, Connor Files, GRFL.

74. NYT, August 29, 1976; Mieczkowski, *The Routledge Historical Atlas*, 130; WSJ, September 21, 1976.

75. NYT, August 10, 1976; Smith, *Events Leading Up to My Death*, 363. Smith applied the same description to Carter.

76. Memorandum, August 1976 (1), National Surveys-Strategy Book, Box 54, 1967–77, Teeter Papers, GRFL.

77. NYT, August 21, September 15, 1976; *The Presidential Campaign 1976*, 2:86, 89.

78. *Public Papers*, 1976–1977, 3:2525.

79. Lynn, interview, October 27, 1994.

80. Drew, *American Journal*, 180.

81. David Kennerly, *Shooter* (New York: Newsweek Books, 1979), 212–13.

82. Buchen, interview, February 28, 1994.

83. Memorandum to Dick Cheney, December 24, 1975, Teeter, Robert-Memoranda and Polling Data (3), Box 4, Chanock Files, GRFL.

84. "Notes on the Campaign," Box 5, Folder: 12/10/75, Connor Files, GRFL; "Themes, 4/21/76," Box 5, Folder: Campaign-Planning, 1976, Connor Files, GRFL.

85. Memorandum to Dick Cheney, August 10, 1976, Box 7, Folder: Campaign-Planning, 1976, Connor Files, GRFL.

86. Seidman, interview, October 18, 1994.

87. Doyle, *Gerald R. Ford*, 44, 70.

88. WP, January 20, 1976.

89. Ford, interview, October 25, 1994.

90. *U.S. News*, August 30, 1976, 29.

91. Ford, *A Time to Heal*, 348.

92. Cheney, "Forming and Managing an Administration," 79.

93. Smith, *The Power Game*, 347, 348.

94. 1980 presidential debate, October 1980, video, Ronald Reagan Presidential Library, Simi Valley, Calif.

95. Gerald R. Ford Museum, Grand Rapids, Mich.; *Public Papers, 1976–1977,* 3:2834.

96. *Public Papers, 1976–1977,* 1:47, 2:1379; *WSJ,* October 26, 1976.

97. Nessen, *It Sure Looks Different,* 319; Osborne, *White House Watch,* xxx.

98. *NYT,* May 29, 1976; *Newsweek,* August 23, 1976, 34, 36; *National Journal,* August 28, 1976, 1210.

99. *Economist,* October 26, 1974, 54; November 9, 1974, 57–58; *Time,* August 23, 1976, 10.

100. Thompson, *Bob Dole,* 94.

101. Ford, interview, August 21, 2003.

102. Thomas Bailey, *Presidential Saints and Sinners* (New York: Free Press, 1981), 275.

103. Harold Stanly and Richard Niemi, *Vital Statistics on American Politics* (Washington, D.C.: Congressional Quarterly Press, 1990), 147.

104. *Time,* January 19, 2004, 21.

105. *Newsweek,* October 22, 1973, 37; *Time,* October 22, 1973, 18; August 23, 1976, 10; *Fortune,* January 1965, 140.

106. Nessen, *It Sure Looks Different,* 320; *The Gallup Opinion Index,* October 1979, 9.

107. *The Gallup Opinion Index,* September 1980, 8.

Conclusion

1. Newspaper clippings, 88:33, General Files, Albert Papers, CACRSC.

2. O'Neill, "Discussant: Paul H. O'Neill," in Firestone and Ugrinsky, *Gerald R. Ford,* 1:312.

3. *U.S. News,* September 20, 1976, 58.

4. NPC, *Factors,* 54; *U.S. News,* March 15, 2004, 56; *NYT,* October 31, 1994.

5. Zarb, interview, September 26, 1994; Dingell, interview, February 14, 1994.

6. *NYT,* October 18, 1976; Frank Zarb, interview by author, September 26, 1994.

7. *NYT,* August 15, 1976; NPC, *Factors,* 49.

8. DiBona, interview, January 23, 2003.

9. *NYT,* April 7, 22, June 18, 26, 1974.

10. Donovan, *Roosevelt to Reagan,* 138; Lovett, *Inflation and Politics,* 22; *Time,* August 23, 1976, 10.

11. Seidman, interview, October 18, 1994.

12. Ford, interview, October 25, 1994.

13. Carroll, "An Economic Record," 72.

14. *NYT,* July 25, 1976;. Nessen, *It Sure Looks Different,* 89–90.

15. American Enterprise Institute, *A Discussion with Gerald R. Ford,* 11. See also *We the People.*

16. Reichley, *Conservatives,* 265. The four shortest presidencies have been, in ascending order of length of service, those of William Henry Harrison, James Abram Garfield, Zachary Taylor, and Warren G. Harding.

17. Ash, interview, January 10, 1994.
18. Seidman, interview, October 18, 1994.
19. Ford, interview, October 25, 1994.
20. Schieffer, *This Just In*, 226–27.
21. *Parade Magazine*, July 5, 1998, 20.
22. Porter, interview, May 8, 1995.
23. Edwards, *The Public Presidency*, 42.
24. Cannon, *Time and Chance*, 412.
25. WP, January 16, 1977.
26. Ford, interview, October 25, 1994.
27. Brent Scowcroft, in Thompson, *The Ford Presidency*, 310.

Bibliography

Documents

The principal source for documents and manuscripts cited in this work is the Gerald R. Ford Presidential Library in Ann Arbor, Michigan. Two commonly used abbreviations for files cited from the library are PHF (Presidential Handwriting File) and WHCF (White House Central File). Other sites consulted were the Carl Albert Congressional Research and Studies Center, the University of Oklahoma at Norman; the Rockefeller Archive Center in Tarrytown, New York; the Birch Bayh Papers at the Lilly Library of Indiana University at Bloomington; the Jacob Javits Papers at Stony Brook University, Stony Brook, New York; and the William Simon Papers at David Bishop Skillman Library, Lafayette College, Easton, Pennsylvania. This work also cites materials from the personal papers of Russell Freeburg, Paul Theis, and Frank Zarb.

Books

Aitken, Jonathan. *Nixon: A Life*. Washington, D.C.: Regnery Pub., 1993.

Ambrose, Stephen E. *Eisenhower: The President*. New York: Simon and Schuster, 1984.

———. *Eisenhower: Soldier and Statesman*. New York: Simon and Schuster, 1991.

———. *Nixon: Ruin and Recovery, 1973–1990*. New York: Touchstone, 1991.

———. *Nixon: Triumph of a Politician, 1962–1972*. New York: Touchstone, 1989.

———. *Rise to Globalism: American Foreign Policy since 1938*. 5th edition. New York: Penguin Books, 1988.

American Enterprise for Public Policy Research. *A Discussion with Gerald R. Ford: The American Presidency*. Washington, D.C.: American Enterprise Institute, 1977.

American Legends. New York: Time, 2001.

Anderson, Annalise, and Dennis Bark, eds. *Thinking about America: The United States in the 1990s*. Stanford, Calif.: Hoover Institution, 1988.

Anderson, Judith. *William Howard Taft: An Intimate History*. New York: W. W. Norton, 1981.

Andrews, Nigel. *Nigel Andrews on Jaws*. New York: Bloomsbury, 1999.

Bailey, Harry, Jr., and Jay Shafritz, eds. *The American Presidency: Historical and*

Contemporary Perspectives. Pacific Grove, Calif.: Brooks/Cole Publishing Company, 1988.

Bailey, Thomas. *Presidential Saints and Sinners*. New York: The Free Press, 1981.

Baker, Russell. *So This Is Depravity*. New York: Washington Square Books, 1980.

Barber, James David. *The Presidential Character: Predicting Performance in the White House*. 4th ed. Englewood Cliffs, N.J.: Prentice Hall, 1992.

Barnet, Richard. *The Lean Years: Politics in the Age of Scarcity*. New York: Simon and Schuster, 1980.

Bell, Daniel. *The Coming of Post-Industrial Society: A Venture in Social Forecasting*. New York: Basic Books, Inc., 1973.

Bellmon, Henry, with Pat Bellmon. *The Life and Times of Henry Bellmon*. Tulsa, Okla.: Council Oak Books, 1992.

Berman, Larry. *The New American Presidency*. Boston, Mass.: Little, Brown, 1987.

Bernstein, Micheal, and David Adler, eds. *Understanding American Economic Decline*. New York: Cambridge University Press, 1994.

Bibby, John, Thomas Mann, and Norman Ornstein. *Vital Statistics of Congress, 1980*. Washington, D.C.: American Enterprise Institute for Public Policy Research, 1980.

Blair, Joan, and Clay Blair Jr. *The Search for JFK*. New York: G.P. Putnam's Sons, 1976.

Blinder, Alan. *Economic Policy and the Great Stagflation*. New York: Academic Press, 1981.

Blum, John Morton. *Years of Discord: American Politics and Society, 1961–1974*. New York: W.W. Norton and Company, 1991.

Boller, Paul F., Jr. *Presidential Anecdotes*. New York: Penguin Books, 1981.

Boyes, William, and Michael Melvin. *Macroeconomics*. 2nd ed. Boston, Mass.: Houghton Mifflin Company, 1994.

Bradlee, Ben. *Conversations with Kennedy*. New York: W.W. Norton and Company, 1976.
——. *A Good Life: Newspapering and Other Adventures*. New York: Simon and Schuster, 1995.

Broder, David. *Changing of the Guard: Power and Leadership in America*. New York: Simon and Schuster, 1980.

Brodnick, Max. *The Jerry Ford Joke Book*. New York: Leisure Books, 1976.

Brooks, Tim, and Earle Marsh. *The Complete Directory to Prime Time Network TV Shows, 1946–Present*. New York: Ballantine Books, 1979.

Burns, Arthur. *Reflections of an Economic Policy Maker: Speeches and Congressional Statements: 1969–1978*. Washington, D.C.: American Enterprise Institute for Public Policy Research, 1978.

The Business Week Team. *The Decline of U.S. Power (and what we can do about it)*. Boston, Mass.: Houghton Mifflin Corp., 1980.

Cader, Michael, ed. *Saturday Night Live: The First Twenty Years*. Boston, Mass.: Houghton Mifflin, 1994.

Calleo, David. *The Imperious Economy*. Cambridge, Mass.: Harvard University Press, 1982.

Campagna, Anthony. *The Economic Consequences of the Vietnam War*. New York: Praeger, 1991.
——. *U.S. National Economic Policy, 1917–1985*. New York: Praeger, 1987.

Cannon, James. *Time and Chance: Gerald Ford's Appointment with History.* New York: HarperCollins, 1994.

Cannon, Lou. *Reagan.* New York: G.P. Putnam's Sons, 1982.

Carbaugh, Robert. *International Economics.* 4th ed. Belmont, Calif.: Wadsworth Publishing Company, 1992.

Carroll, Peter. *It Seemed Like Nothing Happened: America in the 1970s.* New Brunswick, N.J.: Rutgers University Press, 2000.

Carter, Jimmy. *Keeping Faith: Memoirs of a President.* New York: Bantam Books, 1982.

Casserly, John. *The Ford White House: The Diary of a Speechwriter.* Boulder: Colorado Associated University Press, 1977.

Chafe, William. *The Unfinished Journey: America since World War II.* 2nd ed. New York: Oxford University Press, 1991.

Cochran, Thomas. *The Great Depression and World War II: 1929–1945.* Glenview, Ill.: Scott, Foresman, 1968.

Collins, Ace. *Evel Knievel: An American Hero.* New York: St. Martin's Press, 1999.

Combs, Jerald. *The History of American Foreign Policy.* 2nd ed. New York: McGraw-Hill, 1997.

Commager, Henry Steele, and Milton Cantor, eds. *Documents of American History (volume II) since 1898.* 10th ed. Englewood Cliffs, N.J.: Prentice Hall, 1988.

The Conference on Inflation: Transcript, September 27–28, 1974, Washington, D.C. Washington, D.C.: U.S. Government Printing Office, 1974.

Congressional Quarterly Almanac. 1975 and 1976 volumes. Washington, D.C.: Congressional Quarterly, 1976.

Congressional Quarterly's Guide to the Congress of the United States: Origins, History, and Procedure. Washington, D.C.: Congressional Quarterly Press, 1971.

Crabb, Cecil, Jr., and Pat Holt. *Invitation to Struggle: Congress, the President, and Foreign Policy.* 2nd ed. Washington, D.C.: Congressional Quarterly Press, 1984.

Cray, Ed. *Chrome Colossus: General Motors and Its Times.* New York: McGraw-Hill, 1980.

Cronin, Thomas, and Rexford Tugwell, eds. *The Presidency Reappraised.* 2nd ed. New York: Praeger, 1977.

Dallek, Robert. *Hail to the Chief: The Making and Unmaking of Presidents.* New York: Hyperion, 1996.

Davis, David Howard. *Energy Politics.* 4th ed. New York: St. Martin's Press, 1993.

Degler, Carl. *Affluence and Anxiety: 1945–Present.* Glenview, Ill.: Scott, Foresman, 1968.

A Discussion with Gerald R. Ford: The American Presidency. Washington, D.C.: The American Enterprise Institute, 1977.

Dobrynin, Anatoly. *In Confidence: Moscow's Ambassador to America's Six Cold War Presidents (1962–1986).* New York: Times Books, 1995.

Dolce, Philip, and George Skau, eds. *Power and the Presidency.* New York: Charles Scribner's Sons, 1976.

Donaldson, Gary. *Truman Defeats Dewey.* Lexington: The University Press of Kentucky, 1999.

Donovan, Hedley. *Roosevelt to Reagan: A Reporter's Encounters with Nine Presidents.* New York: Harper and Row, 1985.

Doyle, Michael, ed. *Gerald R. Ford: Selected Speeches.* Arlington, Va.: R. W. Beatty, Ltd., 1973.

Bibliography

Drew, Elizabeth. *American Journal: The Events of 1976*. New York: Random House, 1977.

Dumbrell, John. *The Carter Presidency: A Re-Evaluation*. Manchester, United Kingdom: Manchester University Press, 1993.

Eckstein, Otto. *Core Inflation*. Englewood Cliffs, N.J.: Prentice Hall, 1981.

———. *The Great Recession*. New York: North Holland Publishing Company, 1978.

Edwards, George, III. *At the Margins: Presidential Leadership of Congress*. New Haven, Conn.: Yale University Press, 1989.

———. *Presidential Influence in Congress*. San Francisco, Calif.: W.H. Freeman and Company, 1983.

———. *The Public Presidency: The Pursuit of Popular Support*. New York: St. Martin's Press, 1983.

Edwards, Lee. *Goldwater: The Man Who Made a Revolution*. Washington, D.C.: Regnery Pub., 1995.

Ehrlich, Paul, and Anne Ehrlich. *The End of Affluence: A Blueprint for Your Future*. New York: Ballantine Books, 1974.

Ellis, Howard. *Notes on Stagflation*. Washington, D.C.: American Enterprise Institute for Public Policy Research, 1978.

Eisenhower, Dwight D. *The White House Years, vol. 1: Mandate for Change: 1953–1956*. Garden City, N.Y.: Doubleday, 1963.

Firestone, Bernard, and Alexej Ugrinsky. *Gerald Ford and the Politics of Post-Watergate America*. 2 vols. Westport, Conn.: Greenwood Press, 1993.

Fisher, Louis. *The Politics of Shared Power: Congress and the Executive*. 2nd ed. Washington, D.C.: Congressional Quarterly Press, 1987.

Ford, Betty, with Chris Chase. *The Times of My Life*. New York: Harper and Row, 1978.

Ford, Gerald R. *Humor and the Presidency*. New York: Random House, 1987.

———. *The Presidential Campaign 1976*. 3 vols. Washington, D.C.: U.S. Government Printing Office, 1979.

———. *A Time to Heal: The Autobiography of Gerald R. Ford*. New York: Random House, 1979.

Fox, Harrison, Jr., and Susan Webb Hammond. *Congressional Staffs: The Invisible Force in American Lawmaking*. New York: The Free Press, 1977.

Franklin, Daniel. *Making Ends Meet: Congressional Budgeting in the Age of Deficits*. Washington, D.C.: Congressional Quarterly Press, 1993.

Freeman, S. David. *Energy: The New Era*. New York: Walker and Company, 1974.

Frum, David. *How We Got Here, The 70s: The Decade That Brought You Modern Life— For Better or Worse*. New York: Basic Books, 2000.

Fuller, Robert. *Inflation: The Rising Cost of Living on a Small Planet*. Washington, D.C.: WorldWatch Institute, 1980.

Gallup, George. *The Gallup Poll: Public Opinion, 1935–1971*. 3 vols. New York: Random House, 1972.

———. *The Gallup Poll: Public Opinion, 1972–1977*. 2 vols. Wilmington, Del.: Scholarly Resources, Inc., 1978.

Gallup Opinion Index. Princeton, N.J.: Institute of Public Opinion, 1965–.

The Gannett Center for Media Studies. *The Press, the Presidency, and the First Hundred Days*. New York: Gannett Center for Media Studies, 1989.

Garraty, John A. *The Great Depression*. New York: Harcourt Brace Jovanovich, 1986.

Gelderman, Carol. *All the President's Words: The Bully Pulpit and the Creation of the Virtual Presidency*. New York: Walker and Company, 1997.

Genovese, Micheal. *The Presidency in an Age of Limits*. Westport, Conn.: Greenwood, 1993.

Gergen, David. *Eyewitness to Power: The Essence of Leadership, Nixon to Clinton*. New York: Simon and Schuster, 2000.

Ghosh, Arabinda. *OPEC, the Petroleum Industry, and United States Energy Policy*. Westport, Conn.: Quorum Books,1983.

Goldwater, Barry, with John Casserly. *Goldwater*. New York: Doubleday, 1988.

Graff, Henry, ed. *The Presidents: A Reference History*. New York: Charles Scribner's Sons, 1984.

Greene, John R. *The Limits of Power: The Nixon and Ford Administrations*. Bloomington: Indiana University Press, 1992.

——. *The Presidency of Gerald R. Ford*. Lawrence: University Press of Kansas, 1995.

Greenstein, Fred, ed. *Leadership in the Modern Presidency*. Cambridge, Mass.: Harvard University Press, 1988.

Griffin, James, and Henry Steele. *Energy Economics and Policy*. New York: Academic Press, 1980.

Gulley, Bill, with Mary Ellen Reese. *Breaking Cover*. New York: Simon and Schuster, 1980.

Hargreaves, Robert. *Superpower: A Portrait of America in the 70s*. New York: St. Martin's Press, 1973.

Hargrove, Erwin, and Samuel Morley, eds. *The President and the Council of Economic Advisors: Interviews with CEA Chairmen*. Boulder. Colo.: Westview Press, 1984.

Hartmann, Robert. *Palace Politics: An Inside Account of the Ford Years*. New York: McGraw-Hill, 1980.

Heller, Walter. *The Economy: Old Myths and New Realities*. New York: W.W. Norton and Comp., 1976.

Herbers, John. *No Thank You, Mr. President*. New York: Norton, 1976.

Hersey, John. *The President*. New York: Alfred Knopf, 1975.

Hill, Doug, and Jeff Weingrad. *Saturday Night: A Backstage History of Saturday Night Live*. New York: Beech Tree Books, 1986.

Hirschfield, Robert S., ed. *The Power of the Presidency: Concepts and Controversy*. 3rd ed. New York: Aldine Pub. Co., 1982.

Hodgson, Godfrey. *All Things to All Men: The False Promise of the Modern American Presidency*. New York: Simon and Schuster, 1980.

——. *America in Our Time*. New York: Vintage Books, 1976.

Howell, David, Margaret-Mary Howell, and Robert Dronman. *Gentlemanly Attitudes: Jerry Ford and the Campaign of '76*. Washington, D.C.: HKJV Publications, 1980.

Humphrey, Hubert. *The Education of a Public Man: My Life in Politics*, edited by Norman Sherman. Garden City, N.Y.: Doubleday and Company, 1976.

Ippolito, Dennis. *Uncertain Legacies: Federal Budget Policy from Roosevelt through Reagan*. Charlottesville: University Press of Virginia, 1990.

Isaacson, Walter. *Kissinger: A Biography*. New York: Simon and Schuster, 1992.

Bibliography

Johnson, Haynes. *In the Absence of Power: Governing America*. New York: Viking Press, 1980.

Kalt, Joseph. *The Economics and Politics of Oil Price Regulation: Federal Policy in the Post-Embargo Era*. Cambridge, Mass.: The MIT Press, 1981.

Katona, George, and Burkhard Strumpel. *A New Economic Era*. New York: Elsevier North-Holland, Inc., 1978.

Katz, James. *Congress and National Energy Policy*. New Brunswick, N.J.: Transaction Books, 1984.

Kellerman, Barbara. *The Political Presidency: The Practice of Leadership*. New York: Oxford, 1984.

Kennedy, Caroline, ed. *Profiles in Courage for Our Time*. New York: Hyperion, 2002.

Kennerly, David. *Shooter*. New York: Newsweek Books, 1979.

Kissinger, Henry. *Years of Renewal*. New York: Simon and Schuster, 1999.

Kregel, J. A., ed. *Inflation and Income Distribution in Capitalist Crisis: Essays in Memory of Sidney Weintraub*. New York: New York University Press, 1989.

Kutler, Stanley. *The Wars of Watergate: The Last Crisis of Richard Nixon*. New York: Alfred Knopf, 1990.

Lee, Thomas, et al. *Energy Aftermath*. Boston, Mass.: Harvard Business School Press, 1990.

LeRoy, David. *Gerald Ford: Untold Story*. Arlington, Va.: R.W. Beatty, Ltd., 1974.

Leuchterburg, William E. *A Troubled Feast: American Society since 1945*. Boston: Little, Brown, 1973.

Lovett, William. *Inflation and Politics: Fiscal, Monetary, and Wage-Price Discipline*. Lanham, Md.: Lexington Books, 1982.

MacAvoy, Paul, ed. *Deregulation of Cable Television*. Washington, D.C.: American Enterprise Institute, 1977.

——. *Federal Energy Administration Regulation: Report of the Presidential Task Force*. Washington, D.C.: American Enterprise Institute, 1977.

MacAvoy, Paul, and John Snow, eds. *Regulation of Entry and Pricing in Truck Transportation*. Washington, D.C.: American Enterprise Institute, 1977.

——. *Regulation of Passenger Fares and Competition among the Airlines*. Washington, D.C.: American Enterprise Institute, 1977.

MacDougall, Malcolm. *We Almost Made It*. New York: Crown Publishers, Inc., 1977.

MacKenzie, G. Calvin. *The Politics of Presidential Appointments*. New York: The Free Press, 1981.

Mancke, Richard. *Squeaking By: U.S. Energy Policy since the Embargo*. New York: Columbia University Press, 1976.

Marcus, Alfred. *Controversial Issues in Energy Policy*. Newbury Park, Calif.: Sage Publications, 1992.

Martin, Justin. *Greenspan: The Man behind the Money*. Cambridge, Mass.: Perseus, 2000.

Matusow, Allen J. *Nixon's Economy: Booms, Busts, Dollars, and Votes*. Lawrence: University Press of Kansas.

McClendon, Sarah. *My Eight Presidents*. New York: Wyden Books, 1978.

McConnell, Campbell. *Economics: Principles, Problems, and Policies*. 9th ed. New York: McGraw-Hill, 1984.

———. *Economics: Principles, Problems, and Policies.* 12th ed. New York: McGraw-Hill, 1993.

Meadows, Donella, et al. *The Limits to Growth; A Report for the Club of Rome's Project on the Predicament of Mankind.* New York: Universe Books, 1972.

Mears, Walter. *Deadlines Past: Forty Years of Presidential Campaigning: A Reporter's Story.* Kansas City, Mo.: Andrews McMeel, 2003.

Melloan, George, and Joan Melloan. *The Carter Economy.* New York: John Wiley and Sons, 1978.

Mieczkowski, Yanek. *The Routledge Historical Atlas of Presidential Elections.* New York: Routledge Press, 2001.

Mollenhoff, Clark. *The Man Who Pardoned Nixon.* New York: St. Martin's Press, 1976.

Morris, Edmund. *Dutch: A Memoir of Ronald Reagan.* New York: Random House, 1999.

Murphy, Thomas. *The New Politics Congress.* Lanham, Md.: Lexington Books, 1974.

National Petroleum Council. *Factors Affecting U.S. Oil and Gas Outlook: A Report of the National Petroleum Council.* Washington, D.C.: National Petroleum Council, 1987.

Nessen, Ron. *It Sure Looks Different from the Inside.* New York: Playboy Books, 1978.

Nester, William. *American Power, the New World Order and the Japanese Challenge.* New York: St. Martin's Press, 1993.

Neustadt, Richard. *Presidential Power and the Modern Presidents: The Politics of Leadership from Roosevelt to Reagan.* New York: The Free Press, 1990.

Novick, David, et al. *A World of Scarcities: Critical Issues in Public Policy.* New York: John Wiley and Sons, 1976.

O'Neill, Thomas P., with William Novak. *Man of the House: The Life and Political Memoirs of Speaker Tip O'Neill.* New York: Random House, 1987.

Osborne, John. *White House Watch: The Ford Years.* Washington, D.C.: New Republic Books, 1977.

Paarlberg, Don. *An Analysis and History of Inflation.* Westport, Conn.: Praeger, 1993.

Paper, Lewis. *The Promise and the Performance: The Leadership of John F. Kennedy.* New York: Crown Publishers, Inc., 1975.

Pater, Alan, and James Pater, eds. *What They Said in 1974: The Yearbook of Public Opinion.* Beverly Hills, Calif.: Monitor Book Co., 1975.

Paterson, Thomas, and J. Garry Clifford. *America Ascendant: U.S. Foreign Relations since 1939.* Boston, Mass.: D.C. Heath and Company, 1997.

Peters, Ronald, Jr. *The American Speakership: The Office in Historical Perspective.* Baltimore, Md.: Johns Hopkins University Press, 1990.

Peterson, Wallace. *Silent Depression: The Fate of the American Dream.* New York: W.W. Norton, 1994.

Pfiffner, James, ed. *The President and Economic Policy.* Philadelphia, Pa.: Institute for the Study of Human Issues, 1986.

Pomper, Gerald, et al. *The Election of 1976: Reports and Interpretations.* New York: Longman, 1977.

Porter, Roger. *Presidential Decision Making: The Economic Policy Board.* Cambridge: Cambridge University Press, 1980.

Potter, David. *People of Plenty: Economic Abundance and the American Character.* Chicago, Ill.: University of Chicago Press, 1954.

Bibliography

President Ford: The Man and His Record. Washington, D.C.: Congressional Quarterly, 1974.

Prochnow, Herbert, ed. *Dilemmas Facing the Nation.* New York: Harper and Row, 1979.

Public Agenda Foundation. *Moral Leadership in Government.* New York: The Public Agenda Foundation, 1976.

Public Papers of the President: Gerald R. Ford, 1974–1977. 6 vols. Washington, D.C.: U.S. Government Printing Office.

Reagan, Ronald. *An American Life.* New York: Simon and Schuster, 1990.

Reedy, George. *The Twilight of the Presidency,* revised ed. New York: New American Library, 1987.

Reeves, Richard. *A Ford, Not a Lincoln.* New York: Harcourt Brace Jovanovich, 1975.

Reichley, James. *Conservatives in an Age of Change: The Nixon and Ford Administrations.* Washington, D.C.: The Brookings Institution, 1981.

Reinhard, David. *The Republican Right since 1945.* Lanham, Md.: Lexington Books, 1983.

Ribuffo, Leo. *Right Center Left: Essays in American History.* New Brunswick, N.J.: Rutgers University Press, 1992.

Richardson, Elliot. *The Creative Balance: Government, Politics, and the Individual in America's Third Century.* New York: Holt, Rinehart, and Winston, 1976.

Richardson, Elmo. *The Presidency of Dwight D. Eisenhower.* Lawrence: The Regents Press of Kansas, 1979.

Rowan, Hobart. *Self-Inflicted Wounds: From LBJ's Guns and Butter to Reagan's Voodoo Economics.* New York: Times Books, 1994.

Rozell, Mark. *The Press and the Ford Presidency.* Ann Arbor: The University of Michigan Press, 1993.

Saulnier, Raymond. *Constructive Years: The U.S. Economy under Eisenhower.* Lanham, Md.: University Press of America, 1991.

Schapsmeier, Edward, and Frederick Schapsmeier. *Gerald R. Ford's Date with Destiny: A Political Biography.* New York: Peter Lang, 1989.

Schieffer, Bob. *This Just In: What I Couldn't Tell You on TV.* New York: G.P. Putnam's Sons, 2003.

Schlesinger, Arthur M. Jr. *The Imperial Presidency, with a new epilogue by the author.* Boston, Mass.: Houghton Mifflin, 1989.

Schoenebaum, Elenora, ed. *Profiles of an Era: The Nixon/Ford Years.* New York: Harcourt Brace Jovanovich, 1979.

Schram, Martin. *Running for President, 1976: The Carter Campaign.* New York: Stein and Day, 1977.

Schulman, Bruce. *The Seventies: The Great Change in American Culture, Politics, and Society.* New York: The Free Press, 2001.

Schumacher, E. F. *Small Is Beautiful: Economics as if People Mattered.* New York: Perennial Library, 1973.

Schweizer, Peter, and Rochelle Schweizer. *The Bushes: Portrait of a Dynasty.* New York: Doubleday, 2004.

Seidman, William. *Full Faith and Credit: The Great S&L Debacle and Other Washington Sagas.* New York: Times Books, 1993.

Shapiro, Max. *The Penniless Billionaires.* New York: Times Books, 1980.

Shogan, Robert. *The Double-Edged Sword: How Character Makes and Ruins Presidents, from Washington to Clinton.* Boulder, Colo.: Westview Press, 1999.

———. *None of the Above: Why Presidents Fail—And What Can Be Done about It.* New York: New American Library Books, 1982.

———. *The Riddle of Power: Presidential Leadership from Truman to Bush.* New York: Dutton Books, 1991.

Shultz, George, and Kenneth Dam. *Economic Policy beyond the Headlines.* New York: W.W. Norton, 1977.

Sidey, Hugh. *Portrait of a President.* New York: Harper and Row, 1975.

Simon, William. *A Time for Truth.* New York: Reader's Digest Press, 1978.

Small, Melvin. *The Presidency of Richard Nixon.* Lawrence: University Press of Kansas, 1999.

Smith, Hedrick. *The Power Game: How Washington Works.* New York: Ballantine Books, 1989.

Smith, Howard K. *Events Leading Up to My Death: The Life of a Twentieth-Century Reporter.* New York: St. Martin's Press, 1996.

Sobel, Lester, ed. *Energy Crisis: 1974–75.* vol. II. New York: Facts on File, 1975.

Solomon, Ezra. *Beyond the Turning Point: The U.S. Economy in the 1980s.* San Francisco, Calif.: W.H. Freeman, 1982.

Spear, Joseph. *Presidents and the Press: The Nixon Legacy.* Cambridge, Mass.: The MIT Press, 1984.

Spitzer, Robert. *The Preidential Veto: Touchstone of the American Presidency.* Albany: State University of New York Press, 1988.

Stanly, Harold, and Richard Niemi. *Vital Statistics on American Politics.* Washington, D.C.: Congressional Quarterly Press, 1990.

Stein, Herbert. *Presidential Economics.* New York: Simon and Schuster, 1984.

Stroud, Kandy. *How Jimmy Won.* New York: Morrow, 1977.

Sundquist, James. *The Decline and Resurgence of Congress.* Washington, D.C.: The Brookings Institution, 1981.

Takenaka, Heizo. *Contemporary Japanese Economy and Economic Policy.* Ann Arbor: University of Michigan Press, 1991.

terHorst, Jerald. *Gerald Ford and the Future of the Presidency.* New York: The Third Press, 1974.

Thompson, Jake. *Bob Dole: The Republicans' Man for All Seasons.* New York: Donald Fine Books, 1994.

Thompson, Kenneth, ed. *The Ford Presidency: Twenty-two Intimate Portraits of Gerald R. Ford.* Lanham, Md.: University Press of America, 1988.

Thurber, James, ed. *Divided Democracy: Cooperation and Conflict between the President and Congress.* Washington, D.C.: Congressional Quarterly Press, 1991.

Tributes to the Honorable Gerald R. Ford, President of the United States. Washington, D.C.: U.S. Government Printing Office, 1977.

Tugwell, Franklin. *The Energy Crisis and the American Political Economy: Politics and Markets in the Management of Natural Resources.* Stanford, Calif.: Stanford University Press, 1988.

Bibliography

U.S. Bureau of the Census. *Statistical Abstract of the United States.* Washington, D.C.: U.S. Government Printing Office.

Uslander, Eric. *The Decline of Comity in Congress.* Ann Arbor: The University of Michigan Press, 1993.

Vestal, Bud. *Jerry Ford, Up Close: An Investigative Biography.* New York: Coward, McCann, and Geoghegan, 1974.

Vietor, Richard. *Energy Policy in America since 1945: A Study of Business-Government Relations.* Cambridge; New York: Cambridge University Press, 1984.

Viguerie, Richard. *The New Right: We're Ready to Lead.* Falls Church, Va.: The Viguerie Company, 1981.

Wallis, W. Allen. *An Overgoverned Society.* New York: The Free Press, 1976.

Washington Post Staff. *The Fall of a President.* New York: Dell Publishing, 1974.

Waugh, John C. *Reelecting Lincoln: The Battle for the 1864 Presidency.* New York: Crown Publishers, Inc., 1997.

Wayne, Stephen. *The Legislative Presidency.* New York: Harper and Row, 1978.

Wells, Wyatt. *Economist in an Uncertain World: Arthur Burns and the Federal Reserve, 1970–1978.* New York: Columbia University Press, 1994.

Wetterhahn, Ralph. *The Last Battle: The Mayaguez Incident and the End of the Vietnam War.* New York: Carroll and Graf, 2001.

White, Theodore. *America in Search of Itself: The Making of the President, 1956–1980.* New York: Warner Books, 1982.

Whitney, Simon. *Inflation since 1945: Facts and Theories.* New York: Praeger, 1982.

Wicker, Tom. *On Press.* New York: Viking Press, 1978.

Wildavsky, Aaron. *The Beleaguered Presidency.* New Brunswick, N.J.: Transaction Publishers, 1991.

Witcover, Jules. *Marathon: The Pursuit of the Presidency, 1972–1976.* New York: Viking, 1977.

Woodward, Bob. *Shadow: Five Presidents and the Legacy of Watergate.* New York: Simon and Schuster, 1999.

The World Almanac and Book of Facts: 1977. New York: Newspaper Enterprise Association, 1977.

Yergin, Daniel. *The Prize: The Epic Quest for Oil, Money, and Power.* New York: Touchstone, 1992.

Articles, Papers, Audio-visuals, and Other Sources

Baroody, William. "Gerald Ford and the New Politics." *Presidential Studies Quarterly* 7 (Spring and Summer 1977): 91–95.

Bohi, Douglas, and Joel Darmstadter. "The Energy Upheavals of the 1970s: Socioeconomic Watershed or Aberration?" Paper presented at the symposium, "Twenty Years after the Energy Shock—How Far Have We Come? Where Are We Headed?" at the University of Tennesee–Knoxville, April 19, 1994.

Buchen, Phil. "Reflection on a Politician's President," in Thompson, *The Ford Presidency.*

Carroll, Richard. "An Economic Record of Presidential Performance: From Truman to Bush," (unpublished manuscript), 1994.

Cheney, Richard. "Forming and Managing an Administration," in Thompson, *The Ford Presidency.*

Cronin, Thomas. "An Imperiled Presidency," in Davis, *The Post-Imperial Presidency.*

Davidson, Roger. "The President and Congress," in Bailey and Shafritz, *The American Presidency.*

Dudden, Arthur. "Not a Lincoln But a Ford," in Firestone and Ugrinsky, *Gerald R. Ford.*

Ford, Gerald R. Acceptance speech to Republican National Convention (August 19, 1976). Video, Gerald R. Ford Library.

———. Address to a Joint Session of Congress on the Economy (October 8, 1974). Video, Gerald R. Ford Library.

———. "Challenge to American Policy," in Anderson and Bark, *Thinking about America*, 535–44.

———. Energy Address to the Nation (May 27, 1975). Video, Gerald R. Ford Library.

———. Interview on ABC-TV's "Good Morning America," April 22, 1994.

———. State of the Union Address (January 15, 1975). Video, Gerald R. Ford Library.

———. State of the Union preview (January 13, 1975). Video, Gerald R. Ford Library.

Friedman, Irving. "Democracy and Persistent Inflation," in Prochnow, *Dilemmas Facing the Nation*, 55–81.

Gerald Ford's America. Produced by TVTV and the Television Laboratory at WNET-13. Video, Gerald R. Ford Library.

Goodwin, Craufurd, et al. "Energy: 1945–1980." *Wilson Quarterly* 5 (Spring 1981): 54–97.

Gordon, David. "Chickens Home to Roost: From Prosperity to Stagnation in the Postwar U.S. Economy," in Bernstein and Adler, *Understanding American Economic Decline.*

Great Speeches of the 20th Century, Volume One: Presidential Addresses. Rhino Records, 1994 (compact disc).

"Happy Days," *A&E Biography.* Produced by Kevin Bachar and Whiz Iiames-Damutz, 2001.

Hersh, Seymour. "The Pardon: Nixon, Ford, Haig, and the Orderly Transfer of Power." *The Atlantic* 252 (August 1983): 55–78.

Jaws: The E! True Hollywood Story. Produced by E! Entertainment Television, 2002.

Klein, Lawrence R. "The Restructuring of the American Economy," in Kregel, *Inflation and Income Distribution in Capitalist Crisis*, 25–45.

Lamm, Robert. "Harry Truman," from the album *Chicago VIII* (Columbia Records, 1974).

Marcus, Alfred, and Mark Jankus. "The Auto Emissions Debate during the Ford Administration: The Role of Scientific Knowledge," in Firestone and Ugrinsky, *Gerald R. Ford.*

Mieczkowski, Yanek. "President Eisenhower's Reaction to *Sputnik*: Presidential Calm and National Panic" (unpublished master's thesis, Columbia University, 1989).

1980 presidential campaign debate, Jimmy Carter and Ronald Reagan (October 28, 1980). Video, Ronald Reagan Presidential Library.

1976 presidential campaign debates, Gerald R. Ford and Jimmy Carter (September 23, 1976; October 6, 1976; October 23, 1976). Video, Gerald R. Ford Library.

1976 vice-presidential campaign debate, Bob Dole and Walter Mondale (October 15, 1976). Video, Gerald R. Ford Library.

Nessen, Ron. "The Ford Presidency and the Press," in Thompson, *The Ford Presidency.*

Bibliography

Nocera, Joseph. "America's Inflation Anxiety." *Worth* (July/August 1994): 98–104.

Orben, Robert. "Speeches, Humor, and the Public," in Thompson, *The Ford Presidency.*

Parmet, Herbert. "Gerald R. Ford," in Graff, *The Presidents: A Reference History*, 639–58.

Porter, Roger. "Gerald R. Ford: A Healing Presidency," in Greenstein, *Leadership in the Modern Presidency*, 199–227.

Ranney, Austin. "The President and His Party," in Bailey and Shafritz, *The American Presidency.*

Schleede, Glenn. "Predictions, Prescriptions, and Policy: Lessons from the Record," a paper presented at the symposium "Twenty Years after the Energy Shock—How Far Have We Come? Where Are We Headed?" at the University of Tennessee–Knoxville, April 19, 1994.

——. "Updating Energy Market Expectations Unerlying EIA's Annual Energy Outlook (AEO) and National Energy Modeling System (NEMS)," comments prepared for the U.S. Energy Information Administration's National Energy Modeling System/ Annual Energy Outlook Conference, Arlington, Va., April 18, 1994.

Shabecoff, Philip. "Appraising Presidential Power: The Ford Presidency," in Cronin and Tugwell, *The Presidency Reappraised.*

Sloan, John. "Economic Policymaking in the Johnson and Ford Administrations." *Presidential Studies Quarterly* 20 (Winter 1990).

"State of the Union." *Weekly Compilation of Presidential Documents*, vol. 10 (February 4, 1974): 103–59.

Taylor, Timothy. "The War Against Inflation." *Classrooms and Lunchrooms: A Journal for Teachers of Economics* (Fall/Winter 1992–1993): 9.

The Trust for the Bicentennial of the U.S. Constitution. *We the People: The President and the Constitution, Part I: President Ford* (video). 1991.

The Trust for the Bicentennial of the U.S. Constitution. *We the People: The President and the Constitution, Part II: President Carter* (video). 1991.

Vietnam: A Television History. PBS American Experience, 1996 (video).

Vietnam: The 10,000-Day War. BWE Video, 1980 (video).

Wayne, Stephen. "Running the White House: The Ford Experience." *Presidential Studies Quarterly* 7 (Spring and Summer 1977): 95–101.

Woodward, Bob. "Gerald R. Ford," in Kennedy, *Profiles in Courage for Our Time.*

Zarb, Frank. "Discussant: Frank Zarb," in Firestone and Ugrinsk, *Gerald R. Ford.*

Interviews by Author

Personal Interviews

Ash, Roy (August 21, 2001)
Bellmon, Henry (September 21, 1995)
Bennett, Douglas (October 19, 1994)
Buchen, Philip (February 25, 1994)
Bumpers, Dale (June 17, 2003)
Cannon, James (October 19, 1994)
Cavanaugh, James (April 17, 2003)
Coleman, William (September 16, 2003)

Conable, Barber B., Jr. (February 9, 1994)
Curtis, Charles (January 22, 2003)
DiBona, Charles (January 23, 2003; May 20, 2004)
Duval, Michael (March 8, 1994)
Eberle, William (March 29, 2002)
Ford, Gerald (March 30, 1994; October 25, 1994; August 21, 2003)
Freeburg, Russell W. (August 31, 2001)
Friedersdorf, Max (August 14, 2001)
Glozer, Ken (April 22, 2004)
Goldwin, Robert (March 3, 1994)
Goodpaster, Andrew J. (June 15, 2000)
Green, William J. (February 28, 1994)
Hartmann, Robert (October 17, 1994; September 17, 2003)
Hill, John A. (September 19, 2002; May 11, 2004)
Johnson, William A. (April 20, 2004)
Lynn, James (March 3, 1994; October 27, 1994)
MacAvoy, Paul (May 2, 2002)
McCracken, Paul (February 8, 1994)
Nessen, Ron (January 29, 2002)
Nordhaus, Robert (September 18, 2003)
Pasternack, Bruce (March 21, 1994)
Percy, Charles (March 1, 1994)
Schleede, Glenn (March 1, 1994; October 20, 1994; August 28, 2002)
Seevers, Gary (January 16, 2003)
Seidman, L. William (October 18, 1994; May 19, 2004)
Theis, Paul (October 20, 1994; September 17, 2003)
Zarb, Frank (September 26, 1994; February 6, 2003)

Telephone Interviews

Anderson, John B. (May 5, 1994)
Ash, Roy (January 10, 1994; February 8, 1994)
Cederburg, Elford (July 20, 2003)
Dingell, John (February 14, 1994)
Ford, Gerald (January 24, 2002)
Hanley, James (June 14, 1994)
Lynn, James (February 2, 1995; February 14, 2002)
Malkiel, Burton (February 23, 2002)
Mathias, Charles (May 26, 2004)
O'Neill, Paul (August 17, 1994)
Porter, Roger (May 8, 1995)
Van Ness, William (August 28, 2003; September 3, 2003)

Index